Financial Condition Examiners Handbook

2005 Edition

This guidance is as adopted by the NAIC as of December 2004. Please note that there will be modifications to the chapters that should be included in this handbook from year to year as such guidance is subject to the maintenance process. To address this, the NAIC has a website dedicated to providing the holder of this manual with the latest information impacting financial examinations.

The holder of this manual may enter a password-protected NAIC Website at www.naic.org.

- Select the Members drop down menu
- Select Financial Regulatory Services
- Select Solvency Regulation
- Select Financial Examiners Handbook Technical Group
- Select FEH Updates

Regulators can access this information from I-SITE using their I-SITE login credentials.

- Choose StateNet from the Log-in Categories
- Select the Financial Condition E Committee link
- Select Financial Examiners Handbook Updates

Password Information
Although not unique to user, this password should only be used by persons who have obtained the 2005 Financial Examiners Handbook from the NAIC. Please note these are case sensitive:

User ID: **FEHuser05**
Password: **D45BM6ZR**

NAIC
making progress . . . together

ISBN 0-89382-109-8

National Association of Insurance Commissioners
Insurance Products & Services Division
816-783-8300
Fax 816-460-7593
www.naic.org/insprod
prodserv@naic.org

Printed in the United States of America

Executive Headquarters
2301 McGee Street, Suite 800
Kansas City, MO 64108-2662
816-842-3600

Securities Valuation Office
48 Wall Street, 6th Floor
New York, NY 10005-2906
212-398-9000

Government Relations
Hall of States Bldg.
444 North Capitol NW, Suite 701
Washington, DC 20001-1509
202-624-7790

Summary of Substantive Changes

The following represents a summary of the substantive changes that were made to the 2004 version of the Financial Examiners Handbook and are included in this 2005 version. This summary depicts the substantial revisions to the manual therefore, grammatical, formatting, or changes which do not alter the intent of the existing guidance are not included in this summary.

Section	Description of Change
Part 1	**General**
Section III	Use of SAS 70 Reports – Incorporated in accordance with the charge to provide guidance regarding the use of SAS 70 Reports. (Fall 2004)
Section IV	Custodial or Safekeeping Agreements - In response to a referral by the Custodial Assets Working Group, the Financial Examiners Handbook Technical Group made revisions to include broker/dealers as authorized custodians for insurance company securities. (Summer 2004)
Section V	Electronic Distribution of Reports - Revised by the Financial Examiner Handbook Technical Group to permit the electronic distribution of examination reports. (Summer 2004)
Exhibit I	Fidelity Insurance - Revised by the Financial Examiner Handbook Technical Group to clearly define fidelity insurance and identify the types of employees that should be covered by fidelity bonds. (Fall 2004)
Exhibit M	Consideration of Fraud - Revised by the Financial Examiner Handbook Technical Group in accordance with guidance adopted by the American Institute of Certified Public Accountants and included in *Statement on Auditing Standards* (SAS) 99 – *Consideration of Fraud in a Financial Statement Audit.* (Summer 2004)
Part II	**Specific Risk Analysis**
Investment Cycle	Investment Cycle – The Investment Cycle SRA was updated to reflect the changes in the filing requirements for the NAIC SVO.
All Cycles	SAP Reference Update – All SRAs were revised to update references to the NAIC *Accounting Practices and Procedure Manual.*

INDEX OF CONTENTS

PART 1 — GENERAL

INDEX OF CONTENTS

INDEX OF CONTENTS

PART 2 – SPECIFIC RISK ANALYSIS

PART 3 – AUDIT SAMPLING AND CONTROL AND SUBSTANTIVE TESTING PROCEDURES

INDEX OF CONTENTS

PART 4 – REINSURANCE

INDEX OF CONTENTS

PART 1 — GENERAL

TABLE OF CONTENTS

PART 1 — GENERAL

INTRODUCTION

This *Handbook* provides a "guide" to assist state insurance departments in establishing and operating an effective examination system. The basic purposes of an examination system are (1) to detect as early as possible those insurers with potential financial trouble; (2) to determine compliance with state statutes and regulations; and (3) to compile the information needed for timely, appropriate regulatory action. To conduct effective examinations of financial condition, examiners must be qualified by having adequate training and experience since sound judgment must be exercised at every stage of the examination process.

The concepts and procedures presented in this *Handbook* can be applied to all examinations, however, modifications may be warranted based upon the nature and size of specific entities. The *Handbook* procedures should be modified, supplemented or reduced, as appropriate. Nonetheless, it is acknowledged that considerable judgment will be required of the examiner. Such judgment will likely include, among many other matters, the application of the *Handbook* concepts and principles to examinations of small companies such as county mutuals, specialized insurers such as mortgage guaranty companies, and multiple company groups with consolidated accounting systems. For example, the planning concepts described herein are equally applicable to small county mutuals, however the examiner may decide to simplify the documentation of that process to a memorandum and supplemental checklists.

In addition to providing instructions and suggestions for carrying out various phases of examination work, this *Handbook* intends to convey the entire examination process. Items that are discussed throughout this *Handbook* include:

- Limited-scope examinations;
- Examination planning techniques including: internal and external environmental considerations, analytical review procedures, evaluation of internal controls including computer controls, formal planning meetings with company management prior to the start of fieldwork, an assessment of materiality, risk analysis, formal planning documentation, the consideration of fraud in financial condition examinations, and the development of a written examination program;
- Minimum standards for examination administration including: budgeting/monitoring of time, communications with insurance company personnel, use of standardized examination workpapers, use and reliance on Certified Public Accountant (CPA) and internal audit workpapers, examination workpaper review, exit conferences and the supervision of examiners/evaluation of examiner performance;
- Interim reporting to the chief examiner; and
- Post examination follow-up procedures.

A. Key Elements of the System

An examination system should use the examination resources as effectively and efficiently as possible. Focus first should be concentrated on those insurers most likely to be the subject of significant actual or potential problems. Once a company is identified for an examination, a risk analysis methodology should be used to focus on the combined impact of the environment in which the company operates, the company's financial and operating results, and the extent and effectiveness of the company's internal controls. The risk analysis methodology enables the examination team to design an examination program that includes the most effective and efficient combination of tests responsive to a company's unique circumstances.

The four key elements of an effective examination system are: an early warning system, a system for scheduling examinations, a system for planning and conducting examinations, and a proper determination of the necessary scope of examination.

1. An Early Warning System

The National Association of Insurance Commissioners (NAIC) has created Financial Analysis Solvency Tools (FAST), a collection of analytical tools to provide state insurance departments with an integrated approach to screening and analyzing the financial condition of insurance companies to assist the state insurance departments in targeting resources to those insurers in greatest need of regulatory attention. FAST includes the Insurance Regulatory Information System (IRIS), the Scoring System (Annual and Quarterly), and Company Profiles. FAST has two primary components: screening and analysis.

The screening component consists of the Annual Scoring System and IRIS. The Annual Scoring System consists of a series of ratios for which an insurer scores a given number of points based on certain parameters set for each ratio. These ratios generally focus on an insurer's leverage, operations, profitability, liquidity and asset quality. The IRIS utilizes a series of tests applied to published financial statements. It provides state insurance departments with IRIS test results for insurers in their jurisdictions. The IRIS, along with evaluations performed by independent rating agencies, provides timely information that may indicate the need for an increased level of regulatory surveillance.

The analysis component of FAST consists of many profile reports generated from Annual and Quarterly Statement data. Company profile reports can assist the analyst in identifying unusual fluctuations or trends in, or changes in the mix of, an insurer's assets, liabilities, capital and surplus, and operations. The analysis component also includes the NAIC *Financial Analysis Handbooks*.

In addition to FAST, other resources are available for the examiner to utilize. The examiner should evaluate Risk-Based Capital ratios, CPA Audits, Management Discussion & Analysis (MD&A), SEC filings, Jumpstart reports, and financial strength ratings when determining the initial assessment of the company's financial condition.

2. A System for Scheduling Examinations

Scheduling examinations should provide the insurance department with a systematic approach to classify insurers according to priority. Considerable judgment is required to determine an insurer's priority classification. Items to consider include changes in management, IRIS test results, results of prior financial condition and market conduct examinations, information from other sources, and the elapsed time since the last examination.

3. A System for Planning and Conducting Examinations

In the examination planning process, the chief examiner or designee, examiner-in-charge and examination team members should assign priority to accounts or operating cycles that are most likely to affect solvency. The order of priority, or extent of procedures performed on each account, should be based on the risk assessment for each transaction cycle as outlined by the Specific Risk Analysis (SRA) workpapers provided in Part 2. This risk analysis includes consideration of environmental factors, analytical reviews, adequacy of internal controls and work performed by independent CPAs and actuaries.

4. Scope of Examination

Examinations are classified as full-scope or limited-scope. Full-scope examinations are considered comprehensive examinations because their objective is the reporting by the examiner on the company's financial position and affairs. A full-scope examination does not mean necessarily that the examination team would review every area of the company. Planning decisions would be made concerning the use of work of internal and external auditors, and other factors inherent in the risk analysis process. A full-scope examination would still focus on certain cycles based on the risk analysis methodology and the determination of the most effective and efficient combination of tests responsive to audit risk. Conversely, certain cycles may be de-emphasized because of the examiner's assessment of low risk of error. However, assessment of low risk and rationale behind the assessment should be documented in the examination workpapers.

Limited-scope examinations target specific financial accounts and/or areas of a company's operations (e.g., loss reserves). Limited-scope examinations do not employ the comprehensive risk analysis methodology of all accounts and areas of a company's operations that are used in full-scope examinations. The objective of a limited-scope examination is to review specific accounts and processes and report on the findings noted.

With increased use of independent accountants' and actuaries' reports and financial analysis, insurance departments have flexibility in full-scope examinations, as well as through limited-scope examinations. Insurance departments should focus more of their efforts directly on sensitive and judgmental areas that have a material bearing on the determination of a company's solvency.

B. Relationship to the Market Conduct Surveillance System

The financial condition examination system focuses on financial and corporate matters. The market conduct portion of the examination system focuses on such areas as sales, advertising, rating, and the handling of claims. Guidance over market conduct examinations is provided in the NAIC *Market Conduct Examiners Handbook* and is available through the Insurance Products and Services Division of the NAIC.

C. Updating the *Handbook*

The *Handbook* will be updated and bound each year for distribution. Updates to the *Handbook* that are made periodically throughout the year will be posted on the NAIC Website. Instructions for accessing the updates on the Website are located at the front of the *Handbook*. In addition to this bound book, the NAIC *Financial Condition Examiners Handbook* is available on a Folio-View CD-ROM and certain segments of the *Handbook* are included within NAIC developed TeamMate TeamStores. Updates to these sources will be completed annually.

Examiners faced with the day-to-day responsibility for detecting financial difficulties can make a valuable contribution to the continuing improvement of the *Handbook* by submitting recommendations for consideration to the NAIC Financial Examination Manager. Furthermore, changes in the NAIC *Accounting Practices and Procedures Manual* and NAIC Model Laws may require periodic *Handbook* revisions. The NAIC Financial Condition (E) Committee is responsible for considering revisions to the *Handbook*, and recommending them to the members of the NAIC.

I. ASSOCIATION EXAMINATIONS

The Association Examination System is not intended to preempt states' legislative and regulatory authority in conducting financial examinations. The Association Examination System creates a vehicle for conducting financial examinations of multi-state licensed insurers. It allows a representative number of states to adequately plan and devote resources to the financial examination of multi-state licensed insurers. It also allows an independent perspective on examination issues by those participating in the financial examination.

A. Criteria for Calling Association Examinations

The NAIC officially favors the Association plan of examination for all companies licensed in more than one zone or in more than three states in a single zone. Such examinations shall include verification of the payment of taxes by the company to the respective states in which it is licensed, in addition to determining the solvency of the company and the manner in which it conducts its affairs.

In order for these examinations to be accepted by other states, the NAIC's Accreditation Program and Examination Tracking System requires that at least one accredited state participate in each Association examination.

The NAIC has adopted the full use of the NAIC Examination Tracking System (ETS) for all examinations regardless of the number of states in which a company is licensed.

The NAIC has adopted the requirement for EDP assisted examinations on zone examinations when audit software is compatible with the insurer's hardware.

An EDP assisted examination is defined as the use of a software package that will facilitate the examination by providing:

1. The capability of direct retrieval of information from company electronic files to achieve:

   a. reliability of information accumulation;

   b. efficiency of information accumulation;

   c. flexibility of information accumulation (i.e., degree of selectivity or comprehensiveness desired); and

   d. expeditious and extensive analysis of data accumulations.

2. The adaptability to allow the examiner-in-charge the discretion to determine the appropriate information accumulation so that such accumulation will be beneficial for that particular examination.

The NAIC has adopted the Association plan of examination for rating, advisory, service or statistical organizations operating in more than one zone.

The NAIC zone examination system functions in accordance with the policy adopted by the NAIC and implemented under the jurisdiction and supervision of the Financial Condition (E) Committee.

Acting under instructions of the NAIC, the Financial Condition (E) Committee divided the country into four zones:

STATES BY ASSOCIATION EXAMINATION ZONES

NORTHEASTERN ZONE—ZONE I

Connecticut	New Jersey
Delaware	New York
District of Columbia	Pennsylvania
Maine	Rhode Island
Maryland	Vermont
Massachusetts	Virgin Islands
New Hampshire	

SOUTHEASTERN ZONE—ZONE II

Alabama	Mississippi
Arkansas	North Carolina
Florida	Puerto Rico
Georgia	South Carolina
Kentucky	Tennessee
Louisiana	Virginia
	West Virginia

MIDWESTERN ZONE—ZONE III

Iowa	Missouri
Illinois	Nebraska
Indiana	North Dakota
Kansas	Ohio
Michigan	Oklahoma
Minnesota	South Dakota
	Wisconsin

WESTERN ZONE—ZONE IV

Alaska	Montana
American Samoa	Nevada
Arizona	New Mexico
California	Oregon
Colorado	Texas
Guam	Utah
Hawaii	Washington
Idaho	Wyoming

On all Association examinations where a company has annual direct premium writings (or, in the case of a company whose principal business is reinsurance, reinsurance premiums assumed) totaling $15,000,000 or more in a zone, based upon the most recent annual statement, or where such writings in a zone are less than $15,000,000 but 30 percent of its writings are within a zone, such zone shall be invited to participate in the examination. Said zone participation shall not be waived by the zone chair without consent of the majority of the states in the zone. In the event of such waiver, the examiners participating in such examination shall be considered as representing the states in that zone or zones.

On all examinations of rating, advisory, service or statistical organizations, where members and subscribers have annual direct premium writings totaling $100,000,000 or more in a zone, or where such writings in a zone are less than $100,000,000 but 15 percent of its writings are within a zone, such zone shall be invited to participate in such examination. Said zone participation shall not be waived by the zone chair without consent of the majority of states in the zone. In the event of such waiver, the examiners participating in such examination shall be considered as representing the states in that zone or zones.

In any other situation, regardless of the amount of premium writings within a zone, upon request of a majority of states within a zone, the zone chair shall designate an examiner to represent the zone in an examination.

B. Procedures for Calling Association Examinations

The domiciliary or lead state determines the need for an examination. No association examination shall be called with less than thirty-days notice prior to the commencement date.

Use of the ETS is required. The state calling an examination inputs the requisite data into the Exam Detail and subsequent input screens of the ETS, which creates an Examination Call Letter and Premium Schedule that indicates:

1. Name and address of contact person;
2. Name and address of company to be examined;
3. Examination type, examination commencement date and estimated duration of examination, examination site and examination call number;
4. Specific zones to be invited and, where special interests warrant, particular state/states; and
5. Distribution of examination letters to: NAIC Examination Tracking System, concerned states/zone secretaries.

States receive an Examination Call Letter and Premium Schedule from the calling state and must make a decision to participate. If the state does not wish to participate, no action is required.

If the receiving state determines there is a need to participate, it creates Intent to Participate Letter, which indicates:

1. Current date;
2. Name, zone number and address of zone secretary being advised of intent;
3. Name, address and examination call number of company to be examined;
4. Name of examiner to be assigned; and
5. Distribution of Intent to Participate Letter to zone secretary.

So that all states have ample time to review an Examination Call Letter, evaluate their staffing resources, and note the premium volume and/or consumer complaints on the insurer to be examined, each zone secretary shall impose a seven calendar day waiting period before assigning an examiner from a state that wishes to participate. This waiting period may be waived by the zone secretary if the state calling the examination transmits the Examination Call Letter less than fifteen days prior to the commencement of the examination.

Procedures for the zone secretaries (of the invited zones) to communicate which examiner has been selected to represent the zone in an examination are:

1. Review Intent to Participate Letters and select examination participant, primary basis of selection being the state with the highest premium volume.
2. If Intent to Participate Letter is received after commencement of examination, the zone secretary shall inquire of domiciliary insurance department of insurer to be examined, whether additional participation is needed before assigning an examiner.

3. Create an Examination Participation Letter which indicates:
    a. Current date;
    b. Name and zone number of zone secretary;
    c. Examination call number and name and address of company to be examined; and
    d. Name and state of examiner to be assigned.
4. Distribution of Examination Participation Letter to: Examination Tracking System, the state of domicile, the states participating on the examination, and all the states within the zone that were invited to participate.

If a state has a concern with a zone examiner either before the examination commences or during the examination, the domiciliary state should speak to the Chief Examiner of the state in which the examiner is employed. If the concern is not resolved, the domestic state should express its concerns to the zone secretary. The zone secretary will make the final determination. If the domestic state and the zone secretary are one in the same, the zone vice chair will make the final determination.

Participation on Association examinations will be determined and implemented only in accordance with the preceding procedures established in this section of the NAIC *Examiners Handbook.*

If the starting date of a called examination is either postponed or canceled, the state calling the examination shall immediately notify the concerned states/zone secretaries through the Exam Tracking System. Such notification should include comments relative to the postponement or cancellation.

C. Limited-scope Examinations

Often an insurance department may find it advisable to conduct financial examinations that are limited in scope. While the reasons for such a situation are numerous, ordinarily such an examination will be convened in the following circumstances:

1. Unusual values identified through the Insurance Regulatory Information System (IRIS);
2. Internal department analysis of NAIC annual or quarterly statement;
3. Follow-up from a prior report of examination;
4. Request from another insurance department;
5. To provide information necessary for the examination of another insurer;
6. Unusual complaint volume;
7. Transactions disclosed under the Holding Company Act;
8. Preliminary investigations;
9. Limited purpose examinations required by statute; or
10. Examination planning and risk assessment analysis.

The NAIC encourages an efficient determination of a company's financial position, with special emphasis on troubled companies. Therefore, each financial condition examination is not conducted necessarily in exactly the same degree of detail or with the same emphasis on all aspects of a particular insurer's operations. Limited-scope examinations can be very effective in focusing examination resources quickly on those areas requiring immediate attention. Nonetheless, statutes in some states may require a full-scope examination at regular intervals. In addition, states have discretion to determine the appropriate audit scope, and the fact that an independent accountant is engaged by the company does not, by itself, preclude the necessity for a separate full-scope examination by the state.

If the state of domicile determines a particular insurer is the proper subject of a limited-scope, rather than full-scope examination, the notice of convening such an examination should clearly indicate its limited nature, the basis for convening a limited-scope exam, and an identification of the specific areas to be reviewed by the examiners in the Report of Examination. Should any state desire additional examination procedures, it should communicate such requests through its zone secretary, who will inform the examiner representing the zone of the request.

When a limited-scope exam is convened, the primary responsibility for determining the scope and depth of examination procedures rests with the examiner-in-charge who, presumably, has been closely connected with the preliminary determination of the examination focus. The examiner-in-charge must also coordinate the requests from other states for additional examination procedures. While those requests are to be honored, it is the ultimate responsibility of the examiner-in-charge to effectively manage the resources available, so that the initial reasons for a limited-scope examination and its objectives remain intact.

The examiner-in-charge should be able to accommodate reasonable specific requests without causing any disruption of the schedule. With the assistance of examiners from other states who take an active interest in planning and regularly evaluating the exam progress with the examiner-in-charge, the important regulatory goals of solvency, compliance and fairness should be achieved.

The unique nature of each limited-scope examination makes promulgation of a comprehensive reporting format or guideline herein of limited value. Nonetheless, such a report should describe at a minimum the limited objective of the examination noting the scope restriction in the Report of Examination, the overall scope of procedures applied, and the examiner's findings from performing those procedures. However, any state convening such an examination (other than one that is investigatory or preliminary in nature) should distribute the examination report upon its completion, subject to any hearing or other due process requirements of the state initiating the exam.

The matter of prior notice through the zone system, or even the advisability of the same, will depend upon the circumstances under which the limited-scope exam is convened. However, it is NAIC policy that when a limited-scope examination is convened that would otherwise require notification to the NAIC and the zone secretaries, and which is not preliminary in nature, such notice should be in accordance with the timing and distribution requirements of this *Handbook*. If the convening authority determines such notification is not practical or advisable in the circumstances, notice shall be given contemporaneously with the examiners' date of entry.

D. Special Association Examinations

1. A special Association examination may be called by the NAIC Financial Condition (E) Committee if:

   a. Written reports from the zone examiners indicate the examination conducted by the company's state of domicile is inadequate;
   b. The home state is reluctant to schedule an examination when IRIS results or other information indicate the need; or
   c. A state in which a company is licensed requests a special Association examination.

2. Special Association examinations are staffed with personnel selected from state insurance departments by the NAIC Financial Condition (E) Committee.

3. Special Association examination reports should be addressed directly to the Financial Condition (E) Committee.

E. Authority and Responsibility of the Examiner-in-Charge

The examiner-in-charge has the following authority and responsibilities:

1. Planning the examination

   a. Develop initial written plans;
   b. Update written plans periodically to reflect progress;
   c. Advise all other examiners of all current examination developments; and
   d. Confer with all other examiners on all major examination problems on a current basis.

2. Supervision of examiners, including zone examiners

   a. Supervise the conduct of the examination;
   b. Allocate work assignments;
   c. Review each examiner's detailed work plan and revise where necessary;
   d. Monitor progress against plans regularly and initiate necessary corrective action to ensure the examination is completed in a timely manner;
   e. Provide on-the-job training of examiners;
   f. Ensure professional conduct of examiners;
   g. Review each examiner's workpapers to see that they support the examiner's conclusions and findings;
   h. Prepare and deliver performance reviews of domestic examination staff and zone examiners on a timely basis and in accordance with the procedures set forth in the Classifications, Minimum Qualifications, and Suggested Compensation for Zone Examiners Document, Attachment B (Refer to www.naic.org at http://www.naic.org/frs/solvency_regulation/financial_exam_qual_comp_tg/index.htm); and
   i. Monitor the hours worked.

3. Maintain liaison with company management

   a. Conferences or other communications with company officials, except regarding minor matters, should be made only with the full knowledge of all participating zone examiners.
   b. The hours during which an examination should be conducted shall, except where different hours are prescribed by the state department in charge of the examination, correspond as closely as possible to the working hours of the organization being examined.

4. Provide for the security of company records and information.

5. Prepare examination report

   a. Develop report in consultation with all other examiners before completion of fieldwork;
   b. If a disagreement among the examiners (including the examiner-in-charge) cannot be resolved, e.g., by the procedure established in Section V.G., include in the report the comments of the dissenter(s) and indicate which are the majority and minority opinions. (If there is an even split of opinion, so indicate.); and
   c. The preparation of examination report should be developed in consultation with all other examiners. (The examiner-in-charge or domiciliary state insurance

department shall not change or amend a final work copy of any zone examination report without prior advice, consultation and approval of the participating zone examiners.)

6. Maintain summary of actual hours spent on each examination activity.

7. Conduct the examination in a manner consistent with the standards set out in F.3-F.5.

F. Duties and Responsibility of Zone Examiners

1. Cooperate with the examiner-in-charge and other examiners in the conduct of the examination:
   a. Assume responsibility to perform the duties assigned to examiner by the examiner-in-charge;
   b. Take an active interest in the examination as a whole; and
   c. Inform the examiner-in-charge of examination developments on a current basis.

2. Make appropriate arrangements with examiner-in-charge for carrying out specific instructions given to the examiner and for obtaining specifically requested information.

3. Devote full time to examination duties and responsibilities.

4. Adopt the rules of conduct established for the examination team.

5. Observe professional standards of conduct free from any impropriety and appearance of impropriety, and avoid any situations or circumstances that may reasonably appear to influence independence, judgment or discretion.

6. Respect the confidentiality of information developed or received during the course of an examination.

7. In addition to performing duties assigned by the examiner-in-charge, perform such other work as the examiner deems necessary to obtain assurance that major solvency risk areas, specific concerns expressed by the zone he/she represents, and other concerns arising during the examination have been addressed in the examination. This objective can normally be met by reviewing the critical cycles. (Note that the zone examiner should not duplicate the work of the examiner-in-charge.)

8. In addition to performing duties assigned by the examiner-in-charge, perform such other work as the examiner deems necessary for a fair and complete examination.

9. Submit to a performance evaluation by the examiner-in-charge in accordance with the procedures set forth in Part 8 Appendix C. (Refer to www.naic.org. at http://www.naic.org/frs/solvency_regulation/financial_exam_qual_comp_tg/index.htm)

10. Prepare for inclusion in the examination report dissenting opinions, if any, with respect to each issue the examiner deems significant and which is not reflected in the majority report.

11. Items of importance discovered during the examination shall not be considered confidential when reporting to commissioners in the zone represented by the examiner either during or after the completion of the examination.

12. In general, the examiner should remain on the examination until he/she receives a draft copy of the examination report. (Note that the zone examiner should not duplicate the work of the examiner-in-charge.)

13. No examiner shall communicate any information developed during the course of an examination to any person other than a chief examiner (or designee), or through the medium of the examination report after adoption of such report.

14. Remain on the examination until it is completed and a rough draft of the report is in possession. Signed signature sheets may be left with the examiner-in-charge. However, this procedure may be varied for justifiable reasons.

15. Any major difference arising during the course of an examination that is not resolved after thorough discussion with the examiner-in-charge and the participating examiners should be reported by the examiner involved to the examiner's chief examiner and zone secretary.

II. SCHEDULING FINANCIAL CONDITION EXAMINATIONS

Within the time framework established by state law, financial condition examinations should be scheduled to assure more frequent examinations of companies that are likely to be financially troubled or in violation of laws relating to financial condition or corporate conduct. In many cases, the increased frequency will be accomplished by use of limited-scope examinations, which focus directly on areas of concern. Such scheduling embraces the following elements:

A. Responsibility for Scheduling

1. Examinations of domestic companies (not members of a holding company group). Examinations of domestic companies are scheduled by the domiciliary state, except where the company is a member of a holding company group consisting of at least one other insurance company.

2. Examination of insurance holding company groups:

   a. Definitions:

      (1) Subsidiary or controlled company - A subsidiary is an entity that is, directly or indirectly, owned and controlled by the reporting entity. Control shall be presumed to exist if a reporting entity and its affiliates directly or indirectly, own, control, hold with the power to vote, or hold proxies representing 10% or more of the voting interest of the entity.

      (2) Lead state – Typically, the lead state is the state where the parent company is domiciled or, if there is no insurance parent, the state where the largest (by direct written premium volume as shown by the last filed Annual Statement) insurance subsidiary is domiciled.

      (3) Affiliated and or other involved companies - A company owned directly, beneficially, or indirectly in common with that of another and/or a company where substantial reinsurance exists between companies with such ownership affiliations. Substantial means 35 percent or more of policyholder surplus is derived from the reinsurance, or where assets totaling 50 percent or more of policyholder surplus have been transferred, or credit for liabilities and reserve aggregating 50 percent or more of policyholder surplus exists, or any other standard deemed substantial by the regulator.

   b. Procedure for calling joint examinations of member insurers of an insurance holding company system:

      (1) The chief examiner of the lead state is responsible for placing the joint examination call (after prior consultation and notification of all involved states) to simultaneously examine the entire group of insurance companies involved in an insurance holding company group. Also to be considered are unaffiliated insurers that have, through reinsurance affiliations, provided 35 percent or more of existing surplus support at the examination date. The examination of companies that are members of a holding company system having only a reinsurance relationship with the company under the examination may be conducted on a limited basis, to

verify the complete nature of transactions (obligations, liabilities and assets transferred between parties).

States are encouraged to coordinate examinations of property and casualty insurers that operate pursuant to an intercompany reinsurance pooling agreement. Coordination among states includes the timing, scope and extent of examination procedures, utilization of specialists (e.g., information systems and actuarial) and their work products, and allocation of work among examiners. This coordination promotes communication among states, the efficient use of resources, and minimizes the duplication of work.

(2) Where a state of domicile does not desire to call a joint examination or participate in the examination of its domestic in such joint call, the examination may be called by another state, providing any of the following criteria are met:

- The value claimed for the subject insurer represents 50 percent or more of the policyholder surplus of any insurer above it in the insurance holding company system;
- Thirty percent or $5,000,000, whichever is less, of the direct business of the company is within the state desiring to place the call or within a zone of the NAIC, and a joint call by affected states is made or desired; or
- A company in the insurance holding company system has developed by reinsurance, or otherwise, 35 percent or more of its policyholder surplus from the subject affiliated insurer. In this case, it is recommended that the costs of examination should be assessed to the insurer receiving the surplus aid. This examination may be conducted on a limited basis, to verify the complete nature of transactions (obligations, assets, and liabilities transferred between parties).

3. Examinations of underwriting pools, syndicates and associations.

a. The examination of an underwriting pool, syndicate or association is the responsibility of the state in which the organization operates and, if it operates in more than one state, its examination should be coordinated by the lead state through the use of the ETS.

b. The lead state of an underwriting pool, syndicate or association is the one in which the organization's principal office is located. The lead state shall set the time and supervise the conduct of the examinations, shall have discretion in inviting other states to participate in the examination and in defining their participation. The lead state shall input the report on examination into the ETS to insure each interested insurance department, each company which is a subscriber or member of the examined organization and the chair of the Financial Condition (E) Committee has a copy of the report. Each state in which an organization operates, however, shall have the right to examine it, and any such state may commence its own examination, if it deems necessary to do so, upon notice to the lead state.

c. Each state is encouraged to recognize such reports on examination as official state documents, obviating the need for duplicative examinations, to establish procedures for reviewing these reports and to investigate and act upon any violations of law that they may disclose.

d. Where explicit regulatory authority does not exist over an underwriting pool, syndicate, or association, each state in which it operates should negotiate with the organization itself, or with its subscribing members, to obtain an agreement that the organization will submit to the insurance department's examination and will pay examination fees and charges assessed against it.

B. Timing of Schedule Preparation

The scheduling of examinations is a continuous process with a fundamental objective, subject to the time framework established by state law, to apply more examination resources at more frequent intervals to companies (and within companies by specific cycle, account or control objectives) that are more likely to be financially troubled or in violation of laws relating to financial condition or corporate conduct.

C. Procedures for Scheduling

1. Set examination priorities. Subject to state law, insurance departments have some discretion as to the timing, frequency and scope of examinations. It is imperative that the examination schedule be balanced to focus resources on companies that are likely to be financially troubled. This can be reasonably accomplished by taking advantage of other techniques, information and resources available to the insurance department, including but not limited to the following:

    a. Increased the number of limited-scope examinations;
    b. Use of IRIS results, Examination Jumpstart, and Analyst Team Reports, etc.;
    c. Use of reports and working papers from the company's independent accounting firm and actuary;
    d. Reference to audit adjustments recognized by the company's independent accounting firm. (Documentation of CPA identified adjustments may be obtained directly from the company.);
    e. References to any internal control letters furnished by the company's CPAs; and
    f. Findings of reviews of company financial statements performed by other department or NAIC personnel. The department may have a financial analysis team that reviews filed annual and quarterly financial statements and performs analytical procedures such as those indicated in the NAIC Troubled Company Handbook and NAIC Financial Analysis Handbook. Any significant findings from this process should be added to the examination scheduling criteria.

Considerable judgment will always be needed to determine the optimal timing, frequency, and scope of examinations. The following additional items, though not all-inclusive, should be considered:

a. Has a change in management occurred since the last full-scope examination?
b. Has the company been identified as a "priority" company by the IRIS results or supplemental internal department or NAIC financial analytical reviews? Has there

been a significant adverse shift in the results of these tests? (Unless further analysis indicates the results are misleading for some clearly identified reason.);

c. Results of past full-scope, limited-scope and market conduct examinations, including recommendations for timing and extent of follow-up procedures contained therein;
d. Information from other states or outside sources;
e. Concentration of business in high-risk lines, or concentration of assets;
f. Significant changes in operating results or mix of business;
g. Unusual disclosures in the independent accountant or actuary's report;
h. Evidence of surplus aid other than financial reinsurance agreements;
i. Unusual disclosures in the notes to the filed statutory financial statements or the audited financial statements, Form 10K, or other filings, particularly regarding loss contingencies;
j. Nature of any items communicated in material misstatement letters furnished by independent accountants;
k. External environmental considerations, such as a significant downturn in a regional real estate market or securities markets, or the insolvency of a significant reinsurer that may have assumed business from companies operating in the states. Reference should be made to the AICPA's Audit Risk Alert and similar publications for items of current significance regarding audits of insurance companies; and
l. Other non-financial criteria, such as input from other areas within the department including consumer complaints, market conduct, legal, etc.

2. Estimate staffing requirements for each examination:

a. Project total hours based on previous experience and current issues that have been identified.

(1) To facilitate future estimates, a record of examination hours should be filed with the department at the completion of the examination.

(2) The chief examiner or designee should review the previous experience when scheduling a new examination and estimate the total person days required, adjusting for:

- Variance between budgeted and actual time required to complete tasks;

- Special circumstances affecting the new or previous examination. Particular consideration should be given to savings in time that will be realized from risk analysis methodology that will emphasize audit effort on cycles where there is a high likelihood of material error to the financial statements, and may considerably decrease audit effort in other cycles. Consideration should also be given to the time savings anticipated by increased use of reports and working papers from independent accountants and actuaries, as well as company internal audit department and direct assistance from company personnel preparing schedules and pulling documents. In addition, the scope of the current examination may be different (limited vs. full-scope); and

- Changes in the company's size or recordkeeping systems.

b. Determine the staff size and skills required, considering:

(1) Staff needed to complete the examination in a reasonable period of time;

(2) Technical skills required to:

- Apply statistical sampling techniques;
- Evaluate and work with computer-based record systems;
- Examine reserves and reinsurance contracts;
- Deal with problems related to other areas demanding specialized knowledge; and
- Deal with limited-scope examinations that will likely be focused solely on areas that are more complex and more judgmental, and therefore require more expertise.

3. Estimate the time required to complete the examination by dividing the total number of person days plus administrative (e.g., training plus vacation) by the staff size.

4. Project start and completion dates of each examination.

a. List all companies by priority classification and determine the appropriate scope of examination (full-scope vs. limited-scope). A company may not be considered high priority for a full-scope examination, but may receive high priority as a limited-scope examination because of particular circumstances, such as a large receivable from a troubled reinsurer, or a significant contingency such as outstanding litigation;
b. Project available staff by month;
c. Record time and staffing required to complete examinations already in progress; and
d. Record time and staffing required for examinations of holding company units called by the lead state.

D. Quarterly Updating of the Schedule

1. Adjust priorities, if necessary, to reflect additional information on the likely financial condition of domestic companies.

2. Adjust scheduling of examinations to reflect:

a. Updated projection of available staff; and
b. Differences between actual and previously projected time required to complete in progress examinations.

III. PLANNING THE EXAMINATION

A. Objective

The objective of examination planning is to determine the scope of an examination and to design examination procedures based upon the examiner's risk assessment of the company. In order to comply with this objective, the examiner is required to obtain a thorough understanding of an insurer's business operations, which includes assessing the company's internal control structure, lines of business, corporate hierarchy, risk management programs, and any environmental conditions or factors that may affect the current or prospective solvency of the insurer. The examination planning is highly affected by the examiner's judgment and experience in assessing the insurer's risk profile. The nature, extent and timing of examination procedures will be directly affected by the size, complexity and risks of the insurer.

B. Introduction

The following pages discuss how to plan an insurance company examination. The methodology emphasizes a "risk-based" approach whereby resulting examination fieldwork will emphasize the analysis of an insurer's current or prospective solvency risk areas and the fair presentation of surplus. The planning phase of an examination incorporates the analytical work performed by the department's and the NAIC's financial analysts and further enhances such information via on-site discussions and more detailed analytical work by the examiner-in-charge (EIC) during the planning process. The planning process is most effective when accomplished before the general examination fieldwork begins. A more effective and efficient examination process will be achieved by:

1. Increasing the EIC's understanding of Company's management and operations thereby providing better on-site supervision of staff examiners and evaluation of key solvency risk areas;

2. Identifying key solvency risk areas of a Company and emphasizing work effort on those particular areas (and, conversely, de-emphasizing work effort in areas perceived to have lower solvency risk); and

3. Providing improved documentation of the key solvency risk areas and the extent/scope of examination procedures performed in such areas. This improved documentation will facilitate quality reviews and further regulatory action when necessary.

This section provides the framework for the examination planning process. The result of the planning analysis should be to obtain an overall understanding of the company's operations, the industry factors impacting the company, and to determine a preliminary risk assessment and overall examination approach to present to the supervisor in the planning meeting. The goal should be the establishment of a planning schedule and format responsive to the unique aspects of the company's operations and industry factors impacting it.

C. Planning Process Steps and Discussion

1. Review and Analysis

   The EIC should strive to become familiar with the unique aspects of the company's operations/products, and the risk management programs/techniques. Initial steps in the planning process include reviewing the following documents to obtain an overview of the company's general regulatory posture with the department, and to identify existing areas of regulatory focus:

a. General correspondence and other files – Review for significant current period events that may have an impact on assessing comparative prior period work, account balances or future operations;

b. Financial Analysis Annual Statement Review Package, including Examination Jumpstart Profile Report and Analyst Team Reports – These are key pre-planning documents. Review for significant trends, key solvency ratios (including the IRIS ratios) and financial results since the date of the last examination, holding company filings, 10Ks, etc. If significant or unusual solvency results or trends occur, the EIC may want to discuss the analytical results (including follow-up correspondence with the company, if any) with the financial analyst prior to the initial planning meeting with the company. In reviewing the company's IRIS ratios, the examiner should focus on understanding what gave rise to the variances, not simply the fact that certain ratios are outside the norms; and

c. Prior period workpapers/reports – A brief review should be performed to obtain a general understanding of work performed in prior periods, overall scope of work, perceived risk areas, and specific findings. Review should focus on key solvency trends and results from previous steps.

Other key planning steps the EIC should perform are as follows:

a. Evaluate the impact of pervasive factors and perform analyses, as well as hold discussions with management of the company, to gain a better understanding of the following:

(1) Significant Current Events – Significant developments such as a new acquisition, change in key management, litigation, results of revenue agent review (RAR), or other items that may affect the company's solvency should be identified and addressed.

(2) Company Conditions and Issues – The examination team should adequately understand the structure and manner in which the Company conducts its business to evaluate its solvency. Items such as the following should be considered:

- Organizational structure of the entity
- Key markets and product lines
- Key customers and major competitors
- Key solvency risk factors (i.e., holding significant amounts of low grade bonds and/or troubled real estate)

(3) The examination team should also evaluate industry conditions that could adversely affect the company's prospective ability to remain solvent. Such conditions might include the following areas:

- Business and economic trends
- Competitive environment
- Regulatory changes

(4) Obtain an understanding of the company's operations by line or book of business based on discussion with management.

b. Evaluate further specific planning steps to be performed internally at the department and during the site visit to assess the company's solvency risk both globally and with respect to specific areas identified.

c. Consider which individuals should be interviewed and the sources of data to be evaluated to complete each planning step.

d. Document on an informal basis in a format facilitating discussion with the supervisor.

2. In-House Planning Meeting

a. A planning meeting should be arranged prior to the EIC's field-site visit. The EIC, Examination Supervisor, the Financial Analyst and key exam staff who performed the statutory financial analysis should discuss current trends, operations, materiality and key solvency risks. Specific inquiries should be posed to the Financial Analyst to obtain an understanding and concerns of current company trends and financial condition. These inquiries might include comparison of current operating results and financial condition to prior periods, actual results to budget, and to corresponding industry data.

b. Additional items to consider may include the following:

(1) Current events
(2) Results of financial analysis
(3) Industry conditions
(4) Management quality and control environment
(5) EDP issues
(6) Materiality risk and tolerable error
(7) Audit risk alerts published by the AICPA

c. The result of the meeting should include the following:

(1) A common understanding between Supervisor and EIC concerning key examination risk areas and development of rough examination approach;
(2) Specific action steps to be completed during the planning process and scope of that work;
(3) Timing of work to be completed; and
(4) Additional individuals and data sources to be reviewed, interviewed, and/or assessed prior to completion of planning.

3. Management Assessment

This section's purpose is to assist the examiner in documenting the understanding and assessment of an insurer's quality of management. This is accomplished through analysis of two different characteristics of management: competence and performance. Competence attempts to measure the experience, education and historical background, not of specific individuals but of management in general. Performance measures the effectiveness and attitudes of management within the company. Both are needed for effective management. Good managers without the insurance and educational background may not understand industry and pricing implications. Well-educated, experienced managers who do not manage the company well and have limited controls over operations may not have sufficient understanding and control to make effective and good decisions.

A favorable overall assessment of management or the control environment does not, by itself, serve to reduce the scope or extent of examination procedures; rather, control environment issues are considered in context with external environmental, internal control, and analytical review in the Specific Risk Analysis (SRA) process. A quality assessment of management may be determined through discussion with management and observation of key control and management techniques. As a general guideline, the following areas should be considered in the assessment of management (this section is not intended to be all inclusive):

a. Management Competence

(1) How long has key management been with the company in their current positions, and what specific industry experience do they have?
(2) Has there been significant turnover in management?
(3) Have members of management ever been an officer, director, trustee, key employee or controlling stockholder of an insurance company which, while they occupied any such position or served in any such capacity with respect to it,

- Became insolvent or was placed in conservation?
- Was enjoined from or ordered to cease and desist from violating any securities or insurance law or regulation?
- Suffered the suspension or revocation of its certificate of authority or license to do business in any state?

b. Board of Directors

(1) Are Board membership criteria and terms sufficient to enable the effective monitoring and oversight of management?
(2) Does the Board effectively monitor and oversee management activities?

c. Management Performance Evaluation

(1) Does management periodically review information to adequately assess the impact of changes in competition, technology, regulation, environment and general economic trends that may impact the company's business?
(2) Does management have adequate financial and operating information to identify trends or variations from budgets that may impact the statutory financial statements?
(3) Does management effectively analyze and investigate financial and operating information and trends such that significant adverse trends or misstatements in the Annual Statement could reasonably be expected to be identified and rectified on a timely basis?
(4) Do management, supervisors and agents have appropriate knowledge and experience to capably and effectively administer management's policies and procedures?
(5) Does the Company maintain effective controls to ensure potential short-term liquidity problems, long-term capital needs, and other significant

capital and fund management variations or needs are identified and rectified on a timely basis?

(6) Do adequate physical safeguards exist over company assets and are all officers and their employees appropriately bonded (Exhibit I)?

(7) Does management have a positive attitude toward internal controls (including controls over the electronic data processing function)?

(8) Does management have adequate financial and operating information to identify, on a timely basis, potential liabilities, commitments and/or contingencies that may require recording and/or disclosure in the Annual Statement?

The examination team should document its overall assessment of the quality of management, as well as a summary of the supporting rationale and related impact on examination scope based on such assessment. The summary should include a description of any unique examination procedures, including special inquiries that are considered necessary to respond to any significant risks identified as a result of the assessment.

The format for documentation of this assessment is at the discretion of the examiner. For example, a memorandum could summarize the attributes and techniques supporting the examiner's overall evaluation, any resulting examination scope implications, and the approach used to validate the more significant attributes and techniques. For low risk insurance companies, a memorandum may be sufficient documentation.

4. Understanding Materiality and Risk

The examiners should consider materiality and risk when planning the nature and extent of examination procedures and when evaluating the results of those procedures.

a. Materiality

Materiality is defined as the dollar amount above which the examiner's perspective of the company's financial position will be influenced. It is determined at two levels during the initial planning stage: (1) an overall level as it relates to the annual statement taken as a whole; (2) an individual balance (annual statement line item) level.

b. Risk

Risk is defined as the probability that an examiner may unknowingly fail to modify an opinion on an annual statement that is materially misstated or on a company that has a high likelihood of becoming insolvent. Materiality and risk are addressed at an overall level to help develop a strategy that will provide sufficient evidence to enable the examiner to reasonably evaluate whether the annual statement is materially misstated or whether the company has a high likelihood of becoming insolvent.

At the account balance level, risk is the product of the risks that (1) factors in a company's internal or external environment, before considering the functioning of internal controls, will lead to a material error (inherent risk); (2) a material error will not be prevented or detected on a timely basis by the system of internal control (control risk); and (3) the examiner's procedures will fail to detect a material error not detected by the system of internal control (detection risk).

c. Defining Materiality

Planning Materiality (PM) is the examiner's preliminary judgment of materiality made during initial planning. It is used in developing the overall scope of the examination procedures.

At the examination's conclusion, the examiner evaluates whether the total effect of differences identified is material to the annual statement. Thus, the examiner needs to develop the scope of the procedures with a materiality consideration in mind. PM is used for that purpose. The amount considered material at the end of the examination may differ from PM since it ordinarily is not feasible to anticipate all the circumstances that may ultimately influence the examiner's judgment about materiality used in evaluating the overall effect of differences on the annual statement. If the examiner determines that a significantly lower level of materiality is appropriate in evaluating the overall effect of examination differences, the examiner should reconsider the sufficiency of examination procedures.

The estimate of PM requires professional judgment, based on the examiner's understanding of the company's operations. The examiner needs to consider the (1) nature of the business, (2) operating results (e.g., stable earnings, consistently near break-even, volatile results), and (3) financial position. Consideration should also be given to how close the company's surplus is to levels that would trigger regulatory action.

5. Setting Materiality Levels

Some of the factors that should be considered in determining PM are discussed below, along with examples of some measures that might be used. These are not the only measures or percentages that may be used – others may be appropriate based on professional judgment in particular circumstances. If a combination of measures is considered appropriate, the examiner should identify a range from which PM can be derived.

a. PM based on Capital & Surplus Levels - Typically, fair presentation of capital & surplus levels is of primary importance in an examination. Generally, an appropriate starting point in computing PM is 1 percent to 5 percent of capital & surplus. What percent of surplus to use depends on the circumstances of the examination. For example, as a company's capital & surplus declines toward minimum levels, the percentage used probably would be at the lower end of the range. Alternatively, for a strong, well-capitalized insurer with no apparent concerns, the percentage likely would be at the high end.

b. PM based on Operating Results - Another important financial measure is operating results, often the gain from operations. An appropriate starting point in computing PM is 5 percent of the pretax gain from operations. Whether to use current year income or an average of previous years' income is a judgmental decision based on current economic conditions and earnings trends. In many situations, it will be appropriate to challenge the reasonableness of the different methods by computing income several ways.

It also is appropriate to consider the effective tax rate in setting PM. In some situations, the effective tax rate differs from the statutory rate due to a large capital gain, high level of tax credits, or nontaxable income. The starting point from PM assumes that a 5 percent change in pretax income will cause a 5 percent change in taxes and result in a 5 percent change in net income. Accordingly, PM may be at a different amount in situations where the effective rate is significantly different from the statutory rate.

If the company operates at or near break-even or fluctuates between gain and loss from operations from year to year, pretax income may not be the most appropriate basis for computing PM. Also, because statutory accounting requires certain items to be reflected directly in surplus, statutory operating results may not be a good indicator of materiality. Premium volume or total revenue measures may be more appropriate. Again, it may be preferable to use more than one measure to identify a range from which PM can be derived.

c. PM Based on Financial Position – Another measure to consider in determining PM may be one-half of 1 percent of total assets. As gains from operations diminish and become minimal, their usefulness as a point of reference for computing PM also diminishes. In those situations, a smaller percentage of total assets (e.g., one-fourth of 1 percent) may be the most appropriate base.

d. Other Considerations – The general guidelines discussed above should apply to most examinations. However, in special situations the examiner may need to consider additional factors. In all cases, the estimate of PM requires professional judgment and consideration of a variety of factors – as no set of general guidelines can be all encompassing.

Documenting PM. – The examiner should document in the Examination Planning Memorandum the reasons underlying the determination of PM and the amount established as PM.

6. Tolerable Error

Tolerable Error (TE) is the materiality for a particular account balance (annual statement line item) affected by a specific examination objective. It is the amount of monetary error that can exist in a specific account balance without causing the financial statements as a whole to be materially misstated when added to errors in other account balances. TE is determined during the initial planning phase and used in the specific risk analysis process as the basis for (1) assessing the likelihood of material error in each separate account, and (2) planning the nature and extent of examination procedures for such accounts.

Setting TE – When examining an account balance based on a specified level of materiality, it is possible that some amount of error below that level is present, even if no errors are observed. As a result, if PM is used as the materiality level for specific examination tests, no margin is left for the aggregate effect of undetected errors. Thus, it is logical that the amount of TE set for each annual statement line item should be less than PM.

a. TE is a planning concept used to determine the amount of error that the examiner's testing is designed to detect. When the results of such tests detect an amount of error approaching or exceeding TE in that account, the examiner should evaluate the cause of the error and consider performing additional procedures to refine the estimate of acceptable error.

Tolerable error is related to the preliminary estimate of materiality in such a way that, when combined for the entire examination plan, it does not exceed PM. In other words, TE should be set for each account so the probability is remote that the total of undetected errors, detected errors, and judgmental differences from all accounts will exceed PM.

There are various statistical approaches to setting TE. These approaches result in TEs for various accounts that when simply added together exceed PM. However, when aggregated according to statistical formulas, those individual TEs result in an overall level of materiality that approximates PM. In other words, not all errors will move in the same direction. Therefore, the TE assigned to all accounts need not be so low that the sum of all TEs is less than PM. The appropriate level for setting TE will vary by examination. However, as a general guideline, TE can be set at fifty percent (50%) of PM for each particular annual statement line item.

b. Considerations in Changing TE from 50 Percent – There are some typical situations where it is appropriate to set TE at other than 50 percent of PM. In considering these situations, the examiner should be aware of the implicit judgment made when adjusting TE. As TE is increased, the examiner is implying that more risk can be accepted in the related account. This implication follows from the inverse relationship between TE and the extent of the examination procedures: The higher the TE, the smaller the sample size. Conversely, the lower the TE, the larger the sample size.

A higher TE also may be appropriate to use when the test's purpose is to detect errors that would result in balance sheet reclassifications (e.g., misclassification of investments or policyholder deposits).

The examiner may wish to increase the nature or extent of the examination procedures in initial examinations or in examining the recently acquired operations of a company. Reducing TE in these situations is appropriate because the examiner would not have any experience on which to base expectation of errors.

As a result of setting TE at 50 percent of PM, there will likely be various account balances that fall below the indicated threshold of tolerable error. For such accounts, the examiner should consider performing minimum procedures to detect inappropriate statutory accounting treatment, obvious errors and regulatory violations. Such procedures would entail one or a combination of the following:

(1) Obtain an understanding of the account's use;
(2) Perform a cursory review of the account's activity for the preceding 12 months for unusual transactions; and
(3) Perform analytical review procedures to test the reasonableness of the account balance.

7. Specific Risk Analysis (SRA)

The initial draft of SRA workpapers should be started specifying work to be accomplished for each material financial statement account and the scope of that work. Work should be defined on a general basis with emphasis on the scope of work to be completed.

The SRA workpapers are a key component of documentation to be completed in the final planning stages of an examination. The document's purpose is to comprehensively and concisely detail the examination risk associated with each material financial statement caption and the related examination procedures required given the level of risk involved. The document prepared should link the information obtained and documented in other planning forms with the EIC's final assessment of the specific examination procedures to be completed on the examination.

An overview of the preparation of the SRA workpapers is as follows:

a. All of the material financial statement account descriptions and balances should be included and addressed. An important early consideration will be to determine how many specific risk analyses to prepare in a given situation. For example, in evaluating the adequacy of property/casualty loss reserves, one such analysis may suffice. Alternatively, the company's business may consist of several distinctly different blocks of business, operated with fundamentally different management techniques, and thus, very different risk profiles. In this situation, several different risk analyses may be helpful in focusing an examination effort on these blocks of business with greater risk.

   Another common situation is in a multi-company environment where different subsidiaries write similar business using essentially identical systems and management. In this situation, one SRA may be sufficient to evaluate examination risks for each such company involved.

   The number of SRA cycles completed and the extent of substantive testing will be determined by the examiner's risk assessment, which should be thoroughly documented in the SRA workpapers. Through the risk assessment, the examiner determines which cycles are significant as related to the major transaction cycles and material accounts within those cycles. However, if certain SRA cycles are not completed the examiner is required to document, in a memorandum to the file, the basis for this risk assessment and lack of substantive testing.

b. The examiner should identify the risks associated with the accounts. Risk characteristics represent the examiner's evaluation and assessment of the specific risks associated with each material statutory financial statement account. This risk is based on the inherent risks of the account together with risks specific to the company's internal control environment and/or business. Once identified, a risk characteristic should be evaluated as to whether it increases or decreases overall account risk.

   Inherent risks exist because of the nature of the account. For example, cash and short-term investments may have a relatively low inherent risk because of their ease of valuation. Alternatively, inadequate internal controls increase control risk associated with such liquid assets because of increased accessibility.

   Specific risks are those which, due to the unique operations of the company or nature of business being written, either increase or decrease the potential risk of the account.

   Mitigating Controls – The examiner should identify the controls in place at the company or the examination work that may mitigate risk.

   Risk Assessment (High, Medium, Low) – Risk assessment represents the final overall risk rating assigned by the EIC on the account description based on the completion of the previous analysis. The rating given will determine the nature and extent of work to be performed for each material statutory account and SRA cycle.

The overall risk assessment is a matter of professional judgment, and is not merely an exercise in summing or weighing the inherent, control, and/or detection risks. The fundamental principle involved is to focus examination effort where risk is increased. For example, a low-risk assessment might be assigned to recording of investments because of excellent controls and systems, whereas a medium or high-risk assessment might be assigned to investment valuation because of the extent of investments in private placements or CMOs.

c. Work to be Performed and Scope – The examiner should note in the SRA the significant specific work to be performed on each account during the examination. Work included should reflect the overall risk rating for each caption. This should not be an exhaustive listing of work to be performed, but rather the significant tests and the scopes of those tests (e.g., dollar coverage of receivable confirmation). The examiner-in-charge should then utilize their assessment as a basis for developing detailed work programs that define examination procedures and assign work by experience levels.

8. Analytical Review

Analytical review involves the study and comparison of relationships among data at a point in time and the trend in those relationships over periods of time. Based on an understanding of a company's business, the examiner develops certain expectations about important financial and operating relationships. Analytical review results that support these expectations increase the level of confidence and may lead to examination efficiencies by changing the nature of our tests or by reducing the extent of other procedures. Conversely, analytical review results that differ from expectations should increase overall skepticism and may require additional procedures to explain significant variations from expectations.

The overall analytical review is used during the initial planning phase to help understand the impact of changes in environmental factors and to provide a preliminary indication of the company's overall financial condition, including areas that might require emphasis. The detail analytical review, which generally is performed in the program development phase, is more comprehensive than the overall analytical review and is directed to individual accounts or classes of transactions affected by specific audit objectives. In the program execution phase, analytical review procedures can be the primary direct test of an account balance or class of transactions, or they can be used in combination with other direct tests to support the reasonableness of annual statement amounts. The extent to which these analytical review procedures can be substituted for, or can reduce other procedures, will depend on the quality of the evidence (i.e., persuasive, corroborative, or minimal) obtained from the analytical review procedures. At or near the conclusion of an examination, the analytical review is used to assess the overall reasonableness of the financial statements. Exhibit E summarizes the use of analytical review procedures. A sample analytical review template is also provided for the examiner in Exhibit E.

To maximize effectiveness and efficiency, the examiner should select only those relationships that will assist in drawing meaningful conclusions. In designing analytical review procedures, the same procedure often can be used to achieve different examination objectives. A procedure used in one phase to identify potential problems also could be used to help determine the reasonableness of the balance. The uses of analytical review procedures are limited only by the availability of reliable information and by creativity.

During initial planning, analytical review procedures are directed toward overall financial condition and profitability rather than specific accounts. These procedures are directed toward identifying such things as (1) changes in profitability trends; (2) deterioration in asset quality, liquidity, or capital adequacy; (3) changes in investment strategies; and (4) changes in key annual statement balances.

An overall analytical review of annual statement amounts and relationships is one way to update the examiner's understanding of external and internal factors that influence the environment in which the company operates. Among other things, this review should focus attention on significant environmental pressures. An example of an environmental pressure would be changes in levels of overall interest rates and corresponding deficiency reserve considerations for interest-sensitive products. Asking management to respond to such conditions is a significant part of the review process. These analyses should assist in identifying the overall potential for examination problems and in developing the examination plan.

Types of Analytical Review Procedures:

a. Comparisons to Prior Periods

Analysis of a company's financial characteristics and operating results over a period of time provides information useful in evaluating operating performance and assessing expected current-year financial condition and results of operations. Two-year comparisons (e.g., a comparative analysis of current and prior-year operating expenses) may be sufficient to identify changes requiring follow-up with the company. However, comparisons over a number of years (i.e., trend analysis) often can be more informative. Therefore, comparisons of certain key financial statement amounts, ratios and other relationships should cover a three to five year period. To obtain the most benefit from the comparisons, they should be made by line of business. In addition, the comparisons related to results of operations should be made using comparable periods.

Many factors can affect comparisons. For example, changes in price levels or the overall industry trend (growth or decline) may distort comparisons between periods. Therefore, annual statement comparisons should include both dollar amounts and percentage of total assets and income statement classifications as a percentage of total premiums. Financial statements presenting only percentage relationships (sometimes called "common-size statements") can provide a quick indication of fluctuations and trends that may require further investigation or explanation.

When making comparisons over a period of years, trends may be distorted by significant non-recurring events or transactions. Factors that may affect interperiod comparability include:

(1) Changes in product design, customers, marketing strategy or capitalization;
(2) Disposal or acquisition of a line of business;
(3) Accounting changes or account reclassifications;
(4) Unusual charges or credits to operations; and
(5) Significant reinsurance transactions.

The examiner should understand the effects of such events in performing and evaluating trend analysis and in developing expectations about the company's financial data.

b. Comparisons to Budgets or Forecasts

Comparisons of actual operating results to budget or forecasted amounts often can provide important analytical review evidence. However, before making budget or forecast comparisons and investigating variances, the examiner should understand the company's budget or forecast preparation process and the significant underlying assumptions. For example, if the budgetary process includes a study of both present and past operating experience of the company and of general and industry economic conditions, and if past budgets have proven to be realistic, comparison to budgeted amounts can be useful. But if budgets are simply motivational tools (i.e., "stretch goals" rather than management's best estimates) or historically have been prepared inadequately, they may be subject to large variances. In these cases, comparisons with budgets for analytical review purposes should be limited.

Certain components of the annual statement lend themselves more readily to budget comparisons. Examples are investment income and general and administrative expenses. Other financial information such as benefits and claims are influenced by factors difficult to quantify when preparing a budget.

When budgets or forecasts are used in performing analytical review procedures, the examiner should (1) compare them to prior years' operating results and to the current year's financial information, and (2) analyze major revisions made to them during the year.

c. Comparisons to Industry and Competitor Data

Comparisons of annual statement amounts and relationships for the company or its segments to competitor or industry statistics can facilitate an understanding of the company's business environment by showing the impact on the company of emerging trends or structural changes in the industry. By highlighting the company's financial performance relative to the industry, these comparisons also help to identify areas requiring attention on areas where procedures may be limited. Comparisons can be performed by identifying peer groups of companies with similar characteristics and comparing the company's performance to the group, or by comparing the company to industry averages.

An industry average is not a "magic number" indicating ideal or even acceptable performance. However, industry statistics can serve as effective benchmarks for evaluating a company's operations. Therefore, significant variances from industry norms may indicate problems and should be understood. Industry comparisons can identify possible examination problems or management concerns.

While comparisons to industry statistics can provide useful information, the data must be comparable. Meaningful comparisons can be difficult for a variety of reasons, including the fact that each company has unique characteristics, such as product design, target customers, location, corporate structure and capitalization. The variability of industry data does not mean that comparisons with industry norms will not be useful. On the contrary, their principle value may be the questions they raise. However, the examiner should always use judgment in selecting industry data for analytical review purposes, and in evaluating the comparisons. In using peer group comparisons, it is important to select insurance companies that are comparable in size, financial structure, locality and market emphasis (e.g., lines of business) because those factors will affect performance indicators.

While caution should be used, comparisons between peer companies may be useful in determining the aggressiveness or conservatism of the company's investment policies, tax practices and pricing strategies.

An abundance of statistical information exists for the insurance industry. Several industry publications, most notably *Best's Insurance Management Reports* and *Best's Review*, provide certain comparative and pooled statistics. (See "Regulatory Analytical Review" in this part.)

d. Use of Analytical Review in Specific Risk Analysis

While the overall analytical review procedures emphasize general financial condition and trends, the detail analytical review procedures are directed to specific accounts and transactions. The primary purpose is to obtain comfort that the numbers "make sense" in view of the examiner's understanding of the company's operations and evaluation of the accounting system. These procedures usually are performed concurrently with the system evaluation. To determine the reasons for unexpected fluctuations, it may be necessary to investigate the details of specific transactions that constitute an account balance.

The results of detail analytical review procedures may confirm and quantify expected problems (e.g., as a result of certain environmental considerations or inadequate controls noted), or they may indicate that problems are not as significant as expected. Thus, the results of the detail analytical review may decrease the amount of work indicated by the interaction of other inputs to the Specific Risk Analysis or result in an expansion of planned effort.

The difference in focus between overall and detail analytical review is in (1) the nature of the information used, (2) the extent of comparisons, and (3) the period covered by those comparisons, as illustrated in the following table:

	Overall	**Detail**
Information	"Top-level" interim financial statements and overall financial and operating ratios	Various levels of detail (line of business)
Extent of Comparisons	Comparisons of annual statement line items	Details of annual statement line items (e.g., Annual Statement Expense Exhibits)
Period Covered	Year-to-year comparisons and trends over a three to five year period	Quarter-to-quarter month-to-month comparison of current and prior year activity

For many examinations, the difference between the overall and the detail analytical review is not always clear-cut. As a practical matter, the overall and the detail analytical review often are performed at the same time. For example, various ratios are analyzed during initial planning to make a preliminary assessment of the company's financial condition (i.e., overall analytical review evidence). Because those ratios also apply to specific accounts, observations about fluctuations or trends also will provide input to the SRA for the related specific objectives (i.e., detail analytical review evidence).

Operating relationships that could be used in the detail analytical review for each specific objective are included in Exhibit E. Judgment should be used in selecting detail analytical review relationships; some procedures will not be helpful. Each detail analytical review procedure should provide useful evidence that will help (1) assess the likelihood of material error for the accounts or transactions affected by the specific objective, and (2) develop efficient procedures based on the SRA that are responsive to our assessment of risk for a particular examination area.

e. Analytical Review Procedures as Direct Tests

Direct tests fall into three categories – (1) analytical review procedures, (2) tests of key items, and (3) tests of representative samples. Judgment is used to determine the most effective and efficient combination of those tests responsive to the assessment of the likelihood of material error. This section discusses analytical review procedures as direct tests of balances, and provides guidance on the level of persuasiveness and the need to test the underlying data.

Analytical review procedures may be used (1) as primary direct tests of balances, (2) as corroborative tests in combination with other procedures, or (3) to provide at least some minimal level of support for conclusions. Analytical review procedures provide an efficient alternative to detail tests of account balances and allow the examiner to consider whether the numbers make sense in view of expectations. In some cases, analytical review procedures may effectively be used as the only test.

As a first step in planning, the examiner should consider what analytical review procedures are available. The extent to which analytical review procedures can be substituted for, or can reduce other procedures, will depend on the persuasiveness of the analytical review procedures.

Analytical review procedures can be the primary direct test, i.e., the primary basis for conclusions, if they provide persuasive evidence. That would be the case if the procedures generate an amount believed to be a reasonable estimate of the account balance and is consistent with expectations.

Analytical review procedures provide corroborative evidence if they (1) confirm findings from other tests and (2) support management's representations, or otherwise decrease the level of skepticism. Corroborative analytical review procedures cannot serve as the primary basis for a conclusion that an account balance or class of transactions is free of material error.

Analytical review procedures that do not provide persuasive evidence and provide only limited corroborative evidence contribute only minimal support for conclusions. In deciding whether a particular analytical review procedure or combination of procedures provides corroborative evidence or only minimal support for conclusions, the examiner should evaluate both the extent of analytical review procedures and the quality of the evidence expected to be obtained. For example, if the examiner simply compares a current year overall balance (e.g., reserves) to the prior-year balance, and does not supplement that comparison with any other analytical review procedures (e.g., lapses, cash surrenders, new issues, loss ratios, premium volume), the examiner would obtain only minimal support for a conclusion.

Analytical review procedures might provide different levels of persuasiveness for different companies. To illustrate, the SRA for the examination objective "accrued and unearned income on real estate are recorded correctly as to account, amount and period" might indicate a low likelihood of material error. If a company has a stable real estate portfolio, a comparison of the current year accrual to the prior year accrual may provide corroborative evidence if the rental or lease rates have not changed. If the portfolio is constantly changing, a comparison of the current year to the prior year will provide only minimal evidence.

f. Evaluating Analytical Review Results

An understanding of the company's business may identify likely fluctuations in the financial data. These fluctuations may be caused by (1) trends – general changes in business conditions; (2) seasonal patterns – changes in business activity caused by weather or other seasonal changes; (3) cycle patterns – changes in overall economic activity; or (4) dependent relationships – changes related to movements in other financial data.

Fluctuations that cannot be explained from knowledge of the company's business or by known relationships with other financial data may result from non-recurring transactions, erroneous accounting procedures or practices, or other factors. When unexpected significant fluctuations in amounts or key relationships occur, or when expected ones do not, the examiner should find out why. Initial follow-up procedures should include discussions with operating executives and financial management. Management may have already determined the cause of the variations, or if not, may save time by pursuing these matters. The examiner should challenge the reasonableness of management explanations in view of the examiner's understanding of the business and the examiner's expectations.

g. Examples of Analytical Review Procedures

Examples of detail analytical review procedures that can be used in the Specific Risk Analysis and/or as direct tests of balances are discussed below. The examiner should consider analytical review information that has already been prepared by management. Examples include exhibits, charts, graphs and similar analyses included in the company's internal management reports, board reports, divisions or line of business statistics, and similar documents. The key is not to calculate all the ratios possible, but to identify those few key relationships that best satisfy the examiners' objective of substantiating or corroborating the account balance. When deciding whether to incorporate analytical review procedures into the examination program as direct tests of balances, the examiner should consider the extent to which the underlying data should be tested. This is discussed in the next section.

- Operating Results – Life and A&H

Life and A&H premium revenues change as a result of changes in premium rates, volume of risks insured, and extent of coverage per risk insured. Life insurance benefits paid change primarily because of better-or-worse-than expected mortality or surrender experience. A&H loss ratios change as a result of changes in both the incidence and severity of claims.

One measure of life and A&H operating results is the relationship of benefits paid and provided to premium income. Benefits paid and provided can be broken down into various components, depending on the line of business involved. For ordinary life and A&H, these components can be (1) increases in reserves as a percent of premiums and (2) claims incurred as a percent of premiums. Credit life and A&H business is measured by the ratio of claims incurred to premiums earned. Group life and A&H insurance also are measured by this ratio.

Several analytical ratios and relationships can be used to measure the operating results of life and A&H insurance. The ratios and relationships should be prepared by line of business and compared with prior years and, if available, comparable industry data. Examples of some of the more common ratios and relationships include:

(1) Life Insurance

- Prior year total premiums to current year renewal premiums
- Average first-year premiums per policy to average renewal premiums for flexible premium and universal life business
- Benefits paid or provided to premium income
- Claims incurred to premium income
- Cash surrender expense to premium income
- Policyholder dividends to participating premium income and income before dividends to policyholders
- Commission expense to premium income, by first year and renewal business
- General and administrative expenses to premium income
- Premium taxes to premium income
- Investment income to total income
- Investment expenses to investment income

(2) A&H Insurance

- Benefits paid or provided to premium income
- Benefits paid or provided to prior year reserves
- Increase in reserves to premium income
- Claims incurred to premium income
- Commission expense to premium income
- General and administrative expenses to premium income
- Premium taxes to premium income
- Investment income to total income
- Investment expenses to investment income

- Policy Benefits Reserves

In addition to the various ratios and relationships that may be used to analyze operating results, various carry forward schedules and comparative analyses can be used as direct tests of balances or to help support the reasonableness of ordinary life and annuity benefit reserves. Some of the most common ratios and relationships include:

(1) Reserves per $1,000 of in force by line of business and/or significant product; and

(2) Dividend expense per $1,000 of participating in force by line of business and/or significant product.

- Claim Reserves

In addition to the various ratios that may be used to analyze operating results, the following relationships may be used to help support the reasonableness of A&H claim reserves.

(1) Claim reserves (current year to prior years)
(2) Claim reserves to premium income or annualized premiums
(3) Claim incurred to claim reserves
(4) Average claim reserves (current year to prior years)
(5) Average paid claim severity (current year to prior years)
(6) Average paid claim severity to average claim reserves (year-to-year changes in this ratio measure whether reserve level increases correspond to current severity increases)
(7) Historical development of the adequacy of claim reserves

- Underwriting Results – Property/Casualty

A commonly used measurement of property/casualty underwriting results is the "combined ratio," that is, the ratio of losses, loss adjustment expenses and underwriting expenses to premiums. (All general and administrative expenses, other than those allocated to investment operations, are considered underwriting expenses.) The combined ratio is further broken down into two components – the loss ratio and the underwriting expense ratio.

The loss ratio includes both losses and loss expenses incurred as a percentage of premiums earned. The underwriting expense ratio is underwriting expenses incurred to premiums earned. On a statutory basis, the ratio is statutory underwriting expenses incurred to premiums written. GAAP and statutory underwriting expenses differ in that under GAAP, acquisition expenses are deferred and amortized as the related premiums are earned. Under statutory accounting, acquisition expenses are charged as expenses when incurred.

(1) Loss Ratios

The loss ratio changes from period to period because of changes in the relationship between losses and premiums. Losses change as a result of changes in exposures, frequency and severity-of-loss occurrences. Changes in loss adjustment expense levels also affect the loss ratio. Premiums change because of changes in premium rates, in the volume of risks insured and in the extent of exposure per risk insured. Several analytical relationships exist between losses and premiums and their components. Particular effort should be made to obtain these statistics by accident year, if available, to eliminate the distortion of revisions in reserve estimates of prior years. These analytical relationships include:

- Number of claims reported to number of earned exposure units. (This relationship measures loss frequency. For many lines of business, a suitable basis for measuring earned exposure units may not exist. For these lines of business, some other suitable measure of exposure may be substituted.) An "exposure unit" is generally defined as the subject of the insurance coverage. For example, in the case of auto insurance, the exposure unit would be a vehicle or automobile that presents certain risks to the automobile's owner, which risks are mitigated by, among other means, procuring insurance coverage. An "earned exposure unit" is an exposure unit for which coverage is in force for an entire policy year. If a policy is in force for only a fractional year, a fractional earned exposure unit would be recorded based on the portion of the year the policy is in force. When premiums are stated on a unit basis, the effects of changes in premium rates are eliminated, and exposure is presented on a comparable basis. However, a reasonable unit measure of exposure does not exist for many lines of business.

- Average premiums written or earned per policy or per exposure unit.
- In force policies stratified by policy limits. (This is a useful indicator of changing levels of exposure for lines of business for which the calculation can be made.)
- Historical loss development data. (This provides information as to whether the company has historically provided adequate reserves for losses; it can be useful in evaluating the adequacy of current reserves. However, the data is useful only when proper consideration is given to current circumstances affecting loss reserves (e.g., premium rate increases, changes in policy coverage, inflation, etc.).)
- Losses incurred per earned exposure unit. (This relationship measures the "pure premium," the portion of the premium required to cover losses. Again, exposure unit data may not be available for all lines of business.)
- Average loss reserve. (When related to average loss reserves in prior periods, this ratio serves as a current measure of comparative loss reserve adequacy.)
- Average paid claim severity.
- Average paid claim severity to average loss reserve. (On a comparative basis, this ratio measures whether reserve level increases have corresponded with current paid severity increases.)
- Losses incurred to loss reserves. (This ratio measures how rapidly loss reserve levels are changing in relation to loss volume.)
- IBNR loss reserves to various measures of exposure to loss (premiums earned, exposure units earned, premiums written, premiums in force, losses incurred, claims reported, etc.). The ratio measures comparative IBNR reserve adequacy.
- Loss Adjustment expense (LAE) reserves to loss reserves.
- Allocated LAE paid to losses paid.
- Unallocated LAE paid to losses paid.

These relationships can provide some indication of the adequacy of loss reserves. If these relationships are reasonable in view of the examiner's expectations, the extent of loss reserve projections may be minimized. Further, the results of these detail analytical review procedures may aid in the selection of reserve projection methods for direct tests of the reserves (e.g., severity projection method may be selected if average severity shows large fluctuations).

(2) Underwriting Expense Ratios

The underwriting expense ratios change from period to period because of a change in the relationship between underwriting expenses and premiums. A significant portion of underwriting expenses is made up of costs that vary directly with premiums (e.g., commissions and premium taxes). Other costs, principally salaries, may be fixed or semi-fixed. The ratio of these other costs to premiums may also vary as premium levels fluctuate.

Various analytical ratios can be used to review the reasonableness of the relationships between underwriting expenses and written, earned and unearned premiums. These include:

- Commissions to premiums (This ratio can be measured based on either statutory commission expense to premiums written or GAAP commission expense to premiums earned. For most companies, separate calculations of this ratio should be made by line of business for direct, assumed, and ceded business.)
- Commissions netted against agents' balances to agents' balances (Agents' balances are recorded net of the related commissions due to the agents. The amount of commissions netted, if available, should be compared to the grossed-up amount of agents' balances. The resulting ratio should be compared to the ratio of commission expense to premiums.)
- Premium taxes to premiums written (This ratio is a measure of statutory premium tax expense to premiums written. In the absence of a significant shift in the mix of business or in premium tax rates or taxability, this ratio should be quite stable from period to period.)
- Unearned premium reserve to in-force premiums and unearned premium reserve to written premiums (These ratios are measures of the unexpired portion of premiums to total premium volume.)

Four other ratios relate to underwriting and, more specifically, to premiums receivable or agents' balances:

- Agents' or premium balances charged off to premiums written;
- Agents' or premium balances charged off to premiums earned;
- Premium or agent receivables to in-force premiums; and
- Aging of premium or agent receivables. (These ratios will take on varying significance in different situations. Often, premium collection problems and bad debts are minimal because premiums are collected in advance of providing the policy coverage. However, if an insured has paid the premium to an agent of the company, the company must provide coverage even if the agent does not transmit premiums to the company. Therefore, the reliability of agents is of concern.)

(3) Reinsurance

For companies that assume significant amounts of reinsurance, analytical schedules that summarize significant balance sheet and income statement accounts by each major treaty allow analysis of the underwriting results assumed under each major treaty. Their results should be compared with expectations developed through an understanding of the related treaty and environmental considerations.

(4) Investments

In addition to various ratios that may be used to analyze operating results, the following ratios may be used to measure investment operations:

- Individual investment asset categories to total assets (These relationships can be an important indicator of a company's investment philosophy and liquidity, and a key to evaluating a company's compliance with statutory investment limitations.)
- Investment yield – in total and by investment category (This ratio can be based on investment income to average invested assets, in total and by investment category. This ratio can be an important indicator of profit margins on interest-sensitive products and an overall indicator of investment performance.)
- Bond maturity schedule (This may be an important indicator of liquidity – especially for companies in a weak cash flow position.)
- Ratio of market to book value of stocks (This is basically a measure of stock market performance. When the ratio differs from expectations based on overall market trends, further investigation is warranted.)

h. Regulatory Analytical Reviews

The NAIC has developed a series of ratios and trends intended to identify insurance companies that have a statistically high probability of insolvency. The ratios are used to identify companies that require additional analytical review or inquiry by insurance department analysts. If a company has four or more ratios outside the standard range, it becomes subject to further analytical reviews to determine if immediate attention or supervision is required. Manuals describing the IRIS ratios are available from the NAIC.

i. Testing Underlying Data Used In Analytical Review

When should the examiner test the underlying data used in analytical review procedures? It is not necessary to test the data used in overall and detail analytical reviews during initial planning and program development. These reviews are only to increase the examiner's understanding of the company's business, provide a basis for developing examination scope, and identify areas that require further investigation. However, if the analytical review procedures are to be persuasive and be the primary direct test of a balance, the reliability of the data being used must be tested.

If analytical review procedures are used to corroborate the results of other procedures, judgment should be used in determining the need for, or the extent of, tests of the underlying data. Operating data generated independently of the accounting system may not need to be tested as extensively as data generated by the accounting system. The examiner also should keep in mind that computer generated data used in corroborative analytical review procedures may need to be tested to avoid unwarranted reliance on the computer.

j. Final Overall Annual Statement Review

The examiner should perform a final overall review of the annual statement near the conclusion of fieldwork. If the examiner identifies any key trends or relationships that do not make sense based on the examiner's understanding of the business, the examiner should obtain explanations and, if necessary, perform additional procedures.

9. Internal Control and Compliance Testing

A preliminary assessment of the overall internal control environment should be made during the initial planning stage. Management's attitude and understanding of internal controls is the initial requirement in an effective control environment. An evaluation of internal controls relating to each transaction cycle is an important component of the risk assessment for each cycle. The focus of this evaluation is to identify weaknesses in the system of controls that may contribute to the risk of a material financial statement error occurring and failing detection. Making such an assessment is the principal step in designing an effective examination program. Evaluation of internal controls in this context should be performed whether or not reliance on internal controls is contemplated. In addition, an evaluation of good internal controls is not sufficient to establish reliance and thereby reduce the amount of substantive testing. Compliance testing must be performed if reliance on internal controls is planned.

Although examinations to determine solvency of the company are performed emphasizing a balance sheet approach, understanding and testing the internal control structure may be necessary to obtain comfort on significant accounts and transactions. Specifically, high-volume, low-dollar transactions are difficult to test substantively. Analytical review and compliance work are helpful in these situations. The insurance operations contain several significant areas of high-volume, low-dollar transactions which should be addressed: premiums, claims processing and expenditure, or cash disbursements.

Internal control testing is required to be completed by the examiner during examination fieldwork. Consideration should be given to work performed by the CPA auditor to minimize work completed. If reliance on the CPA workpapers is utilized, some testing should also be performed by the examiner to further substantiate whether controls are adequate and effectively operating. This can be in the form of testing the work performed by the CPA, original testing, or a combination thereof. Testing and scopes should be determined based upon materiality of the account and the risk of insolvency of a company. A low or medium risk company may require as little as a memorandum covering controls and a walk through of controls to ensure they are operating effectively. The EIC or supervisor should be contacted for scopes. The intent of such compliance work is to minimize substantive testing.

In each SRA, there is a dedicated section to internal control testing. Internal control procedural questionnaires are provided for the examiner in each SRA cycle. These questionnaires help facilitate the examiner's review and evaluation of control risk for each examination objective. These questionnaires should be completed for all applicable SRA cycles. If the examiner determines that internal control testing need not be completed for a particular cycle, the examiner must document the basis for this assessment within the SRA cycle. It is highly recommended that the examiner complete the internal control procedures themselves or leverage off the work of the independent auditors. However, if company personnel assist in the completion of the internal control questionnaires, and the examiner relies on the internal control procedures when determining the extent and nature of the examination procedures, the examiner must perform additional procedures to substantiate the integrity of these responses.

a. The controls within the SRA questionnaire are grouped into the following objectives:

(1) Authorization – All transactions recorded were reviewed and approved by designated personnel;
(2) Completeness – All transactions that occurred are initially entered into the accounting records, accepted for processing, and generated data files and reports reflect that all transactions have occurred;
(3) Accuracy – Transactions are initially recorded correctly, timely, and accurately; and
(4) Asset Protection – Adequate safeguards over access to and use of assets and records, including the appropriate segregation of duties among company personnel.

b. Testing should be sufficient to obtain comfort that the control is adequate and functioning properly.

The presence of computer processing in the accounting system usually has a significant impact on the examiner's evaluation. Computer-generated data and reports may form the basis for recorded annual statement balances. The accuracy of this information depends on the programs and the data files from which they are produced. Accordingly, an evaluation should consider the elements of internal control in a computerized accounting system, including general controls over development of and changes to computer programs and data file access, and application controls over the results of computer processing. See Exhibit C: Evaluation of Controls in Information Systems (IS) Questionnaire for a sample template to begin testing computer controls.

10. The Use of SAS 70 Reports

(a) SAS 70 Overview

Many insurance companies use non-affiliated organizations to perform such services as data processing or claims processing. As part of the planning process for a financial statement audit or examination of an insurer that uses a third party service provider, the auditor or examiner should consider the internal control environment at this service organization. The Statement on Auditing Standards (SAS) No. 70, *Service Organizations* can assist the auditor or examiner in gaining an understanding of the internal control environment of the service provider.

SAS 70 is an internationally recognized auditing standard developed by the American Institute of Certified Public Accountants (AICPA). The SAS 70 standard provides guidance to enable an independent auditor to issue an opinion on an organization's description of controls. The standard does not include pre-determined control objectives or control activities that organizations must achieve. It is designed to provide information about the service organization's internal control environment to user organizations and user auditors. One of the most effective ways an organization can communicate information about its controls is through a Service Auditor's Report (often referred to as a SAS 70 Report). A SAS 70 audit or examination report signifies that an audit has been performed on a service organization's control objectives and control activities. A SAS 70 report allows organizations to disclose information about their control processes to their customers and their customer's auditors in a uniform format.

When discussing SAS 70 reports, it is important to be familiar with the following terms:

- User organization – The entity that has engaged a service organization and whose financial statements are being audited. In the context of this Handbook, the user organization would be the insurer.
- User auditor – The auditor who reports on the financial statements of the user organization. In the context of this Handbook, the user auditor could be the insurer's independent CPA and/or the state regulator.
- Service organization – The entity (or segment of an entity) that provides services to a user organization that are part of the user organization's information system.
- Service auditor – The auditor who reports on controls of a service organization that may be relevant to a user organization's internal control as it relates to an audit of financial statements.

A service organization may provide services ranging from performing specific tasks, such as maintaining custody of marketable securities, to replacing entire departments. Examples of service organizations are:

- Data processing organizations that perform services such as payroll, billing, general ledger accounting and other administrative functions;
- Trust departments of financial service companies;
- Mortgage loan services; and
- Organizations providing services for employee benefit plans, such as investment management, custody of investments, record keeping of employee or participant data, processing employee benefit claims and other accounting or administrative functions.

These services are typically found with companies that operate either exclusively, or to more than a minor extent, through MGA and/or TPA relationships.

(b) When to use a SAS 70 Report

The SAS 70 standard provides guidance for auditing an entity when an organization's services are part of the user organization's controls. A service organization is part of an insurer's controls if it affects any of the following:

- How the user organization's transactions are initiated;
- The accounting records, supporting information and specific accounts in the financial statements involved in the processing and reporting of the user organization transactions;
- The accounting processing involved from the initiation of the transactions to their inclusion in the financial statements; or
- The financial reporting process used to prepare the user organization's financial statements, including significant accounting estimates and disclosures.

The significance of the service organization's controls depends primarily on the nature and materiality of the transactions it processes for the user organization and the degree of interaction between its activities and those of the user organization. Generally, the user can identify relevant controls at an organization by reading the auditor's SAS 70 report. SAS 70 reports can be classified as a Type I or a Type II report. Information about the operating effectiveness of the controls at the organization are only included in a Type II report.

(c) SAS 70 Reports

A SAS 70 audit can only be performed by an independent certified public accountant (CPA). The auditor is generally a control-oriented professional who has experience in accounting, auditing, and information security. There are two types of SAS 70 Reports: Type I and Type II.

i) Type I SAS 70 Report

A Type I SAS 70 report describes the organization's controls at a specific point in time and includes the independent auditor's report (i.e., opinion). The auditor will express an opinion on (1) whether the organization's description of controls present the relevant aspects of the organization's actual controls in operation as of a specific date, and (2) whether the controls were suitably designed to achieve specified controls objectives.

A Type I SAS 70 report could be helpful in providing a sufficient understanding to plan the audit of the user organization. Such a report, however, is not intended to provide any evidence of the operating effectiveness of the relevant controls that would allow the user auditor to reduce the assessed level of control risk below the maximum. Since no tests were performed on the controls, no reliance can be placed on a Type I report and therefore does not satisfy the needs of outside external auditors or state regulators.

ii) Type II SAS 70 Report

A Type II SAS 70 report not only includes the organization's description of controls and auditor's opinion, but also includes detailed testing of the organization's controls over a minimum of six months. The auditor will express an opinion on the same items noted in a Type I report, and (3) whether the controls that were tested were operating with sufficient effectiveness to provide reasonable, but not absolute, assurance that the control objectives were achieved during the period specified.

The Type II SAS 70 report is the report that should be requested and obtained by state regulators. Since testing of controls has been performed, state regulators may decide to place reliance on the report and reduce testing of internal controls. It should be noted that the state regulator remains responsible for evaluating the evidence presented by the service auditor and for determining its effect on the assessment of control risk at the service organization. The user auditor's assessment of control risk is based on the combined evidence provided by the service auditor's report and the user auditor's own procedures.

The following chart identifies the key components of Type I and Type II reports:

Report Content		Type I	Type II
1.	Independent service auditor's report (opinion)	Included	Included
2.	Organization's description of controls	Included	Included
3.	Information provided by the independent service auditor: includes a description of the service auditor's tests of operating effectiveness and the results of those tests	Optional	Included

(d) SAS 70 Report Section Contents

SAS 70 reports are generally divided into three or four sections depending upon the type of report:

i) Independent auditor's report (i.e. opinion)

ii) Organization's description of controls

iii) Information provided by the service auditor

iv) Other information provided by the organization

Each of these sections are described below:

i) Independent Auditor's Report (Opinion)

This report is characteristically a one to two page letter from the independent auditors to the management of the organization. The language of the opinion generally follows explicit guidelines as determined by the AICPA. The opinion describes the auditor's approach and the scope of the audit. An important item to look for is the date the controls were evaluated and the date(s) the controls were placed into operation.

Components of the Independent Auditor's Report for Type I and Type II reports:

Opinion	Type I	Type II
Whether the organization's description of controls presents fairly, in all material respects, the relevant aspects of the organization's controls that had been placed in operation as of a specific date.	Included	Included
Whether the controls were suitably designed to achieve the specific control objectives.	Included	Included
Whether the controls that were tested were operating with sufficient effectiveness to provide reasonable, but not absolute, assurance that the control objectives were achieved during the period specified.	Not Included	Included

ii) Organization's Description of Controls

The organization's description of controls is the responsibility of the organization. In many cases, the auditor will assist the organization in preparing the descriptions. The description of controls should generally contain the following information:

- Aspects of the organization's control environment; risk assessment process; information and communication process; and monitoring processes that may affect the services provided to user organizations, as it relates to an audit of financial statements;

- Control objectives and related controls; and

- Complimentary controls that may be required at user organizations.

Most of the above items are presented in a narrative format accompanied by flowcharts or diagrams to illustrate the control activities. The organization may also provide background information on the services they provide and the type of processing environment they maintain.

iii) Information Provided by the Service Auditor

This section of the SAS 70 report features a description of the auditor's tests of operating effectiveness of controls and the results of those tests. The following elements should be included in the description:

- The controls tested;

- The objectives the controls were designed to achieve; and

- An indication of the nature, timing, extent and the results of the tests supplied in sufficient detail to enable user auditors to determine the effect of such tests on their assessment of control risk. In evaluating these factors, user auditors should also keep in mind that, for certain assumptions, the shorter the period covered by a specific test and the longer the time elapsed since the performance of the test, the less support of control risk reduction the test may provide.

This information is only presented in a Type II report. Because the report may be intended to satisfy the needs of several different user auditors, a user auditor should determine whether the specific tests of controls and results in the service auditor's report are relevant to assertions that are significant in the user organization's financial statements.

The service auditor may also provide recommendations for improving the organization's controls in this section of the report.

iv) Other Information Provided by the Organization

An organization may want to present other information that is not part of the description of controls. This type of information would be included in a separate section and would not be covered by the auditor's opinion.

(e) Considerations in using SAS 70 Reports

Examination use of this report falls into three general categories:

i. Improve understanding of the servicing entity's role and the impact of its internal controls on the insurer's operations. Note: this review may lead to further inquiries regarding the insurer's ability to manage the risk posed by utilizing a servicing entity.

ii. Evaluating the report's sufficiency to meet examination objectives regarding the adequacy of internal control design and effectiveness testing.

iii. Assessing the external auditor's use (and reliance) of the report within their audit workpapers to facilitate the examination process.

Contact with the servicing entity's auditor may be considered to better understand the scope and results of the auditor's work. If necessary, the examination team may need to contact the servicing entity to perform additional work regarding specific controls and/or their effectiveness.

11. Consideration of the Work Performed by Independent Auditors

a. Introduction

One of this *Handbook*'s objectives is to develop an efficient risk-based examination approach that provides for more timely detection of potentially troubled insurance companies by focusing examination resources on those companies, or areas within companies, that have a higher likelihood of material adjustment to surplus. Examiners can often, but not always, cnhancc efficiency in the examination through appropriate communications with the company's independent auditor. The extent to which the examiner chooses to consider the work of an independent auditor in performance of the examination is a matter of judgment by the examiner.

This section of the *Handbook* discusses why such communications are helpful, how and when they should be conducted, and documentation considerations. It is important to first have a basic understanding of an independent auditors work, the environment in which the independent auditor operates, and the potential similarities and differences between the audit approach of an independent auditor and of an examiner.

b. Differing Objectives of Examiners and CPAs

Independent auditors, sometimes referred to as Certified Public Accountants or CPAs, may be engaged by their insurance company clients to perform, among other services, independent audits of the company in accordance with generally accepted auditing standards (GAAS) as promulgated by the American Institute of Certified Public Accountants (AICPA). The body of knowledge that constitutes GAAS is set forth in auditing standards and interpretations issued by the AICPA. Such standards state "the objective of the ordinary audit of financial statements by the independent auditor is the expression of an opinion on the fairness with which they present fairly, in all material respects, financial position, results of operations, and its cash flows in conformity with generally accepted accounting principles." In many instances states require that the audit be performed on statutory financial statements in conformity with accounting practices prescribed or permitted by the domiciliary state.

Although there are certain similarities between the objectives of an independent auditor and an examiner, differences may also exist. Depending on the company involved and the nature of the CPA's engagement, such differences may be significant, even in those situations where the CPA is reporting pursuant to a state audit rule that may otherwise minimize such differences by requiring a separate company (as opposed to consolidated) audit report on statutory-basis (as opposed to generally accepted accounting principles, or "GAAP") financial statements. For example:

- The examiner may focus more directly on the balance sheet and, in particular, on reported surplus of the company; CPAs may also focus on the other basic financial statements, namely, the income statement and the cash flow statement.

- The examiner may perform virtually all of the examination work after the financial statement date; CPAs may perform a large portion of their audit work prior to the end of the period under audit, particularly in situations involving publicly traded companies that report to shareholders shortly after year end.

- Also, with respect to the difference in timing of work performed, the examiner may focus on substantive tests of year end reported balances; the CPA may focus on tests of internal controls and systems that produce such balances.

- The examiner may review or test the company's compliance with numerous statutes and regulations, dealing with matters such as limitations on investments and other activities, and matters relating to market conduct; such matters often are not a primary objective of the CPA's audit.

- The examiner will have different tools available to help in attaining certain examination objectives, such as Operation Jumpstart, that can, among other tasks, compare a company's investment portfolio as reported in Schedule D of its annual statement with the NAIC's SVO file for cusip number and market value matches; such tools may not be readily available to CPAs, or not available at the time they are performing audit procedures.

- In situations where the independent accountant has extensively tested and relied on work of the company's internal auditors, the examiner may make similar tests and reliance, albeit focusing on those areas of principal concern to the examiner.

- Perhaps the most pervasive difference of all is professional judgment. Both the examiner and the independent auditor will need to assess the internal and external environmental risks affecting the company (inherent risk), the ability of the company's internal controls to identify and rectify potential material errors in account balances or transactions (control risk), and the adequacy of their respective audit or examination procedures to identify such material errors that may exist (detection risk). How the examiner or independent auditor addresses these issues during an examination or audit, and the resulting impact on their assessment of materiality and their determination of examination or audit procedures, will reflect their respective experience, training, and professional judgment. As an extreme case, both can take radically different approaches in addressing such situations, and not necessarily be inconsistent with each other.

c. Similarities – Opportunities for Efficiencies

Given the substantial differences that may exist between an independent auditor and an examiner and how they may apply their respective professional skills in a given insurance company situation, there may be areas nonetheless where their approach, scope of work, procedures, and desired documentation will converge. Such areas provide opportunities for efficiencies that the examiner should consider.

To identify areas for potential examination efficiencies relating to work performed by an independent auditor, the examiner should have an adequate understanding of the overall audit scope and, for areas identified by either the examiner or the CPA as having a higher likelihood of material error, an understanding of the CPA's procedures and results thereof. Given the substantial differences between the professional requirements of independent auditors and examiners, it is presumed that an overall qualitative assessment of one's work by the other would not necessarily be meaningful. However, an "adequate understanding" by the examiner of the CPA's work is realistically attainable and relevant, to the extent that it sheds light on the performance of audit procedures, whether such procedures are substantially similar to procedures contemplated by the examiner and, if so, the nature of related findings and documentation.

d. Meetings with the CPA

The independent accountant's work may be informative to the examiner in efficiently obtaining an understanding of the following matters:

- The internal control structure: This *Handbook* requires an understanding of control risk, as it relates to specific control objectives for an insurer. To the extent that the CPA may have also reviewed and documented internal controls or flowcharted a particular system, such work could be useful to the examiner;

- Risk assessment: At the financial statement level or account-balance or class-of-transaction level, the CPA's work may provide information about the effectiveness of internal control structure policies and procedures that might affect the nature or extent of testing the examiner would otherwise need to perform; and

- Substantive procedures: Some procedures performed by the CPA may provide direct evidence about material misstatements in specific account balances or classes of transactions. The results of these procedures can provide evidence the examiner may consider in restricting detection risk for the related areas.

Communications with the CPA will be helpful in the initial planning process and during the examination program development stage. In the initial planning process, information is obtained regarding the CPA's assessment of risk and materiality, overall audit scope, and findings. Dialogue at this point with the CPA may be helpful in identifying additional areas of risk, mitigating factors that would indicate less risk, and generally confirm the examiner's understanding of such matters from the CPA's perspective.

A good way to start is for the examiner to meet with the independent auditor and inquire directly about such matters. To prepare for the meeting, the examiner should have read the audited financial statements and the independent auditor's report thereon, and management letters (if any). It would be helpful to be far enough along in the examination planning process for the examiner to have formed some tentative conclusions as to which areas of the company may have a higher likelihood of material error in surplus, but not so far along so as to preclude any value from efficiencies that might be gained by learning about the independent auditor's work.

It would also be helpful to have the CPA's working papers available at this meeting, for an overall cursory review by the examiner. This overall review's purpose would be for the examiner to confirm an understanding of matters discussed with the CPA, the overall CPA audit scope, and the nature and extent of the underlying documentation. The working papers would also be available at a later date for a more detailed review by the examiner of those audit areas that the examiner intends to consider using, with appropriate testing if deemed necessary by the examiner (see "Testing the Work of the CPA," "f").

With respect to program development, other sections of this *Handbook* describe this phase of the examination. That phase is summarized through the specific risk analysis process, as follows:

- An assessment of the internal and external environmental factors affecting the company's operations and business (inherent risk);
- An overall analytical review and assessment of whether the company's financial results make sense;
- An assessment of the internal controls at the company, and the ability of the internal control structure to identify and rectify material errors affecting such financial results on a timely basis (control risk);
- Based on the foregoing inputs, an overall assessment of likelihood of material error affecting surplus of the company for the control objective; and
- Determination of examination procedures responsive to the examiner's assessment of the likelihood of material error.

Once the examiner has determined the examination procedures to be performed in the foregoing manner, consideration may be given to the work that the CPA may have already performed and documented substantially similar procedures, and to the extent that the examiner determines such procedures, as documented by the CPA, can be utilized after reviewing the applicable CPA working papers (see "Using the Work of the CPA" and "Testing the Work of the CPA," below). Another meeting or call to the CPA may be appropriate at this point to determine if this is the case.

From these communications with the CPA, the examiner should have obtained an adequate understanding of the CPA's overall audit scope, a tentative list of areas where the CPA's procedures are substantially similar to those contemplated by the examiner, and a list of any areas resulting in material audit adjustments. To document the process, the examiner should prepare a memorandum summarizing the examiner's understanding of the overall audit scope. As discussed below, if consideration by the examiner of the CPA's work significantly affects the nature and extent of the examiner's procedures, copies should be requested of those working papers that support the performance of procedures and findings in such areas.

e. Using the Work of the CPA

Even though the CPA's work may affect the examiner's procedures, the examiner should perform procedures to obtain adequate support for the examiner's report. Evidence obtained through the examiner's direct personal knowledge, including physical examination, observation, computation and inspection, is generally more persuasive than information obtained indirectly.

The responsibility to report on the company's statutory examination rests solely with the examiner. Because the examiner has the ultimate responsibility to report on the examination, judgments about assessments of inherent and control risks, the materiality of misstatements, the sufficiency of tests performed, the evaluation of significant accounting estimates and other matters affecting the examiner's report should always be the examiner's.

In making judgments about the extent of the effect of the CPA's work on the examiner's procedures, the examiner considers:

- The materiality of financial statement amounts;
- The risk (inherent and control risk) of material misstatement related to these financial statement amounts; and
- The degree of subjectivity involved in the evaluation of the audit evidence gathered.

As the materiality of the financial statement amount increases or the risk of material misstatement or the degree of subjectivity increases, the need for the examiner to perform tests may increase. Similarly, as those factors decrease, the need for the examiner to perform tests decreases.

For some financial statement areas, the consideration of the CPA's work solely may not reduce examination risk to an acceptable level to eliminate the necessity of performing tests of those areas directly by the examiner. Valuation of assets and liabilities involving significant accounting estimates, related party transactions, contingencies, and uncertainties are examples of areas that might have a high risk of material misstatement or involve a high degree of subjectivity in the evaluation of audit evidence.

For certain areas related to less material financial statement amounts where the risk of material misstatement or the degree of subjectivity involved in the evaluation of the audit evidence is low, after considering the circumstances and the results of work performed by the CPA, the examiner may decide the risk of material misstatement has been reduced to an acceptable level and that testing directly by the examiner may not be necessary. Cash balances and certain investments are examples that might have a low risk of material misstatement or involve a low degree of subjectivity in the evaluation of audit evidence.

f. Testing the Work of the CPA

The examiner should request the workpapers of the independent CPA for the year under examination and perform a review of these workpapers. The examiner should give the CPA at least two weeks notice to provide the workpapers requested for review. It is preferable that the workpapers are reviewed in conjunction with the examination planning. The review of the CPA workpapers and the meeting with the independent CPA should be coordinated accordingly. The examiner should perform procedures that, in the examiner's judgment, are adequate to evaluate the CPA's work. The examiner should strive to understand the areas tested by the CPA and all respective findings and conclusions. The examiner should utilize these findings and conclusions when determining the nature and extent of the examiner's procedures. Conversely, if the examiner has conducted a risk assessment and does not plan to perform any procedures over certain areas of the company's balance sheet, the examiner does not need to exert significant review over those aspects of the CPA's workpapers. When conducting an evaluation of the CPA's workpapers, the examiner should consider:

- The scope of CPA's work relative to the examiner's objectives;
- The adequacy of the CPA's audit procedures;
- The appropriateness of the CPA's conclusions in the circumstances;
- The consistency of the CPA's reports with the results of the work performed; and
- The identification of any noted issues of deliberate improper financial reporting identified by the CPA's according to SAS 99, Consideration of Fraud in a Financial Statement Audit.

The examiner must exercise sound professional judgment in utilizing the work of the CPAs to alter the nature and extent of the examination procedures. Any reperformance of the CPA's work will depend on the circumstances and will be a matter of the examiner's professional judgment.

12. Examination Planning Memorandum

Proper risk analysis and planning of an examination are essential to the development of an effective examination plan. A thorough understanding of the company's businesses and of the effects of significant changes, trends and current events is critical to properly planning an examination.

A memorandum should be prepared that summarizes the examination planning process. This memorandum should adequately discuss the following:

a. Impact of Pervasive Items

(1) Significant current events.

(2) Industry conditions and issues.

(3) Industry conditions that could have a potential adverse affect on the company's prospective ability to remain solvent.

b. Management Environment – brief discussion based on Examination Team assessment

c. Summary of Examination Approach & Timing

Results of Review of Financial Analysis Package – Discuss significant items or trends noted by Financial Analyst during these reviews, as well as follow-up responses received from company. Document/discuss procedures responsive to these findings to be performed during examination.

This section should also briefly discuss the examination approach (i.e., the nature, timing and extent of procedures to be performed to address the related solvency risk) to be used in each significant area of the examination (i.e., reserves, reinsurance, etc.). For example, for the reserve area, the examiner team would discuss the level of reliance to be placed on the company's internal actuaries (based upon their qualifications, etc.) and how that relates to the specific procedures the examiner intends to perform.

Timing – briefly discuss the anticipated level of staff examiners required to conduct examination and the timetable for completion.

d. Preliminary calculation of planning materiality

13. Complete Specific Risk Analysis (SRA) workpapers documenting the impact of planning results and the specific testing to be performed by the Examining Team on specific accounts. The EIC or supervisor should approve the SRA workpapers before testing begins in that area.

14. EIC Completion of Planning Documentation

Ensure all information forms and assessments have been completed and that the conclusions reached in the forms are appropriate in the circumstances and are properly reflected in work programs and scopes:

a. Examination Planning Questionnaire (Exhibit B)
b. Evaluation of Controls in Information Systems Questionnaire (Exhibit C)

15. A planning file including all documents noted above and any additional supporting workpapers should be compiled and forwarded to the examination supervisor. The planning file should include the following:

a. Examination Planning Checklist (Exhibit A)
b. Examination Planning Questionnaire (Exhibit B)
c. Evaluation of Controls in Information Systems Questionnaire (Exhibit C)
d. CPA Review Checklist (Exhibit D)
e. Analysis of Statutory Financials (e.g., financial analysis workbench)
f. Supporting analytical and background documents
g. Examination Planning Memorandum
h. SRA Documents (preferable but may be completed later)

16. Review of Planning

a. Completed planning documentation should be forwarded to the examination supervisor for review. A planning meeting should be considered especially for larger and higher risk companies. The planning meeting between the EIC and supervisor may be helpful to obtain an agreement and understanding of the examination approach. This meeting should be held subsequent to the supervisor's review of the completed planning package.

The purpose of the meeting is:

(1) To discuss follow-up points proposed by the supervisor based on the review.

(2) To assure that both the EIC and supervisor have the same understanding of examination approach and scopes to avoid miscommunication, especially on the high-risk areas.

(3) To discuss and finalize timing of the examination and any administrative issues.

b. Subsequent to the meeting, the EIC should revise and finalize the planning documents.

c. Note: for all high-risk examinations, a planning package is to be reviewed or discussed with senior department personnel.

IV. CONDUCTING EXAMINATIONS

This section covers procedures and considerations that are important when conducting financial condition examinations. The discussion here is divided as follows:

A. General Examination Procedures
B. Examination of Computer-Based Operations
C. Sampling
D. Using the Work of an Outside Specialist
E. Reinsurance
F. Uniform Accounting for Insurers
G. Managing General Agents
H. Insurance Producers
I. Controlling Producers and Controlled Insurers
J. Custodial or Safekeeping Agreements
K. Use of Independent Certified Public Accountants (CPA) on Multi-state Examinations
L. TeamMate

A. General Examination Procedures

Summary

Certain general procedures, many of which do not result from a SRA, should be considered on all examinations. The examination program should include a section that explains the nature and extent of these general examination procedures. This part of the *Handbook* addresses the following subjects, which are applicable to most examinations:

1. Review of General Ledger and Journal Entries
2. Review of Board of Director and Committee Meeting Minutes
3. Review of Subsequent Events
4. Review of Affiliated Transactions
5. Review of CPA Workpapers
6. Working with Internal Auditors
7. Letters of Representations
8. Other Procedures
9. Consideration of Fraud
10. Examination Review Responsibilities

1. Review of General Ledger and Journal Entries

The examination team should review the general ledger, all significant nonstandard journal entries, and any company workpaper entries made solely to prepare the annual statement. The purpose of this review is to identify any significant or unusual postings from unfamiliar sources, and other unusual entries that might not have been identified through other audit procedures (e.g., the purchase and sale of a significant block of business in the same year).

This review should be performed by an individual sufficiently familiar with the recurring journal entries and other posting sources so that unusual items will be detected. It usually is beneficial to set a dollar limit below which entries need not be investigated.

2. Review of Board of Director and Committee Meeting Minutes

The examination team should read the minutes of all meetings of the board of directors, shareholders, executive committees and other important committees for the entire examination period through the end of fieldwork. Matters affecting the annual statement should be cross-referenced to the appropriate workpapers. As to any recent meetings for which minutes have not yet been prepared, examiners should ask management about matters dealt with at such meetings and request and review written summaries of actions.

3. Review of Subsequent Events

Some events or transactions that occur after the balance sheet date may have an important bearing on the financial statements. The "Review of Events Subsequent to the Balance Sheet Date" checklist (Exhibit G) covers the procedures that should be used in all examinations.

4. Review of Affiliated Transactions

This section provides guidance for identifying and examining affiliated transactions. There are two broad categories of affiliated transactions:

a. Transactions having implications as to potentially misleading the presentation of the annual statement. Such transactions frequently have involved questionable dealings, including management fraud. This type of affiliated transactions occurs infrequently but constitutes a very difficult area.
b. Transactions occurring in the ordinary course of business are considered affiliated transactions only because of an existing relationship between the transacting parties.

Generally, examiners are more concerned with detecting and disclosing those affiliated transactions in the first category than with those affiliated transactions that are transacted in the ordinary course of business. Even though the greatest exposure is focused on only a relatively few affiliated transactions, procedures are performed to encompass the broad definitions of affiliates and affiliated transactions.

a. Affiliates Defined

Affiliates exist when there is a relationship that offers the potential for self-dealing, transactions at less than arm's length, favorable treatment, or the ability to direct the outcome of events differently from what might result in the absence of that relationship. Some examples of affiliates are:

- A company's affiliates
- Principal owners
- Management (including directors)
- Entities for which investments are accounted for by the equity method
- Pension and profit sharing trusts managed by or under the trusteeship of management

An affiliate also includes any other person with which the reporting entity may deal if one party controls or can significantly influence the management or operating policies of the other to an extent that one of the transacting parties might be prevented from fully pursuing its own separate interests. A third person also is affiliated if it can significantly influence the management or operating policies of the transacting parties or if it has an ownership interest in one of the transacting parties and can significantly influence the other to an extent that one or more of the transacting parties might be prevented from fully pursuing its own separate interests.

b. Affiliated Transactions Defined

An affiliated transaction is any direct or indirect transaction between the reporting entity and an affiliate. Affiliated transactions include transactions between:

(1) A parent company and its subsidiaries
(2) Subsidiaries of a common parent
(3) The reporting entity and:
- Other affiliated businesses
- Management (including directors)
- Principal owners
- Pension and profit sharing trusts managed by or under the trusteeship of management
- Other parties having the ability to exert significant influence

Affiliated transactions also may include other transactions in which the reporting entity may not appear to be involved. Identifying these affiliated transactions is frequently difficult, if not impossible, because (1) examiners ordinarily must rely on oral representations to obtain an awareness that a relationship exists and a transaction has occurred; and (2) the parties to the transaction may be adverse to disclosing the motives, facts and circumstances surrounding the transaction.

Transactions that, after study, cannot be understood as to their apparent motivation or appear to be commercially unreasonable raise the presumption that an affiliate transaction exists.

Where subtle affiliated relationships are known or believed to exist, examiners should perform procedures to determine whether an affiliated transaction classification is appropriate. Although oral representations of management or others often are required to understand the business purpose of the transaction, such representations should be evaluated in light of apparent motives and the weight of other evidence. Important oral representations should be confirmed in writing either in the letter of representations or in a separate letter.

There are a number of conditions that may create motivation for affiliated transactions that are designed to alleviate or forestall circumstances management perceived would adversely affect the company. Some examples are:

- Lack of sufficient surplus to continue the business;
- An urgent desire for a continued favorable earnings record in the hope of supporting the price of the company's stock;
- An overly optimistic earnings forecast;
- Dependence on a single or relatively few products for the ongoing success of the company; and
- Significant litigation, especially between shareholders and management.

Absent contrary circumstances, transactions with affiliates should not be assumed to be outside the ordinary course of business. However, affiliated transactions are occasionally deliberately obscured by using devices such as business structure or management operating style.

Circumstances such as these should increase the examiner's skepticism of management. These circumstances may illustrate a manager determined to attain its objectives regardless of the means required to do so.

c. Affiliated Transactions with Partial or No Accounting Recognition

Transactions by or among affiliates are considered to be affiliated transactions even though they may be given partial or no accounting recognition. For example, an entity that provides significant services to an affiliate without charge, or at charges that do not appear normal, may be involved in an affiliated transaction.

d. Affiliates Without Transactions

Sometimes two or more entities are under common ownership or management control, but do not transact business between or among themselves. The mere existence of common control may result in operating results or a financial position significantly different from what would have occurred if the entities were autonomous. For example, two or more entities in the same line of business may be commonly controlled by a party with the ability to increase or decrease the volume of business done by each (i.e., the ability to exercise significant influence over the operations of each entity).

e. Typical Examination Procedures

The following examination procedures typically are considered to identify affiliates and affiliated transactions.

- The review and evaluation of internal accounting control and an understanding of the entity's business and operating environment should be sufficient to recognize whether significant transactions are occurring and are not being given accounting recognition. Examples: a company provides accounting and management services to an affiliate at no charge; a major shareholder absorbs corporate expenses.
- The review and evaluation of the entity's procedures for identifying and properly accounting for affiliated transactions.
- The review and evaluation of the entity's procedures, if any, that prohibit individual directors or other members of management from exercising significant influence over transactions in which that person is an affiliate.

One means used by many entities to preclude significant affiliate influence is to prohibit a director or other member of management from voting or otherwise participating in any business decisions in which that individual is an affiliate. In some cases, an affiliate may have participated in a business decision and it may not be practical for the board to reconsider a previously approved transaction solely so that person can abstain from voting. In these instances, it usually is acceptable to obtain written representation from appropriate management and the affiliate that significant influence was not exercised, provided that by reference to the entity's minutes or otherwise, the examiners are able to satisfy themselves that the affiliate's vote did not influence the outcome of the board's decision (e.g., the resolution was unanimously approved). If examiners have been unable to satisfy themselves as to the absence of significant influence, or conclude that a relationship or transaction merits attention of the board of directors, they may recommend subsequent reconsideration of an issue by the board of directors, with any affiliates abstaining from voting.

The following procedures provide an approach for detecting abuses that sometimes result from holding company or affiliated relationships:

Potential abuses:

(1) Misuse of insurance company assets through:

i. Shifting assets (particularly securities) from one affiliate to another for window-dressing purposes during examinations or at the financial statement date;
ii. Making unsecured loans or advances to affiliates;
iii. Maintaining compensating bank balances for the benefit of an affiliate;
iv. Making inappropriate loans to affiliates or purchases of affiliate securities; or
v. Pledging assets to secure loans for affiliates.

(2) Siphoning of insurance company funds through:

i. Dividends;
ii. Management or service fees;
iii. Payment of exorbitant reinsurance premiums to affiliates;
iv. Inappropriate payment of the expense of affiliates; or
v. Misdirection of premiums or commissions to affiliate insurance companies or agencies.

(3) Other forms of misrepresentation:

i. Creating nonexistent receivables due from affiliates for window-dressing purposes during examination, or at the financial statement date;
ii. Assuming the liabilities by/for an affiliate.

Techniques for deterring abuses:

(1) Examine affiliates simultaneously;
(2) Appoint an affiliate coordinator for large or difficult examinations. The coordinator should be an experienced examiner and capable of supervising others. The coordinator may be either the examiner-in-charge or, in the case of a very large group, an examiner appointed by the examiner-in-charge;
(3) The coordinator's duties include:
i. Reviewing and verifying the propriety of all legal documents (supplied by management) supporting inter affiliate agreements or transactions (e.g., management or service contracts, guarantees or pledges of assets, intercompany loan agreements, agency contracts, inter affiliate reinsurance contracts, and current reports to the Securities and Exchange Commission);
ii. Where necessary, coordinating the investigation of intercompany transactions with the teams that are examining other affiliates;
iii. Compiling a list of all entities that are affiliated with the company and developing an organization (intercompany) chart that includes:

- Any company holding a controlling interest in the company being examined;

- Companies that are controlled by a common holding company;
- Companies in which a director or officer has a substantial interest; and
- Companies controlled by the company being examined.

iv. Supervising the examiners in the investigation of inter affiliate relationships.

(4) Define the duties of examiners to include the development of a list of all significant inter affiliate transactions or balances encountered during the selection and evaluation of data used in the examination of the individual balance sheet accounts and to evaluate compliance with appropriate insurance laws. The developed list should show:

- The nature of the transaction or balance;
- The amount;
- The date of transaction; and
- The record (and page number) from which the sample was taken.

If many transactions of a particular type occur (e.g., premium transactions between the company and an affiliated agent) the examiner should select sample transactions to be included in the inter affiliate transaction list.

(5) Investigate the propriety of inter affiliate transactions and balances that have been identified.

Guidelines for investigating inter affiliate relationships affecting individual balance sheet accounts:

(1) Cash:

i. Determine whether transfers to affiliate bank accounts and cash disbursements to affiliates are supported by legitimate arm's length transactions. Many of the abuses listed above can be detected through careful examination of inter affiliate cash transactions.

ii. If the company maintains large balances in banks that also serve affiliates, verify that the company is not supplying compensating balances for the benefit of the affiliate.

(2) Securities:

i. Check for illegal transfers. Possession of bearer bonds or securities registered in the name of any entity other than the company is a possible indication of the illegal transfer of securities for window-dressing purposes. To detect illegal transfers:

- Examine logs to determine who had access to company and custodian-held securities;

- Confirm registration with issuing entities;
- Check securities transaction records for the period immediately preceding the examination; and
- Compare transfer prices with prevailing market prices of the transfer date.

ii. Investigate all securities that may represent pledges of assets for the benefit of an affiliate.

(3) Dividends:

i. Evaluate the effect of dividends paid to a holding company on the financial condition of the affiliate.

(4) Reinsurance transactions with affiliates:

i Look for inappropriate shifting of reserves from one affiliate to another.

ii. Examine excessive reinsurance premiums to affiliates.

(5) Premiums due (life) and agents' balances (property/casualty):

i. Examine related records to detect possible misdirection of premium income to affiliated agents or companies.

ii. Recompute and evaluate commissions paid to affiliated agents.

(6) General expense records:

i. Determine whether affiliate expenses have been inappropriately allocated to the company.

Regarding affiliates:

Ask appropriate management personnel for the names of all affiliates (including all pension and other trusts established for the benefit of employees) and whether there were any transactions with these parties during the period.

Provide personnel involved in the examination with a list of known affiliates so they may become aware of transactions with such parties during their work. The affiliates list should be updated throughout the examination.

Prepare or obtain a schedule or summary of all known affiliated transactions or transactions believed to be affiliated transactions.

Regularly recurring transactions with affiliates may be reasonably summarized and tested for accuracy. If transactions represent goods and services that clearly are identifiable as to their nature, verification requirements may be satisfied by the review of internal accounting control and transaction tests that are regularly performed in connection with other areas of the examination. However, because transactions include a variety of items, documentation and tests thereof should be expanded to identify the nature of the transactions.

Review accounting records for significant, unusual, or nonrecurring transactions or balances, paying particular attention to transactions recorded at or near the end of the reporting period.

Large and unusual transactions, particularly those settled in cash and those executed at or around year-end, should convey a warning to examiners. Where transactions of this nature have occurred, refer to the following section, "Procedures for Identified Affiliated Transactions," for guidance on procedures that may be appropriate to understand and examine these transactions.

Note that the definition of affiliates (e.g., immediate family, including affiliates and companies controlled by those persons) is considerably broader than the affiliates list that usually is provided to examination personnel.

Certain procedures that usually are performed to achieve other examination objectives also are used in identifying affiliates and affiliated transactions. These procedures include, but are not limited to:

- Considering guarantees indicated by confirmations of cash, investments, loans receivable and payable;
- Examining invoices from law firms;
- Reviewing minutes;
- Reviewing year-end trial balance;
- Reviewing selected operations accounts;
- Reviewing shareholder listings of closely held companies to identify principal shareholders;
- Reviewing material investment transactions during the period under examination to determine whether they cause another entity to become a related party; and
- Reviewing conflict-of-interest statements obtained by the entity from management and directors (covered in Exhibit B: Examination Planning Questionnaire). Conflict-of-interest statements provide the board of directors with information about the existence of relationships between persons completing the statement and parties with whom the entity transacts business.

Procedures for Identified Affiliated Transactions

Where affiliated transactions are identified, or there is reason to believe they exist, the following procedures should be considered. The nature and extent of these procedures should be determined after appropriate consideration of the facts and circumstances. Unusual transactions typically require more extensive examination procedures than do affiliated transactions made in the ordinary course of business.

- Obtain an understanding of the business purpose of the transaction.
- Examine invoices, executed copies of agreements, contracts and other pertinent documents.
- Consider whether the transaction should have been brought to the attention of, and received approval from, the board of directors or other appropriate officials.
- Inspect or confirm collateral; determine whether it can be transferred; evaluate evidence of its fair market value.
- Confirm transaction amount and terms, including guarantees and other significant data, with other parties to the transaction.
- Inspect evidence in possession of the parties to the transaction.
- Confirm or discuss significant information with intermediaries, such as banks, guarantors, agents or attorney, to obtain a better understanding of the transaction.
- Refer to financial publications, trade journals, credit agencies and other information sources when there is reason to believe that material transactions with other business enterprises may lack substance.

- Regarding material uncollected balances, guarantees and other obligations, obtain information as to the financial capability of the other parties to the transaction. This information may be obtained from financial statements, income tax returns, reports issued by other regulatory agencies, taxing authorities, financial publications or credit agencies.

f. Workpaper Documentation

At a minimum, the examiner's workpapers should include the following:

- A list of affiliates;
- A schedule or summary of identified affiliated transactions;
- An item in the company's letter of representations regarding affiliates and affiliated transactions; and
- An indication in the Examination Planning Memorandum as to whether any affiliated transactions were detected, and a description of any identified affiliated transactions that were not in the ordinary course of business or otherwise that required consideration of disclosure.

5. Review of CPA Workpapers

A review of CPA workpapers is performed to identify additional solvency risk areas and other issues that may have been evaluated by the CPA, and to determine the extent of work performed on high risk areas that may provide insight and efficiencies into the current examination. The CPA Checklist provides guidelines and standard documentation for the performance of the review of CPA workpapers. The following items should be considered in such a review:

a. Work performed on high risk areas preliminarily identified in the planning process should be reviewed for actual work performed and any exceptions in testing;

b. The EIC should read carefully the previous period's CPA reports emphasizing review on the footnote disclosures and opinion. Notes should be taken on significant changes to footnotes, unusual disclosures or qualified or modified opinions and discussed with the CPA;

c. A CPA Review Checklist should be completed;

d. The scope of all work to be completed in the current period examination should be reevaluated, based upon the actual work completed by the CPA; and

e. Work performed to satisfy the AICPA's Statement of Auditing Standard (SAS) 99: Consideration of Fraud in a Financial Statement Audit. Independent auditors are required by the AICPA to plan and perform audits in order to obtain reasonable assurance that the financial statements are free of material misstatement, whether caused by error or fraud. The documentation completed by the auditors to satisfy the AICPA guidance is required to be included in the workpapers. The examiner should obtain and review this information when conducting an examination. (Exhibit M: Consideration of Fraud provides guidance to the examiner when reviewing the CPA's consideration of fraud.)

The extent of the review of CPA workpapers will vary between companies depending on the number of high-risk areas identified in the initial planning process, the assigned risk rating and the quality of CPA workpapers.

6. Working With Internal Auditors

Management often establishes an internal audit function to assist in fulfilling such responsibilities as safeguarding assets, ensuring reliability of financial records and efficiency of internal control. Specific responsibilities depend on the size and structure of the entity and the requirements of its management. Although the scope and objectives of internal audit functions vary widely, internal audit departments are normally responsible for one or more of the following areas:

a. Reviewing the internal control structure. The internal audit function is often assigned specific responsibilities by management to review the control environment, accounting system, and control procedures, monitor their operation and recommend improvements;

b. Examining financial and operating information. This may include both reviewing the methods used to identify, measure, classify and report such information, and detailed testing of transactions, balances and procedures; and

c. Reviewing the efficiency and effectiveness of operational controls, as well as the internal control structure.

Internal auditors' work may affect the nature and extent of the examination, including:

a. Procedures performed in obtaining an understanding of the internal control structure;

b. Procedures performed in assessing control risk for specific audit objectives; and

c. Substantive procedures.

When a company has an internal audit department, the examiner should understand its role in the internal control structure, especially where its work may have an effect on the nature and extent of examination work. The examiner should keep up-to-date with changes that take place in the internal audit department (e.g., personnel, approach, reporting relationships and performance).

A statutory examination is focused on the financial statements whereas the work of internal auditors is frequently directed toward the entity's segments (e.g., departments, branches and so forth) and operational matters rather than statutory financial statement reporting. Relevant internal audit activities are those that provide evidence about the design and effectiveness of internal control policies and procedures pertaining to the entity's ability to record, process, summarize and report financial data consistent with the assertions embodied in the financial statements, or that provide direct evidence about potential misstatements of such data. The following procedures will help to assess the relevancy of internal audit activities:

a. Consider knowledge from prior examinations;

b. Review how the internal auditors allocate their audit resources to financial or operating areas in response to their risk assessment process; and

c. Read internal audit reports to obtain detailed information about the scope of internal audit activities.

If, after obtaining an understanding of the internal audit function, the examiner concludes that internal auditors' activities are not relevant to the financial statement audit, the examiner does not have to give further consideration to the internal audit function unless the examiner requests direct assistance from the internal auditors.

The examiner may conclude that the work of internal audit provides substantive audit evidence about specific audit objectives, or provides audit evidence about effective design or operation or other controls that are the basis for assessments of control risk for specific audit objectives. The examiner would need to evaluate the effectiveness of the internal audit department prior to relying on its work. This is usually accomplished by evaluating the internal audit function with respect to organization, planning, performance, and documentation and/or performing tests of its work.

If reliance on the internal audit function is planned, or internal audit is to provide direct assistance in completing the exam, the objectivity and competence of the internal auditors should be considered. The key factors to evaluate and document include:

a. Organizational status - The internal auditors' status in the organization can affect their ability to be objective. Ideally they should report to top management and have access to the board of directors or its audit committee. Internal auditors should be free of other operating responsibility. There should be no constraints or restrictions placed on their work by management, and normally the examiner would expect them to be free to communicate directly;

b. Scope of the function - The examiner should ascertain the nature and depth of coverage of internal auditors' assignments and whether management considers and acts on their recommendations, when appropriate;

c. Technical competence - The examiner should ascertain the qualification of personnel, including the relative depth of their technical training and proficiency, including EDP experience. This might include a review of the policies for hiring and training of internal audit staff, their experience and professional qualifications;

d. Due care - The examiner should ascertain whether internal audit work is appropriately planned, supervised, reviewed and documented. For example, the appropriateness, quality, and extent of audit manuals, work programs, and workpapers used or prepared by internal auditors should be considered; and

e. Coordination - If an examiner decides to use the work of the internal auditors, the examiner should discuss at an early date the areas where the internal auditors may be used. When internal audit work is a factor in determining the nature, and extent of procedures, it is desirable to agree in advance on the extent of participation and supervision, the extent of audit coverage (including sample sizes), and review and reporting procedures.

The examiner should test the work of the internal auditors on which reliance is planned. The extent of the tests depends on judgment about the importance of the audit objectives. The tests may include examination of other similar items, and observation of the internal auditors' procedures. In developing the test procedures, the examiner should consider such factors as whether the internal auditors':

a. Scope of work is appropriate to meet the objectives;

b. Audit programs are adequate;

c. Workpapers adequately document the work performed, including evidence of supervision and review;

d. Conclusions are appropriate in the circumstances; and

e. Reports are consistent with the results of the work performed.

7. Letters of Representations

a. Reliance on Management Representations

During the course of an examination, a company's management makes many representations to examiners in response to specific inquiries and through the financial statements. Management representations, either oral or written, generally should not be taken as the only support for important examination judgments and conclusions. These representations should corroborate information obtained from applying other examination procedures. In certain situations, however, corroborating information that can be obtained from applying examination procedures other than inquiry are limited. For example, when a company plans to take future action that has an impact on the annual statement under examination, the expression of that intention may be the only evidence available. In these situations, a written representation should be obtained to confirm management's plans.

b. Obtaining the Letter

As part of every examination, a letter of representation should be obtained from management. The representations included in such a letter are management's statements obtained to provide evidence, avoid misunderstanding and secure the active cooperation of the company in the performance of procedures. A sample letter is included as Exhibit K.

The sample letter includes typical language that may apply to property/casualty and/or life/health insurance companies, title companies, mortgage guaranty insurers, as well as health maintenance organizations. The actual letter of representation used in a particular examination should be tailored for the company under examination based on the facts and circumstances surrounding that examination. The examiner should be alert for areas of significance that should be included in the company's letter in addition to those provided in the sample letter. Conversely, many of the items included in the sample letter will not be applicable to the company under examination and should be omitted from the actual letter of representation used for that examination. Generally, such letters are no more than a few pages in length, confirming in broad terms the significant representations of management.

c. Signing and Dating Requirements

Letters of representations should bear the same date as the examination report and should be signed by the company's chief executive, financial and accounting officers. Other officers and employees whose functions include significant responsibility for the financial reporting process also should be asked to sign the letter.

d. Review with Management

For convenience, a letter of representation usually is drafted by the examiner and given to the company's management for signature. As a matter of courtesy, and for letters to accomplish their purpose, the representations should be discussed with the individuals who will be asked to sign the letter. Making a draft of the letter available for management's review well ahead of the completion of the examination generally facilitates management's understanding of the purpose and content of the letter and will allow the examiner to obtain the required signatures on a timely basis.

8. Other Procedures

Other procedures examiners should consider include an examination of certificates of authority, a review of the Company's conflict-of-interest policy, and a review of resisted claims.

Examiners should examine certificates of authority to ensure that all certificates of authority are valid and inquire about the status of those that are not valid.

The company's conflict of interest policy should be reviewed for adequacy. Examiners should examine any conflict of interest statements from officers to ensure they are complete and that all applicable employees have completed one.

Examiners should also review resisted claims for period under review, noting the reason for resisting, whether the reason was appropriate, how it was settled, and whether the insurance company's action was timely under all circumstances. This review is performed to evaluate the adequacy of claim reserves and for market practices evaluation.

9. Consideration of Fraud

Examiners should consider the impact and possibility of fraudulent activity while conducting financial condition examinations. In order to effectively complete this task, the examiner should obtain and review the documentation provided by the independent CPA that illustrates their consideration of fraudulent activity. Additionally, the examiners should perform a preliminary fraud risk assessment in order to obtain reasonable assurance that the financial statements do not contain misstatements due to fraud. The examiner should consider the risk of fraud for both fraudulent company reporting and fraudulent claims incurred by the company.

a. Fraudulent Company Reporting – Occurs as a misstatement or omission of amounts or disclosures in the financial statements (fraudulent financial reporting) or with the theft of assets (misappropriation of assets) that results in the financial statements being improperly stated. Fraudulent company reporting is instigated within a company. It is important for the examiner to understand the controls established within a company to determine whether proper control procedures and supervisory techniques have been implemented to mitigate the risk of this type of fraud. Although, proper control procedures may assist in reducing the risk of this fraud, due to collusion and other factors, the risk of fraudulent company reporting can never be totally eliminated.

b. Fraudulent Claims – Occurs when improper or unsupported insurance claims are submitted to the company. These types of claims are more difficult to identify than fraudulent financial reporting as they typically occur through the collusion of outside individuals (i.e., claimant and doctor). However, the company should have controls and documentation procedures established for claim processing that mitigate these fraud occurrences. The examiner will want to identify the processes in place and verify that they are properly being followed. Additionally, the examiner will want to ascertain the company's methods on addressing those identified instances of fraudulent activity and those who perpetrate them.

The use of fraud risk factors assists the examiners in determining whether fraudulent activity exists. Fraud risk factors are items dealing with management characteristics, industry conditions, or the company operating characteristics or financial stability that may indicate an environment for fraud. Fraud risk factors do not indicate that fraud has been perpetrated on or within the company, but they promote the identification of situations or company circumstances that are typically conducive in fraudulent schemes. Typically, fraud occurs when there has been an incentive, opportunity or attitude that permits the occurrence of fraud. Although fraud can occur when only one of these characteristics is present, fraud is most likely to occur when more than one of these conditions is a factor. For example, the more incentives or pressure an employee has to achieve a specific financial statement result, the more likely the employee will be able to rationalize the acceptability of fraudulent activity.

Some examples of fraud risk factors include:

- Management compensation tied to company performance – (Incentive)
- Insufficient supervisory review of controls – (Opportunity)
- Failure to respond to noted accounting/operating irregularities – (Attitude)
- Extraordinary growth or profitability – (Incentive)
- Complex organization structures – (Opportunity)
- Threat of regulatory action – (Incentive)
- Missing accounting transactions or unavailable original documents – (Attitude)
- Unusual delays for requested information – (Attitude)

Exhibit M, included within this *Handbook*, provides a detailed checklist of common risk factors and fraud characteristics (incentive, opportunity or attitude) identified in known fraudulent occurrences. The examiner should utilize this checklist when assessing the company's fraud risk factors.

The examiner should be cognizant of fraud risk factors during the planning, testing, and reporting phases of the examination and structure the examination accordingly to verify that the risk factors identified do not indicate the occurrence of fraud. Additionally, the examiner should consider the fraud risk factors identified during the planning phase in order to adequately determine the overall risk assessment of the examination. Experienced examiners should complete those examinations that appear to have a higher level of fraud risk factors.

In addition to the identification and review of fraud risk factors, the examiner-in-charge should hold discussions with company management to ascertain the occurrence of any known fraudulent activity perpetrated on or within the company. In accordance with these conversations, the examiner should also determine whether the company has an established program for the prevention and detection of fraud. If the company does have a fraud program implemented, the examiner should determine the company's standard procedures to deal with those individuals who commit fraud.

Exhibit M provides the examiner with the suggested format to use for conducting and documenting fraud risk factors as well as the overall consideration of fraud.

10. Examination Review Responsibilities

Workpapers are reviewed principally to assure that the work performed is in accordance with appropriate standards and that the report is appropriate in the circumstances. Other benefits of the review process include the ability to provide members of the professional staff with on-the-job training and to assess their performance.

The review of workpapers is carried out at two distinct levels – detailed and general. Each of these levels of review is intended to accomplish specific objectives. As a result, reviewers at each level have specifically designated responsibilities.

This section sets forth considerations regarding the review of workpapers. It includes guidelines for the nature and extent of the review and the completion of a Review and Approval Summary form.

a. Objectives of Workpaper Review

The review of workpapers is an integral part of complying with appropriate standards. The primary objectives of review procedures are to determine whether:

- The work has been appropriately planned;

- The scope of work is sufficient to support the findings or conclusions contained in the report;
- The work has been performed in accordance with the standards of the department and NAIC; and
- The examination report is supported by the work performed as documented in the examination workpapers.

In addition to these primary objectives, the review also allows the assessment of individual performance, provides on-the-job training, and evaluates the progress of the examination. The goal should be to perform as much of the review as possible in the field and before the completion of field work.

b. Levels of Review

To accomplish the review objectives, two categories of review procedures have been established. The detailed review covers the technical accuracy and completeness of the workpapers. A detailed review of each work area should be performed by the examiner-in-charge. In larger examinations, detailed review responsibilities may be shared by two or more people. The general review focuses on the adequacy of the work as a whole. This review should be performed by the chief examiner or designee.

c. Review of Planning Workpapers

Before any significant work begins, a detailed review of the planning workpapers and examination program should be performed by someone at a level higher than the preparer.

On some examinations, it may not be practical to perform the detailed review of the SRA workpapers and examination program for all areas before field work begins. In these cases, the SRA workpapers and examination program sections applicable to the areas in which work is to commence should be reviewed before any examination procedures are performed.

In many cases, efficiency can be significantly improved by reviewing the SRA workpapers before the examination program is prepared. For example, if the reviewer concludes that the preliminary examination approach should be different, the preliminary examination approach can be changed before the examination program is compiled, thus avoiding changes in the examination program and the related cross-references.

Involvement by experienced examiners in planning meetings and in early review of the documentation of the planning effort will enhance the efficiency of the examination. The chief examiner or designee should approve the Examination Planning Memorandum before the program begins.

The chief examiner or designee also should approve on a timely basis the staffing plan, time budget and assignment of the detailed review responsibilities, considering the level of risk associated with the various work areas.

d. Detailed Review

All workpapers require a detailed review. On larger examinations, there may be two or more detailed reviewers, each with responsibilities for particular areas. On smaller examinations, typically there will be only one detailed reviewer.

The Specific Risk Analysis enables examiners to plan the review to be proportionate to the risk of material error in specific accounts and transactions. This risk of material error and the technical competence and experience of the assigned staff personnel will influence who should perform the procedures in each area. These same factors should influence the selection of the detailed reviewer for each area.

For example, an examiner-in-charge ordinarily will perform procedures in areas requiring significant subjective judgments. As a result, the chief examiner or designee would perform a detailed review of the work in these areas.

The emphasis of a detailed review is on the technical accuracy and completeness of the workpapers. A detailed reviewer should determine whether:

- Procedures in the examination program were properly performed. These procedures should be cross-referenced from the examination program to the workpapers where the work is evidenced.
- Conclusions are clearly documented and adequately supported by the workpapers. A detailed reviewer should determine whether all tick marks are clearly explained, all significant or unusual amounts are appropriately supported and explained, and any ambiguous comments are clarified or removed.
- Procedures performed were sufficient in view of the examination findings and any changes in conditions occurring since the procedures were planned. The examination program is developed from expectations based on conditions existing during the planning process. Therefore, examiners should evaluate the results of procedures against those expectations, considering any subsequent changes in conditions.

In connection with the detailed review, a Summary Review Memorandum (SRM) may be prepared covering all important accounting, examination and reporting issues. All program changes and other issues warranting attention by the chief examiner should be included in the SRM. The SRM should be prepared by the examiner-in-charge.

The Summary Review Memorandum should not repeat comments made in the examination report itself. Rather, the SRM should discuss interpretative analyses by the examiners relative to significant examination areas and issues:

- A final reassessment of materiality and adequacy of overall examination scope in light of known examination adjustments made and current knowledge of the company;
- An overall review, in the aggregate, of any passed adjustment as judgmental difference to the adjusted financial position of the company based on the examination procedures thus far;
- Any other significant factors to be brought to the general reviewer's attention; and
- Each detailed reviewer should read the EPM and relevant sections of the SRA workpaper and examination program to determine whether appropriate recognition has been given to program changes and areas of moderate or high risk (or areas where the initial assessment of low risk was changed).

e. General Review

The general review, which focuses on the adequacy of the examination work as a whole, should be performed by the chief examiner or designee. The general reviewer's responsibilities are to determine whether:

- An adequate detailed review has been performed for all work areas. If any workpapers have not had a detailed review, the general reviewer should perform that review or see that it is done.
- The examination has been performed in accordance with this *Handbook.*
- The statutory financial statement has been prepared in conformity with accounting practices prescribed or permitted by the Department.
- The SRM covers all important examination issues.

The general reviewer's responsibilities may be fulfilled without reviewing all workpapers. This means that workpapers relating to low risk areas ordinarily need only be scanned, while other workpapers should be read more closely. Duplication of the work of the detailed reviewer should be avoided, except to the extent considered necessary to evaluate the adequacy of the detailed review. The extent of the general review is a matter of judgment and will vary among examinations. Ordinarily, the direction and extent of the general review will be influenced by the:

- Risk of material error evaluated on the SRA workpaper;
- Items covered in the SRM; and
- Technical competence and experience of the personnel who performed the work and made the detailed review.

The general review should include the workpapers relating to important examination issues. Typically, such workpapers document:

- Complex or unusual transactions, including affiliated transactions;
- Areas where problems were encountered, expected or unexpected; and
- Changes in accounting policies.

The general reviewer should be satisfied that the annual statement review procedures as described below have been performed. The final overall review of the annual statement may indicate a need for the general reviewer to focus on particular workpapers to understand the reasons for fluctuations or unusual relationships.

f. Actuarial Review

The workpapers or supporting documentation of the actuarial examiner or consulting actuary should also be reviewed. Those performing this review could include the EIC, Chief Examiner or Department Actuary.

g. Annual Statement Review Procedures

Examiners should perform a final overall review of the comparative annual statements near the conclusion of field work. The purpose is to ensure that (1) explanations for fluctuations between years have been obtained, (2) the numbers make sense in light of the understanding of the company, and (3) they are satisfied with the sufficiency of the examination procedures.

h. Documentation of Review

Reviewers should document their review by signing or initialing and dating each workpaper. General reviewers should sign or initial workpapers they have read, but need not document their review of workpapers they have merely scanned to determine whether previous reviews were performed adequately.

If there are several workpapers comprising one account analysis or documenting one procedure, it is sufficient to sign or initial and date only the first page. Reviewers also are encouraged to add their own explanations or rationale in support of conclusions to the workpapers they review.

i. Review and Approval Summary

The Review and Approval Summary for Financial Examinations ("RAS") is applicable to all examinations. Completion of this form documents the performance of the review requirements of this part.

It is the responsibility of the Chief Examiner or designee to be satisfied that all required review procedures are performed and are documented before authorizing the release of the report. An example of such documentation is included in Exhibit H.

B. Examination of Computer-Based Operations

The examiner is faced with special problems when dealing with companies that have computerized record keeping systems. In these situations, a computer audit specialist can provide valuable assistance.

1. Typical problems encountered when examining computer-based operations:

   a. The record keeping system is difficult to understand because of:

      (1) Complexity;
      (2) Insufficient documentation; and
      (3) Unfamiliar terminology.

   b. Key records (e.g., transactions records and detailed inventories of in-force policies, liabilities, and assets) are unavailable as of the balance sheet date because they have been continuously updated since that date.

   c. It is often hard to identify and obtain records with the required information.

   d. The examiner lacks confidence in the completeness and accuracy of printouts produced by company personnel.

   e. Reliance on computer dependent controls and edits with reduced availability of traditional "paper-trails."

2. Duties of a computer audit specialist:

   a. Review the company's record keeping system to determine what it does and how it works.

   b. Review the company's response to the Information System Questionnaire (ISQ) – Understand the controls and the effectiveness of the controls.

c. Properly interface the insurance department's software package (if available) with the company's system.

d. Determine the specific needs of the examiners and arrange for production of the required computer printouts.

e. Remain available to the examiners throughout the examination for consultation on computer-related problems.

f. Provide the examiners with on-the-job training of computer methods and techniques.

3. Duties of examiners relating to computer applications:

a. Provide the computer audit specialist with specific requirements for printouts of company records and files:

- Information required for each item;
- Number of items in the sample;
- Instructions for selecting the sample items; and
- Any operations or calculations required (e.g., matching one record with another).

b. Provide the computer audit specialist with an understanding of examination objectives and the work plan.

4. Computer Audit Procedures for Examinations without a Computer Audit Specialist

The audit procedures listed below is the minimum that should be completed by the examiners if a Computer Audit Specialist is unable to assist on the examination. In addition, review any independent accountant work papers (if available) and/or internal audit work papers and reports to determine where the problem areas have been in the past.

a. Review prior examination report for comments and recommendations.

- The practices and procedures that resulted in adverse comments in the previous examination report should be reevaluated to see whether they have been corrected or not; and
- Review the corrective actions the company has taken.

b. Review the company's response to the ISQ to gain an understanding of its EDP environment and its control consciousness. If the company's controls over the system are weak then the integrity of the data cannot be depended on. In an insurance company, especially, it is critical to have a competent database manager and a well-designed database system with strict access controls.

c. Management Controls

- Review the data processing department's policies and procedures for adequacy and completeness;
- Review the job descriptions for the data processing department to ensure that they are accurate and are up to date;

- Compare the data processing department's organizational charts and job descriptions to determine whether the segregation of duties is adequate within the data processing department. Also determine whether there is a separation of duties between the data processing department and the departments it provides services for;
- Review the termination policies and procedures to ensure that when employees leave, the data processing department is notified so the computer security system can be updated. In addition, verify that terminated employees physical access security rights are revoked;
- Determine whether an independent group, such as an internal or external auditor, conducts control reviews of the computer processing activities;
- Whether internal audit does work in this area or not is determined by whether its staff has sufficient background or knowledge of the areas being reviewed; and
- Determine whether internal audit issues a report to management disclosing its findings and recommendations upon completion of each audit.

d. Information system development and acquisition.

(1) Review the company's new systems development policies and procedures (this applies to acquired systems as well as in-house developed systems);

(2) Determine whether systems are developed in a systematic and logical manner including proper review and sign-off at each of the following phases. The current phase should be completed before beginning the next phase:
  - Project initiation
  - Feasibility study
  - Design phase
  - Development and implementation
  - Post implementation review

(3) Determine the extent to which the users participate in the development of new systems;

(4) Determine to what extent internal audit participates in the development of new systems; and

(5) Determine whether the software acquisition process follow the company's procurement policies. In addition, ascertain whether these products are tested and reviewed prior to being purchased.

e. Information systems operations controls

- Determine whether any reports are generated that identify work that was processed on a non-scheduled basis;
- Determine if an operator's log is maintained for each shift of operations. This log should indicate any problems encountered and any pertinent shift notes;
- Determine if any preventive maintenance is regularly performed on the computer hardware;
- Determine whether the computer operators are allowed to make decisions on distribution of errors and discrepancies based on their severity; and
- Determine whether the MIS manager should review control log entry printout on a daily basis.

f. Logical and physical security

- Review the company's information security policy to determine whether it clearly defines the responsibilities of users versus the responsibility of the management and security administrators;
- Interview the security administrator to determine if their duties are consistent with the company's security policies and procedures;
- Determine if a written policy has been issued that explains the restrictions of who is allowed access to the computer facility;
- Determine if the procedures that prevent unauthorized persons from gaining physical access to the computer facility are adequate;
- Observe computer facility activities to verify that only authorized personnel are being permitted to enter the facility;
- Review the data processing department's procedures for adding, changing, and deleting individuals access rights to the computer resources;
- Determine if there is a minimum length requirement for user's passwords (i.e., five characters). Passwords should be generated by the individual user and not be assigned by the company;
- Determine if passwords are required to be changed periodically and that the same password cannot be immediately reused by that user;
- Verify that passwords are not displayed during the logon process and that they are not printed on the output;
- Determine if the user community management periodically reviews the access rights currently provided to the users in their respective departments;
- Determine if there are procedures for the prompt cancellation of user IDs and passwords when the employee/employer relationship has been terminated;
- Evaluate the procedures for reviewing the security violations reports and verify that this activity is being performed;
- Determine if procedures exist that state authorized computer resource users must be given special permission to access particular resources, such as data files, application processing programs, the operating system, and various commands;
- Determine whether procedures exist for authorizing access to the online data processing environment on an as needed basis. This includes who can view, add, change and delete data and also who has access to which systems;
- Inspect the computer room to determine if the fire protection system is adequate;
- Verify that the computer operations staff is periodically trained in the proper procedures to deal with emergency situations such as fire, water, and alarm incidents;
- Ensure that fire drills are performed on a regular basis by the data processing staff; and
- Terminals should have an automatic log off feature for when they are unattended.

g. Contingency planning

- Evaluate the data processing disaster recovery plan to make sure it is complete and up to date;
- Determine if copies of the plan are being stored off-site;
- Ensure that all critical data processing applications have been identified and that a restoration priority has been assigned to them;
- Review the list of critical computer application programs, operating systems and data files and determine if it is reasonable;
- Determine if copies of the critical data files are rotated to the off-site storage location on a regular basis;
- Ensure that the copies of the application and system programs along with the source and object codes that are stored at the off-site location are kept current and up to date;
- Evaluate the telecommunications disaster recovery plan to make sure it is complete and up to date;
- Determine if the company has negotiated the use of either a hot site or a cold site in the event of a disaster. This should be accompanied with written contracts from all the vendors that will be involved in the restoration process (i.e., hardware, software, forms, etc.);
- Determine whether they are using an uninterruptible power supply;
- Determine whether the company has an inventory list of the supplies that would be needed in the event of a disaster. A list of the vendors names, contacts, and phone numbers should also be included;
- Determine whether the disaster recovery plan is tested periodically to verify its adequacy. If the company has a hot site, this test should include restoring the backup tapes to the backup computer system and testing their accuracy and functionality;
- Determine whether the user departments have developed a manual processing plan that they could use until the computer center can be restored; and
- Determine if the data center has proper fire protection (i.e., a Halon system) and also if there are moisture sensors in the raised floor.

h. Service Bureau Operations

- Determine whether a contract exists between the company being examined and the company providing the data processing services; and
- Review the contract to determine whether it details costs, rights, responsibilities, ownership and length of term for the two parties involved.

i. Local Area Networks

- Determine if the company uses a standard form for requesting the addition, change or deletion of local area network access capabilities;
- Determine whether the security management process for making changes to the local area network user profiles is adequate;
- Determine whether network user access is based on the need-to-know basis;
- Determine whether the local area network's server is connected to an uninterruptible power supply (UPS);

- Verify whether the file server has been secured and cannot be accessed by any unauthorized individuals;
- Determine whether the process used for changing the network configuration is documented; and
- Verify that the network servers are backed-up on a regular basis and that those copies are stored off-site.

j. Personal Computers

- Obtain an inventory list of the microcomputer hardware and software used by the company;
- Determine whether the company has distributed written policies and procedures regarding the acquisition of microcomputer equipment;
- Determine whether the company has distributed written policies and procedures regarding the use of microcomputers. These should cover the following topics:
  (1) Development and testing;
  (2) Documentation;
  (3) Input, processing and output controls;
  (4) Back-up and recovery of programs and data; and
  (5) Security over the custody and use of the microcomputer assets including hardware, software and data.

- Determine whether the company has issued written policies and procedures on the develop-or-buy alternatives for microcomputer application software;
- Determine whether the physical protection provided for the microcomputers is adequate; and
- Verify that there is an appropriate sign-out procedure for microcomputer equipment that is taken off of the company's property.

k. Requirements of companies with computer-based systems:

- Insurers must advise the home state insurance department when computer record keeping equipment is initially installed or substantially changed;
- All transactions and other input data should be printed out or available for printout to allow tracing to original records;
- The detailed files as of each year end must be printed out or available for printout; and
- All record keeping systems should be fully documented.

C. Sampling

Statistical sampling techniques enable an examiner to examine an account without reviewing each of its individual elements. By drawing a sample of individual elements, the examiner can obtain, with predetermined accuracy, information about the whole account.

All examiners should be familiar with sampling techniques. Use of sampling should be considered whenever the examination of material account is susceptible to sampling.

Part 3 of this *Handbook* contains an explanation of sampling theory and techniques for the use of insurance examiners.

D. Using the Work of an Outside Specialist

Decision to Use the Work of an Outside Specialist

Education and experience enable the examiner to be knowledgeable about insurance matters in general, but the examiner is not expected to have the expertise of a person trained for or qualified to engage in the practice of another profession or occupation. During the examination, however, an examiner may encounter matters potentially material to the fair presentation of financial statements that require special knowledge and that in the examiner's judgment require using the work of a specialist. The department should have on staff or be able to contract the requisite expertise to examine effectively any insurer.

Examples of matters that require the work of a specialist include, but are not limited to, the following:

1. Computer applications (e.g., EDP environment and controls, computer audit techniques and expert systems).

2. Valuation (e.g., real estate, restricted securities and other investments).

3. Determination of amounts derived by using specialized techniques or methods (e.g., certain actuarial determinations).

4. Interpretation of technical requirements, regulations, or agreements (e.g., the potential significance of reinsurance and other contracts or other legal documents, or legal title to property).

In performing a financial condition examination, the department may use the work of a specialist as a procedure to obtain competent evidential matter. The circumstances surrounding the use of a specialist differ. Although the familiarity of individual examiners with the work performed by certain types of specialists may differ, the procedures necessary to comply with examination standards need not vary because of the extent of the examiner's knowledge.

Selecting a Specialist

The Department should obtain satisfaction concerning the professional qualifications and reputation of the specialist by inquiry or other procedures, as appropriate. The department should consider the following:

1. The professional certification, license, or other recognition of the competence of the specialist in his/her field, as appropriate.

2. The reputation and standing of the specialist in the views of his/her peers and others familiar with his/her capability or performance.

3. The relationship, if any, of the specialist to the company.

An understanding should exist among the department, including the EIC, the company and the specialist about the nature of the work to be performed by the specialist. Preferably, the understanding should be documented and should cover the following:

1. The objectives and scope of the specialist's work.

2. The specialist's representations as to his relationship, if any, to the company.

3. The methods or assumptions to be used.

4. A comparison of the methods or assumptions to be used with those used in the preceding period.

5. The specialist's understanding of the examiner's corroborative use of the specialist's findings in relation to the representations in the financial statements and examination report.

6. The form and content of the specialist's report that would enable the examiner to make the evaluation described in the following paragraph.

Using the Findings of the Specialist

Although the appropriateness and reasonableness of methods or assumptions used and their application are the responsibility of the specialist, the examiner should obtain an understanding of the methods or assumptions used by the specialist to determine whether the findings are suitable for corroborating the representations in the financial statements. The examiner should consider whether the specialist's findings support the related representations in the financial statements and make appropriate tests of accounting data provided by the company to the specialist. Ordinarily, the examiner would use the work of the specialist unless his/her procedures lead to a belief that the findings are unreasonable in the circumstances. If the specialist is related to the company, the examiner should consider performing additional procedures with respect to some or all of the related specialist's assumptions, methods, or findings to determine whether the findings are not unreasonable or engage an outside specialist for that purpose.

E. Reinsurance

Because of some highly technical aspects of reinsurance, reinsurance receives detailed treatment under Part 4 of this *Handbook.*

F. Uniform Accounting for Insurers

Uniform accounting rules applicable to life insurance are printed in the NAIC *Quarterly and Annual Statement Instructions – Life, Accident & Health.* These should be used in determining the accuracy and appropriateness of expense classification and allocation.

G. Managing General Agents

1. Review the licenses of all managing general agents (MGA):

   a. Note the effective and expiration dates of licenses; and

   b. Note if the MGA is licensed to represent the insurer domiciled in this state.

2. Review all contracts between MGAs and insurance companies:

   a. Each contract must contain a clause that the insurance company may cancel the contract for any reason, upon written notice to the MGA;

   b. Note the limitations each contract places on the MGA with respect to amount of risk insured, geographical location of risk or any other limitations detailed in contract; and

   c. The contract should specifically prohibit the MGA from binding the insurance company to any reinsurance.

3. Sample policies produced by each MGA:

   Each policy must fall within the financial and geographical limitations imposed by each contract with the respective insurance companies.

4. Sample financial accounts submitted by the MGA:

   a. All accounts must be submitted quarterly and within a reasonable amount of time after the end of each quarter; and

   b. All accounts should be in a format and contain such information that will enable an insurance company to use the accounts to properly complete its annual statement.

5. Review internal controls over cash transactions between insurance companies and MGAs:

   a. All funds collected by the MGA on behalf of the insurance company must be deposited in a separate fiduciary account in a bank that is a member of the Federal Reserve System. This account should be owned and controlled by the insurance company;

   b. All funds owed to the insurance company by the MGA should be paid on a timely basis; and

   c. The MGA may retain no more than three months worth of loss and allocated loss expense payments in the fiduciary account owned and operated by the insurance company.

6. Review the insurance company's procedures for monitoring each MGA's activities:

   a. The insurance company should obtain, at least annually, a certified public accountant's report on the business produced by each MGA as well as an opinion of an actuary attesting to the adequacy of loss reserves on business produced by each MGA;

   b. The insurance company should periodically conduct an audit of each MGA's operations; and

   c. The insurance company should make sure that only an officer of the company, who is not affiliated with an MGA, has the authority to bind the insurer to any reinsurance on any participation with syndicates.

H. Insurance Producers

An insurance producer sells, solicits or negotiates insurance on behalf of an insurer and receives compensation or commission. Individuals who are officers, directors, employees and subsidiaries, or affiliates of a company, who do not receive commission from policies written or sold and perform duties unrelated or only indirectly related to the sale, solicitation or negotiation of insurance, are not considered to be insurance producers. Individuals or business entities practicing as insurance producers must maintain a resident or nonresident producer license, when mandated by state law. In order to receive an insurance producer license, individual applicants must pass a written examination that tests: the lines of authority for which application is made, the duties and responsibilities of insurance producers and the state's insurance laws and regulations.

Insurance producers may receive a license in one or more of the following lines of authority or in any other insurance type permitted under state law:

- Life
- Accident and Health or Sickness
- Property
- Casualty
- Variable Life or Variable Annuity Products
- Personal Lines
- Credit

Once an individual or company receives an insurance producer license, the license will remain in effect, unless revoked or suspended, as long as the correlating fees are paid and education requirements are met. Licensed producers are maintained on the NAIC's Producer Database.

If insurance producers violate the governing provisions in the Producer Licensing Model Act, the insurance commissioner may terminate, suspend, or non-renew the insurance producer license. Insurance commissioners may also levy civil penalties against insurance producers if considered necessary.

Notification should be provided to the commissioner when insurers terminate relationships (i.e., agency contracts) with insurance producers either with or without cause. The insurer is required to provide information to the commissioner, if requested, regarding the relationship termination and activity of the producer.

HMO Producers

Health Maintenance Organizations (HMOs) are also permitted to have insurance producers if appropriately licensed. To receive an HMO insurance producer license, in addition to the basic requirements of insurance producers, the HMO producer is required to demonstrate financial responsibility and the reasonable protection of customers. The HMO producer usually completes this requirement by issuing bonds, deposits or other means as specified by the department. Like insurance producers, the licensure of a HMO producer can be denied, suspended or terminated by the state department.

If required by the state, HMO licensed producers shall be appointed to solicit, negotiate, procure or renew HMO membership contracts on behalf of a HMO. Notification of HMO producer appointments is required to be communicated to the state's insurance department. Termination of HMO appointments may occur upon written notification to the state insurance department by either the HMO producer or the HMO.

I. Controlling Producers and Controlled Insurers

Controlling producers are licensed producers, (see above H) who through contracts are able to directly and/or indirectly influence the direction of the controlled insurers management and policies. As with insurance producers, controlling producers receive compensation, commission, or other forms of monetary payment from controlled insurers in return for soliciting, negotiating, or procuring insurance contracts on behalf of the insurer. In accordance with the Business Transacted with Producer Controlled Property/Casualty Insurer Act, with few exceptions, controlling producers who provide gross written premiums equal to or greater than 5% of the controlled insurers admitted assets as reported on the controlled insurers quarterly statement filed as of September 30 of the prior year, are required to maintain compliance with specific contract guidelines, obtain requisite commissioner approval, and provide disclosure to the insured prior to the policy's effective date. Failing to comply with the established requirements may result with the commissioner terminating the relationship between the controlling producer and the controlled insurer and a civil action to establish compensatory damages for the insurer or policyholder.

1. Requirements of Controlling Producers and Controlled Insurers

Contracts between controlling producers and controlled insurers are required to be in writing, contain specific contract provisions if deemed necessary, and be approved by the insurers board of directors. Furthermore, the controlled insurer's audit committee is required to be comprised of independent directors who annually meet with management, CPAs, and casualty actuaries and/or loss reserve specialists to review the sufficiency of the insurer's loss reserves. The findings of the reserve specialists, with regards to the loss ratios and loss reserves established for incurred and outstanding losses for business placed by the producer, has to be reported to the controlled insurer's commissioner by April 1 every year. In order to verify that the controlling producer is not receiving unduly high commissions, the commissioner must also receive detail of the commissions paid and the percentage of the respective paid commissions to the net premiums written, along with comparable data for non-controlling producers placing the same type of business.

2. Specific Contract Provisions

Specific contract provisions between the controlling producer and the controlled insurer are required if the controlling producer meets the 5% written premium threshold as previously indicated. However, the specific contract provisions are not required if the controlling producer does not receive compensation based on the amount of premiums written, or the controlled insurer accepts insurance business only from a controlling producer.

The specific contract provisions are as follows:

a. Upon written notice to the controlling producer, the controlled insurer may terminate the contract for cause. The controlled insurer is entitled to suspend the controlling producer's authority to write business during the duration of any dispute regarding the cause for the termination.

b. The controlling producer shall render accounts including detail of all material transactions to the controlled insurer. This includes information necessary to support all commissions, charges and other fees received by, or owed to, the controlling producer.

c. The controlling producer shall remit all funds due under the terms of the contract to the controlled insurer on at least a monthly basis. Additionally, premiums or installments collected by the controlling producer shall be remitted no later than 90 days after the effective date of a policy placed with the controlled insurer.

d. The controlling producer shall hold all funds collected on behalf of the controlled insurer in a fiduciary capacity, in banks that are members of the Federal Reserve System, and in appropriately identified bank accounts.

e. Separate, identifiable records of business written for the controlled insurer shall be maintained by the controlling producer.

f. The controlling producer shall not assign the contract in whole or in part.

g. The controlled insurer shall provide the controlling producer with its underwriting standards, rules and procedures, manuals setting forth the rates to be charged, and the conditions for the acceptance or rejection of risks. The controlling producer shall adhere to the standards, rules, procedures, rates and conditions. The standards, rules, procedures, rates and conditions shall be the same as those applicable to comparable business placed with the controlled insurer by a producer other than the controlling producer.

h. The contract shall specify the rates and terms of the controlling producer's commissions, charges or other fees and the purposes for those charges or fees. The rates of the commissions, charges and other fees shall not be greater than those applicable to non-controlling producers for comparable business (i.e., same kinds of insurance and risks, similar policy limits, and quality of business) placed with the controlled insurer.

i. Controlling producer compensation based on insurer profits shall not be determined or paid until at least five years after the premiums on liability insurance are earned and at least one year after the premiums are earned on any other type of insurance. Commissions shall not be paid until an independent casualty actuary or loss reserve specialist has confirmed the sufficiency of the controlled insurer's reserves on remaining claims, including incurred but not reported (IBNR).

j. The contract shall specify a percentage limit of writings the controlling producer is entitled to make relative to the controlled insurer's surplus and total writings. The insurer may establish a different limit for each line or subline of business. Notification by the controlled insurer to the controlling producer is required when the established limit is approached. Once the limit has been reached, the controlled insurer is prohibited from accepting business from the controlling producer. The controlling producer shall not attempt to place business with the controlled insurer if it has been notified that the limit has been reached.

k. The controlling producer may bind facultative reinsurance contracts pursuant to obligatory facultative agreements if the contract with the controlled insurer contains underwriting guidelines for assumed and ceded business that includes a list of reinsurers with which automatic agreements are in effect, the coverages and amounts or percentages that may be reinsured, and commission schedules. Otherwise, for business placed by the producer, the controlling producer is entitled to negotiate but is unable to bind reinsurance on behalf of the controlled insurer.

J. Custodial or Safekeeping Agreements

When conducting financial examinations, the custodial or safekeeping agreements should be considered and evaluated with this guidance.

1. An insurance company may by written agreement provide for the custody of its securities with a custodian. If permitted by the state of domicile, the custodian must either be a broker/dealer that is registered with and subject to jurisdiction of the Securities and Exchange Commission, maintains membership in the Securities Investor Protection Corporation, and has a tangible net worth equal to or greater than $250,000,000; or a national bank, state bank, or trust company adequately capitalized and qualified to accept

securities as determined by the standards adopted by the U.S. banking regulators and regulated by state banking laws or a member of the Federal Reserve system. Custodial agreements shall be authorized by a resolution on behalf of the board of directors or an authorized committee of the insurance company. The agreement should state that certificated securities of the insurance company shall be held separate from all other securities. Those securities held indirectly by a custodian or in a clearing corporation shall be separately identified on the custodian's official records as being owned by the insurance company. Registered custodial securities shall be registered in the name of the company, in the name of a nominee of the company, in the name of the custodian or its nominee, or clearing corporation or its nominee. The securities, other than those held to meet deposit requirements, shall be held subject to the instructions of the insurance company, and shall be withdrawable upon the demand of the insurance company. Confirmation of all transfers should be provided to the insurance company in hard-copy or in electronic format.

2. Custodial or safekeeping agreements with an agent, or clearing corporation meeting the requirements herein should contain satisfactory safeguards and controls, including but not limited to the provisions provided below. For the purpose of this guidance, an agent is a national bank, state bank, trust company or broker/dealer with an account in a clearing corporation or a member of the Federal Reserve System. A clearing corporation is a corporation as defined in Article 8 of the Uniform Commercial Code that is organized for the purpose of effecting transactions in securities by computerized book-entry, including the Treasury/Reserve Automated Debt Entry Securities System (TRADES) and Treasury Direct book entry securities systems, except those securities issued under the laws of a foreign country.

   a. The custodian is obligated to indemnify the insurance company for any insurance company's loss of securities in the custodian's custody, except that, unless domiciliary state law, regulation or administrative action otherwise require a stricter standard (Section 2.b. sets forth an example of such a stricter standard), the custodian shall not be so obligated to the extent that such loss was caused by other than the negligence or dishonesty of the custodian;

   b. If domiciliary state law, regulation or administrative action requires a stricter standard of liability for custodians of insurance company securities than that set forth in Section 2.a., then such stricter standard shall apply. An example of a stricter standard that may be used is that the custodian is obligated to indemnify the insurance company for any loss of securities of the insurance company in the custodian's custody occasioned by the negligence or dishonesty of the custodian's officers or employees, or burglary, robbery, holdup, theft, or mysterious disappearance, including loss by damage or destruction;

   c. In the event of a loss of the securities for which the custodian is obligated to indemnify the insurance company, the securities shall be promptly replaced or the value of the securities and the value of any loss of rights or privileges resulting from said loss of securities shall be promptly replaced;

   d. The custodian shall not be liable for any failure to take any action required to be taken hereunder in the event and to the extent that the taking of such action is prevented or delayed by war (whether declared or not and including existing wars), revolution, insurrection, riot, civil commotion, act of God, accident, fire, explosions, stoppage of labor, strikes or other differences with employees, laws, regulations, orders or other acts of any governmental authority, or any other cause whatever beyond its reasonable control;

e. In the event that the custodian gains entry in a clearing corporation through an agent, there should be a written agreement between the custodian and the agent that the agent shall be subjected to the same liability for loss of securities as the custodian. If the agent is governed by laws that differ from the regulation of the custodian, the Commissioner of Insurance of the state of domicile may accept a standard of liability applicable to the agent that is different from the standard liability;

f. If the custodial agreement has been terminated or if 100% of the account assets in any one custody account have been withdrawn, the custodian shall provide written notification, within three business days of termination or withdrawal, to the insurer's domiciliary commissioner;

g. During regular business hours, and upon reasonable notice, an officer or employee of the insurance company, an independent accountant selected by the insurance company and a representative of an appropriate regulatory body shall be entitled to examine, on the premises of the custodian, its records relating to securities, if the custodian is given written instructions to that effect from an authorized officer of the insurance company;

h. The custodian and its agents, upon reasonable request, shall be required to send all reports which they receive from a clearing corporation, which the clearing corporation permits to be redistributed including reports prepared by the custodian's outside auditors, to the insurance company on their respective systems of internal control;

i. To the extent that certain information maintained by the custodian is relied upon by the insurance company in preparation of its annual statement and supporting schedules, the custodian agrees to maintain records sufficient to determine and verify such information.

j. The custodian shall provide, upon written request from a regulator or an authorized officer of the insurance company, the appropriate affidavits, with respect to the insurance company's securities held by the custodian;

k. The custodian shall secure and maintain insurance protection in an adequate amount; and

l. The foreign bank acting as a custodian, or a U.S. custodian's foreign agent, or a foreign clearing corporation is only holding foreign securities or securities required by the foreign country in order for the insurer to do business in that country. A U.S. custodian must hold all other securities.

3. Except as provided below, the examiner shall verify such securities by actual inspection and count, and whenever necessary ascertain whether the securities are the specific ones acquired by the company:

a. Securities on deposit with state officials need not be counted [provided] if a certificate of verification is secured directly from the custodian or insurance commissioner.

b. Where domiciliary state law, regulation, or administrative action does not prohibit the use of custodial arrangements under which actual inspection or count of specific securities acquired is not possible, and the insurance company uses such an arrangement, the examiners shall:

- Apply the provisions of Sections d. and g. below, in cases where the custodian, under the controlling custodial or safekeeping agreement, is permitted to carry securities indirectly or otherwise commingled form;
- Apply the provisions of Sections e. and g. below, in cases where the custodian, under the controlling custodial or safekeeping agreement, directly or indirectly participates in the Treasury Reserve Automated Debt Entry Securities System (TRADES) or Treasury Direct system. These systems are computerized programs sponsored by the United States department of the Treasury and certain agencies and instrumentalities of the United States for holding and transferring securities of the United States government and the agencies and instrumentalities, respectively, in Federal Reserve Banks through banks which are members of the Federal Reserve System or which otherwise have access to such computerized systems; and
- Apply the provisions of Section f. and g. below, in cases where the facilities of a clearing corporation are used, either directly or indirectly through a custodian, under the controlling custodial or safekeeping agreement.

c. Securities held by a custodian under other custodial or safekeeping arrangements need not be counted, at the discretion of the examiner-in-charge, if the following criteria [is] are met (provided the domiciliary state laws do not require that such securities be counted and inspected during an examination):

- Examiners are furnished a copy of the custodial or safekeeping agreements;
- They are satisfied such agreement has the necessary safeguards and controls;
- The securities are held by a custodian licensed by the United States or any state thereof, and such custodian is regularly examined by the applicable licensing authority;
- The securities so deposited are at all times kept separate and apart from other deposit accounts with the custodian, so that at all times they may be identified as belonging solely to the company for which they are held;
- If such a deposit is not counted, a verification certificate signed by an authorized signatory of the custodian holding the deposit shall be secured by the examiners directly;
- Such certificate shall be in sufficient detail to permit adequate identification of the securities; and
- Such certificate may be accepted in lieu of actual count provided it meets the above requirements and the examiners are satisfied that the representation thus made is in accordance with the facts.

d. Where not prohibited by domiciliary state law and if permitted by the terms of the controlling custodial or safekeeping agreement containing satisfactory safeguards and controls, securities held by a custodian that meets the requirements of Section c. above, may be held by the custodian, in bulk as a part of a "jumbo" certificate, or other system under which there is a commingling of securities held in custody. In such cases, the examiners shall:

- Obtain directly from the custodian a certified listing of the securities held as of the date of examination for the account of the insurance company under examination;
- Obtain a copy of the insurance company's listing of the securities held by the custodian for the insurance company's account as of the date of examination; and
- Match the positions shown on the custodian's listing to the positions shown on the company's listing, and reconcile any differences.

e. Custodians which meet the requirements of Section c. above, and which either are members of the Federal Reserve System or non member banks redepositing securities with a member bank, may, when acting as custodians for insurance companies, use the Treasury/Reserve Automated Debt Entry Securities System (TRADES) or the Treasury Direct book entry securities systems under a written agreement with the insurance company permitting such utilization. In such cases, the examiners shall follow the procedures set forth in Sections c. above.

f. Where not prohibited by domiciliary state law, an insurance company may, under a written agreement, use the facilities of a clearing corporation, either directly or through a custodian, subject to the requirements of Section c. above. In such cases, the examiners shall:

- Obtain directly from the depository if direct deposit is used, or from the custodian if indirect deposit is used, a certified listing of the securities held in the clearing corporation as of the date of examination for the account of the insurance company under examination;
- Obtain a copy of the insurance company's listing of its securities held by the clearing corporation as of the date of examination;
- Match the positions shown on the clearing corporation's or custodian's listing to the positions shown on the company's listing, and reconcile any differences; and
- Ascertain that the securities are held by a clearing corporation regulated by the Securities and Exchange Commission, the Federal Reserve System, or the banking authorities in its state of domicile.

g. In carrying out their responsibilities under Section d, e, and f above, it is important that the examiners satisfy themselves as to the integrity of the accounting controls and verification and security procedures of the custodian and/or the clearing corporation, as the case may be. This satisfaction may be obtained by securing the most recent report on the review of the custodian's system of internal controls pertaining to custodian record keeping issued by the respective organization's independent auditors.

K. Use of Independent Certified Public Accountants (CPA) on Multi-state Examinations

When evaluating staffing needs to schedule examinations of domestic insurers, licensed in multiple states, state insurance departments may find it necessary to engage an independent certified public accountant or accounting firm, hereinafter referred to as CPA, to participate in an examination. An insurance department's decision to engage a CPA may arise due to, among other things, insufficient examination staff or the need to meet statutory mandates. While the foregoing circumstances may lead an insurance department to contract the services of a CPA, the department should consider the long term effects of not maintaining an appropriate level of qualified staff. Maintaining competent examiners on examinations and during interim periods enhances the department's ability to effectively regulate domestic insurers and foreign insurers with substantial state premium writings. Through the examination process, examiners develop expertise in, and knowledge of state laws and regulations, various types of insurance products, investment practices, loss/benefits reserving techniques, reinsurance transactions etc., that are useful in effectively and efficiently assessing a domestic company's reports of financial condition and results of operations. This internal expertise is particularly important in handling troubled insurance companies.

The use of a CPA on an examination, where the insurer is licensed in more than one state, will vary by examination and according to each state's circumstances. While there exists many different levels of service that a CPA may provide an insurance department, the use of a CPA in an examination is typically accomplished through an "agreed-upon procedures engagement." Other levels of service, such as an audit of a company's financial statements performed in accordance with generally accepted auditing standards, is not considered, on a stand alone basis, an acceptable substitute for a statutory examination because of its nature and limited examination of compliance with statutory requirements. The following establishes guidelines and standards for engaging a CPA to perform agreed-upon procedures.

1. Engaging a CPA to Perform Agreed-Upon Procedures

The American Institute of Certified Public Accountants (AICPA) Statement on Auditing Standards (SAS) No. 75, *Engagements to Apply Agreed-Upon Procedures to Specified Elements, Accounts, or Items of a Financial Statement*, sets forth the standards and provides guidance to the CPA when performing and reporting on engagements to apply agreed-upon procedures. This Statement allows an independent CPA to accept an engagement where the scope is limited to applying agreed-upon procedures to accounting information that is part of, but significantly less than a financial statement. In an agreed-upon procedures engagement, the CPA performs specific procedures on specific elements, accounts or items of a financial statement and issues a report of findings based on those procedures. The insurance department and the CPA agree upon the procedures to be performed by the CPA that the insurance department believes are appropriate. Therefore, the insurance department assumes all responsibility for the sufficiency of the procedures and the risk that those procedures might be insufficient for their purposes. Because the CPA will only report on the findings of the procedures performed, any conclusions regarding the findings, and disposition thereof, must be made by the department. Additionally, the CPA has no responsibility to determine the differences between the agreed-upon procedures to be performed and the procedures that the CPA would have determined necessary had he or she been engaged to perform another form of engagement, such as an audit under generally accepted auditing standards. The department should review SAS No. 75, and consider the CPA's professional standards prior to engaging an accounting firm to provide this type of service.

The insurance department must attain certain standards relative to the examination report, planning and field work that are in accordance with the NAIC *Financial Condition Examiners Handbook.* These standards relate to the responsibilities of the insurance department and the utility of the examination report in achieving regulatory objectives when engaging a CPA to perform agreed-upon procedures.

The standards for engaging a CPA to perform agreed-upon procedures in examinations are as follows:

Standards of Examination Planning and Field Work

a. The agreed-upon procedures shall be planned and developed according to the NAIC *Financial Condition Examiners Handbook* under the supervision and with the participation of the insurance department's designee, who shall be certified by the Society of Financial Examiners to hold, or be eligible to hold, the title of Certified Financial Examiner (CFE).
b. The agreed-upon procedures, including the examination planning memorandum, applicable risk analysis workpapers and related materials if applicable to the engagement, shall be reviewed and approved by the insurance department's designee.
c. The insurance department's designee shall supervise all significant field work activities.
d. The results and findings of the agreed-upon procedures shall be reviewed for reasonableness and sufficiency, and accompanying workpapers shall be reviewed for adequacy of documentation by the insurance department's designee.

Standards of Examination Reports

a. The report shall be prepared by the insurance department in accordance with the NAIC *Financial Condition Examiners Handbook* and departmental policy.
b. The report shall not include as attachments, reports or letters prepared by the CPA in connection with the engagement.
c. The report shall be signed by the insurance department's designee.

The following amplifies the standards outlined above and provides guidance for meeting the standards.

Standards of Examination Planning and Field Work

The first standard of examination planning and field work requires that the agreed-upon procedures be planned and developed according to the NAIC *Financial Condition Examiners Handbook* under the supervision and with the participation of the insurance department's designee, who must be certified by the Society of Financial Examiners to hold, or be eligible to hold, the title of Certified Financial Examiner (CFE). In addition, since the CPA performing an agreed-upon procedures engagement is only responsible for the procedures performed and therefore has a limited obligation to the commissioner and policyholders, the insurance department's designee must be an employee of the insurance department, or be employed on a contract basis with the insurance department.

Utilizing a CPA to assist in the planning process is at the discretion of the insurance department and will likely depend on the department's examination staffing level and required expertise for the examination. In situations where the CPA is used in the planning process, the insurance department's designee shall ensure that the planning is done in accordance with this *Handbook.*

The second standard of examination planning and field work requires that the agreed-upon procedures, including the examination planning memorandum, applicable specific risk analysis workpapers and related materials if performed as part of the agreed-upon procedures, be reviewed and approved by the insurance department's designee. This is a substantive review of the agreed-upon procedures for all accounts and regulatory compliance issues and shall be evidenced by the insurance department's designee's initials and date on all relevant planning documents. Performing a substantive review of the procedures is necessary because of the department's responsibility for the procedures.

The third standard of examination planning and field work requires that the insurance department's designee supervise all significant field work activities. These activities include, but are not limited to, communications with the company's independent auditors and senior management, application and interpretations of statutory accounting principles, application of the insurance laws and regulations for compliance and any significant modifications to the agreed-upon procedures.

The fourth standard of examination planning and field work requires that the insurance department's designee review the results and findings of the agreed-upon procedures for reasonableness and sufficiency, and workpaper documentation for adequacy. As in an examination performed by insurance department employees, the insurance department's designee shall perform a "detailed review," as defined in this *Handbook*, of the results and findings of the procedures performed. This review should focus primarily on the technical accuracy of the work performed (e.g., the procedures were performed correctly and results correctly interpreted) and the results and findings of the procedures and whether additional procedures should be performed. In addition, the designee should perform a "general review," as defined in this *Handbook*, to ensure that examination risk has been reduced to an acceptable level.

The third and fourth standards of examination planning and field work both recognize planning as an evolving process and that modifications to the agreed-upon procedures may be necessary. Under an agreed-upon procedures arrangement, the insurance department should remain cognizant of its responsibilities and those of the CPA. Regulatory supervision is critical to identifying examination procedures that are sufficient for identifying material financial errors or violations of state requirements. Where examination procedures are found to be insufficient, the insurance department's designee shall take the necessary action to redirect the nature and extent of those procedures to ensure the responsibilities of the commissioner to the policyholders are met on the examination.

Standards of Examination Reports

The first standard of examination reports requires that the report be prepared by the insurance department in accordance with the NAIC *Financial Condition Examiners Handbook* and departmental policy. Since the report is the responsibility and property of the insurance department, the department is to be directly and actively involved in developing the contents of the examination report. This standard would not preclude a CPA from participating in drafting a Report on Examination, so long as the report form complies with this *Handbook* and meets the second standard of examination reports (i.e., does not include CPA's Agreed-Upon Procedures Report).

The second standard of examination reports provides that the examination report not include reports prepared by the CPA in connection with the engagement including the CPA's Agreed-Upon Procedures Report and related letters, appendices and any other documents, which are not the product of the insurance department. The CPA's Agreed-Upon Procedures Report, letters and other documentation provided to the insurance department constitute workpapers supporting the examination report. This standard ensures that reports are prepared in accordance with the NAIC *Financial Condition Examiners Handbook* and provide the necessary information to assist other state insurance regulators in assessing the company's solvency.

The third standard of examination reports requires that the report be signed by the insurance department's designee. As defined in the first standard of planning and field work, this person shall be certified by the Society of Financial Examiners to hold, or be eligible to hold, the title of CFE. Such person has demonstrated proficiency in their knowledge of statutory accounting principles and other procedures and tools utilized to examine insurance companies. In addition this individual has specialized regulatory expertise resulting from their required experience as a financial regulator. This qualification helps ensure the examination was conducted in accordance with the state's statutory requirements and that the financial statements were prepared in accordance with the state's accounting rules. Because the insurance department is solely responsible for the examination and report thereon, a standard requiring the signature of the department's designee is considered necessary and appropriate given the nature of an agreed-upon procedures engagement. Requiring that the department's designee sign the examination report helps ensure the examination was conducted in accordance with the standards set forth in this *Handbook* and is equivalent, in substance, to an examination solely performed by the department's employees.

2. Conflicts-of-Interest

A conflict-of-interest may occur if an examination of a company is performed by a CPA who has a significant relationship with the company, its affiliates or their management (financial or non-financial) that may impair in fact or appearance, the CPA's independence. To evaluate any such conflicts of interest, the insurance department should request a disclosure letter from the prospective CPA regarding the CPA's past, present or planned relationships, both financial and non-financial, with the examined company or its affiliates. The disclosure letter should discuss the nature of the services provided by the CPA and the amount of fees paid to the CPA by the company over the preceding five years.

Determining whether a potential conflict of interest exists is a matter of considerable judgment. As CPAs provide many different types of services (e.g., accounting, auditing, actuarial, management and tax consulting), it will be necessary to evaluate the nature of services provided and the amount of fees involved when determining whether a potential conflict of interest exist.

3. Maintenance of working papers

The insurance department should maintain, at a minimum, a complete photocopied set of the CPA's original workpapers.

Contract Examiners' Immunity Privileges

When hiring contract examiners to perform all or portions of a state insurance examination, the state insurance department should consider the following items related to contract examiners' immunity prior to finalizing an agreement.

- Review the NAIC's Model Examination Law, Section 8 to determine if your state has adopted these provisions in its statutes. If your state has not adopted the Model Law confirm if it has adopted similar language which grants immunity to any examiner appointed by a Commissioner.

- Determine if there are any relevant court decisions or opinions, which hold that an examiner appointed by the Commissioner is, granted immunity under common law from liability in the performance of his/her duties.

- Verify if contract examiners in your state are required to carry liability insurance coverage for work performed. Determine if your state provides insurance coverage to these contract examiners in the performance of their duties.

L. TeamMate

TeamMate is an electronic document organizer software package that the states have the option to purchase to assist them in conducting examinations. This software enables the examiners to compile examination workpaper documentation into a centralized paperless electronic file. The software package tracks completion and review of examination procedures and is capable of including the examination documentation (Word documents, spreadsheets, Watermark images, etc.) entirely within the program. To assist in the utilization of TeamMate, the NAIC has developed TeamMate TeamStores for incorporation into this program. The NAIC TeamStores were developed to provide the states with uniform procedures that mirror the recommended internal control and examination procedures and exhibits included within this *Handbook*.

TeamStores, which are available on StateNet, have been developed for the Specific Risk Analyses (SRAs) included in Part 2, as well as certain workpaper exhibits. The TeamStores will be updated by the NAIC on an annual basis to incorporate any changes. Periodic updates may also occur throughout the year. All significant annual and periodic updates will be provided in new TeamStores, so that the original TeamStores are preserved. The NAIC TeamStores will be clearly marked to indicate the most recent version, and all TeamStore versions posted will continue to be available from StateNet through the TeamStore Archives link. Additionally, a summary of all the annual and periodic revisions will be provided to clearly indicate the incurred revisions. It is recommended that each state designate one individual to retrieve the NAIC provided TeamStores and make any state specific alterations or customizations, reducing the possibility of maintaining numerous versions. Information on how to obtain, import, customize and use the NAIC TeamMate TeamStores is available on the NAIC I-Site and within Exhibit N.

V. REPORTING EXAMINATION PROGRESS AND FINDINGS

This section provides some general guidelines on procedures in reporting examination progress and findings.

A. Interim Reporting to Chief Examiner

At intervals during the examination, not less than monthly, the examiner-in-charge should address a memorandum to the Chief Examiner setting forth:

1. Any significant issues and the EIC's proposed resolution; and
2. Current assignment of each examiner.

B. Interim Reporting by Zone Examiner to their Respective Zones

The requirement of periodic status reports and their confidentiality will be determined on a zone basis.

If the zone determines that the examiner representing the zone be required to prepare and submit status reports on the progress of the examination, the following reporting format is suggested. The reports shall include information on the progress made in addressing the concerns expressed by the zone when the examiner was assigned to the examination, any significant issues disclosed and proposed resolutions. The examiner-in-charge should be given the opportunity to comment and sign the status reports; however, the signature of the examiner-in-charge does not necessarily convey agreement with the information disclosed in the status report. The reports should be prepared not less frequently than monthly, and should be submitted to the zone secretary, the chief examiner of the participating state and the chief examiner of the domiciliary state. The responsibility for requiring the zone examiner to prepare and submit periodic status reports rests with each individual zone. Other states in the zone may request copies of the status reports from the zone secretary. However, states should be aware that the issues disclosed in the status reports are preliminary in nature, and should not take action based on the preliminary findings.

C. The Report on a Full-scope Examination

1. Purpose

The fundamental purposes of a financial condition examination report are (1) to assess the financial condition of the company, and (2) to set forth findings of fact (together with citations of pertinent laws, regulations, and rules) with regard to any material adverse findings disclosed by the examination.

The report should communicate to the appropriate regulatory officials information needed to fulfill their regulatory responsibilities, including information needed by regulatory personnel involved in the admission of companies. Whenever an examiner develops and communicates unessential information, it results in the waste of limited examination resources. The same is true whenever the format and content of an examination report fail to provide specific information needed for any disciplinary or other regulatory action. Consequently, an examination report should focus on problem areas. It should not refer to matters that are immaterial or not of regulatory concern. It should not be directed to company management and should not contain minor unenforceable "housekeeping" recommendations.

2. Format

The report on examination should be structured and written to communicate to regulatory officials examination findings of regulatory importance. It should be written in a manner understandable by someone who is unfamiliar with the company examined. Thus, when discussing certain findings, it may be necessary to provide some background information. However, such information should be limited to data relevant to the issue involved and should be presented as succinctly as possible.

Each report on examination should contain the following sections:

a. Table of Contents (with contents and pages denoted);

b. Salutation (addressing the report to (1) the chair of the NAIC Financial Condition (E) Committee, (2) the secretary of each zone, represented by participating examiners, and (3) the commissioner of the domiciliary state);

c. Description of the company (including the last examination date and a discussion of the important information concerning the examined company's management and control, territory and plan of operation, and reinsurance). If the company is a member of a holding company system, a chart should be presented depicting the company's relationship to the system; and

d. Scope of the examination (summarize the reasons for examining the company, the accounts and activities that were examined, and the emphasis placed on the audit of these accounts and activities).

In general, a financial condition examination shall at least encompass a review of all of the following matters to assess their impact on financial condition and their conformity with related laws. Each of these matters should be appropriately noted in the scope section:

(1) company history;
(2) management and control;
(3) corporate records;
(4) fidelity bonds and other insurance;
(5) officers,' employees,' and agents' welfare and pension plans;
(6) territory and plan of operation;
(7) growth of company;
(8) business in force by states;
(9) mortality and loss experience;
(10) reinsurance;
(11) accounts and records; and
(12) financial statements
- statement of assets and liabilities
- statement of operations
- supporting schedules and exhibits to the extent deemed desirable
- reconciliation of surplus for the period since the last examination
- analysis of changes in financial statements resulting from the examination

In addition, if any other accounts or activities were reviewed during the examination, these matters should appropriately be noted in the "scope" section.

e. Body of Report. The body shall contain the financial statements consisting of a statement of assets and liabilities, statement of operations, reconciliation of surplus and analysis of changes resulting from the examination. The financial statements shall be followed by a discussion of adverse findings, material changes in the financial statements, and other important regulatory information disclosed by the examination.

The discussion of these matters shall be presented in the following manner: Information relating to areas listed above, which generally should be reviewed in every financial condition examination, shall be presented in the order that these areas are listed above. The discussion of any other important findings shall follow and shall be arranged in a logical and understandable manner.

If the examination of any account or activity listed in the "scope" section fails to disclose either a significant adverse finding, a material change in the financial statements, or other information of regulatory significance or requiring regulatory action, it is not necessary to comment on the account or activity in the "body" of the report.

If the examination report contains a critical finding in reference to any part of the company's activities, the finding should be supported adequately by evidence set forth in, or appended to the report, or in the workpapers. This evidence would be available to support the findings if a hearing is called on the report or if a disciplinary proceeding is based upon it.

Any transaction consummated by a company subsequent to the effective date of an examination, which is for the purpose of adjusting the company's previously reported financial condition, shall not be recognized in the preparation of the examiners' financial statement in the report of examination.

Such transaction may be described by a qualifying statement, or statements, when supported by a reference to the original minutes or document evidencing such subsequent transaction or transactions. Such supporting data shall be set forth in a clearly captioned appendix or appendices to the report.

The size of examination report should depend upon the number and importance of the adverse findings disclosed by the examination. If there are few or no adverse findings, the report should be very short, even though the company examined may be very large and complex. On the other hand, if serious adverse findings are disclosed, the report may be relatively long and detailed.

f. Performance Audit Comments. In addition to including comments in the report that directly relate to the solvency of the company, examiners may also make performance audit comments, where appropriate. These comments may be similar to the management letter comments frequently made by CPA firms.

Generally, standard examination techniques involve identifying a problem and reporting on it in the examination report. Performance auditing techniques require examiners to determine why something is a problem, what caused the problem, and how the problem can be corrected. When examiners include performance audit comments in the examination report, the report generally is more informative and it gives readers a better understanding of how well the company is managed.

Many insolvencies are caused by mismanagement. When examiners identify systems, operational and management problems, they may have an opportunity to alert management to problems that, if left uncorrected, could ultimately lead to insolvency. Consequently, examiners should report on and constructively suggest how management should correct these problems identified during the examination.

Performance audit comments usually should contain these attributes:

- The condition. This is a concise statement of the problem found;
- The cause. Report on what factors caused or created the problem;
- The effect. Examiners should determine how material the problem is and report on what effect the problem has on the financial statements, financial condition of the company, or the company's operations;
- The criteria. Relate the examination finding to the criteria that makes the "condition" a problem. For example, if a company violated an investment statute, it is the statute that the examiner uses as a standard to determine that a problem exists. It is the criteria that explains to the reader why something is a problem; and
- The recommendation. In this attribute, the examiner recommends to the company what it should do to correct the problem. If a company has already implemented the recommendation, also mention that fact.

3. Alternate Format

The following is a recommended format and contents summary for association financial condition examination reports. Report comments should be brief, objective and void of unessential information. Each report should contain a minimum of the following sections:

a. Table of Contents (with contents and pages denoted)

b. Salutation (addressing the report to (1) the chair of the NAIC Financial Condition (E) Committee, (2) the secretary of each zone represented, and (3) the commissioner of the domiciliary state)

c. Scope of Examination

- Period covered by examination – suggested additional wording, "including any material transactions and/or events occurring subsequent to the examination date and noted during the course of this examination."
- Examination procedure employed – state any reliance upon IRIS reports, independent audit reports, Internal Revenue Service audit reports, internal audit department reports, etc.
- Status of adverse findings, material changes in the financial statement, and other significant regulatory information disclosed in the previous examination – update of previous examination findings.

d. History

- General – state company's organization date, authorized lines of insurance, and amendments to articles of incorporation and bylaws during the examination period.
- Capital Stock – state the number of authorized and issued/outstanding shares, related par values and, if company is a controlled insurer, the controlling person.
- Dividends to Stockholders – schedule of dividends declared and/or paid during the examination period. Comment on extraordinary dividends.
- Management – list directors by name, location and principal occupation; senior officers by name and title; and principal internal committees and members.

- Conflict of Interest Procedure – state any exceptions noted in a review of such forms completed by management during the examination period.
- Corporate Records – state whether minutes of meetings of stockholders, directors, and committees adequately approve and support company transactions and events. State whether the previous examination report was reviewed by company directors.
- Acquisitions, Mergers, Disposals, Dissolutions, and Purchases or Sales though Reinsurance – include appropriate comments for any such major corporate event in which the company is involved during the examination period.
- Surplus Debentures – comment on debentures issued or retired during the examination period and on those outstanding at the current examination date.

e. Affiliated Companies – include holding company organization chart, summary of cost-sharing agreements, and any significant regulatory information concerning parent, subsidiaries and affiliates.

f. Fidelity Bond and Other Insurance – state the amount of such bond and whether it meets the NAIC suggested minimum. A general comment concerning other coverages should be sufficient unless there is reason to be more specific.

g. Pension, Stock Ownership, and Insurance Plans – state briefly the type of plans offered by the company, omitting details concerning eligibility requirements and benefits available to company employees and agents. State whether the provision was made in the financial statement for company obligations under such plans.

h. Statutory Deposits – schedule by state, type of asset on deposit and corresponding aggregate deposit, and market values.

i. Insurance Products and Related Practices

- Policy Forms and Underwriting – state exceptions noted in a comparison of form stock to approved forms. State risk retention limits.
- Territory and Plan of Operation – list or make exception comments concerning licensing authorities. Comment on marketing system employed.
- Advertising and Sales Material – compare sales material to related policies and comment on any material exceptions.
- Treatment of Policyholders – include comments or statistical summaries concerning claim settlement practices consistent with the review of claims. State whether the company maintains some control over policyholder complaints.

j. Reinsurance – comment on treaties containing unusual provisions, particularly those where a projected final accounting fails to show a transfer of risk. Financial statement adjustments may be necessary to properly account for the actual intent of a treaty.

k. Accounts and Records – comment on system employed by company, any related deficiencies, and significant delays encountered in obtaining examination-requested information.

l. Financial Statement – include a balance sheet, a summary of operations or an underwriting and investment exhibit, a capital and surplus account, and an analysis of surplus.

m. Comments on Financial Statement – the examination report should focus on problem areas and should not refer to matters that are immaterial or not of regulatory concern. Include in this section only those balance sheet captions under which comments are to be made relative to adverse findings, material changes in financials, and other significant regulatory information disclosed by the examination.

n. Capital and Surplus – statement of examination findings of capital paid up, gross paid-in and contributed surplus, and unassigned funds (surplus). Include a comparative analysis of changes in the financial statement resulting from examination findings.

o. Conclusion – an acknowledgment of participating examiners and signature page for zone examiners.

D. The Report on a Limited-scope Examination

1. Purpose

The full-scope examination is just one of many tools available to state insurance departments to monitor the solvency of insurance companies. By definition, the full-scope examination is comprehensive, and limitations on resources generally preclude performing a full-scope examination at frequent intervals. Therefore, an important aspect of the full-scope examination process is the recommendations of the examiners regarding areas of the company that should be scheduled for some type of specific follow-up action by the department, such as a limited-scope examination, correspondence from the chief examiner, meeting with the company, or other matters.

The following examples are by no means all-inclusive, and are submitted to illustrate examiner findings that should be noted for some sort of follow-up activity by the Department:

- The examiner does not note any adverse findings regarding reinsurance balances, but observes that there is a working layer treaty with heavy losses ceded that is coming up for renewal on January 1. The examiner notes that follow-up procedures are recommended shortly after the beginning of the year to determine whether the new treaty terms will materially impact the operations of the company; and

- The examiners learn that the company has scheduled to implement a significant system conversion to a new policy management system. Follow-up procedures are recommended for one year from the date of the report to determine whether the system conversion occurred smoothly, and review the impact on internal controls of the company;

- The examiners learn that the company will begin writing a new line of long-tailed business that involves use of third party administrators for handling the underwriting and claims management functions. Follow-up procedures are recommended to be scheduled for the following year to review the progress of this new book of business, and determine the adequacy of the internal controls the company has put in place.

A limited-scope examination's purpose is to review specific aspects of the company's operations or financial statements, to perform specific procedures with respect to those aspects, and to report as to the examiners' findings thereon. By definition, a limited-scope examination is less comprehensive than a full-scope examination. A limited-scope examination will generally focus on areas currently perceived by the department to be problem areas or potential problem areas. Consequently, the limited-scope examination report should provide specific information for any disciplinary or other regulatory action.

2. Format

The report on a limited-scope examination should be structured and written to communicate to regulatory officials the findings of specific areas reviewed. In many instances, a limited-scope examination report will be a follow-up to a finding of a recent full-scope examination. It may be appropriate to refer to the full-scope examination report for general background information about the company. However, with regard to the specific areas covered by the limited-scope examination, information should be provided to clearly set forth those areas, background as to why such areas are the subject of the report if not otherwise evident, a brief description of the procedures performed, and the examiner's findings.

Each report on a limited-scope examination should contain the following section:

a. Table of Contents (with contents and pages denoted)

b. Salutation

c. An identification of the company, the date of the last full-scope examination that was performed at the company, and a description of the concerns that gave rise to the need for the subject limited-scope examination.

d. A disclosure that the report is a limited-scope examination, and is not intended to communicate all matters of importance for an understanding of the company's financial condition.

e. Scope of the Examination, identifying those areas that were specifically reviewed and a brief description of the procedures performed. For example, a limited-scope examination could review specifically the collectibility of certain reinsurance balances. The description of the procedures would not entail each and every step that was performed but would describe generally whether the procedures were limited to inquiry of company officials, included more substantive tests such as independent verification, confirmation with third parties or other procedures.

f. The examiners' findings should be presented, with an indication for each area examined that the issue or concern that gave rise to the need for the limited-scope examination has now been resolved, has yet to be resolved and its current status, and other information necessary for further regulatory action. Unlike a full-scope examination for which it is not necessary to comment on areas that do not result in significant adverse findings, a limited-scope examination report should include an affirmative statement, if such is the case, that no significant adjustments or adverse findings were identified for the area reviewed.

g. An important aspect of the full-scope examination process is the recommendations of the examiners regarding areas of the company that should be scheduled for further follow-up action by the department, such as another limited-scope examination, correspondence from the chief examiner, meeting with the company, and other matters.

h. Performance Audit Comments. As with a full-scope examination, the body of the limited-scope examination report should communicate any recommendations that came to the examiners' attention.

E. Discussion of Report Findings with Company Officials

Periodically, during an examination, it will be necessary for examiners to discuss tentative findings or other matters with company officials. Examiners are encouraged to initiate such discussions.

However, discussions with company officials, except regarding minor matters, should be held only with the knowledge of the examiner-in-charge.

The purpose of discussions with company officials concerning report findings should be limited to assisting the examiners in ascertaining facts and in verifying the accuracy of the findings. Whenever the examiners have doubt as to the accuracy of an examination finding, they should give the company an opportunity to review the finding and the material supporting it.

F. Typing of Reports, and Draft Reports for Participating Zone Examiners

Procedures adopted by the home state for the typing, printing and reproduction of the report on examination are to be followed. All participating zone examiners shall be furnished a draft of the report prior to leaving the assignment.

G. Coordination of Association Examination Reports and Resolution of Report Conflicts

1. Where no controversy exists and the Report of Examination has been agreed upon and signed by the participating examiners and adopted by the domiciliary state, it shall be the duty of the said domiciliary state to immediately distribute a copy of the Report of Examination to each of the states in which the company is licensed to transact business. Examination reports may be mailed in hard copy form to the other states, sent in an electronic format or posted to the Internet. If the report is posted to the Internet, the state must proactively communicate the availability of the report to the other state insurance departments. If a state requests a hard copy of the examination report, such must be sent to the state in a timely manner. If the department has the company mail out the reports to other states in which it does business, the department should have an established procedure to obtain evidence from the company that such reports were mailed.

2. If the participating examiners do not agree and cannot sign a unanimous report of examination, it shall then be the duty of the commissioner of the domiciliary state to call a conference with the commissioners of the states of the participating examiners in an effort to settle differences. If no agreement results from the conference, majority and one or more minority reports shall be made, and it shall then be the duty of the commissioner of the domiciliary state to distribute copies of the majority and minority reports to those states in which the company is licensed to transact business.

3. In those instances in which the company under examination shall request a hearing on the report of examination, it shall be the duty of the commissioner of the domiciliary state to call a hearing in accordance with the laws of that state, request the attendance of the participating examiners, and invite the attendance of commissioners whose examiners participated in such examination including the respective zone secretaries; thereafter, the

supervisory official of the home state shall notify, at least once in each ninety days, the supervisory official of each participating state, the secretary of each participating zone and the chair of the Financial Condition (E) Committee, of the progress of the hearing and the reasons for any delay or postponement in the release of the examination report.

4. If the report of an association examination is not released within three months after completion and signature by a majority of the participating states, the secretary of any zone participating in the examination may make such report, or any part thereof, available to the individual states in his zone.

5. When an association examination has been called, which call covers a group of companies, the examination reports of the companies in the group are to be handled in accordance with subparagraph 1 above, and should not be delayed only because the examination of the remainder of the companies in the group has not been completed.

H. Post Examination Follow-up Procedures

The effectiveness of the examination system would be enhanced if effective follow-up procedures are instituted by the home state insurance department. Periodically, after the report has been submitted, inquiries should be made to the company to elicit the extent of corrective action, not otherwise known, on report recommendations and criticisms. The timing and extent of these inquiries or other follow-up action may be determined based upon recommendations of examiners during a full-scope or limited examination. A lack of satisfactory corrective action by the company may be cause for consideration of official proceedings against the directors and officers.

VI. COMMENTS AND GRIEVANCE PROCEDURE REGARDING COMPLIANCE WITH EXAMINATION STANDARDS

This section covers procedures to be followed by industry and regulators relating to comments and grievances involving compliance with examination standards.

Each comment or grievance must be put in writing and presented in the following format. The matter is to be addressed to the Examination Oversight (E) Task Force.

The resolution of each submission either will be made or administered by the Task Force with ratification by the parent committee of the NAIC. Subsequent to ratification of action taken, the person making the submission will be notified.

The above procedure should suffice to receive and properly respond to any and all matters involving compliance with examination standards.

COMPLIANCE WITH EXAMINATION STANDARDS

COMMENTS AND GRIEVANCES

Date:

To: Chair, Examination Oversight (E) Task Force

From:

Nature of Comment and/or Grievance and Proposed Method for Resolution, if any. (Please submit complete particulars together with any references, etc.)

EXHIBIT A
EXAMINATION PLANNING PROCEDURES CHECKLIST

Company Name ____

____

Period of Examination ____

	Done By	Date
A. Gather Necessary Planning Information		
1. Complete, or have company personnel complete, as early as practical the Examination Planning Questionnaire (EPQ) and Evaluation of Controls in Information Systems Questionnaire (ISQ).		
2. Request a copy of the in-house financial analyst's reports on the company's financial condition and operating results since the last examination.		
3. Request copies or originals of relevant information filed with the department for review and analysis. Such information generally includes:		
a. Annual statements for the years under review.		
b. Previous examination report and supporting workpapers.		
c. Market conduct report.		
d. CPA audit report.		
e. Actuarial opinion, for years under review.		
f. Independent loss reserve analysis report, if done.		
g. Management's discussion and analysis letter.		
h. Risk-based capital report.		
i. Holding company registration statements, for years under review.		
j. SEC registration statements, latest 10K & 10Q.		
Other relevant information may include:		
k. Examination jumpstart reports.		
l. IRIS reports.		
m. Department's correspondence file.		
n. Inter-divisional memorandum.		
o. NAIC database reports (SAD, RIRS, CDS).		

Done By	Date

p. Credit rating agency reports.

q. Articles of incorporation, by-laws and amendments.

r. Recently approved agreements or contracts (e.g., expense sharing agreements, assumption reinsurance contracts, custodial agreements).

B. Obtain an Understanding of Company's Business

1. Utilizing the information obtained in steps 1, 2 and 3 above, obtain an understanding of the company's business. Knowledge of the company's business should encompass areas such as:

a. Company background (e.g., organization and formation, principal lines of business, capital structure, ownership, last financial condition and market conduct examinations, etc.).

b. Pending matters (e.g., request for rate increases, approval of custodial agreement and market conduct examinations, etc.).

c. Related party relationships and transactions (e.g., identify parent, affiliates, subsidiaries and ultimate controlling person, principal owners, large shareholders, board of directors, officers, etc.).

d. Management and control environment (see Exhibit B & C) (e.g., stable management, role of the board of directors, management's response to examination inquiries, etc.).

Other items to review include the company's methods of: producing business, underwriting and processing claims and use of third party organizations. In addition, information obtained in Steps C and G below will aid in obtaining an understanding of the company's business. (This procedure is performed to provide the examiner with a basis for making materiality judgments and for assessing inherent and control risks.)

C. Identify Significant Examination Issues

1. Identify significant examination, accounting and reporting issues affecting the examination. Consider the impact of changes in the NAIC Accounting Practices and Procedures Manual, Annual Statement Instructions, state statutes, and department rulings. Also consider company departures from Statutory Accounting Principles, permitted practices, significant accounting transactions (e.g., loss portfolio transfers, financial reinsurance, assumption reinsurance, loss reserve discounting), and entry into new types of investments (e.g., derivatives, private placements, etc.).

	Done By	Date
D. Meet with Designated Department Personnel		
1. Meet with the in-house financial analyst to discuss the company's financial condition and operating results since the last examination. Ascertain the reasons for unusual trends, abnormal ratios and transactions that are not easily discernible. This step should be performed in the early stages of planning.		
2. Meet with the in-house actuary to discuss the company's historical reserving issues and extent of data validation required.		
3. Meet with the chief examiner or designee to discuss the use of a specialist (e.g., actuary, appraiser, EDP examiner, reinsurance expert), planning materiality and the preliminary examination approach. This step is performed in the later stages of planning once an understanding of the company has been obtained.		
a. Coordinate the use of an EDP examiner on the examination, if appropriate.		
b. Prepare "request for bid" letters for use of a specialist.		
c. Inquire of significant events (e.g., pending merger/acquisition) and department concerns.		
d. Discuss impact of conditions present in the industry and economy relative to the examination plan.		
e. Discuss staff experience requirements.		
E. Meet with Company Representatives		
1. Meet with company personnel to discuss relevant examination issues such as the following:		
a. Discuss thoroughly all significant changes in the company's operations or major lines of business.		
b. Inquire as to whether the company had made personnel or systems changes that would significantly affect the areas of accounting controls, procedures, systems, or approval authorities. The same inquiries should be made of the electronic data processing (EDP) department and the internal audit department's procedures and scope.		
c. Arrange access to CPA workpapers.		
d. Arrange access to SAS 70 reports. (Refer to the 'Use of SAS 70 Reports' section of this *Handbook* for further guidance on SAS 70 reports.)		
e. Other examination arrangements.		

	Done By	Date
2. Make request for required reports, records, etc. not gathered in Step A.		
3. Obtain internal audit reports for review and consideration.		
4. Request trial balance in PC compatible files and other accounting records used to prepare annual statements.		
5. Request pertinent information to confirm investment and bank accounts.		
F. Perform Preliminary Analytical Review Procedures		
1. Utilizing the “5 year profile report,” IRIS reports and in-house financial analyst’s work, perform and/or review trend analysis and financial and health company, focus on investment quality, liquidity and related party transactions.		
G. Assess the Effects of External Environmental Conditions		
1. Assess the effects of external environmental conditions and factors. (Focus on conditions which affect the company’s primary lines of business, increase solvency risk or increase the risk of material misstatements. For example, competition, inflation or other economic/market factors, new regulatory requirements, recent catastrophes, pollution and asbestos liabilities, etc. There are resources that provide this type of information on an annual basis, such as, the AICPA Audit Risk Alert for Insurance Companies.)		
H. Set Planning Materiality Levels		
1. Based on the preliminary analytical review and understanding of the company’s business, determine planning materiality and tolerable error.		
a. Policyholders’ surplus relative to state’s minimum financial requirements.		
Consider:		
b. Policyholders’ surplus relative to Risk-Based Capital action levels.		
c. Stability of operations.		
d. Quality of policyholders’ surplus.		
e. Nature of the principal lines of business.		

Done By	Date

I. Meet with Company's Independent Auditors

1. Arrange a meeting with the independent auditors through company management to review workpapers and discuss the scope of the audit (i.e., materiality, risk assessment and significant accounts). (Reviewing the CPA's workpapers early in the planning phase enhances the EIC's understanding of the company's operations and increases examination efficiency by identifying similar work that may be relied upon (subject to examiner testing) in reducing control and substantive tests.)

   Consider:

   a. Reviewing relevant prior year audit workpapers if current year audit is in progress.

   b. Reviewing Management Letter and Internal Control Letter.

J. Meet with the Company's Independent Actuaries

1. Arrange a meeting with the independent actuaries to review the objectives and scope of the actuary's work and to obtain an understanding of the methods and assumptions used in establishing the actuarially determined asset or liability.

   Consider:

   a. The materiality and risks (i.e., nature and type of business, loss development, reinsurance, etc.) associated with the accounts.

   b. The actuaries' professional qualifications (i.e., FCAS or ACAS for casualty insurance), reputation and relationship with the insurer.

   c. Any changes in methodology or assumptions from the prior examination.

K. Assess Control Environment

1. Evaluate the company's overall control environment utilizing the EPQ, ISQ, CPA workpapers, prior examination workpapers and through follow up meetings with company representatives. (This procedure is performed to determine whether the control environment can adequately support specific controls and produce reliable accounting records.)

	Done By	Date
L. Perform Specific Risk Analysis Process		
1. Determine significant cycles (e.g., premiums, claims, investments) and the material accounts within those cycles. Complete applicable SRA workpapers (including internal control questionnaires) only for those cycles determined to be significant. Significance should be considered in terms of major transaction cycles.		
2. Review examination objectives in the NAIC *Financial Condition Examiners Handbook* and modify where appropriate.		
3. Assess inherent risks for examination cycles.		
Note – Inherent risk is the risk that a material misstatement will occur in the account balance before considering specific internal control procedures. The examiner should consider these risks whether or not specific control reliance is contemplated for a given examination objective.		
4. Assess the impact that external environmental factors/conditions will have upon specific account balances.		
Note - These factors/conditions exist outside the control of management but impact a company's solvency, and in some cases, account balances. The examiner should consider these factors/conditions when determining an acceptable level of examination risk.		
5. Perform detail analytical review procedures.		
a. Compare details of individual accounts or annual statement balances and operating and financial ratios related to specific accounts to previous years to identify unusual or unexpected relationships among accounts. (Sources: Trial Balances, IRIS ratios, Examiner Team Synopsis, NAIC Profile Reports, Management's Discussion & Analysis Letter, A.M. Best's Aggregates & Averages Publication.)		
b. Identify account balances or areas requiring additional emphasis or where procedures maybe limited because of the materiality of the amount.		
6. Assess the level of control risks and the intended degree of reliance on internal controls for examination objectives.		

	Done By	Date
a. For each examination objective, assess the level of control risk as high, medium or low and document the basis for these assessments. Assessing the level of control risk involves identifying specific internal control structure policies and procedures and determining whether the control environment and the various control procedures “placed in operation” result in a high, medium or low risk that material errors may exist.		
b. For each examination objective, assess the intended degree of control reliance as high, medium or low and document the basis for these assessments. Assessing the intended degree of reliance on internal controls involves determining whether the anticipated result of performing test of controls to evaluate the “operating effectiveness” of actual policies and procedures will support a high, medium or low degree of reliance.		
Note - Consider the most efficient and effective means to meet the examination objectives. The examiner may assess the level of control risk as high if the examiner believes policies and procedures in place are unlikely to pertain to an objective. Similarly, the examiner may assess the intended degree of control reliance as low if the examiner believes procedures are unlikely to be effective, or because evaluating their effectiveness would be inefficient. Therefore, although a company may appear to have controls in place over a specific account, it may by less efficient to spend time evaluating and testing the controls effectiveness.		
7. Consider CPA’s work for examination objectives.		
a. Consider using the CPA’s work to reduce control and/or substantive tests for a particular examination objective, where appropriate.		
b. Document the nature and extent of the CPA’s work and testing of CPA’s work for the examination objective in the SRA workpapers or in other appropriate work papers.		
8. Assess overall risk (examination risk) of material adjustment to policyholders’ surplus for individual account balances (Note – this is referred to as the Risk of Material Misstatement in Part 3 of the *Handbook*).		
a. Based on your judgment of materiality, assessments of inherent risk and control risk, determine the overall risk associated with the account by indicating high, medium or low.		

	Done By	Date
9. Prepare examination programs.		
a. Based on the level of control risk and the intended reliance on internal controls, design appropriate tests of specific internal controls identified in the SRAs and the ISQ in accordance with Part 3 of the *Handbook* – I. Control Testing.		
b. Based on the overall risk assessment (risk of material misstatement) and the degree of reliance on internal controls (control reliance) select the appropriate substantive examination testing procedures and design others as necessary in accordance with Part 3 of the *Handbook* – II. Substantive Testing.		
10. For cycles determined to be less significant, complete only the Examination Procedures Documentation portion of the SRA workpapers and obtain the chief examiner or designee's approval before procedures are performed.		
M. Prepare Time Budget		
1. Prepare time budget and allocate work assignments for the examination and obtain the chief examiner or designee's approval.		
N. Complete Examination Planning Memorandum		
1. Complete the EPM and applicable SRA documentation and obtain the chief examiner's or designee's approval before detailed procedures are performed. See Exhibit L for suggested elements to be included in an EPM.		

EXHIBIT B
EXAMINATION PLANNING QUESTIONNAIRE

	Yes	No	Comments
Please provide complete responses, using additional sheets if necessary.			
I. OWNERSHIP AND MANAGEMENT INFLUENCES			
A. Concentration of Ownership In a separate memorandum, describe the concentration of ownership including approximate number of shareholders, any significant shareholders, whether shares are actively traded, and extent of management's ownership interest.			
B. Board of Directors In a separate memorandum, describe the make-up of the board of directors, including number of directors, affiliations of outside directors, relationship of each director to the organization, and number of years as a director. Include board members who served at any time during the period under examination.			
C. Is there an audit committee?			
How many members serve on the committee?			
How many are outside directors?			
How often does the committee meet?			
Are minutes of meetings prepared and retained?			
D. Duties of the Board and its Committees Excerpt from the articles of incorporation and bylaws a description of the duties assigned and performed by the board of directors, its audit committee, and any other committees of the board. Include a current list of committees and the members as of the examination date.			
E. Corporate Planning			
Has the company developed a long-term strategic plan?			
How often is it reviewed and updated?			

	Yes	No	Comments
Does management obtain and use information to stay abreast of changes in the competitive, technological and regulatory environments? What resources are used?			
F. List any key consultants whose services were used during the examination period. State the specialist's relationship, if any, to the company.			
II. ORGANIZATION AND PERSONNEL PRACTICES			
ORGANIZATION			
A. Include current copies of each: Corporate structure chart Personnel organization chart			
B. Do the charts clearly reflect areas of responsibility and lines of reporting and communication? If not, explain.			
C. Are there formal position descriptions for administrative and financial personnel? Provide copies.			
D. Is there a formal conflict of interest policy or code of conduct in effect? Provide a copy.			
Does it require periodic declarations by officers, directors, and key employees?			
In a separate memorandum, describe the system used to monitor compliance with the conflict of interest policy and/or code of conduct.			
PERSONNEL			
E. Does the recruitment and selection process for new employees in the administrative and financial areas require investigation of background and references?			
F. Has there been significant turnover in management? If yes, document the reason(s).			
G. How long has key management been with the company in their current position, and what specific industry experience do they have?			

	Yes	No	Comments
H. Have any officers been associated with a company that became insolvent or placed in conservatorship, suffered a revocation of license, or ordered to cease and desist from violations of insurance law or regulations?			
I. Are personnel policies, including hiring, evaluation and termination, documented and communicated to employees?			
J. Are employees who handle cash, securities, and other valuable assets bonded? List the amount of coverage and deductible.			
K. Are any related persons employed within the company? If yes, provide their names, job titles and relationship.			
L. Is rotation of duties enforced by mandatory vacations?			
M. Is job performance periodically evaluated and reviewed with each employee?			
N. Are there formal training programs for administrative and financial personnel? In a separate memorandum, describe the training program(s).			
III. INTERNAL AUDIT ACTIVITIES AND INTERNAL CONTROLS			
Is an internal audit department used? If yes, please complete the following:			
A. Do internal auditors prepare and follow written audit programs?			
Is the scope of internal audit activities planned in advance with:			
Senior management?			
Board of directors?			
Audit committee?			
B. In a separate memorandum, describe the normal duties of the internal auditors including extent of financial audits and operational audits.			

			Yes	No	Comments
		Indicate the following:			
		Size and organization of the staff (including ratio of supervisors to staff)			
		Prior experience of staff members			
		Number of CPAs and CIAs			
		Scope restrictions			
	C.	Do internal auditors have direct access to:			
		Senior management?			
		Board of directors?			
		Audit committee?			
		Appropriate executives?			
		Are responses to recommendations documented?			
		Is implementation of internal audit recommendations monitored?			
		Are there training programs for internal auditors?			
		Describe the training programs.			
		Describe any established continuing education requirements.			
		Are any internal auditors or members of their families related to other employees?			
IV.	**MONITORING PROCEDURES**				
	BUDGETS				
	A.	Does management develop an annual budget and financial plan based on corporate goals and objectives?			
		Are budget expectations communicated to those affected?			
	B.	Are estimates included in financial data and statements reviewed by knowledgeable individuals independent of the estimation process?			
		Who performs the review?			

		Yes	No	Comments
	Are the entries supported by explanation and/or documentation?			
C.	Is financial performance and the status of the company's financial condition periodically reviewed and/or compared to the plan?			
	Are variances between performance vs. plan explained by management?			
	How often are these analyses performed?			
D.	Do budgeting procedures cover all subsidiaries and departments?			
	Do budgets and forecasts cover:			
	Premium income by line of insurance?			
	Policy benefits by line of insurance?			
	General expenses?			
	Investments (allocation of investable funds, and income and expenses)?			
	Statutory surplus?			
	Federal income taxes?			
	Cash flow?			
E.	Does management use financial and other informational reporting to gauge accomplishment to plan and to maintain a controlled environment?			
	Is assessment made of:			
	Profitability?			
	Business growth?			
	Investment of funds, including liquidity?			
	Direct expenses?			
	Capital expenditures?			

	Yes	No	Comments
FINANCIAL PLANNING AND REPORTING			
F. In a separate memorandum, summarize the qualifications of key employees responsible for preparation and issuance of financial statements. Include names, titles, job responsibilities, background, and number of years in present position.			
G. Are financial statements submitted at regular intervals to operating management?			
To the board of directors?			
To the audit committee?			
Are they accompanied by analytical comments?			
Do they show comparisons with:			
Prior periods?			
Budgets or forecasts?			
H. Who reviews and approves financial information for public distribution (e.g., press releases, filings with regulatory bodies, and policyholders' or shareholders' reports)?			
Chief executive officer?			
Chief operating officer?			
Chief financial officer?			
Chief actuary?			
Board of directors?			
Audit committee?			
OPERATIONS			
I. Are operating policies periodically reviewed?			
Does documentation include up-to-date:			
Accounting policies and procedures?			
Chart of accounts describing the nature of each account? If yes, provide a copy.			

		Yes	No	Comments
J.	Operating Analyses In multi-line insurance organizations, are reports on operating results and key financial data provided by major lines of business and/or subsidiary to the home office on a regular and timely basis? In a separate schedule, list the principal operating analyses used (e.g., line of business analyses, loss ratios, in-force and reserve amounts, investment yields). Describe contents and indicate frequency of preparation. Sample analyses may be attached instead of a schedule.			
K.	Investments Is there a policy regarding the investment of the company's assets?			
	How often is it reviewed and updated?			
	Is investment performance periodically reported upon by management?			
	Are all investment activities approved by the board of directors?			
	Are securities kept:			
	On hand?			
	With a non-discretionary custodian?			
	With a discretionary custodian?			
	If discretionary, is there an approved list of investments?			
L.	Are any third-party service organizations used? If yes, please provide a list.			
	Are detail records reconciled? If yes, how often?			
	Are internal audits performed? If yes, how often?			
	Are SAS 70 audits issued? If yes, please provide. (Refer to the 'Use of SAS 70 Reports' section of this *Handbook* for further guidance on SAS 70 reports.)			

	Yes	No	Comments
RECONCILIATIONS			
M. For the following assets indicate how often they are reconciled to the accounting records and the person performing the reconciliation:			
Bonds			
Stocks			
Mortgage loans on real estate			
Collateral loans			
Real estate			
Policy loans			
Certificates of deposit			
Cash			
Office equipment			
N. How often are the following detail and control accounts reconciled and who performs the reconciliation?			
Financial values in master policy file			
Suspense accounts			
Reinsurance assumed			
Investment in bonds			
Stocks			
Mortgage loans on real estate			
Collateral loans			
Policy loans			
Certificates of deposit			
Accrued investment income			
Office equipment			

		Yes	No	Comments
	Debt			
	Equity			
O.	Please indicate how often the following are reconciled and who performs the reconciliation:			
	Information files or registers for agreement of the information base premium, commission, and cash receipts registers			
	Premium billing and in-force files			
	Reserve valuation and master file			
P.	Are changes between beginning and ending balances accounted for:			
	Investments			
	Policy reserves			
	In-force amounts			
	Income tax asset/liability			
	Debt			
	Equity			
Q.	Are the same accounting and closing practices followed at interim dates as at year end?			
	Are current year statements prepared on the same basis (i.e., key accounting principles, actuarial and pricing assumptions) as that used in the prior year?			
	Were the statements prepared in accordance with state statutes?			
R.	Are all general journal entries other than standard entries required to be authorized by a responsible official not involved with the origination of entries?			
S.	Is access to accounting and financial records restricted to authorized personnel?			
	Are internal control procedures written and current to safeguard the company's assets?			

		Yes	No	Comments
REINSURANCE				
T.	Do reinsurance agreements require formal review and approval, prior to execution, by officers?			
	Which officers?			
	By the board of directors?			
	Is regulatory approval (where applicable) of reinsurance agreements documented?			
	Does the documentation include projections of the expected economic results and the accounting for the transactions?			
U.	Are all amendments and changes to reinsurance agreements supported by written documentation?			
	Discuss any major changes in terms (e.g., commission, percent participation, limits or retentions) or conditions of contracts with significant management companies, agents or on reinsurance layers. Document in detail significant specific arrangements with agents, MGAs or others.			
V.	With respect to reinsurance assumed:			
	Are ceding companies required to submit appropriate periodic reports on the reinsured business? Indicate the frequency of these reports.			
	Are such periodic reports compared to projections made at the date of the agreement?			
	If yes, are material deviations investigated?			
	Does your company periodically review or inspect ceding company records and changes therein (premiums, terminations, benefits or claims)? If yes, how often?			
	Are these reviews performed as of the assumption date and periodically thereafter?			

		Yes	No	Comments
W.	With respect to reinsurance ceded: Is the financial stability of assuming companies reviewed to ascertain whether such companies are solvent and have the ability meet liabilities assumed under the reinsurance agreement?			
X.	Are the results of reinsurance agreements monitored to permit timely recapture of ceded premium or cancellation of assumed reinsurance?			
	Who reviews and approves the decision to recapture or cancel the treaties?			
V.	**LEGAL AND REGULATORY REQUIREMENTS**			
A.	Where are current copies of insurance company and/or insurance holding company laws, Internal Revenue Service tax laws and other regulations maintained?			
B.	Describe the procedures to assure that management is informed of changes in laws.			
C.	Are the following specific areas of company activities regularly reviewed for compliance with regulatory requirements? If yes, how often?			
	Capital requirements and dividend restrictions			
	Transactions with employees, directors, and officers			
	Permitted ratios of categories of qualified investments to statutory capital and/or surplus			
	Prohibitions or restrictions as to particular kinds of investments			
	Prescribed loan-to-value ratios for mortgage loans and similar credit-type investments			
	Policy form approval			
	Treatment of policyholders in benefit settlement matters			
	Disposal of real estate acquired by foreclosure			
	Permitted non-insurance activities			

	Yes	No	Comments
Foreign operations			
Reporting			
Describe documentation procedures and indicate who is responsible for regulatory requirement.			
D. State any government restrictions or regulatory requirements that pertain specifically to the company.			
Provide copies of any limited scope examinations, audits by regulatory or other government agencies. Discuss any IRS revenue agents' reports, deficiency assessments and developments in IRS examinations in progress.			
Has the company complied with all debt covenants and other agreements?			
E. Are there any material contingent liabilities or commitments?			

EXHIBIT C
EVALUATION OF CONTROLS IN INFORMATION SYSTEMS (IS) QUESTIONNAIRE

INSTRUCTION NOTE 1: In order to expedite the IS controls evaluation process, this questionnaire is designed to be completed by the insurance company's information systems management before the IS specialist(s) assigned to the examination begin(s) fieldwork. Accordingly, the tone of the questionnaire is directed to the insurance company's IS managers. The examiners recognize the wide variation in the size (e.g., large mainframe vs. small network) and structure (e.g., centralized vs. decentralized) of the many processing environments in place at company's throughout the insurance industry. Therefore, several sections of the questionnaire contain a "Scoping Note," which is designed to be answered by the insurance company's IS managers and evaluated by the examiner to determine whether or not the particular section of the questionnaire needs to be completed by the company and tested by the examiner. For those sections that will be completed, the answers to each question should be made in a manner that reflects an understanding of the company's particular control environment, as well as an understanding of the audit intent of each question. This can generally be achieved if the company involves an internal information systems auditor in the question answering process. Specific "Guidance Points" have also been included in the more technical areas of the questionnaire to help facilitate its completion by the company's IS managers.

INSTRUCTION NOTE 2: Every question includes a description of particular test documentation that should be provided by the insurance company. In those cases where documentation does not exist or is not otherwise available, the insurance company should provide examples of processes that can be observed and/or the individuals who can be interviewed to corroborate the presence of controls that are not formally documented.

INSTRUCTION NOTE 3: Due to the inherently high degree of change in information technology, the period under review for this questionnaire should generally range from the latest 12 to 18 months of the overall financial condition examination time period. The period under review should generally encompass the last year of the examination period and the period of time up to and including the actual examination fieldwork. The period under review for this information systems evaluation is ____________________ through ____________________.

INSTRUCTION NOTE 4: The questions must only be answered for all **financially significant information systems**. For the purposes of this questionnaire, financially significant information systems are defined as the computer hardware and software, including system programs and application programs, which are used to perform automated processing of a financially significant account balance or set of transactions. This includes financially significant e-business systems. Financially significant information systems are normally identified as "critical" in the insurance company's business continuity plan.

INSTRUCTION NOTE 5: After the examiners have reviewed the company's narrative response to each question within each relevant section, along with the appropriate sample test documentation gathered by the company and available on the company premises, the examiners may determine that information systems controls appear to be in place at the company. If this is the case, it may be efficient for the examiners to test the information systems controls to determine whether the controls are operating effectively, thereby allowing the examiners to rely on the results of the control tests to reduce the level of substantive testing. Specific "test procedures" have been included throughout the questionnaire to help facilitate the nature and extent of the test procedures to be performed. In accordance with the control testing guidance contained in Part 3 of the *Financial Condition Examiners Handbook*, the control tests will consist of either judgmental sampling or attribute sampling. Some controls, such as information systems management controls, will be more subject to judgmental sampling, whereby the examiner inspects a judgmental number of information systems management reports issued during the period under review. Other controls, such as programming controls, will be more subject to attribute sampling, whereby the examiner would select as few as 11 program change documents, if the level of risk initially identified from the responses to the questionnaire was determined to be low and the level of intended reliance on the controls is low, or as many as

76 program change documents, if the level of risk initially identified from the responses to the questionnaire was determined to be high and the level of intended reliance on the controls is high.

INSTRUCTION NOTE 6: IS testing should be performed across all financially significant applications. Only one IS questionnaire may typically be completed by a company because many companies implement common controls across all applications. However, a company may not consistently apply and enforce the common controls across all applications. Some controls, such as inspection of the data center, are conducive to observation and are not subject to sampling. Other controls, such as programming and security authorization, are conducive to audit trail inspection and are subject to sampling. For those controls subject to sampling, the examiner should determine the appropriate sample size to be used based upon the level of inherent risk and the intended level of control risk applied against the compliance sample size table contained in Part 3 of the *Financial Condition Examiners Handbook*. For example, if the sample size is determined to be 70 and the company operates 7 financially significant applications within a common control infrastructure whereby only one IS questionnaire has been completed, the examiner should test 10 program changes for each application.

SUMMARY OF SCOPING NOTES:

Section A – No scoping note included, as completion of this section is required for all companies.

Section B – No scoping note included, as completion of this section is required for all companies.

Section C – This scoping note considers the conditions under which computer programs may undergo change.

Section D – This scoping note considers the conditions under which new computer systems may be developed and/or implemented.

Section E – No scoping note included, as completion of this section is required for all companies.

Section F and G – This scoping note considers the conditions under which the company would make changes to end of day, end of month, or end of year processes within financially significant computer systems.

Section H – This scoping note considers whether the company has ever used or currently intends to use an outside computer processing service organization.

Section I – No scoping note included, as completion of this section is required for all companies.

Section J – No scoping note included, as completion of this section is required for all companies.

Section K – This scoping note considers the status of current or planned e-business initiatives.

Section L – This scoping note considers whether the company has ever used or currently intends to use the public Internet or any WANs.

A. MANAGEMENT CONTROL

The name, title and phone number of the insurance company's contact person responsible for providing the answers to this set of questions is:

Guidance Point: Question K1 in Section K focuses specifically on top management's involvement in e-business

	Yes	No	Attachment
A1. Is there an IS steering committee or other evidence that top management is involved in the IS function and, if so, who are the members? Please provide copies of the steering committee meeting minutes or other evidence (e.g., memos or agendas) of steering committee meetings held during the period under review. *Test procedure: the examiner's evaluation of the minutes or other evidence provided, along with a judgmental sample of minutes or other evidence issued within the past 12 to 18 months, will generally be sufficient for this test.*			
A2. Is the IS department fully staffed and, if not, list the significant vacancies? Please provide an organization chart that identifies significant vacancies. *Test procedure: the examiner's evaluation of the chart provided will generally be sufficient for this test.*			
A3. Is there an internal audit function? Please refer to question B5 under Organization Controls. If so, is an IS division or specialist on the staff? Please provide the name and phone number of the internal audit contact person or senior IS specialist responsible for providing assistance to the IS examiners. *Test procedure: the examiner's evaluation of the contact person's ability and availability to assist with the examination will be sufficient for this test.*			
A4. Are periodic tests or reviews of the system made by the internal audit staff to ensure that controls are functioning in accordance with established standards? Please provide a list of system reviews performed during the period under review over each financially significant system, along with copies of system review reports and/or test results. *Test procedure: the examiner's evaluation of the review documentation provided will generally be sufficient for this test.*			
Guidance Point: Question K2 in Section K focuses specifically on the e-business strategy.			
A5. Is there an IS strategy consistent with the business strategy and, if so, has it been communicated by senior management to the rest of the individuals in the company? Please provide the table of contents or executive overview of the strategic plan for the business and information systems. *Test procedure: the examiner's evaluation of the table of contents or executive overview provided will generally be sufficient for this test.*			

B. ORGANIZATION CONTROLS

NOTE: Organization Control questions must be completed for each of the insurance company's financially significant organizational units that are directly responsible for maintenance or development, operation or security of financially significant production systems. Organization Control questions will typically be answered only once for centralized computer processing environments. In decentralized environments the questions may need to be answered more than once because separate organizational units may effectively have separate information systems departments.

The name, title and phone number of the insurance company's contact person responsible for providing the answers to this set of questions is:

____

***Guidance Point*: Segregation of incompatible duties is an important element of the system of internal control. Appropriate segregation of duties helps to prevent mistakes, errors or potential fraud. Segregation of duties in smaller organizations may be difficult to achieve, because of a limited number of personnel. Compensating controls will be needed, such as assigning non-technical duties (e.g., data entry, input/reconciliation of control totals, etc.) to someone outside the data processing department. Likewise, strong data processing management and reporting controls, as well as proactive user involvement with the data processing function, may mitigate segregation of duties concerns.**

		Yes	No	Attachment
B1.	Is the IS department independent of all operating units for which it performs data processing functions? Please provide evidence (e.g., from the organization chart) that data processing functions are independent from end user operating units. *Test procedure: the examiner's evaluation of the evidence provided will be sufficient for this test.*			
B2.	Are the IS roles and responsibilities clearly defined? Please provide a copy of a job function/description from each IS area (e.g., one from system maintenance and development, one from computer operations and one from computer security). *Test procedure: the examiner's evaluation of the job functions/descriptions provided will generally be sufficient for this test.*			
B3.	Are all incompatible functions, such as the initiation and authorization of transactions, or the custody of assets, performed outside the IS department? Please provide a copy of a description of the functions performed by the IS department. *Test procedure: the examiner's evaluation of the descriptions provided will be sufficient for this test.*			
B4.	Are the functions of system design and programming adequately segregated from computer operations and data entry functions? Please provide a copy of these function descriptions. *Test procedure: the examiner's evaluation of the descriptions provided will generally be sufficient for this test.*			

	Question	Yes	No	Attachment
B5.	If the number of employees in the IS department prevents separation of duties, are detailed procedures maintained outside the IS department to safeguard assets and data? Please provide copies of documented mitigating control procedures for any incompatible duties. *Test procedure: the examiner's evaluation of the procedures provided will generally be sufficient for this test.*			

Scoping Note – Section C	YES	NO
Can the company make changes to the program source code, either in-house developed software or vendor developed packages, which comprise the financially significant information systems identified through INSTRUCTION NOTE 4 in the front of the questionnaire?		
Have any changes, other than vendor installed updates, been made to financially significant computer programs (e.g., in-house enhancements, vendor changes for company specifications, bug fixes, etc.) during the period identified in INSTRUCTION NOTE 3 in the front of the questionnaire?		

If the answer to either of the above questions is YES, the company's respective IS manager should complete section C of the questionnaire. If the answer to BOTH questions is NO, the company's respective IS manager should not complete section C of the questionnaire, but should describe below, or in an attachment, the conditions under which computer programs may undergo change at the company. This information will be evaluated by the examiner to confirm whether or not this section should be completed and tested.

C. CHANGES TO APPLICATIONS

NOTE: Changes to Applications questions must be completed for financially significant production applications, both internally developed and purchased packages, which were changed during the period under review.

The name, title and phone number of the insurance company's contact person responsible for providing the answers to this set of questions is:

____

	Yes	No	Attachment
C1. Does management monitor the level of open requests for changes to applications and the satisfaction of users with changes made? Please provide a copy of reports on application performance, which have been reviewed and approved by management and include information regarding the volume of changes made to applications, application problems, emergency fixes, application related help desk calls, backlog of requests from users for application changes and users' views on the functional and operational quality of applications. *Test procedure: the examiner's evaluation of the reports and evidence provided will generally be sufficient for this test.*			
C2. Is there a control that ensures that user needs result in appropriate program change requests and the requests are properly evaluated, authorized and tested? Please provide a list of program changes made during the period under review, evidence of cost justification for the most significant program change from each system, evidence of user and IS management written authorization of the most significant change from each system and evidence of user and IS management review and approval of each of the most significant program changes completed for each system. Include evidence that management reviewed the test plans to see that the level of testing was appropriate for the risk involved in the application change. Also, include evidence that management reviewed the final test results. If all financially significant information systems reside on the same computer platform or essentially similar computer platforms that are subject to the same or similar program change controls, it is sensible to select a single attribute sample from the population of program changes made on these platforms. However, if financially significant information systems reside on separate or essentially dissimilar computer platforms that are not subject to the same or similar program change controls, an attribute sample should be selected from each computer platform. *Test procedure: the examiner's evaluation of the list of program changes and the related evidence provided, along with an attribute sample of between 11 and 76 program changes made within the past 12 to 18 months on each computer processing platform that contains a financially significant information system, will generally be sufficient for this test.*			

		Yes	No	Attachment
C3.	Is there a control that ensures that change requests are appropriately prioritized and monitored? Please provide a log of change requests, including evidence of management review, which shows the priority of each request and shows budget to actual time comparisons with explanations for significant budget to actual variances or changes in priority. *Test procedure: the examiner's evaluation of the log and evidence provided will generally be sufficient for this test.*			
C4.	Is there a control that would prevent or detect unauthorized changes made after the completion of testing but before transfer to the live environment? Please provide a description of the control and the name and phone number of the person who can demonstrate or validate the control. *Test procedure: the examiner's evaluation of the control description, corroborating inquiry with the person identified and observation of the control, if possible, will generally be sufficient for this test.*			
C5.	When program changes are made in-house, is there a control that ensures that the source code used corresponds to the most recent version of the program and modifications to a program by more than one programmer are coordinated? Please provide a description of the control and the name and phone number of the person who can demonstrate or validate the control. *Test procedure: the examiner's evaluation of the control description, corroborating inquiry with the person identified and observation of the control, if possible, will generally be sufficient for this test.*			
C6.	Is there a control that ensures that only properly tested, reviewed and approved changes are transferred into the live environment? Please provide a description of the control and the name and phone number of the person who can demonstrate or validate the control. *Test procedure: the examiner's evaluation of the control description, corroborating inquiry with the person identified and observation of the control, if possible, will generally be sufficient for this test.*			
C7.	Is there a control that ensures that the correct program libraries are updated with the most recent version of the program? Please provide a description of the control and the name and phone number of the person who can demonstrate or validate the control. *Test procedure: the examiner's evaluation of the control description, corroborating inquiry with the person identified and observation of the control, if possible, will generally be sufficient for this test.*			
C8.	Where applications run at multiple sites, is there a control that ensures that all copies of live programs are updated? Please provide a description of the control and the name and phone number of the person who can demonstrate or validate the control. *Test procedure: the examiner's evaluation of the control description, corroborating inquiry with the person identified and observation of the control, if possible, will generally be sufficient for this test.*			

	Yes	No	Attachment
C9. Is application documentation appropriately updated and distributed to affected users and IS staff? Please provide a copy of updated application documentation for the most significant program change made from question C2. Test procedure: the examiner's evaluation of the *individual attachments provided will generally be sufficient for this test.*			
C10. Is technical documentation updated to reflect program or database structural changes? Please provide a copy of updated technical documentation for the most significant program and/or database changes made from question C2. *Test procedure: the examiner's evaluation of the individual attachments provided will generally be sufficient for this test.*			

Scoping Note – Section D	**YES**	**NO**
Have any financially significant information systems, including new vendor packages, been developed and/or implemented during the period identified in INSTRUCTION NOTE 3 in the front of the questionnaire?		
Have any financially significant information systems, including new vendor packages, been in the process of development and/or implementation during the period identified in INSTRUCTION NOTE 3 in the front of the questionnaire?		

If the answer to either of the above questions is YES, the company's respective IS manager should complete section D of the questionnaire. If the answer to BOTH questions is NO, the company's respective IS manager should not complete section D of the questionnaire, but should describe below or in an attachment the conditions under which new computer systems may be developed and/or implemented at the company. This information will be evaluated by the examiner to confirm whether or not this section should be completed and tested.

D. SYSTEM AND PROGRAM DEVELOPMENT

NOTE: System and Program Development questions must be completed for financially significant production applications that were developed in-house during the period under review or purchased and modified during the period under review.

The name, title and phone number of the insurance company's contact person responsible for providing the answers to this set of questions is:

____

	Yes	No	Attachment
D1. Is there a control that ensures that all necessary steps are appropriately included in a project plan (e.g., use of a system development methodology)? Please provide a copy of an overview of the current system development life cycle methodology (SDLC) and a copy of the policy that requires development projects to have a clear sponsor at the senior management level. *Test procedure: the examiner's evaluation of the documentation provided will generally be sufficient for this test.*			
D2. Does management monitor the development and implementation of new applications? Please provide copies of reports which show evidence of management's review and show documentation of the status of the application(s) during and after development and implementation, including information regarding assessments from quality assurance reviews, actual completion of tasks against plan (e.g., design, testing and conversion of data), actual delivery dates against milestones and deadlines, actual project costs against budgets, and the extent of problems incurred after the application(s) go(es) live. *Test procedure: the examiner's evaluation of the reports and evidence provided will generally be sufficient for this test.*			
Guidance Point: **A well-controlled company performs feasibility studies, including cost benefit analyses to determine the effects on existing hardware (e.g., processing and storage capacity) and system software of new or significantly enhanced applications. These studies also determine whether the existing hardware and system software configuration is compatible with the application. For example, a company may use an IBM mainframe computer to process their financial applications, however, they are considering the purchase of financial application software that was designed to be processed using a HP computer.**			
D3. Do implementation plans include cost justification? Please provide a list of projects completed during the period under review and a copy of a project cost justification for the most significant project from each system (e.g., most significant in terms of cost or business impact). *Test procedure: the examiner's evaluation of the individual attachments provided will generally be sufficient for this test.*			
D4. Does senior management approve the plan before work commences? Please provide evidence of senior management approval of the project plan for the most significant projects identified in question D3. *Test procedure: the examiner's evaluation of the evidence provided will generally be sufficient for this test.*			

	Yes	No	Attachment
***Guidance Point*: In any new or significantly enhanced application, some desired features are likely to be overlooked during the initial stages of design and development. As these features are identified, modifications to the initial specifications should be documented and subject to the same request, feasibility and design procedures as the initial application.**			
D5. Is there a procedure that provides for senior management's review of progress on the project at critical stages of its development and, if so, does the procedure provide that work cannot progress to the next phase (systems design, programming, testing, conversion, etc.) until and unless approval has been given? Please provide evidence of senior management's review of progress for each significant project identified in question D3. *Test procedure: the examiner's evaluation of the evidence provided will generally be sufficient for this test.*			
D6. Do user departments (e.g., accounting department), auditors (e.g., external and internal), and computer operations personnel participate in the early stages of planning and development of new systems? Please provide evidence of user department, auditor, and computer operations involvement throughout each significant project identified in question D3 (e.g., documented attendance at project review meetings and/or memo's documenting involvement). *Test procedure: the examiner's evaluation of the evidence provided will generally be sufficient for this test.*			
D7. Is there a systems design standards manual? Please provide a copy of the index from the manual. Test procedure: the examiner's evaluation of the index provided will generally be sufficient for this test.			
D8. Is there a programming standards manual? Please provide a copy of the index from the manual. Test procedure: the examiner's evaluation of the index provided will generally be sufficient for this test.			
D9. Does "computer operations" have the authority to refuse to make systems software changes that have not been properly approved? Please provide evidence of the authority (e.g., a policy or computer operations job description). *Test procedure: the examiner's evaluation of the evidence provided will generally be sufficient for this test.*			
***Guidance Point*: A well-controlled company has policies that require test plans to be developed for new or significantly enhanced applications. The planning documentation should include tests to be performed, expected results, and how test data will be developed. Normally, the test plan is reviewed and approved by the application owners and data processing management. Depending on the complexity of the application, the level and extent of testing may vary. For example, when a single application is implemented, such as payroll, testing would normally be performed to ensure programs work individually and in conjunction with each other, and interface appropriately with existing applications. In a highly integrated application, such as claims processing, testing would tend to cover the areas noted above, as well as between specific subsystems, such as the general ledger.**			

	Yes	No	Attachment
D10. Is there a control that prevents testing from being performed on "live" data files? Please provide a description of the control and the name and phone number of the person who can demonstrate or validate the control. *Test procedure: the examiner's evaluation of the control description, corroborating inquiry with the person identified and observation of the control, if possible, will generally be sufficient for this test.*			
D11. Is appropriate program testing performed by the IS staff and users to prevent or detect errors in program coding and ensure that the application operates as intended in the live environment? Please provide evidence of program test results for each major project identified in question D3. *Test procedure: the examiner's evaluation of the evidence provided will generally be sufficient for this test.*			
D12. Is there a control that ensures that when modifications are made subsequent to initial testing they are also subject to appropriate program testing procedures? Please provide a description of the control and the name and phone number of the person who can demonstrate or validate the control. *Test procedure: the examiner's evaluation of the control description, corroborating inquiry with the person identified and observation of the control, if possible, will generally be sufficient for this test.*			
D13. Is there a control that ensures that unauthorized changes cannot be made after the completion of program testing but before transfer into the live environment? Please provide a description of the control and the name and phone number of the person who can demonstrate or validate the control. *Test procedure: the examiner's evaluation of the control description, corroborating inquiry with the person identified and observation of the control, if possible, will generally be sufficient for this test.*			
D14. Is an effort made to perform a parallel run by program and by system, where possible? Please provide for each project identified in question D3, evidence of parallel test results, if any, including evidence of management's review. *Test procedure: the examiner's evaluation of the evidence provided will generally be sufficient for this test.*			
D15. Is there a control that ensures that purchased software packages are subject to adequate selection procedures, such as a thorough investigation of package capabilities compared to business needs and a thorough comparison of several packages to one another? Please provide a list of financial software packages that were purchased during the period under review and evidence of management's justification for each purchase. *Test procedure: the examiner's evaluation of the list and evidence provided will generally be sufficient for this test.*			
***Guidance Point*: Vendor application software generally provides options that allow the user, to some extent, to customize the application for their unique purposes. These options are often called parameters, and, for example, can be used to alter aging categories, prepare customized trial balances, or modify the selection criteria for reporting.**			

	Yes	No	Attachment
D16. Is there a control that ensures that packaged software options selected and parameters set are appropriate to achieve business and application control requirements? Please provide evidence of management's review of options selected and parameters set for each project identified in question D3. *Test procedure: the examiner's evaluation of the evidence provided will generally be sufficient for this test.*			
D17. Is the conversion process controlled for old transaction data, standing data and establishment of data not used by the old application? Please provide evidence of management's review and approval of the data conversion plan and data conversion results for each major project identified in question D3. *Test procedure: the examiner's evaluation of the evidence provided will generally be sufficient for this test.*			
D18. Is there a control that ensures that test plans require users and IS staff to perform an appropriate evaluation of data output? Please provide evidence of management's review and approval of the data test plans and data test results for each major project identified in question D3. *Test procedure: the examiner's evaluation of the evidence provided will generally be sufficient for this test.*			
D19. Are users appropriately trained? Please provide evidence of user attendance at training sessions that relate to the most significant project identified in question D3. *Test procedure: the examiner's evaluation of the evidence provided will generally be sufficient for this test.*			
D20. Is user documentation available to users at implementation? Please provide a copy of the index to user documentation manuals prepared as part of the most significant project identified in question D3. *Test procedure: the examiner's evaluation of the index will generally be sufficient for this test.*			
D21. Is the technical documentation available to technical staff at implementation? Please provide a copy of the index to technical documentation manuals prepared as part of the most significant project identified in question D3. *Test procedure: the examiner's evaluation of the evidence provided will generally be sufficient for this test.*			
D22. Is program code secured for access by only authorized individuals? Please describe procedures to secure directories, datasets or other containers of source code, code being tested, tested code awaiting movement to production areas, and live object code for financially significant systems. *Test procedure: the examiner's evaluation of the list provided, corroborating inquiry with the person identified and observation of the storage areas, if practical, will generally be sufficient for this test.*			

E. OPERATIONS

NOTE: Operations questions will typically be answered only once for centralized computer processing environments. In decentralized environments the questions may need to be answered more than once because separate organizational units may effectively have separate operations environments.

The name, title and phone number of the insurance company's contact person responsible for providing the answers to this set of questions is:

		Yes	No	Attachment
E1.	Is an inventory of hardware and software maintained? Please provide an inventory of hardware and software on spreadsheet provided (Attachment A).			
E2.	Does management make use of automated tools to record mainframe, server and network performance and use the output of these tools to proactively upgrade or replace components when they approach their operating capacity or show signs of imminent failure? Please provide the name and phone number of the person(s) who can confirm the use of mainframe, server and network monitoring tools. *Test Procedure: The examiner's evaluation of the evidence provided will generally be sufficient for this test.*			
E3.	Is there a control that ensures the prior release of a program can be restored if an upgrade causes a problem in the live environment? Please provide a description of the control and the name and phone number of the person who can demonstrate or validate the control. *Test procedure: the examiner's evaluation of the control description, corroborating inquiry with the person identified and observation of the control, if possible, will generally be sufficient for this test.*			
E4.	Is there a standard operations procedures manual that is current and enforced? Please provide a copy of the index from the manual. *Test procedure: the examiner's evaluation of the index will generally be sufficient for this test.*			
E5.	Does batch scheduling software allow for the creation of triggers and dependencies that start, stop, or pause batch cycles based on the availability of resources and data and the successful completion of prerequisite jobs? Please provide a description of the batch scheduling controls and the name and phone number of the person who can demonstrate or validate the function. *Test procedure: the examiner's evaluation of the function, corroborating inquiry with the person identified and observation of the function, if possible, will generally be sufficient for this test.*			

	Yes	No	Attachment
E6. Are operators and programmers restricted from physical access to the tape library? Please provide a list of all personnel, identified by name and job title, who have access to the tape library. *Test procedure: the examiner's evaluation of the list and corroborating inquiry with a judgmental sample of people on the list will generally be sufficient for this test.*			
***Guidance Point*: Question E7 applies specifically to the computer room. Question I7 in Section I addresses this for all types of restricted facilities and asks about monitoring controls.**			
E7. Is physical access to the computer room restricted to operations personnel? Please provide a list of all personnel, identified by name and job title, who have security access privileges to the computer room. *Test procedure: the examiner's evaluation of the list and corroborating inquiry with a judgmental sample of people on the list will generally be sufficient for this test.*			
E8. Are computer operators supervised at all times and are computer operators rotated periodically so no one person is continuously responsible for the running of a specific program? Please provide a copy of operations personnel shift assignments for the last month of the period under review. *Test procedure: the examiner's evaluation of the shift assignments and corroborating inquiry with a judgmental sample of computer operators identified on the shift assignments will generally be sufficient for this test.*			
E9. Is there a control that ensures application programs are run in accordance with a preapproved job schedule? Please provide a description of the control and evidence of management's approval of the existing job schedule. *Test procedure: the examiner's evaluation of the control and evidence provided will generally be sufficient for this test.*			
E10. Is there a control that ensures that all changes to preapproved job schedules are appropriate and authorized? Please provide a description of the control and evidence of management's approval of the last job schedule change made during the period under review. *Test procedure: the examiner's evaluation of the control and evidence provided will generally be sufficient for this test.*			
E11. Is there a control that ensures that departures from pre-approved job schedules are identified and approved? Please provide a description of the control and evidence of management's approval of the last departure that occurred during the period under review. *Test procedure: the examiner's evaluation of the control and evidence provided will generally be sufficient for this test.*			

Item	Question	Yes	No	Attachment
E12.	What control ensures that data required for a job execution is available (e.g., transmissions from other locations are received prior to job execution)? Please provide a description of the control and the name and phone number of the person who can demonstrate or validate the control. *Test procedure: the examiner's evaluation of the control, corroborating inquiry with the person identified and observation of the control, if possible, will generally be sufficient for this test.*			
E13.	Is the execution of jobs logged or otherwise documented, and if so, is the ability to alter the log controlled? Test procedure: the examiner should review and evaluate a sample of logs produced and determine what logical and/or physical security measures protect them.			
E14.	Is machine operation activity captured on the system and is there an independent reporting and examination of machine activity to check operator performance and machine efficiency and, if so, by whom? Please provide for the period under review, evidence of the latest IS review of operation activity or error reports and subsequent investigation and resolution of operation problems. *Test procedure: the examiner's evaluation of the evidence provided, including evidence of the subsequent investigation and resolution of the problems, will generally be sufficient for this test.*			
E15.	Is the computer center located out of the main flow of traffic, away from public view and behind substantial walls and does the center have a fire detection system and a fire suppression system, such as sprinklers charged with water at points outside the computer room? Please provide the name and phone number of the person who can arrange a tour of the computer center. *Test procedure: the examiner's observation of the data center will generally be sufficient for this test.*			
E16.	Are backup copies of data files and programs maintained in a locked waterproof and fireproof storage area? Please provide an inventory of the contents of the storage area and the name and phone number of the person who can arrange a tour of the storage area. *Test procedure: the examiner's evaluation of the inventory, corroborating inquiry with the person identified and observation of the storage area, if practical, will generally be sufficient for this test.*			
E17.	Are internal file labels used on all magnetic tape files? Please provide the name and phone number of the person who can demonstrate or validate the use of internal file labels. *Test procedure: the examiner's corroborating inquiry with the person identified and observation of the use of internal file labels, if possible, will generally be sufficient for this test.*			

	Yes	No	Attachment
E18. Are console operators permitted to override operating system label error messages (such as unexpired file) and, if so, under what circumstances? Please provide a description of the circumstances and the name and phone number of the person who can demonstrate or validate the circumstances. *Test procedure: the examiner's evaluation of the circumstances, corroborating inquiry with the person identified, and observation of the circumstances, if possible, will generally be sufficient for this test.*			
E19. Are copies of programs, essential documents, records and files updated periodically and stored in an off-premises location? Please provide an inventory of the contents of off-premises locations and the name and phone number of the person who can be contacted to verify the contents of the off-premises locations. *Test procedure: the examiner's evaluation of the inventory list and corroborating inquiry with the person identified will generally be sufficient for this test.*			
E20. Is a records retention program in effect to define how long data and backups must be retained? If so, what considerations were used in devising it? Please provide a copy of record retention policies and procedures and an assessment of whether they are in compliance with IRS Revenue Procedure 1998-25. *Test procedure: the examiner's evaluation and assessment of the policies and procedures will generally be sufficient for this test.*			
Guidance Point: **Operational failures can include network failures. This Guidance Point applies to Questions E21 through E25.**			
E21. Are there appropriate escalation procedures in place to resolve operational failures in a timely manner? Please provide a copy of the escalation procedures and evidence of compliance with the escalation procedures during the last operational failure. *Test procedure: the examiner's evaluation of the escalation procedures and evidence of compliance during the latest failure or major processing disruption will generally be sufficient for this test.*			
E22. Are appropriate IS staff and, where appropriate, users involved in the resolution of operational failures? Please provide evidence of IS staff and user involvement in the resolution of operational failures that occurred during the last month of the period under review. *Test procedure: the examiner's evaluation of the evidence provided, along with a judgmental sample of evidence selected over the past 12 to 18 months, will generally be sufficient for this test.*			
E23. Is there appropriate reporting of operational failures? Please provide a copy of the latest operational failure reports for the period under review. *Test procedure: the examiner's evaluation of the evidence provided, along with a judgmental sample of reports available over the past 12 to 18 months, will generally be sufficient for this test.*			

		Yes	No	Attachment
E24.	Are procedures in place to identify an operational point of failure? Please provide a copy of the procedures and the name and phone number of the person who can demonstrate or validate the procedures. *Test procedure: the examiner's evaluation of the procedures and corroborating inquiry with the person identified will generally be sufficient for this test.*			
E25.	Is there a control that ensures that the underlying causes of operational failures are identified and addressed (as opposed to applying short-term fixes)? Please provide evidence of the investigation and resolution of the operational failures reported in question E26. *Test procedure: the examiner's evaluation of the evidence provided, along with a judgmental sample of evidence selected over the past 12 to 18 months, will generally be sufficient for this test.*			
E26.	Is there a control that prevents the corruption of databases (e.g., is there database integrity checking)? Please provide a description of the control and the name and phone number of the person who can demonstrate or validate the control. *Test procedure: the examiner's evaluation of the control, corroborating inquiry with the person identified and observation of the control, if possible, will generally be sufficient for this test.*			
E27.	Is there a control that ensures the effective administration of databases (e.g., is it the responsibility of a database administrator)? Please provide a job description for the database administrator and the name and phone number of the administrator. *Test procedure: the examiner's evaluation of the job description and corroborating inquiry with the person identified will generally be sufficient for this test.*			
E28.	Does insurance coverage exist to protect against loss of equipment, programs and data? Please provide a copy of the insurance policy. *Test procedure: the examiner's evaluation of the coverage provided for in the insurance policy will generally be sufficient for this test.*			
E29.	If the company provides data processing services for others, is there insurance to protect it from liability for errors and omissions? Please provide a copy of the insurance policy. *Test procedure: the examiner's evaluation of the coverage provided for in the insurance policy will generally be sufficient for this test.*			
E30.	Does IS management provide a periodic maintenance schedule for changes to computer systems and infrastructure as well as a mechanism by which the ramifications of these changes can be considered by all impacted groups? Please provide a log of all significant systems and infrastructure changes implemented during the last year of the period under review, including evidence of the review of these changes by impacted groups. *Test procedure: the examiner's evaluation of the evidence provided will generally be sufficient for this test.*			

	Yes	No	Attachment
E31. Are system patches monitored to ensure that all systems are updated in a timely manner? Please provide a description of the technology used to keep system patches up-to-date, e.g., Software Update Service (SUS). If a manual system is used to maintain system patches, please provide a description of the manual procedures. *Test procedure: the examiner's evaluation of the evidence provided will generally be sufficient for this test.*			
E32. Is a control in place to ensure programs running longer than 30 minutes have checkpoint/restart facilities? Please provide a description of the control and the name and phone number of the person who can demonstrate or validate the control. *Test procedure: the examiner's evaluation of the control, corroborating inquiry with the person identified and observation of the control, if possible, will generally be sufficient for this test.*			
***Guidance Point*:** **System software is the computer programs and related procedures that control the processing of the computer hardware and non-application-related functions. Examples of system software include the operating system, security software, tape management system, job scheduling software, telecommunications and network software, and the underlying database management software.**			
E33. Is the selection of system software and related options controlled? Please provide a copy of system software selection and option review procedures. *Test procedure: the examiner's evaluation of the procedures provided will generally be sufficient for this test.*			
E34. Are new system software or upgrades to existing system software appropriately tested before being moved to the live environment? Please provide a description of the control, a list of all system software changes made during the period under review, and a copy of the most significant change, including test results and IS management approval. *Test procedure: the examiner's evaluation of the control and list provided, test results and evidence of management's approval provided, along with the same information for a judgmental sample of system software changes made over the past 12 to 18 months, will generally be sufficient for this test.*			
E35. Is computer equipment protected from damage resulting from electronic power interruption, surges and spikes? Please provide the name and phone number of the persons who can arrange a tour of the server area, including an examination of the surge protection equipment/facility. *Test procedure: the examiner's observation of the server area will generally be sufficient for this test.*			

	Question	Yes	No	Attachment
E36.	Is the process used in changing the network configuration documented? Please provide a copy of the documented process and the name and phone number of the person who can demonstrate or validate the process. *Test procedure: the examiner's evaluation of the process, corroborating inquiry with the person identified and observation of the process, if possible, will generally be sufficient for this test.*			
E37.	Is the network monitored for failed nodes, circuits or segments? Please provide a copy of the network monitoring process and management documentation and the name and phone number of the person who can demonstrate this process. *Test procedure: the examiner's evaluation of the documentation and observation of the process will generally be sufficient for this test.*			

Scoping Note – Section F and G	Yes	No
Can the company make changes to end of day, end of month, or end of year processes within the financially significant computer systems identified through INSTRUCTION NOTE 4 in the front of the questionnaire?		

If the answer to the above question is YES, the company's respective IS manager should complete sections F and G of the questionnaire. If the answer to the above question is NO, the company's respective IS manager should not complete sections F and G of the questionnaire, but should describe below, or in an attachment, the following: Under what conditions would the company ever make changes to end of day, end of month or end of year processes. This information will be evaluated by the examiner to confirm whether or not this section should be completed and tested.

F. PROCESSING CONTROLS

The name, title and phone number of the insurance company's contact person responsible for providing the answers to this set of questions is:

***Guidance Point*: Consider the response to question F1 in conjunction with the responses to question L4 in Section L if the transmissions pass over the Internet**

	Yes	No	Attachment
F1. Are there control procedures in place to ensure electronic data transmissions are transmitted and received completely and accurately? Please provide a copy of the control procedures and the name and phone number of the person who can demonstrate or validate the procedures. *Test procedure: the examiner's evaluation of the control, corroborating inquiry with the person identified and observation of the control, if possible, will generally be sufficient for this test.*			
F2. Are there control procedures in place to detect data that is input inaccurately or incompletely? Please provide a description of the control and the name and phone number of the people who can demonstrate or validate the control for each financially significant application. *Test procedure: the examiner's evaluation of the control, corroborating inquiry with the people identified and observation of the control, if possible, will generally be sufficient for this test.*			
F3. If there are any negotiable continuous forms, such as checks, are they kept under strict inventory control? Please provide the name and phone number of the person who can demonstrate or validate inventory control. *Test procedure: the examiner's corroborating inquiry with the person identified and observation of the control, if possible, will generally be sufficient for this test.*			
F4. Does the audit trail of records and reference provide the means to adequately trace any transaction forward to the final total, trace any transaction back to the original source document or input and trace any final total back to the component transactions? Please provide audit trail documentation for one transaction from each financially significant application. *Test procedure: the examiner's evaluation of the audit trail for the transaction provided from each financially significant application, as well as a judgmental test of at least one more transaction for each financially significant application, will generally be sufficient for this test.*			

G. DOCUMENTATION

The name, title and phone number of the insurance company's contact person responsible for providing the answers to this set of questions is:

____

	Yes	No	Attachment
G1. Is a documentation standards manual in existence and is it enforced? Please provide a copy of the table of contents from the manual. *Test procedure: the examiner's evaluation of the table of contents will generally be sufficient for this test.*			
G2. Is a documentation check-off list used to ensure all required documentation is prepared and approved for all new systems and for changes to existing systems and/or programs? Please provide a copy of the documentation check-off list for each financially significant application. *Test procedure: the examiner's evaluation of the check-off list will generally be sufficient for this test.*			
G3. As a minimum, are the following types of documentation prepared for every application and, if so, provide a copy of each type of documentation for each financially significant application:			
(a) Systems program definitions, a high level systems flow chart, narratives, etc.?			
(b) Programs file definitions, program flow charts, narratives, etc.?			
Test procedure: the examiner's evaluation of the documentation provided will generally be sufficient for this test.			

Scoping Note – Section H

Does the company use an outside service organization for any financially significant transaction processing?	YES	NO

If the answer to the above question is YES, the company's respective IS manager should complete section H of the questionnaire. If the answer is NO, the company's respective IS manager should not complete section H of the questionnaire, but should describe below, or in an attachment, whether the company has ever used or currently intends to use an outside computer processing service organization. This information will be evaluated by the examiner to confirm whether or not any part of this section should be completed and tested.

____

____

____

____

____

____

____

____

H. OUTSIDE SERVICE CENTER CONTROLS

NOTE: Outside Service Center Control questions must only be completed for outside service centers that performed computer processing of the insurance company's financially significant transactions **and** had responsibility for authorizing the transactions **or** maintained the related accountability of the transactions during the period under review. Be sure to consider web hosting vendors and application service providers (ASPs).

The name, title and phone number of the insurance company's contact person responsible for providing the answers to this set of questions is:

____

	Yes	No	Attachment
H1. Document the following general information:			
(a) Service center name:____________			
(b) Number of years in business:____________			
(c) Dunn and Bradstreet rating:____________			
(d) Managing executive of the service center:____________			

		Yes	No	Attachment
	(e) Name and title of the insurance company contact at the service center:			
	(f) Name and title of the individual within the insurance company designated to be the liaison with service center:____________			
	(g) Attach copies of all executed contracts (current contracts) between the service center and the company.			
	(h) Does the service center have an outside auditor and, if so, provide a copy of the most recent SAS-70 audit report, management letters, and the service center's response.			
	(i) Does the service have an internal audit function and, if so, provide a copy of the most recent IS internal audit report and the service center's response.			
H2.	Does the service center provide any of the following services for the insurance company?			
	(a) Processing?			
	(b) Data preparation?			
	(c) Program development?			
	(d) Program maintenance?			
	(e) Systems analysis?			
	(f) Other (explain)?			
H3.	Does the service center's blanket bond (fidelity insurance) cover losses due to actions by their personnel? Please provide a copy of the service center's blanket bond or evidence that auditing and testing of the bond is included in the SAS-70 report completed by the service center's external auditors. *Test procedure: the examiner's evaluation of the bond or evidence from the SAS-70 report will generally be sufficient for this test.*			
H4.	Does the service center carry insurance adequate to restore loss of company records due to mishap? Please provide a copy of the service center's insurance policy covering the loss of company records due to mishap or evidence that auditing and testing of the policy is included in the SAS-70 report completed by the service center's external auditors. *Test procedure: the examiner's evaluation of the insurance policy or evidence from the SAS-70 report will generally be sufficient for this test.*			

	Yes	No	Attachment
H5. Does the insurance company carry insurance of its own to compensate for losses caused by the service center? Please provide a copy of the insurance company's policy covering potential losses caused by the service center. *Test procedure: the examiner's evaluation of the insurance policy will generally be sufficient for this test.*			
H6. Is the insurance company the legal owner of all programs as well as tapes, disks, documentation, etc., used in the processing of its applications and is the insurance company the legal owner of data records created exclusively for the insurance company and/or the company's affiliate? Please provide same as question H1g. *Test procedure: the examiner's evaluation of the documentation provided in question H 1g will generally be sufficient for this test.*			
H7. Can the service center legally confiscate the insurance company's data, data recording media, or programs? Please provide same as question H1g. *Test procedure: the examiner's evaluation of the documentation provided in question H1g will generally be sufficient for this test.*			
H8. Is the service center adequately protected by a disaster plan and, if so, is it up-to-date and tested? Please provide a copy of the service center's disaster recovery plan and related test results or evidence that auditing and testing of the disaster plan and related test results is included in the SAS-70 report completed by the service center's external auditors. *Test procedure: the examiner's evaluation of the disaster recovery plan and related test results or evidence from the SAS-70 report will generally be sufficient for this test.*			
H9. Have provisions been made for backup of critical files away from the service center premises? Please provide a copy of the service center's backup procedures or evidence that auditing and testing of the backup procedures is included in the SAS-70 report completed by the service center's external auditors. *Test procedure: the examiner's evaluation of the backup procedures or evidence from the SAS-70 report will generally be sufficient for this test.*			
H10. Is the original or a copy kept of all source documents transmitted to the service center? Please provide a copy of the source documents for the last transmission to the service center that occurred during the period under review. *Test procedure: the examiner's evaluation of the source documents provided, as well as source documents for a judgmental sample of transactions processed within the past 12 to 18 months, will generally be sufficient for this test.*			

	Yes	No	Attachment
H11. Are controls, such as document count, transaction count, or other control totals, established for all documents sent to the service center? Please provide a description of the controls and the name and phone number of the person who can validate the controls. *Test procedure: the examiner's evaluation of the controls, corroborating inquiry with the person identified and observation of the controls, if possible, will generally be sufficient for this test.*			
H12. Are input control figures reconciled with the control figures furnished by the service center? Please provide a copy of the reconciliation for the last input to the service center that occurred during the period under review. *Test procedure: the examiner's evaluation of the reconciliation provided, as well as a judgmental sample of reconciliations performed within the past 12 to 18 months, will generally be sufficient for this test.*			
H13. Are all rejected transactions clearly identified and listed on an error report or file ? Please provide a copy of the last printout made during the period under review. *Test procedure: the examiner's evaluation of the printout provided will generally be sufficient for this test.*			
H14. Are there methods to ensure that errors are corrected within the system? Please provide a copy of the error resolution procedures and the name and phone number of the person who can demonstrate or validate the methods. *Test procedure: the examiner's evaluation of the controls ,corroborating inquiry with the person identified and observation of the controls, if possible, will generally be sufficient for this test.*			

I. LOGICAL AND PHYSICAL SECURITY

<u>NOTE 1:</u> Logical and Physical Security questions will typically be answered only once for centralized computer processing environments. In decentralized environments the questions may need to be answered more than once because separate organizational units may effectively have separate processing environments (i.e., each unit may have its own systems and local area networks).

<u>NOTE 2:</u> Virtually all insurance companies use some type of system-based logical security software, such as RACF, in the mainframe environment or system-level security from the operating systems, such as Windows NT or UNIX, to restrict access to financially significant information systems. However, some insurance companies rely upon application-based security to restrict access to appropriate functions within financially significant applications while other insurance companies rely upon system-based security to secure both system access and application access. If the insurance company under examination relies upon system-based security to secure both system access and application access, questions I21 through I24 do **not** have to be answered.

The name, title and phone number of the insurance company's contact person responsible for providing the answers to this set of questions is:

____

	Yes	No	Attachment
<u>Guidance Point:</u> **Well controlled companies have reporting mechanisms in place that allow management to monitor both authorized and unauthorized attempts to access sensitive computer facilities. These reports are reviewed regularly by security administration personnel. Persistent attempts by individuals to gain unauthorized access to these facilities are reported to senior data processing management. Additionally, access by individuals to these facilities that appears inappropriate is investigated to determine whether it is consistent with the individual's job responsibilities.**			
I1. Does management demonstrate an awareness of security risks, recognize that security is both a technical and operational, as well as a cultural issue, and promote security awareness across all levels of the organization? Please provide a copy of security awareness training material, including the company security policy. *Test procedure: the examiner's evaluation of the material provided.*			
<u>Guidance Point:</u> **The security administrator's role is to ensure that only appropriately authorized individuals are granted access to system and application resources. The security officer's role is responsible for the monitoring, modification, and enforcement of the access control strategy as well as the overall security strategy for the organization. The security function should be positioned within the company's structure in a location that enables it to be an adequate control function. It should be segregated from other departments that may affect its objectivity. Security can be accomplished successfully from either a centralized or decentralized location. Although neither approach is better than the other, the type selected must fit the company's structure. If the company is relatively small to medium in size, it may not have both a full-time security administrator and security officer.**			

	Yes	No	Attachment
I2. Does the company's information security policy clearly define the responsibilities of users, management and security personnel? Please provide a copy of the policy. *Test procedure: the examiner's evaluation of the policy provided will generally be sufficient for this test.*			
I3. Are the assigned tasks of the individual responsible for information security consistent with the company's security policy statement? Please provide a copy of the job description for the person responsible for information security. *Test procedure: the examiner's evaluation of the job description provided will generally be sufficient for this test.*			
Guidance Point: **Well-controlled companies restrict physical access to sensitive computer facilities (e.g., the computer room and the network operations center) using many methods, which include: smart cards, combination numbers and keys. These control procedures operate at all times, including evenings, weekends, and holidays.**			
I4. Has a written statement been issued that defines the restrictions on access to the computer facility? Please provide a copy of the statement. *Test procedure: the examiner's evaluation of the written statement provided will generally be sufficient for this test.*			
I5. Are procedures in effect in the computer facility to verify that only authorized individuals are being permitted to enter the facility? Please provide a copy of the procedures and the name and phone number of the person who can demonstrate or validate the procedures. *Test procedure: the examiner's evaluation of the procedures provided, corroborating inquiry with the person identified, and observation of the procedures, if possible, will generally be sufficient for this test.*			
I6. Does the IS department have procedures for adding individuals to the list of those authorized to have access to computer resources, changing their access capabilities, and deleting them from this list? Please provide a copy of the procedures and the list of authorized personnel, including their access capabilities. *Test procedure: the examiner's evaluation of the procedures and the list provided, along with corroborating inquiry with a judgmental sample of people included on the list, will generally be sufficient for this test.*			
I7. Does the system that controls access to restricted facilities keep a log of which badges enter the facilities? Is this log reviewed daily, weekly, monthly? How long are logs retained for and where? Please provide a copy of the log(s) and a copy of the procedures that govern its review. Please provide contact information for the person responsible for the log review. *Test procedure: the examiners review of the log review procedure, the existing log report and spot checks of the accuracy of the report will be sufficient for this examination.*			

Question	Yes	No	Attachment
Guidance Point: **Only appropriately authorized individuals should be granted access to system and application resources. Access should be granted by the security administrator after the appropriate approvals have been obtained from data processing management or application owners. For example, permitting an individual to pay claims using the claims application should only be granted if approval has been obtained from senior claims management. Likewise, update access to the claims master data file, outside of the application software (e.g., by writing independent programs), should only be granted if approval has been obtained from appropriate management. Finally, the company's management should expressly prohibit the sharing of user IDs and passwords.**			
I8. Is there a control that ensures the effectiveness of financially significant system password controls (e.g., unique user IDs, password disciplines)? Please provide a copy of the logical security procedures used to determine the structure and use of system passwords (e.g., password expiration, password composition and password confidentiality) and the name and number of the person who can provide the state examiner with a system logon ID and password in order to test questions I8 through I10. *Test procedure: the examiner's evaluation of the procedures provided, corroborating inquiry with the person identified, and execution of the procedures necessary to test questions I8 through I11, will generally be sufficient for this test.*			
I9. Are passwords generated by each user rather than assigned by the company? Please provide same as question I8. *Test procedure: same as question I7.*			
I10. Are passwords properly not displayed during the logon process and properly omitted from printed output, are they stored in an encrypted state and are they transmitted in that state across the network during the authentication and authorization process? Please provide same as question I8. *Test procedure: same as question I8.*			
I11. Does the system automatically prompt users to change their passwords at least quarterly and prevent passwords from being reused by the same individual? Please provide a printout of the security parameters, such as password aging and password history. *Test procedure: the examiner's evaluation of the parameters provided will generally be sufficient for this test.*			
I12. Are operating system security authorization forms completed and approved by management to ensure that system access granted to users and IS staff is commensurate with their job responsibilities? Please provide a list of all authorized system users, including system or application account IDs, for each platform on which financially significant applications reside. If one platform (e.g., Windows or Novell) is used to authenticate all users to the Company network, then one list will be sufficient, so long as all users, from all significant			

	Yes	No	Attachment
computer systems, are included on this list. *Test procedure: The examiner should select an attribute sample of forms for between 11 and 76 employees form the list provided by the company. If all financially significant information systems reside on the same computer platform or essentially similar computer platforms that are subject to the same or similar logical security controls, it is sensible to select a single attribute sample. If not, an attribute sample should be selected from the population of employees who have security access accounts on each disimilar computer platform.*			
Guidance Point: **Well-controlled companies periodically verify that access to application resources is appropriate. Typically, this is accomplished by distributing lists of the individuals with access privileges to application functions and features, program libraries and data files to application owners and data processing management to confirm that such access is appropriate.**			
I13. Does user department management periodically validate the access capabilities currently provided to individuals in their department? Please provide evidence of the last user access review performed during the period under review. *Test procedure: the examiner's evaluation of the evidence provided will generally be sufficient for this test.*			
I14. Is there a control that ensures that users are restricted to their applications (e.g., preventing users from escaping from application menus)? Please provide a description of the control and the name and phone number of the person who can demonstrate or validate the control. *Test procedure: the examiner's evaluation of the control, corroborating inquiry with the person identified and observation of the control, if possible, will generally be sufficient for this test.*			
Guidance Point: **When employees are transferred between departments, their access privileges to system and application resources should be updated accordingly. For example, if an employee is transferred from the claims department to the general ledger department, his or her claims application access privileges should be revoked. When employees are terminated, all system access privileges should be revoked immediately.**			
I15. Do procedures provide for prompt cancellation of identification codes and passwords when the employment of the individual to whom they were assigned has been terminated? Please provide a copy of the procedures and evidence that the procedures were followed for the last IS person or user terminated, if any, during the period under review. *Test procedure: the examiner's evaluation of the procedures and evidence provided will generally be sufficient for this test.*			

Question	Yes	No	Attachment
Guidance Point: **Well-controlled companies have reporting mechanisms in place to monitor security events (e.g., invalid logon attempts, unauthorized attempts to access data and programs, changes to software security values and rules). These reports are reviewed regularly by security personnel. Persistent attempts by individuals to gain unauthorized access to resources are reported to the applicable application owners (e.g., the manager of the claims department) and/or senior management**			
I16. Does management review and resolve reports of security violations? Please provide evidence of IS management's review of security violation reports and subsequent resolution of violations. *Test procedure: the examiner's evaluation of the evidence provided will generally be sufficient for this test.*			
I17. Do procedures exist which require authorized users of computing resources to be given specific permission to access particular resources, including data files, application processing programs, the operating system and various commands? Please provide a copy of the procedures. *Test procedure: the examiner's evaluation of the procedures provided will generally be sufficient for this test.*			
I18. Is there a control that ensures appropriate restriction of remote access (e.g., through networks or using dial-up facilities)? Please provide a description of the control and the name and phone number of the person who can demonstrate or validate the control. *Test procedure: the examiner's evaluation of the control, corroborating inquiry with the person identified and observation of the control, if possible, will generally be sufficient for this test.*			
Guidance Point: **The more secure the computer system, the less flexible it will be in responding to unusual circumstances, which may make it necessary to bypass some of the security protection. A policy for dealing with emergencies should be prepared. Activities during the emergency should be logged carefully. Once the emergency is over, security protection should be reinstated immediately. The impact of the activities during the emergency should be assessed and authorized retrospectively, and appropriate corrective action should be taken. Emergencies during the day can be corrected by a responsible technical support person with a user-ID with special privileges. If a problem occurs outside of normal working hours, the off-shift personnel (e.g., on-call programmer) may need a special user-ID.**			
I19. Is there a control over administrator level access to the operating system that ensures access to sensitive software utilities is appropriately restricted and monitored (consider the use of these sensitive facilities during an emergency situation)? Please provide a list of the sensitive software utilities commonly used by the company and evidence that the last use of each utility during the period under review was approved.			

		Yes	No	Attachment
I20.	If applicable, are personnel with access to sensitive software utilities restricted access to physical financially significant assets? Please provide a copy of the job description for the last person who executed each of the utilities identified in question I19. *Test procedure: the examiner's evaluation of the job description provided will generally be sufficient for this test.*			
I21.	Is there a control that ensures the effectiveness of financially significant application password controls (e.g., unique user IDs and password disciplines)? Please provide a copy of the logical security procedures used to determine the structure and use of application passwords (e.g., password expiration and password confidentiality) and the name and number of the person who can demonstrate or validate the procedures. *Test procedure: the examiner's evaluation of the procedures, corroborating inquiry with the person identified and observation of the procedures, if possible, will generally be sufficient for this test.*			
I22.	Are application security authorization forms completed and approved by management to ensure system access granted to users is commensurate with their job responsibilities? Please provide a copy of a completed and approved application security authorization form for one user from each financially significant application. *Test procedure: the examiner's evaluation of the application security authorization forms provided, along with the application security authorization forms on file for the employees selected from the attribute sample selected for question I12 above, should be sufficient for this test.*			
I23.	Are there procedures that ensure that application access is appropriately changed on a timely basis when employees transfer or terminate? Please provide a copy of the procedures and evidence that the procedures were followed for the last user terminated, if any, during the period under review. *Test procedure: the examiner's evaluation of the procedures and related evidence will generally be sufficient for this test.*			
I24.	Are periodic checks carried out to confirm that employees' current application access is commensurate with their job responsibilities? Please provide evidence of the last check performed during the period under review. *Test procedure: the examiner's evaluation of the evidence provided will generally be sufficient for this test.*			

Item	Question	Yes	No	Attachment
I25.	Is there an appropriate sign-out procedure for computer equipment that is removed from the company's offices? Does the equipment have asset management tags affixed and recorded in an asset management system? Please provide a copy of the procedure and the name and phone number of the person who can demonstrate and validate the procedure. *Test procedure: the examiner's evaluation of the procedure, corroborating inquiry with the person identified, and observation of the procedure, if possible, will generally be sufficient for this test.*			
I26.	Has the company issued written policy statements regarding the use of personal computers and, if so, do the statements include appropriate requirements for development and testing, documentation, input, processing and output controls, back-up and recovery of programs and data and security over custody and use of personal computer assets, including hardware, software and data? Please provide copies of the policy statements. *Test procedure: the examiner's evaluation of the statements provided will generally be sufficient for this test.*			
I27.	Does the company have formal monitoring procedures and systems to detect unauthorized access attempts from either outside or inside the company? Please provide copies of the intrusion detection policy, documentation of the systems in place and the review process followed. Please provide the name and phone number of the person who can provide evidence of the use of intrusion detection systems. *Test procedure: the examiners review of the documentation and corroborating inquiry with the person identified and observation of the technology in use will be sufficient evidence for this test.*			
I28.	Does the company have formal emergency response procedures to follow if a computer security incident occurs? Please provide a copy of the incident response procedure. *Test procedure: the examiner's evaluation of the procedures will generally be sufficient for this test.*			
	Guidance Point: **Such procedures typically include notifying management, including the legal and public relations department. These procedures may also include guidelines for contacting law enforcement at the discretion of senior corporate management.**			
I29.	Does the company utilize a virus detection system on personal computers that is regularly updated and, if yes, does it have a disinfecting feature (e.g., the ability to restore files to a healthy state)? Please provide the name of the virus detection and/or anti-virus software and the name and phone number of the person who can provide evidence of the mandatory, periodic use and update of the anti-virus software across the network. *Test procedure: the examiner's corroborating inquiry with the person identified and observation of the software in use will generally be sufficient for this test.*			

	Yes	No	Attachment
I30. Has management developed a comprehensive policy addressing the unique security risks associated with wireless technologies? Please provide a copy of policies addressing wireless technology risks.			

J. CONTINGENCY PLANNING

The name, title and phone number of the insurance company's contact person responsible for providing the answers to this set of questions is:

____

	Question	Yes	No	Attachment
J1.	Is the business contingency plan a) current, b) based on a business impact analysis, c) been tested and d) address all significant business activities, including financial functions, telecommunication services, data processing and network services? Please provide a copy of the plan and evidence of test results, including management's resolution of test discrepancies. *Test procedure: the examiner's evaluation of the plan and evidence provided will generally be sufficient for this test.*			
J2.	Are copies of the plan kept in relevant off-site locations? Please provide a list of the locations and the name and phone number of the person who can validate the existence of the copies at the off-site locations. *Test procedure: the examiner's evaluation of the list and corroborating inquiry with the person identified will generally be sufficient for this test.*			
J3.	Has a restoration priority been assigned to all significant business activities? Please provide a copy of the prioritized business activities. *Test procedure: the examiner's evaluation of the activities provided will generally be sufficient for this test.*			
J4.	Does the plan contain a list of critical computer application programs, operating systems and data files? Please provide same as question J1. *Test procedure: same as question J1.*			
J5.	Does a written agreement or contract exist for use by IS of a specific alternate site and computer hardware to restore data processing operations after a disaster occurs and does the site have a backup generator in place in case of local power outages, a fire detection and suppression system and moisture sensors in place under the raised floor? Please provide a copy of the agreement and the name and phone number of the person who can validate the existence of the equipment at the alternate site. *Test procedure: the examiner's evaluation of the agreement and corroborating inquiry with the person identified will generally be sufficient for this test.*			
J6.	Does the plan contain a list of the supplies that would be needed in the event of a disaster, together with names and phone numbers of the suppliers? Please provide same as question J1. *Test procedure: same as question J1.*			

		Yes	No	Attachment
J7.	Have user departments developed adequate manual processing procedures for use until the electronic data processing function can be restored? Please provide the name and phone number of one person from each financially significant user area who can demonstrate the procedures. *Test procedure: the examiner's corroborating inquiry with the people identified and observation of the procedures, if possible, will generally be sufficient for this test.*			
J8.	Is there a disaster recovery plan in effect and, if so, is it up to date and has it been tested? Please provide a copy of the disaster recovery plan and evidence of results for the last test conducted during the period under review. *Test procedure: the examiner's evaluation of the disaster recovery plan and evidence of the latest test results will generally be sufficient for this test.*			
J9.	Does the business continuity plan clearly describe senior management roles and responsibilities associated with the declaration of a emergency and implementation of the business continuity and disaster recovery plans? Does the plan clearly identify the general process by which the threat will be assessed and the specific individuals who are authorized to declare an emergency? Please indicate where individuals with the authority to declare an emergency are listed within the plan document. *Test procedure: the examiner's evaluation of the evidence provided will generally be sufficient for this test.*			

Scoping Note – Section K	YES	NO
NOTE: The company should describe the status of current or planned e-business initiatives. This information will be evaluated by the examiner to confirm whether or not this section should be completed and tested and whether additional examination procedures may be required.		
Do user authorization or authentication controls depend on computer security (e.g., user IDs and passwords)?		
Does the company utilize e-channels for the marketing of the company's insurance or annuity products?		
Does the company utilize e-channels for the submission, acceptance and/or administration of policies?		
Does the company utilize e-channels for the submission, acceptance and/or the processing of claims and/or annuity products?		
Does the company utilize e-channels in the processing, or to supplement the processing of any other financially significant account balances or sets of transactions described in Instruction Note 4, such as investments, reinsurance, procurement, employee benefits, etc.		
Guidance Point: **E-channels include voice recognition units (VRUs), the Internet, third-party extranets and wireless and broadband communications media.**		
NOTE: If the answer to any of the above questions is YES and the transactions are material, as defined in Instruction Note 4 to this questionnaire the company should complete section K of the questionnaire. If the answer to ALL questions is NO, the company should not complete section K of the questionnaire.		

K. E-BUSINESS CONTROLS

The name, title and phone number of the insurance company's contact person responsible for providing the answers to this set of questions is:

____

	Yes	No	Attachment
K1. Are the company's e-business initiatives led by a knowledgeable team that includes top executive management? Please provide the organizational chart for e-business initiatives and the job descriptions and resumes for key e-business leaders. *Test procedure: the examiner's evaluation of the e-business organization chart, job descriptions and resumes will generally be sufficient for this test.*			
Guidance Point: **The e-business strategy should be closely linked to the overall corporate strategy. Personnel documentation could include a mapping of the required skill set to the current employee skill set inventory, a document outlining the company's criteria for outsourcing or hiring personnel with requisite skills or a description of the company's e-business training program.**			
K2. Is a formal e-business strategy in place at the company and does the strategy include consideration of the availability of appropriate technology, as well as technically competent personnel, necessary to support the company's e-business initiatives? Please provide a copy of the strategy. *Test procedure: the examiner's evaluation of the strategy document will generally be sufficient for this test.*			
K3. Has company management developed a formal document that clearly defines the tactical methods and technologies for implementing the company's e-business strategy? Please provide a copy of this document. *Test procedure: the examiner's evaluation of the implementation document (typically a tactical or project plan) explaining how the e-business strategy should be executed will generally be sufficient for this test.*			
Guidance Point: **A knowledge management methodology should include training programs, formal training documentation or a web enabled knowledge repository.**			
K4. Does the company have a methodology in place for knowledge transfer to or among employees to facilitate ongoing improvement of key e-business processes? Please provide evidence of this process. *Test procedure: the examiner's evaluation of the methodology documentation will generally be sufficient for this test.*			

	Yes	No	Attachment
Guidance Point: **The responsibility for monitoring pending regulations and compliance with new regulations should be formally assigned, typically to a compliance function or a risk management function. Consider whether the company has assigned responsibility for relevant regulations, such as the Gramm-Leach-Bliley Act, the Health Insurance Portability and Accountability Act, the Electronic Signature in Global and National Commerce Act (e-sign), and the European Union Safe-Harbor Agreement.**			
K5. Are appropriate company personnel knowledgeable of e-business specific industry regulations and international regulations (e.g., data privacy acts, electronic signature laws, and encryption regulations) and have internal controls been established at the company to help ensure compliance with applicable regulations? Please provide evidence of the controls. *Test procedure: the examiner's evaluation of the controls documentation will generally be sufficient for this test.*			
Guidance Point: **The company's legal or compliance function should review the company's insurance coverage to ensure it covers e-business transactions. For example, the company needs to determine whether its insurance covers lost business due to web site failures, the penalties from unauthorized disclosure of customer or business partner information, fines from violating privacy regulations and the costs associated with prosecuting security break-ins.**			
K6. Are the company's e-business transactions covered by an insurance policy? Please provide evidence of the insurance coverage. *Test procedure: the examiner's evaluation of the coverage will generally be sufficient for this test.*			
K7. Are controls in place at the company to help ensure proper monitoring of where the company is liable for taxes associated with the company's e-business activities? Please provide evidence of this monitoring control. *Test procedure: the examiner's evaluation of the monitoring control will generally be sufficient for this test.*			
Guidance Point: **Alliance management controls include the assignment of resources to manage the alliance, definition of the company's and the alliance partner(s) roles and responsibilities, maintenance of service level agreements (SLAs), and management of problem identification, investigation and resolution.**			
K8. Have alliance management controls, such as service level agreements ("SLAs"), been established for all e-business partnerships and strategic alliances? If so, please provide a copy of the SLAs and a copy of alliance management policies and procedures. *Test procedure: the examiner's evaluation of the controls documentation will generally be sufficient for this test.*			

Guidance Point: **Operational resilience – effective operational resilience allows a company to significantly reduce business risk and avoid operational failure, including failure in operational process or strategy and operational lapses in control that endanger the company's ability to achieve its strategic objectives. Operational failures can include the unavailability of operations or services and the inability to meet customer demands.**

Scalability of architecture – the ability to increase or decrease the network architecture, including software and hardware components, to meet changes in demand. The scalability of the company's business model needs to be considered in conjunction with scalability of its e-business technical architecture. A scalable network architecture means the architecture can be changed in size and configuration without major changes needing to be made.

Redundancy – means that if a primary component failure occurs, there is a redundant component that can take over in the event the primary component fails.

Load balancing – is the concept of distributing of processing across a network so that that no one device bears too much of the workload. Load balancing becomes more important in situations where web site traffic is difficult to predict. If the load is not balanced, network failures or delayed response time can occur. There are several methods of load balancing, e.g., hardware based, software based.

Performance monitoring – is the process in which key resources of a system are identified and then monitored on a continuous basis. Typically, the company should monitor network capacity, server capacity (CPU, memory, I/O capacity) and storage capacity. The company should have the ability to take snapshots of current performance in the environment (i.e., snapshot of a systems CPU utilization at x time) and the ability to trend key measurements over a period of time (i.e., intra-day CPU utilization, weekly CPU utilization, monthly CPU utilization, etc).

Note: Capacity planning is directly related to performance monitoring. With capacity planning, baseline values are derived from performance monitoring activities. These baselines are indicators of performance under normal loads as well as upper-level thresholds. The actual planning exercises use this information, gathered from performance monitoring, and input from business units on expected changes to the current volumes (i.e., from a marketing campaign or general market change) to create capacity planning models. These models are then used to determine if the current environment needs to be enhanced to support the future business needs.

	Yes	No	Attachment
K9. Have the following operational resilience elements been addressed for e-business initiatives?			
(a) Scalability of architecture?			

	Yes	No	Attachment
(b) Redundancy?			
(c) Load balancing?			
(d) Performance monitoring?			
(e) Business continuity?			
Please provide evidence, including a network topology diagram, showing that these elements have been addressed. *Test procedure: the examiner's evaluation of the documentation will generally be sufficient for this test.*			
Guidance Point: **Authentication is the verification of a user's identity. Confidentiality is the assurance that stored and transmitted data can only be viewed by those people who are specifically authorized. Integrity is the assurance that stored and transmitted data is accurate and can only be modified by those people who are specifically authorized. Auditability is the ability of systems and applications to create and maintain useable records for all user actions and system events.** **By definition, non-repudiation is the strength and accuracy of authentication, integrity, confidentiality and audit controls so users can or cannot deny the validity of their transaction. This is becoming a hot topic as the use of the Internet for electronic commerce increases. An example of non-repudiation occurs when you go to a grocery store and sign your check in front of the cashier. The cashier looks at the picture and signature on your driver's license and then compares them to your face and signature on the check. As a result, you cannot deny that you signed the check. (This example assumes that you can rely on the integrity of the driver's license and the integrity of the review performed by the clerk.)**			
K10. Has company management assessed the company's e-business security risks in terms of authentication, confidentiality, integrity, auditability and non-repudiation? Please provide a copy of this assessment. *Test procedure: the examiner's evaluation of the assessment documentation will generally be sufficient for this test.*			
K11. Has company management considered, documented and implemented a process for the creation, maintainability, and archiving of all the company's web content? Please provide a copy of the process. *Test procedure: the examiner's evaluation of the process documentation will generally be sufficient for this test.*			
Guidance Point: **The company should address intellectual property rights in its contracts with third party consultants. In addition, employee contracts should address intellectual property rights.**			

	Yes	No	Attachment
K12. Has the company established a strategy and supporting procedures to ensure that its intellectual property is adequately protected? Has management taken precautions through legal and technical means to protect the company's web content and does management ensure contracts with IT vendors and partners address intellectual property rights? Please provide a copy of the procedures document that describes management's approach to these issues. *Test procedure: the examiner's evaluation of the documentation will generally be sufficient for this test.*			
K13. Does company management take reasonable security precautions to ensure that personal data about the company's web site visitors is not accessible by unauthorized persons? Please provide a copy of the policy and procedures document describing management's approach to this issue. *Test procedure: the examiner's evaluation of the policy and procedures documentation will generally be sufficient for this test.*			
K14. Is a privacy policy in place at the company? If yes, are the following issues addressed in the privacy policy and in practice?			
(a) Notice / awareness? Customers should be given notice of a company's information collection and usage practices in order to make informed decisions as to whether, and to what extent, to disclose personal information.			
(b) Choice / consent? Data subjects should be given options as to how any personal information collected from them may be used. A degree of choice can be provided through mandatory and optional data elements or opt-in and opt-out methods.			
(c) Access / participation? Data subjects must have the ability to access, correct or update data about themselves and to contest the data's accuracy and completeness.			
(d) Ongoing Compliance Monitoring? The company should have a compliance-monitoring program in place to help ensure that the practices disclosed in the company's online privacy policy are complied with on an ongoing basis.			
Please provide a copy of the company's corporate or divisional privacy policies. Test procedure: the examiner's evaluation of the documentation will generally be sufficient for this test.			
K15. Has company management created channels for the company's customers to provide electronic feedback about the company's products and services? Please provide a copy of the most recent summarization of electronic customer feedback. *Test procedure: the examiner's evaluation of the feedback documentation will generally be sufficient for this test.*			

Yes	No	Attachment

***Guidance Point** (Source: PricewaterhouseCoopers E-Business Technology Forecast):* **PGP – stands for Pretty Good Privacy and is a type of public key encryption. A public key is essentially a binary number algorithm that locks and unlocks data. Public-key encryption is based on two keys: one to encrypt the message and another to decrypt it. Public key cryptosystems are also referred to as asymmetric key encryption, which means that knowing the public encryption key is no help in being able to decrypt a message. Users wanting to receive confidential information can freely announce their public key, which then is used by the sender to encrypt data to be sent to them. (Typically, public keys are stored in a publicly accessible standardized directory.) The data can be decrypted only by the holder of the corresponding private key.**

Public Key Infrastructure (PKI) – "A PKI is the underlying technical and institutional framework that allows public-key encryption technology to be deployed widely…Integral to a PKI are a means of authentication and encryption, secure directory services, secure interoperation of directory servers and client access to directories, and the Simple Distributed Security Infrastructure (SDSI), a system that uses public-key cryptography combined with mechanisms for defining groups and group membership certificates. A PKI is designed to solve the problem of trustworthiness."

Symmetric Key Encryption – "In the shared single-key method, the same key is used to encrypt and decrypt the message. However, this method requires that the sender and recipient both have the same key and that no one else does. Transmitting the key over the same insecure channel as the encrypted message is not acceptable, so a secure out-of-band communications method is required. (Even more critical to such an exchange is a preexisting relationship between the two parties that creates a secure context within which the secret-key can be exchanged.) Moreover, each pair of parties requires a unique key. The number of keys increases rapidly as the number of transactions grows. The most commonly used symmetric-key algorithms are the Data Encryption Standard (DES), the International Data Encryption Algorithm (IDEA), or Triple-DES."

SSL – "The most popular process in use today to protect sensitive information such as payment data uses the Secure Sockets Layer (SSL) protocol, which was developed by Netscape and is now a de facto standard. SSL encrypts data sent between Customer Alice's browser and Merchant Bob's server. SSL constructs a communication connection where all data is encrypted before being transmitted over the Internet. Handshake routines at the onset of an SSL session share identifying information between the two parties, select one of several encryption algorithms to be used, and create the necessary session-specific encryption keys.

Alice's browser, for example, must locate Bob's public key, which is stored at Bob's Web commerce site. Using Bob's public key, Alice's browser can create an encrypted message only Bob can read containing a unique, session-specific key that will be used to encrypt messages exchanged between the two parties for the duration of this transaction. After the handshake is completed, Alice's

	Yes	No	Attachment
browser and Bob's server exchange data that is encrypted using conventional secret-key encryption before being transported over the insecure network. The entire process is transparent to Alice and Bob because the complex SSL technology has been embedded successfully in browsers and servers without burdening users with the need to understand or be involved in the setup of the secure data transfer."			
K16. Does the company utilize encryption technology for securing its e-business transactions? If yes, what forms of encryption and how are they used? Please provide documentation of the types of transactions and the types of encryption used, such as simple PGP, Secure Socket Layer (SSL), point-to-point hardware encryption or digital certificates in a Public Key Infrastructure (PKI). Please provide the contact information for a person responsible for encryption of e-business transactions. *Test procedure: the examiner's evaluation of the documentation, review of selected transactions and corroborating interviews will generally be sufficient for this test.*			
Guidance Point: **(Source: PricewaterhouseCoopers E-Business Technology Forecast) If the company uses digital certificates in any form then question K17 needs to be answered regarding the issuance, maintenance and deletion of certificates.** **A certification authority is also referred to as a CA. "Certification authorities address the PKI problem by supplying authentication as a service from a trusted third party. The certification authority vouches for the authenticity of a public key either by storing it in a centralized, online database or by distributing it with a certificate, which is basically a copy of the user's public key that has been digitally signed by the certification authority. An enterprise may operate its own certification authority.** **A certificate is similar to an identity card with a notary seal on it. It is valid for a stated period of time and is subject to cancellation by being included on a certificate revocation list (CRL). CRLs basically are "hot lists" that identify certificates that have been withdrawn, canceled, or compromised or that should not be trusted for other specified reasons."**			
K17. Does the company operate its own digital certificate authority (CA) or has it outsourced that function? Please provide documentation regarding all certificate management processes including a copy of the certificate practice statement and certificate policies. Please provide the contact information for a person responsible for management of digital certificates. *Test procedure: the examiner's evaluation of the documentation, review of selected transactions, and corroborating interviews will generally be sufficient for this test.*			

	Yes	No	Attachment
Guidance Point: **The examiner should consider the response to Question K18 in conjunction with the understanding of the control environment obtained in the SRAs. The risks identified in Question K10 should be managed through the establishment of both technical and business process and financial controls. Question K18 is focusing on the business process and financial controls that the company has implemented to ensure the accuracy, completeness, authorization and existence of e-business transactions.**			
K18. Has the company reviewed its legacy business process and financial controls, and updated them where necessary, to ensure that they are appropriate for ensuring the confidentiality, integrity, and non–repudiation of electronic communications and transactions? Please provide documentation describing these controls and the contact information for a person responsible for managing the e-business controls environment. *Test procedure: the examiner's evaluation of the documentation, review of selected transactions, and corroborating interviews will generally be sufficient for this test.*			
Guidance Point: **The examiner should consider the response to Question K19 in conjunction with the response to Question E22 in Section E.**			
K19. Does the company have a formal policy for electronic record retention? Consider whether the company has addressed the following:			
(a) its electronic records are acceptable to its national tax authorities and other governmental or regulatory bodies to which information must be provided.			
(b) its electronic records are generated and maintained using a system that is likely to produce acceptable evidence in legal proceedings.			
(c) content on the web site is archived for possible legal use in accordance with the rules of each jurisdiction, as to length of time and detail of the archive.			
(d) usability and readability of electronic records as the company's systems migrate from one version to another.			
Please provide a copy of the e-business electronic record keeping policy and the contact information for a person responsible for ensuring compliance with this policy. *Test procedure: the examiner's evaluation of the documentation and corroborating interviews will generally be sufficient for this test.*			

Scoping Note - Section L	**YES**	**NO**
Does the company use the public Internet or any Wide Area Networks (WANs)?		

If the answer to the above question is YES, the company's respective IS manager should complete section L of the questionnaire. If the answer is NO, the company's respective IS manager should not complete section L of the questionnaire, but should describe below, or in an attachment, whether the company has ever used or currently intends to use the public Internet or any WANs. This information will be evaluated by the examiner to confirm whether or not any part of this section should be completed and tested.

____

____

____

____

____

____

____

____

L. WIDE AREA NETWORK (WAN) AND INTERNET CONTROLS

The name, title and phone number of the insurance company's contact person responsible for providing the answers to this set of questions is:

____

		Yes	**No**	**Attachment**
L1.	Does the company use Wide Area Networks (WANs) and, if yes, do information systems personnel have documentation to identify and describe network nodes and network configurations? Please provide copies of historical and current network design and network configuration, and/or narratives describing network design and configuration. *Test procedure: the examiner's evaluation of the documentation provided will generally be sufficient for this test.*			
L2.	Does the company use the public Internet and, if yes, has management outside of information systems supported the overall direction of the company's use of the Internet? Please provide a copy of the company's policy regarding Internet usage. *Test procedure: the examiner's evaluation of the policy provided will generally be sufficient for this test.*			

		Yes	No	Attachment
L3.	Are controls in place to help ensure employee Internet usage is commensurate with the Internet Usage Policy? Is access to the Internet restricted so that inappropriate locations may not be accessed? *Test procedure: the examiner's evaluation of the evidence provided will generally be sufficient for this test.*			
L4.	Are appropriate management, users and information systems personnel involved in the specification of the Internet control facility design? Please provide evidence of approval by appropriate management, users and information systems personnel of the Internet control facility design. *Test procedure: the examiner's evaluation of the evidence provided will generally be sufficient for this test.*			
L5.	Does the company allow access to the WAN or Internet (e.g., - direct dial-in access, access via a local on-site server or both)? Are controls in place to ensure access is appropriately authorized? Are periodic checks carried out to ensure access is appropriately maintained? Please provide a copy of a completed authorization form for one user from each major line of business, a description of the periodic checks performed and evidence of the last check performed during the period under examination. *Test procedure: the examiner's evaluation of the forms and evidence provided will generally be sufficient for this test.*			
L6.	Is financially significant accounting information or sensitive management information transmitted across the WAN or Internet and, if yes, is a data encryption feature in place and functioning? Please provide the name of the data encryption package, the name of the person who has access to the keys and the name and phone number of the person who can demonstrate the feature. *Test procedure: the examiner's corroborating inquiry with the person identified and observation of the feature in use will generally be sufficient for this test.*			
L7.	Is financially significant accounting information or sensitive management information stored on company computer systems or servers which are connected via an intra-company network to any network outside the company and, if so, does the company use firewall technology to protect its internal network from the external ones? Please provide the name and phone number of the person who can provide evidence of the use of firewall technology, including diagrams that show the firewall's location within the network infrastructure as well as the protection rules for the firewall. *Test procedure: the examiner's corroborating inquiry with the person identified and observation of the technology in use will generally be sufficient for this test.*			

	Yes	No	Attachment
L8. Does the company utilize a virus detection system on the network and, if yes, does it have a disinfecting feature (e.g., the ability to restore files to a healthy state)? Please provide the name of the virus detection and/or anti-virus software and the name and phone number of the person who can provide evidence of the use of anti-virus software. *Test procedure: the examiner's corroborating inquiry with the person identified and observation of the software in use will generally be sufficient for this test.*			
L9. Does the company scan all incoming e-mail and files for viruses concealed in attachments and if yes, does it disinfect said attachments? Please provide the name of the e-mail and file scanning program and the name and contact information for the person who can demonstrate its use. *Test procedure: the examiner's corroborating inquiry with the person identified and observation of the software in use will generally be sufficient for this test.*			
L10. Does the company scan or filter outbound e-mail for either offensive or potentially damaging content? Please provide the name of the content filtering program and the name and contact information for the person who can demonstrate its use. *Test procedure: the examiner's corroborating inquiry with the person identified and observation of the software in use will generally be sufficient for this test.*			
L11. Does the disaster recovery plan (previously covered in Section J) encompass recovery of the WAN? Please provide a copy of the plan and evidence of test results, including management's resolution of test discrepancies. *Test procedure: the examiner's evaluation of the plan and evidence provided will generally be sufficient for this test.*			

ATTACHMENT A – SIGNIFICANT COMPUTER APPLICATIONS

Complete this schedule for all financially significant computer hardware and software.

Application Name	Application Function[1]	Computing Platform[2]	Application Software Source[3]	Date of application installation	Are changes made to this application	Team Supporting Application[4]	Location(s) of Business Users	Location(s) of Computer Systems

[1] At a minimum, include systems responsible for general ledger functions, policy issuance, policy administration, and claims/payment processing.
[2] Each unique computing platform should have a separate row entry in the table below.
[3] Application software source could be in-house development, external custom development, package, or customized package.
[4] Please indicate if this application is outsourced, supported in a remote data center, or completed by a separate IS organization.

Operating System	Platform	OS Security Software[5]	Hardware Location

[5] e.g., RACF, ACF2, Top Secret, OS400, Windows 2000, Novell, Linux, Unix, etc.

EXHIBIT D
CPA REVIEW CHECKLIST

COMPANY NAME ______________________________

PERIOD OF EXAMINATION ______________________________

EXAMINATION FIELD DATE ______________________________

PREPARED BY ______________________________

DATE ______________________________

A. REVIEW GUIDELINES AND INSTRUCTIONS

This form's purpose is to provide guidance for the review of CPA audit workpapers in conjunction with the Department's examination of an insurer and guidelines for the documentation of that review. Outside auditor work can provide insight into off examination period company activity and provide additional assurance as to the propriety of amounts per the statutory return under examination, as well as assurances to the ultimate solvency of the company.

CAUTION should be taken when relying on third party auditors to limit the Department's examination scope. The quality and effectiveness of audits varies significantly between auditing firms and between engagements within the same firm. Quality may vary due to the experience of the performing engagement team, to time or fee restrictions and so on.

This form provides the examiner with a checklist to facilitate both the planning and performing of the CPA workpaper review. Other areas that should be reviewed very closely include loss reserves, underwriting results and the profit and loss accounts. These areas are generally considered to be higher risk in most examination situations and, accordingly, will be tested thoroughly during the Department's examination. As such, a detailed discussion of what should be done when reviewing these areas has not been included since reliance on the CPA's work to reduce work performed by the examination team will generally be minimal.

Timing – Review of CPA workpapers and the completion of this form should be done subsequent to the initial planning visit to the company but before determination of scope of the examination and drafting of specific work programs.

B. SUMMARY OF WORK PERFORMED AND AUDIT INFORMATION

Note: The following section is to be completed 1) to aid in the assessment and documentation of both the scope of the audit performed and 2) to determine what workpapers have been provided (and not provided) for our review. To fully assess the quality and completeness of work performed, it is essential to determine what information and workpapers have not been provided for the review. This can be done through discussion with the manager or partner in charge of the engagement.

Indicate the names and titles of those to whom the inquiries below were directed and the dates the inquiries were made:

NAME	TITLE	DATE
__________	__________	__________
__________	__________	__________
__________	__________	__________

1. What is the name of the accounting or auditing firm that performed the audit under review?

   ____

2. How many years has this firm been performing this engagement?

   ____

3. Was the company audited individually or was the audit performed in conjunction with a consolidated entity? If audited in conjunction with a consolidated entity, were there any scope limitations on work performed?

   ____

   ____

   ____

4. What is the reporting date of the audit?

   ____

5. What workpapers have been removed and are not accessible for Department review?

   ____

   ____

6. Obtain a copy of company's management letter from outside auditors and discuss significant or unusual comments. Document any items below.

____

7. Was the audit a GAAP or STAT audit? If GAAP, was a STAT/GAAP reconciliation of earnings and retained earnings performed? Obtain a copy of the reconciliation and obtain an understanding of the reconciling items and the impact on the Department's scope for the examination.

____

8. Was a clean opinion provided? If not, explain.

____

9. Obtain a copy of the proposed adjusting and reclassifying journal entries. Obtain an understanding of each entry and discuss the implications with auditors. Determine the impact on the examination and review planning as necessary.

____

10. Obtain copies of the responses to audit inquiry letters from law firms or outside counsel. Review each response to determine the scope of further communication with legal counsel regarding litigation, claims, assessments and unasserted claims.

11. Discuss with auditors any significant audit issues or concerns that they may have. Determine the impact on the Department's examination, if any, and document below.

____

____

12. Please provide on this and subsequent pages a description of the following for each significant account or cycle for which the independent auditor's work was reviewed and/or relied upon:

- A description of the independent auditor's approach to testing the account or cycle;
- A description of how the independent auditor's work was tested for accuracy and propriety;
- A description of the extent to which the independent auditor's work was relied upon;
- A description of how the examination approach was modified as a result of the reliance placed on the independent auditor's work.

13. COMMENTS

____

____

EXHIBIT E
ANALYTICAL REVIEW PROCEDURES IN THE EXAMINATION APPROACH

I. Overall Analytical Review

A. Timing

During the development of our overall strategy in the initial planning phase.

B. Objectives and Documentation

Develop expectations about financial statement amounts and other financial relationships in light of the review of current developments and knowledge of the company's business. Helps in developing the overall strategy by identifying potential problem areas (e.g., unexpected fluctuations or the absence of expected fluctuations). Pertinent matters (including expectations) documented in planning workpapers, "Examination Planning Memorandum" (EPM), and Inherent Risk Section of SRA.

C. Procedures

Review of annual statements for trends or changes in general financial condition and profitability. Comparison of certain operating and financial ratios to prior years, to budgets, and, if available, to major competitors and the industry as a whole. Annual statement analysis supplement with inquiries of financial and operating management to develop expected financial relationships.

II. Detail Analytical Review

A. Timing

Concurrent with the system evaluation during the program development phase. For many examinations, may be done concurrently with the overall analytical review.

B. Objectives and Documentation

Determine whether annual statement amounts and relationships make sense in view of expectations. Allows measurement of effects of changes in conditions or circumstances. Helps identify key items and areas requiring additional emphasis or areas where procedures may be limited because of the reasonableness of the amounts. Documented in detail analytical review workpapers and Inherent Risk section of SRAs.

C. Procedures

Comparisons of details of individual accounts or annual statement classifications and analysis of operating and financial ratios related to specific accounts. Analysis based on expectations and further inquiry of operating and financial management.

III. Direct Tests

A. Timing

During balance verification work as part of the program execution phase.

B. Objectives and Documentation

Used as the primary direct test or in combination with other procedures to support the reasonableness of an account balance or class of transactions. Provides an efficient alternative to detail testing and allows consideration of whether the numbers make sense in light of expectations. Leads to amendment of Examination Planning Memorandum if expectations are not met. Documented in various workpapers related to the account or class of transaction being tested.

C. Procedures

Various procedures based on the nature of the account or class of transactions being tested. Procedures designed to support the reasonableness of a balance by reference to related financial or operating information. Analysis based on support of underlying data, expectations developed from the Specific Risk Analysis, and investigation of responses to inquiries of management.

IV. Final Overall Annual Statement Review

A. Timing

At or near conclusion of our fieldwork.

B. Objectives and Documentation

Determine whether the final financial statement amounts make sense in view of results and understanding of the business.

C. Procedures

Review of annual statement and selected ratios.

EXHIBIT F
EXAMPLES OF KEY DATA AND RELATIONSHIPS RELATED TO SPECIFIC AUDIT OBJECTIVES

The following list describes key data and relationships that could be used in performing detail analytical review procedures for certain audit objectives. These ratios also may be used as direct tests of account balances. Fluctuations in these relationships may indicate changes in operating policies, accounting methods, business mix, or other conditions or circumstances (e.g., a change in benefit ratios may indicate a shift in line of business or product mix, or changes in costs or premium rates).

To make the most effective use of analytical review procedures, it is important that the key data and relationships be calculated for specific lines of business or insurance products.

The list is not exhaustive, nor does it represent required procedures for all insurance examinations. To avoid repetition, year-to-year (or other period) comparisons and comparisons to budget are not included in this list.

Audit Objectives		Key Data/Relationships
Stocks and bonds are authorized and are recorded correctly as to account, amount, and period.		Amounts of security type and changes from period to period. Scheduled maturities. Level of purchase and sales activity.
Accrued and unearned income on stocks and bonds is recorded correctly as to account, amount and period.		Accrued investment income as stocks and bonds as a percentage of stocks and bonds. Accrued investment expense to accrued investment income. Accrued investment income as a percentage of investment income.
Stocks and bonds are properly valued and loss in value is promptly identified and provided for.		Relationship of cost and market values by category. Scheduled bond maturities.
Mortgage loans are authorized and are recorded correctly as to account, amount and period.		Composition of portfolio regarding loan size (e.g., 50% > $1 million). Scheduled maturities.
Accrued and unearned income on mortgage loans is recorded correctly as to account, amount and period.		Accrued income as a percent of total portfolio. Accrued income on mortgage loans as a percent of total investment income.
Mortgage loans are properly valued and admitted and loss in value is promptly identified and provided for.		Ratio of nonadmitted loans to total loan portfolio.
Real estate holdings are authorized and are properly recorded as to account, amount and period.		Real estate to total investments.

Audit Objectives		Key Data/Relationships
Accrued and unearned income on real estate holding is recorded correctly as to account, amount and period.		Accrued expense to accrued income. Accrued income to total real estate portfolio. Accrued income from real estate as a percentage of total investment income.
Real estate holdings are protected by insurance and any loss in value is promptly identified and provided for.		Loss to total portfolio - Insurance proceeds from losses to book value - Insurance policy face value to book value.
Policy loans are authorized and are recorded correctly as to account, amount and period.		Policy loan balances to total investments - Policy loan balance to total cash value of policies in-force.
Accrued and unearned policy loan income is recorded correctly as to account, amount and period.		Accrued interest on policy loans to total policy loans. Accrued interest on policy loans to total investment income.
Policy loans are properly valued and nonadmitted assets are promptly identified and provided for.		Overloans to total policy loans.
Short-term investments are authorized, properly valued and recorded correctly as to account, amount and period.		Scheduled maturity dates. Short-term investments to total investments. Composition of short-term investment (e.g., CDs are 50%).
Accrued and unearned income on short-term investments is properly recorded as to account, amount and period.		Accrued interest on short-term investments to total short-term investments. Accrued interest on short-term investments to total investment income.
Other assets are properly valued and recorded correctly as to account, amount and period.		Amortization/depreciation to asset cost.
Reinsurance assumed and ceded transactions are authorized and recorded correctly as to account, amount and period.		Reinsurance premiums assumed to premium income. Reinsurance premiums ceded to premium income. Comparison of assumed and ceded in-force in total and by line to total in-force and to prior periods.
Provisions for income taxes and related assets and liabilities are recorded correctly as to account, amount and period.		Income tax provision to pre-tax income.

Audit Objectives		Key Data/Relationships
Due, deferred and advance premiums are calculated correctly and recorded properly as to account, amount and period.		Due and deferred premiums to total premiums. Advance premiums to total premiums.
Life policy benefit reserves are complete and are recorded correctly as to account, amount and period.		Increase in reserves to premium income. Reserves per $1,000 of in-force by line of business.
Policies with deficiency reserve situations are identified and properly provided for.		Net premiums to gross premiums. Loss ratios and results of operations for A&H and credit business.
Accident and health reserves are properly calculated and recorded correctly as to account, amount and period.		Unearned premiums to written premiums.
Other reserves and policy liabilities are complete and are recorded properly as to account, amount and period.		Reserves per $1,000 of in-force. Credit unearned premiums per $1,000 of life and indemnity in-force. Increase in reserves to premium income.
Claim liabilities are complete and reasonable and are recorded correctly as to account, amount and period.		Numbers and total amounts of due and unpaid and in course of settlement claims. Due and unpaid and in course of settlement amount to total claim reserves. Average claim reserves to average benefit payment amount.
Other liabilities are complete and reasonable and are recorded properly as to account, amount and period.		Accrued salary-to-salary expense. Accrued commission-to-commission expense. Accrued salary per employee. Total other accruals to total other expenses.
Remittances and unallocated items are reasonable and current.		Total suspense account to premium income.
Borrowed money is authorized and recorded properly as to account, amount and period.		Interest expense to average borrowing rate by outstanding debt.

EXHIBIT G
REVIEW OF EVENTS SUBSEQUENT TO THE BALANCE SHEET DATE

Company_________________Examination Date________________Approved by______________________

Generally, the period of review of post-balance sheet events extends from the date of the balance sheet to the date of the examination report, which in most cases is the date of substantial completion of the fieldwork. It is usually not possible, however, to extend all procedures to the same date. If delivery of the examination report is unduly delayed, consideration should be given to extending the review to a later date.

The workpaper should contain specific information as to the scope of the investigation of subsequent events and the consideration given to each of them. Procedures related to subsequent events that extend into the subsequent period include, but are not necessarily limited to, the items described below.

	Done By	Date
1. Scan cash receipt records for evidence of proceeds of loans, significant sales of productive assets or other unusual items. Amounts over $__________ Date through ___________		
2. Scan cash disbursement records for unusual payments and payment of liabilities not recorded as of balance-sheet date. Amounts over $__________ Date through ___________		
3. Review general journal entries for entries that would have a material effect upon the financial statements as of balance sheet date. Amounts over $__________ Date through ___________		
4. Read minutes of meetings to directors, stockholders and important committees up to the report date. If minutes have not been prepared, obtain a written representation from the secretary about matters dealt with at such meetings. Review draft (if any) of proxy statement to be issued to shareholders for matters that may affect the financial statements.		
5. Read latest available interim financial statements. Compare them with the financial statements being reported on and obtain explanations for any unusual items noted as a result of the comparison. Amounts over $__________ Date through ___________		

	Done By	Date
6. Inquire of officers and other executives having responsibility for financial and accounting matters as to whether the interim statements have been prepared on the same basis as that used for the statements under examination. (Indicate identity of statements and periods covered.) Amounts over $___________ Date through ____________		
7. Inquire of officers and other executives having responsibility for financial and accounting matters (limited where appropriate to major locations) as to: (Note: Indicate persons with whom discussions were held and date and attach memoranda or comments regarding significant matters discussed. Corporate office inquiries should extend to the report date.) a. Whether any substantial contingent liabilities or commitments existed at the balance-sheet date or at the date of inquiry. b. Whether there was any significant change in the capital stock or debt to the date of inquiry. c. The current status of items in the financial statements being reported on that were accounted for on the basis of tentative, preliminary or inconclusive data. d. Whether any other matters had occurred that would materially affect the financial statements or operations of the company. This includes appropriate inquiries as to subsequent events of material affiliates accounted for by the equity method. Amounts over $___________ Date through ____________		
8. If the above procedures produce responses that significantly affect the financial statements, they should be confirmed in writing. This may be done in the letter of representations. Amounts over $___________ Date through ____________		

EXHIBIT H
REVIEW AND APPROVAL SUMMARY (RAS) FOR EXAMINATIONS

NAME OF COMPANY ______________________________

EXAMINATION DATE ______________________________

EXAMINER-IN-CHARGE ______________________________

SUPERVISING EXAMINER ______________________________

Detailed Review	**Done By**	**Date**
1. I have read the Examination Planning Memorandum, SRA workpapers, and examination program insofar as they relate to the areas of the examination I reviewed.		
2. I have reviewed all workpapers and am satisfied that the planned procedures were performed, results of work were adequately documented, and procedures performed were sufficient considering the results obtained and any changes in conditions occurring since the procedures were planned.		
3. I have compared the accounts in the general ledger trial balance or examination workpapers with the summarizations, classifications, and descriptions of them in the annual statement.		
4. I am satisfied that the examination was conducted in accordance with appropriate professional standards, Department policies, and the procedures set forth in the NAIC *Financial Condition Examiners Handbook.*		
5. I have prepared the Summary Review Memorandum and it covers all important accounting and examination issues.		
General Review		
1. I have reviewed the Examination Planning Memorandum, SRA workpapers, and examination program.		
2. I have reviewed the workpapers for this examination and am satisfied that the planned procedures were performed, results of work were adequately documented, and procedures performed were sufficient.		
3. I have reviewed the Summary Review Memorandum and concur with the conclusions therein.		
4. I am satisfied that the examination was conducted in accordance with appropriate professional standards, Department policies, and the procedures set forth in the NAIC *Financial Condition Examiners Handbook.*		

	Done By	Date
5. I have reviewed the Report of Examination and am satisfied that it was prepared in conformity with statutory accounting principals as prescribed in the NAIC *Accounting Practices and Procedures Manual* or as permitted by the Department.		

Note: Completion of procedures should be indicated by dating and initialing the space provided. Any exceptions (e.g., Not Applicable) should be explained either in this RAS or in an attached memorandum.

EXHIBIT I
SUGGESTED MINIMUM AMOUNTS OF FIDELITY INSURANCE

Fidelity Bonds provide coverage to the insured business or individual for money or other property lost because of dishonest acts of its bonded employees. While the need for fidelity bond coverage can vary from company to company, it is recommended that those who have access to cash and investments be bonded. This includes the people who have the ability to authorize wire transfers, write checks and those who can buy, sell, or transfer investments. The terms of each policy may vary, however, it is recommended that the policy be written to cover material acts of theft or dishonesty by bonded employees.

The following table indicates the exposure index amount with the recommended fidelity bond amount:

Exposure Index		Bracket No. *	Amount of Bond		
$1,000 -	$25,000	1	$15,000	-	$25,000
25,000 -	125,000	2	25,000	-	50,000
125,000 -	250,000	3	50,000	-	75,000
250,000 -	500,000	4	75,000	-	100,000
500,000 -	750,000	5	100,000	-	125,000
750,000 -	1,000,000	6	125,000	-	150,000
1,000,000 -	1,375,000	7	150,000	-	175,000
1,375,000 -	1,750,000	8	175,000	-	200,000
1,750,000 -	2,125,000	9	200,000	-	225,000
2,125,000 -	2,500,000	10	225,000	-	250,000
2,500,000 -	3,325,000	11	250,000	-	300,000
3,325,000 -	4,175,000	12	300,000	-	350,000
4,175,000 -	5,000,000	13	350,000	-	400,000
5,000,000 -	6,075,000	14	400,000	-	450,000
6,075,000 -	7,150,000	15	450,000	-	500,000
7,150,000 -	9,275,000	16	500,000	-	600,000
9,275,000 -	11,425,000	17	600,000	-	700,000
11,425,000 -	15,000,000	18	700,000	-	800,000
15,000,000 -	20,000,000	19	800,000	-	900,000
20,000,000 -	25,000,000	20	900,000	-	1,000,000
25,000,000 -	50,000,000	21	1,000,000	-	1,250,000
50,000,000 -	87,500,000	22	1,250,000	-	1,500,000
87,500,000 -	125,000,000	23	1,500,000	-	1,750,000
125,000,000 -	187,500,000	24	1,750,000	-	2,000,000
187,500,000 -	250,000,000	25	2,000,000	-	2,250,000
250,000,000 -	333,325,000	26	2,250,000	-	2,500,000
333,325,000 -	500,000,000	27	2,500,000	-	3,000,000
500,000,000 -	750,000,000	28	3,300,000	-	3,500,000
750,000,000 -	1,000,000,000	29	3,500,000	-	4,000,000
1,000,000,000 -	1,250,000,000	30	4,000,000	-	4,500,000
1,250,000,000 -	1,500,000,000	31	4,500,000	-	5,000,000

Calculation of Bond Amount

1. Total Admitted Assets

   $_______X5%=$________

2. Gross Income*

   $_______X10%=$_______

   Exposure Index =$_____**

3. Minimum Amount of Bond

   Bracket No.______$______

*Include gross premium written and assumed plus interest and dividend income.

**Amount is calculated by adding the results of number 1 and 2 above.

The exposure index is calculated using all insured companies named on the fidelity bond. The fidelity bond policy limits listed above are not a substitute for the risk assessment that should be made by company management in establishing a reasonable level of insurance coverage. Similarly, company management should evaluate its business needs for other insurance coverages such as general liability and property, if applicable.

The insurance examiner, therefore, in evaluating the amount of the fidelity bond coverage amount, should not rely on the schedule above as an absolute guide, but instead, should review the internal controls that serve to mitigate the exposures covered by such insurance policies. In evaluating the fidelity bond the examiner should also consider if the reporting entity has the ability to meet the deductible.

Note: Fidelity bonds are written to cover material acts of theft or dishonesty by bonded employees. Thus, if a crime is committed by an employee who is not bonded, the company may have to bear the costs of that loss. Alternatively, companies may buy a general fidelity insurance policy commonly referred to as crime coverage. Crime coverage is an acceptable alternative to fidelity bonds if it provides coverage that is at least as broad as the coverage provided by a fidelity bond. Keep in mind that both fidelity bonds and crime coverage will vary from policy to policy, so the examiner should use professional judgment when analyzing the individual policy and the risk that the policy hedges.

EXHIBIT J
EXAMINER'S AFFIDAVIT AS TO STANDARDS AND PROCEDURES USED IN AN EXAMINATION

State of ______________________,

County of _____________________,

_______________, being duly sworn, states as follows:

1. I have authority to represent _________________ in the examination of _________________.

2. ______________________ is accredited under the National Association of Insurance Commissioners Financial Regulation Standards and Accreditation.

3. I have reviewed the examination work papers and examination report, and the examination of ______________________ was performed in a manner consistent with the standards and procedures required by ___________________.

   The affiant says nothing further.

____
Examiner's Signature

Subscribed and sworn before me by _____________________ on this __________ day of ________, 20_______.

(SEAL)

____
Notary Public

My commission expires _______________________[date].

EXHIBIT K
SAMPLE LETTER OF REPRESENTATION

An illustrative management representation letter for the property and casualty, mortgage guaranty, title company, health, and life, accident and health entities is presented in Exhibit K. The sample letters incorporate representations that should ordinarily be obtained by the examiner as well as clauses for specific issues. The management representation letter should be modified by the regulator to meet the circumstances of the particular examination and the nature of the company being examined.

Modifications or special representations relating to management's knowledge or intent should be obtained when the examiner believes that they are necessary to complement other examination procedures or when corroborating evidential matter is limited. It would be unusual to obtain a representation letter that did not include some special representations to cover individual company circumstances.

Certain representations may be limited to matters that may have a material effect on the statutory financial statements, as indicated in the illustrative letter. It is preferable for management to specify the agreed-on materiality limits in the representation letter. Illustrative language for this materiality purpose is included in the sample letter. When evaluating the materiality threshold to be included in the letter, the examiner should consider the nature of the company under examination and the extent of detail desired in management's representations. In no event shall the materiality threshold included in the letter exceed planning materiality levels as this level relates to the examiner's overall perspective of the financial statements rather than a particular account balance or cycle. The illustrative letter also contains qualitative criterion of materiality, which is required in all representation letters.

(On Company Letterhead)

Date (date should agree with report of examination)

Name of Examiner
Examiner-In-Charge
(Name of State) Department of Insurance
Address
City, State Zip Code

We are providing this letter in connection with your examination of the statutory financial statements of *(Name of Insurance Company)* as of (*Month, Date, Year*) and for the period from (*Month, Date, Year*) to (*Month, Date, Year*). We are responsible for the preparation of the statutory financial statements of financial position, results of operations, and changes in statutory financial position in conformity with the accounting practices prescribed or permitted by the (Name of State) Department of Insurance.

Certain representations in this letter are described as being limited to those matters that are material. Solely for the purpose of preparing this letter, the term "material," when used in this letter, means any item or group of similar items involving potential amounts of more than $_________. These amounts are not intended to represent the materiality threshold for financial reporting and disclosure purposes. Notwithstanding this, an item is considered material, regardless of size, if it involves an omission or misstatement of accounting information that, in the light of surrounding circumstances, makes it probable that the judgment of a reasonable person relying on the information would have been changed or influenced by the omission or misstatement.

We confirm, to the best of our knowledge and belief, the following representations made to you during the examination.

1. We have made available to you all:

   - Statutory financial records and related data; and
   - Minutes of meetings of stockholders/policyholders (if a mutual company), directors and committees, or summaries of actions of recent meetings for which minutes have not yet been prepared.

2. There have been no:

   - Fraud or other irregularities involving management or employees who have significant roles in the internal control structure;
   - Fraud or other irregularities involving other employees that have or may have a material effect on the statutory financial statements;
   - Fraud or other irregularities involving agents, MGAs, third party administrators, independent contractors, holding companies or other individuals or parties that have or may have a material impact on the statutory financial position of the Company; or
   - Communications from regulatory agencies concerning noncompliance with, or deficiencies in, statutory financial reporting practices.

3. We have no plans or intentions that may materially affect the carrying value or classification of assets and liabilities.

4. The financial statements are free of material and intentional immaterial misstatements.

5. The following have been properly recorded or disclosed in the statutory financial statements:

- Any related party transactions and related amounts receivable or payable, including sales, purchases, loans, transfers, leasing arrangements, and guarantees.
- All liabilities, both actual and contingent.
- Guarantees whether written or oral, under which the Company is contingently liable.
- Capital stock (N/A for mutual companies) repurchase options or agreements on capital stock reserved for options, warrants, conversions, or other requirements.
- Arrangements with financial institutions involving compensating balances or other arrangements involving restrictions on cash balances and line-of-credit or similar arrangements.
- Significant estimates and material concentrations known to management that are required to be disclosed in accordance with SSAP No. 1, *Disclosure of Accounting Policies, Risks & Uncertainties, and Other Disclosures*.
- Amount of credit risk and extent, nature, and terms of financial instruments with off-balance-sheet risk in accordance with SSAP No. 27.
- Agreements to repurchase assets previously sold.

6. We confirm the completeness of the information provided regarding the identification of related parties.

7. There are no violation or possible violations of laws or regulations whose effects should be considered for disclosure in the statutory financial statements or as a basis for recording a loss contingency.

8. Contingent Liabilities:

- There are no other liabilities or gain or loss contingencies that are required to be accrued or disclosed by SSAP No. 5.
- There is no litigation against the Company that is considered material in relation to the statutory financial position of the Company. For purposes of this section, the Company has excluded litigation for which the only amounts sought relate to benefits within the normal terms of coverage under contracts of insurance issued by the Company, and which are otherwise considered in the actuarial determination of the Company's unpaid claim reserves.
- *In the occurrence of a contingent liability noted by management the following should be included in the management representation letter*: Except for the contingent liability disclosed in Note X of the financial statements, there are no contingent liabilities which require disclosure in the financial statements or notes thereto.
- *(If applicable)* The …litigation by XYZ Company has been settled for the total sum of XXX that has been properly reflected in the financial statements. No other claims in connection with this litigation have been or are expected to be received.

9. Adequate provision has been made for adjustments and losses in collection of receivables.

10. Provision has been made for estimated retroactive adjustments by third-party payors under reimbursement agreements.

11. The Company is in compliance with bond indentures or other debt instruments.

12. Pending changes in the organizational structure, financing arrangements, or other matters that could have a material effect on the financial statements of the Company are properly disclosed.

13. The Company has properly classified all assets as admitted or nonadmitted in accordance with SSAP No. 4.

14. The Company has free and clear title to all owned assets, and there are no liens or encumbrances on such assets nor has any asset been pledged except as disclosed in the annual statement.

15. We have reviewed long-lived assets and certain identifiable intangibles whenever changes in circumstances have indicated that the carrying amount of these assets might not be recoverable and have recorded the adjustment in accordance with SSAP No. 5.

16. Deferred tax assets and liabilities as reported in the financial statements comply and have been valued in accordance with SSAP No. 10, *Income Taxes.*

17. The Company has properly disclosed and recorded any premium deficiency reserves in accordance with SSAP No. 53.

18. Investments are appropriately recorded and valued as follows:

    - Bonds – are recorded and disclosed in accordance with SSAP No. 26 and interpretations thereof.
    - Preferred stocks – are recorded and disclosed in accordance with SSAP No. 32 and interpretations thereof.
    - Common stocks - are recorded and disclosed in accordance with SSAP No. 30 and interpretations thereof. Common stock of subsidiaries and affiliated or controlled companies are recorded and disclosed in accordance with SSAP No. 46 and interpretations thereof.
    - Short-term investments – are recorded and disclosed in accordance with SSAP No. 2 and interpretations thereof.
    - Mortgage loans and collateral loans – are recorded and disclosed in accordance with SSAP's No. 37 & 21 and interpretations thereof.
    - Real estate – are recorded and disclosed in accordance with SSAP No. 40 and interpretations thereof.

19. The Company's liabilities for unpaid losses and loss adjustment expenses are based on and recorded at management's best estimate in accordance with SSAP No. 55.

20. Agents' balances or uncollected premiums have been recorded and disclosed in accordance with SSAP No. 6.

21. There were no material commitments for construction or acquisition of property, plant and equipment, or to acquire other noncurrent assets, such as investments or intangibles.

22. *In the event of a material commitment replace clause #21 with the following*: Other than the commitment described in Note *X* of the financial statements, there are no material commitments for construction, or acquisition of property, plant and equipment, or to acquire other noncurrent assets, such as investments or intangibles which require disclosure in the financial statements.

23. We have complied with all aspects of contractual agreements that would have a material effect on the statutory financial statement in the event of noncompliance.

24. There are no material transactions that have not been properly recorded in the accounting records underlying the statutory financial statements.

25. All required returns and statutory reporting requirements have been filed on a timely basis with the appropriate regulatory bodies.

26. All material reinsurance transactions have been recorded and disclosed in accordance with SSAP No. 62.

27. The Company has properly disclosed and recorded all changes in accounting principles in accordance with SSAP No. 3.

28. The Company has recorded and disclosed subsequent events in accordance with SSAP No. 9.

29. *In the event of a subsequent event, the following should replace clause #28 in the Management Representations Letter:* Other than…. described in Note X to the financial statements, there have been no events subsequent to period end which require adjustment of or disclosure in the financial statements or notes thereto.

30. The Company is not aware of the employment of or a business relationship with a "prohibited person" as defined in The Violent Crime Control and Law Enforcement Act of 1994: United States Code, Section 1033 (e)(1)(A).

31. Note *X* to the financial statements discloses all of the matters of which we are aware that are relevant to the Company's ability to continue as a going concern, including significant conditions and events, and management's plans.

32. We agree with the findings of specialists in evaluating the (describe the assertion) and have adequately considered the qualifications of the specialists in determining the amounts and disclosures used in the financial statements and underlying accounting records. We did not give or cause any instructions to be given to specialists with respect to the values or amounts derived in an attempt to bias their work.

33. The valuation of securities X is unavailable from the NAIC Securities Valuation Office; therefore, the Company has determined a value for this financial instrument. The methods and significant assumptions used to determine this value are in accordance with SSAP No. 27.

34. The Company has recorded and disclosed defined benefit plans and defined contribution plans in accordance with SSAP No. 89.

35. The Company has recorded and disclosed postretirement benefits other than pensions in accordance with SSAP No. 14.

We understand that your examination was made in accordance with standards established by the (Name of State) Department of Insurance, and procedures established by *the National Association of Insurance Commissioners*, and accordingly included such tests of the accounting records and such other procedures as considered necessary under the circumstances.

Name of Insurance Company

_________________________ _______________

Chief Executive Officer Date

_________________________ _______________

Chief Financial Officer Date

(On Company Letterhead)

Date (date should agree with report of examination)

Name of Examiner
Examiner-In-Charge
(Name of State) Department of Insurance
Address
City, State Zip Code

We are providing this letter in connection with your examination of the statutory financial statements of *(Name of Insurance Company)* as of (*Month, Date, Year*), and for the period from (*Month, Date, Year*) to (*Month, Date, Year*). We are responsible for the preparation of the statutory financial statements of financial position, results of operations, and changes in statutory financial position in conformity with the accounting practices prescribed or permitted by the (Name of State) Department of Insurance.

Certain representations in this letter are described as being limited to those matters that are material. Solely for the purpose of preparing this letter, the term "material," when used in this letter, means any item or group of similar items involving potential amounts of more than $___________. These amounts are not intended to represent the materiality threshold for financial reporting and disclosure purposes. Notwithstanding this, an item is considered material, regardless of size, if it involves an omission or misstatement of accounting information that, in the light of surrounding circumstances, makes it probable that the judgment of a reasonable person relying on the information would have been changed or influenced by the omission or misstatement.

We confirm, to the best of our knowledge and belief, the following representations made to you during the examination.

1. We have made available to you all:

    - Statutory financial records and related data; and
    - Minutes of meetings of stockholders/policyholders (if a mutual company), directors and committees, or summaries of actions of recent meetings for which minutes have not yet been prepared.

2. There have been no:

    - Fraud or other irregularities involving management or employees who have significant roles in the internal control structure;
    - Fraud or other irregularities involving other employees that have or may have a material effect on the statutory financial statements;
    - Fraud or other irregularities involving agents, MGAs, third party administrators, independent contractors, holding companies or other individuals or parties that have or may have a material effect on the statutory financial position of the Company; or
    - Communications from regulatory agencies concerning noncompliance with, or deficiencies in, statutory financial reporting practices.

3. We have no plans or intentions that may materially affect the carrying value or classification of assets and liabilities.

4. The financial statements are free of material and intentional immaterial misstatements.

5. The following have been properly recorded or disclosed in the statutory financial statements:

   - Any related party transactions and related amounts receivable or payable, including sales, purchases, loans, transfers, leasing arrangements, and guarantees.

   - All liabilities, both actual and contingent.

   - Guarantees whether written or oral, under which the Company is contingently liable.

   - Capital stock (N/A for mutual companies) repurchase options or agreements on capital stock reserved for options, warrants, conversions, or other requirements.

   - Arrangements with financial institutions involving compensating balances or other arrangements involving restrictions on cash balances and line-of-credit or similar arrangements.

   - Significant estimates and material concentrations known to management that are required to be disclosed in accordance with SSAP No. 1, *Disclosure of Accounting Policies, Risks & Uncertainties, and Other Disclosures.*

   - Amount of credit risk and extent, nature, and terms of financial instruments with off-balance-sheet risk to be disclosed in accordance with SSAP No. 27.

   - Agreements to repurchase assets previously sold.

6. We confirm the completeness of the information provided regarding the identification of related parties.

7. There are no violation or possible violations of laws or regulations whose effects should be considered for disclosure in the statutory financial statements or as a basis for recording a loss contingency.

8. Contingent Liabilities:

   - There are no other liabilities or gain or loss contingencies that are required to be accrued or disclosed by SSAP No. 5.

   - There is no litigation against the Company that is considered material in relation to the statutory financial position of the Company. For purposes of this section, the Company has excluded litigation for which the only amounts sought relate to benefits within the normal terms of coverage under contracts of insurance issued by the Company, and which are otherwise considered in the actuarial determination of the Company's unpaid claim reserves.

   - *In the occurrence of a contingent liability noted by management the following should be included in the management representation letter*: Except for the contingent liability disclosed in Note X of the financial statements, there are no contingent liabilities which require disclosure in the financial statements or notes thereto.

   - (*If applicable*) The … litigation by XYZ Company has been settled for the total sum of XXX that has been properly reflected in the financial statements. No other claims in connection with litigation have been or are expected to be received.

9. Adequate provision has been made for adjustments and losses in collection of receivables.

10. Provision has been made for estimated retroactive adjustments by third-party payors under reimbursement agreements.

11. The Company is in compliance with bond indentures or other debt instruments.

12. Pending changes in the organizational structure, financing arrangements, or other matters that could have a material effect on the financial statements of the Company are properly disclosed.

13. The Company has properly classified all assets as admitted or nonadmitted in accordance with SSAP No. 4.

14. The Company has free and clear title to all owned assets, and there are no liens or encumbrances on such assets nor has any asset been pledged except as disclosed in the annual statement.

15. We have reviewed long-lived assets and certain identifiable intangibles whenever changes in circumstances have indicated that the carrying amount of these assets might not be recoverable and have recorded the adjustment in accordance with SSAP No. 5.

16. Deferred tax assets and liabilities as reported in the financial statements comply and have been valued in accordance with SSAP No. 10, *Income Taxes.*

17. Investments are appropriately recorded and valued as follows:

   - Bonds – are recorded and disclosed in accordance with SSAP No. 26 and interpretations thereof.
   - Preferred stocks – are recorded and disclosed in accordance with SSAP No. 32 and interpretations thereof.
   - Common stocks – are recorded and disclosed in accordance with SSAP No. 30 and interpretations thereof. Common stock of subsidiaries and affiliated or controlled companies are recorded and disclosed in accordance with SSAP No. 46 and interpretations thereof.
   - Short-term investments – are recorded and disclosed in accordance with SSAP No. 2 and interpretations thereof.
   - Mortgage loans and collateral loans – are recorded and disclosed in accordance with SSAP's No. 37 & 21 and interpretations thereof.
   - Real estate – are recorded and disclosed in accordance with SSAP No. 40 and interpretations thereof.
   - Policy loans – are recorded and disclosed in accordance with SSAP No. 49 and interpretations thereof.

18. Cost Reports filed with third parties:

   - All required Medicare, Medicaid, and similar reports have been properly filed.
   - Management is responsible for accuracy and propriety of all cost records filed.
   - All costs reflected on such reports are appropriate and allowable under applicable reimbursement rules and regulations and are patient-related and properly allocated to applicable payors.

- The reimbursement methodologies and principles employed are in accordance with applicable rules and regulations.

- Adequate consideration has been given to, and appropriate provision made for, audit adjustments by intermediaries, third-party payors, or other regulatory agencies.

- All items required to be disclosed, including disputed costs that are being claimed to establish a basis for subsequent appeal, have been fully disclosed in the cost report.

- Recorded third-party settlements include differences between filed (and to be filed) cost reports and calculated settlements, which are necessary based on historical experience or new or ambiguous regulations that may be subject to differing interpretations.

19. The Company has properly disclosed and recorded policy reserves in accordance with SSAP's No. 51, 52, 54 and 59. The Company's liabilities for unpaid claims and claim adjustment expenses are based upon and recorded at management's best extimate in accordance with SSAP No. 55.

20. The Company has properly disclosed and recorded separate account transactions in accordance with SSAP No. 56.

21. The Company's actuary has certified as to the propriety of the basis and amounts at which the deferred and uncollected premiums, the reserve for life policies and contracts (including deposit-like contracts; SSAP No. 52), and the reserve for accident and health policies are stated.

22. The Company has computed the asset valuation reserve and interest maintenance reserve in accordance with methods prescribed by the Annual Statement Instructions of the National Association of Insurance Commissioners.

23. There were no material commitments for construction or acquisition of property, plant and equipment, or to acquire other noncurrent assets, such as investments or intangibles.

24. *In the event of a material commitment replace clause #23 with the following*: Other than the commitment described in Note *X* of the financial statements, there are no material commitments for construction, or acquisition of property, plant and equipment, or to acquire other noncurrent assets, such as investments or intangibles which require disclosure in the financial statements.

25. We have complied with all aspects of contractual agreements that would have a material effect on the statutory financial statement in the event of noncompliance.

26. There are no material transactions that have not been properly recorded in the accounting records underlying the statutory financial statements.

27. All required returns and statutory reporting requirements have been filed on a timely basis with the appropriate regulatory bodies.

28. All material reinsurance transactions have been recorded and disclosed in accordance with SSAP No. 61.

29. The Company has properly disclosed and recorded all changes in accounting principles in accordance with SSAP No. 3.

30. The Company has recorded and disclosed subsequent events in accordance with SSAP No. 9.

31. *In the event of a subsequent event, the following should replace clause #30 in the Management Representations Letter:* Other than…. described in Note X to the financial statements, there have been no events subsequent to period end which require adjustment of or disclosure in the financial statements or notes thereto.

32. The Company is not aware of the employment of or a business relationship with a "prohibited person" as defined in The Violent Crime Control and Law Enforcement Act of 1994: United States Code, Section 1033 (e)(1)(A).

33. Note *X* to the financial statements discloses all of the matters of which we are aware that are relevant to the Company's ability to continue as a going concern, including significant conditions and events, and management's plans.

34. We agree with the findings of specialists in evaluating the (describe the assertion) and have adequately considered the qualifications of the specialists in determining the amounts and disclosures used in the financial statements and underlying accounting records. We did not give or cause any instructions to be given to specialists with respect to the values or amounts derived in an attempt to bias their work.

35. The valuation of securities X is unavailable from the NAIC Securities Valuation Office; therefore, the Company has determined a value for this financial instrument. The methods and significant assumptions used to determine this value are in accordance with SSAP No. 27.

36. The Company has recorded and disclosed defined benefit plans and defined contribution plans in accordance with SSAP No. 89.

37. The Company has recorded and disclosed postretirement benefits other than pensions in accordance with SSAP No. 14.

We understand that your examination was made in accordance with standards established by the (Name of State) Department of Insurance, and procedures established by *the National Association of Insurance Commissioners*, and accordingly included such tests of the accounting records and such other procedures as considered necessary under the circumstances.

Name of Insurance Company

______________________________ __________________

Chief Executive Officer Date

______________________________ __________________

Chief Financial Officer Date

(On Company Letterhead)

Date (date should agree with report of examination)

Name of Examiner
Examiner-In-Charge
(Name of State) Department of Insurance
Address
City, State Zip Code

We are providing this letter in connection with your examination of the statutory financial statements of *(Name of Insurance Company*) as of (*Month, Date, Year*), and for the period from (*Month, Date, Year*) to (*Month, Date, Year*). We are responsible for the preparation in the statutory financial statements of financial position, results of operations, and changes in statutory financial position in conformity with the accounting practices prescribed or permitted by the (Name of State) Department of Insurance.

Certain representations in this letter are described as being limited to those matters that are material. Solely for the purpose of preparing this letter, the term "material," when used in this letter, means any item or group of similar items involving potential amounts of more than $___________. These amounts are not intended to represent the materiality threshold for financial reporting and disclosure purposes. Notwithstanding this, an item is considered material, regardless of size, if it involves an omission or misstatement of accounting information that, in the light of surrounding circumstances, makes it probable that the judgment of a reasonable person relying on the information would have been changed or influenced by the omission or misstatement.

We confirm, to the best of our knowledge and belief, the following representations made to you during the examination.

1. We have made available to you all:

    - Statutory financial records and related data; and
    - Minutes of meetings of stockholders/policyholders (if a mutual company), directors and committees, or summaries of actions of recent meetings for which minutes have not yet been prepared.

2. There have been no:

    - Fraud or other irregularities involving management or employees who have significant roles in the internal control structure;
    - Fraud or other irregularities involving other employees that have or may have a material effect on the statutory financial statements;
    - Fraud or other irregularities involving agents, MGAs, third party administrators, independent contractors, holding companies or other individuals or parties that have or may have a material effect on the statutory financial position of the Company; or
    - Communications from regulatory agencies concerning noncompliance with, or deficiencies in, statutory financial reporting practices. This includes those related to Medicare and Medicaid antifraud and abuse statutes.

3. We have no plans or intentions that may materially affect the carrying value or classification of assets and liabilities.

4. The financial statements are free of material and intentional immaterial misstatements.

5. The following have been properly recorded or disclosed in the statutory financial statements:

- Any related party transactions and related amounts receivable or payable, including sales, purchases, loans, transfers, leasing arrangements, and guarantees.
- All liabilities, both actual and contingent.
- Guarantees whether written or oral, under which the company is contingently liable.
- Capital stock (N/A for mutual companies) repurchase options or agreements on capital stock reserved for options, warrants, conversions, or other requirements.
- Arrangements with financial institutions involving compensating balances or other arrangements involving restrictions on cash balances and line-of-credit or similar arrangements.
- Significant estimates and material concentrations known to management that are required to be disclosed in accordance with SSAP No. 1, *Disclosure of Accounting Policies, Risks & Uncertainties, and Other Disclosures.*
- Amount of credit risk and extent, nature, and terms of financial instruments with off-balance-sheet risk to be disclosed in accordance with SSAP No. 27.
- Agreements to repurchase assets previously sold.

6. We confirm the completeness of the information provided regarding the identification of related parties.

7. There are no violations or possible violations of laws or regulations whose effects should be considered for disclosure in the statutory financial statements or as a basis for recording a loss contingency. This includes those related to Medicare and Medicaid antifraud and abuse statutes, including but not limited to the Medicare and Medicaid anti-Kickback Statutes, Limitations on Certain Physical Referrals (the Stark law), and the False Claims Act, in any jurisdiction, whose effects should be considered for disclosure in the financial statements or as a basis for recording a loss contingency other than those disclosed or accrued in the financial statements.

8. Billings to third party payors comply in all material respects with diagnostic and procedure coding guidelines (for example ICD-9-CM and CPT-4) and laws and regulations (including those dealing with Medicare and Medicaid antifraud and abuse), and billings reflect only charges for goods and services that were medically necessary; properly approved by regulatory bodies (i.e., Food and Drug Administration), if required and properly rendered.

9. Contingent Liabilities:

- There are no other liabilities or gain or loss contingencies that are required to be accrued or disclosed by SSAP No. 5.
- There is no litigation against the Company that is considered material in relation to the statutory financial position of the Company. For purposes of this section, the company has excluded litigation for which the only amounts sought relate to benefits within the normal terms of coverage under

contracts of insurance issued by the company, and which are otherwise considered in the actuarial determination of the company's unpaid claim reserves.

- *In the occurrence of a contingent liability noted by management the following should be included in the management representation letter*: Except for the contingent liability disclosed in Note X of the financial statements, there are no contingent liabilities that require disclosure in the financial statements or notes thereto.

- (*If applicable*) The … litigation by XYZ Company has been settled for the total sum of XXX that has been properly reflected in the financial statements. No other claims in connection with litigation have been or are expected to be received.

10. Adequate provision has been made for adjustments and losses in collection of receivables.

11. Provision has been made for estimated retroactive adjustments by third-party payors under reimbursement agreements.

12. The Company is in compliance with bond indentures or other debt instruments.

13. Pending changes in the organizational structure, financing arrangements, or other matters that could have a material effect on the financial statements of the Company are properly disclosed.

14. The Company has properly classified all assets as admitted or nonadmitted in accordance with SSAP No. 4.

15. The Company has free and clear title to all owned assets, and there are no liens or encumbrances on such assets nor has any asset been pledged except as disclosed in the annual statement.

16. We have reviewed long-lived assets and certain identifiable intangibles whenever changes in circumstances have indicated that the carrying amount of these assets might not be recoverable and have recorded the adjustment in accordance with SSAP No. 5.

17. Deferred tax assets and liabilities as reported in the financial statements comply and have been valued in accordance with SSAP No. 10, *Income Taxes*.

18. Investments are appropriately recorded and valued as follows:

    - Bonds – are recorded and disclosed in accordance with SSAP No. 26 and interpretations thereof.
    - Preferred stocks – are recorded and disclosed in accordance with SSAP No. 32 and interpretations thereof.
    - Common stocks – are recorded and disclosed in accordance with SSAP No. 30 and interpretations thereof. Common stock of subsidiaries and affiliated or controlled companies are recorded and disclosed in accordance with SSAP No. 46 and interpretations thereof.
    - Short-term investments – are recorded and disclosed in accordance with SSAP No. 2 and interpretations thereof.
    - Mortgage loans and collateral loans – are recorded and disclosed in accordance with SSAP's No. 37 & 21 and interpretations thereof.
    - Real estate – are recorded and disclosed in accordance with SSAP No. 40 and interpretations thereof.
    - Health Care Delivery Assets – are recorded and disclosed in accordance with SSAP No. 73

19. Accident and Health Premiums Due and Unpaid – Premiums are recognized and reported in accordance with SSAP No. 54. Uncollected premiums are reported in accordance with SSAP No. 6.

20. Adequate Consideration has been given to, and appropriate provision made for, estimated adjustments to revenue, such as for denied claims and changes to diagnosis- related group (DRG) assignments.

21. All peer review organizations, fiscal intermediary, and third-party payor reports and information have been made available.

22. Cost Reports filed with third parties:

- All required Medicare, Medicaid, and similar reports have been properly filed.
- Management is responsible for accuracy and propriety of all cost records filed.
- All costs reflected on such reports are appropriate and allowable under applicable reimbursement rules and regulations and are patient-related and properly allocated to applicable payors.
- The reimbursement methodologies and principles employed are in accordance with applicable rules and regulations.
- Adequate consideration has been given to, and appropriate provision made for, audit adjustments by intermediaries, third-party payors, or other regulatory agencies.
- All items required to be disclosed, including disputed costs that are being claimed to establish a basis for subsequent appeal, have been fully disclosed in the cost report.
- Recorded third-party settlements include differences between filed (and to be filed) cost reports and calculated settlements, which are necessary based on historical experience or new or ambiguous regulations that may be subject to differing interpretations.

23. The Company's actuary has certified to the propriety of the basis and amounts at which the claim reserves and all actuarial liabilities are stated at *(Month, Date, Year)*.

24. The Company has recorded individual and group accident and health reserves in accordance with SSAP No. 54.

25. The Company's liabilities for unpaid claims and claim adjustment expenses are based on and recorded at management's best estimate in accordance with SSAP No. 55.

26. Utilization Data has been properly determined and included in the statutory financial statement.

27. Covered liabilities are properly stated in the statutory financial statement and are determined as health care services covered through "hold harmless" clauses in the provider contracts which state that providers will not bill enrollees even though the provided has not been paid by the HMO.

28. The Company is in compliance with contractual agreements, grants, and donor restrictions.

29. There were no material commitments for construction or acquisition of property, plant and equipment, or to acquire other noncurrent assets, such as investments or intangibles.

30. In the event of a material commitment replace clause #29 with the following: Other than the commitment described in Note X of the financial statements, there are no material commitments for construction, or acquisition of property, plant and equipment, or to acquire other noncurrent assets, such as investments or intangibles which require disclosure in the financial statements.

31. We have complied with all aspects of contractual agreements that would have a material effect on the statutory financial statement in the event of noncompliance.

32. There are no material transactions that have not been properly recorded in the accounting records underlying the statutory financial statements.

33. All required returns and statutory reporting requirements have been filed on a timely basis with the appropriate regulatory bodies.

34. All material reinsurance transactions have been recorded and disclosed in accordance with SSAP No. 61.

35. The Company has properly disclosed and recorded all changes in accounting principles in accordance with SSAP No. 3.

36. The Company has recorded and disclosed subsequent events in accordance with SSAP No. 9.

37. In the event of a subsequent event, the following should replace clause #36 in the Management Representations Letter: Other than.... described in Note X to the financial statements, there have been no events subsequent to period end which require adjustment of or disclosure in the financial statements or notes thereto.

38. The Company is not aware of the employment of or a business relationship with a "prohibited person" as defined in The Violent Crime Control and Law Enforcement Act of 1994: United States Code, Section 1033 (e)(1)(A).

39. Note *X* to the financial statements discloses all of the matters of which we are aware that are relevant to the company's ability to continue as a going concern, including significant conditions and events, and management's plans.

40. We agree with the findings of specialists in evaluating the (describe the assertion) and have adequately considered the qualifications of the specialists in determining the amounts and disclosures used in the financial statements and underlying accounting records. We did not give or cause any instructions to be given to specialists with respect to the values or amounts derived in an attempt to bias their work.

41. The valuation of securities X is unavailable from the NAIC Securities Valuation Office; therefore, the Company has determined a value for this financial instrument. The methods and significant assumptions used to determine this value are in accordance with SSAP No. 27.

42. The Company has recorded and disclosed defined benefit plans and defined contribution plans in accordance with SSAP No. 89.

43. The Company has recorded and disclosed postretirement benefits other than pensions in accordance with SSAP No. 14.

We understand that your examination was made in accordance with standards established by the (Name of State) Department of Insurance, and procedures established by *the National Association of Insurance Commissioners*, and accordingly included such tests of the accounting records and such other procedures as considered necessary under the circumstances.

Name of Insurance Company

____________________________________ ______________________

Chief Executive Officer Date

____________________________________ ______________________

Chief Financial Officer Date

(On Company Letterhead)

Date (date should agree with report of examination)

Name of Examiner
Examiner-In-Charge
(Name of State) Department of Insurance
Address
City, State Zip Code

We are providing this letter in connection with your examination of the statutory financial statements of *(Name of Mortgage Guaranty*) as of (*Month, Date, Year*), and for the period from (*Month, Date, Year*) to (*Month, Date, Year*). We are responsible for the preparation of the statutory financial statements of financial position, results of operations, and changes in statutory financial position in conformity with the accounting practices prescribed or permitted by the (Name of State) Department of Insurance.

Certain representations in this letter are described as being limited to those matters that are material. Solely for the purpose of preparing this letter, the term "material," when used in this letter, means any item or group of similar items involving potential amounts of more than $___________. These amounts are not intended to represent the materiality threshold for financial reporting and disclosure purposes. Notwithstanding this, an item is considered material, regardless of size, if it involves an omission or misstatement of accounting information that, in the light of surrounding circumstances, makes it probable that the judgment of a reasonable person relying on the information would have been changed or influenced by the omission or misstatement.

We confirm, to the best of our knowledge and belief, the following representations made to you during the examination.

1. We have made available to you all:

   - Statutory financial records and related data; and
   - Minutes of meetings of stockholders/policyholders (if a mutual company), directors and committees, or summaries of actions of recent meetings for which minutes have not yet been prepared.

2. There have been no:

   - Fraud or other irregularities involving management or employees who have significant roles in the internal control structure;
   - Fraud or other irregularities involving other employees that have or may have a material effect on the statutory financial statements;
   - Fraud or other irregularities involving agents, MGAs, third party administrators, independent contractors, holding companies or other individuals or parties that have or may have a material effect on the statutory financial position of the Company; or
   - Communications from regulatory agencies concerning noncompliance with, or deficiencies in, statutory financial reporting practices.

3. We have no plans or intentions that may materially affect the carrying value or classification of assets and liabilities.

4. The financial statements are free of material and intentional immaterial misstatements.

5. The following have been properly recorded or disclosed in the statutory financial statements:

- Any related party transactions and related amounts receivable or payable, including sales, purchases, loans, transfers, leasing arrangements, and guarantees.

- All liabilities, both actual and contingent.

- Guarantees whether written or oral, under which the Company is contingently liable.

- Capital stock (N/A for mutual companies) repurchase options or agreements on capital stock reserved for options, warrants, conversions, or other requirements.

- Arrangements with financial institutions involving compensating balances or other arrangements involving restrictions on cash balances and line-of-credit or similar arrangements.

- Significant estimates and material concentrations known to management that are required to be disclosed in accordance with SSAP No. 1, *Disclosure of Accounting Policies, Risks & Uncertainties, and Other Disclosures.*

- Amount of credit risk and extent, nature, and terms of financial instruments with off-balance-sheet risk to be disclosed in accordance with SSAP No. 27.

- Agreements to repurchase assets previously sold.

6. We confirm the completeness of the information provided regarding the identification of related parties.

7. There are no violation or possible violations of laws or regulations whose effects should be considered for disclosure in the statutory financial statements or as a basis for recording a loss contingency.

8. Contingent Liabilities:

- There are no other liabilities or gain or loss contingencies that are required to be accrued or disclosed by SSAP No. 5.

- There is no litigation against the Company that is considered material in relation to the statutory financial position of the Company. For purposes of this section, the Company has excluded litigation for which the only amounts sought relate to benefits within the normal terms of coverage under contracts of insurance issued by the Company, and which are otherwise considered in the actuarial determination of the Company's unpaid claim reserves.

- *In the occurrence of a contingent liability noted by management the following should be included in the management representation letter*: Except for the contingent liability disclosed in Note X of the financial statements, there are no contingent liabilities that require disclosure in the financial statements or notes thereto.

- (*If applicable*) The … litigation by XYZ Company has been settled for the total sum of XXX that has been properly reflected in the financial statements. No other claims in connection with litigation have been or are expected to be received.

9. Adequate provision has been made for adjustments and losses in collection of receivables.

10. Provision has been made for estimated retroactive adjustments by third-party payors under reimbursement agreements.

11. The Company is in compliance with bond indentures or other debt instruments.

12. Pending changes in the organizational structure, financing arrangements, or other matters that could have a material effect on the financial statements of the Company are properly disclosed.

13. The Company has properly classified all assets as admitted or nonadmitted in accordance with SSAP No. 4.

14. The Company has free and clear title to all owned assets, and there are no liens or encumbrances on such assets nor has any asset been pledged except as disclosed in the annual statement.

15. We have reviewed long-lived assets and certain identifiable intangibles whenever changes in circumstances have indicated that the carrying amount of these assets might not be recoverable and have recorded the adjustment in accordance with SSAP No. 5.

16. Deferred tax assets and liabilities as reported in the financial statements comply and have been valued in accordance with SSAP No. 10, *Income Taxes*.

17. Investments are appropriately recorded and valued as follows:

    - Bonds – are recorded and disclosed in accordance with SSAP No. 26 and interpretations thereof.
    - Preferred stocks – are recorded and disclosed in accordance with SSAP No. 32 and interpretations thereof.
    - Common stocks – are recorded and disclosed in accordance with SSAP No. 30 and interpretations thereof. Common stock of subsidiaries and affiliated or controlled companies are recorded and disclosed in accordance with SSAP No. 46 and interpretations thereof.
    - Short-term investments – are recorded and disclosed in accordance with SSAP No. 2 and interpretations thereof.
    - Mortgage loans and collateral loans – are recorded and disclosed in accordance with SSAP's No. 37 & 21 and interpretations thereof.
    - Real estate – are recorded and disclosed in accordance with SSAP No. 40 and interpretations thereof.

18. The Statutory Contingency Reserve and applicable supplementary reserve has been properly recorded and disclosed in accordance with SSAP No. 58.

19. The Company's liabilities for unpaid losses and loss adjustment expenses are based on and recorded at management's best estimate in accordance with SSAP No. 55.

20. Agents' balances or uncollected premiums have been recorded and disclosed in accordance with SSAP No. 6.

21. There were no material commitments for construction or acquisition of property, plant and equipment, or to acquire other noncurrent assets, such as investments or intangibles.

22. *In the event of a material commitment replace clause #21 with the following*: Other than the commitment described in Note *X* of the financial statements, there are no material commitments for construction, or acquisition of property, plant and equipment, or to acquire other noncurrent assets, such as investments or intangibles which require disclosure in the financial statements.

23. We have complied with all aspects of contractual agreements that would have a material effect on the statutory financial statement in the event of noncompliance.

24. There are no material transactions that have not been properly recorded in the accounting records underlying the statutory financial statements.

25. All required returns and statutory reporting requirements have been filed on a timely basis with the appropriate regulatory bodies.

26. All material reinsurance transactions have been recorded and disclosed in accordance with SSAP No. 62.

27. The Company has properly disclosed and recorded all changes in accounting principles in accordance with SSAP No. 3.

28. The Company has recorded and disclosed subsequent events in accordance with SSAP No. 9.

29. *In the event of a subsequent event, the following should replace clause #28 in the Management Representations Letter:* Other than.... described in Note X to the financial statements, there have been no events subsequent to period end which require adjustment of or disclosure in the financial statements or notes thereto.

30. The Company is not aware of the employment of or a business relationship with a "prohibited person" as defined in The Violent Crime Control and Law Enforcement Act of 1994: United States Code, Section 1033 (e)(1)(A).

31. Note *X* to the financial statements discloses all of the matters of which we are aware that are relevant to the Company's ability to continue as a going concern, including significant conditions and events, and management's plans.

32. We agree with the findings of specialists in evaluating the (describe the assertion) and have adequately considered the qualifications of the specialists in determining the amounts and disclosures used in the financial statements and underlying accounting records. We did not give or cause any instructions to be given to specialists with respect to the values or amounts derived in an attempt to bias their work.

33. The valuation of securities X is unavailable from the NAIC Securities Valuation Office; therefore, the Company has determined a value for this financial instrument. The methods and significant assumptions used to determine this value are in accordance with SSAP No. 27.

34. The Company has recorded and disclosed defined benefit plans and defined contribution plans in accordance with SSAP No. 89.

35. The Company has recorded and disclosed postretirement benefits other than pensions in accordance with SSAP No. 14.

We understand that your examination was made in accordance with standards established by the (Name of State) Department of Insurance, and procedures established by *the National Association of Insurance Commissioners*, and accordingly included such tests of the accounting records and such other procedures as considered necessary under the circumstances.

Name of Insurance Company

__________________________________ ____________________

Chief Executive Officer Date

__________________________________ ____________________

Chief Financial Officer Date

(On Company Letterhead)

Date (date should agree with report of examination)

Name of Examiner
Examiner-In-Charge
(Name of State) Department of Insurance
Address
City, State Zip Code

We are providing this letter in connection with your examination of the statutory financial statements of *(Name of Title Company*) as of (*Month, Date, Year*), and for the period from (*Month, Date, Year*) to (*Month, Date, Year*). We are responsible for the preparation of the statutory financial statements of financial position, results of operations, and changes in statutory financial position in conformity with the accounting practices prescribed or permitted by the (Name of State) Department of Insurance.

Certain representations in this letter are described as being limited to those matters that are material. Solely for the purpose of preparing this letter, the term "material," when used in this letter, means any item or group of similar items involving potential amounts of more than $___________. These amounts are not intended to represent the materiality threshold for financial reporting and disclosure purposes. Notwithstanding this, an item is considered material, regardless of size, if it involves an omission or misstatement of accounting information that, in the light of surrounding circumstances, makes it probable that the judgment of a reasonable person relying on the information would have been changed or influenced by the omission or misstatement.

We confirm, to the best of our knowledge and belief, the following representations made to you during the examination.

1. We have made available to you all:

   - Statutory financial records and related data; and
   - Minutes of meetings of stockholders/policyholders (if a mutual company), directors and committees, or summaries of actions of recent meetings for which minutes have not yet been prepared.

2. There have been no:

   - Fraud or other irregularities involving management or employees who have significant roles in the internal control structure;
   - Fraud or other irregularities involving other employees that have or may have a material effect on the statutory financial statements;
   - Fraud or other irregularities involving agents, MGAs, third party administrators, independent contractors, holding companies or other individuals or parties that have or may have a material effect on the statutory financial position of the Company; or
   - Communications from regulatory agencies concerning noncompliance with, or deficiencies in, statutory financial reporting practices.

3. We have no plans or intentions that may materially affect the carrying value or classification of assets and liabilities.

4. The financial statements are free of material and intentional immaterial misstatements.

5. The following have been properly recorded or disclosed in the statutory financial statements:

- Any related party transactions and related amounts receivable or payable, including sales, purchases, loans, transfers, leasing arrangements, and guarantees.
- All liabilities, both actual and contingent.
- Guarantees whether written or oral, under which the Company is contingently liable.
- Capital stock (N/A for mutual companies) repurchase options or agreements on capital stock reserved for options, warrants, conversions, or other requirements.
- Arrangements with financial institutions involving compensating balances or other arrangements involving restrictions on cash balances and line-of-credit or similar arrangements.
- Significant estimates and material concentrations known to management that are required to be disclosed in accordance with SSAP No. 1, *Disclosure of Accounting Policies, Risks & Uncertainties, and Other Disclosures.*
- Amount of credit risk and extent, nature, and terms of financial instruments with off-balance-sheet risk to be disclosed in accordance with SSAP No. 27.
- Agreements to repurchase assets previously sold.

6. We confirm the completeness of the information provided regarding the identification of related parties.

7. There are no violation or possible violations of laws or regulations whose effects should be considered for disclosure in the statutory financial statements or as a basis for recording a loss contingency.

8. Contingent Liabilities:

- There are no other liabilities or gain or loss contingencies that are required to be accrued or disclosed by SSAP No. 5.
- There is no litigation against the Company that is considered material in relation to the statutory financial position of the Company. For purposes of this section, the Company has excluded litigation for which the only amounts sought relate to benefits within the normal terms of coverage under contracts of insurance issued by the Company, and which are otherwise considered in the actuarial determination of the Company's unpaid claim reserves.
- *In the occurrence of a contingent liability noted by management the following should be included in the management representation letter*: Except for the contingent liability disclosed in Note X of the financial statements, there are no contingent liabilities that require disclosure in the financial statements or notes thereto.
- (*If applicable*) The … litigation by XYZ Company has been settled for the total sum of XXX that has been properly reflected in the financial statements. No other claims in connection with litigation have been or are expected to be received.

9. Adequate provision has been made for adjustments and losses in collection of receivables.

10. Provision has been made for estimated retroactive adjustments by third-party payors under reimbursement agreements.

11. The Company is in compliance with bond indentures or other debt instruments.

12. Pending changes in the organizational structure, financing arrangements, or other matters that could have a material effect on the financial statements of the Company are properly disclosed.

13. The Company has properly classified all assets as admitted or nonadmitted in accordance with SSAP No. 4.

14. The Company has free and clear title to all owned assets, and there are no liens or encumbrances on such assets nor has any asset been pledged except as disclosed in the annual statement.

15. We have reviewed long-lived assets and certain identifiable intangibles whenever changes in circumstances have indicated that the carrying amount of these assets might not be recoverable and have recorded the adjustment in accordance with SSAP No. 5.

16. Deferred tax assets and liabilities as reported in the financial statements comply and have been valued in accordance with SSAP No. 10, *Income Taxes*.

17. Investments are appropriately recorded and valued as follows:

- Bonds – are recorded and disclosed in accordance with SSAP No. 26 and interpretations thereof.
- Preferred stocks – are recorded and disclosed in accordance with SSAP No. 32 and interpretations thereof.
- Common stocks – are recorded and disclosed in accordance with SSAP No. 30 and interpretations thereof. Common stock of subsidiaries and affiliated or controlled companies are recorded and disclosed in accordance with SSAP No. 46 and interpretations thereof.
- Short-term investments – are recorded and disclosed in accordance with SSAP No. 2 and interpretations thereof.
- Mortgage loans and collateral loans – are recorded and disclosed in accordance with SSAP's No. 37 & 21 and interpretations thereof.
- Real estate – are recorded and disclosed in accordance with SSAP No. 40 and interpretations thereof.

18. The Statutory Premium Reserve and applicable supplemental reserve has been properly recorded and disclosed in accordance with SSAP No. 57.

19. Title Plants have been recorded and disclosed in accordance with SSAP No. 57.

20. The Company's liabilities for unpaid claims and claim adjustment expenses are based upon and recorded at management's best estimate in accordance with SSAP No. 55.

21. Agents' balances or uncollected premiums have been recorded and disclosed in accordance with SSAP No. 6.

22. There were no material commitments for construction or acquisition of property, plant and equipment, or to acquire other noncurrent assets, such as investments or intangibles.

23. *In the event of a material commitment replace clause #22 with the following*: Other than the commitment described in Note *X* of the financial statements, there are no material commitments for construction, or acquisition of property, plant and equipment, or to acquire other noncurrent assets, such as investments or intangibles which require disclosure in the financial statements.

24. We have complied with all aspects of contractual agreements that would have a material effect on the statutory financial statement in the event of noncompliance.

25. There are no material transactions that have not been properly recorded in the accounting records underlying the statutory financial statements.

26. All required returns and statutory reporting requirements have been filed on a timely basis with the appropriate regulatory bodies.

27. All material reinsurance transactions have been recorded and disclosed in accordance with SSAP No. 62.

28. The Company has properly disclosed and recorded all changes in accounting principles in accordance with SSAP No. 3.

29. The Company has recorded and disclosed subsequent events in accordance with SSAP No. 9.

30. *In the event of a subsequent event, the following should replace clause #29 in the Management Representations Letter:* Other than…. described in Note X to the financial statements, there have been no events subsequent to period end which require adjustment of or disclosure in the financial statements or notes thereto.

31. The Company is not aware of the employment of or a business relationship with a "prohibited person" as defined in The Violent Crime Control and Law Enforcement Act of 1994: United States Code, Section 1033 (e)(1)(A).

32. Note *X* to the financial statements discloses all of the matters of which we are aware that are relevant to the Company's ability to continue as a going concern, including significant conditions and events, and management's plans.

33. We agree with the findings of specialists in evaluating the (describe the assertion) and have adequately considered the qualifications of the specialists in determining the amounts and disclosures used in the financial statements and underlying accounting records. We did not give or cause any instructions to be given to specialists with respect to the values or amounts derived in an attempt to bias their work.

34. The valuation of securities X is unavailable from the NAIC Securities Valuation Office; therefore, the Company has determined a value for this financial instrument. The methods and significant assumptions used to determine this value are in accordance with SSAP No. 27.

35. The Company has recorded and disclosed defined benefit plans and defined contribution plans in accordance with SSAP No. 89.

36. The Company has recorded and disclosed postretirement benefits other than pensions in accordance with SSAP No. 14.

We understand that your examination was made in accordance with standards established by the (Name of State) Department of Insurance, and procedures established by *the National Association of Insurance Commissioners*, and accordingly included such tests of the accounting records and such other procedures as considered necessary under the circumstances.

Name of Title Company

______________________________ __________________

Chief Executive Officer Date

______________________________ __________________

Chief Financial Officer Date

EXHIBIT L
EXAMINATION PLANNING MEMORANDUM

The following is an illustration of an examination planning memorandum to assist examiners in documenting the planning process. The illustration includes those areas discussed in the Examination Planning Memorandum, plus additional areas including examination goals, zone activities, related parties, pending matters, communications with CPAs, department and company personnel, use of work performed by others and accounting and reporting issues that may be necessary to adequately document the examination plan.

This exhibit is an illustration, and is not intended to be all inclusive and should be tailored to each examination. It is not necessary for every examination's planning memorandum to address each of the areas and points discussed herein. Therefore, the examiner-in-charge should use his or her judgment in determining which sections of this illustration are applicable and document any other pertinent information considered. In making these judgments the examiner should bear in mind the purpose of the planning memorandum, which is to provide a concise summary of examination risks, significant examination activities and the overall examination approach. Where feasible, the planning memorandum should incorporate key documents by reference and attach detail reports and information as exhibits. Examples of the latter are details of preliminary analytical review, annual statement jurat page, Schedule Y and ETS Premium Schedule.

COMPANY NAME:

EXAMINATION DATE:

This planning memorandum is intended to document our examination plan as it relates to (Name of Insurance Company), as of December 31, 20XX.

EXAMINATION GOALS

The department may consider establishing specific or general goals for the examination. Following are examples of general examination goals:

- Perform an examination that identifies significant deviations from statutory accounting practices that affect solvency;
- Perform an examination that identifies significant deviations from (state) insurance laws, regulations and department directives;
- Perform the examination in accordance with standards prescribed in the revised NAIC *Financial Condition Examiners Handbook*, NAIC Accreditation Standards and department policy;
- Identify and report on significant operational and internal control deficiencies;
- Complete the examination efficiently within the budgeted time and within scheduling requirements; and
- Provide on-the-job training and professional development of department staff.

COMPANY BACKGROUND

Document significant operating characteristics of the company, including the type of company (e.g., Mutual, Stock, Title, HMO, Captive), its principal line(s) of business, capital structure, ownership and the as of date of the last financial condition and market conduct examinations.

ZONE ACTIVITIES

This section documents relevant correspondence with a zone(s) and zone participant(s). Document whether the examination was called through the NAIC's Exam Tracking System (ETS), invited zone(s), correspondence from such zone(s) and/or participating examiners, and to what extent the zone representative(s) will be involved in planning the examination and developing the scope of procedures.

PENDING MATTERS

List matters identified in planning meetings and review of department correspondence that are outstanding or pending approval (e.g., request for rate increase/decrease, real estate appraisal, custodial agreement) and briefly discuss follow-up procedures planned.

SIGNIFICANT CURRENT EVENTS

Significant current events are events or conditions that may have an impact on or influence the scope of the examination or determination to rely on specific controls. Examples of significant current events are as follows:

- Turnover in key management, particularly financial or actuarial personnel;
- Entry into or departure from a significant line(s) of business;
- Recent acquisition or merger;
- Issuance of surplus notes, common stock or debt; and
- Recent regulatory actions (financial and/or market).

RELATED PARTIES

Identify:

- Parent, affiliates, subsidiaries and ultimate controlling person;
- Principal owners;
- Controlling shareholders (10% and greater); and
- Board of directors & officers.

RESULTS OF PRELIMINARY ANALYTICAL REVIEW

Briefly summarize your preliminary observations as they relate to the company's overall financial condition and operations since the last examination. Such observations would be made from reviewing the financial analyst's work, meetings with the analyst and performing other analytical review procedures. Details of this review may be attached as an exhibit to the planning memo. Examples of preliminary analytical review results would entail identifying unusual IRIS results and explanations thereof, profitability of underwriting and overall operations, the level to which the company has leveraged policyholders' surplus, composition of investment portfolio and Jumpstart exceptions.

EXTERNAL ENVIRONMENTAL CONSIDERATIONS

Identify external environmental factors or conditions pertinent to the company's operations, investments and/or line(s) of business. Following are examples of such factors or conditions that could affect or influence an examination approach.

- Commercial real estate markets in many parts of the country are experiencing high vacancy rates, adding to an already illiquid asset;

- Upward trending interest rates lowers market value on debt securities. If a company has failed to match its assets to liabilities, the company may be forced to sell its debt securities at a loss;
- The increased use of loan backed securities and structured securities, such as Government Pass-Throughs, collateralized mortgage obligations (CMOs), principal only (POs) and interest only (IOs) certificates, to enhance portfolio yields. The investment risks of these securities can be difficult to evaluate; and
- RBC requirements.

MANAGEMENT ENVIRONMENT

Briefly discuss your evaluation of the company's overall control (internal) environment, including assessment of management and the board of directors. Document your assessment of the company's overall operating environment and whether there is planned reliance on specific internal controls.

DEPARTMENT ACTIVITIES

Summarize what the examination team has done to coordinate with department personnel, such as meetings with chief examiner, financial analyst, department actuary, etc.

OUTSIDE ACTIVITIES

Summarize what the examination team has done to coordinate with company personnel and other outside parties including the company's independent auditors and consulting actuary. Consider attaching as exhibits to the planning memo copies of the independent auditors' report and actuarial opinion.

Consider identifying company contact persons in personnel in accounting, actuarial, investment, underwriting, claims, marketing, information systems, etc.

SUMMARY OF THE EXAMINATION APPROACH

1. Provide background information on material accounts and discuss assessed level of control risk.

2. Discuss overall examination approach for material accounts and regulatory compliance testing.

3. Outline in bullet point format the nature of examination procedures for material accounts.

Sections 1, 2 and 3 above may be summarized by transaction cycle, annual statement line item or other format. The examiner should use his or her judgment in determining the format best suited for the examination. For example, the summary examination approach for a large life insurance company may be grouped as Investment Cycle, Reserves and Benefits Cycle, Premium Cycle, Reinsurance Cycle, Other Assets, Other Liabilities and Regulatory Compliance.

Document planning materiality and tolerable error thresholds and briefly explain the basis for planning materiality.

USE OF WORK PERFORMED BY OTHERS

Where the examination utilizes the work performed by others (e.g., internal auditors, independent auditors, consulting actuaries), briefly describe how you plan to rely on such work and how the underlying data was tested.

ACCOUNTING AND REPORTING ISSUES

Identify any significant accounting or reporting issues relevant to the company's business. Following are examples:

- Permitted statutory accounting practices;
- Significant accounting transactions such as a loss portfolio transfer, merger or financial reinsurance;
- Recently adopted statutory accounting or reporting rules; and
- Accounting for new types of investments such as derivatives and private placements.

EXAMINATION TEAM

Include names and positions of team members. Include any specialist or consultants utilized.

TIME BUDGET AND WORK ASSIGNMENTS

Attach time budget and work assignment worksheet as an exhibit.

EXHIBITS

List all exhibits attached to planning memorandum. An example listing might include:

Exhibit 1 Details of Preliminary Analytical Review

Exhibit 2 Examination Planning Checklist

Exhibit 3 CPA Report

Exhibit 4 Actuarial Opinion

Exhibit 5 CPA Letter Confirming Permitted Practices

Exhibit 6 List of Items and Schedules Requested from Company

Exhibit 7 Examination Planning Questionnaire

Exhibit 8 Time Budget

Exhibit 9 Planning Memo Amendment #1

Exhibit 10 Planning Memo Amendment #2

EXAMINATION PLAN APPROVAL

The chief examiner or designee should review and approve the planning memo and evidence such by signing and dating. The examiner-in-charge should sign and date the planning memo as well.

EXHIBIT M
CONSIDERATION OF FRAUD

COMPANY NAME ______________________________

PERIOD OF EXAMINATION ______________________________

EXAMINER-IN-CHARGE ______________________________

The consideration of fraud in financial condition examinations should occur during the planning, testing, and reporting phases of the examination. The examiner needs to consider fraud risk factors and develop examination procedures in order to adequately obtain reasonable assurance that misstatements due to fraud are not included in the financial statements. The independent CPA's are required by Statement on Auditing Standards (SAS) No. 99 *Consideration of Fraud in a Financial Statement Audit* to complete and document consideration of fraud. The examiner should obtain and review this information in accordance with the review of the CPA workpapers. Although the examiner should utilize the CPA workpaper documentation to the extent deemed reasonable, reliance on the CPA workpapers does not preclude the examiner from identifying and inquiring about fraud risk factors noted during the examination or interviewing company management regarding the possibility of fraud, or known fraud occurrences.

The examiner should utilize this exhibit in order to adequately document the consideration of fraud for financial condition examinations. This exhibit has been divided into two different sections. The first section includes a summary of the fraud consideration and the second section includes the examiners actual documentation of fraud consideration. Once the examiner has completed the fraud consideration for a particular phase (planning, testing or reporting) he or she should sign-off the summary page. This enables the examiner-in-charge to be aware of when fraud consideration for the various phases has been completed. The entire exhibit and any supplemental attachments should be included in the working papers.

The consideration of fraud is primarily completed through the identification and examination of fraud risk factors. Fraud risk factors are conditions that may indicate the occurrence of fraud. Some examples include the insufficient review of controls, failure to respond to known accounting irregularities, extraordinary growth or profitability, threat of regulatory action, and missing accounting documentation. This exhibit includes a detailed checklist of fraud risk factors identified in previously detected fraudulent incidences to assist the examiner in determining applicable fraud risk factors.

By properly considering and attesting to fraud risk factors, the examiner is able to obtain reasonable assurance that the financial statements are free from material misstatement due to fraud. Completion and approval of this document does not indicate that fraud has not been perpetrated on or within the company nor does it provide absolute assurance that committed frauds have been detected. It is possible to complete a properly planned and performed examination and not discover occurrences of perpetrated fraudulent activity.

Note: Any examiner may complete the consideration of fraud during the examination, but the Examiner-In-Charge is required to review and sign-off the prepared workpapers.

SUMMARY OF THE CONSIDERATION OF FRAUD - PLANNING PHASE

Note: The following section should be completed in accordance with the consideration of fraud during the planning phase of the examination. The examiner should provide documentation of the actual review during the planning phase as indicated throughout this exhibit.

PLANNING PHASE PROCEDURES	COMPLETED BY	DATE
1. Obtain and review the independent CPA workpapers detailing the fraud consideration documentation. Identify any fraud risk factors or other items noted that might be indicative of fraudulent activity by either fraudulent financial reporting, the misappropriation of assets, or through fraudulent claims.		
a. Document any fraud risk factors noted and procedures performed by the CPA to mitigate fraud risk.		
b. Document the results of communications amongst the independent CPAs, company officials, or others with respect to the risk of fraud in the entity and known fraudulent activity perpetrated on or within the company.		
c. Review and evaluate the other information documented by the independent CPA with respect to their consideration of fraud and utilize this information, if applicable, to develop and further enhance the planned examination procedures.		
2. Review the company's operations, both financial and operative, to identify any additional fraud risk factors. Review and adjust the planned examination procedures according to the noted risk factors. Use the CPA workpapers to facilitate this review.		
a. Document the fraud risk factors identified and the examination procedures designed to mitigate the fraud risk.		
3. Meet with company management to discuss the risk of fraud in the entity and to inquire whether management is aware of any fraudulent activity that has been conducted on or within the company and if the company is maintaining compliance with Federal Anti-money Laundering requirements. Determine that the company has established antifraud initiatives reasonably calculated to detect, prosecute and prevent fraudulent insurance acts.		
a. Identify the company managers utilized for this discussion and summarize the dialogue results. Include the discussion results in a memorandum for inclusion in the workpapers.		

SUMMARY OF THE CONSIDERATION OF FRAUD - TESTING PHASE

Note: The following section should be completed in accordance with the consideration of fraud during the testing phase of the examination. The examiner should provide documentation of the actual review during the testing phase as indicated throughout this exhibit.

TESTING PHASE PROCEDURES	COMPLETED BY	DATE
1. Continue to identify fraud risk factors during the examination process. Adapt the planned examination procedures as necessary to mitigate fraud risk.		
a. Review the planned examination approach to determine if modification is necessary in accordance with the additional identified fraud risk factors.		
b. Evaluate the assessed materiality levels as well as the overall risk assessment to adequately reflect the discovery of additional fraud risk factors.		
c. Document any changes to the planned examination approach, materiality levels, or the overall risk assessments in a memorandum for inclusion in the examination workpapers.		
2. Review the fraud initiatives established by the company to advertise, identify, investigate and report fraudulent acts.		
a. Verify that the established fraud program is advertised and promoted to the company's insured.		
i. Determine whether claim forms and applications indicate that any person who knowingly presents a false or fraudulent claim for payment of a loss or benefit or knowingly presents false information in an application for insurance is guilty of a crime and may be subject to fines and confinement in prison.		
b. Verify that the company has established a procedure to report fraudulent insurance acts to the commissioner in the manner prescribed by the commissioner.		

TESTING PHASE PROCEDURES			COMPLETED BY	DATE
3.	Verify that the company has implemented an anti-money laundering program in compliance with the USA PATRIOT Act. *Note: The U.S. Treasury has not yet issued final implementation rules under the USA PATRIOT Act, though the proposed rules did exempt property and casualty insurers and health insurers. Since the final rules have not been issued yet, no examination procedures have been created and no further examination work is considered necessary. The NAIC has established an Ad Hoc Task Force on USA PATRIOT Act Compliance to address the concerns of insurance regulators with respect to the Act.*			
4.	Document the investigation of any potential fraudulent activity noted during the examination process. *(Note: This does not refer to additional fraud risk factors identified.)*			
	a.	If, after completing the review of fraud risk factors and examination procedures, the examiner identifies a potential fraud situation, the examiner and EIC, depending on state guidelines, should either inform the appropriate state insurance department division responsible for investigating potential fraudulent activity, or perform procedures to further investigate the potential fraudulent activity. If the examiner is investigating the potential fraud, the examiner should:		
		i. Discuss the nature and effect of the fraudulent activity with the appropriate level of management.		
		ii. Attempt to obtain additional evidential matter regarding the fraudulent activity to determine the overall effect on the financial statements and the company operations.		
	b.	Verify that necessary information regarding the knowledge or reasonable belief that a fraudulent act has been, will be, or is being committed has been communicated to the commissioner as required. *(Note: If the state has adopted the Insurance Fraud Prevention Model Act, information obtained by the commissioner in an investigation of a suspected or known fraudulent act is confidential by law and is not subject to subpoena. Additionally, the commissioner or individual gathering the information on behalf of the commissioner is not permitted or required to testify in a private civil action with regards to the confidential documents.)*		

SUMMARY OF THE CONSIDERATION OF FRAUD - REPORTING PHASE

Note: The following section should be completed in accordance with the consideration of fraud during the reporting phase of the examination. The examiner should provide documentation of the actual review during the completion phase as indicated throughout this exhibit.

REPORTING PHASE PROCEDURES		COMPLETED BY	DATE
1.	Review the fraud risk factors identified throughout the planning and testing phases of the examination and the examination procedures completed to verify that the noted fraud risk factors have been adequately considered throughout the examination process.		
2.	Although the focus of the examination is not to detect fraud, verify that the examination has been conducted in a manner to alleviate the risk of fraud through the consideration of fraud risk factors.		
3.	Verify that the report of examination properly presents the financial condition of the company with regards to any known instances of fraud perpetrated on or within the company.		

DOCUMENTATION OF FRAUD CONSIDERATION – PLANNING PHASE

The examiner should document the evidence of the consideration of fraud during the planning phase of the examination as indicated below.

A. Review and Consideration of Independent CPA workpapers:

In accordance with the AICPA 2002 'Consideration of Fraud in a Financial Statement Audit,' external auditors are required to perform specific procedures to ensure that the audit has been responsibly planned and performed to obtain reasonable assurance that the financial statements are free of material misstatement. In accordance with the AICPA guidance, documentation of the auditor's consideration should be included in the CPA workpapers. The examiner should review the work performed by the auditor and consider the auditor's documentation and findings. *For the items included under this section, the examiner may choose to copy and include the CPA workpapers as a supplement to this workpaper.*

Note: If the independent CPA has performed a fraud risk assessment at the holding company level rather than the insurance company entity level, the CPA workpapers may not provide enough information to warrant a thorough review as outlined in the steps below. In this instance, the examiner may choose not to rely on the CPA's consideration of fraud and should document the rationale in the workpapers. The examiner may continue the consideration of fraud in Part B – Review Company Operations and Identify Fraud Risk Factors.

1. Summarize the discussions held amongst the external audit team regarding how and where the company's financial statements might be susceptible to material misstatement due to fraud. The examiner should identify when this discussion occurred, the audit team members involved, and the items discussed.

   ____

   ____

   ____

2. Document the procedures performed by the external auditors to identify and assess the risk of material misstatement due to fraud. These procedures typically entail inquiring of management and others about the risk or occurrence of fraud, performing an evaluation of analytical procedures, considering fraud risk factors, and considering other information considered pertinent for the determination of fraud.

   a. Inquires of management and others on the risk of fraud:

      Document conversations the external auditor held with management to determine:

      (1) Known occurrences of fraud perpetrated on or within the company;

      (2) Any allegations of fraudulent activity;

      (3) Management's understanding of the risk of fraud in the company;

      (4) Whether the company has established programs for the prevention and detection of fraud or whether specific fraud mitigators have been implemented;

      (5) Management's established process to monitor multiple locations and whether any specific location poses an increase risk of fraud;

      (6) How management communicates the company's view of ethical behavior and business practices to employees.

Document other conversations held by the external auditor with regards to:

(1) Communications with the audit committee regarding internal controls;

(2) Communications with internal auditors regarding the risks of fraud, procedures performed to identify or detect fraud, management responses to internal auditor requests, and any known or suspected fraud;

(3) Conversations held with others outside the financial reporting division regarding suspicious or inappropriate activities;

(4) Inquiries made to other department personnel, employees or legal council regarding the risk of fraud or related topics.

____

____

____

____

b. Evaluation of Analytical Procedures During Planning:

Document the steps performed and findings noted by the auditor with regards to the analytical procedures executed during the planning phase of the examination. Identify results noted from these analytical procedures that indicate unusual or unexpected relationships as well as the auditor's consideration of these occurrences in determining risk from material misstatement due to fraud.

____

____

____

____

c. Consideration of Fraud Risk Factors:

Document the consideration of fraud risk factors by the external auditor. Detail the auditor's identified specific risks of fraud and the procedures employed to investigate/mitigate the fraud risk factors. Evaluate the auditor's consideration on the type, significance, likelihood, and pervasiveness of the identified risks as well as the auditor's overall response to the risk.

____

____

____

d. Consideration of Other Information Utilized in Identifying Risks:

Review and summarize other information considered by the auditor in their process to identify risks of material misstatement due to fraud. Items that may be considered include identified inherent risks and established procedures over the acceptance and/or continuation of audit clients.

3. Summarize the auditor's consideration with regards to the ability of management to override controls. Evaluate and document the auditor's determination to perform (or not perform) additional procedures to address the risk of control deviations due to management overrides.

4. Document other risks or conditions noted by the auditor that resulted in the auditor completing additional auditing procedures or documenting added responses.

5. Document communications the external auditor had regarding fraud, or the risk of fraud, with the company's management, audit committee, or other individuals. The examiner should consider the level of management informed for all known fraudulent acts.

B. Review Company Operations and Identify Fraud Risk Factors:

1. Review the company's operations, both financial and operative, to identify fraud risk factors. Common fraud risk factors are indicated in the following chart. The fraud risk factors are categorized according to the three conditions typically present when fraud occurs:

- Incentives/Pressures to commit fraud
- Opportunities exist to perpetrate fraud
- Attitudes/Rationalizations that fraud is ethical or acceptable

FRAUD RISK FACTORS	COMPANY APPLICABILITY			
	Y	N	N/A	COMMENTS
Misstatements From Fraudulent Financial Reporting				
Incentives / Pressures				
1. Are any of the following conditions present that may indicate a personal incentive for management to engage in fraudulent financial reporting?				
a. Are compensatory management bonuses and incentives derived from the company's ability to accomplish aggressive operating or performance results?				
b. Do any other conditions exist that may indicate a motivation for management to engage in fraudulent financial reporting?				
c. Are unduly aggressive financial targets and expectations for operating personnel established by management?				
d. Is management or the board of directors' personal financial situation threatened by their financial interests in the entity?				
2 Is the financial stability or profitability of the company threatened by economic, industry or entity operating conditions?				
a. Is the company subject to new accounting, statutory or regulatory pronouncements that could hinder the company's profitability or financial stability?				
b. Is the company encountering a significant competition or market saturation and declining margins?				

FRAUD RISK FACTORS		COMPANY APPLICABILITY			
		Y	N	N/A	COMMENTS
c.	Is the insurance industry experiencing an increase in the number of insolvencies?				
d.	Is the industry experiencing rapid changes in technology?				
e.	Is the holding company's ability to meet its debt service requirements contingent upon increased profits and/or dividends from the insurance subsidiaries?				
f.	Has the company experienced unusually rapid growth or profitability when compared with other companies in the same industry?				
3.	Does company management have substantial pressure to acquire additional operating capital?				
4.	Is management subject to excessive pressure to meet expectations or requirements of third parties?				
a.	Is the company highly vulnerable to changes in interest rates?				
b.	Does the company need to obtain debt financing or does the company have a marginal ability to meet debt repayment requirements? Are the debt covenants difficult to maintain?				
c.	Could the company face adverse consequences on a significant pending transaction (such as a business combination, financing arrangement, or contract award) if poor financial results are reported?				
5.	Has the company set unrealistically aggressive sales or profitability incentive programs?				
6.	Is the company facing the threat of insolvency?				
Opportunities					
1.	Do the company's operations provide opportunities to engage in fraudulent activity:				
a.	Does the company engage in significant related-party transactions that are not considered to be in the ordinary course of business or with companies not subject to the examination process or audited by an independent accounting firm?				

FRAUD RISK FACTORS		COMPANY APPLICABILITY Y	N	N/A	COMMENTS
b.	Are the company's financial statements subject to significant estimates that were determined by subjective judgments or uncertainties, or that can adversely impact the financials if changed?				
c.	Does the company have unusual or highly complex transactions (particularly those close to year-end) that are difficult to assess for substance over form?				
d.	Does the company have significant bank accounts or subsidiary or branch operations in tax-haven jurisdictions for which there appears to be no clear business justification?				
2.	Does the company have appropriate monitoring controls over management?				
a.	Is the overall management of the company dominated by a single person or small group without compensating controls (i.e., appropriate oversight by the board of directors or audit committee)?				
b.	Is the board of directors actively involved in the oversight of the financial reporting process and internal control?				
3.	Does the company have a complex or unstable organizational structure?				
a.	Is it difficult to determine the organization or individual(s) that control(s) the entity?				
b.	Does the company have an overly complex organizational structure involving numerous or unusual legal entities or managerial lines of authority?				
c.	Is there a high turnover within senior management, the audit committee, board members or legal counsel?				
4.	Does the company have suffient internal controls and are they operating properly?				
a.	Has the company been observed to employ an ineffective accounting, internal auditing or information technology staff?				
b.	Is there a high turnover rate in accounting, internal audit, or information technology staff?				

	COMPANY APPLICABILITY			
FRAUD RISK FACTORS	**Y**	**N**	**N/A**	**COMMENTS**
Attitudes				
1. Does company management convey an improper attitude regarding internal controls and the financial reporting process?				
a. Does management neglect to effectively communicate and encourage the company's values or ethics?				
b. Does management have an excessive interest in preserving or increasing the earning's trend through the use of aggressive accounting practices?				
c. Does management have an interest in engaging inappropriate methods to diminish reported earnings on a tax-motivated basis?				
d. Are there instances of management failing to correct known reportable conditions within an appropriate time frame?				
e. Does management illustrate a substantial disregard for regulatory authorities?				
2. Are management and employees employed in a non-financial department utilized to determine (or demonstrate an interest in) the accounting practices and financial estimates?				
3. Do related or competing businesses consider the management to have a poor reputation?				
4. Have any of the following situations occurred illustrating a strained relationship with either the current or predecessor auditor?				
a. Are there frequent disputes regarding accounting, auditing, or reporting matters?				
b. Is the auditor limited to specific individuals or sources of information while conducting the audit?				
c. Are auditor communications with the board of directors or the audit committee restricted?				
d. Does management attempt to influence the auditor, and/or the scope of the auditor's work?				

FRAUD RISK FACTORS	COMPANY APPLICABILITY			
	Y	N	N/A	COMMENTS
5. Are there any instances of fraud claims against the company or management or any recognized violations of security laws?				
Misstatements from Misappropriation of Assets				
Incentives / Pressures				
1. Are personal financial obligations of management or employees with access to cash and other assets creating pressure to misappropriate assets?				
2. Do adverse relationships exist between the company and employees (i.e., anticipated layoffs, compensation issues) that may motivate an employee to misappropriate assets?				
Opportunities				
1. Does the company maintain or process large amounts of cash?				
2. Does the company have fixed assets that are easily susceptible to misappropriation (i.e., small size, portability, marketability, lack of ownership identification, etc.)?				
3. Is the company susceptible to fraudulent, unauthorized disbursements (i.e., claim payments or payroll disbursements) being made in amounts that are material to the financial statements?				
4. Do any of the conditions listed below, that may indicate possible deficiencies in the company's internal controls over assets susceptible to misappropriation, exist?				
a. Is there a lack of appropriate management oversight of assets that are susceptible for misappropriation (for example, inadequate supervision or monitoring of remote locations)?				
b. Is there inadequate record-keeping with respect to assets susceptible to misappropriation?				
c. Is there a lack of appropriate segregation of duties or independent checks not mitigated by other factors?				
d. Does the company lack an appropriate system of authorization and approval of transactions (i.e., benefit or loss payments)?				

	COMPANY APPLICABILITY			
FRAUD RISK FACTORS	**Y**	**N**	**N/A**	**COMMENTS**
e. Are there inadequate physical safeguards over cash, investments, inventory, or fixed assets?				
f. Is there a lack of timely and appropriate documentation for transactions affecting assets susceptible for misappropriation (i.e., rejected claims, benefit payments, etc.)?				
g. Has the company failed to require mandatory vacations for employees in key control functions?				
h. Does management have an inadequate understanding of information technology, which enables IT employees to misappropriate assets?				
i. Are there adequate access controls over automated records including control over and review of computer systems event logs?				
Attitudes / Rationalizations				
1. Does management display a disregard for internal controls by overriding controls or failing to correct control deficiencies?				
2. Is there disregard for the need to monitor and reduce risks relating to the misappropriation of assets?				
3. Has there been any behavioral or lifestyle changes for management or employees that may indicate that assets have been misappropriated?				
4. Has there been behavior indicating displeasure or dissatisfaction with the company or its treatment of employees?				
Fraudulent Claims				
Note: The following risk factors indicate possible warning signs for fraudulent claims. Although the examiner should not evaluate all submitted claims for fraud, the examiner should verify that the company has established control procedures to mitigate related risk factors. If the company has experienced a significant number of fraudulent claims, the examiner should perform additional procedures to determine the company's actions to prevent and detect fraudulent claims.				
1. Does the company have several claims within the first 6 months of a coverage period or during the policy's contestable period?				

FRAUD RISK FACTORS	COMPANY APPLICABILITY			
	Y	N	N/A	COMMENTS
2. Does the company typically accept photocopied claim forms?				
3. Does the company usually write insurance policies with excessive coverage limits for the type of risk insured?				
4. Does the company fail to adequately review submitted claims and therefore inadvertently process claims with the following characteristics?				
a. Write-outs, type-overs, and erasures;				
b. Misspelled medical terms, and terms inconsistent with the diagnosis or treatment;				
c. Suspiciously detailed or extremely vague information concerning the claim;				
d. Stamped or photocopied physician/lawyer approval;				
e. Claimant address is a post office box;				
f. Subjective diagnosis or general statement of diagnosis rather than actual records;				
g. Omitted or different personal information on the claim form;				
h. Claim indicates physicians, attorneys, or employers who are outside the claimant's geographical area, or who have been included on other questionable claims.				

B. Review Company Operations and Identify Fraud Risk Factors (Cont'd):

2. Document any identified risk factors related to fraudulent financial reporting, misappropriation of assets, or fraudulent claims noted by the examiner not included on the aforementioned list:

____

____

____

____

3. For those fraud risk factors identified, document the examination procedures or steps the examiner will perform to mitigate fraud risk. Summarize the procedures below:

Fraud Risk Factor		**Examination Procedure**
Example – Company had several significant transactions at year-end		*Example - The examiner will perform substantive examination procedures on these transactions to mitigate associated risks.*

C. Obtain Understanding of Management's Consideration of Fraud

1. Inquire of management about its understanding of the risk of material misstatement due to fraud and its knowledge of fraudulent activity.

a. Identify the members of management utilized for this discussion:

NAME		**TITLE**

b. Summarize management's indication of the risk of fraud within the company:

____

____

____

____

____

c. Summarize the responses of management with respect to any known occurrences of fraud perpetrated on or within the entity:

d. Determine whether the company has an established program for awareness, prevention, detection and reporting of fraud. Provide details of this established program, as well as management's assessment of the effectiveness and the overseeing individual:

DOCUMENTATION OF FRAUD CONSIDERATION – TESTING PHASE

Note: The examiner should document the evidence of the consideration of fraud during the testing phase of the examination as indicated below.

A. Continue to Identify Fraud Risk Factors

Review the listing of possible fraud risk factors to determine if any other factors have been discovered while performing examination testwork. Document these additional fraud risk factors and the procedures taken by the examiner to mitigate the risk of fraud.

Fraud Risk Factor		Examination Procedure

B. Review and Document Indications of Fraud

1. Throughout the examination process the examiner should document any instances of potential fraud identified or brought to the attention of the examiner. In accordance with the state's guidelines, the examiner and EIC should either report the potential fraudulent activity to the designated state insurance department division responsible for investigating potential fraudulent activity or perform procedures to further investigate the potential fraud.

   Provide a brief summary of any noted potential fraudulent activity and the process for further investigating the potential fraud.

   ____

   ____

   ____

   ____

   ____

DOCUMENTATION OF FRAUD CONSIDERATION – REPORTING PHASE

(This phase should be completed by the Examiner-In-Charge)

Note: The examiner-in-charge should document the evidence of the consideration of fraud during the reporting phase of the examination as indicated below.

A. Consideration of Fraud Risk Factors and Examination Procedures

1. Review the fraud risk factors and the examination procedures utilized to mitigate or investigate the risk of fraud. Verify that the examination procedures employed provide the examiner with reasonable assurance that the financial statements are free of material misstatement with regards to fraud. Document any additional examination procedures completed to obtain such assurance. *(Please note that the object of this examination is not to detect fraud, but the examiner should obtain reasonable assurance.)*

____

____

____

____

____

EXHIBIT N
AUTOMATING EXAMINATIONS TOOLS AND TECHNIQUES

This chapter provides guidance to financial examiners and promotes the use of automation tools during financial examinations. A variety of software tools are referenced to assist examiners with the implementation of automated procedures.

I. Purpose of Automated Examinations

Primary incentives for the use of automated examination processes are to shorten the length of an examination (which can contribute to reduced examination expenses) and allow the examiner to test entire populations of data for compliance with statutes, rules and regulations. By testing the entire population, a reliable statement of compliance can be made and trends of compliance (or noncompliance) more easily identified. As electronic examination data is collected and archived by states, information about the company's data and prior examination results may become useful for new examinations. Examiners may perform portions of an automated examination before traveling to the company or individual's location. Automation facilitates sharing of data and examination results between regulators as appropriate.

II. Automation Tools

A. NAIC Resources

1. I-SITE

The NAIC systems contain a variety of data related to companies and individuals operating in the insurance industry. An examiner can look up a company or individual and readily identify which applications contain information about the entity. The NAIC I-SITE system provides a way for examiners to access this information.

I-SITE is used to report financial, market conduct and producer information housed in the NAIC databases.

Users in the state insurance departments can access I-SITE at http://i-site-state.naic.org/. Remote users, such as examiners in the field, can access I-SITE through state-obtained Internet service providers at http://i-site.naic.org/.

To access the application you will need an I-SITE user name and password. Contact the NAIC Data Processing Coordinator in your state to obtain your user name and password.

The following is a list of the reports and utilities that are currently available within I-SITE:

a. Financial Applications

Analyst Team Report: Replaces the Exam Team Synopsis currently available for Life, Property and Fraternal companies and uses Financial Analysis and Solvency Tracking (FAST) ratios and Risk-Based Capital (RBC) ratios. This report also provides the Analyst Team Summary (ATS) level assigned to the Company (A-F). This analysis process improves on the Exam Team Synopsis by providing a clearly-defined prioritization system and incorporating regulator analysis.

Company Demographics: Information from the company master file, an accumulation of data gathered from various forms of the annual financial statement, including company name, company code, financial data year, business type, filing status, filing type, other names, company contacts, all addresses, officers, filing by state and waivers and extensions.

Exam Jumpstart: Reports that provide preliminary examination information to allow examiners a head-start on the examination process. Information available through Jumpstart includes exception reports relating to Reinsurance and Investments (including PE exceptions). Reports may also be customized to fit individual needs.

Exam Team: Provides documents written by the NAIC Examiner Team after they have reviewed the company that provide various financial information and points out possible areas of concern with respect to the company.

Exam Tracking System (ETS): Allows financial and market conduct examiners to communicate examination schedules and results; includes functions for calling financial, market conduct and combined examinations, reporting dates and easy access to information about the people involved in the examination; can also be used to view or update examination information.

Financial Analysis Handbook: Provides annual and quarterly reports used to answer many questions contained in a series of checklists designed to help with the financial analysis process.

Insurance Regulatory Information System (IRIS) Worksheet: Displays IRIS results specific to a company for a given year and contains company demographic information, summarized IRIS ratios results, key annual statement information and detailed IRIS ratio information, including the values of the inputs to each ratio's calculation.

Line Reports: Compare the data from one line of the annual statement for several companies (for example, "Total Assets" listed in the Current Year field of the Assets Page for all the same business type companies domiciled in a specified state).

Loss Reserve Analysis: Allows the examiner to perform a quick analysis of the company's loss and loss adjustment expense reserves by line of business using various standard actuarial methods. The analysis uses annual statement year data from Schedule P. The examiner may also obtain data triangles and loss development factors.

Pick-A-Page (Annual Statement data): Financial and demographic information obtained from annual and quarterly financial statements filed by insurance companies. Risk-Based Capital (RBC) detail calculations are also available.

Profiles: Reports that provide quarterly and five-year "snapshots" of a company's financial information.

Scoring: Provides annual and quarterly reports of weighted financial ratios that allow an analyst to prioritize companies based on profitability, leverage, assets and liquidity, cash flow and changes in surplus (FAST scores).

Scoring Worksheet: Provides details of each Scoring ratio component for a single company, including the values of the inputs to each ratio's calculation (FAST scores and Quarterly Scoring System).

b. **State and Public Access/Compliance Applications**

Analyst Notes: Provides access to information entered by the NAIC analyst assigned to each company, including any pertinent information about a filing not captured by other means, such as records from telephone conversations, electronic mail messages, compliance and financial data reporting issues, summaries of conversations with state regulators regarding a company's filing, etc. Analyst notes are available for the 1999 data year for "small" business types only. Property and Life data is available for 2000 data year and forward.

Audit Trail: Provides access to all changes (edits, inserts and deletes) to a company's financial data and demographics information housed in the NAIC databases, including detailed information about why, when and who made the edit, insert or delete to the database. Audit trail reports are available for the 1999 data year for "small" business types: HMO, HMDI, Fraternal and Title. Property and Life data is available for 2000 data year and forward.

Filing-at-a-Glance: Provides regulators the details of the status of an individual company's filing, receive dates and whether the filing passed all minimum standards. Annual and quarterly filings include SVO Compliance Certificates, Statement of Actuarial Opinions, State Pages, RBC Reports, Insurance Expense Exhibit, Management Discussion & Analysis (MD&A) Reports, and Annual Audited Financial Statements. Filing-at-a-Glance reports are available for the 1999 data year for "small" business types: HMO, HMDI, Fraternal and Title. Property and Life data is available for 2000 data year and forward.

Personalized Information Capture System (PICS): Provides a customized notification system for NAIC databases, where users can establish a profile of selected events indicating the type of information of interest and receive e-mail notification (Alert) if/when the information changes in the NAIC databases.

Validation Exceptions: Provides information regarding errors related to an insurance company's financial statement filing. Users may select any individual company, and assuming the company has filed with the NAIC, validation exceptions associated with that filing will be reported. These errors may have prevented the filing from loading to the database, or they may provide an indication of data quality.

View Documents: Provides access to electronic documents stored by the NAIC for a specific filing, including a printable version of a company's data as filed, and electronic access to free-form text portions of the annual statement filing (SVO Compliance, Statement of Actuarial Opinion, Management Discussion and Analysis and Annual Audited Financial Statements) These reports are available for the 1999 data year for "small" business types: HMO, HMDI, Fraternal and Title. Property and Life data is available for 2000 data year and forward.

c. **Market Applications**

Complaints Database System (CDS): Provides information about closed complaints filed by consumers against insurance entities and National Producer Numbers.

Directors and Officers: Listing of the officers and directors for a company or a listing of companies for which an individual serves as an officer or director. This information is available from 1997 through the current annual statement data.

Relationships: Displays the entities and National Producer Numbers related to the original entity or National Producer Number requested, as well as a list of information available.

Exam Tracking System (ETS): Allows market conduct and financial examiners to communicate examination schedules and results; includes functions for calling financial, market conduct and combined examinations, reporting dates and easy access to information about the people involved in the examination; can also be used to view or update examination information.

Licensing/Internet PDB: A database that links state regulatory licensing systems into one common system and establishes a repository of producer information that aids states and industry in the producer licensing process.

Market Demographics: Demographic information for insurance producers (companies, agencies, agents, etc.) such as addresses, date of birth, social security number, entity number, National Producer Number, primary and alias names.

Regulatory Information Retrieval System (RIRS): Contains regulatory actions taken by participating state insurance departments against insurance producers, companies and other entities engaged in the business of insurance.

Special Activities Database (SAD): Contains information related to market and civil activities and legal actions involving entities or National Producer Numbers engaged in the business of insurance.

Form A Filings: State Insurance Departments can voluntarily submit Form A filings to be included in the NAIC database.

d. **Securities and Subsidiaries**

Securities (Valuation of Securities Database): Provides the capability to view current valuations information for securities (assets that represent a company's stock ownership of another company) in the NAIC database.

Subsidiaries (Valuation of Securities Database): Provides the capability to view current valuations information for subsidiaries (a company in which more than 10 percent of the company's common stock is owned by a parent company) in the NAIC database.

e. **Summary Reports**

Analyst Team Summary: Provides the Analyst Team Level assigned to all companies of a specified statement type, data year and state. This report is available for the 1999 data year and forward for Property, Life and Fraternal companies.

Examination Tracking (ETS) Summary: Provides a history of examinations that match specified criteria, such as all financial examinations called in a specified state for a specified date range.

Filing Submission Status: Provides a listing of received or missing financial filings for all companies of a specified year and statement type based on whether the company is domiciled, licensed, and/or writing business in a particular state.

Insurance Regulatory Information System (IRIS) Summary: Provides IRIS ratio results for all companies of a specified business type and data year based on whether the company is domiciled, licensed and/or writing business in a particular state.

Regulatory Information Retrieval System (RIRS) Summary: Provides a listing of entities, and National Producer Numbers (firms and individuals) that have common regulatory action elements such as the same action state, a common penalty amount range or a common date range.

Special Activities Database (SAD) Summary: Generates a list of entities and National Producer Numbers with one or more common SAD activity elements, such as the same activity code or the activity within the same state.

Scoring Summary: Provides Scoring information for a specified group of companies, such as all property companies licensed in a particular state.

State Page Summary: Based on data from the Schedule D, Schedule T, State Page and Credit Life and Accident & Health Experience Exhibit. You can obtain detail reports, which show figures by company, or aggregate reports, which show totals for all companies for a line or lines of business.

Financial Analysis Handbook (FAH) Summary: Provides a summary of the company's responses to questions in the Financial Analysis Handbook.

Schedule T Exceptions: Provides exceptions to state Schedule T information.

f. **Utilities**

Closed Complaint Filing Status: Lists by state/territory the number of closed complaints entered in the Complaints Database System, the earliest date a complaint was closed, and the most recent date a complaint was closed. Sorting options are available.

Codelist Generator: Allows users to view and/or update the licensing records of businesses operating in their state, which allows states to maintain current records to ensure the accuracy of licensing data in reports referencing this information.

Data Models: Describes the table structures and the business rules that apply in defining the requirements controlling the design and implementation of the NAIC databases.

Data Reference Manual: Details how annual statement data is stored within the NAIC database tables.

Financial Analysis Handbook (FAH) File Download: Allows users to download the Program Automator Checklists and/or the corresponding Microsoft Word documents for the Financial Analysis Handbook (FAH).

File Repository: Allows state users to share files with each other. Users can submit files to the repository so others can use or view their files, or download files currently available in the repository.

Participating State Report: Provides information regarding states that are participating in the Producer Database (PDB), including the last date the PDB was updated for each state, PDB implementation date, earliest original license issue date, number of active appointments, number of active resident producers, number of active non-resident producers and total number of unique producers listed in the PDB.

RIRS/SAD Batch Inquiry: Allows users to submit a list of entities, and National Producer Numbers to query against the SAD and/or RIRS database(s) to facilitate the due diligence requirement for producer licensing.

State Contact Viewer: Displays the persons designated by the users I-SITE (Oracle) User ID, as the point of contact for Market Conduct data including Regulatory Actions, Special Activities, Relationships and Examinations, as well as persons designated as contact for Financial Examinations.

State Offerings: Provides a method for each state to view license classes, lines of authority, assignments and statuses for the Producer Database.

System Usage Report: A report that displays information about I-SITE access by a specified state, including a breakdown of usage by application and user id, as well as totals for the time period selected.

Transmission Viewer: Displays the status of transmissions and transaction errors that have been sent to the Producer Database by the state insurance departments.

2. NAIC SERFF System

The NAIC SERFF (System Electronic Rate & Forms Filing) System is designed to enable companies to send and states to receive, comment on, and approve or reject insurance industry rate and form filings. SERFF streamlines and accelerates the rate and form filing process. SERFF identifies state filing submission requirements and through the use of checklists and checks, and balances within the system, ensures greater accuracy and completeness during the filing process. SERFF's workflow features assist the states in review process and filings are typically reviewed in less time, with fewer problems for companies to resolve.

3. Market Conduct Statistical Utilities Program (MCSU)

MSCU is an Access program designed to support the sampling process. Determinations of sample size and probability of the accuracy of sampling results are easily calculated. In addition an option is available to perform working days calculations.

B. NAIC Recommended Resources

1. ACL for Windows

ACL for Windows is the NAIC recommended software to assist with the audit and evaluation of electronic data during an examination. ACL is best suited for large volumes of data such as losses and premiums. Entire populations can be tested for data accuracy and completeness. In addition, files can be sorted for totaling, sampling, and other examination procedures.

The URL for this site is: http://www.acl.com/.

2. TeamMate

TeamMate is an electronic document organizer software package that the states have the option to purchase to assist them in conducting examinations. This software enables the examiners to compile examination workpaper documentation into a centralized paperless electronic file. The software package tracks completion and review of examination procedures and is capable of including the examination documentation (Word documents, spreadsheets, etc.) entirely within the program. To assist in the utilization of TeamMate, the NAIC has developed TeamMate TeamStores for incorporation into this program. The NAIC TeamStores were developed to provide the states with uniform procedures that mirror the recommended internal control and examination procedures and exhibits included within this Handbook.

TeamStores, which are available on I-SITE, have been developed for the Specific Risk Analyses (SRAs) included in Part 2, as well as certain workpaper exhibits. The TeamStores will be updated by the NAIC on an annual basis to incorporate any changes. Periodic updates may also occur throughout the year.

3. U.S. Insurance Reports

U.S. Insurance reports, from Thompson Financial Insurance Solutions, are available to all states on a subscription basis. These reports include information on all insurance companies that file their annual and quarterly financial statements with the NAIC. U.S. Insurance reports are contained on a Compact Disk (CD) and include Market Share information, financial statement historical data, and the ability to use standard quick reports or customized reports for individual needs.

C. Other Data Resources

1. State Systems

The examiner should identify what information is stored electronically in their state systems and whether it can be extracted for automated testing. If a company's data will be tested against the state's data, the initial request for data sent to the company should consider the state's data format to simplify testing.

2. A.M. Best Reports

The objective of Best's rating system is to evaluate the factors affecting the overall performance of an insurance company in order to provide an opinion of the company's financial strength, operating performance and ability to meet its obligations to policyholders. The procedure includes quantitative and qualitative evaluations of the company's financial condition and operating performance.

Best's Ratings of life/health insurance companies are formally evaluated on an annual and quarterly basis and following any significant event (i.e., catastrophe, lawsuit, management or ownership change, etc.). The annual review, which includes an analysis of the current first quarter results, is performed following a comprehensive collection of information by A.M. Best. This includes a company's state filing of the National Association of Insurance Commissioners (NAIC) annual statement, required to be filed by March 1 in most states, along with many other documents such as Best's supplemental rating questionnaires.

In addition to the extensive documentation, an important component of the company evaluation is the frequent meetings, phone calls and correspondence between A.M. Best's analysts and company management, which provide crucial information and understanding of the company's operations, financial condition and future business plans. This unique step allows A.M. Best to make a comprehensive qualitative evaluation of a company's overall operations.

While the information contained in the reports was obtained from sources believed to be reliable, its accuracy is not guaranteed. A.M. Best submits company NAIC statement data to a rigorous, computerized cross-checking routine to verify its arithmetic accuracy. However, they do not audit the companies' financial records or statements and, therefore, cannot attest as to the accuracy of the data provided to A.M. Best.

The URL for this site is: http://www.ambest.com/.

D. Other Software Tools

1. Spreadsheets

Spreadsheet applications are computer programs that let you create and manipulate data. Data in a spreadsheet can be defined and formulas created for calculations, analysis, etc. The most common spreadsheet software is Excel. Lotus 123 is another very common spreadsheet software.

Expert systems using spreadsheet software have been created over the years by many regulators and other industry individuals. These systems allow the examiner to input or download data to the spreadsheet, which then automatically performs all the necessary calculations and analysis. Some of the expert systems available include Schedule P Analysis, Provision for Reinsurance, Financial Statements, AVR, IMR, Bond Amortization, Excess of Statutory Reserves over Statement Reserves, Sampling, etc.

2. Word Processors

Word processors facilitate the creation of letters, reports, working papers, labels, and other documents.

3. Databases

Database software provides for queries and reports to be created against a database. Database examples are included utilizing Access. Paradox is another popular database product.

III. Reference Tools, Training and Assistance

A. NAIC Resources

1. Sponsored Training

The NAIC provides a variety of training opportunities and educational events which may prove beneficial to examiners. Available training includes classes for Introductory ACL, Introductory Market Conduct ACL, Advanced ACL, and TeamMate. In addition, instruction for NAIC systems is available as well as regularly scheduled events such as the E-Regulation Conference.

2. Help Desk

The NAIC Help Desk is available to assist regulators as needed. Their phone number is (816) 783-8500.

3. ExecuTrain Virtual Campus

ExecuTrain Virtual Campus provides training for various software packages through the Internet. The courses are interactive and allow individuals to learn at their own pace.

B. Other Resources

1. StateNet

This web site has information about the NAIC, direct links to many of its applications, calendar of events, training information, discussion forums and the committee activities. This web site is intended for NAIC staff members and State Department of Insurance Employees only. This site is confidential and requires an I.D. and password that may be obtained for State Users through their DP Coordinator. The URL for this site is: http://www.naic.org/state/. If you already have an I-SITE Log-in ID and password, you can get directly into StateNet from the I-SITE Log-in page. The two available I-SITE locations are http://i-site-state.naic.org/ and http://i-site.naic.org/.

2. Internet

The Internet has a wealth of information related to the insurance industry. SEC reports are available for publicly traded companies. Many companies as well as insurance departments and other regulatory bodies have their own web sites. State web sites may contain information such as state insurance codes, regulatory orders and bulletins, examination procedures and reports, complaints and other publicly available information about companies doing business in the state.

PART 2—
SPECIFIC RISK ANALYSIS WORKPAPERS

TABLE OF CONTENTS

PART 2 — SPECIFIC RISK ANALYSIS WORKPAPERS

SPECIFIC RISK ANALYSIS

This summary was added to this *Handbook* to clarify and provide additional guidance for completing the revised Specific Risk Analysis (SRA) workpapers. The revised workpapers contain a new format as well as additional examination objectives, internal control questions and examination procedures. Since it is only a summary, Part 1 of the *Handbook* as well as Part 3 on sampling and Part 4 on reinsurance should be referenced for more specific guidance.

INTRODUCTION

Effective July 1, 1997, the new risk-based examination approach, as contained in this *Handbook*, was required by the NAIC for accreditation. The central objective of the risk-based approach is to focus examination resources on those high-risk areas of a company's operations and lessen resources on those areas that generally pose little or no risk. This is accomplished primarily through completing the SRA process.

Initial Steps in the Planning Phase

The planning phase of the examination lays the foundation for determining the nature and extent of examination procedures and provides the examination team with a guide to follow throughout the examination. Therefore, sufficient time and resources should be allocated to the planning phase of the examination.

There are a number of steps that must be completed during the planning phase. These steps are documented in Exhibit A – Examination Planning Procedures Checklist. The main steps are to: gather necessary planning information; obtain an understanding of the company's business; identify significant examination issues; meet with designated insurance department personnel; meet with company representatives including internal auditors; perform preliminary analytical review procedures; assess the effects of the external environmental conditions; set preliminary materiality levels; meet with the independent auditors; meet with independent actuaries; assess the control environment; perform the SRA process; prepare time budget and complete the examination planning memorandum.

The degree of work required for each of these steps will depend on the risk profile and organizational structure of the company being examined, the perceived financial condition of the company and the examiner's knowledge of the company and its business. When evaluating the company, it may be decided that performing one or more of the above steps does not improve the efficiency and effectiveness of the examination. Therefore, the examiner-in-charge should always use professional judgment when determining the extent of planning and use of the SRA approach. In addition, these steps are presented in Exhibit A in a logical order for completion, however, circumstances may arise that requires the steps to be completed in a different sequence.

Completion of the SRAs

Once a thorough understanding of the company and its business has been obtained, preliminary materiality levels have been established and a general understanding of the internal control environment (See Exhibit B – Examination Planning Questionnaire & Exhibit C – Evaluation of Controls in Information Systems (IS) Questionnaire) has been attained, the examiner may begin completing the SRAs.

The examiner should determine which cycles are significant based in terms of major transaction cycles and should also determine the material accounts within those cycles. With few exceptions, the premium, investment and loss/benefit cycles will be material to the ongoing solvency of the company and therefore considered significant. For individual annual statement balances, materiality is evaluated against tolerable error (see Planning the Examination in Part 1 of this *Handbook*). If the account is determined to be immaterial, the examiner should consider performing minimal procedures to detect inappropriate statutory accounting treatment, errors and regulatory violations.

The first step in completing the SRAs is to review the examination objectives and the related financial statement assertion(s) and modify where appropriate. There are eight financial statement assertions, and they are as follows: accuracy, completeness, compliance, cutoff, existence, obligation and ownership, valuation and presentation and disclosure. Financial statement assertions are representations by management which include: account balances, transaction classes and disclosure components of annual statements. The examiner should consider that while examination objectives and related financial statement assertion(s) remain constant from company to company they are not equally relevant to a given company and cycle. Therefore, adjustments may need to be made to the examination objectives before proceeding to the next step.

Next, the examiner should identify and assess the inherent risks for each cycle, regardless of whether specific control reliance is contemplated for a given examination objective. Inherent risk is the susceptibility of an annual statement balance to material misstatement before considering related internal controls. The examiner assesses inherent risks to identify potential sources of material financial statement misstatements and to assist in the nature and extent of examination procedures. The inherent risks should be documented within the SRA workpapers.

The examiner should also consider the impact of industry and economic conditions on the operations of the company and particular areas of the company's financial statements. Such external environmental conditions should be documented within the SRA workpapers if relevant and material to the examination plan.

Performing a detailed analytical review is also a component of the SRA process. This review is directed toward specific annual statement balances. The review is primarily performed to obtain a comfort level concerning the annual statement account balances in view of the examiner's understanding of the company's operations and evaluation of the accounting system. The examiner should use judgment when selecting the accounts for analytical review. Based upon the results, the examiner should identify balances or areas that may require additional emphasis or where procedures can be limited. Analytical review procedures and conclusions should be documented in the SRA workpapers.

Central to the SRA process is the evaluation of a company's internal controls over significant transaction cycles. The internal control questionnaires are part of all SRA workpapers to help facilitate the examiner's review and assessment of control risk. The questionnaires may be completed by company personnel or examination staff. When company personnel are utilized, greater care should be taken by the examiner to ensure the results are accurate. The internal control questions included in the questionnaire are marked with control objectives. A company's control structure should address four primary control objectives: authorization, completeness, accuracy and asset protection. The control objectives assist the examiner in determining the strength of the internal control as well as any risks that are not addressed by the control procedure.

Once the questionnaire is complete, the examiner should evaluate the responses to the internal control questions and assess the level of control risk and the intended degree of reliance. If control risk is assessed as less than high for a particular examination objective, then those controls must be tested. The controls should be tested to determine whether the procedure is operating as expected, applied throughout the entire period of reliance, performed on a timely basis, and encompasses all transactions and identifying errors. The types of testing procedure methods include inquiry, inspection, observation and reperformance. Part 3 of this *Handbook* provides specific guidance for control testing and audit sampling. To adequately document the control testing process, the examiner should indicate on the SRA his or her initials, workpaper reference and any comments regarding the results of the control procedure. In addition, the amount of reliance (i.e., Low, Medium or High) should be documented. The examiner may not assess risk at less than high on the basis of controls without performing control testwork. Based upon the testing results, the examiner should determine whether the preliminary assessment of control risk is confirmed or needs to be revised. The SRA workpapers have been revised to include an "Overall Risk Assessment" which enables the examiner to fully document the final risk assessment for each annual statement line item.

After control procedures are identified and tested and the risk assessment is completed, the examiner-in-charge should then decide what substantive examination procedures will be performed. By this point in the planning phase, the examiner should have a good understanding of the company and know which areas will be emphasized. The first step is to decide whether substantive testing may be reduced based upon their reliance on controls. For example, if the company has strong controls over bonds in the area of completeness, then the examiner should use professional judgment when evaluating the completeness examination procedures for bonds to determine which substantive procedures should be reduced. The examination procedures contained herein are also divided by examination objectives to help with this process. The examiner should modify any of the existing procedures or develop additional procedures based on professional judgment and specific knowledge of the company.

SECTION A — PREMIUM CYCLE: LIFE

Listed below are the corresponding Annual Statement line items that are related to the procedures contained in this Premium Specific Risk Analysis:

Annual Statement Blank Line Items

Life Insurance Premiums and Annuity Considerations Deferred and Uncollected on In Force Business (Less Premiums on Reinsurance Ceded and Less Loading)
Accident and Health Premiums Due and Unpaid
Amounts Receivable Relating to Uninsured Accident and Health Plans
Amounts Due From Agents
Detail of Write-Ins (Accrued Additional Retrospective Premiums)
Premiums and Annuity Considerations for Life and Accident and Health Contracts Received in Advance Less Discount; Including Accident and Health Premiums
Contract Liabilities Not Included Elsewhere – Provision for Experience Rating Refunds, Including Accident and Health Experience Rating Refunds
Commissions to Agents Due or Accrued – Life and Annuity Contracts, Accident and Health, and Deposit-Type Contract Funds
Amounts Held for Agents' Account, Including Agents' Credit Balances
Remittances and Items Not Allocated
Liability for Amounts Held Under Uninsured Accident and Health Plans
Detail of Write-Ins (Rate Credits to Group Policyholders)

Relevant SSAP's Include:

#6, Uncollected Premium Balances, Bills Receivable for Premiums, and Amounts Due from Agents and Brokers
#18, Transfers and Servicing of Financial Assets and Extinguishments of Liabilities
#42, Sale of Premium Receivables
#47, Uninsured Plans
#51, Life Contracts
#54, Individual and Group Accident and Health Contracts
#66, Retrospectively Rated Contracts
#67, Other Liabilities
#71, Policy Acquisition Costs and Commissions

SPECIFIC RISK ANALYSIS WORKPAPERS

Risk Analysis Prepared By/Date ______________________________

Planning Exam Analysis Prepared By/Date ______________________________

Reviewed By/Date ______________________________

EXAMINATION OBJECTIVES:

1. Insurance contracts and related premiums were properly executed, authorized, and in-force. (Existence and Compliance)

2. Premiums and commissions are calculated, valued, and recorded accurately and properly reflected in the financial statements. (Valuation, Compliance, Accuracy, Completeness and Cutoff)

3. The company properly records the recognition of premiums in accordance with contract guidelines and the NAIC *Accounting Practices and Procedures Manual.* (Ownership and Obligation)

4. The premiums are presented in accordance with the NAIC *Annual Statement Instructions* and the NAIC *Accounting Practices and Procedures Manual.* (Presentation and Disclosure)

INHERENT RISKS

____

____

____

____

INTERNAL AND EXTERNAL ENVIRONMENTAL CONDITIONS/FACTORS

____

____

____

____

RESULTS OF DETAIL ANALYTICAL REVIEW PROCEDURES

____

____

____

____

CONTROL RISK — PREMIUM CYCLE: LIFE

This questionnaire is designed to assist the examiner in assessing control risk for life premium cycles. Part 1, Section III and Part 3 of this *Handbook* provide guidance in consideration of an insurer's internal control structure for use when designing substantive examination procedures.

This questionnaire includes examples of internal control procedures and policies that are commonly utilized by insurers to achieve internal control objectives. For each control procedure listed below, indicate by placing a check mark in the yes or no box whether or not the insurer employs such a procedure, or other similar practice (include a description of the similar procedure). To the extent the control procedure is not applicable, indicate N/A. If other relevant control procedures are in place, list them in the space that follows. Control procedures that are tested by the examiner should be documented by including the workpaper reference in the comment section and the examiner's initials in the reliance column.

For each individual control procedure there is a control objective listed that satisfies the procedure.

If the examiner initially assesses control risk as low or medium for a particular account balance, then those controls must be tested. The controls should be tested to determine whether the procedure is operating as expected, applied throughout the entire period of reliance, performed on a timely basis, encompassing all transactions and identifying errors. Some examples of testing procedures are inquiry, observation, reperformance and examination of documents. The level of reliance, if any, should be indicated in the applicable column along with any comments the examiner may have regarding the procedure.

Based upon the testing results, the examiner should determine whether the preliminary control risk assessment is confirmed or should be revised.

CONTROL OBJECTIVES

Authorization (AU) – All transactions recorded were reviewed and approved by designated personnel.

Completeness (CO) – All transactions that occurred are initially entered into the accounting records, accepted for processing and generated data files and reports reflect that all transactions have occurred.

Accuracy (AC) – Transactions are initially recorded correctly, timely and accurately.

Asset Protection (AP) – Adequate safeguards over access to and use of assets and records, including the appropriate segregation of duties among company personnel.

	Control Obj.	Y	N	Work Paper Ref.	Reliance
General Control Procedures					
The examiner should determine the amount of documentation necessary for each control procedure. If the examiner intends to place substantial reliance on the established controls, the examiner should explain the control procedure in a workpaper and document the individual responsible for supervising the control activity as well as the frequency of the control activity.					
1. Are policy applications checked independently for compliance with company underwriting standards?	AC				
2. Does management periodically review the underwriting performance of agents, brokers and sales personnel?	AC				
3. Does the company have procedures in place that comply with state requirements over the licensing and appointing of agents?	AC				
4. Does management periodically evaluate the financial condition of outside agents or others (MGAs) who handle the premiums?	AC				
5. Are underwriting standards approved by management on a current basis?	AU				
6. Are premium and commission discrepancy write-offs reviewed and approved independently?	AU				
7. Are policy term, effective/expiration dates, and lines of insurance tested? Are exceptions independently investigated?	AC				
8. Are renewal listings reconciled and/or matched to billing, cancellation and expiration listings?	AC				
9. Are policy forms approved, pre-numbered and sequence of policies issued verified independently?	AC AP				
10. Are premium adjustments resulting from endorsements, cancellations and audits checked independently for accuracy?	AC AU				

		Control Obj.	Y	N	Work Paper Ref.	Reliance
11.	Is there a procedure for approval of deletions other than expirations?	AC AU				
12.	Are premium billings and rate determinations periodically tested for accuracy and agreement with rate books, contracts or other supporting documentation?	AC				
13.	Are commission statements periodically tested for accuracy and agreement with commission schedules?	AC				
14.	Is the accuracy of agents' balances/premiums receivable aging independently checked?	AC				
15.	Is the detail of agents' balances/premiums receivable records and the premiums written per premium register reconciled to general ledger control accounts regularly?	AC CO				
16.	Does someone independent of the actual transaction function review the recorded receivable transactions?	AU AP				
17.	Are follow-ups conducted for past due accounts and are these accounts independently monitored for potential write-offs?	CO				
18.	Are all billing records reconciled to premium registers?	AC CO				
19.	Do procedures exist that restrict access of in-force files to unauthorized personnel?	AU AP				
20.	Are procedures to review suspense accounts established to ensure they are properly cleared?	AC				

OTHER KEY CONTROLS EXISTING FOR THIS CONTROL OBJECTIVE:

SUMMARY EVALUATION OF CONTROL RISK:

EVALUATION OF INDEPENDENT CPA'S WORK FOR THIS EXAMINATION (CPA REVIEW CHECKLIST):

OVERALL RISK ASSESSMENT

Balance Sheet Evaluation of the Likelihood of a Material Adjustment to Surplus:

The evaluation of the likelihood of a material adjustment to surplus should be based on the following criteria:

- Inherent Risk
- Internal & External Environmental Factors
- Control Risk
- Materiality Consideration

The examiner should rate each item as to the likelihood of a material misstatement. All items are assumed as "High" prior to any examiner evaluation. A "High" assessment requires the examiner to perform substantive examination procedures over that account area. A lower assessment allows the examiner to perform analytical or fewer substantive procedures to satisfy the examination requirements. If an assessment other than "High" is selected for any of the accounts, the examiner needs to document the basis for the assessment. If the assessment is based on control testwork, the documentation should include results of control procedures and related workpaper references.

1) "Life Insurance Premiums and Annuity Considerations Deferred and Uncollected on In Force Business (Less Premiums on Reinsurance Ceded and Less Loading)"

____________ High ____________ Medium ___________Low

Basis for Assessment:

____

____

____

2) "Accident and Health Premiums Due and Unpaid"

____________ High ____________ Medium ___________Low

Basis for Assessment:

____

____

____

3) "Amounts Receivable Relating to Uninsured Accident and Health Plans"

___________ High ___________ Medium ___________ Low

Basis for Assessment:

____

____

____

4) "Amounts Due From Agents"

___________ High ___________Medium ___________ Low

Basis for Assessment:

____

____

____

5) "Detail of Write-Ins (Accrued Additional Retrospective Premiums)"

___________ High ___________ Medium ___________ Low

Basis for Assessment:

____

____

____

6) "Premiums and Annuity Considerations for Life and Accident and Health Contracts Received in Advance Less Discount; Including Accident and Health Premiums"

___________ High ___________ Medium ___________ Low

Basis for Assessment:

____

____

____

7) "Contract Liabilities Not Included Elsewhere – Provision for Experience Rating Refunds, Including Accident and Health Experience Rating Refunds"

____________ High ____________ Medium ___________ Low

Basis for Assessment:

____

____

____

8) "Commissions to Agents Due or Accrued – Life and Annuity Contracts, Accident and Health, and Deposit-Type Contract Funds"

____________ High ____________ Medium ___________ Low

Basis for Assessment:

____

____

____

9) "Amounts Held for Agents' Account, Including Agents' Credit Balances"

____________ High ____________ Medium ___________ Low

Basis for Assessment:

____

____

____

10) "Remittances and Items Not Allocated"

____________ High ____________ Medium ___________ Low

Basis for Assessment:

____

____

____

11) "Liability for Amounts Held Under Uninsured Accident and Health Plans"

____________ High ____________ Medium ___________ Low

Basis for Assessment:

---

12) "Detail of Write-Ins (Rate Credits to Group Policyholders)"

____________ High ____________ Medium ___________ Low

Basis for Assessment:

PRELIMINARY EXAMINATION APPROACH — PREMIUM CYCLE: LIFE

Listed below are the corresponding Annual Statement line items that are related to the procedures contained in this Premium Specific Risk Analysis:

Life Insurance Premiums and Annuity Considerations Deferred and Uncollected on In Force Business (Less Premiums on Reinsurance Ceded and Less Loading)
Accident and Health Premiums Due and Unpaid
Amounts Receivable Relating to Uninsured Accident and Health Plans
Amounts Due From Agents
Detail of Write-Ins (Accrued Additional Retrospective Premiums)
Premiums and Annuity Considerations for Life and Accident and Health Contracts Received in Advance Less Discount; Including Accident and Health Premiums
Contract Liabilities Not Included Elsewhere – Provision for Experience Rating Refunds, Including Accident and Health Experience Rating Refunds
Commissions to Agents Due or Accrued – Life and Annuity Contracts, Accident and Health, and Deposit-Type Contract Funds
Amounts Held for Agents' Account, Including Agents' Credit Balances
Remittances and Items Not Allocated
Liability for Amounts Held Under Uninsured Accident and Health Plans
Detail of Write-Ins (Rate Credits to Group Policyholders)

The actual examination procedures selected to be performed are a matter of considerable judgment by the examiner. The following "Examination Program" includes examples of procedures commonly used.

To the extent that the examiner judgmentally determines whether it is appropriate to use the following procedures, that selection can be documented by checking the space next to such procedure, with modifications noted in the margin. The examiner may determine that alternative or additional procedures are required. If so, those procedures can be added on a supplemental sheet. The examiner performing the procedure should indicate satisfactory completion by initialing and dating in the space provided, and referencing the workpapers where the procedures and findings are documented.

The examiner may choose to apply the examination procedures to less than 100% of the items comprising an account balance. Guidance for audit sampling and control and substantive procedures can be found in Part 3 of the NAIC *Financial Condition Examiners Handbook.*

After each examination procedure, the examination objective that the procedure satisfies is indicated. The examination objectives are accuracy, completeness, compliance, cutoff, existence, obligation and ownership, valuation and presentation and disclosure.

EXAMINATION OBJECTIVES

Accuracy (AC) – Recorded transactions and account balances are mathematically accurate, are based on correct amounts and have been classified into the correct account.

Completeness (CO) – All transactions and account balances that should be recorded in the annual financial statement were recorded.

Compliance (CM) – Business transactions and affairs have been conducted in accordance with state insurance codes, other state laws or department directives.

Cutoff (CT) – All transactions are recorded in the correct accounting period.

Existence (EX) – Recorded transactions occurred and are not fictitious and recorded assets and liabilities existed as of the balance sheet date.

Obligation (OB) and Ownership (OW) – Recorded liabilities are obligations of the company and recorded assets are the rights of the company at the balance sheet date.

Valuation (VA) – Assets and liabilities are valued in accordance with state statute and NAIC accounting guidance.

Presentation and Disclosure (PD) – The elements of the Annual Statement are properly classified and all disclosures are accurately included in the Annual Statement.

Procedure	Exam Obj.	Completion Date	Examiner	Work Paper Ref.
EXAMINATION PROCEDURES				
<u>General Procedures</u>				
1. Through discussions with management and review of the company's overall insurance transactions, obtain an understanding of the company's policy for premiums and annuity considerations. Document this understanding in a narrative and include in the workpapers. This narrative should include:	CM OB/OW			
a. Types of insurance contracts in-force at the company;	CM OB/OW			
b. Process of recording and recognizing premiums: Life: **SSAP No. 51, paragraphs 2-12**; Accident and Health: **SSAP No. 54, paragraphs 2-7**;	CM OB/OW			
c. Method for calculating deferred premiums or unearned premium reserve (Mean Reserve Method or Mid-Terminal Reserve Method), **SSAP No. 51, paragraphs 21-24**; and	CM VA			
d. Premium due dates (Original and deposit premiums, Endorsement premiums, Installment premiums, and Audit premiums and retrospective premiums, **SSAP No. 6, paragraph 7**).	CM			
2. Reconcile the database to applicable general ledger accounts or Annual Statement reports by query of database components such as:	CO AC EX			
a. Premium income; and	CO AC EX			
b. Aging elements (Due date for premium balances should be determined in accordance with **SSAP No. 6, paragraph 7**).	CO AC EX			

	Exam Obj.	Completion Date	Examiner	Work Paper Ref.
3. Verify and validate individual determinants by tracing a sample of the following attributes from the policy application to the database and from the database to the policy application:	CO AC EX			
a. Effective date;	CO AC EX			
b. Policy type;	CO AC EX			
c. Policy or contract number;	CO AC EX			
d. Premium amount and premium mode; and	CO AC EX			
e. Issue age.	CO AC EX			
4. Scan the database to review for internal inconsistencies such as:	CO AC EX			
a. Missing or negative premium amounts;	CO AC EX			
b. Unusually small or large amounts; and	CO AC EX			
c. Contracts misclassified by type (e.g., annuity versus deposit), effective date, term and expiration date.	CO AC EX			
5. Review audits and evaluations by government bodies concerning the entity.	CO AC EX			
6. Determine the date of the last Quality of Care/Market Conduct examination and review the report for applicable matters.	CO AC EX			

	Exam Obj.	Completion Date	Examiner	Work Paper Ref.
7. For business subject to redetermination (e.g., Federal Groups, Medicare), review the recent premium audit available from the following:	CO AC EX			
a. Office of Personnel Management;	CO AC EX			
b. Centers for Medicare & Medicaid Services (CMS); and	CO AC EX			
c. Other Federal or state agencies.	CO AC EX			
8. Determine the status of any ongoing audits or reviews.	CO AC EX			
9. Verify that accounting for contracts subject to redetermination by other entities follows the guidelines in **SSAP No. 54, paragraphs 26-31**.	CO AC EX			
10. Review a sample of reports the company produces from the database to ensure they are logical.	CO AC EX			
a. Verify that elements contained in the reports are available from the database(s).	CO AC EX			
b. Trace a sample of the report elements from the source documents to the database.	CO AC EX			
11. Review the method of marketing and, if applicable, the agency sales force makeup.	CM			
a. Review managing general agent, third party administrator and general agency agreements to insure inclusion to required regulatory clauses and that regulatory filings were made.	CM			

	Exam Obj.	Completion Date	Examiner	Work Paper Ref.
b. Examine the documentation relating to the method used to monitor its outside representatives to ensure their compliance with contractual and regulatory provisions.	CM			
<u>**Life Insurance Premiums and Annuity Considerations Deferred and Uncollected on In Force Business (Less Premiums on Reinsurance and Less Loading)**</u>				
1. Obtain the detail of the life insurance premiums and annuity considerations deferred and uncollected on in-force business. Agree this detail to the company's general ledger and Annual Statement.	AC EX			
2. Verify that the company uses the Mean Reserve Method in calculating policy reserves in accordance with **SSAP No. 51, paragraph 21-23**. (Note: The Mid-Terminal Method as described in **SSAP No. 51, paragraph 24** utilizes an unearned premium reserve.)	AC EX			
3. Verify that the deferred premiums are properly calculated in accordance with **SSAP No. 51, paragraph 23**. Select a sample of contracts included in the calculation and perform procedures to verify the information utilized in the calculation.	AC VA			
a. Gross Premium – Agree to contract terms.	AC			
b. Policy Execution Date – Review the contract terms to verify that the policy was in-force.	AC			
c. Modal Premium Due Date and Policy Anniversary Date – Agree to contract terms.	AC			
d. Deferred Collected Premiums – Agree to policyholder remittances.	AC			

	Exam Obj.	Completion Date	Examiner	Work Paper Ref.
e. Loading – Loading is the difference between gross and net premiums as indicated in **SSAP No. 51, paragraph 4**. Verify that the net premium has been calculated in accordance with **SSAP No. 51, paragraph 3**.	AC VA			
4. Verify that premiums related to reinsurance are properly excluded.	CM			
5. Verify that the life insurance premiums and annuity considerations deferred and uncollected on in-force business is properly included as an admitted asset in accordance with **SSAP No. 51, paragraph 23**.	CM			
6. Verify that all required disclosures in accordance with **SSAP No. 51, paragraphs 39 and 40** have been properly made.	PD			
<u>Accident and Health Premiums Due and Unpaid</u>				
1. Obtain an aging detail of the accident and health premiums due and unpaid. Agree this detail to the company's general ledger and Annual Statement.	AC EX			
2. Perform procedures to ascertain the existence and valuation of these receivables.	EX VA			
a. Perform subsequent receipt testwork.	EX VA			
b. Confirm significant balances directly.	EX VA			
3. Verify that the due date for aging was determined in accordance with **SSAP No. 6, paragraphs 7 and 8**. For original and deposit premiums the due date is the effective date of the underlying contract, not the agent/reporting entity contractual relationship.	AC EX VA			
4. Review the assets to determine whether they should be classified as non-admitted in accordance with **SSAP No. 6, paragraphs 9 and 11**.	VA PD			

	Exam Obj.	Completion Date	Examiner	Work Paper Ref.
a. Verify that amounts classified as non-admitted collected subsequent to the date of the statutory financial statements are not used to adjust the non-admitted assets otherwise calculated.	VA			
5. Review the admitted assets for collectibility. If an amount due is considered uncollectible, the amount should be written off and charged to income in accordance with **SSAP No. 6, paragraph 10**.	VA			
a. Perform procedures to identify those premium receivables collected subsequent to year-end in order to ascertain the collectiblilty of the premium receivables.	VA			
6. Inquire of the company's management to determine whether any agent's balances or uncollected premiums have been transferred or sold (factored) with or without recourse.	EX			
a. For those receivables that have been transferred or sold, verify that the company has properly recorded the transaction and removed the receivable in accordance with **SSAP No. 42, paragraphs 3-7**.	AC VA			
Amounts Receivable Relating to Uninsured Accident and Health Plans				
1. Obtain an aging detail of the accounts receivable relating to uninsured accident and health plans. Agree this detail to the company's general ledger and Annual Statement.	AC EX			

	Exam Obj.	Completion Date	Examiner	Work Paper Ref.
2. Determine whether the plans are properly classified according to contract type, as described in **SSAP No. 47, paragraphs 2-4**. Uninsured plans include Administrative Services Only (ASO) plans, Administrative Services Contracts (ASC), and Federal, state or other governmental funded programs where there is no underwriting risk. Partially insured or combination plans should be accounted for as two plans, an insured plan and an uninsured plan.	AC EX			
3. Review the account and verify that the balance is consistent with the items permitted under **SSAP No. 47, paragraph 8**. Permitted items include claims and other costs by the administrator on behalf of the third party at risk and/or fees related to the services provided by the administrator. Verify that receivables are not recorded for unpaid claims.	AC EX			
4. Perform procedures to ascertain the existence and valuation of these receivables.	EX VA			
a. Perform subsequent receipt testwork.	EX VA			
b. Confirm receivables directly.	EX VA			
5. Evaluate the account receivables to determine any non-admitted amounts in accordance with **SSAP No. 47, paragraphs 9 and 10**:	VA			
a. Uncollected uninsured plan receivables over ninety days, excluding Medicare and similar government plans, due shall be accounted for as a non-admitted asset;	VA			
b. Other amounts that are deemed probable for uncollectibility should be written off and charged to operations.	VA			
6. Verify that disclosures required by **SSAP No. 47, paragraphs 12 and 13** have been properly made.	PD			

	Exam Obj.	Completion Date	Examiner	Work Paper Ref.
<u>Amounts Due From Agents</u>				
1. Obtain an aging detail of the amounts due from agents and agree it to the company's general ledger and Annual Statement.	AC EX			
2. Perform procedures to ascertain the existence and valuation of these amounts due:	EX VA			
a. Test the agents' balances due by verifying the amounts due with contract terms or other supporting documentation;	EX VA			
b. Perform subsequent receipt procedures; and	EX VA			
c. Confirm the amount due directly with the agent.	EX VA			
3. Verify that the assets are properly recorded as admitted unless specifically non-admitted in accordance with **SSAP No. 6, paragraph 6**:	VA PD			
a. Amounts are in the form of unsecured loans or advances;	VA PD			
b. Contractual terms for repayment are through application of future renewal commissions and/or other credits; and	VA PD			
c. Terms of repayment do not provide readily available cash for the satisfaction of policyholder liabilities.	VA PD			
4. Determine if any wash transactions as described in **SSAP No. 6, paragraphs 12 and 13** exist and if they have been properly recorded.	VA			
5. Review the aging detail to determine any amounts due that are over 90 days past due. Verify that those amounts due are non-admitted in accordance with **SSAP No. 6, paragraph 9**.	VA			

	Exam Obj.	Completion Date	Examiner	Work Paper Ref.
a. Verify that amounts classified as non-admitted assets collected subsequent to the date of the statutory financial statements are not used to adjust the non-admitted asset in accordance with **SSAP No. 6, paragraph 11**.	VA			
6. Review the remaining admitted assets for collectibility. If an amount due is considered uncollectible, the amount should be written off and charged to income in accordance with **SSAP No. 6, paragraph 10**.	VA			
a. Perform procedures to identify those amounts due collected subsequent to year-end in order to ascertain the collectibility of the amounts due.	VA			
7. Inquire of the company's management to determine whether any amounts due from agents have been transferred or sold (factored) with or without recourse.	EX			
a. For those amounts due that have been transferred or sold, verify that the company has properly recorded the transfer and removed the receivable in accordance with **SSAP No. 18, paragraphs 3-5 and 34-35**.	AC VA			
<u>Detail of Write-Ins (Accrued Additional Retrospective Premiums)</u>				
1. Obtain the detail of the accrued additional retrospective premiums. Agree the detail to the company's general ledger and Annual Statement.	AC EX			
2. Select a sample of contracts included on the accrued additional retrospective detail. Verify that the contract specifications allow for accrued additional retrospective premiums.	EX			

	Exam Obj.	Completion Date	Examiner	Work Paper Ref.
3. Review the calculation for the accrued additional retrospective premiums and verify that the methodology utilized to determine the accrued additional retrospective premium is in accordance with **SSAP No. 66, paragraph 6** and is properly disclosed in accordance with **SSAP No. 66, paragraph 12**.	AC VA			
4. Verify that the company has properly recorded the accrued additional retrospective premium as a write-in for invested assets with a corresponding entry to premiums in accordance with **SSAP No. 66, paragraph 8**.	PD			
5. For those retrospective premiums that have been billed, verify that those premiums greater than 90 days past due are properly non-admitted in accordance with **SSAP No. 66, paragraph 10**.	VA			
6. Verify that any uncollectible additional accrued retrospective premiums have been properly written off in accordance with **SSAP No. 66, paragraph 11**.	VA			
<u>Premium and Annuity Considerations for Life and Accident and Health Contracts Received in Advance Less Discount, Including Accident and Health Premiums</u>				
1. Obtain the detail of the premium and annuity considerations for life and health contracts received in advance. Agree this schedule to the company's general ledger and Annual Statement.	AC EX			
2. Compare the payment remittance for advance premiums to the detail noting that the full amount of the premium paid is included in the advance premiums. Investigate any discrepancies.	AC VA			
3. Review the contract specifications and compare the premium payment remittance to the insurance contract premium terms. Identify whether discounts are provided for advance payments in accordance with **SSAP No. 51, paragraph 25**.	AC EX VA			

	Exam Obj.	Completion Date	Examiner	Work Paper Ref.
a. Through discussions with management, obtain an understanding of the insurance company's policies with regards to granting discounts for advance premiums.	AC VA OB/OW			
b. Perform procedures to recalculate the permitted discount in accordance with the specific policy terms.	AC VA			
c. Verify that advance premium discounts are properly charged to interest from the date of the payment to the premium due date in accordance with **SSAP No. 51, paragraph 25**.	AC VA PD			
4. Verify that the gross advance premium, less any discount, is reported as a liability in the financial statements and is not considered premium income until due in accordance with **SSAP No. 51, paragraph 25**.	AC VA PD			
5. Perform procedures to verify that the advance premiums are properly recorded.	AC VA CO			
a. Select a sample of premium remittances and determine the policy year to which they apply. For those premiums that are due on or after the next policy anniversary date, verify that they are included on the advance premium detail.	AC VA CO			
b. Obtain the detail of 'new' policies with effective dates subsequent to year-end. Select a sample and trace the contract to the premium remittance. Verify that the remittance was received subsequent to year-end or properly included in the advance premium detail.	AC VA CO			

	Exam Obj.	Completion Date	Examiner	Work Paper Ref.
Contract Liabilities Not Included Elsewhere – Provision for Experience Rating Refunds, Including Accident and Health Experience Rating Refunds				
1. Obtain the detail of the provision for experience rating refunds. Agree this detail to the company's general ledger and Annual Statement.	AC EX			
2. Select a sample of contracts included on the experience rating refund detail. Verify that the contract specifications allow for retrospective rating.	AC EX			
3. Review the calculation for the experience rating refunds and verify that the methodology utilized to determine the accrued retrospective premium is in accordance with **SSAP No. 66, paragraph 6** and is properly disclosed in accordance with **SSAP No. 66, paragraph 12**.	AC VA			
4. Perform a search for unrecorded experience rating refunds. Obtain the detail of the experience rating refunds issued after year-end. Compare this detail to the year-end liability detail. Identify and investigate any refunds issued subsequent to year-end that were excluded from the detail or significant discrepancies.	CO EX VA			
5. In accordance with other examination procedures performed, identify any experience rating refunds that have not been properly recorded.	CO EX VA			
6. Verify that the company has properly recorded the accrued retrospective premium as an experience rating refund liability with a corresponding entry to premiums in accordance with **SSAP No. 66, paragraph 8**.	PD			

	Exam Obj.	Completion Date	Examiner	Work Paper Ref.
Commissions to Agents Due or Accrued – Life and Annuity Contracts, Accident and Health, and Deposit-Type Contract Funds				
1. Obtain the detail of the commissions to agents and override commissions to general agents due or accrued. Agree this detail to the company's general ledger and Annual Statement.	AC EX			
2. From the detail select a sample and trace the payable to a commission agreement. Perform procedures to verify the accuracy of this information:	AC VA			
a. Recalculate the commission payable based on the commission agreement specifications (**SSAP No. 71, paragraph 3**); and	VA			
b. Review the commissions paid subsequent to year-end. Verify that those commissions were properly valued and included on the year-end liability. Investigate any subsequent payments not included on the detail or payments, which were undervalued at year-end.	VA CO			
Amounts Held for Agents' Account, Including Agents' Credit Balances				
1. Obtain the detail of the amounts held for agents' account and agents' credit balances. Agree this detail to the company's general ledger and Annual Statement.	AC EX			
2. Through discussion with management, obtain an understanding of the items that are included in this account. Verify that commissions due to agents are excluded from this account and properly included within Commissions to Agents Due or Accrued.	AC			
3. Perform procedures to verify the accuracy and completeness of this account.	AC CO			

	Exam Obj.	Completion Date	Examiner	Work Paper Ref.
a. Identify any agents excluded from the current year detail, which were included on the prior year detail. Verify that the amounts held and/or credit balances have been properly returned or applied to the agents account.	AC CO			
b. Confirm directly with agents the amounts held or credit balances with the company.	CO			
Remittances and Items Not Allocated				
1. Obtain the detail of the remittances and items not allocated and agree it to the company's general ledger and Annual Statement.	AC EX			
2. Review the detail provided by the company and identify the items included in this detail as specified in **SSAP No. 67, paragraph 9**:	EX			
a. Premium payments received with the application for policies which have not yet been issued;	EX			
b. Premium payments in an amount different than the amount billed by the reporting entity; and	EX			
c. Unidentified cash receipts.	EX			
3. Verify that the company is clearing and reconciling this account in a timely manner.	AC EX			
Liability for Amounts Held Under Uninsured Accident and Health Plans				
1. Obtain the detail of the liability for amounts held under uninsured accident and health plans. Agree this detail to the company's general ledger and Annual Statement.	AC EX			
2. Verify that the liability has been established for funds held by an administrator for the benefit of an uninsured plan or for funds that may be owed by the administrator in connection with the administration of an uninsured plan in accordance with **SSAP No. 47, paragraph 11**.	AC EX CO VA			

Procedure	Exam Obj.	Completion Date	Examiner	Work Paper Ref.
a. Obtain the detail of all uninsured plans in-force at the company. Perform procedures to verify that a correlating liability has been established as required in step #2.	AC EX CO			
b. Verify that a liability pertaining to one uninsured plan has not been offset by an asset relating to a different plan in accordance with **SSAP No. 47, paragraph 11**.	AC EX VA			
3. Ascertain that administrators have not recorded aggregate reserves, claim/loss reserves or liabilities (except for Medicare or similarly structures cost based reimbursement) for any other claim costs paid by the administrator on behalf of uninsured plans in accordance with **SSAP No. 47, paragraph 11**.	AC EX			
Detail of Write-Ins (Rate Credits to Group Policyholders)				
1. Obtain the detail of the rate credits to group policyholders. Agree this detail to the company's general ledger and Annual Statement.	AC EX			
2. Review the insurance contract terms and related rate credit calculation to verify the reported liability.	AC EX			
3. Verify significant decreases in the liability by determining whether established insurance contracts have been terminated or undergone contract revision in the current year.	AC			
4. Ascertain that all related rate credits are properly recorded by identifying significant in-force group contracts at the company.	AC CO			

SECTION B — PREMIUM CYCLE: PROPERTY & CASUALTY

Listed below are the corresponding Annual Statement line items that are related to the procedures contained in this Premium Specific Risk Analysis:

Annual Statement Blank Line Items

Agents' Balances or Uncollected Premiums
Bills Receivable, Taken for Premiums
Commissions Payable, Contingent Commissions and Other Similar Charges
Unearned Premiums
Advance Premiums
Dividends Declared and Unpaid - Policyholders
Remittances and Items Not Allocated
Detail of Write-Ins (Premium Deficiency Reserve)

Relevant SSAP's Include:

#6, Uncollected Premium Balances, Bills Receivable for Premiums, and Amounts Due from Agents and Brokers
#18, Transfers and Servicing of Financial Assets and Extinguishments of Liabilities
#42, Sale of Premium Receivables
#53, Property and Casualty Contracts – Premiums
#65, Property and Casualty Contracts
#66, Retrospectively Rated Contracts
#67, Other Liabilities
#71, Policy Acquisition Costs and Commissions

SPECIFIC RISK ANALYSIS WORKPAPERS

Risk Analysis Prepared By/Date ______________________________

Planning Exam Analysis Prepared By/Date ______________________________

Reviewed By/Date ______________________________

EXAMINATION OBJECTIVES:

1. Insurance contracts and related premiums were properly executed, authorized and in-force. (Existence and Compliance)

2. Premiums and commissions are calculated, valued and recorded accurately and properly reflected in the financial statements. (Valuation, Compliance, Accuracy, Completeness and Cutoff)

3. The company properly records the recognition of premiums in accordance with contract guidelines and the NAIC *Accounting Practices and Procedures Manual*. (Ownership and Obligation)

4. The premiums are presented in accordance with the NAIC *Annual Statement Instructions* and the NAIC *Accounting Practices and Procedures Manual*. (Presentation and Disclosure)

INHERENT RISKS

____

____

____

____

INTERNAL AND EXTERNAL ENVIRONMENTAL CONDITIONS/FACTORS

____

____

____

____

RESULTS OF DETAIL ANALYTICAL REVIEW PROCEDURES

____

____

____

____

CONTROL RISK — PREMIUM CYCLE: PROPERTY & CASUALTY

This questionnaire is designed to assist the examiner in assessing control risk for property and casualty premium cycles. Part 1, Section III and Part 3 of this *Handbook* provide guidance in consideration of an insurer's internal control structure for use when designing substantive examination procedures.

This questionnaire includes examples of internal control procedures and policies that are commonly utilized by insurers to achieve internal control objectives. For each control procedure listed below, indicate by placing a check mark in the yes or no box whether or not the insurer employs such a procedure, or other similar practice (include a description of the similar procedure). To the extent the control procedure is not applicable, indicate N/A. If other relevant control procedures are in place, list them in the space that follows. Control procedures that are tested by the examiner should be documented by including the workpaper reference in the comment section and the examiner's initials in the reliance column.

For each individual control procedure there is a control objective listed that satisfies the procedure.

If the examiner initially assesses control risk as low or medium for a particular account balance, then those controls must be tested. The controls should be tested to determine whether the procedure is operating as expected, applied throughout the entire period of reliance, performed on a timely basis, encompassing all transactions and identifying errors. Some examples of testing procedures are inquiry, observation, re-performance and examination of documents. The level of reliance, if any, should be indicated in the applicable column along with any comments the examiner may have regarding the procedure.

Based upon the testing results, the examiner should determine whether the preliminary control risk assessment is confirmed or should be revised.

CONTROL OBJECTIVES

Authorization (AU) – All transactions recorded were reviewed and approved by designated personnel.

Completeness (CO) – All transactions that occurred are initially entered into the accounting records, accepted for processing and generated data files and reports reflect that all transactions have occurred.

Accuracy (AC) – Transactions are initially recorded correctly, timely and accurately.

Asset Protection (AP) – Adequate safeguards over access to and use of assets and records, including the appropriate segregation of duties among company personnel.

	Control Obj.	Y	N	Work Paper Ref.	Reliance
General Control Procedures					
The examiner should determine the amount of documentation necessary for each control procedure. If the examiner intends to place substantial reliance on the established controls, the examiner should explain the control procedure in a workpaper and document the individual responsible for supervising the control activity as well as the frequency of the control activity.					
1. Are policy applications checked independently for compliance with company underwriting standards?	AC				
2. Does management periodically review the underwriting performance of agents, brokers and sales personnel?	AC				
3. Does management periodically evaluate and review the financial condition and controls of outside agents or others (MGAs) who handle the premiums of insurers?	AC				
4. Are underwriting standards approved by management on a regular basis?	AU				
5. Are premium and commission discrepancy write-offs reviewed and approved by someone independent of the function?	AU				
6. Are policy term, effective/expiration dates and lines of insurance verified to contract terms? Are exceptions independently investigated?	AC				
7. Are renewal listings reconciled and/or matched to billing, cancellation and expiration listings?	AC				
8. Are policy forms approved, pre-numbered and sequence of policies issued verified by someone independent of the function?	AC AP				
9. Is access to unused forms and policy application/dailies restricted?	AU AP				

		Control Obj.	Y	N	Work Paper Ref.	Reliance
10.	Are premium adjustments resulting from endorsements, cancellations and audits checked independently for accuracy?	AC AU				
11.	Is there a procedure for approval of deletions other than expirations?	AC AU				
12.	Are premium billings and rate determinations periodically tested for accuracy and agreement with ratebooks, contracts or other supporting documentation?	AC				
13.	Are commission statements periodically tested for accuracy and agreement with commission schedules?	AC				
14.	Is the accuracy of agents' balances/premiums receivable aging independently checked?	AC				
15.	Is the detail of agents' balances/premiums receivable records and the premiums written per premium register reconciled to general ledger control accounts regularly?	AC CO				
16.	Does someone independent of the actual transaction function review the recorded receivable transactions?	AU AP				
17.	Are follow-ups conducted for past due accounts and are these accounts independently monitored for potential write-offs?	CO				
18.	Are all billing records reconciled to premium registers?	AC CO				
19.	Are procedures in place that monitor installment receivables to ensure the remaining installments due are less than applicable unearned premiums?	AC CO				
20.	Do procedures exist that restrict access of in-force files to unauthorized personnel?	AU AP				
21.	Are procedures to review suspense accounts established to ensure they are properly cleared?	AC				

OTHER KEY CONTROLS EXISTING FOR THIS CONTROL OBJECTIVE:

SUMMARY EVALUATION OF CONTROL RISK:

EVALUATION OF INDEPENDENT CPA'S WORK FOR THIS EXAMINATION (CPA REVIEW CHECKLIST):

OVERALL RISK ASSESSMENT

Balance Sheet Evaluation of the Likelihood of a Material Adjustment to Surplus:

The evaluation of the likelihood of a material adjustment to surplus should be based on the following criteria:

- Inherent Risk
- Internal & External Environmental Factors
- Control Risk
- Materiality Consideration

The examiner should rate each item as to the likelihood of a material misstatement. All items are assumed as "High" prior to any examiner evaluation. A "High" assessment requires the examiner to perform substantive examination procedures over that account area. A lower assessment allows the examiner to perform analytical or fewer substantive procedures to satisfy the examination requirements. If an assessment other than "High" is selected for any of the accounts, the examiner needs to document the basis for the assessment. If the assessment is based on control testwork, the documentation should include results of control procedures and related workpaper references.

1) "Agents' Balances or Uncollected Premiums"

__________ High __________ Medium __________ Low

Basis for Assessment:

____

____

____

2) "Bills Receivable, Taken for Premiums"

__________ High __________ Medium __________ Low

Basis for Assessment:

____

____

____

3) "Commissions Payable, Contingent Commissions and Other Similar Charges"

___________ High ___________Medium ___________Low

Basis for Assessment:

____

____

____

4) "Unearned Premiums"

___________ High ___________Medium ___________ Low

Basis for Assessment:

____

____

____

5) "Advance Premiums"

___________ High ___________ Medium ___________ Low

Basis for Assessment:

____

____

____

6) "Dividends Declared and Unpaid - Policyholders"

___________ High ___________ Medium ___________ Low

Basis for Assessment:

____

____

____

7) "Remittances and Items Not Allocated"

___________ High ___________ Medium __________ Low

Basis for Assessment:

____

____

____

8) "Detail of Write-Ins (Premium Deficiency Reserve)"

___________ High ___________ Medium __________ Low

Basis for Assessment:

____

____

____

PRELIMINARY EXAMINATION APPROACH — PREMIUM CYCLE: PROPERTY & CASUALTY

Listed below are the corresponding Annual Statement line items that are related to the procedures contained in this Premium Specific Risk Analysis:

Agents' Balances or Uncollected Premiums
Bills Receivable, Taken for Premiums
Commissions Payable, Contingent Commissions and Other Similar Charges
Unearned Premiums
Advance Premiums
Dividends Declared and Unpaid - Policyholders
Remittances and Items Not Allocated
Detail of Write-Ins (Premium Deficiency Reserve)

The actual examination procedures selected to be performed are a matter of considerable judgment by the examiner. The following "Examination Program" includes examples of procedures commonly used.

To the extent that the examiner judgmentally determines whether it is appropriate to use the following procedures, that selection can be documented by checking the space next to such procedure, with modifications noted in the margin. The examiner may determine that alternative or additional procedures are required. If so, those procedures can be added on a supplemental sheet. The examiner performing the procedure should indicate satisfactory completion by initialing and dating in the space provided, and referencing the workpapers where the procedures and findings are documented.

The examiner may choose to apply the examination procedures to less than 100% of the items comprising an account balance. Guidance for audit sampling and control and substantive procedures can be found in Part 3 of the NAIC *Financial Condition Examiners Handbook.*

After each examination procedure, the examination objective that the procedure satisfies is indicated. The examination objectives are accuracy, completeness, compliance, cutoff, existence, obligation and ownership, valuation and presentation and disclosure.

EXAMINATION OBJECTIVES

Accuracy (AC) – Recorded transactions and account balances are mathematically accurate, are based on correct amounts and have been classified into the correct account.

Completeness (CO) – All transactions and account balances that should be recorded in the annual financial statement were recorded.

Compliance (CM) – Business transactions and affairs have been conducted in accordance with state insurance codes, other state laws or department directives.

Cutoff (CT) – All transactions are recorded in the correct accounting period.

Existence (EX) – Recorded transactions occurred and are not fictitious and recorded assets and liabilities existed as of the balance sheet date.

Obligation (OB) and Ownership (OW) – Recorded liabilities are obligations of the company and recorded assets are the rights of the company at the balance sheet date.

Valuation (VA) – Assets and liabilities are valued in accordance with state statute and NAIC accounting guidance.

Presentation and Disclosure (PD) – The elements of the Annual Statement are properly classified and all disclosures are accurately included in the Annual Statement.

	Exam Obj.	Completion Date	Examiner	Work Paper Ref.
EXAMINATION PROCEDURES				
General Procedures				
1. Through discussions with management and review of the company's overall insurance transactions, obtain an understanding of the company's policy for written premiums. Document this understanding in a narrative and include in the workpapers. This narrative should include:	CM OB/OW VA			
a. Types of insurance contracts in-force at the company;	CM OB/OW			
b. Basis for recording premiums per contract type (Indefinite – premium and expense recognized immediately or Fixed – premium earned over term, **SSAP No. 65, paragraph 7**);	CM OB/OW			
c. Method for calculating unearned premium reserve (Daily Pro Rata Method or Monthly Pro Rata Method, **SSAP No. 53, paragraph 7**);	CM VA			
d. Premium due dates (Original and deposit premiums, Endorsement premiums, Installment premiums and Audit premiums and retrospect premiums, **SSAP No. 6, paragraph 7**); and	CM			
e. Duration of contracts in-force (Annual, Semi-annual, or Quarterly).	CM			
2. Review the company's premium database(s) to ensure the database(s) is complete and accurate. Reconcile the database to applicable general ledger accounts or Annual Statement reports by query of database components such as:	CO AC EX			
a. Premium income; and	CO AC EX			

	Exam Obj.	Completion Date	Examiner	Work Paper Ref.
b. Aging elements (due date for premium balances should be determined in accordance with **SSAP No. 6, paragraph 7**).	CO AC EX			
3. Trace a sample of records from the application or report of the agent to the database and from the database to the application or report of the agent; verify and validate individual determinants such as:	CO AC EX			
a. Effective date, term and expiration date of the coverage;	CO AC EX			
b. Contract or identification number;	CO AC EX			
c. Premium amount; and	CO AC EX			
d. Negative amounts.	CO AC EX			
4. Scan the database to review for internal inconsistencies such as:	CO AC EX			
a. Missing or negative premium amounts;	CO AC EX			
b. Unusually small amounts; and	CO AC EX			
c. Contracts misclassified by type (e.g., homeowner's reported as auto), effective date, term and expiration date.	CO AC EX			
5. Review a sample of reports the company produces from the database to ensure they are logical. Verify:	CO AC EX			
a. Elements contained in the reports are available from the database(s); and	CO AC EX			
b. Trace a sample of the report elements from the source documents to the database.	CO AC EX			

	Exam Obj.	Completion Date	Examiner	Work Paper Ref.
6. Are premiums in-force reconciled to premiums written and regularly reviewed?	CO AC			
7. Review the method of marketing and, if applicable, the agency sales force makeup.	CM			
a. Review the managing general agent, the third party administrator and the general agency agreements to insure inclusion to required regulatory clauses and that regulatory filings were made.	CM			
b. Examine the documentation relating to the method used to monitor its outside representatives to ensure their compliance with contractual and regulatory provisions.	CM			
<u>**Agents' Balances or Uncollected Premiums**</u>				
Premiums and Agents' Balances in Course of Collection				
1. Obtain the detail of the premiums and agents' balances in course of collection and agree the detail to the company's general ledger and Annual Statement.	EX AC			
2. Obtain an aging detail of the agents' balances due by agent on a policy-by-policy basis and perform procedures to verify the existence and valuation of these assets. Test the agents' balances due by verifying premium obligations in accordance with in-force insurance policy provisions and by verifying the commission calculation.	EX VA			
3. Inquire of the company's management to determine whether any agent's balances or uncollected premiums have been transferred or sold (factored) with or without recourse. For those receivables that have been transferred or sold, verify that the company has properly recorded the transfer and removed the receivable in accordance with **SSAP No. 42, paragraphs 4-7.**	EX AC VA			

	Exam Obj.	Completion Date	Examiner	Work Paper Ref.
4. Review the aging detail to determine any policy premiums that are over 90 days past due. Verify that those premium receivables are non-admitted in accordance with **SSAP No. 6, paragraph 9**.	VA			
5. Review the remaining admitted assets for collectibility. If an amount due is considered uncollectible, the amount should be written off and charged to income in accordance with **SSAP No. 6, paragraph 10**. Perform procedures to identify those premium receivables collected subsequent to year-end in order to ascertain the collectibility of the premium receivables.	VA			
Premiums, Agents' Balances, and Installments Booked but Deferred and Not Yet Due				
6. Obtain the detail of the premiums, agents' balances and installments booked but deferred and not yet due on a policy-by-policy basis. Obtain the detail of the earned but unbilled premiums. Agree both schedules to the company's general ledger and Annual Statement.	EX AC			
7. Review the respective insurance contracts included on the detail. Verify that the contracts are in-force and that installment payments are permitted under the contract provisions.	EX AC			
8. Recalculate the amount included on the detail by agreeing the original premium amount to the respective contract and reviewing the payment remittance and documentation (check copy) for installment payments received.	AC VA			
a. Verify that installments have been made on a timely basis. Identify all installments that are over 90 days due. Verify that the amounts over 90 days due plus all other future installment payments recorded on the policy are non-admitted to the extent there is no related unearned premium in accordance with **SSAP No. 6, paragraph 9**.	VA			

	Exam Obj.	Completion Date	Examiner	Work Paper Ref.
b. For those installments that are considered uncollectible, verify that the receivable has been properly written off in accordance with **SSAP No. 6, paragraph 10**.	VA			
9. Verify that an unearned premium reserve has been properly recorded for items included on the premiums, agents' balances and installment detail.	AC EX VA CO			
10. Ascertain that the company is properly recording premium revenue and eliminating the premiums, agent's balances and installments balance when installment payments are received.	AC VA			
a. Trace the accounting entries for a sample of installment payments from the premiums, agents' balances and installment detail to the cash receipts journal.	AC			
11. Through review of the aging detail for the other receivables recorded by the company (e.g., Agents; Balances or Uncollected Premiums), verify that installment payments are properly included and classified in this account.	CO			
12. Review the calculation detail of the Earned But Unbilled (EBUB) premiums. Identify the types of insurance contracts with EBUB premiums.	EX AC			
13. Through discussions with management and through review of the contracts, determine how the company calculates and records the estimated premiums and the EBUB premium. **SSAP No. 53, paragraph 9** provides guidance on the methods of determining and recording the EBUB premium.	EX AC VA			
14. Recalculate the EBUB premium and verify that the adjustment was properly recorded to premium revenue in accordance **with SSAP No. 53, paragraph 10**. Also, in instances of refunded premiums, verify that earned premiums were properly reduced.	AC VA			

	Exam Obj.	Completion Date	Examiner	Work Paper Ref.
15. Verify that 10% of the EBUB in excess of collateral specifically held and identifiable on a per policy basis is non-admitted in accordance with **SSAP No. 53, paragraph 12**.	VA			
16. Verify that all EBUB premium adjustments that are considered uncollectible are written off in accordance with **SSAP No. 53, paragraph 12**.	VA			
Accrued Retrospective Premiums				
17. Obtain the detail of the accrued retrospective premiums and agree it to the company's general ledger and Annual Statement.	EX AC			
18. Review the contracts included in the detail to verify that the contract specifications allow for retrospective rating.	EX AC			
19. Verify and recalculate that the company's method for estimating retrospective premiums complies with the contract and permitted methods noted in **SSAP No. 66, paragraph 6** and is properly disclosed in accordance with **SSAP No. 66, paragraph 12**.	AC VA			
20. Verify that the company has properly recorded the accrued retrospective premium as a receivable or as a write-in liability in accordance with **SSAP No. 66, paragraph 8.**	AC			
21. Ascertain that the company has properly classified and disclosed the accrued retrospective premium as admitted or non-admitted in accordance with **SSAP No. 66, paragraphs 9 & 13**.	AC			
22. Verify that any uncollectible portion of this asset is properly written off and disclosed in accordance with **SSAP No. 66, paragraph 11**.	VA			
Bills Receivable, Taken for Premiums				
1. Obtain the detail of the bills receivable taken for premiums. Agree this detail to the company's general ledger and Annual Statement. This detail should include:	AC EX			

	Exam Obj.	Completion Date	Examiner	Work Paper Ref.
a. Name of borrower and bill number;	EX			
b. Policy number;	EX			
c. Original amount of indebtedness;	EX			
d. Date of note;	EX			
e. Due date;	EX			
f. Mode of payment (installment or single payment);	EX			
g. Status (current or in arrears);	EX			
h. Interest rate;	EX			
i. Amount paid toward principal and interest to date; and	EX			
j. Interest due or accrued.	EX			
2. Trace the bill number, policy number and borrower's name from the detail to the notes and application files.	AC EX			
a. Verify the propriety of the note agreement and authorization records. Check to verify that the policy is still in-force.	AC EX			
b. Determine unsigned and improperly signed bills.	AC			
c. Trace the amount of original indebtedness to the note. Identify any notes that are incorrectly classified as current.	AC			
d. Trace the amount to the premium income journal.	AC VA			
3. Verify that bill receivable payments have been properly recorded and allocated between principal and interest:	AC VA			

	Exam Obj.	Completion Date	Examiner	Work Paper Ref.
a. Trace payments from the detail to the payment remittance noting any discrepancies between the allocation of principal and interest; and	AC VA			
b. Recalculate interest due or accrued.	EX VA			
4. Inquire of the company's management to determine whether any bill receivables taken for premiums have been transferred or sold (factored) with or without recourse.	EX			
a. For those receivables that have been transferred or sold verify that the company has properly recorded the transfer and removed the receivable in accordance with **SSAP No. 18, paragraphs 3-5 & 34-35**.	AC VA			
5. Review the bill receivable detail to identify any receivables that should be considered nonadmitted in accordance with **SSAP No. 6, paragraph 9**.	AC			
<u>**Commissions Payable, Contingent Commissions and Other Similar Charges**</u>				
1. Obtain the detail of the commissions payable, contingent commissions and other similar charges and agree the detail to the company's general ledger and Annual Statement.	AC EX			
2. From the detail, select a sample and trace the payable to a commission agreement. Perform procedures to verify the accuracy of this information:	AC VA			
a. Recalculate the commission payable based on the commission agreement specifications (**SSAP No. 71, paragraph 3**); and	VA			

	Exam Obj.	Completion Date	Examiner	Work Paper Ref.
b. Review the commissions paid subsequent to year-end. Verify that those commissions were properly valued and included on the year-end liability. Investigate any subsequent payments not included on the detail or payments which were undervalued at year-end.	VA			
3. Review the premium receivables and verify that the correlating commission liabilities have been properly included in the commission payable detail.	CO VA			
4. Conduct a separate review of contingent, retroactive and experience agreements to verify that all commission liabilities in accordance with these agreements are properly recorded.	CO VA			
5. Review and investigate any methodology differences identified between the calculation of various commission levels for financial statements and the methods used to calculate commissions in the actual payment process.	AC VA			
<u>**Unearned Premiums**</u>				
1. Obtain the detail of the unearned premiums and agree it to the company's general ledger and Annual Statement.	AC EX			
2. Through discussions with management, ascertain an understanding of the company's policy of recognizing premiums and recording the unearned premium reserve:	AC CO EX VA			
a. Daily Pro Rata Method **(SSAP No. 53, paragraph 7)**;	AC VA			
b. Monthly Pro Rata Method **(SSAP No. 53, paragraph 7)**; and	AC VA			
c. Contracts equal to or in excess of 13 months **(SSAP No. 65, paragraphs 21-33)**.	AC VA			

	Exam Obj.	Completion Date	Examiner	Work Paper Ref.
Daily Pro Rata and Monthly Pro Rata Methods:				
3. Obtain the detail of unearned premiums calculated by the Daily/Monthly Pro Rata Methods.	AC CO			
4. Select a sample and verify that the following have been properly considered by the company while calculating the unearned premium reserve:	AC			
a. Lines of business, term, and expiration date of the policy;	AC			
b. Policy number;	AC			
c. Premium;	AC			
d. Use of original premium, original terms, and mid-term endorsements; and	AC			
e. Treatment of deposit and audit premiums and late reporting policies.	AC			
5. Obtain the premium deposits register (if applicable). From this register, trace a sample of premium deposits to the unearned premium detail to identify any contract premium payments that have been improperly excluded from the unearned premium reserve.	CO			
6. For items selected in step #4, recalculate the unearned premium reserve. Verify that the calculation utilized by the company is in accordance with the guidance provided in **SSAP No. 53, paragraph 7**.	VA			
Contracts Equal to or in Excess of 13 Months:				
7. Obtain the detail of all unearned premiums calculated for policies equal to or in excess of 13 months.	AC EX			
8. Compare contracts included on this detail to the detail of all long-term in-force contracts to identify any excluded contracts.	CO			

	Exam Obj.	Completion Date	Examiner	Work Paper Ref.
9. Select a sample of contracts included on the detail and verify that they meet the specific characteristics in accordance with **SSAP No. 65, paragraph 23**.	AC			
10. For those contracts selected in step #9, verify that the unearned premium reserve has been appropriately calculated in accordance with the guidelines and tests established in **SSAP No. 65, paragraphs 24-31**.	AC VA			
11. Verify that any reserve credits for ceded reinsurance are appropriately reflected in the financial statements and that the reporting entity properly establishes the resulting net unearned premium reserve in accordance with **SSAP No. 65, paragraph 25**.	AC VA			
12. Verify that all disclosures or required reports are properly obtained and presented in accordance with **SSAP No. 65, paragraph 32**.	PD			
Other Methods Tailored to Specific Types of Insurance:				
13. Discuss with management any other employed methods for calculating the unearned premium reserve and verify that the methods used are in accordance with the NAIC *Accounting Practices and Procedures Manual* for the specific insurance type.	EX AC			
14. Perform procedures to verify the company is properly applying the method to calculate the unearned premium calculation.	AC VA			
<u>Advance Premiums</u>				
1. Obtain the detail of the advance premiums on a policy basis and agree it to the company's general ledger and Annual Statement.	AC EX			
2. Review the respective advance premium contracts and verify that the contracts were not in effect at year-end in accordance with **SSAP No. 53, paragraph 13**.	AC EX			

	Exam Obj.	Completion Date	Examiner	Work Paper Ref.
3. Compare the premium payment remittance to the detail noting that the full amount of the premium paid is properly included in the advance premiums.	AC VA			
4. Verify that the paid premium has been properly excluded from the written premium or the unearned premium reserve in accordance with **SSAP No. 53, paragraph 13**.	AC VA			
5. Obtain the detail of 'new' policies with effective dates subsequent to year-end. Select a sample and trace the contract to the premium payment remittance. Verify that the payment was received subsequent to year-end or properly included in the advance premium detail.	CO			
<u>Dividends Declared and Unpaid - Policyholders</u>				
1. Obtain the detail of the policyholder's dividends declared and unpaid. Agree this detail to the company's general ledger and Annual Statement.	AC EX			
2. Agree the declared dividends to the board of director's minutes. Determine whether these dividends have any dividend restrictions.	AC EX CO			
3. Through review of the board of directors minutes, determine whether all declared policyholder dividends are properly recorded in accordance with **SSAP No. 65, paragraph 45**.	EX CO			
a. Verify that dividends to policyholders immediately become liabilities of the reporting entity when they are declared by the board of directors and should be recorded as a liability.	EX CO			
4. Determine that the company has properly disclosed the terms of any dividend restrictions in accordance with **SSAP No. 65, paragraph 46**.	PD			

	Exam Obj.	Completion Date	Examiner	Work Paper Ref.
Remittances and Items Not Allocated				
1. Obtain the detail of the remittances and items not allocated and agree it the company's general ledger and Annual Statement.	AC EX			
2. Review the detail provided by the company and identify the items included in this detail as specified in **SSAP No. 67, paragraph 9**:	EX			
a. Premium payments received with the application for policies which have not yet been issued;	EX			
b. Premium payments in an amount different than the amount billed by the reporting entity; and	EX			
c. Unidentified cash receipts.	EX			
3. Recalculate amounts included on the detail by verifying the cash receipt, the insurance policy premium amount billed and contract terms (date of issuance). Investigate any discrepancies.	AC VA			
4. In accordance with other premium testwork performed, verify that all noted instances of cash receipts received in excess of the amount billed and cash receipts for policies not in-force are properly included in this liability account.	CO AC			
5. Verify that the company is clearing and reconciling this account in a timely manner.	AC EX			
Detail of Write-Ins (Premium Deficiency Reserve)				
The NAIC Annual Statement Instructions for Property Casualty Companies requires premium deficiency reserves, as defined in ***SSAP No. 53****, to be included as a write-in item. See the Annual Statement instructions for further guidance on the proper reporting of these items.*				
1. Through discussions with management or other examination procedures performed, identify any premium deficiency reserves in accordance with **SSAP No. 53, paragraph 15**.	EX			

	Exam Obj.	Completion Date	Examiner	Work Paper Ref.
2. Verify that the premium deficiency reserve has been properly valued and recorded in accordance with **SSAP No. 53, paragraph 15**.	AC EX VA			
3. Verify that the company has properly disclosed all premium deficiency reserves in accordance with **SSAP No. 53, paragraph 16**.	PD			

SECTION C — PREMIUM CYCLE: HEALTH

Listed below are the corresponding Annual Statement line items that are related to the procedures contained in this Premium Specific Risk Analysis:

Annual Statement Blank Line Items

Accident and Health Premiums Due and Unpaid
Amounts Receivable Relating to Uninsured Accident and Health Plans
Amounts Due From Agents
Detail of Write-Ins (Additional Accrued Retrospective Premiums)
Premiums Received in Advance
General Expenses Due or Accrued (Commissions)
Amounts Withheld or Retained for the Account of Others
Liability for Amounts Held Under Uninsured Accident and Health Plans
Detail of Write-Ins (Accrued Return Retrospective Premiums)
Premium Deficiency Reserves

Relevant SSAP's Include:

#6, Uncollected Premium Balances, Bills Receivable for Premiums, and Amounts Due from Agents and Brokers
#18, Transfers and Servicing of Financial Assets and Extinguishments of Liabilities
#42, Sale of Premium Receivables
#47, Uninsured Plans
#50, Classifications and Definitions of Insurance or Managed Care Contracts In-force
#54, Individual and Group Accident and Health Contracts
#66, Retrospectively Rated Contracts
#67, Other Liabilities
#71, Policy Acquisition Costs and Commissions
#84, Certain Health Care Receivables and Receivables Under Government Insured Plans

Other Relevant Statutory Accounting Guidance

INT 01-01 of the Emerging Accounting Issues Working Group: Application of SSAP No. 6, Paragraph 9 a. to de minimus Receivables Balances of Group Accident and Health Policies

SPECIFIC RISK ANALYSIS WORKPAPERS

Risk Analysis Prepared By/Date ____________________

Planning and Exam Analysis Prepared By/Date ____________________

Reviewed By/Date ____________________

EXAMINATION OBJECTIVES:

1. Insurance contracts and related premiums were properly executed, authorized and in-force. (Existence and Compliance)

2. Premiums and commissions are calculated, valued and recorded accurately and properly reflected in the Financial Statements. (Valuation, Compliance, Accuracy, Completeness, and Cutoff)

3. The company properly records the recognition of premiums in accordance with contract guidelines and the NAIC *Accounting Practices and Procedures Manual*. (Ownership and Obligation)

4. The premiums are presented in accordance with the NAIC *Annual Statement Instructions* and the NAIC *Accounting Practices and Procedures Manual*. (Presentation and Disclosure)

INHERENT RISK

____

____

____

____

INTERNAL AND EXTERNAL ENVIRONMENTAL CONDITIONS/FACTORS

____

____

____

____

RESULTS OF DETAIL ANALYTICAL REVIEW PROCEDURES

____

____

____

____

CONTROL RISK — PREMIUM CYCLE: HEALTH

This questionnaire is designed to assist the examiner in assessing control risk for health premium cycles. Part 1, Section III and Part 3 of this *Handbook* provide guidance in consideration of an insurer's internal control structure for use when designing substantive examination procedures.

This questionnaire includes examples of internal control procedures and policies that are commonly utilized by insurers to achieve internal control objectives. For each control procedure listed below, indicate by placing a check mark in the yes or no box whether or not the insurer employs such a procedure, or other similar practice (include a description of the similar procedure). To the extent the control procedure is not applicable, indicate N/A. If other relevant control procedures are in place, list them in the space that follows. Control procedures that are tested by the examiner should be documented by including the workpaper reference in the comment section and the examiner's initials in the reliance column.

For each individual control procedure there is a control objective listed that satisfies the procedure.

If the examiner initially assesses control risk as low or medium for a particular account balance, then those controls must be tested. The controls should be tested to determine whether the procedure is operating as expected, applied throughout the entire period of reliance, performed on a timely basis, encompassing all transactions and identifying errors. Some examples of testing procedures are inquiry, observation, re-performance and examination of documents. The level of reliance, if any, should be indicated in the applicable column along with any comments the examiner may have regarding the procedure.

Based upon the testing results, the examiner should determine whether the preliminary control risk assessment is confirmed or should be revised.

CONTROL OBJECTIVES

Authorization (AU) – All transactions recorded were reviewed and approved by designated personnel.

Completeness (CO) – All transactions that occurred are initially entered into the accounting records, accepted for processing and generated data files and reports reflect that all transactions have occurred.

Accuracy (AC) – Transactions are initially recorded correctly, timely and accurately.

Asset Protection (AP) – Adequate safeguards over access to and use of assets and records, including the appropriate segregation of duties among company personnel.

	Control Obj.	Y	N	Work Paper Ref.	Reliance
General Control Procedures					
The examiner should determine the amount of documentation necessary for each control procedure. If the examiner intends to place substantial reliance on the established controls, the examiner should explain the control procedure in a workpaper and document the individual responsible for supervising the control activity as well as the frequency of the control activity.					
1. Are policy applications checked independently for compliance with company underwriting standards?	AC				
2. Does management periodically review the underwriting performance and written agreements of agents, brokers and sales personnel?	AC				
3. Does the company have procedures in place that comply with State requirements over the licensing and appointing of agents?	AC				
4. Does management periodically evaluate the financial condition of outside agents or others (MGA's) who handle the premiums?	AC				
5. Are underwriting standards approved by management on a current basis?	AU				
6. Are premium and commission discrepancy write-offs reviewed and approved independently?	AU				
7. Are policy term, effective/expiration dates, and lines of insurance tested? Are exceptions independently investigated?	AC				
8. Are renewal listings reconciled and/or matched to billing, cancellation and expiration listings?	AC				
9. Are policy forms approved, pre-numbered and sequence of policies issued verified independently?	AC AP				
10. Are premium adjustments resulting from endorsements, cancellations and audits checked independently for accuracy?	AC AU				

		Control Obj.	Y	N	Work Paper Ref.	Reliance
11.	Is there a procedure for approval of deletions other than expirations?	AC AU				
12.	Are premium billings and rate determinations periodically tested for accuracy and agreement with rate books, contracts or other supporting documentation?	AC				
13.	Are commission statements periodically tested for accuracy and agreement with commission schedules?	AC				
14.	Is the accuracy of agents' balances/premiums receivable aging independently checked?	AC				
15.	Is the detail of agents' balances/premiums receivable records and the premiums written per premium register reconciled to general ledger control accounts regularly?	AC CO				
16.	Are the retrospective premium calculations reviewed? Are these receivables and liabilities cleared on a timely basis?	AC				
17.	Does someone independent of the actual transaction function review the recorded receivable transactions?	AU AP				
18.	Are follow-ups conducted for past due accounts and are these accounts independently monitored for potential write-offs?	CO				
19.	Are all billing records reconciled to premium registers?	AC CO				
20.	Do procedures exist that restrict access of premium files to unauthorized personnel?	AU AP				
21.	Are procedures to review suspense accounts established to ensure they are properly cleared?	AC				
22.	Is the balance of accident and health premiums due and unpaid periodically matched to the subsequent collection of these items?	AC CO				

	Control Obj.	Y	N	Work Paper Ref.	Reliance
23. Are procedures established to monitor the self-insured groups reimbursements to the company for amounts receivable relating to uninsured accident and health plans?	CO				
24. Are deposits held to ensure payment from self-insured groups properly included in the liability for amounts held under uninsured accident and health plans as required by **SSAP No. 47, paragraph 11**? Are the deposits refunded to the groups after they terminate, provided they are current in paying the amounts receivable relating to uninsured accident and health plans?	AC AP				
25. Are there performance penalties or bonuses incorporated in the administrative agreements for uninsured health plans?	AP AU				
26. Are amounts due from CMS (Centers for Medicare and Medicaid Services) or other federal or state government entities traced to the subsequent collection of these balances?	CO				

OTHER KEY CONTROLS EXISTING FOR THIS CONTROL OBJECTIVE:

SUMMARY EVALUATION OF CONTROL RISK:

EVALUATION OF INDEPENDENT CPA'S WORK FOR THIS EXAMINATION (CPA REVIEW CHECKLIST):

OVERALL RISK ASSESSMENT

Balance Sheet Evaluation of the Likelihood of a Material Adjustment to Surplus:

The evaluation of the likelihood of a material adjustment to surplus should be based on the following criteria:

- Inherent Risk
- Internal & External Environmental Factors
- Control Risk
- Materiality Consideration

The examiner should rate each item as to the likelihood of a material misstatement. All items are assumed as "High" prior to any examiner evaluation. A "High" assessment requires the examiner to perform substantive examination procedures over that account area. A lower assessment allows the examiner to perform analytical or fewer substantive procedures to satisfy the examination requirements. If an assessment other than "High" is selected for any of the accounts, the examiner needs to document the basis for the assessment. If the assessment is based on control testwork, the documentation should include results of control procedures and related workpaper references.

1) "Accident and Health Premiums Due and Unpaid"

__________ High __________ Medium __________ Low

Basis for Assessment:

____

____

____

2) "Amounts Receivable Relating to Uninsured Accident and Health Plans"

__________ High __________ Medium __________ Low

Basis for Assessment:

____

____

____

3) "Amounts Due From Agents"

__________ High __________ Medium __________Low

Basis for Assessment:

____

____

____

4) "Detail of Write-Ins (Additional Accrued Retrospective Premiums)"

__________ High __________ Medium __________Low

Basis for Assessment:

____

____

____

5) "Premiums Received in Advance"

__________ High __________ Medium __________Low

Basis for Assessment:

____

____

____

6) "General Expenses Due or Accrued (Commissions)"

__________ High __________ Medium __________Low

Basis for Assessment:

____

____

____

7) "Amounts Withheld or Retained for the Account of Others"

___________ High ___________ Medium __________Low

Basis for Assessment:

____

____

____

8) "Liability for Amounts Held Under Uninsured Accident and Health Plans"

___________ High ___________ Medium __________Low

Basis for Assessment:

____

____

____

9) "Detail of Write Ins (Accrued Return Retrospective Premiums)"

___________ High ___________ Medium __________Low

Basis for Assessment:

____

____

____

10) "Premium Deficiency Reserves"

___________ High ___________ Medium __________Low

Basis for Assessment:

____

____

____

PRELIMINARY EXAMINATION APPROACH — PREMIUM CYCLE: HEALTH

Listed below are the corresponding Annual Statement line items that are related to the procedures contained in this Premium Specific Risk Analysis:

Accident and Health Premiums Due and Unpaid
Amounts Receivable Relating to Uninsured Accident and Health Plans
Amounts Due From Agents
Detail of Write-Ins (Additional Accrued Retrospective Premiums)
Premiums Received in Advance
General Expenses Due or Accrued (Commissions)
Amounts Withheld or Retained for the Account of Others
Liability for Amounts Held Under Uninsured Accident and Health Plans
Detail of Write-Ins (Accrued Return Retrospective Premiums)
Premium Deficiency Reserves

The actual examination procedures selected to be performed are a matter of considerable judgment by the examiner. The following "Examination Program" includes examples of procedures commonly used.

To the extent that the examiner judgmentally determines whether it is appropriate to use the following procedures, that selection can be documented by checking the space next to such procedure, with modifications noted in the margin. The examiner may determine that alternative or additional procedures are required. If so, those procedures can be added on a supplemental sheet. The examiner performing the procedure should indicate satisfactory completion by initialing and dating in the space provided, and referencing the workpapers where the procedures and findings are documented.

The examiner may choose to apply the examination procedures to less than 100% of the items comprising an account balance. Guidance for audit sampling and control and substantive procedures can be found in Part 3 of the NAIC *Financial Condition Examiners Handbook.*

After each examination procedure, the examination objective that the procedure satisfies is indicated. The examination objectives are accuracy, completeness, compliance, cutoff, existence, obligation and ownership, valuation and presentation and disclosure.

EXAMINATION OBJECTIVES

Accuracy (AC) – Recorded transactions and account balances are mathematically accurate, are based on correct amounts and have been classified into the correct account.

Completeness (CO) – All transactions and account balances that should be recorded in the annual financial statement were recorded.

Compliance (CM) – Business transactions and affairs have been conducted in accordance with state insurance codes, other state laws or department directives.

Cutoff (CT) – All transactions are recorded in the correct accounting period.

Existence (EX) – Recorded transactions occurred and are not fictitious and recorded assets and liabilities existed as of the balance sheet date.

Obligation (OB) and Ownership (OW) – Recorded liabilities are obligations of the company and recorded assets are the rights of the company at the balance sheet date.

Valuation (VA) – Assets and liabilities are valued in accordance with state statute and NAIC accounting guidance.

Presentation and Disclosure (PD) – The elements of the Annual Statement are properly classified and all disclosures are accurately included in the Annual Statement.

	Exam Obj.	Completion Date	Examiner	Work Paper Ref.
EXAMINATION PROCEDURES				
<u>General Procedures</u>				
1. Through discussions with management and review of the company's overall insurance transactions, obtain an understanding of the company's policy for premiums. Document this understanding in a narrative and include in the workpapers. This narrative should include:	CM OB/OW			
a. Types of insurance contracts in-force at the company; (In accordance with **SSAP No. 50, paragraphs 21-31** this may include managed care, income replacement, expense reimbursement, credit accident and health, continuing care, long-term care and accidental death and dismemberment.)	CM OB/OW			
b. Process of recording and recognizing premiums for individual and group accident and health contracts in accordance with **SSAP No. 54, paragraphs 2-7**; and	CM OB/OW			
c. Premium due dates (original and deposit premiums, endorsement premiums, installment premiums and audit premiums and retrospective premiums, **SSAP No. 6, paragraph 7**).	CM			
2. Reconcile the database to applicable general ledger accounts or annual statement reports by query of database components such as:	CO AC EX			
a. Premium income; and	CO AC EX			
b. Aging elements. (Due date for premium balances should be determined in accordance with **SSAP No. 6, paragraph 7.**)	CO AC EX			

	Exam Obj.	Completion Date	Examiner	Work Paper Ref.
3. Verify and validate individual determinants by tracing a sample of the following attributes from the policy application to the database and from the database to the policy application:	CO AC EX			
a. Effective date, term and expiration date of the coverage;	CO AC EX			
b. Contract or identification number;	CO AC EX			
c. Premium Amount; and	CO AC EX			
d. Negative Amounts.	CO AC EX			
4. Scan the database to review for internal inconsistencies such as:	CO AC EX			
a. Missing or negative premium amounts;	CO AC EX			
b. Unusually small or large amounts; and	CO AC EX			
c. Contracts misclassified by type (e.g., Medicare), effective date, term and expiration date.	CO AC EX			
5. Review a sample of reports the company produces from the database to ensure they are logical.	CO AC EX			
a. Verify that elements contained in the reports are available from the database(s).	CO AC EX			
b. Trace a sample of the report elements from the source documents to the database.	CO AC EX			
6. Review audits and evaluations by government bodies concerning the entity.	CO AC EX			
7. Determine the date of the last Quality of Care/Market Conduct examination and review the report for applicable matters.	CO AC EX			

Procedure	Exam Obj.	Completion Date	Examiner	Work Paper Ref.
8. For business subject to redetermination (e.g., Federal Groups, Medicare), review the recent premium audit available from the following:	CO AC EX			
a. Office of Personnel Management;	CO AC EX			
b. Centers for Medicare & Medicaid Services (CMS); and	CO AC EX			
c. Other Federal or state agencies.	CO AC EX			
9. Determine the status of any ongoing audits or reviews.	CO AC EX			
10. Verify that accounting for contracts subject to redetermination by other entities follows the guidelines in **SSAP No. 54, paragraphs 26-31**.	CO AC EX			
11. Review the method of marketing and, if applicable, the agency sales force makeup.	CM			
a. Review managing general agent, third party administrator and general agency agreements to insure inclusion to required regulatory clauses and that regulatory filings were made.	CM			
b. Examine the documentation relating to the method used to monitor its outside representatives to ensure their compliance with contractual and regulatory provisions.	CM			
<u>**Accident and Health Premiums Due and Unpaid**</u>				
1. Obtain an aging detail of the accident and health premiums due and unpaid. Agree this detail to the company's general ledger and Annual Statement.	AC EX			
2. Perform procedures to ascertain the existence and valuation of these receivables.	EX VA			
a. Perform subsequent receipt testwork.	EX VA			

	Exam Obj.	Completion Date	Examiner	Work Paper Ref.
b. Confirm significant balances directly.	EX VA			
3. Verify that the due date for aging was determined in accordance with **SSAP No. 6, paragraphs 7-8**. For original and deposit premiums the due date is the effective date of the underlying contract, not the agent/reporting entity contractual relationship.	AC EX VA			
4. Review the assets to determine whether they should be classified as nonadmitted in accordance with **SSAP No. 6, paragraphs 9 and 11**. Receivables over 90 days due should be nonadmitted and future installments on those policies should also be nonadmitted. (The 90 day rule does not apply to Medicare and similar government funded insured and uninsured plans. Pursuant to INT 01-01 the existence of nonadmitted *de minimus* balances on group accident and health contracts will not cause current premium installment receivables on that contract to be nonadmitted. Agent's balances on a policy-by-policy basis over ninety days overdue should be nonadmitted, regardless of unearned premium.)	VA PD			
a. Verify that amounts classified as nonadmitted collected subsequent to the date of the statutory financial statements are not used to adjust the nonadmitted assets otherwise calculated.	VA			
b. Confirm that amounts more than 90 days past due from Medicare and similar government funded insured plans are valued in accordance with **SSAP No. 84, paragraph 23**.	VA PD			
5. Review the admitted assets for collectibility. If an amount due is considered uncollectible, the amount should be written off and charged to income in accordance with **SSAP No. 6, paragraph 10**.	VA			
a. Perform procedures to identify those premium receivables collected subsequent to year-end in order to ascertain the collectiblilty of the premium receivables.	VA			

	Exam Obj.	Completion Date	Examiner	Work Paper Ref.
6. Inquire of the company's management to determine whether any agent's balances or uncollected premiums have been transferred or sold (factored) with or without recourse.	EX			
a. For those receivables that have been transferred or sold verify that the company has properly recorded the transaction and removed the receivable in accordance with **SSAP No. 42, paragraphs 3-7**.	AC VA			
<u>**Amounts Receivable Relating to Uninsured Accident and Health Plans**</u>				
1. Obtain an aging detail of the accounts receivable relating to uninsured accident and health plans. Agree this detail to the company's general ledger and Annual Statement.	AC EX			
2. Determine whether the plans are properly classified according to contract type, as described in **SSAP No. 47, paragraphs 2-4**. Uninsured plans include Administrative Services Only (ASO) plans, Administrative Services Contracts, (ASC) and federal, state, or other governmental funded programs where there is no underwriting risk. Partially insured or combination plans should be accounted for as two plans, an insured plan and an uninsured plan.	AC EX			
3. Review the account and verify that the balance is consistent with the items permitted under **SSAP No. 47, paragraph 8** and **SSAP No. 84, paragraph 13**. Permitted items include claims and other costs by the administrator on behalf of the third party at risk and/or fees related to the services provided by the administrator. Allowable items also include pharmaceutical rebates of uninsured plans retained by the reporting entity as an administrative fee. Verify that receivables are not recorded for unpaid claims.	AC EX			
4. Perform procedures to ascertain the existence and valuation of these receivables.	EX VA			
a. Perform subsequent receipt testwork.	EX VA			

	Exam Obj.	Completion Date	Examiner	Work Paper Ref.
b. Confirm receivables directly.	EX VA			
5. Evaluate the account receivables to determine any non-admitted amounts in accordance with **SSAP No. 47, paragraphs 9-10**:	VA			
a. Uncollected uninsured plan receivables over ninety days, excluding Medicare and similar government plans, due shall be accounted for as a non-admitted asset; and	VA			
b. Other amounts that are deemed probable for uncollectibility should be written off and charged to operations.	VA			
6. Verify that disclosures required by **SSAP No. 47, paragraphs 12-13** have been properly made.	PD			
7. Review the company's performance reports relative to administering uninsured plans and compare the results to standards established in the underlying administrative service agreement.	PD			
<u>Amounts Due From Agents</u>				
1. Obtain an aging detail of the amounts due from agents and agree it to the company's general ledger and Annual Statement.	AC EX			
2. Perform testwork to ascertain the existence and valuation of these amounts due:	EX VA			
a. Test the agents' balances due by verifying the amounts due with contract terms or other supporting documentation;	EX VA			
b. Perform subsequent receipt procedures; and	EX VA			
c. Confirm the amount due directly with the agent.	EX VA			
3. Verify that the assets are properly recorded as admitted unless specifically nonadmitted in accordance with **SSAP No. 6, paragraph 6**:	VA PD			

	Exam Obj.	Completion Date	Examiner	Work Paper Ref.
a. Amounts are in the form of unsecured loans or advances;	VA PD			
b. Contractual terms for repayment are through application of future renewal commissions and/or other credits; and	VA PD			
c. Terms of repayment do not provide readily available cash for the satisfaction of policyholder liabilities.	VA PD			
4. Determine if any wash transactions as described in **SSAP No. 6, paragraphs 12-13** exist and if they have been properly recorded.	VA			
5. Review the aging detail to determine any amounts due that are over 90 days past due. Verify that those amounts due are non-admitted in accordance with **SSAP No. 6, paragraph 9**.	VA			
a. Verify that amounts classified as nonadmitted assets collected subsequent to the date of the statutory financial statements are not used to adjust the nonadmitted asset in accordance with **SSAP No. 6, paragraph 11**.	VA			
6. Review the remaining admitted assets for collectibility. If an amount due is considered uncollectible, the amount should be written off and charged to income in accordance with **SSAP No. 6, paragraph 10**.	VA			
a. Perform procedures to identify those amounts due collected subsequent to year-end in order to ascertain the collectibility of the amounts due.	VA			
7. Inquire of the company's management to determine whether any amounts due from agents have been transferred or sold (factored) with or without recourse.	EX			

	Exam Obj.	Completion Date	Examiner	Work Paper Ref.
a. For those amounts due that have been transferred or sold verify that the company has properly recorded the transfer and removed the receivable in accordance with **SSAP No. 18, paragraphs 3-5 and 34-35**.	AC VA			
8. Inquire of the company's management to determine whether any amounts due from agents have been offset in accordance with **SSAP No. 6, paragraph 9**.	AC VA			
a. For those amounts that have been offset verify that the guidelines in **SSAP No. 64** have been followed, and all required disclosures have been properly included.	AC VA			
<u>Detail of Write-Ins (Additional Accrued Retrospective Premiums)</u>				
1. Obtain detail of the additional accrued retrospective premiums. Agree the detail to the company's general ledger and Annual Statement.	AC EX			
2. Select a sample of contracts included on the additional accrued retrospective detail. Verify that the contract specifications allow for additional accrued retrospective premiums.	EX			
3. Review the calculation for the additional accrued retrospective premiums and verify that the methodology utilized to determine the additional accrued retrospective premium is in accordance with **SSAP No. 66, paragraph 6** and is properly disclosed in accordance with **SSAP No. 66, paragraph 12**.	AC VA			
4. Verify that the company has properly recorded the additional accrued retrospective premium as a write-in for other than invested assets with a corresponding entry to premiums in accordance with **SSAP No. 66, paragraph 8**.	PD			
5. For those retrospective premiums that have been billed, verify that those premiums greater than 90 days past due are properly non-admitted in accordance with **SSAP No. 66, paragraph 10**.	VA			

	Exam Obj.	Completion Date	Examiner	Work Paper Ref.
6. Verify that any uncollectible additional accrued retrospective premiums have properly written off in accordance with **SSAP No. 66, paragraph 11**.	VA			
<u>Premiums Received in Advance</u>				
1. Obtain detail of the premiums received in advance. Agree this schedule to the company's general ledger and Annual Statement.	AC EX			
2. Compare the payment remittance for advance premiums to the detail noting that the full amount of the premium paid is included in the advance premiums. Investigate any discrepancies.	AC VA			
3. Review the contract specifications and compare the premium payment remittance to the insurance contract premium terms.	AC EX VA			
4. Verify that the premium income is not recognized until due and advance premiums are recognized as a liability in accordance with **SSAP No. 54, paragraphs 2-6**.	AC VA PD			
5. Perform procedures to verify that the advance premiums are properly recorded.	AC VA CO			
a. Select a sample of premium remittances and determine the contract period to which they apply. For those premiums that are due on or after the next contract period anniversary date, verify that they are included on the advance premium detail.	AC VA CO			
b. Obtain detail of 'new' policies with effective dates subsequent to year-end. Select a sample and trace the contract to the premium remittance. Verify that that remittance was received subsequent to year-end or properly included in the advance premium detail.	AC VA CO			

	Exam Obj.	Completion Date	Examiner	Work Paper Ref.
General Expenses Due or Accrued (Commissions)				
1. Obtain detail of the general expenses (commissions) due or accrued. Agree this detail to the company's general ledger and Annual Statement.	AC EX			
2. From the detail select a sample and trace the payable to a commission agreement or other supporting documentation. Perform procedures to verify the accuracy of this information:	AC VA			
a. Recalculate the commission payable based on the commission agreement specifications (**SSAP No. 71, paragraph 3**); and	VA			
b. Review the commissions and other expenses paid subsequent to year-end. Verify that those commissions or expenses were properly valued and included on the year-end liability. Investigate any subsequent payments not included on the detail or payments which were undervalued at year-end.	VA CO			
Amounts Withheld or Retained for the Account of Others				
1. Obtain detail of the amounts withheld or retained for the account of others. Agree this detail to the company's general ledger and Annual Statement.	AC EX			
2. Verify the accuracy of the amounts by tracing individual transactions to supporting records (e.g., cash receipts/disbursements records, payroll records). Verify that amounts withheld or retained are recorded as a liability when the related items are expensed or when funds are received in accordance with **SSAP No. 67, paragraphs 8-9**.	AC EX			
3. Perform procedures to ascertain the accuracy and valuation of these amounts.	AC EX VA			
a. Trace a sample of accounts to subsequent settlement.	AC EX VA			

	Exam Obj.	Completion Date	Examiner	Work Paper Ref.
b. Confirm amounts directly with third parties.	AC EX VA			
Liability for Amounts Held Under Uninsured Accident and Health Plans				
1. Obtain detail of the liability for amounts held under uninsured accident and health plans. Agree this detail to the company's general ledger and Annual Statement.	AC EX			
2. Verify that the liability has been established for funds held by an administrator for the benefit of an uninsured plan or for funds that may be owed by the administrator in connection with the administration of an uninsured plan in accordance with **SSAP No. 47, paragraph 11 and SSAP No. 84, paragraph 13**.	AC EX CO VA			
a. Obtain detail of all uninsured plans in-force at the company. Perform procedures to verify that a correlating liability has been established as required in step #2.	AC EX CO			
b. Verify that a liability pertaining to one uninsured plan has not been offset by an asset relating to a different plan in accordance with **SSAP No. 47, paragraph 11**.	AC EX VA			
3. Ascertain that administrators have not recorded aggregate reserves, claim/loss reserves, or liabilities (except for Medicare or similarly structures cost based reimbursement) for any other claim costs paid by the administrator on behalf of uninsured plans in accordance with **SSAP No. 47, paragraph 11**.	AC EX			
Detail of Write-Ins (Accrued Return Retrospective Premiums)				
1. Obtain detail of the accrued return retrospective premiums. Agree the detail to the company's general ledger and Annual Statement.	AC EX			

	Exam Obj.	Completion Date	Examiner	Work Paper Ref.
2. Select a sample of contracts included on the accrued return retrospective premium detail. Verify that the contract specifications allow for accrued retrospective premiums.	EX			
3. Review the calculation for the accrued return retrospective premiums and verify that the methodology utilized to determine the accrued retrospective premium is in accordance with **SSAP No. 66, paragraph 6** and is properly disclosed in accordance with **SSAP No. 66, paragraph 12**.	AC VA			
4. Verify that the company has properly recorded the accrued return retrospective premium as a liability write-in, provisions for experience rating refunds, with a corresponding entry to premiums in accordance with **SSAP No. 66, paragraph 8**.	PD			
Premium Deficiency Reserves				
Premium Deficiency reserves should be included within the Policy Reserves Annual Statement line item. Procedures pertaining to the other aspects of policy reserves are included in the Loss/Benefits Health SRA. Since the premium deficiency reserve pertains particularly to the company's premiums, this aspect of policy reserves is included in this Premium SRA.				
1. Through discussions with management or other examination procedures performed, identify any premium deficiency reserves in accordance with **SSAP No. 54, paragraph 18** and the **Health Reserves Guidance Manual**.	EX			
a. A premium deficiency reserve occurs when the expected claim payments or incurred costs, claim adjustment expenses and administration costs exceed the premiums for the remainder of the contract. Contracts may be grouped in a manner consistent with how policies are marketed, serviced and measured.	EX			
2. Verify that the premium deficiency reserve has been properly valued and recorded in accordance with **SSAP No. 54, paragraph 18** and the **Health Reserves Guidance Manual**.	AC EX VA			

	Exam Obj.	Completion Date	Examiner	Work Paper Ref.
3. Verify that the company has properly disclosed all premium deficiency reserves in accordance with **SSAP No. 54, paragraph 34** and the **Health Reserves Guidance Manual**.	PD			

SECTION D — LOSSES AND BENEFITS CYCLE: LIFE

Listed below are the corresponding Annual Statement line items that are related to the procedures contained in this Losses and Benefits Specific Risk Analysis:

Annual Statement Blank Line Items

Aggregate Reserve for Life Contracts
Aggregate Reserve for Accident and Health Contracts
Liability for Deposit-Type Contracts
Contract Claims
Policyholders' Dividends and Coupons Due and Unpaid
Provisions for Policyholders' Dividends and Coupons Payable in Following Calendar Year
Amount Provisionally Held for Deferred Dividend Policies
Contract Liabilities Not Included Elsewhere – Surrender Values on Canceled Contracts
Drafts Outstanding

Relevant SSAP's Include:

#2, Cash, Drafts, and Short-term Investments
#3, Accounting Changes and Corrections of Errors
#50, Classifications and Definitions of Insurance or Managed Care Contracts In Force
#51, Life Contracts
#52, Deposit-Type Contracts
#54, Individual and Group Accident and Health Contracts
#55, Unpaid Claims, Losses, and Loss Adjustment Expenses
#61, Life, Deposit-Type and Accident and Health Reinsurance
#65, Property and Casualty Contracts
#80, Life Contracts, Deposit-Type Contracts and Separate Accounts, Amendments to SSAP No. 51 – Life Contracts, SSAP No. 52 – Deposit-Type Contracts, and SSAP No. 56 – Separate Accounts.
#85, Claim Adjustment Expenses, Amendments to SSAP No. 55 (Effective December 31, 2003)

SPECIFIC RISK ANALYSIS WORKPAPERS

Risk Analysis Prepared By/Date ____________________

Planning Exam Analysis Prepared By/Date ____________________

Reviewed By/Date ____________________

EXAMINATION OBJECTIVES:

1. Policy benefits are valid obligations of the company as of the examination date and properly authorized and calculated in accordance with policy provisions. (Ownership and Obligation, Valuation, Accuracy and Compliance)

2. Reserves, liabilities, and policy benefits are complete and are recorded properly as to account, amount and period. (Accuracy, Cutoff and Compliance)

3. Policy reserves are established with appropriate reserving tables and policies with deficiency reserve situations are identified and properly provided for. (Compliance and Valuation)

4. Additions to, deletions from, and changes in policy information on the policy master file are approved and recorded correctly. (Accuracy and Compliance)

INHERENT RISKS

INTERNAL AND EXTERNAL ENVIRONMENTAL CONDITIONS/FACTORS

RESULTS OF DETAIL ANALYTICAL REVIEW PROCEDURES

CONTROL RISK — LOSSES AND BENEFITS CYCLE: LIFE

This questionnaire is designed to assist the examiner in assessing control risk for the losses and benefits life cycle. Part 1, Section III and Part 3 of this *Handbook* provide guidance in consideration of an insurer's internal control structure for use when designing substantive examination procedures.

This questionnaire includes examples of internal control procedures and policies that are commonly utilized by insurers to achieve internal control objectives. For each control procedure listed below, indicate by placing a check mark in the yes or no box whether or not the insurer employs such a procedure, or other similar practice (include a description of the similar procedure). To the extent the control procedure is not applicable, indicate N/A. If other relevant control procedures are in place, list them in the space that follows. Control procedures that are tested by the examiner should be documented by including the workpaper reference in the comment section and the examiner's initials in the reliance column.

For each individual control procedure there is a control objective listed that satisfies the procedure.

If the examiner initially assesses control risk as low or medium for a particular account balance, then those controls must be tested. The controls should be tested to determine whether the procedure is operating as expected, applied throughout the entire period of reliance, performed on a timely basis, encompassing all transactions and identifying errors. Some examples of testing procedures are inquiry, observation, re-performance and examination of documents. The level of reliance, if any, should be indicated in the applicable column along with any comments the examiner may have regarding the procedure.

Based upon the testing results, the examiner should determine whether the preliminary control risk assessment is confirmed or should be revised.

CONTROL OBJECTIVES

Authorization (AU) – All transactions recorded were reviewed and approved by designated personnel.

Completeness (CO) – All transactions that occurred were initially entered into the accounting records, accepted for processing and generated data files and reports reflect that all transactions have occurred.

Accuracy (AC) – Transactions are initially recorded correctly, timely and accurately.

Asset Protection (AP) – Adequate safeguards over access to and use of assets and records, including the appropriate segregation of duties among company personnel.

	Control Obj.	Y	N	Work Paper Ref.	Reliance
General Control Procedures					
The examiner should determine the amount of documentation necessary for each control procedure. If the examiner intends to place substantial reliance on the established controls, the examiner should explain the control procedure in a workpaper and document the individual responsible for supervising the control activity as well as the frequency of the control activity.					
1. Is there an established process that includes verification of the in-force status of the policy before the claim is processed?	AU AP				
2. Are reviews or tests of policy reserves and premium valuation output performed to ensure that in-force policies and related data are included in the proper valuation category (e.g., plan/year/age), appropriate factors have been applied, and calculations are accurate?	AC				
3. Are changes to the master policy file and losses data authorized and approved? Are persons authorized to make additions, deletions, and changes to the master file limited in number and scope of job responsibilities?	AU				
4. Are master file transactions accounted for by input/output reconciliation controls (e.g., batch totals, hash totals, numerical sequence, edit reports)?	AU				
5. Are controls (review, reconciliation or edit) in effect to ensure that master files and other records are updated to reflect benefits paid?	CO				
6. Is the nature and amount of benefits paid authorized and compared to policy coverage, dividend scale, cash value, etc. prior to payment?	AU AC				
7. Are benefit payments and supporting documents reviewed and approved in accordance with established policy provisions (e.g., over a certain amount) prior to issuing a draft or check?	AU AP				

	Control Obj.	Y	N	Work Paper Ref.	Reliance
8. Are reviews performed to determine that continuous claim benefit payments (e.g., disability claims annuity benefits) are valid and supported by appropriate documentation?	AU AC				
9. Are benefit payments subject to independent testing or other periodic quality control checks?	AC				
10. Is there a segregation of duties between those responsible for maintaining the benefit payment records and those responsible for processing cash disbursements?	AP				
11. Do procedures exist to ensure that transactions are recorded in the correct accounting period?	CO				
12. Are benefit disbursement records reconciled to postings for benefit expense, suspense and other general ledger accounts?	AC CO				
13. Is a review for an accurate cut-off of benefit payments made for each accounting period including timely clearance of suspense accounts?	CO				
14. Are actual investment, mortality, morbidity and expense experience compared with assumed experience by lines of insurance to evaluate continued appropriateness of assumptions and whether provisions for losses are required (e.g., actual experience is substituted for assumed experience in the gross premium calculation)?	AC				
15. Do procedures exist to ensure that drafts written were recorded in the correct accounting period and those not presented for payment were recorded as a liability in accordance with **SSAP No. 2, paragraph 8**?	CO				
16. Are inventories of reported and unpaid claims maintained and periodically reconciled to due and unpaid claim liability listings and the general ledger?	AC CO				
17. Are estimated liabilities for resisted and litigated claims reviewed and evaluated for reasonableness?	AC				

	Control Obj.	Y	N	Work Paper Ref.	Reliance
18. Are the reserving methodology and valuation practices reviewed and approved by management?	AU CO				
19. Are processing backlogs compared to normal levels and considered in claim reserving calculations?	CO AC				
20. Are comparisons made to determine that policy reserves are released when death claim liabilities are established?	CO				
21. Are aggregate reserve and reserve changes by line of business reviewed, and are significant fluctuations investigated?	AC				
22. Are policy reserve calculations performed by internal audit or an outside consultant and compared to recorded reserve estimates?	AC				

OTHER KEY CONTROLS EXISTING FOR THIS EXAMINATION OBJECTIVE:

SUMMARY EVALUATION OF CONTROL RISK:

EVALUATION OF INDEPENDENT CPA'S WORK FOR THIS EXAMINATION (CPA REVIEW CHECKLIST):

OVERALL RISK ASSESSMENT

Balance Sheet Evaluation of the Likelihood of a Material Adjustment to Surplus:

The evaluation of the likelihood of a material adjustment to surplus should be based on the following criteria:

- Inherent Risk
- Internal & External Environmental Factors
- Control Risk
- Materiality Consideration

The examiner should rate each item as to the likelihood of a material misstatement. All items are assumed as "High" prior to any examiner evaluation. A "High" assessment requires the examiner to perform substantive examination procedures over that account area. A lower assessment allows the examiner to perform analytical or fewer substantive procedures to satisfy the examination requirements. If an assessment other than "High" is selected for any of the accounts, the examiner needs to document the basis for the assessment. If the assessment is based on control testwork, the documentation should include results of control procedures and related workpaper references.

1) "Aggregate Reserve for Life Contracts"

___________ High ___________ Medium ___________Low

Basis for Assessment:

____

____

____

2) "Aggregate Reserve for Accident and Health Contracts"

___________ High ___________ Medium ___________Low

Basis for Assessment:

____

____

____

3) "Liability for Deposit-Type Contracts"

____________ High ____________ Medium ____________Low

Basis for Assessment:

____

____

____

4) "Contract Claims"

____________ High ____________ Medium ____________Low

Basis for Assessment:

____

____

____

5) "Policyholders' Dividends and Coupons Due and Unpaid"

____________ High ____________ Medium ____________Low

Basis for Assessment:

____

____

____

6) "Provisions for Policyholders' Dividends and Coupons Payable in Following Calendar Year"

____________ High ____________ Medium ____________Low

Basis for Assessment:

____

____

____

7) "Amount Provisionally Held for Deferred Dividend Policies"

___________ High ___________ Medium ___________Low

Basis for Assessment:

____

____

____

8) "Contract Liabilities Not Included Elsewhere – Surrender Values on Cancelled Contracts"

___________ High ___________ Medium ___________Low

Basis for Assessment:

____

____

____

9) "Drafts Outstanding"

___________ High ___________ Medium ___________Low

Basis for Assessment:

____

____

____

PRELIMINARY EXAMINATION APPROACH — LOSSES AND BENEFITS CYCLE: LIFE

Listed below are the corresponding Annual Statement line items that are related to the procedures contained in this Losses and Benefits Specific Risk Analysis:

Aggregate Reserve for Life Contracts
Aggregate Reserve for Accident and Health Contracts
Liability for Deposit-Type Contracts
Contract Claims
Policyholders' Dividends and Coupons Due and Unpaid
Provisions for Policyholders' Dividends and Coupons Payable in Following Calendar Year
Amount Provisionally Held for Deferred Dividend Policies
Contract Liabilities Not Included Elsewhere – Surrender Values on Canceled Contracts
Drafts Outstanding

The actual examination procedures selected to be performed are a matter of considerable judgment by the examiner. The following "Examination Program" includes examples of procedures commonly used.

To the extent that the examiner judgmentally determines whether it is appropriate to use the following procedures, that selection can be documented by checking the space next to such procedure, with modifications noted in the margin. The examiner may determine that alternative or additional procedures are required. If so, those procedures can be added on a supplemental sheet. The examiner performing the procedure should indicate satisfactory completion by initialing and dating in the space provided, and referencing the workpapers where the procedures and findings are documented.

The examiner may choose to apply the examination procedures to less than 100% of the items comprising an account balance. Guidance for audit sampling and control and substantive procedures can be found in Part 3 of the NAIC *Financial Condition Examiners Handbook.* As appropriate, some procedures should be performed by a designated actuary.

After each examination procedure, the examination objective that the procedure satisfies is indicated. The examination objectives are accuracy, completeness, compliance, cutoff, existence, obligation and ownership, valuation and presentation and disclosure.

EXAMINATION OBJECTIVES

Accuracy (AC) – Recorded transactions and account balances are mathematically accurate, are based on correct amounts and have been classified into the correct account.

Completeness (CO) – All transactions and account balances that should be recorded in the Annual Financial Statement were recorded.

Compliance (CM) – Business transactions and affairs have been conducted in accordance with state insurance codes, other state laws or department directives.

Cutoff (CT) – All transactions are recorded in the correct accounting period.

Existence (EX) – Recorded transactions occurred and are not fictitious and recorded assets and liabilities existed as of the balance sheet date.

Obligation (OB) and Ownership (OW) – Recorded liabilities are obligations of the company and recorded assets are the rights of the company at the balance sheet date.

Valuation (VA) – Assets and liabilities are valued in accordance with state statute and NAIC accounting guidance.

Presentation and Disclosure (PD) – The elements of the Annual Statement are properly classified and all disclosures are accurately included in the Annual Statement.

	Exam Obj.	Completion Date	Examiner	Work Paper Ref.
EXAMINATION PROCEDURES				
General Procedures				
1. Through discussions with management and review of the company's overall insurance procedures, obtain an understanding of the company's reserving procedures. Document this understanding in a narrative and include in the workpapers. This narrative should include:	CM OB/OW			
a. Types of life insurance products provided by the company (e.g., whole life, endowment, term life, supplementary, group life, franchise life, universal life, variable life, limited payment, credit life and annuity contracts) in accordance with **SSAP No. 50, paragraphs 10-20**;	CM OB/OW			
b. Reserving methods established for the life insurance products in-force. These methods should include utilization of the guidelines included in Appendixes A-820, A-822, A-585, A-695, A-830 and A-200 as well as Appendix C of the NAIC *Accounting Practices and Procedures Manual* and the Actuarial Standards of Practice in accordance with **SSAP No. 51, paragraphs 14-18** and **SSAP No. 80, paragraphs 2-4**;	CM OB/OW			
c. Types of accident and health contracts provided by the company (e.g., managed care, income replacement, expense reimbursement, credit accident and health, continuing care, long-term care and accidental death and dismemberment contracts) in accordance with **SSAP No. 50, paragraphs 26-31**;	CM OB/OW			

	Exam Obj.	Completion Date	Examiner	Work Paper Ref.
d. Reserving methods established for the accident and health contracts in-force which includes policy reserves, claim reserves and miscellaneous reserves. These methods should include utilization of the guidelines included in Appendixes A-010, A-641, A-820 and A-822 as well as Appendix C of the NAIC *Accounting Practices and Procedures Manual* and the Actuarial Standards of Practice in accordance with **SSAP No. 54, paragraphs 8-11**;	CM OB/OW			
e. Types of deposit-type contracts provided by the company (e.g., supplemental contracts, lottery payouts, structured settlements, guaranteed interest contracts, income settlement options, dividend and coupon accumulations, annuities certain, premium and other deposit funds) in accordance with **SSAP No. 50, paragraphs 43-45**; and	CM OB/OW			
f. Reserving methods established for deposit-type contracts in-force. These methods should include utilization of the guidelines included in Appendixes A-820, A-822, A-695, A-830 and A-200 of the NAIC *Accounting Practices and Procedures Manual* and the Actuarial Standards of Practice as well as other methods described in accordance with **SSAP No. 52, paragraphs 7-10** and **SSAP No. 80, paragraphs 2-4**.	CM OB/OW			
2. Inquire of the company's use of an in-house or outside actuary in determining the reserve amounts.	AC CM			
a. Determine whether the company uses an in-house or outside actuary. Identify any change in actuaries from the last examination.	AC CM			

	Exam Obj.	Completion Date	Examiner	Work Paper Ref.
b. Verify that the actuary is a qualified actuary in accordance with guidelines in accordance with Appendix A-820 of the NAIC *Accounting Practices and Procedures Manual.*	AC CM			
c. Verify that the information provided to the actuary in the policy maintenance system is current and accurate in accordance with the actual policies in-force at the company.	AC CM			
d. Verify that the actuary follows the Actuarial Guidelines established in Appendix C of the NAIC *Accounting Practices and Procedures Manual.*	AC CM			
e. Read the actuarial report and compare it to the prior year actuarial report identifying and investigating significant variations. Inquire as to any world or economic events that have been factored into the current calculation.	AC CM			
f. Agree the actuarial results provided by the actuary to the company's calculation of current year reserves. Identify and investigate any instances in which the actuary's results are not utilized.	AC CM			
<u>Aggregate Reserve for Life Contracts</u>				
1. Obtain the calculation and supporting detail of the aggregate reserve for life contracts. Agree this calculation to the company's general ledger and Annual Statement.	AC EX			
2. Verify that the company has established a statutory policy reserve for all unmatured contractual obligations included in the insurance contract provisions, including separate benefits, in accordance with **SSAP No. 51, paragraph 14**.	AC EX CO			

	Exam Obj.	Completion Date	Examiner	Work Paper Ref.
a. Obtain a copy of the listing detailing in-force insurance contracts provided to the company's actuary. Perform procedures to verify the completeness of this listing by tracing to the database a sample of contracts selected from sources outside the reserve system. Perform procedures to verify the accuracy of this listing by agreeing reserve data to the actual insurance contract provisions.	AC EX CO CT			
3. Identify the assumptions and methodologies utilized in determining the company's life reserve. Verify that these assumptions and methodologies agree with those permitted in accordance with **SSAP No. 51, paragraphs 14-18** and **SSAP No. 80, paragraphs 2-4**:	AC CM			
a. Appendix A-820 – Minimum Life and Annuity Reserve Standards;	AC CM			
b. Appendix A-822 – Asset Adequacy Requirements;	AC CM			
c. Appendix A-825 – Commissioners Annuity Reserve Valuation Method (CARVM);	AC CM			
d. Appendix A-585 – Universal Life Insurance;	AC CM			
e. Appendix A-695 – Synthetic Guaranteed Investment Contracts;	AC CM			
f. Appendix A-830 – Valuation of Life Insurance Policies; and	AC CM			
g. Appendix A-200 – Separate Accounts Funding Guaranteed Minimum Benefits Under Group Contracts.	AC CM			

	Exam Obj.	Completion Date	Examiner	Work Paper Ref.
4. Determine whether the company utilizes the policy anniversary date or the reporting date to calculate the reserves. If the anniversary date is used, verify that the terminal reserve has been adjusted back to the reporting date in accordance with **SSAP No. 51, paragraphs 19-20**. Review the methods utilized in adjusting these reserves and verify that they agree with the methods permitted in accordance with **SSAP No. 51, paragraphs 21-24**.	AC CM			
5. Identify whether the company has any life insurance contracts with supplemental benefits. Perform procedures to verify that these supplemental benefits have been adequately reserved in accordance with **SSAP No. 51, paragraph 33**.	EX AC			
6. Identify whether the company's life insurance contracts have the option of accelerated benefits. Perform procedures to verify that these accelerated benefits and related life contacts have been properly reserved in accordance with **SSAP No. 51, paragraph 35**.	EX AC CM			
7. Identify any changes in the valuation basis in the reserve computation. Verify that these changes have been classified and disclosed as an accounting change in accordance with **SSAP No. 3** and **SSAP No. 51, paragraph 32**.	AC VA PD			
8. Perform procedures to validate the company's recorded life reserve.	AC VA			
a. Recalculate, or have an independent actuary recalculate, the company's life reserve based on the examined methodologies and assumptions.	AC VA			
b. Compare the calculated reserve to the company's recorded life reserve for reasonableness.	AC VA			

	Exam Obj.	Completion Date	Examiner	Work Paper Ref.
c. Investigate any significant differences between the reserve calculations as well as instances in which the company has recorded the minimum or maximum of the reserve range.	AC VA			
9. Identify any additional reserves recorded by the company. Reference **SSAP No. 51, paragraph 36** for a listing of common additional reserves. Perform procedures to ascertain the proper valuation of these liabilities.	EX AC VA			
10. Verify that all required disclosures in accordance with **SSAP No. 51, paragraphs 37-38** have been properly made.	PD			
<u>Aggregate Reserve for Accident and Health Contracts</u>				
1. Obtain the calculation and supporting detail of the aggregate reserve for accident and health contracts. Agree this calculation to the company's general ledger and Annual Statement.	AC EX			
2. Verify that the company has established a statutory policy reserve for all unmatured contractual obligations included in the insurance contract provisions, including separate benefits, in accordance with **SSAP No. 54, paragraph 10**.	AC EX CO			
a. Obtain a copy of the listing detailing in-force insurance contracts provided to the company's actuary. Perform procedures to verify the accuracy of this listing by agreeing a sample of the obligations to the actual insurance contract provisions and from the contract to the database. Verify that contracts established after year-end have been properly excluded from the listing.	AC EX CO CT			

	Exam Obj.	Completion Date	Examiner	Work Paper Ref.
3. Identify the assumptions and methodologies utilized in determining the company's accident and health reserve. Verify that these assumptions and methodologies agree with those permitted in accordance with **SSAP No. 54, paragraphs 10-11**:	AC CM			
a. Appendix A-010 – Minimum Reserve Standards for Individual and Group Health Insurance;	AC CM			
b. Appendix A-641 – Long Term Care Insurance;	AC CM			
c. Appendix A-820 – Minimum Life and Annuity Standards; and	AC CM			
d. Appendix A-822 – Asset Adequacy Analysis Requirements.	AC CM			
4. Identify contract reserves or additional reserves that are recorded on accident and health contracts. Verify that these reserves are recorded in accordance with **SSAP No. 54, paragraphs 13-14**. Perform procedures to ascertain the proper valuation of these reserves.	EX AC			
a. Verify that contract reserves are recorded when premium and benefits are not earned or incurred at the same incidence over the policy period.	EX AC			
b. Verify that contract reserves are recorded when the future benefits exceed the future net premiums or where the contract provides for the extension of benefits after the termination of coverage.	EX AC			
5. Identify any terminal reserves recorded for accident and health contracts. Verify that these reserves are recorded to cover the assumed difference between future benefits and future net premiums in accordance with **SSAP No. 54, paragraphs 15-16**. Perform procedures to ascertain the proper liability of these recorded reserves.	EX AC			

	Exam Obj.	Completion Date	Examiner	Work Paper Ref.
a. Verify that the terminal reserve calculation includes consideration of the interest rate, mortality and/or morbidity table and a valuation method.	EX AC			
b. Verify that the terminal reserves calculated as of the end of the policy year are adjusted to reflect the portion of the net premium that is unearned at the reporting date by either the Mean Reserve Method, Mid-Terminal Reserve Method (**SSAP No. 51, paragraphs 21-24**) or through another method (e.g., Exact Reserve Valuation).	EX AC			
6. Identify any instances in which negative reserves have been used to offset positive reserves for other benefits in the same policy. Verify that in these instances the mean reserve on any policy is not less than half the valuation net premium in accordance with **SSAP No. 54, paragraph 17**.	EX AC			
a. Verify whether contracts with favorable margins in an experience rated package are used to offset the need to establish additional reserves on other contracts in the package.	EX AC			
7. Identify whether the company has any accident or health contracts with supplemental benefits. Perform procedures to verify that these supplemental benefits have been adequately reserved for in accordance with **SSAP No. 54, paragraph 22**.	EX AC			
8. Identify any changes in the valuation basis in the reserve computation. Verify that these changes have been classified and disclosed as an accounting change in accordance with **SSAP No. 3 and SSAP No. 54, paragraph 21**.	AC VA PD			

Procedure	Exam Obj.	Completion Date	Examiner	Work Paper Ref.
9. Determine whether the company has adequately recorded accident and health reserves. In accordance with **SSAP No. 54, paragraph 23**, the prospective gross premium valuation is the ultimate test of reserve adequacy and shall include consideration of unearned premium reserves, contract or additional reserves, claim reserves and miscellaneous reserves. (Each component should be computed separately.) Perform procedures to validate the company's recorded accident and health reserve.	AC VA			
a. Recalculate the company's accident and health reserves based on the examined methodologies and assumptions.	AC VA			
b. Compare the calculated reserve to the company's recorded accident and health reserve for reasonableness.	AC VA			
c. Investigate any significant differences between the reserve calculations as well as instances in which the company has recorded the minimum or maximum of the reserve range.	AC VA			
10. Identify any additional reserves recorded by the company. Reference **SSAP No. 54, paragraph 25** for a listing of common additional reserves. Perform procedures to ascertain the proper valuation of these liabilities.	EX AC VA			
<u>**Liability for Deposit-Type Contracts**</u>				
1. Obtain the calculation detail for the deposit-type contract liability. Agree this detail to the company's general ledger and Annual Statement.	AC EX			
2. Verify that the company has established a statutory policy reserve for all contractual obligations included in the contract provisions, including separate benefits, in accordance with **SSAP No. 52, paragraph 7**.	AC EX CO			

	Exam Obj.	Completion Date	Examiner	Work Paper Ref.
a. Obtain a copy of the listing detailing in-force insurance contracts provided to the company's actuary. Perform procedures to verify the accuracy of this listing by agreeing a sample of the obligations to the actual insurance contract provisions. Verify that contracts established after year-end have been properly excluded from the listing.	AC EX CO CT			
3. Identify the assumptions and methodologies utilized in determining the company's deposit-type contract liability. Verify that these assumptions and methodologies agree with those permitted in accordance with **SSAP No. 52, paragraphs 7-10 and SSAP No. 80, paragraphs 2-4**:	AC CM			
a. Appendix A-820 – Minimum Life and Annuity Standards;	AC CM			
b. Appendix A-822 – Asset Adequacy Analysis Requirements;	AC CM			
c. Appendix A-695 – Synthetic Guaranteed Investment Contracts;	AC CM			
d. Appendix A-830 – Valuation of Life Insurance Policies;	AC CM			
e. Appendix A-200 – Separate Accounts Funding Guaranteed Minimum Benefits Under Group Contracts;	AC CM			
f. Guaranteed Fixed Benefits – Present value of all future guaranteed benefits discounted at the valuation interest rate; and	AC CM			
g. All Other Contracts – Accumulated amounts paid plus an income accumulation, less any withdrawals and surrender charges.	AC CM			

	Exam Obj.	Completion Date	Examiner	Work Paper Ref.
4. Identify any instances in which the policy reserves have been adjusted in accordance with reinsurance assumed or ceded in accordance with **SSAP No. 52, paragraph 10** and **SSAP No. 61, paragraph 27**.	AC EX			
a. Verify that net consideration exchanged is recorded as a contra-liability by the payer of the net considerations and as a liability by the receiver. Throughout the life of the contract, receipts and disbursements shall be recorded through the asset/liability accounts.	AC EX			
5. Identify any instances in which the company has recorded obligations under structured settlements. Verify that these obligations and related annuities have been recorded in accordance with **SSAP No. 52, paragraph 11** and **SSAP No. 65, paragraphs 17-20**.	AC EX VA			
6. Identify any changes in the valuation basis in the reserve computation. Verify that these changes have been classified and disclosed as an accounting change in accordance with **SSAP No. 3 and SSAP No. 52, paragraph 13**.	AC VA PD			
a. Verify that any changes in the actuarial reserves resulting due to a change in valuation basis have been recorded directly to surplus in accordance with **SSAP No. 52, paragraph 13**.	AC VA PD			
7. Determine whether the company has adequately recorded deposit-type contract liabilities.	AC VA			
a. Recalculate the company's deposit-type contract liabilities based on the examined methodologies and assumptions.	AC VA			
b. Compare the calculated liability to the company's recorded deposit-type contract liability for reasonableness.	AC VA			

	Exam Obj.	Completion Date	Examiner	Work Paper Ref.
c. Investigate any significant differences between the liability calculations as well as instances in which the company has recorded the minimum or maximum of the liability range.	AC VA			
8. Identify any additional reserves recorded by the company. Reference **SSAP No. 52, paragraph 15** for a listing of common additional reserves. Perform procedures to ascertain the proper valuation of these liabilities.	EX AC VA			
9. Verify that all required disclosures in accordance with **SSAP No. 52, paragraphs 16-17** have been properly made.	PD			
<u>Contract Claims</u>				
Life Claims				
1. Obtain detail of the liability established for the life contract claims/benefits. Agree this detail to the company's general ledger and Annual Statement. Verify that the liability detail has been categorized in accordance with **SSAP No. 55, paragraph 6** and **SSAP No. 85**:	EX AC			
a. Due and unpaid claims;	EX AC			
b. Resisted claims in course of settlement;	EX AC			
c. Other claims in course of settlement;	EX AC			
d. Incurred but not reported claims (IBNR); and	EX AC			
e. Claim adjustment expenses for life reporting entities.	AC EX			
2. From the detail provided in step #1 of the due and unpaid claims, resisted claims in course of settlement, and other claims in course of settlement, trace and substantiate the claim/benefit details:	EX AC VA OB/OW			
a. Claimant – Agree to insurance contract;	EX			

	Exam Obj.	Completion Date	Examiner	Work Paper Ref.
b. Claim/Benefit Liability – Agree to contract terms and/or supporting documentation;	VA			
c. Policy Term – Agree to insurance contract;	OB/OW			
d. Beneficiary – Agree to insurance contract;	AC			
e. Contract In-force – Review premium receipts to verify proper receipt of premiums and to verify that the contract was in-force at the time of the claim request; and	OB/OW			
f. Supporting Documentation – Review the supporting documentation (e.g., death certificate) obtained by the company to certify the claim/benefit request.	EX			
3. From the testwork performed in step #2, identify any claims included on the detail for which the liability recorded is not consistent with the contract terms. Identify claims that appear to have not been paid in a reasonable or fair time frame. Investigate the status of these claims/benefits with company management.	EX AC			
4. Verify that the claims/benefits liability is complete and properly recorded at year-end.	AC CO VA CM			
a. Obtain the claims/benefits register subsequent to year-end. Select a sample of claims from this register, noting the reported date, and trace them to the year-end claim liability listing. Investigate any instances in which claims were excluded from the year-end detail or in which the liability was materially understated at year-end.	AC CO VA			

	Exam Obj.	Completion Date	Examiner	Work Paper Ref.
b. Select a sample of claims included on the closed claim detail and agree the claim payment to cash disbursements or cancelled checks.	AC CO VA CM			
5. Obtain detail of resisted claims and claims closed without payment. Agree this detail to the company's Annual Statement. Perform procedures to verify the grounds for the resisted claims.	AC EX			
a. Examine the claim applications and claim files as well as the insurance policy. Discuss the rationale of resisting claims with company management.	AC EX			
6. Obtain the calculation for the IBNR claim liability. Perform procedures to ascertain the reasonableness of this established liability.	AC EX VA			
a. Through discussions with management obtain an understanding of the assumptions and methodologies used to estimate the liability for IBNR claims. **SSAP No. 55, paragraph 9** provides general insight to the acceptable techniques used to value these liabilities.	AC EX VA			
b. Verify that the company is utilizing the best estimate for claim liability in accordance with **SSAP No. 55, paragraphs 8-12**.	AC EX VA			
c. Recalculate the IBNR reserve based on the overall life contracts in-force at the company.	AC EX VA			
7. Obtain detail of the claim adjustment expenses for life contracts. Compare the claim adjustment expenses to prior year expenses. Investigate any significant fluctuations.	AC EX VA			

Procedure	Exam Obj.	Completion Date	Examiner	Work Paper Ref.
Accident and Health Claims				
8. Obtain detail of the liability established for the accident and health contract claims. Agree this detail to the company's general ledger and Annual Statement. Verify that the liability detail has been categorized in accordance with **SSAP No. 55, paragraph 6** and **SSAP No. 85**:	EX AC			
a. Due and unpaid claims;	EX AC			
b. Resisted claims in course of settlement;	EX AC			
c. Other claims in course of settlement; and	EX AC			
d. Incurred but not reported claims (IBNR).	EX AC			
9. Identify the claim reserves accrued by the company. Verify that these reserves are appropriately estimated to cover the costs of future health care services currently obligated by the company as a result of premiums earned to date in accordance with **SSAP No. 55, paragraph 6, SSAP No. 85** and **SSAP No. 54, paragraph 19**. The claim reserves should also include a reserve for disability benefits covered under the premium waiver provisions.	EX AC VA			
a. Verify whether disability claims with a duration of less than two years are based on the reporting entry's experience, if credible, or other methods as appropriate.	EX AC VA			
b. Verify that disability claims with durations of greater than two years are determined by a tabular method using the age of the insured at disablement, the number of months the insured has been disabled, and the number of months remaining in the benefit period.	EX AC VA			

	Exam Obj.	Completion Date	Examiner	Work Paper Ref.
10. Through discussions with management and examination procedures performed, determine whether an appropriate claim reserve has been recorded.	EX AC VA CO			
a. Obtain detail of the reported but unpaid claims. Verify that the company has established a claim liability for each of these claims. Identify the methodologies and assumptions used to calculate these claim liabilities. Investigate any claims included on this detail that the company has not reserved for.	EX AC VA CO			
b. Recalculate the claim reserves and disability reserves. Investigate any significant variances between the recalculated reserve and the recorded reserve.	EX AC VA			
11. From the provided detail in step #1 of the due and unpaid claims, resisted claims in course of settlement, and other claims in course of settlement, trace the claim/benefit amount and other information to supporting documentation:	EX AC VA OB/OW			
a. Claimant – Agree to insurance contract;	EX			
b. Claim/Benefit Liability – Agree to contract terms or supporting documentation;	VA			
c. Policy Term – Agree to insurance contract;	OB/OW			
d. Contract In-force – Review premium receipts to verify proper receipt of premiums and to verify that the contract was in-force at the time of the claim request; and	OB/OW			
e. Supporting Documentation – Review the supporting documentation (e.g., doctor invoice) obtained by the company to certify the claim/benefit request.	EX			

	Exam Obj.	Completion Date	Examiner	Work Paper Ref.
12. From the testwork performed in step #2, identify any claims included on the detail for which the liability recorded is not consistent with the contract terms or claims that appear to have not been paid in a reasonable or fair time frame. Investigate the status of these claims/benefits with company management.	EX AC			
13. Verify that the claims liability is complete and properly recorded at year-end.	AC CO VA CM			
a. Obtain the claims paid register subsequent to year-end. Select a sample of claims from this register and trace them to the year-end claim liability listing. Investigate any instances in which claims were excluded from the year-end detail or in which the liability was materially understated at year-end.	AC CO VA CM			
b. Select a sample of claims included on the closed claim detail and agree the claim payment to cash disbursements or cancelled checks.	AC CO VA			
14. Obtain detail of resisted claims and claims closed without payment. Agree this detail to the company's Annual Statement. Perform procedures to verify the grounds for the resisted claims:	AC EX			
a. Examine the claim applications and claim files, as well as the insurance policy. Discuss the rationale of resisting claims with company management.	AC EX			
15. Obtain the calculation for the IBNR claim liability. Perform procedures to ascertain the reasonableness of this established liability.	AC EX VA			

	Exam Obj.	Completion Date	Examiner	Work Paper Ref.
a. Through discussions with management obtain an understanding of the assumptions and methodologies used to estimate the liability for IBNR claims. **SSAP No. 55, paragraph 9** provides general insight to the acceptable techniques used to value these liabilities.	AC EX VA			
b. Verify that the company is utilizing the best estimate for claim liability in accordance with **SSAP No. 55, paragraphs 8-11**.	AC EX VA			
c. Recalculate the IBNR reserve based on the overall life contracts in-force at the company.	AC EX VA			
16. Obtain detail of the claim adjustment expenses for accident and health reporting entities. Compare the claim adjustment expenses to the prior year expenses. Investigate any significant fluctuations.	AC EX VA			
<u>Policyholder's Dividends and Coupons Due and Unpaid</u>				
1. Obtain detail of the policyholder's dividends and coupons due and unpaid. Agree this detail to the company's general ledger and Annual Statement.	AC EX			
2. Verify that the policyholder's dividends due and unpaid liability consists of dividends payable to the policyholder in the current year but that have not been distributed or applied as of the reporting date in accordance with **SSAP No. 51, paragraph 27**.	AC EX CO VA			
a. Review the board of director minutes to verify the amount and timing in which the policyholder's dividends should be paid. Investigate any discrepancies.	AC EX CO VA			

	Exam Obj.	Completion Date	Examiner	Work Paper Ref.
3. In order to verify the coupons due and unpaid, agree the coupons payable to the respective insurance policy. Verify that the insurance policy requires an annual return in the form of coupons.	AC EX CO VA			
a. Recalculate the coupon amount payable considering any discounts for interest or mortality in accordance with **SSAP No. 51, paragraph 30**.	AC EX CO VA			
b. Through other examination procedures performed, identify any insurance contracts whose terms require coupon payments that have been excluded from the year-end liability.	AC EX CO VA			
4. Verify that the required policyholder dividend disclosure noted in **SSAP No. 51, paragraph 41** has been properly made.	PD			
<u>Provision for Policyholder's Dividends and Coupons Payable in Following Calendar Year</u>				
1. Obtain detail of the policyholder's dividend and coupons payable in the following calendar year. Agree this detail to the company's general ledger and Annual Statement. Verify that this liability has been adequately categorized into the following:	AC EX			
a. Dividends apportioned for payment;	AC EX			
b. Dividends not yet apportioned; and	AC EX			
c. Coupons and similar benefits.	AC EX			
Dividends Apportioned for Payment				
2. Review the board of directors minutes to verify the estimated amount of policyholder dividends declared prior to the end of the statement year which are not yet paid or due at the end of the year in accordance with **SSAP No. 51, paragraph 28**.	AC EX VA CO			

	Exam Obj.	Completion Date	Examiner	Work Paper Ref.
Dividends Not Yet Apportioned				
3. Review the estimated amount of dividend liability for dividends not yet apportioned and verify that it meets the criteria established in accordance with **SSAP No. 51, paragraph 28**.	AC EX VA			
a. Verify that liability for individual insurance is equal to the aggregate amount of the dividends estimated to be payable in the following calendar year whether or not declared or apportioned.	AC EX VA			
b. Verify that liability for group insurance and pensions is equal to the portion of the dividend payable in the following calendar year which has been earned in the current calendar year.	AC EX VA			
Coupons and Similar Benefits				
4. Review the estimated liability for coupons and similar benefits and verify it meets the criteria established in **SSAP No. 51, paragraph 30**.	AC EX VA			
a. Verify that liability for accumulated mature coupon payments is determined by the interest accrued from the date of maturity.	AC EX VA			
b. Verify that liability for non-matured policyholder coupons is the face value of the coupon, discounted at interest and mortality.	AC EX VA			
Amount Provisionally Held for Deferred Dividend Policies				
1. Obtain detail of the amount provisionally held for deferred dividend policies. Agree this detail to the company's general ledger and Annual Statement.	AC EX			

Procedure	Exam Obj.	Completion Date	Examiner	Work Paper Ref.
2. Through discussions with the company, ascertain the items included within this account. Verify that the items within this account are properly excluded from the other dividend liability established.	AC EX			
3. Perform procedures to verify the completeness and valuation of the liability established in this account.	CO VA			
<u>**Contract Liabilities Not Included Elsewhere – Surrender Values on Cancelled Contracts**</u>				
1. Obtain detail of the surrender values on cancelled contracts. Agree this detail to the company's general ledger and Annual Statement.	AC EX			
2. Obtain and review a listing of the current year cancelled contracts. Utilizing this listing, verify that the company considered all current year cancelled contracts to determine the respective surrender value liability.	AC CO			
a. Identify those cancelled contracts without surrender values and perform procedures to verify that surrender values were not required in accordance with the actual insurance contract provisions.	AC CO			
3. Verify the recorded liability by recalculating the surrender values in accordance with actual insurance contract specifications. Perform a search for unrecorded surrender values remitted subsequent to year-end to verify the recorded liability and to identify any liability not recorded at year-end.	AC CO VA			
<u>**Drafts Outstanding**</u>				
1. Obtain detail of the drafts outstanding. Agree this detail to the company's general ledger and Annual Statement.	AC EX			

	Exam Obj.	Completion Date	Examiner	Work Paper Ref.
2. Through discussion with management and review of the account activity, develop an understanding of what items are being recorded in this account. **SSAP No. 2, paragraph 6** provides guidance to the definition and characteristics of a draft.	AC EX			
3. For those drafts outstanding pertaining to claims/benefits, verify that the company utilizes the Draft Issue Method in accordance with **SSAP No. 2, paragraph 8**. Determine that these respective drafts outstanding were recorded with corresponding entries to paid losses and loss reserves.	AC EX CM			
a. For companies who do not have drafts outstanding, determine that they appropriately use the Draft Honored Method in accordance with **SSAP No. 2, paragraph 8**.	AC EX CM			
4. Identify those drafts outstanding in excess of six (6) months and verify that the company has properly conducted procedures to locate and notify the beneficiary or claimant of the outstanding draft.	AC CM			
5. For drafts outstanding, verify that the company accurately and timely completes and remits the escheat statement to the appropriate state.	AC EX CO VA			
6. Verify that the method to account for drafts outstanding is consistent with the prior year and that any changes to the method used to account for drafts issued and outstanding has been governed by **SSAP No. 3** in accordance with **SSAP No. 2, paragraph 9**.	AC EX			

SECTION E — LOSSES AND BENEFITS CYCLE: PROPERTY/CASUALTY

Listed below are the corresponding Annual Statement line items that are related to the procedures contained in this Losses and Benefits Specific Risk Analysis:

Annual Statement Blank Line Items

Losses
Loss Adjustment Expenses
Dividends Declared and Unpaid – Policyholders
Drafts Outstanding

Relevant SSAP's include:

#2,	Cash, Drafts, and Short-term Investments
#50,	Classifications and Definitions of Insurance or Managed Care Contracts In-Force
#55,	Unpaid Claims, Losses, and Loss Adjustment Expenses
#65,	Property and Casualty Contracts
#70,	Allocation of Expenses

SPECIFIC RISK ANALYSIS WORKPAPERS

Risk Analysis Prepared By/Date ______________________________

Preliminary Examination Approach Prepared By/Date ______________________________

Reviewed By/Date ______________________________

EXAMINATION OBJECTIVES:

1. All paid and unpaid losses and loss adjustment expenses existed, were obligations of the insurer and were reported correctly during the period under review as to accounts, amounts and period. (Completeness, Accuracy, Existence, Obligation and Ownership and Cutoff)

2. Paid and unpaid losses and loss adjustment expenses were in compliance with state statutes. (Compliance)

3. Provision for unpaid losses and loss adjustment expenses as of the balance sheet date is adequate. (Valuation)

4. Paid and unpaid losses and loss adjustment expenses and related disclosures were reported in accordance with NAIC *Annual Statement Instructions*. (Presentation and Disclosure)

INHERENT RISKS

____

____

____

____

INTERNAL AND EXTERNAL ENVIRONMENTAL CONDITIONS/FACTORS

____

____

____

____

RESULTS OF DETAIL ANALYTICAL REVIEW PROCEDURES

____

____

____

____

CONTROL RISK — LOSSES AND BENEFITS CYCLE: PROPERTY/CASUALTY

This questionnaire is designed to assist the examiner in assessing control risk for property and casualty losses and benefits cycles. Part 1, Section III and Part 3 of this *Handbook* provide guidance in consideration of an insurer's internal control structure for use when designing substantive examination procedures.

This questionnaire includes examples of internal control procedures and policies that are commonly utilized by insurers to achieve internal control objectives. For each control procedure listed below, indicate by placing a check mark in the yes or no box whether or not the insurer employs such a procedure, or other similar practice (include a description of the similar procedure). To the extent the control procedure is not applicable, indicate N/A. If other relevant control procedures are in place, list them in the space that follows. Control procedures that are tested by the examiner should be documented by including the workpaper reference in the comment section and the examiner's initials in the reliance column.

For each individual control procedure there is a control objective listed that satisfies the procedure.

If the examiner initially assesses control risk as low or medium for a particular account balance, then those controls must be tested. The controls should be tested to determine whether the procedure is operating as expected, applied throughout the entire period of reliance, performed on a timely basis, encompassing all transactions and identifying errors. Some examples of testing procedures are inquiry, observation, re-performance and examination of documents. The level of reliance, if any, should be indicated in the applicable column along with any comments the examiner may have regarding the procedure.

Based upon the testing results, the examiner should determine whether the preliminary control risk assessment is confirmed or should be revised.

CONTROL OBJECTIVES

Authorization (AU) – All transactions recorded were reviewed and approved by designated personnel.

Completeness (CO) – All transactions that occurred were initially entered into the accounting records, accepted for processing and generated data files and reports reflect that all transactions have occurred.

Accuracy (AC) – Transactions are initially recorded correctly, timely and accurately.

Asset Protection (AP) – Adequate safeguards over access to and use of assets and records, including the appropriate segregation of duties among company personnel.

	Control Obj.	Y	N	Work Paper Ref.	Reliance
General Control Procedures					
The examiner should determine the amount of documentation necessary for each control procedure. If the examiner intends to place substantial reliance on the established controls, the examiner should explain the control procedure in a workpaper and document the individual responsible for supervising the control activity as well as the frequency of the control activity.					
1. Is the in-force status of the policy verified before the claim is processed?	AU AP				
2. Are changes to the master policy file and losses data authorized and approved?	AU				
3. Are master file transactions accounted for by input/output reconciliation controls (e.g., batch totals, hash totals, numerical sequence, edit reports)?	AU				
4. Are controls (review, reconciliation or edit) in effect to ensure that master files and other records are updated to reflect claims paid?	CO				
5. Are persons authorized to make additions, deletions, and changes to data contained in files, registers, databases, etc. limited in number and scope of job responsibilities?	AU AP				
6. Are claim payments and supporting documents reviewed and approved in accordance with established policy provisions (e.g., over a certain amount) prior to issuing a draft or check?	AU AP				
7. Are loss ratios by line or class of business or other key analytical relationships monitored and unusual fluctuations investigated on a timely basis?	CO				
8. Are claim payments subject to independent testing or other periodic quality control checks?	AC				
9. Is there adequate segregation of duties between loss adjusters, those responsible for maintaining the loss payable records and those responsible for processing cash disbursements?	AP				

	Control Obj.	Y	N	Work Paper Ref.	Reliance
10. Do procedures exist to ensure that transactions are recorded in the correct accounting period and accident year?	CO				
11. Are benefit disbursement records reconciled to postings for benefit expense, suspense, and other general ledger accounts?	AC CO				
12. Are suspense accounts reviewed to ensure that they are cleared of salvage and subrogation receipts, reinsurance recoverable receipts and claim payments in a timely manner?	CO				
13. Do procedures exist to ensure that salvage and subrogation are conducted as arms length transactions?	AU CO AC				
14. Are account and line of insurance distribution independently reviewed and approved or subjected to validity tests (e.g., edit checks, over logical combinations of data) prior to entry into the system, and are exceptions independently investigated?	CO AC				
15. Do procedures exist to ensure that drafts written were recorded in the correct accounting period and those not presented for payment were recorded as a liability in accordance with **SSAP No. 2, paragraph 8**?	CO				
16. Are inventories of reported and unpaid claims maintained and periodically reconciled to unpaid claim liability listings and the general ledger?	AC CO				
17. Are estimated liabilities for resisted and litigated claims reviewed and evaluated for reasonableness?	AC				
18. Is access to unissued checks or drafts limited to authorized personnel?	AP				
19. Does a qualified property/casualty actuary review the internal reserve analyses prepared by the insurer?	AU				
20. Are procedures in place to reconcile actuarial data to Schedule P?	CO AC				

	Control Obj.	Y	N	Work Paper Ref.	Reliance
21. Are processing backlogs compared to normal levels and considered in claim reserving calculations?	CO AC				
22. Does the company periodically review the factors used to establish loss or loss adjustment expense (LAE) reserves?	AC				
23. Are analytical procedures in place to review reserve changes, balances and fluctuations from period to period?	AC				
24. Are independent reserve projections performed periodically throughout the year and compared to recorded reserve estimates?	AC				

OTHER KEY CONTROLS EXISTING FOR THIS CONTROL OBJECTIVES:

SUMMARY EVALUATION OF CONTROL RISK:

EVALUATION OF INDEPENDENT CPA'S WORK FOR EXAMINATION (CPA REVIEW CHECKLIST):

OVERALL RISK ASSESSMENT

Balance Sheet Item Evaluation of Likelihood of Material Adjustment to Surplus:

The evaluation of the likelihood of a material adjustment to surplus should be based on the following criteria:

- Inherent Risk
- Internal & External Environmental Factors
- Control Risk
- Materiality Consideration

The examiner should rate each item as to the likelihood of a material misstatement. All items are assumed as "High" prior to any examiner evaluation. A "High" assessment requires the examiner to perform substantive examination procedures over that account area. A lower assessment allows the examiner to perform analytical or fewer substantive procedures to satisfy the examination requirements. If an assessment other than "High" is selected for any of the accounts, the examiner needs to document the basis for the assessment. If the assessment is based on control testwork, the documentation should include results of control procedures and related workpaper references.

1) "Losses"

___________ High ___________ Medium ___________Low

Basis for Assessment:

____

____

____

2) "Loss Adjustment Expenses"

___________ High ___________ Medium ___________Low

Basis for Assessment:

____

____

____

3) "Dividends Declared and Unpaid - Policyholders"

___________ High ___________ Medium __________Low

Basis for Assessment:

____

____

____

4) "Drafts Outstanding"

___________ High ___________ Medium __________Low

Basis for Assessment:

____

____

____

PRELIMINARY EXAMINATION APPROACH — LOSSES AND BENEFITS: PROPERTY/CASUALTY

Listed below are the corresponding Annual Statement line items that are related to the procedures contained in this Losses/Benefits Specific Risk Analysis:

Losses
Loss Adjustment Expenses
Dividends Declared and Unpaid - Policyholders
Drafts Outstanding

The actual examination procedures selected to be performed are a matter of considerable judgment by the examiner. The following "Examination Program" includes examples of procedures commonly used.

To the extent that the examiner judgmentally determines whether it is appropriate to use the following procedures, that selection can be documented by checking the space next to such procedure, with modifications noted in the margin. The examiner may determine that alternative or additional procedures are required. If so, those procedures can be added on a supplemental sheet. The examiner performing the procedure should indicate satisfactory completion by initialing and dating in the space provided, and referencing the workpapers where the procedures and findings are documented.

The examiner may chose to apply the examination procedures to less than 100% of the items comprising an account balance. Guidance for audit sampling and control and substantive procedures can be found in Part 3 of the NAIC *Financial Condition Examiners Handbook.* As appropriate, some procedures may be performed by a designated actuary.

After each examination procedure, the examination objective that the procedure satisfies is indicated. The examination objectives are accuracy, completeness, compliance, cutoff, existence, obligation & ownership, valuation and presentation and disclosure.

EXAMINATION OBJECTIVES:

Accuracy (AC) – Recorded transactions and account balances are mathematically accurate, are based on correct amounts and have been classified into the correct account.

Completeness (CO) – All transactions and account balances that should be recorded in the Annual Financial Statement were recorded.

Compliance (CM) – Business transactions and affairs have been conducted in accordance with state insurance codes, other state laws or department directives.

Cutoff (CT) – All transactions are recorded in the correct accounting period.

Existence (EX) – Recorded transactions occurred and are not fictitious and recorded assets and liabilities existed as of the balance sheet date.

Obligation (OB) and Ownership (OW) – Recorded liabilities are obligations of the company and recorded assets are the rights of the company at the balance sheet date.

Valuation (VA) – Assets and liabilities are valued in accordance with state statute and NAIC accounting guidance.

Presentation and Disclosure (PD) – The elements of the Annual Statement are properly classified and all disclosures are accurately included in the Annual Statement.

	Exam Obj.	Completion Date	Examiner	Work Paper Ref.
EXAMINATION PROCEDURES				
<u>**General Procedures**</u>				
1. Through discussion with management and review of the company's overall insurance procedures, obtain an understanding of the company's insurance products and possible liabilities. Document this understanding in a memorandum and include in the workpapers. This narrative should include:	CM OB/OW			
a. Types of insurance contracts provided by the company (e.g., traditional property and casualty insurance contracts, title insurance contracts, mortgage and financial guaranty contracts.) in accordance with **SSAP No. 50, paragraphs 32-42**;	CM OB/OW			
b. Types of perils insured under the property and casualty contracts (e.g., fire and allied lines, ocean marine, inland marine, workers' compensation, automobile, multiple peril, professional liability, miscellaneous liability, fidelity bonds and surety bonds) in accordance with SSAP No. 50, paragraph 36; and	CM OB/OW			
c. Specific characteristics of insurance provided (e.g., excess lines, surplus lines, involuntary plans and pools) in accordance with **SSAP No. 50, paragraphs 37-40**.	CM OB/OW			
2. Inquire of the company's use of an in-house actuary or outside actuary in determining the reserve amounts.	AC CM			
a. Determine whether the company uses an in-house or outside actuary. Identify any change in actuaries from the last examination. Note if actuaries have formal designations (e.g., FCAS).	AC CM			

	Exam Obj.	Completion Date	Examiner	Work Paper Ref.
b. Read the actuarial report and compare it to the prior year actuarial report identifying and investigating significant variations. Inquire as to any world or economic events that have been factored into the current calculation.	AC CM			
c. Agree the actuarial results provided by the actuary to the company's calculation of current year reserves. Identify and investigate any instances in which the actuary's results are not utilized.	AC CM			
Data Validation				
3. After discussion with the assigned actuary and supervisor, obtain the company's actuarial report for losses and loss adjustment expenses and reconcile to supporting company reports, general ledger and annual statement schedules and exhibits as of the valuation date. *(Note: The working papers may include Direct & Assumed, Ceded, and Net amounts for payments and reserves. Special attention should be given by the Examiner to separate losses processed on the company's computer system versus off-system (manually recorded) losses. The on-system (control) totals will be important when requesting and reconciling downloaded data from the company.)*	AC CM			
4. Determine if account balances and disclosures comply with the NAIC *Accounting Practices and Procedures Manual* (codification), NAIC *Financial Condition Examiners Handbook*, and NAIC *Annual Statement Instructions.*	AC CM			

	Exam Obj.	Completion Date	Examiner	Work Paper Ref.
5. Develop a detailed download of all claim transactions in the examination period for a selected line(s) of business. (This should be a material line and should be the line chosen for data validation.) *(Note: Discuss with Examiner In-Charge, EDP Specialist, and actuary assigned to the examination prior to requesting download from company. It may be necessary to modify this request depending on the number of claims reported to the company. This may be performed by the company and reviewed by the manager.)* Consider the following information on the download (this may vary depending on what information is captured on the record):	AC			
a. Claim number;	AC			
b. Claimant;	AC			
c. Line of business codes;	AC			
d. Coverage codes;	AC			
e. Branch codes (if applicable);	AC			
f. Report date (mm/dd/yy);	AC			
g. Accident date (mm/dd/yy);	AC			
h. Reinsurance codes (direct and assumed, ceded, net – DAC);	AC			
i. Loss payments (through examination date);	AC			
j. Paid date;	AC			
k. DCC payments (through examination date);	AC			
l. Outstanding loss reserves (as of the examination date); and	AC			
m. Outstanding DCC reserves (as of the examination date).	AC			

	Exam Obj.	Completion Date	Examiner	Work Paper Ref.
6. Reconcile the cumulative payments and outstanding reserves for losses and DCC by line and by accident year from the detail claim download obtained in the previous step to the company's working papers obtained in step #3. *(Note: This may be performed by the company, and reviewed by the examiner.)*	AC			
7. Discuss with actuary which data cells should be selected for data validation. Select a sample of claim transactions from selected data cells. Use Chapter 3 of the NAIC *Financial Condition Examiners Handbook* for guidance in selecting the sample. Include on the sample data elements included on the record (claim number, claimant, accident date, report date, line of business, coverage code, cumulative payments, outstanding reserves, etc.).	AC			
8. Request the claim files from the company based on the sample above. Review the claim file information and verify that the information in the claim file matches the information contained on the sample selected in step #7. (Verify all information including the line of business, accident date, report date, reserves at the examination date, cumulative paid losses and loss adjustment expenses and all other relevant data included in the claim download sample.) Trace selected payments to cash disbursements and cancelled checks.	AC			
9. Perform completeness testing by reviewing subsequent loss and DCC payments. Physically pull claims from the claims department files (if a company's claim department maintains physical files), select a sequence of claim numbers and trace to the detail download; or perform other appropriate procedures.	AC			

	Exam Obj.	Completion Date	Examiner	Work Paper Ref.
10. Document your findings, if exceptions are found discuss results with the assigned actuary and supervisor before considering additional samples. *(Note: It is important that the actuary be notified as early as possible, particularly if the data is not accurate and/or complete. An analysis of the company's reserves is meaningless unless the data used is accurate and complete.)*	AC			
<u>Losses</u>				
1. Obtain the supporting detail of the loss liability established for property and casualty contracts. Agree this detail to the company's general ledger and Annual Statement. Verify that this liability has been categorized in accordance with **SSAP No. 55, paragraph 5**.	EX AC			
a. Reported losses;	EX AC			
b. Incurred but not reported losses (IBNR); and	EX AC			
c. Loss adjustment expenses.	EX AC			
2. Perform procedures to ascertain the reasonableness of the established liabilities.	AC VA			
3. Determine whether any liabilities have been discounted. Verify that the discounted liabilities meet the specific requirements of fixed and reasonably determinable payments as stated in accordance with **SSAP No. 65, paragraph 10**.	EX VA PD			
a. Verify that any tabular or non-tabular discounts have been properly calculated and recorded in accordance with actuarial guidelines and **SSAP No. 65, paragraphs 11-12**.	EX VA			

	Exam Obj.	Completion Date	Examiner	Work Paper Ref.
b. Verify that the required disclosures for tabular and non-tabular discounts, as well as, changes in the discounting rate for reserves have been properly reported in the financial statements in accordance with **SSAP No. 65, paragraphs 13-15**.	PD			
4. Verify that the claim liability is complete and properly recorded at year-end.	AC CO VA CM			
a. Obtain the claims register subsequent to year-end. Select a sample of claims from this register, identify the date they were reported, and trace them to the year-end claim liability listing. Investigate any instances in which claims were reported prior to year-end and excluded from the year-end detail or the established liability was materially understated at year-end.	AC CO VA			
b. Select a sample of claims included on the closed claim detail and agree the claim payment to cash disbursements or cancelled checks.	AC CO VA CM			
5. Identify any instances in which the company has recorded obligations under structured settlements. Verify that these obligations and related annuities have been recorded in accordance with **SSAP No. 65, paragraphs 17-20**.	EX AC PD			
6. Identify any high deductible policies in-force at the company. Verify that the company has properly reserved losses throughout the policy periods and not over the period after the deductible has been reached in accordance with **SSAP No. 65, paragraph 35**.	EX AC PD			
7. Identify asbestos or environmental exposures at the company. Verify that these exposures are properly recorded in accordance with **SSAP No. 55** and disclosed in accordance with **SSAP No. 65, paragraph 42**.	EX AC PD			

	Exam Obj.	Completion Date	Examiner	Work Paper Ref.
Loss Adjustment Expenses				
1. Obtain the supporting detail of the loss adjustment expenses established for property and casualty contracts. Agree this detail to the company's general ledger and Annual Statement.	EX AC			
2. Perform procedures to ascertain the reasonableness of the established liabilities.	AC VA			
3. Through discussion with management and review of the company's insurance practices, obtain an understanding of the types of expenses included in this classification. In accordance with **SSAP No. 70, paragraph 3**, expenses incurred in the adjusting, recording and paying of claims, should be allocated to this specific category. These expenses can then be grouped into two broad categories: Defense and Cost Containment (DCC) and Adjusting and Other (AO) in accordance with **SSAP No. 55, paragraph 5**.	EX AC			
4. Determine that the Defense and Cost Containment (DCC) category includes defense, litigation, and medical cost containment expenses including:	EX AC			
a. Surveillance expenses;	EX AC			
b. Fixed amounts for medical cost containment expenses;	EX AC			
c. Loss adjustment expenses for participation in voluntary and involuntary market pools if reported by accident year;	EX AC			
d. Fees or salaries for appraisers, private investigators, hearing representatives, reinspectors and fraud investigators, if working in defense of a claim and fees or salaries for rehabilitation nurses;	EX AC			
e. Attorney fees incurred owing to a duty to defend even when other coverage does not exist; and	EX AC			
f. Cost of experts.	EX AC			

	Exam Obj.	Completion Date	Examiner	Work Paper Ref.
5. Adjustment and Other (AO) expenses are those not assigned to DCC including:	EX AC			
a. Fees and expenses of adjusters and settling agents;	EX AC			
b. Loss adjustment expenses for participation in voluntary and involuntary market pools if reported by calendar year;	EX AC			
c. Attorney fees incurred in the determination of coverage, including litigation between the reporting entity and the policyholder; and	EX AC			
d. Fees and salaries for appraisers, private investigators, hearing representatives, reinspectors, and fraud investigators, if working in the capacity of an adjuster.	EX AC			
6. From the identification of items included in the loss adjustment expenses in steps 2-4, perform procedures to determine whether the liability is appropriately and properly stated.	VA AC			
a. The liability for loss adjustment expenses should be based upon the ultimate cost for settling the claims (including the effects of inflation and other societal and economic factors) using past experience adjusted for current trends, and any other factors that would modify past experience in accordance with **SSAP No. 55, paragraph 8**.	VA AC			
7. Review the liability for reasonableness by comparing the current year liability to prior year. Investigate any significant fluctuations from prior year.	CO VA AC			
Dividends Declared and Unpaid - Policyholders				
1. Obtain detail of the policyholder's dividends declared and unpaid. Agree this detail to the company's general ledger and Annual Statement.	AC EX			

	Exam Obj.	Completion Date	Examiner	Work Paper Ref.
2. Agree the declared dividends to the board of director's minutes. Determine whether these dividends have any restrictions.	AC EX			
3. Through review of the board of directors minutes determine whether all declared policyholder dividends are properly recorded in accordance with **SSAP No. 65, paragraph 45**.	AC EX CO VA			
a. Verify that dividends to policyholders immediately become liabilities of the reporting entity when declared by the board of directors and are recorded as such.	AC CO			
4. Determine that the company has properly disclosed the terms of any dividend restrictions in accordance with **SSAP No. 65, paragraph 46**.	PD			
Drafts Outstanding				
1. Obtain detail of the drafts outstanding. Agree this detail to the company's general ledger and Annual Statement.	AC EX			
2. Through discussion with management and review of the account activity, develop an understanding of what items are being recorded in this account. **SSAP No. 2, paragraph 6** provides guidance to the definition and characteristics of a draft.	AC EX			
3. For those drafts outstanding pertaining to claims, verify that the company utilizes the Draft Issue Method in accordance with **SSAP No. 2, paragraph 8**. Determine that these respective drafts outstanding were recorded with corresponding entries to paid losses and loss reserves.	AC EX CM			
a. For companies who do not have drafts outstanding, determine that they appropriately use the Draft Honored Method in accordance with **SSAP No. 2, paragraph 8**.	AC EX CM			

	Exam Obj.	Completion Date	Examiner	Work Paper Ref.
4. Identify those drafts outstanding in excess of six (6) months and verify that the company has properly conducted procedures to notify the beneficiary or claimant of the outstanding draft.	AC CM			
5. For drafts outstanding, verify that the company accurately and timely remits these claim payments as escheat payments to the appropriate state.	AC EX CO VA			
6. Verify that the method to account for drafts outstanding is consistent with the prior year and that any changes to the method used to account for drafts issued and outstanding has been governed by **SSAP No. 3** in accordance with **SSAP No. 2, paragraph 9**.	AC EX			

SECTION F — LOSSES AND BENEFITS CYCLE: HEALTH

Listed below are the corresponding Annual Statement line items that are related to the procedures contained in this Losses and Benefits Specific Risk Analysis.

Annual Statement Blank Line Items

Health Care Receivables (Pharmaceutical Rebate Receivables, Claim Overpayment Receivables, Loans and Advances to Providers, and Capitation Arrangement Receivables)
Claims Unpaid (See Actuarial Opinion)
Accrued Medical Incentive Pool and Bonus Payments
Unpaid Claims Adjustment Expenses (See Actuarial Opinion)
Aggregate Policy Reserves (See Actuarial Opinion)
Aggregate Claim Reserves (See Actuarial Opinion)
Aggregate Write-ins for Other Liabilities (Medical Malpractice Liabilities)

Note: The user should be aware that depending on the holding company structure and operations of the entity, that this cycle can also have an impact on other accounts such as Amounts due to Parent, Subsidiaries, and Affiliates and Amounts due from Parent, Subsidiaries and Affiliates.

Relevant SSAP's Include

#3, Accounting Changes and Corrections of Errors
#5, Liabilities, Contingencies and Impairments of Assets
#25, Accounting for and Disclosures about Transactions with Affiliates and Other Related Parties
#50, Classifications and Definitions of Insurance or Managed Care Contracts in Force
#54, Individual and Group Accident and Health Contracts
#55, Unpaid Claims, Losses and Loss Adjustment Expenses
#61, Life, Deposit Type and Accident and Health Reinsurance
#84, Certain Health Care Receivables and Receivables Under Government Insured Plans
#85, Claim Adjustment Expenses, Amendments to SSAP No. 55 (Effective December 31, 2003)

SPECIFIC RISK ANALYSIS WORKPAPERS

Risk Analysis Prepared By/Date ______________________________

Planning Exam Analysis Prepared By/Date ______________________________

Reviewed By/Date ______________________________

Note: Procedures for certain amounts classified as Policy Reserves can be found in other SRAs. Procedures for Premium Deficiency Reserves can be found in the Premium Cycle: Health SRA.

EXAMINATION OBJECTIVES

1. All claims, claim adjustment expenses and withhold/medical incentive liabilities and expenses were adequate, recorded in the proper general ledger accounts and reported in the proper period. (Accuracy, Completeness, Existence and Cutoff)

2. All claims, claim adjustment expenses and withhold/medical incentive liabilities and expenses reported during period under review were actual obligations of the insurer. (Ownership and Obligation)

3. Claims, claim adjustment expenses, and withhold/medical incentive liabilities and expenses were included within the appropriate claim database and were substantiated by the appropriate supporting documents. (Existence, Valuation)

4. Paid and unpaid claims, claim adjustment expenses, IBNR claims and withhold/medical incentive liabilities are recorded in compliance with state statutes. (Compliance)

5. Claims, claim adjustment expenses, and withhold/medical incentive liabilities and expenses and the related disclosures are recorded in compliance with the NAIC *Accounting Practices and Procedures Manual* and *Annual Statement Instructions* (including properly reported as covered/uncovered). (Valuation, Compliance and Presentation and Disclosure)

6. Health care receivables existed and were the legal property of the reporting entity as of the examination date. (Existence and Ownership)

7. Health care receivables existed and are valued and presented in accordance with the NAIC *Accounting Practices and Procedures Manual* and state laws and regulations. (Presentation and Disclosure, Valuation and Compliance)

8. Health care receivables have been accurately accounted for and reported in the reporting entity's records consistent with agreements. (Accuracy and Completeness)

9. Health care receivables transactions have been reported in the appropriate accounting period. (Cutoff)

10. Liability for medical malpractice is complete and recorded properly as to account, amount, and period. (Accuracy, Cutoff and Compliance)

Note: Examination procedures for Health Care Receivables – Risk Sharing Receivables can be found in the Reinsurance and Risk Transfer Instruments Cycle: Health SRA.

INHERENT RISKS

INTERNAL AND EXTERNAL ENVIRONMENTAL CONDITIONS/FACTORS

RESULTS OF DETAIL ANALYTICAL REVIEW PROCEDURES

CONTROL RISK — LOSSES AND BENEFITS CYCLE: HEALTH

This questionnaire is designed to assist the examiner in assessing control risk in loss and benefit related account balances. Part 1, Section III and Part 3 of this *Handbook* provides guidance on considering an insurer's internal control structure in designing substantive examination procedures.

This questionnaire includes examples of internal control procedures and policies that are commonly utilized by insurers to achieve internal control objectives. For each control procedure listed below, indicate by placing a check mark in yes or no box whether or not the insurer employs such a procedure, or other similar practice (include a description of the similar procedure). To the extent the control procedure is not applicable, indicate N/A. If other relevant control procedures are in place, list them in the space that follows. Control procedures that are tested by the examiner should be documented by including the workpaper reference in the comment section and the examiner's initials in the reliance column.

After each individual control procedure there is a control objective listed that satisfies the procedure.

If the examiner initially assesses control risk less than high for a particular account balance, then those controls must be tested. The controls should be tested to determine whether the procedure is: operating as expected, applied throughout the entire period of reliance, performed on a timely basis, encompassing all transactions and identifying errors. Some examples of testing procedures are inquiry, observation, reperformance and examination of documents. The level of reliance, if any, should be indicated in the reliance column along with any comments the examiner may have regarding the procedure.

Based upon the testing results, the examiner should determine whether the preliminary assessment of the control risk is confirmed or needs to be revised.

CONTROL OBJECTIVES

Authorization (AU) – All transactions recorded were reviewed and approved by designated personnel.

Completeness (CO) – All transactions that occurred were initially entered into the accounting records, accepted for processing and generated data files and reports reflect that all transactions have occurred.

Accuracy (AC) – Transactions were initially recorded correctly, timely and accurately.

Asset Protection (AP) – Adequate safeguards over access to and use of assets and records, including the appropriate segregation of duties among company personnel.

	Control Obj.	Y	N	Work Paper Ref.	Reliance
General Control Procedures					
The examiner should determine the amount of documentation necessary for each control procedure. If the examiner intends to place substantial reliance on the established control, the examiner should explain the control procedure in a workpaper and document the individual responsible for supervising the control activity as well as the frequency of the control activity.					
Claims Unpaid and Unpaid Claims Adjustment Expenses					
1. Are claim submissions reviewed and approved or rejected prior to processing the claim for payment?	AU				
2. Do procedures exist to prevent the payment of claims and prevent the initial recording of claims reserves for policies not included in the enrollment listing?	AU				
3. Are changes to the master policy file and claim data authorized and approved?	AU				
4. Do procedures exist to prevent additions/deletions to data contained in files, registers, databases, etc.?	AU				
5. Is the duplication of payment or payment by unauthorized personnel prevented?	AU				
6. Are changes to data on submitted claims permitted in the adjudication process?	AU				
7. Is the use of dummy codes permitted?	AU AC				
8. Are claim reserves established or reviewed by a qualified actuary?	AC				
9. Is the statistical data reviewed for unusual items and relationships (e.g., negative reserves, aged claim with no recent reserve changes or other claim transactions)?	AC				
10. Are prepayments (capitation or other provider advances) approved?	AU CO				

	Control Obj.	Y	N	Work Paper Ref.	Reliance
11. Do procedures exist to ensure that transactions are recorded in the correct accounting period and claim year?	CO				
12. Do procedures exist to ensure that transactions are input and accepted for processing?	CO				
13. Do procedures exist to ensure that rejected or suspended claims are appropriately investigated and resolved?	CO				
14. Are advance or capitation accounts reconciled periodically to ascertain that claims submissions are being properly applied?	CO AC				
15. Do procedures exist to ensure that reported unpaid claims are recorded at the correct rate pursuant to a provider contract or member policy?	CO AC				
16. Is a claim inventory taken periodically to ensure that the detail claim filings agree with recorded claim information in the loss master file and on aging exhibits?	CO AC				
17. Is the general ledger reconciled to the unpaid claims subsidiary ledger?	CO AC				
18. Do procedures exist to ensure that funds received from Coordination of Benefits (C.O.B.) and subrogation are properly recorded?	CO AC				
19. Are suspense accounts reviewed to ensure that they are cleared of C.O.B and subrogation receipts, reinsurance recoverable receipts and claim payments in a timely manner?	CO AC				
20. Do procedures exist to ensure that reinsurance recoverables are properly recorded, billed and received?	AC				
21. Does the company periodically perform quality control reviews to check the accuracy of recorded claim transactions?	AC				
22. Does the company periodically review the factors used to establish loss or Claims/Claim Adjustment Expense (C/CAE) reserves?	AC				

	Control Obj.	Y	N	Work Paper Ref.	Reliance
23. Are independent reserve projections performed periodically throughout the year and compared to recorded reserve estimates?	AC				
24. Is the statistical loss data reconciled to the accounting data?	AP				
25. Is access to unissued checks or drafts and check signing machines limited to authorized personnel?	AP				
26. Is access to claim records restricted?	AP				
27. Do procedures exist to ensure that claims in excess of company's retention limits are reviewed? Do procedures exist to ensure that claims are reported to reinsurers in the appropriate time frame?	CO AC AP				
28. Does the company separately classify its CAE into cost containment expenses and other claim adjustment expenses as required by **SSAP No. 85**?	AC				
<u>Accrued Medical Incentive Pool and Bonus Payments</u>					
1. Are contracts containing medical incentive pool arrangements and amendments properly documented?	AC CO				
2. Do procedures exist to ensure that accounting for medical incentive pool arrangements is reviewed, compared to contract terms and expected results, and approved?	AU				
3. Are medical incentive pool transactions reviewed and approved prior to issuing a draft or check?	AU				
4. Do procedures exist to prevent the payment of medical incentive pool payments to providers who do not have such provision in the contract?	AU				
5. How is the duplication of payment or payment by unauthorized personnel prevented?	AU				
6. Does a qualified actuary review the statistical data and accrual for the company's medical incentive pool arrangements?	AU				

	Control Obj.	Y	N	Work Paper Ref.	Reliance
7. Do procedures exist to ensure that transactions are recorded in the correct accounting period?	CO				
8. Is the medical incentive pool data reconciled to the accounting data?	AC				
9. Are medical incentive pool reserves reviewed for adequacy and adjusted, when appropriate?	AC				
10. Is there adequate segregation of duties between employees responsible for maintaining the medical incentive pool payment records and those responsible for processing cash disbursements?	AP				
<u>Aggregate Policy and Claim Reserves</u>					
1. Are methodology and assumptions used to compute reserves compared to minimum statutory requirements for reasonableness and consistency?	AU AC				
2. Are reserving assumptions and practices periodically reviewed to determine that appropriate recognition has been given to changes in the entity's mix of business, operations philosophy or general procedural policies /practices?	AC CO				
3. Are eligibility or in-force records reconciled to reserve and premium records to assure that all in-force policies are reserved for?	AC CO				
4. Are reconciliations of in-force records from period to period prepared?	AC CO				
5. Is policy information in the master file periodically compared to appropriate guidelines to ensure that policy master file is appropriately updated for cancellations and retroactive eligibility dates?	AC CO				
6. Is policy master file information periodically agreed to other independent sources such as the group application, provider capitation billing, etc.?	AC CO				

	Control Obj.	Y	N	Work Paper Ref.	Reliance
Health Care Receivables					
1. Are written agreements for health care receivables in place?	AU CO				
2. Are the detail listings regarding health care receivables reconciled to the general ledger control accounts regularly?	AC CO				
3. Does someone independent of the actual transaction function review the recorded receivable transactions?	AU AP				
4. Are follow-ups conducted for past due accounts and are these accounts independently monitored for potential write-offs?	CO				
5. Is the balance of health care receivables periodically matched to the subsequent collection of these items?	AC CO				
6. Are all categories of health care receivables reviewed for impairment in compliance with **SSAP No. 5**?	AC				
7. Are write-offs reviewed and approved independently?	AU				
8. Do agreements for health care receivables contain specific provisions to authorize and/or allow accurate identification of the receivable, as **SSAP No. 84** requires?	AU AC				
9. Are periodic reviews or reconciliations made of health care receivables to ensure amounts reported are reasonable, consistent and/or collectible and comply with the requirements of **SSAP No. 84**?	AU AC				
10. Does the reporting entity identify pharmaceutical rebate receivables separately for insured and uninsured business?	AC CO				
11. For pharmaceutical rebates of uninsured plans, are there procedures in place to determine the payable to the uninsured plan?	AC CO				

	Control Obj.	Y	N	Work Paper Ref.	Reliance
12. If the reporting entity utilizes a Pharmacy Benefits Manager (PBM), are written experience reports received periodically and reviewed for accuracy by the reporting entity, meeting with the requirements of **SSAP No. 84, paragraph 10**?	AC AU CO				
13. If the reporting entity contracts directly with a pharmaceutical company, does the reporting entity bill and collect rebates in accordance with **SSAP No. 84, paragraph 10**?	AC				
14. Are claim overpayment receivables specifically identifiable and invoiced before being recorded as an asset as required by **SSAP No. 84, paragraph 14**?	CO AC				
15. Are there follow-up procedures with health care providers to ensure that overpayments are either collected by the reporting entity or used to offset the amounts currently owed the providers in accordance with **SSAP No. 84, paragraph 14**?	CO AC				
16. Are advances to providers under capitation agreements periodically reconciled?	AC				
17. Are loans and advances to non-related hospitals recorded and reconciled periodically in accordance with **SSAP No. 84, paragraphs 16 and 17**?	AC CO				
<u>Aggregate Write-in for Other Liabilities (Medical Malpractice Liabilities)</u>					
1. Does the risk management system identify and monitor potential malpractice incidents as well as evaluate the appropriateness of coverage?	AU CO				
2. Are changes to the risk management system with regard to medical malpractice coverage communicated to the necessary company personnel on a timely basis?	AC AP AU				
3. Is the adequacy of the medical malpractice liability reviewed regularly?	AC CO				
4. Are actuarial assumptions reviewed periodically to determine appropriateness?	AC				

	Control Obj.	Y	N	Work Paper Ref.	Reliance
5. Does outside legal counsel monitor medical malpractice claims?	AC CO				

OTHER KEY CONTROLS EXISTING FOR THIS EXAMINATION OBJECTIVE:

SUMMARY EVALUATION OF CONTROL RISK:

EVALUATION OF INDEPDENT CPA'S WORK FOR THIS EXAMINATION (CPA REVIEW CHECKLIST):

OVERALL RISK ASSESSMENT

Balance Sheet Item Evaluation of Likelihood of Material Adjustment to Surplus:

The evaluation of the likelihood of a material adjustment to surplus should be based on the following criteria:

- Inherent Risk
- Internal & External Environmental Factors
- Control Risk
- Materiality Consideration

The examiner should rate each item as to the likelihood of a material misstatement. All items are assumed as "High" prior to any examiner evaluation. A "High" assessment requires the examiner to perform substantive examination procedures over that account area. A lower assessment allows the examiner to perform analytical or fewer substantive procedures to satisfy the examination requirements. If an assessment other than "High" is selected for any of the accounts, the examiner needs to document the basis for the assessment. If the assessment is based on control testwork, the documentation should include results of control procedures and related workpaper references.

1) "Claims Unpaid"

____________ High ____________ Medium ____________ Low

Basis for Assessment:

____

____

____

2) "Accrued Medical Incentive Pool and Bonus Payments"

____________ High ____________ Medium ____________ Low

Basis for Assessment:

____

____

____

3) "Unpaid Claims Adjustment Expenses"

__________ High __________ Medium __________ Low

Basis for Assessment:

---

4) "Aggregate Policy and Claims Reserves"

__________ High __________ Medium __________ Low

Basis for Assessment:

---

5) "Health Care Receivables"

__________ High __________ Medium __________ Low

Basis for Assessment:

---

6) "Aggregate Write-ins for Other Liabilities (Medical Malpractice Liabilities)"

__________ High __________ Medium __________ Low

Basis for Assessment:

PRELIMINARY EXAMINATION APPROACH — LOSSES AND BENEITS CYCLE: HEALTH

Listed below are the corresponding Annual Statement Line Items that are related to the procedures contained in this Losses and Benefits Specific Risk Analysis:

Health Care Receivables (Pharmaceutical Rebate Receivables, Claim Overpayment Receivables, Loans and Advances to Providers, and Capitation Arrangement Receivables)
Claims Unpaid (See Actuarial Opinion)
Accrued Medical Incentive Pool and Bonus Payments
Unpaid Claims Adjustment Expenses (See Actuarial Opinion)
Aggregate Policy Reserves (See Actuarial Opinion)
Aggregate Claim Reserves (See Actuarial Opinion)
Aggregate Write-ins for Other Liabilities (Medical Malpractice Liabilities)

The actual examination procedures selected to be performed is a matter of considerable judgment by the examiner. The following "Examination Program" includes examples of procedures commonly used.

To the extent that the examiner judgmentally determines whether it is appropriate to use the following procedures, that selection can be documented by checking the space next to such procedure, with modifications noted in the margin. The examiner may determine that alternative or additional procedures are required. If so, those procedures can be added on a supplemental sheet. The examiner performing the procedure should indicate satisfactory completion by initialing and dating in the space provided, and referencing the workpapers where the procedures and findings are documented.

The examiner may chose to apply the examination procedures to less than 100% of the items comprising an account balance. Guidance for audit sampling and control and substantive procedures can be found in Part 3 of the NAIC *Financial Condition Examiners Handbook.*

After each examination procedure, the examination objective that the procedure satisfies is indicated. The examination objectives are accuracy, completeness, compliance, cutoff, existence, obligation and ownership, valuation and presentation and disclosure.

EXAMINATION OBJECTIVES:

Accuracy (AC) – Recorded transactions and account balances are mathematically accurate, are based on correct amounts and have been classified into the correct account.

Completeness (CO) – All transactions and account balances that should be recorded in the annual financial statement were recorded.

Compliance (CM) – Business transactions and affairs have been conducted in accordance with state insurance codes, other state laws or department directives.

Cutoff (CT) – All transactions are recorded in the correct accounting period.

Existence (EX) – Recorded transactions occurred and are not fictitious and recorded assets and liabilities existed as of the balance sheet date.

Obligation (OB) and Ownership (OW) – Recorded liabilities are obligations of the company and recorded assets are the rights of the company at the balance sheet date.

Valuation (VA) – Assets and liabilities are valued in accordance with state statute and NAIC accounting guidance.

Presentation and Disclosure (PD) – The elements of the annual statement are properly classified and all disclosures are accurately included in the annual statement.

	Exam Obj.	Completion Date	Examiner	Work Paper Ref.
EXAMINATION PROCEDURES				
<u>**General Procedures**</u>				
1. Determine the company's Reserving Philosophy by discussing:	PD VA			
a. Methodologies utilized by the company to compute reserves;	PD VA			
b. Possible changes in methodologies as compared to prior years;	PD VA			
c. Possible changes in writings and new lines of business;	PD VA			
d. Reserve treatment of withhold and bonus/incentive programs;	PD VA			
e. Reserve treatment of claims processed for payment including claims, which are applied to advances; and	PD VA			
f. Possible changes in underwriting standards or claims handling procedures and philosophies which could impact reserve projections, such as inflation, changes in provider arrangements, regulation, court decisions, staffing changes, changes in settlement practices or standards, changes in claims processing backlogs and changes in internal or external adjusters.	PD VA			
2. Verify that changes in valuation basis noted above are recorded consistently with **SSAP No. 54, paragraph 21** and **SSAP No. 3**, Accounting Changes and Corrections of Errors.	VA AC PD			
3. Compare company loss ratios to industry norms.	VA CO			
4. Review historical claim counts by line of business for unusual trends.	VA CO			

	Exam Obj.	Completion Date	Examiner	Work Paper Ref.
5. Determine the effect of changes in the company's reinsurance programs including:	CO AC			
a. New contracts;	CO AC			
b. Changes in retention limits; and	CO AC			
c. Changes in contract exclusions or carve outs.	CO AC			
6. Review management reports showing recent trends in utilization and cost by line of business.	VA			
7. Review the entity's claim data base(s) to insure the data base(s) is complete and accurate. Scan the data base(s) for internal inconsistencies such as missing claim amounts; unusually small amounts; claims misclassified by type (e.g., Medicare).	CO AC			
8. Review scope, findings and related reports of external auditors' claim audit.	VA PD			
9. Review selection cycle, scope, findings and related reports of internal auditors' claim audits.	CM AC			
10. Review actuarial reports and reserve opinions for the examination period. Verify that the actuarial opinion was prepared in accordance with the actuarial requirements of **SSAP No. 54, paragraph 11**, and the Actuarial Standards Board.	VA PD			
11. Through discussion with company management and review of the company's insurance practices, obtain an understanding of the types of expenses included within CAE. In accordance with **SSAP No. 85**, costs expected to be incurred in connection with the adjustment and recording of accident and health claims should be classified as CAE. These expenses can then be grouped into two categories: cost containment expenses and other claim adjustment expenses, as set forth in **SSAP No. 85**.	EX AC VA PD			
12. Obtain a summary of claims expenses by line of business for each year under review and:	AC CO EX			

		Exam Obj.	Completion Date	Examiner	Work Paper Ref.
	a. Reconcile to the general ledger; and	AC CO EX			
	b. Reconcile the general ledger to Annual Statement, Underwriting and Investment Exhibit Part 2B, columns 1 and 2.	AC CO EX			
13	Obtain a summary of unpaid claims by line of business for each year under review and:	AC CO EX			
	a. Reconcile to the Annual Statement, Underwriting and Investment Exhibit Part 2B, columns 3 and 4; and	AC CO EX			
	b. Verify that the total of line 11, columns 3 and 4 of the Underwriting and Investment Exhibit Part 2B equals the sum of lines 1 and 2, column 3 on page 3 of the Annual Statement.	AC CO EX			
14.	Verify that claims, losses and claim adjustment expenses are recognized when the insured event occurs in accordance with **SSAP No. 55**.	CT CO			
15.	Verify that claims liabilities include provisions for all components noted in **SSAP No. 55, paragraphs 7 and 8** and **SSAP No. 85**.	CO AC			
16.	Obtain detailed statistical records (paid and reported unpaid), and underlying file layouts of transactions inclusive of the following:	EX CO AC			
	a. Claim number;	EX CO AC			
	b. Insured name;	EX CO AC			
	c. Line of business;	EX CO AC			
	d. Date of service;	EX CO AC			
	e. Received date;	EX CO AC			

	Exam Obj.	Completion Date	Examiner	Work Paper Ref.
f. Check/draft date; and	EX CO AC			
g. Claim amount.	EX CO AC			
17. Determine that all claims are entered on the entity's data base and in the general ledger using the following steps:	CO AC EX OB/OW			
a. Conduct a walkthrough of the claims processing to determine that:	CO AC EX OB/OW			
i) All paper claims are properly entered into claims system; and	CO AC EX OB/OW			
ii) All electronically submitted claims are accounted for.	CO AC EX OB			
b. Obtain detail and explanation of all manual adjustments to the general ledger.	CO AC EX OB			
18. Reconcile database to the general ledger.	CO			
19. Review on-line or paper procedure manuals for processing claims and determine if adequate provision for update distribution and training exist.	AC			
20. Review current year company calendar year and service year claim and claim adjustment expense ratios in total and by line of business and compare with prior three years.	VA CO			
21. Review the health entity's methods of tracking complaint and appeals procedures and method of tracking claims pending.	CM PD			
22. Review a sample of paid and denied claims to ensure compliance with contract provisions with respect to timeliness, payments made to enrollees, doctors or providers (if the doctors or providers are not paid by capitation).	CM			

	Exam Obj.	Completion Date	Examiner	Work Paper Ref.
23. Review reports or reviews conducted by other State or Federal regulatory authorities.	PD CM			
24. Review the health entity's methodology and procedures employed for reporting aged claims on Annual Statement Exhibit 5.	PD VA			
25. Verify that claims are properly classified as covered or uncovered as defined in the NAIC *Annual Statement Instructions.*	PD			
<u>Claims Unpaid and Unpaid Claims Adjustment Expenses</u>				
1. Select a representative sample of claim payments within the lag table cells and verify that payment was made in accordance with contractual terms.	CO CT AC			
2. Check the claim reports for completeness and accuracy of claim amounts by tracing samples of claims to verify statistical coding of claim files with regard to:	AC CO			
a. Insured and policy number;	AC CO			
b. Provider name or code;	AC CO			
c. Service description or code;	AC CO			
d. Line of business;	AC CO			
e. Date(s) of service;	AC CO			
f. Date claim received;	AC CO			
g. Claim amount paid or rejected; and	AC CO			
h. Paid date.	AC CO			
3. Reconcile payments to the cash disbursements journal and trace payments to canceled checks.	CO AC			
4. On a sample basis, confirm payments with payees and compare confirmation signatures with check/draft endorsements.	EX			

	Exam Obj.	Completion Date	Examiner	Work Paper Ref.
5. Confirm unpaid claims and claim advances with major providers. Determine overall collectibility of claim advances to major providers in accordance with **SSAP No. 5, SSAP No. 25** and **SSAP No. 84**.	EX VA			
6. Review projections of company utilization and cost by line of business.	VA			
7. Analyze claim-aging trends during the examination period overall and by provider category (e.g., Hospital, Physician, IPA, other).	CM PD			
8. Test the procedures to determine how the claims received by the entity are posted into the claims processing system for aging including:	AC PD VA			
a. Received date vs. date entered in the system;	AC PD VA			
b. Value of claim entered;	AC PD VA			
c. Accuracy of aging "buckets" and covered vs. uncovered; and	AC PD VA			
d. Separation by business segment (Medicare, Medicaid, Commercial) and exclusion of ASO business.	AC PD VA			
9. Calculate one and two year subsequent net development of claims and claim adjustment expense reserves for the most recent 2 calendar years prior to the examination date and recalculate capital and surplus for each of those years based upon the development results and recalculate leverage ratios.	CO CT PD			
10. Compare examination date liabilities to available subsequent runoff by line of business.	CO EX			
11. Determine the impact of changes in retention or reinsurance coverage on loss reserve projections.	CO OB			

	Exam Obj.	Completion Date	Examiner	Work Paper Ref.
12. Determine if specific types of coverage need to be segregated and analyzed separately within lines of business, such as:	PD			
a. Comprehensive coverage (incl. Medical or hospital only);	PD			
b. Dental coverage;	PD			
c. Medicare supplemental;	PD			
d. Other health coverage (e.g., vision, drug); and	PD			
e. Other "non-health" coverage (e.g., LTC, disability, stop loss).	PD			
13. For contracts (such as Medicare and Medicaid, etc.), which are subject to redetermination by other entities, verify that guidelines **of SSAP No. 54, paragraphs 26-31**, are followed.	VA AC			
14. Determine company procedures as to how and at what amount received unpaid claims are recorded.	AC CM PD			
15. Review calculation of claims and CAE reserves and determine if calculation is equitable and reasonable. Verify that management records its best estimate of its liabilities for unpaid claims, unpaid losses and claims adjustment expenses in accordance with **SSAP No. 55, paragraph 10**.	AC VA PD			
16. In the rare instance when management's estimate is a range with all points equally probable, then the midpoint within the range should be recorded in accordance with **SSAP No. 55, paragraph 11**.	AC VA			
17. Determine the reasonableness of the company's projections of loss and claim adjustment expense reserves, including IBNR:	CM OB			
a. Choose a few methods of projection deemed suitable for particular lines of business utilizing available data;	CM OB			

	Exam Obj.	Completion Date	Examiner	Work Paper Ref.
b. Compare company projections with examination projections and prepare a schedule indicating redundancy or deficiency by line of business; and	CM OB			
c. Review results with management personnel and obtain explanations for significant differences from company-prepared projections.	CM OB			
18. Verify that claims in excess of retention limit are submitted to review and to reinsurer as required by contract.	CO OB			
19. Request claims data in the possession of the health entity that underlie the capitated arrangements if claim payments are made by the health entity.	AC OB			
20. Test that the company has classified claim adjustment expenses according to **SSAP No. 85, paragraph 4**.	EX AC			
21. Review the expenses classified as cost containment and other claim adjustment on Underwriting and Investment Exhibit Part 3 for reasonableness.	AC PD			
22. Perform other analytical review procedures, as appropriate.	OB			
<u>Accrued Medical Incentive Pool and Bonus Payments</u>				
1. Obtain an understanding of the company's withhold, medical incentive pool and bonus payments arrangements by reviewing prior examination and independent audit workpapers and meeting with company personnel.	CO AC			
2. Review the agreements with providers for provisions pertaining to medical incentive pools, withholds and any similar arrangement.	CO OB AC			

	Exam Obj.	Completion Date	Examiner	Work Paper Ref.
a. Inquire into any changes in medical incentive pool and bonus payment arrangements since the previous examination, including new contracts or amendments to existing contracts. If possible, determine the reasons for these changes.	CO OB AC			
b. Ensure these contract provisions comply with the regulatory requirements of the state in which service is provided.	CO OB AC			
3. Obtain a detailed listing of providers with whom the company has withhold or medical incentive pool arrangements. The listing should be in sufficient detail to determine each individual provider's withhold percentage, the amount of the total withhold for the year and the amount of the medical incentive pool liability.	CO EX			
a. Obtain and review the calculation for the amount reported as accrued medical incentive pool at year-end.	CO EX			
b. Consider the reasonableness of the accrual based on a review of **part 2B of the Underwriting and Investment Exhibit** for the prior annual statements, noting the respective accruals and subsequent payments.	PD			
c. Test whether account balances and disclosures comply with **SSAP No. 55, paragraph 7, SSAP No. 85** and the NAIC *Annual Statement Instructions*.	PD CO			
d. Review the Notes to the Financial Statements and General Interrogatories and evaluate the completeness of information (including actuarial opinion).	PD			
4. Review a sample of provider contracts to ensure that withhold percentages and calculations are in accordance with provisions contained in the contracts.	AC			

	Exam Obj.	Completion Date	Examiner	Work Paper Ref.
5. Review withhold retention or disbursement and medical incentive pool transactions occurring subsequent to year-end and compare to year-end accrual for adequacy and adherence to contract terms.	CO AC CT			
6. Perform other analytical review procedures, as appropriate.	OB			
Aggregate Policy and Claim Reserves				
Detecting Insufficient Unearned Premium Reserves				
1. Identify the detailed inventory of individual policies (grouped by plan, term and expiration date) and group policies in-force. The inventory should show for each group:	CO AC OB			
a. Unearned premium amounts; (Recalculate the unearned premium for a representative sample of policies or policy groupings, for selected lines of business using computer audit tools.) Verify that unearned premium is calculated in accordance with the requirements of **SSAP No. 54, paragraph 12**:	VA			
i) Pro rata unearned premium factor; and	VA			
ii) Total premium amount.	VA			
b. For each policy:	VA			
i) Policy number;	VA			
ii) Original premium;	VA			
iii) Any additional premiums (endorsements); and	VA			
iv) Any return premiums.	VA			
2. Check the eligibility/in-force inventory for completeness and accuracy of premium amounts.	VA			

	Exam Obj.	Completion Date	Examiner	Work Paper Ref.
a. Trace a sample of premium payments from the cash receipts journal to the application file and in-force inventory. Verify:	VA			
i) Plan, term and expiration date of policy;	VA			
ii) Policy number; and	VA			
iii) Original premium amount (plus adjustments).	VA			
b. Scan the in-force inventory for internal inconsistencies such as:	VA			
i) Missing premium amounts;	VA			
ii) Unusually small amounts; and	VA			
iii) Policies misclassified by plan, term or expiration date.	VA			
3. Select a sample of individual policy groups and group policies from the in-force inventory; for each group and group policy, verify the correctness of:	VA			
a. The unearned premium factor;	VA			
b. The reinsured premium factor;	VA			
c. The total premium amount for the group; and	VA			
d. The extension of premium amount times the factors.	VA			
Detecting Insufficient Reserves for Guaranteed Renewable Contracts				
4. Identify the detailed inventory of guaranteed renewable and non cancelable contracts, which should include:	AC			
a. Contract number;	AC			

	Exam Obj.	Completion Date	Examiner	Work Paper Ref.
b. Annual premium; and	AC			
c. Reserve factor determinants (plan, issue age, attained age).	AC			
5. Determine if contract or additional reserves required by **SSAP No. 54, paragraphs 9 and 13-18** need to be recorded. This includes the possibility of premium deficiency reserves. (Note: Premium deficiency reserve calculation procedures are included in the Premiums Cycles.)	VA AC CO			
6. From the detailed cash receipts journal, select a sample of premium payments that is representative of all guaranteed renewable and non-cancelable plans.	EX			
7. Trace the sample payments from the receipts journal to the application file and detailed inventory. Verify:	AC VA			
a. Policy number;	AC VA			
b. Annual premium; and	AC VA			
c. Reserve factor determinants.	AC VA			
8. Verify the reserve factor tables.	VA CM			
9. Select a sample of contracts from the detailed inventory. Determine whether reserve factors are properly matched to the sample contracts.	VA AC			
a. For the contracts in the sample, verify the multiplications of annual premium times the reserve factor.	VA AC			
10. Review applicable reinsurance agreements and confirm that reserve reductions for reinsurance are correct.	AC			
Detecting Insufficient Reserves for Claims and Future Contingent Benefits				
11. Verify reserves for reported claims.	CO			

	Exam Obj.	Completion Date	Examiner	Work Paper Ref.
a. Identify the inventory of all outstanding accident and health claims.	CO AC			
b. Select a sample of claim payments from the cash disbursements journal and trace the amount of payment to the inventory.	CO			
c. Select a sample of claims from the claim file and trace the claim number, date of initiation, and policy claim amount to the inventory.	CO			
d. Verify the factor tables used to estimate the present value of expected future claim payments.	VA			
e. Select a sample of claims from the inventory and verify the contributions of each claim-to-claim reserves.	CO			
i) Trace the factor from the inventory to the factor tables.	CO			
ii) Verify the multiplication of the factor times the policy claim amount.	VA			
12. Review applicable reinsurance agreements and confirm that reserve reductions for reinsurance are correct.	VA OB			
13. Obtain the company's workpapers supporting IBNR reserves and evaluate the calculation methods. Determine whether they are reasonable and consistently applied.	VA			
14. Test the reserving method applied to any group policies with future contingent benefits.	VA			
15. Trace total reserve provisions for unearned premiums, guaranteed renewable contracts, claims and future contingent benefits from the detailed inventories and workpapers (verified above) to the balance sheet.	CO			
16. Compare this year's aggregate accident and health reserves with prior year's reserves.	VA			

	Exam Obj.	Completion Date	Examiner	Work Paper Ref.
Health Care Receivables				
1. Obtain copies of agreements related to pharmaceutical rebate receivables, claim overpayment receivables, capitation arrangement receivables and risk sharing receivables. This includes agreements with any pharmacy benefit managers (PBM). Document the individuals who maintain these agreements.	EX			
2. Obtain the aged listing or computation of the health care receivables. Reconcile the aging report(s) to the applicable general ledger accounts and/or Annual Statement.	CO CT			
3. Verify that the health care receivable is properly computed or estimated according to contractual provisions and **SSAP No. 84**. Also verify that the entity has properly non-admitted the various health care receivables in accordance with the **SSAP No. 84**.	AC CM			
4. Select a sample of balances in the aging reports.	EX AC OB/OW VA CT			
a. Obtain supporting documentation to verify the accuracy of the aging of the balances in the sample.	EX AC OB/OW VA CT			
b. Determine the amounts collected subsequent to the examination date for the sample items and compare to the receivables. Investigate significant differences and amounts that remain uncollected.	EX AC OB/OW VA CT			
c. Confirm significant balances directly.	EX VA			
5. Review Exhibit 4 of the reporting entity's annual statement:	AC PD CM			

	Exam Obj.	Completion Date	Examiner	Work Paper Ref.
a. Verify that the aging of health care receivables on Exhibit 4 reconciles to the aging report by aging category and in total.	PD AC			
b. Test Exhibit 4 for verification that all health care receivables with balances greater than $10,000 or those that are 10% of gross health care receivables are properly listed on that exhibit.	PD CM			
6. Verify that health care receivables are reviewed for impairment in compliance with **SSAP No. 5**. Document the frequency of these reviews and the persons responsible for such reviews.	AC VA			
7. Ascertain that accounts relative to health care receivables are reconciled periodically. Document the frequency of these reviews and the persons responsible for such reviews.	VA OW EX			
Pharmaceutical Rebate Receivables				
8. Pharmaceutical rebates receivables consist of reasonably estimated amounts and billed amounts. For pharmaceutical rebate receivables:	CM VA OB/OW			
a. Verify that rebates are billed on at least a quarterly basis.	CM			
b. Confirm that estimated amounts are based on actual prescriptions filled within three months immediately preceding the reporting date.	CM VA			
c. Review the reporting entity's method for estimating its pharmacy rebates. Verify that the methodology is reasonable and is applied consistently.	VA AC			
d. Verify that estimated amounts are invoiced within two months of the reporting date that it was an estimate.	OB/OW			
e. Ascertain that pharmaceutical rebates that have not been collected within 90 days of the invoice/confirmation date have been nonadmitted.	CM VA			

	Exam Obj.	Completion Date	Examiner	Work Paper Ref.
f. Ascertain whether the reporting entity separately identifies pharmaceutical rebate receivables for insured and uninsured business. Document the reporting entity's method of determining these amounts and determine whether such method is reasonable.	AC VA			
9. Verify treatment of pharmacy rebates of uninsured plans is in compliance with **SSAP No. 84, paragraphs 12 and 13**:	CM VA PD			
a. Verify that receivable and payable balances are recorded on the financial statements of the reporting entity; receivables as a Health Care Receivable and the corresponding payable as a Liability for Amounts Held Under Uninsured Accident and Health Plans. Document the reporting entity's method of determining the payable balance and whether the method is reasonable.	PD VA			
b. Verify that amounts collected in excess of amounts to be remitted to the uninsured plan are reported as an Amount Receivable Relating to Uninsured Accident and Health Plans and as a reduction to general expenses.	PD CM			
10. Confirm that income from pharmaceutical rebates is reported as a reduction to claims expense as required by **SSAP No. 84, paragraph 12**.	PD CM			
11. Review the disclosure in the financial statement for the pharmaceutical rebate receivables to ensure the disclosure meets the requirements of **SSAP No. 84, paragraph 24**. For the last three years and for each quarter therein the reporting entity should disclose:	PD			
a. Estimated balance of pharmacy rebates receivable as reported on the financial statements;	PD			

	Exam Obj.	Completion Date	Examiner	Work Paper Ref.
b. Pharmacy rebates as invoiced or confirmed in writing; and	PD			
c. Pharmacy rebates collected.	PD			
12. If the reporting entity utilizes a pharmacy benefits manager, verify that written experience reports are received periodically and reviewed for accuracy by the reporting entity in a timely manner. **SSAP No. 84, paragraph 10** requires this. Document the method used to review such reports and the frequency of such reviews.	CM EX VA OB/OW			
Loans and Advances to Providers, including Capitation Arrangement Receivables				
13. Confirm that loans and advances to affiliated providers follow the guidance in **SSAP No. 25**.	CM			
14. Verify that any receivables for loans and advances to non-affiliated providers meet the setoff conditions in **SSAP No. 64** and are admitted only up to the amount of the payable to that provider for reported claims, e.g., not including IBNR, as set forth by **SSAP No. 84, paragraph 15**.	VA CM			
15. Loans or advances to non-related party hospitals shall be admitted up to the amount of the payable to the hospital for claims incurred, if certain conditions contained in **SSAP No. 84, paragraphs 16 and 17** are met:	CM VA OW/OB EX			
a. Verify that the loan or advance meets the setoff conditions in **SSAP No. 64**;	CM			
b. Verify that the loan or advance is supported by a legally enforceable contract;	EX			
c. Confirm that the loan or advance is administered pursuant to contractual terms and that the contractual terms of the agreement provide for quarterly reconciliations;	CM VA			

	Exam Obj.	Completion Date	Examiner	Work Paper Ref.
d. Ascertain that each quarterly reconciliation is completed within nine months of the end of such quarter;	CM VA			
e. Confirm that all quarterly reconciled differences are settled within 90 days of the date the reconciliation is completed; and	OB/OW VA			
f. If a quarterly reconciliation is not performed or settled in accordance with d. and e. above, all assets for loans or advances to that hospital shall be nonadmitted per **SSAP No. 84, paragraphs 16 and 17**.	VA			
16. Determine the reasonableness of IBNR amounts allocated to hospitals with loans or advances.	AC VA			
17. Advances to providers under capitation arrangements that are made under the terms of an approved provider services contract in anticipation of future services shall be admitted subject to certain conditions, as set forth by **SSAP No. 84, paragraph 14**:	VA OW/OB			
a. Confirm that the advanced amount does not exceed one month of average capitation payments for the subject provider during the preceding twelve months.	VA			
b. Ascertain that the contract cannot be terminated before the end of the month for which the advanced amount was paid.	OW/OB			
Claim Overpayment Receivables				
18. Verify that claim overpayments meet the setoff conditions in **SSAP No. 64** and are admitted only up to the amount of the payable to that provider for reported claims, e.g., not including IBNR.	CM VA			
19. Confirm that claim overpayments are specifically identifiable and are not estimates.	VA EX AC			

	Exam Obj.	Completion Date	Examiner	Work Paper Ref.
20. Ascertain that follow-up procedures with providers regarding overpayments are operating effectively. Document who is responsible for such follow-up procedures.	VA OB/OW			
<u>**Aggregate Write-ins for Other Liabilities (Medical Malpractice Liabilities)**</u>				
1. Determine the type of medical malpractice coverage in place (e.g., occurrence basis or claims-made), and the level of insurance protection obtained.	AC EX			
2. Determine whether such coverage transfers the malpractice risk, considering the viability of the insurance carrier.	AC			
3. Ensure that no gaps in coverage exist or that tail coverage has been purchased, if applicable.	AC CO			
4. If the reporting entity self-insures or has claims made coverages in place, determine whether the related liability is sufficient. Assure that the liability is accrued in accordance with **SSAP No. 5**. Consider the use of a specialist in the evaluation of the liability.	AC CO CM			
a. Obtain an understanding of the assumptions used in determining the liability.	AC CO VA			
b. Determine whether appropriate information is used in calculations, such as historical claim experience, policy terms, and exposure data, (e.g., number of beds, outpatient visits, emergency room visists, etc.)	AC CO VA			
c. Review prior period estimates and subsequent run-out to determine reasonableness.	AC CO			
5. Verify that the company has procedures in place for reporting all asserted claims to the insurer.	AC CO VA			
6. Inquire about the number and amount of medical malpractice claims asserted or settled during the examination period.	AC CO			

	Exam Obj.	Completion Date	Examiner	Work Paper Ref.
7. Review attorney's letters to determine whether asserted claims exist.	CO			
8. Review medical malpractice claims and legal costs incurred during the examination period.	AC CO			
9. For retrospectively rated policies, determine whether an accrual is necessary for losses in excess of the minimum premium. If an accrual currently exists, verify its reasonableness.	AC CO CM			

SECTION G — REINSURANCE AND RISK TRANSFER INSTRUMENTS CYCLE: LIFE

Listed below are the corresponding Annual Statement line items that are related to the procedures contained in this Reinsurance Specific Risk Analysis:

Annual Statement Blank Line Items

Amounts Recoverable from Reinsurers
Commissions and Expense Allowances Due
Experience Rating and Other Refunds Due
Other Amounts Receivable Under Reinsurance Contracts
Life Insurance Premiums and Annuity Considerations Deferred and Uncollected on In-Force Business (Less Premiums on Reinsurance Ceded and Less Loading)
Other Amounts Payable on Reinsurance, Including Assumed and Ceded
Commissions and Expense Allowances Payable on Reinsurance Assumed
Reinsurance in Unauthorized Companies
Funds Held Under Reinsurance Treaties with Unauthorized Reinsurers
Funds Held Under Coinsurance
Reserve Adjustments for Reinsurance Ceded

Relevant SSAP's Include:

#5, Liabilities, Contingencies, and Impairments of Assets
#61, Life, Deposit-Type and Accident and Health Reinsurance
#63, Underwriting Pools and Associations Including Intercompany Pools
#64, Offsetting and Netting of Assets and Liabilities

SPECIFIC RISK ANALYSIS WORKPAPERS

Risk Analysis Prepared By/Date ______________________________

Planning Exam Analysis Prepared By/Date ______________________________

Reviewed By/Date ______________________________

EXAMINATION OBJECTIVES:

1. Reinsurance contract that effectively transfers risk exists between parties and contains provisions mandated through regulation. (Existence and Compliance)

2. Amounts of reinsurance ceded are valued accurately and reflected in the financial statements. (Valuation, Compliance, Accuracy, Cutoff and Presentation and Disclosure)

3. Reinsurance assumed transactions are properly authorized, valued and recorded. (Valuation, Compliance, Accuracy and Cutoff)

4. The insurance company owns, or has appropriate rights to the recorded reinsurance ceded or assumed assets and incurs the reported reinsurance ceded or assumed liabilities. (Ownership and Obligation)

INHERENT RISKS

____

____

____

____

INTERNAL AND EXTERNAL ENVIRONMENTAL CONDITIONS/FACTORS

____

____

____

____

RESULTS OF DETAIL ANALYTICAL REVIEW PROCEDURES

____

____

____

____

CONTROL RISK — REINSURANCE AND RISK TRANSFER INSTRUMENTS CYCLE: LIFE

This questionnaire is designed to assist the examiner in assessing control risk for reinsurance life cycles. Part 1, Section III and Part 3 of this *Handbook* provides guidance in consideration of an insurer's internal control structure for use when designing substantive examination procedures.

This questionnaire includes examples of internal control procedures and policies that are commonly utilized by insurers to achieve internal control objectives. For each control procedure listed below, indicate by placing a check mark in the yes or no box whether or not the insurer employs such a procedure, or other similar practice (include a description of the similar procedure). To the extent the control procedure is not applicable, indicate N/A. If other relevant control procedures are in place, list them in the space that follows. Control procedures that are tested by the examiner should be documented by including the workpaper reference in the comment section and the examiner's initials in the reliance column.

For each individual control procedure there is a control objective listed that satisfies the procedure.

If the examiner initially assesses control risk as low or medium for a particular account balance, then those controls must be tested. The controls should be tested to determine whether the procedure is operating as expected, applied throughout the entire period of reliance, performed on a timely basis, encompassing all transactions and identifying errors. Some examples of testing procedures are inquiry, observation, re-performance and examination of documents. The level of reliance, if any, should be indicated in the applicable column along with any comments the examiner may have regarding the procedure.

Based upon the testing results, the examiner should determine whether the preliminary control risk assessment is confirmed or should be revised.

CONTROL OBJECTIVES

Authorization (AU) – All transactions recorded were reviewed and approved by designated personnel.

Completeness (CO) – All transactions that occurred were initially entered into the accounting records, accepted for processing and generated data files and reports reflect that all transactions have occurred.

Accuracy (AC) – Transactions were initially recorded correctly, timely and accurately.

Asset Protection (AP) – Adequate safeguards over access to and use of assets and records, including the appropriate segregation of duties among company personnel.

	Control Obj.	Y	N	Work Paper Ref.	Reliance
General Control Procedures					
The examiner should determine the amount of documentation necessary for each control procedure. If the examiner intends to place substantial reliance on the established controls, the examiner should explain the control procedure in a workpaper and document the individual responsible for supervising the control activity as well as the frequency of the control activity.					
1. Are reinsurance contracts reviewed for compliance with state regulations?	AU				
2. Are reinsurance contract terms and amendments reviewed for compliance with company guidelines prior to execution?	AU AC				
3. Are reinsurance contract terms and expected results properly documented prior to execution?	AU AP				
4. Do procedures exist to ensure that reinsurance accounting transactions (expense allowances, experience refunds, contingency reserves, mean reserve adjustments, recaptures, etc.) are reviewed, compared to contract terms and expected results, and approved in accordance with **SSAP No. 61, paragraphs 21-55**?	AU AC				
5. Are *ceding* companies and intermediaries approved with regards to business reputation, financial stability, and experience prior to contract execution and monitored on a continuous basis?	AU				
6. Are *assuming* companies and intermediaries approved with regards to business reputation, financial stability, and experience prior to contract execution and monitored on a continuous basis?	AU				
7. Are amounts due from ceding and assuming companies and intermediaries reviewed for collectibility in accordance with **SSAP No. 61, paragraph 41** and **SSAP No. 5**?	CO				

		Control Obj.	Y	N	Work Paper Ref.	Reliance
8.	Are reviews performed to ascertain that timely reports and accounting data are received from ceding companies or intermediaries and used to record transactions?	AC				
9.	Are activity analyses for cumulative reinsurance contracts prepared and reviewed to assist in evaluation of profitability, risk exposure, contract variance and expected results?	AC CO				
10.	Are controls and accounting records for ceding entities independently tested or reviewed to substantiate accounting data provided or to monitor compliance with contract provisions?	AC AP				
11.	Is an independent review conducted of a ceding company's underwriting practices, claims processing, loss reserving and actuarial policies and procedures?	AC AP				
12.	Are recorded amounts of ceded reinsurance reconciled to detailed policy and reinsurance records?	AC CO				
13.	Is an evaluation of the need for adequacy letters of credit or collateral conducted prior to contract execution and monitored on a continuous basis?	AP				
14.	Are reinsurance limitations as well as mortality and morbidity rates considered during the underwriting process?	AU				
15.	Is the assuming company authorized to transact reinsurance within the ceding company's state of domicile? If not, are letters of credit or other means of security provided?	AU				
16.	Are reinsurance transactions, claims processing, premium collection, key information systems functions and general accounting activities appropriately segregated? Are independent reviews conducted of the work performed? Are the reinsurance receivables/payables reviewed by someone independent of the transactional function?	AP				

	Control Obj.	Y	N	Work Paper Ref.	Reliance
17. Do data files and production programs have adequate safeguards against unauthorized access? Are there proper safeguards over access to any collateral held by the ceding entity from the assuming entity, including funds held under coinsurance?	AP				

OTHER KEY CONTROLS EXISTING FOR THIS EXAMINATION OBJECTIVE:

SUMMARY EVALUATION OF CONTROL RISK:

EVALUATION OF INDEPENDENT CPA'S WORK FOR THIS EXAMINATION (CPA REVIEW CHECKLIST):

OVERALL RISK ASSESSMENT

Balance Sheet Evaluation of the Likelihood of a Material Adjustment to Surplus:

The evaluation of the likelihood of a material adjustment to surplus should be based on the following criteria:

- Inherent Risk
- Internal & External Environmental Factors
- Control Risk
- Materiality Consideration

The examiner should rate each item as to the likelihood of a material misstatement. All items are assumed as "High" prior to any examiner evaluation. A "High" assessment requires the examiner to perform substantive examination procedures over that account area. A lower assessment allows the examiner to perform analytical or fewer substantive procedures to satisfy the examination requirements. If an assessment other than "High" is selected for any of the accounts, the examiner needs to document the basis for the assessment. If the assessment is based on control testwork, the documentation should include results of control procedures and related workpaper references.

1) "Amounts Recoverable from Reinsurers"

____________ High ____________ Medium ____________ Low

Basis for Assessment:

____

____

____

2) "Commissions and Expense Allowances Due"

____________ High ____________ Medium ____________ Low

Basis for Assessment:

____

____

____

3) "Experience Rating and Other Refunds Due"

___________ High ___________Medium ___________Low

Basis for Assessment:

____

____

____

4) " Other Amounts Receivable Under Reinsurance Contracts"

___________ High ___________Medium ___________ Low

Basis for Assessment:

____

____

____

5) "Life Insurance Premiums and Annuity Considerations Deferred and Uncollected on In-Force Business (Less Premiums on Reinsurance Ceded and Less Loading)"

___________ High ___________ Medium ___________ Low

Basis for Assessment:

____

____

____

6) "Other Amounts Payable on Reinsurance, Including Assumed and Ceded"

___________ High ___________ Medium ___________ Low

Basis for Assessment:

____

____

____

7) "Commissions and Expense Allowances Payable on Reinsurance Assumed"

___________ High ___________ Medium ___________ Low

Basis for Assessment:

____

____

____

8) "Reinsurance in Unauthorized Companies"

___________ High ___________ Medium ___________ Low

Basis for Assessment:

____

____

____

9) "Funds Held Under Reinsurance Treaties with Unauthorized Reinsurers"

___________ High ___________ Medium ___________ Low

Basis for Assessment:

____

____

____

10) "Funds Held Under Coinsurance"

___________ High ___________ Medium ___________ Low

Basis for Assessment:

____

____

____

11) "Reserve Adjustments for Reinsurance Ceded"

___________ High ___________ Medium __________ Low

Basis for Assessment:

____

____

____

PRELIMINARY EXAMINATION APPROACH — REINSURANCE AND RISK TRANSFER INSTRUMENTS CYCLE: LIFE

Listed below are the corresponding Annual Statement line items that are related to the procedures contained in this Reinsurance Specific Risk Analysis:

Amounts Recoverable from Reinsurers
Commissions and Expense Allowances Due
Experience Rating and Other Refunds Due
Other Amounts Receivable Under Reinsurance Contracts
Life Insurance Premiums and Annuity Considerations Deferred and Uncollected on In-force Business (Less Premiums on Reinsurance Ceded and Less Loading)
Other Amounts Payable on Reinsurance, Including Assumed and Ceded
Commissions and Expense Allowances Payable on Reinsurance Assumed
Reinsurance in Unauthorized Companies
Funds Held Under Reinsurance Treaties with Unauthorized Reinsurers
Funds Held Under Coinsurance
Reserve Adjustments for Reinsurance Ceded

The actual examination procedures selected to be performed is a matter of considerable judgment by the examiner. The following "Examination Program" includes examples of procedures commonly used.

To the extent that the examiner judgmentally determines whether it is appropriate to use the following procedures, that selection can be documented by checking the space next to such procedure, with modifications noted in the margin. The examiner may determine that alternative or additional procedures are required. If so, those procedures can be added on a supplemental sheet. The examiner performing the procedure should indicate satisfactory completion by initialing and dating in the space provided, and referencing the workpapers where the procedures and findings are documented.

The examiner may choose to apply the examination procedures to less than 100% of the items comprising an account balance. Guidance for audit sampling and control and substantive procedures can be found in Part 3 of the NAIC *Financial Condition Examiners Handbook.*

After each examination procedure, the examination objective that the procedure satisfies is indicated. The examination objectives are accuracy, completeness, compliance, cutoff, existence, obligation and ownership, valuation and presentation and disclosure.

EXAMINATION OBJECTIVES

Accuracy (AC) – Recorded transactions and account balances are mathematically accurate, are based on correct amounts and have been classified into the correct account.

Completeness (CO) – All transactions and account balances that should be recorded in the Annual financial statement were recorded.

Compliance (CM) – Business transactions and affairs have been conducted in accordance with state insurance codes, other state laws or department directives.

Cutoff (CT) – All transactions are recorded in the correct accounting period.

Existence (EX) – Recorded transactions occurred and are not fictitious and recorded assets and liabilities existed as of the balance sheet date.

Obligation (OB) and Ownership (OW) – Recorded liabilities are obligations of the company and recorded assets are the rights of the company at the balance sheet date.

Valuation (VA) – Assets and liabilities are valued in accordance with state statute and NAIC accounting guidance.

Presentation and Disclosure (PD) – The elements of the Annual Statement are properly classified and all disclosures are accurately included in the Annual Statement.

	Exam Obj.	Completion Date	Examiner	Work Paper Ref.
EXAMINATION PROCEDURES				
General Procedures				
Assumed and Ceded Reinsurance Transactions				
1. Through discussions with management and review of the company's transactions obtain an understanding of the company's assumed and ceded reinsurance policies. Document this understanding in a narrative and include in the workpapers. This narrative should include:	CM OB/OW VA			
a. A general description of the reinsurance program;	CM OB/OW			
b. The entity's maximum retained liability;	VA			
c. The maximum reinsurance coverage provided by the ceding program; and	VA			
d. Policy and procedure of the ceding program when the maximum coverage allowed is less than the largest risk written.	VA			
2. On a selective basis examine the reinsurance underwriting files relating to anticipated reinsurance contracts loss results. This file should include documentation of:	VA			
a. Historical loss ratios and combined ratios of ceding companies;	VA			
b. Anticipated loss ratios under contract;	VA			
c. Indications of the content and frequency of ceding company reports;	VA			
d. Prior business experience with ceding company;	VA			
e. The assuming company's past experience with similar risks; and	VA			
f. Pricing and ceding commission information.	VA			

	Exam Obj.	Completion Date	Examiner	Work Paper Ref.
3. Obtain copies of all significant assumed and ceded reinsurance treaties in-force for the period under examination. Prepare outlines of each contract showing the following:	EX AC CO			
(Additional information may be necessary based on the reinsurance practices of the individual company.)				
a. Name of reinsurer;	CO AC			
b. Name of reinsured;	CO AC			
c. Type of contract: Automatic or Facultative; Proportional (yearly renewable term, coinsurance, or modified coinsurance) or Nonproportional (catastrophe or stop-loss) **SSAP No. 61, paragraphs 11-16**;	CO AC			
d. Effective date and contract execution date;	EX AC CO			
e. Reporting responsibility;	CO AC			
f. Payment terms;	CO AC			
g. Payment of premium;	CO AC			
h. Termination;	CO AC			
i. Insolvency clause;	CO AC			
j. Policies/lines of business reinsured;	CO AC			
k. Company retention;	CO AC			
l. Reinsurer's limits;	CO AC			
m. Continuation of benefits clause;	CO AC			
n. Any collateral or letters of credit pursuant to the terms of the contract;	CO AC			
o. Experience rating refunds; and	CO AC			

		Exam Obj.	Completion Date	Examiner	Work Paper Ref.
p.	Contract exclusions/exceptions/carve outs. (Note: These exclusions/exceptions/carve outs can best be defined as procedures or other items that are specifically excluded from the reinsurance contract. In effect, the carve out causes the reinsurer to reach or exceed a higher limit.)	CO AC			
4.	Review each contract selected in step #3 to detect any unusual features that may significantly affect the company's financial condition, or that are in violation of laws, regulations, or good practice. Identify any of the following transactions:	CM AC EX CT OB/OW VA			
a.	Cut-through endorsements **(SSAP No. 61, paragraph 3)**;	EX AC			
b.	Reinsurance among affiliated or associated companies (pooling agreements; described in detail by **SSAP No. 63**);	CM AC			
c.	Fronting arrangements;	CM AC			
d.	Guaranteed profit contracts;	CM AC			
e.	Excessive risk assumed under treaty;	CM			
f.	Significant or unexpected changes in the entity's reinsurance programs [retention levels; form of reinsurance (e.g., excess of loss, pro rata, prospective, retrospective); type of reinsurance (e.g., treaty or facultative)];	CM			
g.	Large portfolio reinsurance during the last three months of any calendar year of the period;	EX CT			
h.	Unauthorized reinsurance and funds held;	OB/OW CM			
i.	Excessively high reinsurance commissions;	VA CM			
j.	Liability under expired contracts; and	VA CM			
k.	Retroactive adjustment of premiums.	CT CM			

	Exam Obj.	Completion Date	Examiner	Work Paper Ref.
Assumed Reinsurance				
5. For assumed reinsurance agreements, review and evaluate the company's procedures to assess the internal control environment of the ceding company.	AC EX CM OB/OW PD			
a. Read the reinsurance contract, related correspondence, and underwriting file to obtain an understanding of the contract, its business purpose and its expected impact on operations.	EX AC			
b. Examine documentation of required management review and approval of the contract.	CM			
c. Determine compliance with underwriting guidelines.	CM			
6. Obtain financial information and determine financial strength of all significant reinsurance assumed.	AC CM VA			
a. Obtain and analyze recent financial information, or other available sources of information, of the ceding company, such as financial reports filed with the SEC or with insurance industry reporting and rating services such as IRIS results files with the regulatory authorities.	AC CM VA			
7. Verify that the overall accounting treatment of reinsurance contracts complies with accounting guidelines described in accordance with **SSAP No. 61, paragraphs 21, 23, 39 and 40**.	AC VA			
8. Verify that the company has established policy reserves for assumed reinsurance in accordance with **SSAP No. 61, paragraph 38**.	EX VA			

		Exam Obj.	Completion Date	Examiner	Work Paper Ref.
9.	Obtain detail of assumed reinsurance premium income and agree it to the company's general ledger. Perform procedures to verify that the reinsurance premium income has been properly recorded in accordance with **SSAP No. 61, paragraph 25**. For selected assumed reinsurance transactions, trace recorded transactions to reports from ceding companies or intermediaries (bordereau).	VA AC			
10.	Examine any assumed reinsurance that has been retroceded. Examine supporting documentation of the company's review and request for retrocession.	EX			
11.	Determine that all required disclosures noted in **SSAP No. 61, paragraphs 57-63** are properly included in the financial statements.	PD			
	Ceded Reinsurance				
12.	Identify and obtain detail of the company's ceded reinsurance accounts. Agree the total of each of the accounts to the company's general ledger. Investigate any discrepancies.	EX AC			
13.	Categorize the types of reinsurance contracts and determine if each contract transfers risk in accordance with **SSAP No. 61, paragraphs 17-20**. If a contract does not transfer risk, verify that it has received deposit accounting treatment in accordance with **SSAP No. 61, paragraph 50**. (Consult the NAIC *Life and Health Reinsurance Agreements Model Regulation* (NAIC Model Act No. 791) for additional guidance on the transfer of risk.)	PD VA			
14.	Verify that the overall accounting treatment of reinsurance contracts complies with accounting guidelines described in **SSAP No. 61, paragraphs 21, 22, 39 and 40.**	VA PD			
15.	Obtain financial information and determine financial strength of all significant reinsurers to which business was ceded.	VA AC CM			

	Exam Obj.	Completion Date	Examiner	Work Paper Ref.
a. Obtain and analyze recent financial information, or other available sources of information, of the assuming company; such as financial reports filed with the SEC or with insurance industry reporting and rating services such as the IRIS results filed with the regulatory authorities.	CM			
16. Determine that all required disclosures noted in **SSAP No. 61, paragraphs 57-63** are properly included in the financial statements.	PD			
<u>Amounts Recoverable From Reinsurers</u>				
1. Obtain a detailed listing of the reinsurance recoverables aging and agree the total to the company's general ledger and Annual Statement.	EX AC			
2. Agree the reinsurance recoverables to a valid reinsurance contract noting the following:	EX OB/OW CM			
a. Reinsurance premiums have been paid;	EX			
b. Claim is covered under the reinsurance contract; and	CM			
c. Deductible payments by the ceding company have been met.	OB/OW			
3. Verify that the ceding company has paid the claim by agreeing the reinsurance recoverable to a copy of the claim payment.	AC CO CM			
a. For unpaid reinsurance claims, perform procedures to verify that the claim is valid under the reinsurance contract and not in dispute.	CM			
4. Review the aging detail and identify recoverables aged over 90 days. Discuss with management and perform procedures to ascertain the collectibility of these reinsurance recoverables. All uncollectible recoverables should be written off in accordance with **SSAP No. 61, paragraph 41**.	VA EX			
a. Confirm reinsurance recoverables directly with the assuming company.	EX			

	Exam Obj.	Completion Date	Examiner	Work Paper Ref.
b. Perform subsequent receipt testwork.	VA EX			
5. Verify that all reinsurance recoverables written off or disputed have been properly disclosed in accordance with **SSAP No. 61, paragraph 61**.	PD			
6. With respect to reinsurance effected through an intermediary, review treaties for credit risk assumption provisions. (Consult the NAIC *Reinsurance Intermediary Model Act* (NAIC Model Act No. 790) for additional guidance on reinsurance intermediaries.)	EX			
Commissions and Expense Allowances Due				
1. Obtain detail of the commissions and expense allowances due. Agree the detail to the company's general ledger and Annual Statement.	EX AC			
2. Obtain a schedule detailing the commissions and expense allowances due by reinsurer. Perform procedures to verify the receivables:	EX VA			
a. Recalculate the commissions and expense allowances due by utilizing percentages and amounts specified in the reinsurance contract;	VA			
b. Confirm significant commissions and expense allowances due directly with the reinsurer; and	EX VA			
c. Perform subsequent receipt testwork.	EX VA			
3. Identify any commissions and expense allowances due which are associated with expired or disputed reinsurance contracts. Perform procedures to verify that the commissions and expenses due under these contracts are collectible. Verify that all uncollectible amounts are properly written off and disclosed in the company's financial statements.	EX VA			
4. Verify that all commissions and expense allowances due have been properly recorded in accordance with **SSAP No. 61, paragraphs 28-32**.	AC VA			

	Exam Obj.	Completion Date	Examiner	Work Paper Ref.
Experience Rating and Other Refunds Due				
1. Obtain detail of the experience rating and other refunds due. Agree the detail to the company's general ledger and Annual Statement.	EX AC			
2. Utilizing the detail obtained, perform procedures to verify the receivables:	EX VA			
a. Trace the receivable directly to the reinsurance contract or other source documentation;	EX VA			
b. Confirm any significant experience rating and other refunds due directly with third parties; and	EX			
c. Perform subsequent receipt testwork.	EX VA			
3. Review detail of the experience rating and refunds due for collectibility. Verify that all uncollectible receivables are properly written off and disclosed by the company.	VA			
4. Verify that all experience refunds have been properly recorded in accordance with **SSAP No. 61, paragraphs 33-34**.	AC			
Other Amounts Receivable Under Reinsurance Contracts				
1. Obtain detail of other amounts receivable under reinsurance contracts. Agree the detail to the company's general ledger and Annual Statement.	EX AC			
2. Utilizing the detail obtained, perform procedures to verify the existence and valuation of these receivables:	EX VA			
a. Trace the reinsurance receivable directly to the reinsurance contract or other source documentation;	EX VA			
b. Confirm significant receivables directly with third parties; and	EX VA			
c. Perform subsequent receipt testwork.	EX VA			

	Exam Obj.	Completion Date	Examiner	Work Paper Ref.
3. Review detail of the receivables and identify any receivables that have aged over 90 days. Perform procedures to ascertain the collectibility of these receivables. All receivables deemed uncollectible should be written off and properly disclosed by the company.	EX VA			
Life Insurance Premiums and Annuity Considerations Deferred and Uncollected on In-force Business (Less Premiums on Reinsurance Ceded and Less Loading)				
Ceded Reinsurance Premiums Payable				
1. Obtain detail of ceded reinsurance contracts and premium responsibilities. Obtain a schedule of the ceded reinsurance premiums payable and agree this schedule to the company's general ledger.	EX AC			
2. Recalculate the ceded reinsurance premiums payable based on the reinsurance contract provisions.	VA			
3. Verify the completeness of reinsurance premiums payable by verifying paid premium obligations to payment documentation.	CO			
4. Verify that the company has properly excluded the ceded reinsurance premiums payable from the "Life Insurance Premiums and Annuity Considerations Deferred and Uncollected on In-Force Business (Less Premiums on Reinsurance Ceded and Less Loading)" asset classification on the Annual Statement.	PD			
Other Amounts Payable on Reinsurance, Including Assumed and Ceded				
1. Obtain detail of other amounts payable pertaining to assumed and ceded reinsurance. Agree the detail to the company's general ledger and Annual Statement.	EX AC			
2. Utilizing the detail obtained, recalculate and trace the amounts payable directly to reinsurance contract provisions.	VA			

	Exam Obj.	Completion Date	Examiner	Work Paper Ref.
3. Perform a search for unrecorded liabilities. Obtain the reinsurance disbursements detail and select a sample of disbursements to test for proper accrual.	CO			
Commission and Expense Allowances Payable on Reinsurance Assumed				
1. Obtain detail of commission and expense allowances payable on assumed reinsurance. Agree the detail to the company's general ledger and Annual Statement.	EX AC			
2. Compare the allowances payable to prior year balances. Investigate and document any significant fluctuations.	EX AC			
3. Obtain a schedule of commission and expense payables by reinsurance contract. Recalculate the commission and expense allowance payable based on actual contract provisions.	CO AC			
4. Obtain and review all new assumed reinsurance contracts. Note that all commission and expense allowances for these contracts have been properly recorded in accordance with **SSAP No. 61, paragraphs 33 and 34**.	EX CO AC			
Reinsurance in Unauthorized Companies				
1. Review reinsurance agreements and identify any unauthorized reinsurers in accordance with the definition found in **SSAP No. 61, paragraph 42**.	EX			
2. Obtain a schedule detailing the company's paid and unpaid losses due from unauthorized reinsurance companies. Agree this schedule to the company's general ledger and Annual Statement.	CO EX PD			
3. Verify that the company has properly included or excluded the admitted asset or reduction of liability for the paid and unpaid losses due from unauthorized reinsurance companies based on the criteria established by **Appendix A-785 to the NAIC *Accounting Practices and Procedures Manual*, paragraph 16**.	AC PD			

	Exam Obj.	Completion Date	Examiner	Work Paper Ref.
4. Identify any credits taken in balance sheet accounts for reinsurance ceded to unauthorized reinsurers. Verify that an offsetting liability has been established in accordance with **SSAP No. 61, paragraphs 42-43**.	VA PD			
5. Identify any unauthorized reinsurance funds held by the ceding company or letters of credit that may offset reinsurance recoverables to the extent of the reinsurance recoverable balance, funds held, or to the amount allowable under the letter of credit.	EX VA AC OB/OW			
a. Verify that the letters of credit are clean, irrevocable, and issued by a qualified U.S. financial institution, as defined in **Appendix A-785 to the NAIC *Accounting Practices and Procedures Manual***.	AC OB/OW			
6. Obtain detail of unearned reinsurance premiums in unauthorized companies. Recalculate these unearned premiums and agree the amount to Schedule S on the company's Annual Statement.	AC CO			
7. Identify and reconcile any reductions in reserves for reinsurance in unauthorized companies.	EX			
<u>Funds held Under Reinsurance Treaties with Unauthorized Reinsurers; Funds held under Coinsurance</u>				
1. Obtain detail of funds held under reinsurance treaties with unauthorized reinsurers. Obtain detail of funds held under coinsurance. Agree the detail to the company's general ledger and Annual Statement. Perform analytical procedures comparing the amounts to prior year balances. Investigate and document any significant fluctuations.	CO EX AC			
2. Perform procedures to ascertain to the completeness and accuracy of the recorded liabilities:	CO EX AC CM			

	Exam Obj.	Completion Date	Examiner	Work Paper Ref.
a. Review reinsurance agreements and determine that all funds held by the ceding entity in accordance with the contracts are properly recorded;	AC CO CM			
b. Confirm with reinsurers the funds held by the ceding company; and	EX			
c. Identify new reinsurance contracts for which funds are not held. Review these contracts to verify that the contract does not specify that funds should be transferred and held by the ceding entity.	EX CO			
<u>Reserve Adjustments for Reinsurance Ceded</u>				
1. Obtain a schedule of reserve credits the company has recorded for ceded reinsurance. Verify credits are in accordance with **SSAP No. 61, paragraphs 35-37**.	EX CM			
2. Review the reinsurance contracts for which reserve credits have been taken and verify that they meet the specifications and requirements of a domestic ceding insurer in accordance with **Appendix A-785 'Credit for Reinsurance' of the NAIC *Accounting Practices and Procedures Manual*.**	AC CM			
a. Verify that reserve credits for reinsurers not meeting the requirements of a 'domestic ceded reinsurer' meet the exception criteria established in **Appendix A-785 of the NAIC *Accounting Practices and Procedures Manual*.**	AC CM			
3. Perform procedures to ensure that the reserve credits recorded by the company do not exceed limits imposed by **Appendix A-785 of the NAIC *Accounting Practices and Procedures Manual*.**	CM			
4. Reconcile reserve credits to ceded reinsurance policies when applicable. Identify and document any ceded reinsurance contracts, which do not have recorded credits.	CO			
5. Reconcile the reserve credits to the Schedule S in the company's Annual Statement.	PD AC			

SECTION H — REINSURANCE AND RISK TRANSFER INSTRUMENTS CYCLE: PROPERTY & CASUALTY

Listed below are the corresponding Annual Statement line items that are related to the procedures contained in this Reinsurance Specific Risk Analysis:

Annual Statement Blank Line Items

Funds Held by or Deposited with Reinsured Companies
Reinsurance Recoverables on Loss and Loss Adjustment Expense Payments
Amount Due From/To Protected Cells
Protected Cell Assets
Reinsurance Payable on Paid Loss and Loss Adjustment Expenses
Ceded Reinsurance Premiums Payable (Net of Ceding Commissions)
Funds Held by the Company Under Reinsurance Treaties
Provision for Reinsurance
Protected Cell Liabilities

Relevant SSAP's Include:

#5, Liabilities, Contingencies, and Impairments of Assets
#62, Property and Casualty Reinsurance
#63, Underwriting Pools and Associations Including Intercompany Pools
#64, Offsetting and Netting of Assets and Liabilities
#65, Property and Casualty Contracts
#74, Accounting for the Issuance of Insurance-Linked Securities Issued by a Property and Casualty Insurer through a Protected Cell
#75, Reinsurance Deposit Accounting – An Amendment to SSAP No. 62, Property and Casualty Reinsurance

SPECIFIC RISK ANALYSIS WORKPAPERS

Risk Analysis Prepared By/Date ______________________________

Planning Exam Analysis Prepared By/Date ______________________________

Reviewed By/Date ______________________________

EXAMINATION OBJECTIVES:

1. Reinsurance contract that effectively transfers insurance risk exists between parties and contains provisions mandated through regulation. (Existence and Compliance)

2. Amounts of reinsurance ceded are valued accurately and reflected in the financial statements. (Valuation, Completeness, Compliance, Accuracy, Cutoff and Presentation and Disclosure)

3. Reinsurance assumed transactions are properly authorized, valued and recorded. (Valuation, Compliance, Accuracy and Cutoff)

4. The insurance company owns, or has appropriate rights to the recorded reinsurance ceded or assumed assets and incurs the reported reinsurance ceded or assumed liabilities. (Ownership and Obligation)

INHERENT RISKS

____

____

____

____

INTERNAL AND EXTERNAL ENVIRONMENTAL CONDITIONS/FACTORS

____

____

____

____

RESULTS OF DETAIL ANALYTICAL REVIEW PROCEDURES

____

____

____

____

CONTROL RISK — REINSURANCE AND RISK TRANSFER INSTRUMENTS CYCLE: PROPERTY & CASUALTY

This questionnaire is designed to assist the examiner in assessing control risk for reinsurance property and casualty cycles. Part 1, Section III and Part 3 of this *Handbook* provides guidance in consideration of an insurer's internal control structure for use when designing substantive examination procedures.

This questionnaire includes examples of internal control procedures and policies that are commonly utilized by insurers to achieve internal control objectives. For each control procedure listed below, indicate by placing a check mark in the yes or no box whether or not the insurer employs such a procedure, or other similar practice (include a description of the similar procedure). To the extent the control procedure is not applicable, indicate N/A. If other relevant control procedures are in place, list them in the space that follows. Control procedures that are tested by the examiner should be documented by including the workpaper reference in the comment section and the examiner's initials in the reliance column.

For each individual control procedure there is a control objective listed that satisfies the procedure.

If the examiner initially assesses control risk as low or medium for a particular account balance, then those controls must be tested. The controls should be tested to determine whether the procedure is operating as expected, applied throughout the entire period of reliance, performed on a timely basis, encompassing all transactions and identifying errors. Some examples of testing procedures are inquiry, observation, re-performance and examination of documents. The level of reliance, if any, should be indicated in the applicable column along with any comments the examiner may have regarding the procedure.

Based upon the testing results, the examiner should determine whether the preliminary control risk assessment is confirmed or should be revised.

CONTROL OBJECTIVES

Authorization (AU) – All transactions recorded were reviewed and approved by designated personnel.

Completeness (CO) – All transactions that occurred are initially entered into the accounting records, accepted for processing and generated data files and reports reflect that all transactions have occurred.

Accuracy (AC) – Transactions are initially recorded correctly, timely and accurately.

Asset Protection (AP) – Adequate safeguards over access to and use of assets and records, including the appropriate segregation of duties among company personnel.

	Control Obj.	Y	N	Work Paper Ref.	Reliance
General Control Procedures					
The examiner should determine the amount of documentation necessary for each control procedure. If the examiner intends to place substantial reliance on the established controls, the examiner should explain the control procedure in a workpaper and document the individual responsible for supervising the control activity as well as the frequency of the control activity.					
1. Are reinsurance contracts reviewed for compliance with state regulations?	AU				
2. Are reinsurance contract terms, amendments, and extent of subscription reviewed for compliance with company and reinsurance coverage guidelines prior to execution?	AU AC				
3. Are reinsurance contract terms and expected results properly documented prior to execution?	AU AP				
4. Do procedures exist to ensure that reinsurance accounting transactions (expense allowances, etc.) are reviewed, compared to contract terms and expected results, and approved in accordance with **SSAP No. 62, paragraphs 17-33** and **SSAP No. 75**?	AU AC				
5. Are ceding companies and intermediaries approved with regards to business reputation, financial stability, and experience prior to contract execution and monitored on a continuous basis?	AU				
6. Are assuming companies and intermediaries approved with regards to business reputation, financial stability, and experience prior to contract execution and monitored on a continuous basis?	AU				
7. Are amounts due from ceding and assuming companies and intermediaries reviewed for collectibility in accordance with **SSAP No. 62, paragraph 56** and **SSAP No. 5**?	CO				

		Control Obj.	Y	N	Work Paper Ref.	Reliance
8.	Are reviews performed to ascertain that timely reports and accounting data are received from ceding companies or intermediaries and used to record transactions?	AC				
9.	Are intermediary bonding reviews completed to assure the security of funds that are passed through?	AP				
10.	Are activity analyses for cumulative reinsurance contracts prepared and reviewed to assist in evaluation of profitability, risk exposure, contract variance and expected results?	AC CO				
11.	Are controls and accounting records for ceding entities independently tested or reviewed to substantiate accounting data provided or to monitor compliance with contract provisions?	AC AP				
12.	Is an independent review conducted of a ceding company's underwriting practices, claims processing, loss reserving and actuarial policies and procedures?	AC AP				
13.	Are recorded amounts of ceded reinsurance reconciled to detailed policy and reinsurance records?	AC CO				
14.	Is an evaluation of the need for adequacy letters of credit or collateral conducted prior to contract execution and monitored on a continuous basis?	AP				
15.	Are procedures in place and reviews performed to detect overlapping reinsurance coverage?	AC				
16.	Are reinsurance agreements factored into the underwriting process?	AU				
17.	Are reinsurance retrocession agreements reviewed and authorized prior to execution?	AU				
18.	Are regular reviews conducted to verify that the company's established systems and processes are properly identifying business to be reinsured?	AC				

	Control Obj.	Y	N	Work Paper Ref.	Reliance
19. Is the assuming company authorized to transact reinsurance within the ceding company's state of domicile? If not, are letters of credit or other means of security provided?	AU				
20. Are protected cell agreements (CAT bonds) in accordance with **SSAP No. 74** periodically reviewed to determine compliance with SSAP guidelines? Are these transactions properly approved and authorized?	AU				
21. Verify that the Special Purpose Reinsurance Vehicle (SPRV) transaction has been reviewed by the Commissioner and that he/she notified the domestic regulator of the SPRV in writing that the transaction has not been disapproved. Verify that the SPRV is authorized in its domiciliary US jurisdiction.	AU				
22. Are reinsurance transactions, claims processing, premium collection, key information systems functions and general accounting activities appropriately segregated? Are independent reviews conducted of the work performed? Are the reinsurance receivables/payables reviewed by someone independent of the transactional function?	AP				
23. Do data files and production programs have adequate safeguards against unauthorized access, as well as proper safeguards over access to any collateral held by the ceding entity from the assuming entity?	AP				

OTHER KEY CONTROLS EXISTING FOR THIS EXAMINATION OBJECTIVE:

SUMMARY EVALUATION OF CONTROL RISK:

EVALUATION OF INDEPENDENT CPA'S WORK FOR THIS EXAMINATION (CPA REVIEW CHECKLIST):

OVERALL RISK ASSESSMENT

Balance Sheet Evaluation of the Likelihood of a Material Adjustment to Surplus:

The evaluation of the likelihood of a material adjustment to surplus should be based on the following criteria:

- Inherent Risk
- Internal & External Environmental Factors
- Control Risk
- Materiality Consideration

The examiner should rate each item as to the likelihood of a material misstatement. All items are assumed as "High" prior to any examiner evaluation. A "High" assessment requires the examiner to perform substantive examination procedures over that account area. A lower assessment allows the examiner to perform analytical or fewer substantive procedures to satisfy the examination requirements. If an assessment other than "High" is selected for any of the accounts, the examiner needs to document the basis for the assessment. If the assessment is based on control testwork, the documentation should include results of control procedures and related workpaper references.

1) "Funds Held by or Deposited with Reinsured Companies"

___________ High ___________ Medium ___________ Low

Basis for Assessment:

____

____

____

2) "Reinsurance Recoverables on Loss and Loss Adjustment Expense Payments"

___________ High ___________ Medium ___________ Low

Basis for Assessment:

____

____

____

3) "Amount Due From/To Protected Cells"

__________ High __________ Medium __________ Low

Basis for Assessment:

4) "Protected Cell Assets"

__________ High __________ Medium __________ Low

Basis for Assessment:

5) "Reinsurance Payable on Paid Loss and Loss Adjustment Expenses"

__________ High __________ Medium __________ Low

Basis for Assessment:

6) "Ceded Reinsurance Premiums Payable (Net of Ceding Commissions)"

__________ High __________ Medium __________ Low

Basis for Assessment:

7) "Funds Held by the Company Under Reinsurance Treaties"

___________ High ___________ Medium __________ Low

Basis for Assessment:

---

8) "Provision for Reinsurance"

___________ High ___________ Medium __________ Low

Basis for Assessment:

---

9) "Protected Cell Liabilities"

___________ High ___________ Medium __________ Low

Basis for Assessment:

PRELIMINARY EXAMINATION APPROACH — REINSURANCE AND RISK TRANSFER INSTRUMENTS CYCLE: PROPERTY & CASUALTY

Listed below are the corresponding Annual Statement line items that are related to the procedures contained in this Reinsurance Specific Risk Analysis:

Funds Held by or Deposited with Reinsured Companies
Reinsurance Recoverables on Loss and Loss Adjustment Expense Payments
Amount Due From/To Protected Cells
Protected Cell Assets
Reinsurance Payable on Paid Loss and Loss Adjustment Expenses
Ceded Reinsurance Premiums Payable (Net of Ceding Commissions)
Funds Held by the Company Under Reinsurance Treaties
Provision for Reinsurance
Protected Cell Liabilities

The actual examination procedures selected to be performed is a matter of considerable judgment by the examiner. The following "Examination Program" includes examples of procedures commonly used.

To the extent that the examiner judgmentally determines whether it is appropriate to use the following procedures, that selection can be documented by checking the space next to such procedure, with modifications noted in the margin. The examiner may determine that alternative or additional procedures are required. If so, those procedures can be added on a supplemental sheet. The examiner performing the procedure should indicate satisfactory completion by initialing and dating in the space provided, and referencing the workpapers where the procedures and findings are documented.

The examiner may chose to apply the examination procedures to less than 100% of the items comprising an account balance. Guidance for audit sampling and control and substantive procedures can be found in Part 3 of the NAIC *Financial Condition Examiners Handbook.*

After each examination procedure, the examination objective that the procedure satisfies is indicated. The examination objectives are accuracy, completeness, compliance, cutoff, existence, obligation and ownership, valuation and presentation and disclosure.

EXAMINATION OBJECTIVES

Accuracy (AC) – Recorded transactions and account balances are mathematically accurate, are based on correct amounts and have been classified into the correct account.

Completeness (CO) – All transactions and account balances that should be recorded in the annual financial statement were recorded.

Compliance (CM) – Business transactions and affairs have been conducted in accordance with state insurance codes, other state laws or department directives.

Cutoff (CT) – All transactions are recorded in the correct accounting period.

Existence (EX) – Recorded transactions occurred and are not fictitious and recorded assets and liabilities existed as of the balance sheet date.

Obligation (OB) and Ownership (OW) – Recorded liabilities are obligations of the company and recorded assets are the rights of the company at the balance sheet date.

Valuation (VA) – Assets and liabilities are valued in accordance with state statute and NAIC accounting guidance.

Presentation and Disclosure (PD) – The elements of the Annual Statement are properly classified and all disclosures are accurately included in the Annual Statement.

	Exam Obj.	Completion Date	Examiner	Work Paper Ref.
EXAMINATION PROCEDURES				
<u>**General Procedures**</u>				
Assumed and Ceded Reinsurance Transactions				
1. Through discussions with management and review of the transactions obtain an understanding of the assumed and ceded reinsurance policies. Document this understanding in a narrative and include in the workpapers. This narrative should include:	CM OB/OW VA			
a. A general description of the reinsurance program;	CM OB/OW			
b. The entity's maximum retained liability;	VA			
c. The maximum reinsurance coverage provided by the ceding program; and	VA			
d. Policy and procedure of the ceding program when the maximum coverage allowed is less than the largest risk written.	VA			
2. On a selective basis examine the underwriting files relating to anticipated reinsurance contracts loss results. This file should include documentation of:	VA			
a. Historical loss ratios and combined ratios of ceding companies;	VA			
b. Anticipated loss ratios under contract;	VA			
c. Indications of the content and frequency of ceding company reports;	VA			
d. Prior business experience with ceding company;	VA			
e. The assuming companies past experience with similar risks; and	VA			
f. Pricing and ceding commission information.	VA			

	Exam Obj.	Completion Date	Examiner	Work Paper Ref.
3. Obtain copies of all significant assumed and ceded reinsurance treaties in-force for the period under examination. Prepare outlines of each contract showing the following:	EX AC CO			
(Additional information may be necessary based on the reinsurance practices of the individual company.)				
a. Name of reinsurer;	CO AC			
b. Name of reinsured;	CO AC			
c. Type of contract (Treaty or Facultative; Pro Rata, Excess of Loss, or Catastrophe; Retroactive or Progressive) **SSAP No. 62, paragraphs 4-5**;	CO AC			
d. Effective date and contract execution date (**SSAP No. 62, paragraph 23**);	EX AC CO			
e. Reporting responsibility **(SSAP No. 62, paragraph 6)**;	CO AC			
f. Payment terms **(SSAP No. 62, paragraph 6)**;	CO AC			
g. Payment of premium taxes **(SSAP No. 62, paragraph 6)**;	CO AC			
h. Termination **(SSAP No. 62, paragraph 6)**;	CO AC			
i. Insolvency clause **(SSAP No. 62, paragraph 6)**;	CO AC			
j. Policies/lines of business reinsured;	CO AC			
k. Company retention;	CO AC			
l. Reinsurer's limits;	CO AC			

	Exam Obj.	Completion Date	Examiner	Work Paper Ref.
m. Continuation of benefits clause;	CO AC			
n. Any collateral or letters of credit pursuant to the terms of the contract;	CO AC			
o. Expense allowances;	CO AC			
p. Recapture provisions;	CO AC			
q. Intermediaries;	CO AC			
r. Renewal/recovery provisions;	CO AC			
s. Corridor or offset provisions;	CO AC			
t. Experience rating refunds; and	CO AC			
u. Contract exclusions/exceptions/carve outs. (Note: These exclusions/exceptions/carve outs can best be defined as procedures or other items that are specifically excluded from the reinsurance contract. In effect, the carve out causes the reinsurer to reach or exceed a higher limit.)	CO AC			
4. Review each contract selected in step #3 to verify that they meet the required terms for reinsurance agreements in accordance with **SSAP No. 62, paragraph 8**.	CO AC			
5. Verify that reinsurance intermediaries are properly licensed and have a valid contract with the company. Review the Reinsurance Intermediary Model Act and verify compliance with all required provisions.	CM AC			

	Exam Obj.	Completion Date	Examiner	Work Paper Ref.
6. Review each contract selected in step #3 to detect any unusual features that may significantly affect the financial condition, or that are in violation of laws, regulations, or good practice. Identify any of the following transactions:	CM AC EX CT OB/OW VA			
a. Cut-through endorsements;	EX AC			
b. Reinsurance among affiliated or associated companies. (Pooling agreements are described in detail by **SSAP No. 63**);	CM AC			
c. Fronting arrangements;	CM AC			
d. Guaranteed profit contracts;	CM AC			
e. Excessive risk assumed under treaty;	CM			
f. Significant or unexpected changes in the entity's reinsurance programs [retention levels, form of reinsurance (e.g., excess of loss, pro rata, prospective, retrospective), type of reinsurance (e.g., treaty or facultative)];	CM			
g. Large portfolio reinsurance during the last three months of any calendar year of the period;	EX CT			
h. Unauthorized reinsurance and funds held;	OB/OW CM			
i. Excessively high reinsurance commissions;	VA CM			
j. Liability under expired contracts; and	VA CM			
k. Retroactive adjustment of premiums.	CT CM			
7. For each prospective reinsurance agreement identified in step #3, verify that the agreements have been accounted for in accordance with **SSAP No. 62, paragraphs 25-26**.	CO AC			

	Exam Obj.	Completion Date	Examiner	Work Paper Ref.
a. Verify that amounts paid for prospective reinsurance are reported as a reduction of written and earned premiums and earned over the remaining contract period in proportion to the amount of reinsurance protection provided in accordance with **SSAP No. 62, paragraph 25.**	AC			
8. For each retroactive reinsurance agreement identified in step #3, verify that the agreements have been accounted for in accordance with **SSAP No. 62, paragraphs 27-33**.	CO AC			
a. Review the retroactive reinsurance agreements and verify that structured settlement annuities, novations, terminations, and intercompany reinsurance agreements as detailed in **SSAP No. 62, paragraph 30**, are not included in the specific retrospective reinsurance accounting. Verify that these have been properly classified as prospective agreements.	AC			
9. Identify any protected cell agreements (CAT Bonds) in-force at the company. Review the agreements and verify that they have been properly recorded in accordance with **SSAP No. 74**.	EX AC			
10. Identify any contracts entered into with Special Purpose Reinsurance Vehicles (SPRVs) domiciled in the United States. Review the agreements and verify compliance with standards. (Consult the NAIC Special Purpose Vehicle Model Act.)	EX CM			
11. Through review of the reinsurance contracts, identify any instances in which the property/casualty company is assuming accident and health reinsurance. For those instances, perform procedures to verify that the reinsurance contracts provide sufficient transfer of risk or has been properly recorded in accordance with deposit-type accounting guidelines identified in **SSAP No. 61 and SSAP No. 75**.	CM AC			

	Exam Obj.	Completion Date	Examiner	Work Paper Ref.
Assumed Reinsurance				
12. For reinsurance assumption agreements, review and evaluate the procedures to assess the internal control environment of the ceding company.	AC EX CM OB/OW PD			
a. Read the reinsurance contract, related correspondence, and underwriting file to obtain an understanding of the contract, its business purpose and its expected impact on operations.	EX AC			
b. Examine documentation of required management review and approval of the contract.	CM			
c. Determine compliance with underwriting guidelines.	CM			
13. Obtain financial information and determine financial strength of all significant reinsurance assumed.	VA AC CM			
a. Obtain and analyze recent financial information, or other available sources of information, of the ceding company, such as financial reports filed with the SEC or with insurance industry reporting and rating services such as IRIS results filed with the regulatory authorities.	VA AC CM			
14. Verify that the overall accounting treatment of assumed reinsurance transactions complies with accounting guidelines described in **SSAP No. 62 paragraphs 35-40**.	AC VA			
15. Obtain detail of assumed reinsurance premium income and agree it to the company's general ledger. Perform procedures to verify that premium receivables have been properly recorded in accordance with **SSAP No. 62, paragraphs 35-37**. For selected assumed reinsurance transactions, trace recorded transactions to reports provided from ceding companies or intermediaries (bordereau).	AC VA			

	Exam Obj.	Completion Date	Examiner	Work Paper Ref.
16. Examine any assumed reinsurance that has been retroceded. Examine supporting documentation of the review and request for retrocession.	EX			
17. Determine that all required disclosures noted in **SSAP No. 62, paragraphs 65-72** are properly disclosed.	PD			
Ceded Reinsurance				
18. Identify and obtain detail of the company's ceded reinsurance accounts. Agree the total of each of the accounts to the company's general ledger. Investigate any discrepancies.	EX AC			
19. Categorize the types of reinsurance contracts and determine if the contracts transfer risk in accordance with **SSAP No. 62, paragraphs 9-16**. If a contract does not transfer risk, verify that it has received deposit accounting treatment in accordance with **SSAP No. 75, Reinsurance Deposit Accounting**.	PD VA			
20. Verify that the overall accounting treatment of reinsurance contracts complies with accounting guidelines described in **SSAP No. 62, paragraphs 17-33**.	VA PD			
21. Obtain financial information and determine financial strength of all significant reinsurers to which business was ceded.	VA AC CM			
a. Obtain and analyze recent financial information, or other available sources of information, of the assuming company, such as financial reports filed with the SEC or with insurance industry reporting and rating services such as the IRIS results filed with the regulatory authorities.	CM			
22. Determine that all required disclosures noted in **SSAP No. 62, paragraphs 65-74** are properly included in the financial statements.	PD			

	Exam Obj.	Completion Date	Examiner	Work Paper Ref.
Funds Held by or Deposited with Reinsured Companies				
1. Obtain detail of the funds held by or deposited with reinsured companies and agree it to the general ledger and Annual Statement.	EX AC PD			
2. Verify the existence and ownership of these assets.	EX VA OB/OW			
a. Obtain the respective reinsurance agreements and agree the deposited funds to specific contract provisions.	EX VA OB/OW			
b. Confirm with the reinsurer the reinsurance deposits and related contract terms.	EX VA OB/OW			
Reinsurance Recoverables on Loss and Loss Adjustment Expense Payments				
1. Obtain an aging report of the reinsurance recoverables on loss and loss adjustment expenses and agree the report to the company's general ledger and Annual Statement.	EX AC PD			
2. Agree the reinsurance recoverables to a valid reinsurance contract noting the following:	EX OB/OW CM			
a. Reinsurance premiums have been paid;	EX			
b. Claim is covered under the reinsurance contract; and	CM			
c. Deductible payments by the ceding company have been met.	OB/OW			
3. Verify that the ceding company has paid the claim by agreeing the reinsurance recoverable to a copy of the claim payment.	AC CO CM			

	Exam Obj.	Completion Date	Examiner	Work Paper Ref.
a. For unpaid reinsurance claims, perform procedures to verify that the claim is valid under the reinsurance contract and not in dispute.	CM			
4. Review the aging detail and identify recoverables aged over 90 days. Discuss with management and perform procedures to ascertain the collectibility of these reinsurance recoverables. All uncollectible recoverables should be written off in accordance with **SSAP No. 62 paragraph 56**.	VA EX			
a. Confirm reinsurance recoverables directly with the assuming company.	EX			
b. Perform subsequent receipt testwork.	VA CO			
5. Verify that all uncollectible and disputed receivables have been properly accounted for in accordance with **SSAP No. 62, paragraphs 54-56**.	VA PD			
6. Verify that all reinsurance recoverables written off or disputed have been properly disclosed in accordance with **SSAP No. 62, paragraphs 66-67**.	PD			
7. Verify that the reinsurance recoverables have been recognized and recorded in accordance with **SSAP No. 62 paragraphs 17 and 19**.	AC			
8. With respect to reinsurance affected through an intermediary, review treaties for credit risk assumption provisions. (Consult the NAIC Reinsurance Intermediary Model Act (NAIC Model Act No. 790) for additional guidance on reinsurance intermediaries.)	CM			
<u>Amount Due From/To Protected Cells</u>				
1. Obtain detail of the amount due from/to protected cells and agree the detail to the company's protected cell ledger and Annual Statement.	EX AC PD			
2. From the above detail, obtain and review the protected cell agreements to verify the recoverable or liability reported. Recalculate the recoverable or liability based on the contract specifications.	VA AC			

	Exam Obj.	Completion Date	Examiner	Work Paper Ref.
3. Verify that the protected cell recoverables and liabilities are properly netted and that the recoverables are stated at fair value in accordance with **SSAP No. 74, paragraph 10**.	VA			
<u>**Protected Cell Assets**</u>				
1. Obtain detail of the protected cell assets and agree the detail to the company's protected cell ledger and Annual Statement.	EX AC PD			
2. Review the protected cell asset detail and verify that the assets are properly classified and included with protected cells in accordance with **SSAP No. 74**.	AC CO			
3. Verify that all protected cell assets are properly stated at fair value in accordance with **SSAP No. 74, paragraph 14**.	VA			
4. Verify that the protected cell assets are properly excluded from the other assets of the company and reported separately. Ensure that all disclosures and reports are properly included as required in **SSAP No. 74, paragraphs 18-19**.	PD			
<u>**Reinsurance Payable on Paid Loss and Loss Adjustment Expenses**</u>				
1. Obtain detail of the assumed and ceded reinsurance loss and loss adjustment expenses payable and agree it to the company's general ledger and Annual Statement.	EX AC PD			
2. Perform procedures to verify the completeness of the reinsurance losses payable.	CO VA EX			
a. Perform analytical procedures comparing current year reinsurance payables to prior year balances. Investigate any significant fluctuations.	CO VA			
b. Perform analytical procedures comparing the current year reinsurance payable balance to projected balances. Investigate any significant fluctuations.	CO VA			

	Exam Obj.	Completion Date	Examiner	Work Paper Ref.
c. Perform a search for unrecorded reinsurance payables by obtaining distribution detail of subsequent reinsurance loss payments. Compare this detail to the year-end listing of reinsurance payables established by the company. Identify any losses subsequently paid which were not recorded as a loss payable at year-end. Verify that all liabilities that were in existence at period-end were properly recorded.	CO VA EX			
3. Verify that the assumed reinsurance payables have been recorded in accordance with **SSAP No. 62, paragraph 40**.	AC			
4. Compare the ceded reinsurance payables with the reinsurance recoverables on loss and loss adjustment expense payments.	EX AC VA			
a. Identify and investigate any instances in which the ceded loss payment has been received by the company but not yet paid to the insured.	EX AC			
<u>**Ceded Reinsurance Premiums Payable (Net of Ceding Commissions)**</u>				
1. Obtain detail of ceded reinsurance contracts and premium responsibilities. Obtain a schedule of the ceded reinsurance premiums payable and agree this schedule to the company's general ledger and Annual Statement.	EX AC PD			
2. Recalculate the ceded reinsurance premiums payable based on the reinsurance contract provisions.	VA			
3. Verify the completeness of reinsurance premiums payable by verifying paid premium obligations to payment documentation.	CO			
4. Identify any instances in which ceded reinsurance premium liabilities have been offset by amounts due from reinsurers in accordance with **SSAP No. 62, paragraph 41** and **SSAP No. 64, Offsetting and Netting of Assets and Liabilities**. For those offsets verify the following:	EX VA AC CM PD			

	Exam Obj.	Completion Date	Examiner	Work Paper Ref.
a. Verify that a legal right of offset exists (See **SSAP No. 64, paragraph 2** for the specific criteria);	AC CM			
b. Confirm the amount due from the reinsurer;	VA EX			
c. Recalculate the premium payable; and	VA EX			
d. Verify that the offsetting receivable and payable have been properly netted from the balance sheet. (Note: The examiner needs to clearly document in the workpapers and Financial Statements which receivables and payables have been offset.)	AC PD			
<u>**Funds Held by the Company Under Reinsurance Treaties**</u>				
1. Obtain detail of funds held under reinsurance treaties. Agree the detail to the company's general ledger and Annual Statement. Perform analytical procedures comparing the amounts to prior year balances. Investigate and document any significant fluctuations.	CO EX VA PD			
2. Ascertain to the completeness and accuracy of the recorded liabilities:	CO EX AC CM			
a. Review the reinsurance agreements and determine that all funds held by the company for reinsurance contracts are properly recorded; and	AC CO CM			
b. Identify new reinsurance contracts for which funds are not held. Review these contracts to verify that the contract does not specify that funds should be transferred and held by the company.	CM CO			

	Exam Obj.	Completion Date	Examiner	Work Paper Ref.
Provision for Reinsurance				
(Note: The provision for reinsurance is a calculation in the Annual Statement. Factors for this calculation include the provision for unauthorized reinsurance and the provision for overdue reinsurance. Please refer to the Annual Statement for more guidance with regards to this balance sheet line item.)				
1. Obtain and recalculate the provision for reinsurance. Verify that the provision has been calculated and recorded in compliance with **SSAP No. 62, paragraphs 52-53**. Agree the amounts used in the calculation to previously examined, reconciled balances.	AC CO VA			
2. Identify any significant amounts included in the calculation not previously examined. Perform procedures to ascertain the validity of the amounts and their utilization in the calculation.	EX AC VA			
3. Obtain a schedule of all companies to which insurance is ceded. Identify all reinsurers who do not meet the authorized reinsurer criteria in accordance with **SSAP No. 62, paragraph 53** and **Appendix A-785 to the NAIC *Accounting Practices and Procedures.*** Verify that all unauthorized reinsurers are properly included in the Annual Statement schedule 'Provision for Unauthorized Reinsurance.'	EX			
4. Verify that the company has properly completed the 'Provision for Unauthorized Reinsurance' schedule in the company's Annual Statement. Identify the unauthorized reinsurers who have funds held or letters of credit to substantiate their assumed reinsurance balance.	AC CO EX VA OB/OW			
a. Agree the funds held per the Annual Statement schedule to the listing reconciled in accordance with the 'Funds Held by the Company Under Reinsurance Treaties.' Identify and investigate any discrepancies.	AC EX			

	Exam Obj.	Completion Date	Examiner	Work Paper Ref.
b. Review the letters of credit recorded in the Annual Statement schedule and verify that they are clean, irrevocable, and issued by a qualified U.S. financial institution, as defined in **Appendix A-785 'Credit for Reinsurance' of the NAIC** ***Accounting Practices and Procedures Manual.***	CO OB/OW			
5. Identify any unauthorized reinsurers who have been granted reserve credits and verify that they meet the specifications and requirements of a domestic ceding insurer in accordance with **Appendix A-785 of the NAIC** ***Accounting Practices and Procedures Manual.***	EX AC CM			
a. Verify that reserve credits for reinsurers not meeting the requirements of a 'domestic ceded reinsurer' meet the exception criteria established in **Appendix A-785 of the NAIC** ***Accounting Practices and Procedures Manual***.	AC CM			
b. Perform procedures to ensure that the reserve credits recorded by the company comply with the guidelines established and do not exceed limits imposed by **Appendix A-785 of the NAIC** ***Accounting Practices and Procedures Manual***.	CM			
6. Review the Annual Statement schedule and identify any other material offsets for unauthorized reinsurance recoverables. Perform procedures to ascertain the validity and existence of these offsets.	EX AC VA			
7. Reconcile the 'Provision for Unauthorized Reinsurance' schedule based on the above testwork. Verify the mathematical accuracy of the schedule. Trace the schedule's recalculated total to the 'Provision for Reinsurance' calculation.	AC			
8. Verify that the company has properly completed the 'Provision for Authorized Overdue Reinsurance' schedule in the company's Annual Statement. Agree the reinsurance recoverables (and other related amounts) from this schedule to amounts previously examined in accordance with the 'Reinsurance Payable on Paid Loss and Loss Adjustment Expenses.' Identify and investigate any discrepancies.	AC CO EX VA			

	Exam Obj.	Completion Date	Examiner	Work Paper Ref.
9. Verify the mathematical accuracy of this schedule. Trace the recalculated total to the 'Provision for Reinsurance' calculation.	AC			
10. Verify that the company has properly completed the 'Provision for Overdue Reinsurance' schedule in the company's Annual Statement. Identify the reinsurers included on this schedule who have funds held or letters of credit to substantiate their assumed reinsurance balance.	AC CO EX VA OB/OW			
a. Agree the funds held per the schedule to the listing reconciled in accordance with the 'Funds Held by the Company Under Reinsurance Treaties.' Identify and investigate any discrepancies.	AC EX			
b. Review the letters of credit recorded in the schedule and verify that they are clean, irrevocable, and issued by a qualified U.S. financial institution, as defined in **Appendix A-785 'Credit for Reinsurance' of the NAIC *Accounting Practices and Procedures Manual.***	AC OB/OW			
11. Identify any reinsurers who have been granted reserve credits and verify that they meet the specifications and requirements of a domestic ceding insurer in accordance with **Appendix A-785 of the NAIC *Accounting Practices and Procedures Manual.***	EX AC CM			
a. Verify that reserve credits for reinsurers not meeting the requirements of a 'domestic ceded reinsurer' meet the exception criteria established in **Appendix A-785 of the NAIC *Accounting Practices and Procedures Manual.***	AC CM			
b. Perform procedures to ensure that the reserve credits recorded by the company comply with the guidelines established and do not exceed limits imposed by **Appendix A-785 of the NAIC *Accounting Practices and Procedures Manual.***	CM			

	Exam Obj.	Completion Date	Examiner	Work Paper Ref.
12. Review the schedule and identify any other material offsets for overdue reinsurance recoverables. Perform procedures to ascertain the validity and existence of these offsets.	EX AC VA			
13. Reconcile the 'Provision for Overdue Reinsurance' schedule based on the above testwork. Verify the mathematical accuracy of the schedule. Trace the schedule's recalculated total to the 'Provision for Reinsurance' calculation.	AC PD			
<u>**Protected Cell Liabilities**</u>				
1. Obtain detail of the protected cell liabilities and agree the detail to the company's protected cell ledger and Annual Statement.	EX			
2. Review the protected cell liability detail and verify that the liabilities are properly classified and included with protected cells in accordance with **SSAP No. 74**.	AC			
3. Verify that all protected cell liabilities are properly recorded at either contractual value or fair value in accordance with **SSAP No. 74, paragraph 14**.	VA			
4. Verify that the protected cell liabilities are properly excluded from the other liabilities of the company and reported separately in accordance with **SSAP No. 74, paragraph 11**. Ensure that all disclosures and reports are properly included as required in **SSAP No. 74, paragraphs 18-19**.	PD			

SECTION I — REINSURANCE AND RISK TRANSFER INSTRUMENTS CYCLE: HEALTH

Listed below are the corresponding Annual Statement line items that are related to the procedures contained in this Reinsurance Specific Risk Analysis:

Annual Statement Blank Line Items

Amounts Recoverable from Reinsurers
Funds Held Under Reinsurance Treaties with Authorized and Unauthorized Reinsurers
Reinsurance in Unauthorized Companies
Health Care Receivables (Risk Sharing Receivables)

Relevant SSAP's Include:

#5, Liabilities, Contingencies, and Impairments of Assets
#25, Accounting for and Disclosures about Transactions with Affiliates and Other Related Parties
#61, Life, Deposit-Type and Accident and Health Reinsurance
#63, Underwriting Pools and Associations Including Intercompany Pools
#64, Offsetting and Netting Of Assets and Liabilities
#84, Certain Health Care Receivables and Receivables Under Government Insurers Plans

SPECIFIC RISK ANALYSIS WORKPAPERS

Risk Analysis Prepared By/Date ______________________________

Planning Exam Analysis Prepared By/Date ______________________________

Reviewed By/Date ______________________________

Descriptive Note on Risk Transfer: One of the principles of managed care is to contract for services at a fixed price. Some managed care entities transfer a significant portion of their risks to Organized Delivery Systems such as Independent Practice Associations (IPAs), Integrated Delivery Systems (IDSs) and Provider HMOs. Because this risk transfer method functions similar to reinsurance, the normal reinsurance cycle was expanded to include the review of Organized Delivery Systems. Abbreviated examination procedures related to risk transfer receivables can be found in the Health Care Receivables section of the Premium Cycle-Health SRA.

EXAMINATION OBJECTIVES:

1. Reinsurance contract that effectively transfers risk exists between parties and contains provisions mandated through regulation. (Existence and Compliance)

2. Amounts of reinsurance ceded are valued accurately and reflected in the financial statements. (Valuation, Compliance, Accuracy, Cutoff and Presentation and Disclosure)

3. Reinsurance assumed transactions are properly authorized, valued and recorded. (Valuation, Compliance, Accuracy, and Cutoff)

4. The insurance company owns, or has appropriate rights to the recorded reinsurance ceded or assumed assets and incurs the reported reinsurance ceded or assumed liabilities. (Ownership and Obligation)

5. Contracts with Organized Delivery Systems (risk bearing entities) such as Independent Practice Associations (IPAs), Integrated Delivery Systems (IDSs), and Provider HMOs are properly authorized and recorded. (Compliance and Accuracy)

INHERENT RISKS

INTERNAL AND EXTERNAL ENVIRONMENTAL CONDITIONS/FACTORS

RESULTS OF DETAIL ANALYTICAL REVIEW PROCEDURES

CONTROL RISK — REINSURANCE AND RISK TRANSFER INSTRUMENTS CYCLE: HEALTH

This questionnaire is designed to assist the examiner in assessing control risk for reinsurance health cycles. Part 1, Section III and Part 3 of this *Handbook* provides guidance in consideration of an insurer's internal control structure for use when designing substantive examination procedures.

This questionnaire includes examples of internal control procedures and policies that are commonly utilized by insurers to achieve internal control objectives. For each control procedure listed below, indicate by placing a check mark in the yes or no box whether or not the insurer employs such a procedure, or other similar practice (include a description of the similar procedure). To the extent the control procedure is not applicable, indicate N/A. If other relevant control procedures are in place, list them in the space that follows. Control procedures that are tested by the examiner should be documented by including the workpaper reference in the comment section and the examiner's initials in the reliance column.

For each individual control procedure there is a control objective listed that satisfies the procedure.

If the examiner initially assesses control risk as low or medium for a particular account balance, then those controls must be tested. The controls should be tested to determine whether the procedure is operating as expected, applied throughout the entire period of reliance, performed on a timely basis, encompassing all transactions, and identifying errors. Some examples of testing procedures are inquiry, observation, re-performance, and examination of documents. The level of reliance, if any, should be indicated in the applicable column along with any comments the examiner may have regarding the procedure.

Based upon the testing results, the examiner should determine whether the preliminary control risk assessment is confirmed or should be revised.

CONTROL OBJECTIVES

Authorization (AU) – All transactions recorded were reviewed and approved by designated personnel.

Completeness (CO) – All transactions that occurred were initially entered into the accounting records, accepted for processing, and generated data files and reports reflect that all transactions have occurred.

Accuracy (AC) – Transactions are initially recorded correctly, timely and accurately.

Asset Protection (AP) – Adequate safeguards over access to and use of assets and records, including the appropriate segregation of duties among company personnel.

	Control Obj.	Y	N	Work Paper Ref.	Reliance
General Control Procedures					
The examiner should determine the amount of documentation necessary for each control procedure. If the examiner intends to place substantial reliance on the established controls, the examiner should explain the control procedures in a workpaper and document the individual responsible for supervising the control activity as well as the frequency of the control activity.					
1. Are reinsurance contracts reviewed for compliance with state regulations?	AU				
2. Are reinsurance contract terms and amendments reviewed for compliance with company guidelines prior to execution?	AU AC				
3. Are reinsurance contract terms and expected results properly documented prior to execution?	AU AP				
4. Is the financial stability of Organized Delivery Systems reviewed prior to contract execution and monitored on a continuing basis?	AU				
5. Do procedures exist to ensure that reinsurance accounting transactions (expense allowances, experience refunds, contingency reserves, mean reserve adjustments, recaptures, etc.) are reviewed, compared to contract terms and expected results, and approved in accordance with **SSAP No. 61, paragraphs 21-55**?	AU AC				
6. Are *ceding* companies and intermediaries approved with regards to business reputation, financial stability and experience prior to contract execution and monitored on a continuous basis?	AU				
7. Are *assuming* companies and intermediaries approved with regards to business reputation, financial stability and experience prior to contract execution and monitored on a continuous basis?	AU				
8. Are amounts due from ceding and assuming companies, Organized Delivery Systems (risk bearing entities) and intermediaries reviewed for collectibility in accordance with **SSAP No. 61, paragraph 41** and **SSAP No. 5**?	CO				

	Control Obj.	Y	N	Work Paper Ref.	Reliance
9. Are reviews performed to ascertain that timely reports and accounting data are received from ceding companies or intermediaries and used to record transactions?	AC				
10. Are activity analyses for cumulative reinsurance contracts prepared and reviewed to assist in evaluation of profitability, risk exposure, contract variance and expected results?	AC CO				
11. Are controls and accounting records for ceding entities independently tested or reviewed to substantiate accounting data provided or to monitor compliance with contract provisions?	AC AP				
12. Is an independent review conducted of a ceding company's underwriting practices, claims processing, loss reserving and actuarial policies and procedures?	AC AP				
13. Are recorded amounts of ceded reinsurance reconciled to detailed policy and reinsurance records?	AC CO				
14. Is an evaluation of the need for adequacy letters of credit or collateral conducted prior to contract execution and monitored on a continuous basis?	AP				
15. Are reinsurance limitations as well as mortality and morbidity rates considered during the underwriting process?	AU				
16. Is the assuming company authorized to transact reinsurance within the ceding company's state of domicile? If not, are letters of credit or other means of security provided?	AU				
17. Are reinsurance transactions, claims processing, premium collection, key information systems functions, and general accounting activities appropriately segregated? Are independent reviews conducted of the work performed? Are the reinsurance receivables/payables reviewed by someone independent of the transactional function?	AP				

	Control Obj.	Y	N	Work Paper Ref.	Reliance
18. Do data files and production programs have adequate safeguards against unauthorized access? Are there proper safeguards over access to any collateral held by the ceding entity from the assuming entity, including funds held under coinsurance?	AP				
19. Are contracts with Organized Delivery Systems (risk bearing entities) reviewed for compliance with the entity's and regulatory guidelines and approved prior to execution as well as on an annual basis?	AU				
Health Care Receivables					
The examiner should determine the amount of documentation necessary for each control procedure. If the examiner intends to place substantial reliance on the established controls, the examiner should explain the control procedures in a workpaper and document the individual responsible for supervising the control activity as well as the frequency of the control activity.					
1. Are risk-sharing contracts reviewed for compliance with **SSAP No. 84** prior to execution?	AU AC				
2. Does the reporting entity perform evaluations of the receivable and payables in relation to the actual claims experience by contract? Who performs these reviews?	AC CO				
3. Does the reporting entity ensure that adequate experience exists for each contract when determining its estimates?	AC CO				
4. Are risk-sharing receivables determined and billed in accordance with **SSAP No. 84, paragraphs 20a and 20b**?	AC CO				

OTHER KEY CONTROLS EXISTING FOR THIS EXAMINATION OBJECTIVE:

SUMMARY EVALUATION OF CONTROL RISK:

EVALUATION OF INDEPENDENT CPA'S WORK FOR THIS EXAMINATION (CPA REVIEW CHECKLIST):

OVERALL RISK ASSESSMENT

Balance Sheet Evaluation of the Likelihood of a Material Adjustment to Surplus:

The evaluation of the likelihood of a material adjustment to surplus should be based on the following criteria:

- Inherent Risk
- Internal & External Environmental Factors
- Control Risk
- Materiality Consideration

The examiner should rate each item as to the likelihood of a material misstatement. All items are assumed as 'High' prior to any examiner evaluation. A 'High' assessment requires the examiner to perform substantive examination procedures over that account area. A lower assessment allows the examiner to perform analytical or fewer substantive procedures to satisfy the examination requirements. If an assessment other than 'High' is selected for any of the accounts, the examiner needs to document the basis for the assessment. If the assessment is based on control testwork, the documentation should include results of control procedures and related workpaper references.

1) "Amounts Recoverable from Reinsurers"

___________ High ___________ Medium ___________Low

Basis for Assessment:

____

____

____

2) "Funds Held Under Reinsurance Treaties with Authorized and Unauthorized Reinsurers"

___________ High ___________ Medium ___________ Low

Basis for Assessment:

____

____

____

3) "Reinsurance in Unauthorized Companies"

___________ High ___________ Medium __________ Low

Basis for Assessment:

____

____

____

4) "Health Care Receivables (Risk Sharing Receivables)"

___________ High ___________ Medium __________ Low

Basis for Assessment:

____

____

____

PRELIMINARY EXAMINATION APPROACH — REINSURANCE AND RISK TRANSFER INSTRUMENTS CYCLE: HEALTH

Listed below are the corresponding Annual Statement line items that are related to the procedures contained in this Reinsurance Specific Risk Analysis:

Amounts Recoverable from Reinsurers
Funds Held Under Reinsurance Treaties with Authorized and Unauthorized Reinsurers
Reinsurance in Unauthorized Companies
Health Care Receivables (Risk Sharing Receivables)

The actual examination procedures selected to be performed is a matter of considerable judgment by the examiner. The following "Examination Program" includes examples of procedures commonly used.

To the extent that the examiner judgmentally determines whether it is appropriate to use the following procedures, that selection can be documented by checking the space next to such procedure, with modifications noted in the margin. The examiner may determine that alternative or additional procedures are required. If so, those procedures can be added on a supplemental sheet. The examiner performing the procedure should indicate satisfactory completion by initialing and dating in the space provided, and referencing the workpapers where the procedures and findings are documented.

The examiner may choose to apply the examination procedures to less than 100% of the items comprising an account balance. Guidance for audit sampling and control and substantive procedures can be found in Part 3 of the NAIC *Financial Condition Examiners Handbook.*

After each examination procedure, the examination objective that the procedure satisfies is indicated. The examination objectives are accuracy, completeness, compliance, cutoff, existence, obligation and ownership, valuation and presentation and disclosure.

EXAMINATION OBJECTIVES

Accuracy (AC) – Recorded transactions and account balances are mathematically accurate, are based on correct amounts and have been classified into the correct account.

Completeness (CO) – All transactions and account balances that should be recorded in the annual financial statement were recorded.

Compliance (CM) – Business transactions and affairs have been conducted in accordance with state insurance codes, other state laws or department directives.

Cutoff (CT) – All transactions are recorded in the correct accounting period.

Existence (EX) – Recorded transactions occurred and are not fictitious and recorded assets and liabilities existed as of the balance sheet date.

Obligation (OB) and Ownership (OW) – Recorded liabilities are obligations of the company and recorded assets are the rights of the company at the balance sheet date.

Valuation (VA) – Assets and liabilities are valued in accordance with state statute and NAIC accounting guidance.

Presentation and Disclosure (PD) – The elements of the Annual Statement are properly classified and all disclosures are accurately included in the Annual Statement.

	Exam Obj.	Completion Date	Examiner	Work Paper Ref.
EXAMINATION PROCEDURES				
General Procedures				
Assumed and Ceded Reinsurance Transactions				
1. Through discussions with management and review of the company's transactions obtain an understanding of the company's assumed and ceded reinsurance policies. Document this understanding in a narrative and include in the workpapers. This narrative should include:	CM OB/OW VA			
a. A general description of the reinsurance program;	CM OB/OW			
b. The entity's maximum retained liability;	VA			
c. The maximum reinsurance coverage provided by the ceding program; and	VA			
d. Policy and procedure of the ceding program when the maximum coverage allowed is less than the largest risk written.	VA			
2. On a selective basis examine the reinsurance underwriting files relating to anticipated reinsurance contracts loss results. This file should include documentation of:	VA			
a. Historical loss ratios and combined ratios of ceding companies;	VA			
b. Anticipated loss ratios under contract;	VA			
c. Indications of the content and frequency of ceding company reports;	VA			
d. Prior business experience with ceding company;	VA			
e. The assuming company's past experience with similar risks; and	VA			

	Exam Obj.	Completion Date	Examiner	Work Paper Ref.
f. Pricing and ceding commission information.	VA			
3. Obtain copies of all significant reinsurance treaties and Organized Delivery Systems (risk bearing entities) in-force as of the date of examination. Prepare outlines of each contract showing the following:	EX AC CO			
(Additional information may be necessary based on the reinsurance practices of the individual company.)				
a. Name of reinsurer/Organized Delivery Systems;	CO AC			
b. Name of reinsured;	CO AC			
c. Type of contract: Automatic or Facultative; Proportional (yearly renewable term, coinsurance, or modified coinsurance) or Nonproportional (catastrophe or stop-loss) **SSAP No. 61, paragraphs 11-16**;	CO AC			
d. Effective date and contract execution date;	CO EX AC			
e. Reporting responsibility;	CO AC			
f. Payment terms;	CO AC			
g. Payment of premium taxes;	CO AC			
h. Termination;	CO AC			
i. Insolvency clause;	CO AC			
j. Payment of premium taxes;	CO AC			

	Exam Obj.	Completion Date	Examiner	Work Paper Ref.
k. Policies/lines of business reinsured;	CO AC			
l. Company retention;	CO AC			
m. Reinsurer's limits;	CO AC			
n. Continuation of benefits clause;	CO AC			
o. Any collateral or letters of credit pursuant to the terms of the contract;	CO AC			
p. Experience rating refunds; and	CO AC			
q. Contract exclusions/exceptions/carve outs. (Note: These exclusions/ exceptions/ carve outs can best be defined as procedures or other items that are specifically excluded from the reinsurance contract. In effect, the carve out causes the reinsurer to reach or exceed a higher limit.)	CO AC			
4. Review each contract selected in step #3 to detect any unusual features that may significantly affect the company's financial condition, or that are in violation of laws, regulations, or good practice. Identify any of the following transactions:	CM AC EX CT OB/OW VA			
a. Cut-through endorsements **(SSAP No. 61, paragraph 3)**;	EX AC			
b. Reinsurance among affiliated or associated companies (pooling agreements; described in detail by **SSAP No. 63**);	CM AC			
c. Fronting arrangements;	CM AC			

	Exam Obj.	Completion Date	Examiner	Work Paper Ref.
d. Guaranteed profit contracts;	CM AC			
e. Excessive risk assumed under treaty;	CM			
f. Significant or unexpected changes in the entity's reinsurance programs [retention levels; form of reinsurance (e.g., excess of loss, pro rata, prospective, retrospective); type of reinsurance (e.g., treaty or facultative)];	CM			
g. Large portfolio reinsurance during the last three months of any calendar year of the period;	EX CT			
h. Unauthorized reinsurance and funds held;	OB/OW CM			
i. Excessively high reinsurance commissions;	VA CM			
j. Liability under expired contracts; and	VA CM			
k. Retroactive adjustment of premiums.	CT CM			
5. Review a sample of receivables and settlements of the major Organized Delivery Systems to insure proper execution and settlement of the terms of the agreements.	AC VA			
6. Review overall collectibility of receivables from Organized Delivery Systems in accordance with **SSAP No. 5** and **SSAP No. 25** and any other applicable SSAPs. Uncollectible amounts should be written off through a charge to the statement of operations.	AC VA			
7. Verify that the entity reports all administrative and medical costs as "uncovered" unless guaranteed by a financially qualified sponsoring organization or services are rendered by a doctor or provider, under contract with the entity whose contract contains an acceptable "hold harmless" clause. (Uncovered is defined in the Annual Statement Instructions.)	AC			

	Exam Obj.	Completion Date	Examiner	Work Paper Ref.
8. Verify that the entity's method of calculating "uncovered" medical expenses and liabilities as defined in the Annual Statement Instructions involves taking an accurate inventory using its own claims history files and that the HMO accurately identifies the paid claims as "covered" or "uncovered." (This section should be coordinated with the underlying data testing.) The classification of "covered" or "uncovered" claims should also comply with any applicable regulatory guidelines.	AC			
Assumed Reinsurance				
9. For assumed reinsurance agreements, review and evaluate the company's procedures to assess the internal control environment of the ceding company. This could include the following:	AC EX CM OB/OW PD			
a. Read the reinsurance contract, related correspondence, and underwriting file to obtain an understanding of the contract, its business purpose and its expected impact on operations;	EX AC			
b. Examine documentation of required management review and approval of the contract; and	CM			
c. Determine compliance with underwriting guidelines.	CM			
10. Obtain financial information and determine financial strength of all significant reinsurance assumed:	AC CM VA			
a. Obtain and analyze recent financial information, or other available sources of information, of the ceding company, such as financial reports filed with the SEC or with insurance industry reporting and rating services such as IRIS results filed with the regulatory authorities.	AC CM VA			

	Exam Obj.	Completion Date	Examiner	Work Paper Ref.
11. Verify that the overall accounting treatment of reinsurance contracts complies with accounting guidelines described in accordance with **SSAP No. 61, paragraphs 21, 23, 39 & 40**.	AC VA			
12. Verify that the company has established policy reserves for assumed reinsurance in accordance with **SSAP No. 61, paragraph 38**.	EX VA			
13. Obtain detail of assumed reinsurance premium income and agree it to the company's general ledger. Perform procedures to verify that the reinsurance premium income has been properly recorded in accordance with **SSAP No. 61, paragraph 25**. For selected assumed reinsurance transactions, trace recorded transactions to reports from ceding companies or intermediaries (bordereau).	VA AC			
14. Examine any assumed reinsurance that has been retroceded. Examine supporting documentation of the company's review and request for retrocession.	EX			
15. Determine that all required disclosures noted in **SSAP No. 61, paragraphs 57-63** are properly disclosed.	PD			
Ceded Reinsurance				
16. Identify and obtain detail of the company's ceded reinsurance accounts. Agree the total of each of the accounts to the company's general ledger. Investigate any discrepancies.	EX AC			
17. Categorize the types of reinsurance contracts and determine if the contracts transfer risk in accordance with **SSAP No. 61, paragraphs 17-20**. If a contract does not transfer risk, verify that it has received deposit accounting treatment in accordance with **SSAP No. 61, paragraph 50**. (Consult the NAIC Life and Health Reinsurance Agreements Model Regulation (NAIC Model Act No. 791) for additional guidance on the transfer of risk.)	PD VA			

	Exam Obj.	Completion Date	Examiner	Work Paper Ref.
18. Verify that contracts with organized delivery systems qualify for risk transfer treatment by containing all of the following characteristics:	AC VA			
a. Payment is based upon a fixed amount per month, either as a percentage of premium or a fixed dollar amount;	AC VA			
b. Payment is fixed for a period no less than twelve months; and	AC VA			
c. The arrangement contains no provision for retroactive adjustment either within or beyond a 12 month period.	AC VA			
19. Verify that the overall accounting treatment of reinsurance contracts complies with accounting guidelines described in **SSAP No. 61, paragraphs 21-22, 39 & 40**.	VA PD			
20. Obtain financial information and determine financial strength of all significant reinsurers (from Annual Statement Schedule S) / Organized Delivery Systems (from Annual Statement Exhibit 8, Part 2 – Intermediaries) to which risk was ceded/transferred.	VA AC CM			
a. Obtain and analyze recent financial information, or other available sources of information, of the assuming company; such as financial reports filed with the SEC or with insurance industry reporting and rating services such as the IRIS results filed with the regulatory authorities. For Organized Delivery Systems (risk bearing entities) request periodic audited financial statements and financial projections as required by the state of domicile.	CM AC VA			
21. Determine that all required disclosures noted in **SSAP No. 61, paragraphs 57-63** are properly included in the financial statements.	PD			

	Exam Obj.	Completion Date	Examiner	Work Paper Ref.
<u>Amounts Recoverable From Reinsurers</u>				
1. Obtain a detailed listing of the reinsurance recoverables aging and agree the total to the company's general ledger and Annual Statement.	EX			
2. Agree the reinsurance recoverables to a valid reinsurance contract noting the following:	EX OB/OW CM			
a. Reinsurance premiums have been paid;	EX			
b. Claim is covered under the reinsurance contract; and	CM			
c. Deductible payments by the ceding company have been met.	OB/OW			
3. Verify that the ceding company has paid the claim by agreeing the reinsurance recoverable to a copy of the claim payment.	AC CO CM			
a. For unpaid reinsurance claims, perform procedures to verify that the claim is valid under the reinsurance contract and not in dispute.	CM			
4. Review the aging detail and identify recoverables aged over 90 days. Discuss with management and perform procedures to ascertain the collectibility of these reinsurance recoverables. All uncollectible recoverables should be written off in accordance with **SSAP No. 61, paragraph 41**.	VA EX			
a. Confirm reinsurance recoverables directly with the assuming company.	EX			
b. Perform subsequent receipt testwork.	EX VA			
5. Verify that all reinsurance recoverables written off or disputed have been properly disclosed in accordance with **SSAP No. 61, paragraph 61**.	PD			

	Exam Obj.	Completion Date	Examiner	Work Paper Ref.
6. With respect to reinsurance effected through an intermediary and Organized Delivery Systems (risk bearing entities), review treaties for credit risk assumption provisions. (Consult the NAIC Reinsurance Intermediary Model Act (NAIC Model Act No. 790) for additional guidance on reinsurance intermediaries.)	EX			
<u>Funds held Under Reinsurance Treaties with Authorized and Unauthorized Reinsurers</u>				
1. Obtain detail of funds held under reinsurance treaties with authorized and unauthorized reinsurers. Agree the detail to the company's general ledger and Annual Statement. Compare the amounts to prior year balances. Investigate and document any significant fluctuations.	CO EX AC			
2. Perform procedures to ascertain to the completeness and accuracy of the recorded liabilities:	CO EX AC CM			
a. Review reinsurance agreements and determine that all funds held by the ceding entity in accordance with the contracts are properly recorded;	AC CO CM			
b. Confirm with reinsurers the funds held by the ceding company; and	EX			
c. Identify new reinsurance contracts for which funds are not held. Review these contracts to verify that the contract does not specify that funds should be transferred and held by the ceding entity.	EX CO			
<u>Reinsurance in Unauthorized Companies</u>				
1. Review reinsurance agreements and identify any unauthorized reinsurers in accordance with the definition found in **SSAP No. 61, paragraph 42** and **Appendix A-785 to the NAIC** ***Accounting Practices and Procedures Manual***.	EX			

		Exam Obj.	Completion Date	Examiner	Work Paper Ref.
2.	Obtain a schedule detailing the company's paid and unpaid losses due from unauthorized reinsurance companies. Agree this schedule to the company's general ledger.	CO EX			
3.	Verify that the company has properly included or excluded the admitted asset or reduction of liability for the paid and unpaid losses due from unauthorized reinsurance companies based on the criteria established by **Appendix A-785 to the NAIC *Accounting Practices and Procedures Manual* paragraph 16**.	AC PD			
4.	Identify any credits taken in balance sheet accounts for reinsurance ceded to unauthorized reinsurers. Verify that an offsetting liability has been established in accordance with **SSAP No. 61, paragraphs 42-43**.	VA PD			
5.	Identify any unauthorized reinsurance funds held by the ceding company or letters of credit that may offset reinsurance recoverables to the extent of the reinsurance recoverable balance, funds held, or to the amount allowable under the letter of credit.	EX VA AC OB/OW			
	a. Verify that the letters of credit are clean, irrevocable, and issued by a qualified U.S financial institution, as defined in **Appendix A-785 to the NAIC *Accounting Practices and Procedures Manual***.	AC OB/OW			
6.	Obtain detail of unearned reinsurance premiums in unauthorized companies. Recalculate these unearned premiums and agree the amount to the company's Annual Statement.	AC CO			
7.	Identify and reconcile any reductions in reserves for reinsurance in unauthorized companies.	EX			
8.	Trace the unauthorized reinsurance detail to the company's Annual Statement.	PD			

	Exam Obj.	Completion Date	Examiner	Work Paper Ref.
Health Care Receivables (Risk Sharing Receivables)				
1. Confirm that all risk-sharing agreements include a clause that will provide for evaluation of the receivables and payables with relation to the actual claims experience at least annually as required by **SSAP No. 84, paragraph 20a**.	CM			
2. Ensure risk receivables and payables are only recorded when reasonably estimated or billed. Estimates of risk sharing receivables can be admitted if based on at least six months of actual claims experience for each risk-sharing contract, pursuant to **SSAP No. 84, paragraph 20a**.	VA CM			
3. Review the reporting entity's method for estimating its risk sharing receivables. Verify that the methodology is reasonable and is applied consistently from period to period, as required by **SSAP No. 84, paragraph 21**.	AC			
4. Test risk sharing receivables and payables to ensure they are billed or refunded in accordance with the contractual provisions in a timely manner. Verify that the determination of the final risk sharing balance began no later than 6 months following the end of the contract period with billing occurring no later than 8 months after the end of the contract period in accordance with **SSAP No. 84, paragraph 20a.**	EX CM VA AC			
5. Verify that risk-sharing receivables that have not been collected within 90 days of the date of billing are nonadmitted, as required by **SSAP No. 84, paragraph 20b**.	CM VA			
6. Verify that an evaluation for collectibility has been made at least quarterly, as required by **SSAP No. 84, paragraph 20d**. Uncollectible amounts should be written off in accordance with **SSAP No. 5**.	VA			

	Exam Obj.	Completion Date	Examiner	Work Paper Ref.
7. Ensure risk sharing receivables and payables are reported gross rather than netted on the balance sheet. Receivable and payable balances from the same provider whose balances meet the setoff conditions in **SSAP No. 64** shall be netted per **SSAP No. 84, paragraph 20c**.	PD			
8. Review the disclosure in the notes to the financial statement to determine that all required information has been disclosed relative to risk sharing contracts as required by **SSAP No. 84, paragraph 25**.	PD			
9. Verify that the method to estimate the receivable during interim periods is reasonable and is applied consistently from period to period.	CM			

SECTION J — INVESTMENT CYCLE

Listed below are the corresponding Annual Statement line items that are related to the procedures contained in this Investment Specific Risk Analysis:

Annual Statement Blank Line Items

Bonds, Stocks, and Short Term Investments
Securities Lending, Repurchase and Reverse Repurchase Agreements
Insurer Investment Pools
Cash on Hand and on Deposit
Derivative Transactions
Policy Loans and Premium Notes
Real Estate, Mortgage Loans, and Collateral Loans
Investment Income Due and Accrued
Separate Accounts
Interest Maintenance Reserve/Asset Valuation Reserve
Receivable/Payable for Securities
Aggregate Write-Ins for Invested Assets

Relevant SSAP's Include:

#2, Cash, Drafts and Short Term Investments
#7, Asset Valuation Reserve and Interest Maintenance Reserve
#18, Transfers and Servicing of Financial Assets and Extinguishments of Liabilities
#21, Other Admitted Assets
#23, Foreign Currency Transactions and Translations
#26, Bonds, excluding Loan-backed and Structured Securities
#30, Investments in Common Stock
#32, Investments in Preferred Stock
#33, Securitization
#34, Investment Income Due and Accrued
#37, Mortgage Loans
#38, Acquisition, Development, and Construction Arrangements
#39, Reverse Mortgages
#40, Real Estate Investments
#41, Surplus Notes
#43, Loan-backed and Structured Securities
#44, Capitalization of Interest
#45, Repurchase Agreements, Reverse Repurchase Agreements and Dollar Repurchase Agreements
#46, Investments in Subsidiary, Controlled and Affiliated Entities
#48, Investments in Joint Ventures, Partnerships and Limited Liability Companies
#49, Policy Loans
#56, Separate Accounts
#77, Real Estate Sales
86, Accounting for Derivative Instruments and Hedging Activities

SPECIFIC RISK ANALYSIS WORK PAPERS

Risk Analysis Prepared By/Date ______________________________

Planning Exam Analysis Prepared By/Date ______________________________

Reviewed By/Date ______________________________

EXAMINATION OBJECTIVES:

Securities and Invested Assets (Note: this includes bonds, stocks, short term investments, mortgage loans, real estate, collateral loans, cash on hand and on deposit, and other invested assets)

1. Securities and invested assets existed and were the legal property of the insurer as of the examination date. (Existence and Ownership)

2. Securities and invested assets are valued in accordance with the SVO's *Purposes and Procedures Manual*, valuation guidance and state laws and regulations. (Valuation)

3. All securities and invested asset transactions have been accurately accounted for and reported in the insurer's records. (Accuracy and Completeness)

4. All securities and invested asset transactions have been reported in the appropriate accounting period. (Cutoff)

5. Investments and related disclosures were presented in the Annual Statement in accordance with NAIC *Annual Statement Instructions* and *Accounting Practices and Procedures Manual*. (Presentation and Disclosure)

6. Investments and investment practices conform to the statutory provisions of the state's investment code (e.g., board approval of investments and custodial agreements). (Compliance)

Policy Loans and Premium Notes

1. Policy loans and premium notes existed as of the examination date. (Existence)

2. Policy loans and premium notes are valued in accordance with state laws and regulations. (Valuation)

3. All policy loans and premium note transactions have been accurately accounted for and reported in the insurer's records. (Accuracy, Completeness and Cutoff)

Investment Income Due and Accrued

1. Investment income due and accrued has been valued in accordance with NAIC *Accounting Practices and Procedures Manual* and state laws and regulations. (Valuation)

2. All investment income due and accrued has been accurately computed and recorded as of the examination date. (Accuracy and Completeness)

3. Investment income due and accrued has been reported in the appropriate accounting period. (Cutoff)

4. Investment income due and accrued and related disclosures were presented in the Annual Statement in accordance with the NAIC *Annual Statement Instructions* and *Accounting Practices and Procedures Manual*. (Presentation and Disclosure)

Separate Accounts (Life Companies Only)

1. All separate account balances existed and were the legal property of the insurer as of the examination date. (Existence and Ownership)

2. Separate accounts have been valued in accordance with the NAIC *Accounting Practices and Procedures Manual*, the SVO's *Purposes and Procedures Manual* and state laws and regulations. (Valuation)

3. All separate accounts have been correctly recorded as of the examination date. (Completeness and Accuracy)

4. Separate accounts and any related disclosures were presented in the Annual Statement in accordance with the NAIC *Annual Statement Instructions* and the NAIC *Accounting Practices and Procedures Manual.* (Presentation and Disclosure)

Interest Maintenance Reserve/Asset Valuation Reserve (Life Companies Only)

1. Interest maintenance and asset valuation reserves include all applicable values required to calculate the reserve. (Completeness)

2. Interest maintenance and asset valuation reserves are computed in accordance with the NAIC *Annual Statement Instructions.* (Accuracy, Completeness and Valuation)

3. Interest maintenance and asset valuation reserves were presented in the Annual Statement in accordance with the NAIC *Annual Statement Instructions.* (Presentation and Disclosure)

Receivable/Payable for Securities

1. Receivables/Payables for securities were valid and were the legal right/obligation of the insurer as of the examination date. (Existence and Ownership/Obligation)

2. All Receivables/Payables for securities have been accurately accounted for and reported in the insurer records. (Accuracy, Completeness, Cutoff and Valuation)

3. Receivables/Payables for securities were presented in the Annual Statement in accordance with the NAIC *Annual Statement Instructions* and *Accounting Practices and Procedures Manual.* (Presentation and Disclosure)

Aggregate Write-Ins For Invested Assets

1. Aggregate write-ins for invested assets existed and were the legal property of the insurer as of the examination date. (Existence and Ownership)

2. Aggregate write-ins for invested assets are valued in accordance with the NAIC *Accounting Practices and Procedures Manual* and state laws and regulations. (Valuation)

3. All aggregate write-ins for invested assets have been accurately accounted for and reported in the insured's records. (Accuracy, Completeness and Cutoff)

4. Aggregate write-ins for invested assets were presented in the Annual Statement in accordance with the NAIC *Annual Statement Instructions* and *Accounting Practices and Procedures Manual.* (Presentation and Disclosure)

INHERENT RISKS

INTERNAL AND EXTERNAL ENVIRONMENTAL CONDITIONS/FACTORS

RESULTS OF DETAIL ANALYTICAL REVIEW PROCEDURES

CONTROL RISK — INVESTMENT CYCLE*

*Note: Due to the various types of investments included within the Other Invested Assets section, the investment control risk cycle contains additional investments other than what is included under the examination objectives.

This questionnaire is designed to assist the examiner in assessing control risk for investment account balances. Part 1, Section III and Part 3 of this *Handbook* provides guidance in consideration of an insurer's internal control structure for use when designing substantive examination procedures.

This questionnaire includes examples of internal control procedures and policies that are commonly utilized by insurers to achieve internal control objectives. For each control procedure listed below, indicate by placing a check mark in the yes or no box whether or not the insurer employs such a procedure, or other similar practice (include a description of the similar procedure). To the extent the control procedure is not applicable, indicate N/A. If other relevant control procedures are in place, list them in the space that follows. Control procedures that are tested by the examiner should be documented by including the workpaper reference in the comment section and the examiner's initials in the reliance column.

For each individual control procedure there is a control objective listed that satisfies the procedure.

If the examiner initially assesses control risk as low or medium for a particular account balance, then those controls must be tested. The controls should be tested to determine whether the procedure is operating as expected, applied throughout the entire period of reliance, performed on a timely basis, encompassing all transactions and identifying errors. Some examples of testing procedures are inquiry, observation, re-performance and examination of documents. The level of reliance, if any, should be indicated in the applicable column along with any comments the examiner may have regarding the procedure.

Based upon the testing results, the examiner should determine whether the preliminary control risk assessment is confirmed or should be revised.

CONTROL OBJECTIVES

Authorization (AU) – All transactions recorded were reviewed and approved by designated personnel.

Completeness (CO) – All transactions that occurred are initially entered into the accounting records, accepted for processing and generated data files and reports reflect that all transactions have occurred.

Accuracy (AC) – Transactions are initially recorded correctly, timely and accurately.

Asset Protection (AP) – Adequate safeguards over access to and use of assets and records, including the appropriate segregation of duties among company personnel.

	Control Obj.	Y	N	Work Paper Ref.	Reliance
General Control Procedures					
The examiner should determine the amount of documentation necessary for each control procedure. If the examiner intends to place substantial reliance on the established controls, the examiner should explain the control procedure in a workpaper and document the indiviudal responsible for supervising the control activity as well as the frequency of the control activity.					
1. Has the board of directors adopted a written investment plan with specific guidelines as to the quality, maturity and diversification of investments?	AU				
2. Does management review investment valuation methods for compliance with company policies and regulatory requirements?	AU				
3. Does management review investments for compliance with the authorized investment plans, including quality, maturity, dollar limits and regulatory requirements?	AU				
4. Does the board of directors or authorized committee approve all investment transactions?	AU				
5. Are changes made to the investment master file data to ensure that authorized and approved transactions are timely and accurately updated? Are adjustments properly recorded in the subsidiary ledgers and general ledger?	AU CO				
6. Are the custodian's account statements and invested asset records periodically inspected and reconciled to investment ledgers by an individual independent of the custodial function?	CO AC				
7. Does management have a written process in place to assure compliance with the NAIC Securities Valuation Office (SVO) filing requirements set forth in the *Purposes and Procedures Manual of the NAIC SVO*?	AC				

		Control Obj.	Y	N	Work Paper Ref.	Reliance
8.	Does management have a written process in place to actively monitor Nationally Recognized Statistical Rating Organization (NRSRO) ratings to ascertain that securities not filed with the NAIC Securities Valuation Office (SVO) meet the 'filing exempt' requirements as stated in Part Four of the *Purposes and Procedures Manual of the NAIC SVO*? Per the NAIC SVO filing exempt requirements, bonds and preferred stock rated and monitered by at least one NRSRO with a rating equivelant to the NAIC 1 throuh 6 designation categories are considered 'filing exempt.' In the event that security has multiple ratings, the second-highest rating becomes the basis for the designation translation. Public Common Stock is considered filing exempt if it is not restricted to transferability and is listed on the New York Stock Exchange, American Stock Exchange or traded on the NASDAQ National Market System (Filing exempt securities will be given an NAIC SVO rating equivelant to the NRSRO ratings received. A comparison of NRSRO ratings and their SVO equivalent designations are included in the Appendix in the Purposes and Procedures Manual of the NAIC SVO.)	CO AC				
9.	Does the insurer have mechanisms in place to subsequently monitor 'filing exempt' securities to properly and timely react if NAIC SVO filing becomes required?	AC				
10.	Does management periodically review the security files to determine proper filing with the NAIC SVO for those securities that have lost their filing exemption?	AU AC				
11.	Does management perform periodic investment reviews to identify and record other than temporary impairments?	AC				
12.	Is access to securities, investment accounts, and records limited to authorized personnel, including custodians?	AP				

	Control Obj.	Y	N	Work Paper Ref.	Reliance
13. Is there separation of duties between employees accounting for investments and those employees authorizing investments decisions?	AP				
14. Are foreign currency translation calculations periodically reviewed by management?	AC				
15. Does management periodically evaluate the financial condition and capabilities of bank custodians, broker/dealers, servicing agents, property managers, and others with whom the insurer has established business relationships?	AP				
Note: *The following control policies and procedures, while they are generally considered specific to the investment(s) listed, may extend to other asset types.*					
Bonds, Stocks and Short Term Investments					
1. Does management review the unrealized and realized gains or losses of investment calculations?	AU				
2. Are assumptions for future cash flow projections on mortgage-backed securities reviewed and monitored by investment management?	AU				
3. Are daily security transaction reports reviewed by someone independent of the processing of the transactions?	AU				
4. Are proper period reviews completed for those securities and other investment transactions settling after year-end review?	CO				
5. Do procedures exist to ensure that investment transactions have been accurately processed and recorded in the investment master file and not duplicated elsewhere?	CO AC				
6. Are buy and sell orders to brokers periodically compared to broker advice?	AC				
7. Are quoted market prices on investment transaction dates compared periodically to purchase/sale prices by persons independent of those executing and approving transactions?	AC				

	Control Obj.	Y	N	Work Paper Ref.	Reliance
8. Do procedures exist to prevent unauthorized individuals from trading securities?	AP				
Securities Lending, Repurchase and Reverse Repurchase Agreements					
Securities Lending					
1. Has the board of directors or appointed committee developed a written plan for securities lending transactions?	AU				
2. Are the employees involved in the credit analysis of security borrowers different from those participating in the management and documentation of the securities lending program activities?	AP				
3. Are written agreements maintained with those parties borrowing securities from the insurer that specify the duties and responsibilities of each party which include, but are not limited to, acceptable types of collateral, standards for collateral custody and control, collateral valuation and initial margin, accrued interest, market value, margin calls, methods for transmitting coupon or dividend payments received if the security is on loan on the payment date, conditions which will trigger the termination of the loan (including events of default) and acceptable methods of delivery for loaned securities and collateral?	AP				
4. Does a record-keeping system exist to produce daily reports showing: the lending status of securities, outstanding loans by borrower and returns of loaned securities?	AU AP				
5. Do procedures exist to ensure that the delivery of loaned securities is not made unless adequate collateral has been received or will be received simultaneously with the securities delivery?	AP				
6. Are safekeeping facilities maintained for collateral received on securities loaned?	AP				

	Control Obj.	Y	N	Work Paper Ref.	Reliance
7. If the company administers its securities lending program through an authorized financial institution, has the company:	AP				
a. Obtained a written agreement with the financial institution in which the financial institution assumes liability for any and all losses, claims and other expenses arising out of negligence or willful misconduct with respect to the duties it performs in relation to the securities lending program?	AP				
b. Contractually obligated its custodian to provide records and reports which support the accounting and Annual Statement requirements?	AU AC				
8. Do procedures exist to track the daily market value of securities loaned and collateral held to ensure that any calls for additional collateral are made on a timely basis, minimum collateral level are maintained and approved credit limits are not exceeded?	AP AU				
9. Are securities lending activities periodically audited internally to assess the accuracy of the accounting records, the timeliness of reports and the company's overall compliance with established policies and procedures?	AC				
10. Does the company's written securities lending plan describe how cash received will be invested?	AP				
11. Do procedures exist to establish limit approvals and monitor credit risk of parties borrowing securities from the insurer?	AP				
Repurchase and Reverse Repurchase Agreements					
12. Has the board of directors or appointed committee developed a written plan for repurchase transactions?	AU				

	Control Obj.	Y	N	Work Paper Ref.	Reliance
13. Are employees involved in the credit analysis of a party entering into a repurchase agreement with the insurer different from those participating in the management and recording of the agreements and activities?	AP				
14. Are written agreements maintained with parties who enter into repurchase agreements with the insurer that specify the duties and responsibilities of each party which include, but are not limited to, acceptable types of collateral, standards for collateral custody and control, collateral valuation and initial margin, accrued interest, market tracking, margin calls, methods for transmitting/receiving coupon or dividend payments, conditions which will trigger the termination of the repurchase agreement (including events of default) and acceptable methods of delivery for securities and collateral?	AP				
15. Does a record-keeping system exists to produce daily reports showing the status of securities held for collateral?	AU AP				
16. Do procedures exist to ensure that the delivery of securities is not made unless adequate collateral has been received or will be received simultaneously with the security delivery?	AP				
17. Are facilities maintained for the safekeeping of collateral held in conjunction with a repurchase agreement?	AP				
18. If the company administers its securities repurchase agreement program through an authorized financial institution, has the company:	AP				
a. Obtained a written agreement with the financial institution in which the financial institution assumes liability for any and all losses, claims, and other expenses arising out of negligence or willful misconduct with respect to the duties it performs in relation to the repurchase agreement program?	AP				

	Control Obj.	Y	N	Work Paper Ref.	Reliance
b. Contractually obligated its custodian to provide records and reports, which support the accounting and Annual Statement requirements?	AU AC				
19. Do procedures exist to track the daily market value of securities held as collateral to ensure that any calls for additional collateral are made on a timely basis, minimum collateral levels are maintained and approved credit limits are not exceeded?	CO AC				
20. Are repurchase agreement activities periodically audited internally to assess the accuracy of the accounting records, the timeliness of reports and the company's overall compliance with established policies and procedures?	AC				
21. Do procedures exist to establish limit approvals and monitor credit risk of parties who enter into repurchase agreement with the insurance company?	AP				
<u>Insurer Investment Pools</u>					
1. Are there written guidelines for the investment pool that specify the duties and responsibilities of each party involved?	AU				
2. Does the investment pool have a designated manager?	AU				
3. Are detailed accounting records maintained for all cash receipts and disbursements?	CO AC				
4. Do the investment pool accounting records reflect the types of securities and maturities underlying the investment pool?	CO				
5. Is each participant's proportionate share in the investment pool readily identified in the accounting records?	AP				

	Control Obj.	Y	N	Work Paper Ref.	Reliance
Cash on Hand and on Deposit					
1. Is the bank reconciliation function separate from the issuance of checks and cash receipts function?	AC				
2. Is there a responsible official that regularly reviews the company's cash position and approves investment of excess cash?	AU AP				
3. Do funds moved electronically require the use of code words, number codes, callbacks or other security procedures?	AP				
4. Do procedures exist to account and safeguard cash and assets that are not deposited when received?	AP				
Derivative Transactions					
1. Has management established written guidelines for entering into derivative transactions?	AU				
2. Do the guidelines address investment objectives and risk constraints, permissible transactions and the relationship of those transactions to its operations?	AU				
3. Do procedures exist to ensure that purchase transactions do not exceed limitations promulgated by the insurer's state of domicile?	AU				
4. Does the company have a monitoring system for determining whether a derivative instrument used for hedging has been effective?	AU				
5. Do procedures exist to ensure that derivative transactions have been accurately documented?	AC CO				
6. Do procedures exist to prevent unauthorized personnel from engaging in derivative transactions?	AP AU				
7. Do procedures exist to measure credit risk?	AP				

	Control Obj.	Y	N	Work Paper Ref.	Reliance
8. Does the board of directors or the investment committee determine whether there are adequate professional personnel and adequate systems to engage in derivative transactions?	AP				
Policy Loans and Premium Notes					
1. Are policy loans/premium notes reconciled to the policy loan inventory balance in the general ledger periodically?	CO				
2. Are policy loans periodically compared to cash surrender values?	AC				
3. Are available policy loan values recomputed and compared to automatic premium loan amounts?	AC				
4. Are policy loan applications compared to policy applications and terms prior to issuing new loans?	AP				
Real Estate, Mortgage Loans and Collateral Loans					
1. Has the company instituted underwriting policies and guidelines (e.g., title searches, appraisals) for accepting liens against property? If yes, have the policies and guidelines been periodically evaluated?	AU				
2. Are new mortgage loans reviewed and monitored for compliance with authorized investment objectives, dollar limits and regulatory requirements?	AU				
3. Are the perfection of deed, status of existing loans, hazard insurance and property tax payments monitored?	AU				
4. Is loan information entered into the processing system monitored by someone independent of the processing function to ensure accuracy and completeness?	CO AC				
5. Are reclassifications of foreclosed mortgage loans reviewed and approved by management?	AU				

	Control Obj.	Y	N	Work Paper Ref.	Reliance
6. Are internal and external appraisals periodically reviewed by investment personnel as to methodology, review of assumptions, and capitalization rates, in accordance with **SSAP No. 40, paragraph 11**?	AU				
7. Are current appraisals obtained for loans in foreclosure, real estate held for sale and impaired real estate properties (as described in **SSAP No. 40, paragraph 9**)?	AC				
<u>Investment Income Due and Accrued</u>					
1. Is expected investment income compared with actual amounts received and reviewed by management?	AC				
2. Are investment yield reports regularly prepared and fluctuations investigated by appropriate officials?	AU				
3. Is the investment income received/receivable detail regularly reconciled to the general ledger control accounts by employees having no access to investments or cash receipts?	CO AP				
4. Are investment income accruals, amortization of premiums, accretion of discounts and interest purchased and sold recomputed for clerical accuracy?	AC				
<u>Separate Accounts</u>					
1. Does management approve the fund transfers between the separate account and general account functions?	AU				
2. Are separate account transactions settled after year-end reviewed for proper period entry?	CO				
3. Do procedures exist to ensure that separate account transactions have been accurately processed and reconciled to the general ledger?	AC CO				

	Control Obj.	Y	N	Work Paper Ref.	Reliance
Interest Maintenance Reserve/Asset Valuation Reserve					
1. Are the interest maintenance reserve and asset valuation reserve calculations reviewed by financial management?	AU				
2. Do procedures exist to ensure that the realized capital gains/losses used to compute the interest maintenance reserve are accurate and complete?	AC CO				
Receivable/Payable for Securities					
1. Are the recorded receivables/payables reviewed by someone independent of the transactional function?	AU				
2. Do procedures exist to ensure that receivables/payables have been completely processed and recorded?	CO				
3. Are sell/buy orders to brokers compared to recorded receivable/payable transactions?	AC				

OTHER KEY CONTROLS EXISTING FOR THIS CONTROL OBJECTIVE:

SUMMARY EVALUATION OF CONTROL RISK:

EVALUATION OF INDEPENDENT CPA'S WORK FOR THIS EXAMINATION (CPA REVIEW CHECKLIST):

OVERALL RISK ASSESSMENT

Balance Sheet Evaluation of the Likelihood of a Material Adjustment to Surplus:

The evaluation of the likelihood of a material adjustment to surplus should be based on the following criteria:

Inherent Risk

Internal & External Environmental Factors

Control Risk

Materiality Consideration

The examiner should rate each item as to the likelihood of a material misstatement. All items are assumed as "High" prior to any examiner evaluation. A "High" assessment requires the examiner to perform substantive examination procedures over that account area. A lower assessment allows the examiner to perform analytical or fewer substantive procedures to satisfy the examination requirements. If an assessment other than "High" is selected for any of the accounts, the examiner needs to document the basis for the assessment. If the assessment is based on control testwork, the documentation should include results of control procedures and related workpaper references.

1) "Bonds, Stocks, and Short Term Investments"

___________ High ___________ Medium ___________ Low

Basis for Assessment:

____

____

____

2) "Securities Lending, Repurchase and Reverse Repurchase Agreements"

___________ High ___________ Medium ___________ Low

Basis for Assessment:

____

____

____

3) "Insurer Investment Pools"

___________ High ___________ Medium __________ Low

Basis for Assessment:

____

____

____

4) "Cash on Hand and on Deposit"

___________ High ___________ Medium _________ Low

Basis for Assessment:

____

____

____

5) "Derivative Transactions"

___________ High ___________ Medium __________ Low

Basis for Assessment:

____

____

____

6) "Policy Loans and Premium Notes"

___________ High ___________ Medium __________ Low

Basis for Assessment:

____

____

____

7) "Real Estate, Mortgage Loans, and Collateral Loans"

___________ High ___________ Medium ___________ Low

Basis for Assessment:

8) "Investment Income Due and Accrued"

___________ High ___________ Medium ___________ Low

Basis for Assessment:

9) "Separate Accounts"

___________ High ___________ Medium ___________ Low

Basis for Assessment:

10) "Interest Maintenance Reserve/Asset Valuation Reserve"

___________ High ___________ Medium ___________ Low

Basis for Assessment:

11) "Receivable/Payable for Securities"

___________ High ___________ Medium __________ Low

Basis for Assessment:

____

____

____

12) "Aggregate Write-Ins for Invested Assets"

___________ High ___________ Medium __________ Low

Basis for Assessment:

____

____

____

PRELIMINARY EXAMINATION APPROACH — INVESTMENT CYCLE

Listed below are the corresponding Annual Statement line items that are related to the procedures contained in this Investment Specific Risk Analysis:

Bonds, Stocks, and Short Term Investments
Securities Lending, Repurchase and Reverse Repurchase Agreements
Insurer Investment Pools
Cash on Hand and on Deposit
Derivative Transactions
Policy Loans and Premium Notes
Real Estate, Mortgage Loans, and Collateral Loans
Investment Income Due and Accrued
Separate Accounts
Interest Maintenance Reserve/Asset Valuation Reserve
Receivable/Payable for Securities
Aggregate Write-Ins for Invested Assets

The actual examination procedures selected to be performed is a matter of considerable judgment by the examiner. The following "Examination Program" includes examples of procedures commonly used.

To the extent that the examiner judgmentally determines whether it is appropriate to use the following procedures, that selection can be documented by checking the space next to such procedure, with modifications noted in the margin. The examiner may determine that alternative or additional procedures are required. If so, those procedures can be added on a supplemental sheet. The examiner performing the procedure should indicate satisfactory completion by initialing and dating in the space provided, and referencing the work papers where the procedures and findings are documented.

The examiner may choose to apply the examination procedures to less than 100% of the items comprising an account balance. Guidance for audit sampling and control and substantive procedures can be found in Part 3 of the NAIC *Financial Condition Examiners Handbook.*

After each examination procedure, the examination objective that the procedure satisfies is indicated. The examination objectives are accuracy, completeness, compliance, cutoff, existence, obligation and ownership, valuation and presentation and disclosure.

EXAMINATION OBJECTIVES

Accuracy (AC) – Recorded transactions and account balances are mathematically accurate, are based on correct amounts and have been classified into the correct account.

Completeness (CO) – All transactions and account balances that should be recorded in the annual financial statement were recorded.

Compliance (CM) – Business transactions and affairs have been conducted in accordance with state insurance codes, other state laws or department directives.

Cutoff (CT) – All transactions are recorded in the correct accounting period.

Existence (EX) – Recorded transactions occurred and are not fictitious and recorded assets and liabilities existed as of the balance sheet date.

Obligation (OB) and Ownership (OW) – Recorded liabilities are obligations of the company and recorded assets are the rights of the company at the balance sheet date.

Valuation (VA) – Assets and liabilities are valued in accordance with state statute and NAIC accounting guidance.

Presentation and Disclosure (PD) – The elements of the Annual Statement are properly classified and all disclosures are accurately included in the Annual Statement.

EXAMINATION PROCEDURES

Bonds, Stocks, and Short Term Investments

Procedure	Exam Obj.	Completion Date	Examiner	Work Paper Ref.
1. Review custodial and safekeeping agreements for proper controls and safeguards.	CM			
2. Determine that any custodial or safekeeping agreement with a bank, trust company, or securities depository has been submitted to, and approved by, the insurance department and meets the criteria set forth in Part 1, Section IV, of this *Handbook.*	CM			
3. If available, review the independent audit or other reports on the custodian's system of internal control and assess the custodian's financial stability (e.g., SAS 70 report).	AC			
4. Review investment committee minutes and determine whether investment transactions have been properly authorized on a timely basis and whether the use of investment managers and advisors have been properly authorized.	CM			
5. Review arrangements with brokers and dealers, investment managers and advisors to assess their qualifications and independence.	AC			
6. Obtain an understanding of relevant accounting practices and procedures for unusual securities and security transactions (e.g., asset-backed securities and agreements, stripped securities and securities lending).	AC			
7. Consider the reasonableness of commissions and other fees paid to security brokers and dealers, investment managers and advisors.	AC			
8. Make inquiries to ascertain any conflicts of interest or improprieties affecting the directors, officers or employees of the company. (Review conflict of interest statements.)	OB/OW			
9. Obtain affidavits from company's management that securities are held free and clear.	OB/OW			

	Exam Obj.	Completion Date	Examiner	Work Paper Ref.
10. Inspect and count security certificates kept on company premises.	OB/OW EX AC CM			
a. Reconcile security certificates from count date to examination date.	EX			
b. Compare securities with applicable Schedule D data and investigate discrepancies.	AC			
c. Determine whether securities are adequately safeguarded against unauthorized access and destruction.	CM			
11. As of the examination date, obtain direct confirmation(s) of securities on deposit with state insurance departments from custodian or insurance department's security division. (Inspect and count such securities where confirmation is not obtained.)	OB/OW EX AC			
a. Compare confirmed securities listing (e.g., description, par value, number of shares, cost) with applicable Schedule D parts and investigate discrepancies.	AC			
12. As of the examination date, obtain direct confirmation(s) signed by an authorized signatory of the custodian holding securities on deposit directly or indirectly through a securities depository. (Perform alternative procedures on securities where confirmation is not obtained.)	OB/OW EX AC			
a. Request security confirmation by location (e.g., security depository, federal book-entry system, bank held).	EX			
b. Confirm existence of borrowed money or any other form of indebtedness to the custodian.	EX			
c. Ascertain whether securities deposited are subject to any liens, claims, or held as collateral for any loans made to an officer, director, or employee of the company.	OB/OW			
d. Ascertain how securities are registered (e.g., company name, company's nominee name, or custodian's nominee name).	OB/OW			

Procedure	Exam Obj.	Completion Date	Examiner	Work Paper Ref.
e. Compare confirmed security listing (e.g., description, par value, number of shares, cost) with applicable Schedule D parts and investigate discrepancies.	AC			
Note: At the domiciliary state's discretion, bonds and stocks may be counted before, after, or at year-end.				
13. If interim testing is performed:	AC CO CM			
a. Obtain brokers' advice for transactions that occurred between the interim date and examination date.	CO			
b. Reconcile the securities inventory back to the examination date, using the interim transaction records.	AC			
c. Inquire of, and observe, the company's procedures to physically examine securities held under the company's control.	CM			
14. Examine a sample of the custodians' and company's logs to determine who had access to securities (and why) since the examination was announced.	EX OB/OW			
15. Utilize NAIC Jumpstart reports to identify and clear all designation and valuation exceptions.	VA			
16. Verify that the insurer has certified in its annual/quarterly statements that all requirements of the NAIC Securities Valuation Office (SVO) have been met. (See NAIC *Annual Statement Instructions.*)	VA			
17. Perform procedures to ascertain that the insurer has properly complied with the SVO filing guidelines as stated in the *Purposes and Procedres Manual of the NAIC SVO* and that all securities not considered 'filing exempt' have been filed with the NAIC SVO.	VA			

	Exam Obj.	Completion Date	Examiner	Work Paper Ref.
18. If applicable, perform procedures to verify compliance with state specific mechanisms to ensure that insurers have filed all securities required to filed with the SVO. (As the SVO filing exempt provisions do not have a compliance mechanism, it is recommended for states to develop such mechanisms to protect interests relative to domiciliary insurers.)				
19. Review the insurer's exemption reports for securities that lost their NAIC SVO filing exemption to verify timely compliance with the NAIC SVO filing requirements as stated in the *Purposes and Procedures Manual of the NAIC SVO*. If action did not occur timely, review the securitiy file for documentation of adverse effects on RBC, FAST Ratios and AVR.	VA			
20. Select a sample of 'filing exempt' securities to determine that the selected securities properly and continuously met the NAIC SVO filing exemption requirements stated in Part Four of the *Purposes and Procedures Manual of the NAIC SVO*.	VA			
21. Select a sample of amortized bonds from Schedule D. Test the amortization of the discount or premium on the bonds and determine the appropriateness of the amortization method utilized. **SSAP No. 26, paragraph 6**, states that amortization of bond premium or discount shall be calculated using the scientific (constant yield) method. Bonds containing call provisions shall be amortized to the call or maturity value/date which produces the lowest asset value (yield to worst).	VA			
22. Ensure that any impaired securities are properly written down to fair value as a new cost basis and that the amount of the write down is accounted for as a realized loss in accordance with **SSAP No. 26, paragraph 8**, for bonds, **SSAP No. 30, paragraph 9**, for common stocks, **SSAP No. 32, paragraphs 21-23** for preferred stocks, **SSAP No. 43, paragraph 15**, for loan-backed and structured securities, and **SSAP No. 46, paragraphs 16 and 17**, for subsidiary, controlled, or affiliated (SCA) investments.	VA			

	Exam Obj.	Completion Date	Examiner	Work Paper Ref.
23. Determine the company's method of determining prepayment assumptions for loan-backed securities and evaluate proper valuation. Ensure that changes in prepayment assumptions and the resulting cash flows are reviewed periodically in accordance with **SSAP No. 43, paragraphs 9-14**.	VA			
24. For loan-backed securities, analyze yields for indications of unusually high or low yields or yields that differ significantly from expectations.	VA			
25. Review purchases and sales for indications of possible wash sales. Ensure that wash sales are disclosed in accordance with **SSAP No. 18, paragraph 37**.	VA			
26. For SCA investments, evaluate the appropriateness of the accounting method used for valuation. **SSAP No. 46, paragraph 7**, states that investments in SCA entities shall be recorded using (1) the market valuation approach, (2) the statutory equity method, or (3) the audited GAAP equity method.	VA			
27. Ensure that the reporting entity's share of the undistributed earnings and losses of the SCA are included in unrealized gains and losses of the reporting entity. Recalculate the unrealized gain or loss for each SCA investment.	PD VA			
28. For foreign securities recalculate the currency conversion in accordance with **SSAP No. 23**.	VA			
29. Review the state investment statutes for compliance. Utilize the company's "Summary Investment Schedule" as required by A-001 to perform this review.	CM			
30. For private placements obtain the listing of private placements with location of supporting documentation (e.g., indenture, deed of trust).	EX OB/OW			
a. Select a sample of private placements and confirm with the issuing company.	EX OB/OW			
31. Compare investment information, including a description of securities, from the bank confirmation and other security confirmations received to Schedule D and DA for significant discrepancies.	CO AC CT			

		Exam Obj.	Completion Date	Examiner	Work Paper Ref.
32.	Reconcile Schedule D and DA – Bonds, Stocks, and Short Term Investments as of the examination date to the previous examination date.	CO AC CT			
33.	Compare investment totals in Schedule D and DA to the insurer's reconciliation of the investment ledgers to the general ledger control accounts and balance sheet. Investigate significant discrepancies and any unusual reconciling items.	CO AC CT			
34.	Select a sample of purchases and sales of securities from Schedule D and DA – Bonds, Stocks, and Short Term Investments.	CO AC CT			
	a. Ascertain that securities are recorded on their trade date, not the settlement date, except for the acquisition of private placement securities, which should be recorded on their funding date, in accordance with **SSAP No. 26, paragraph 4**, for bonds, **SSAP No. 30, paragraph 5**, for common stocks, **SSAP No. 32, paragraph 10**, for preferred stocks and **SSAP No. 43, paragraph 6**, for loan-backed and structured securities.	CO			
	b. Compare description, CUSIP, par value, interest rate, maturity date, cost, interest paid on purchase (or sales price) and acquisition date (or trade date) to broker's advice.	AC			
	c. Compare net amount of funds paid to the bank or custodian statement.	AC			
	d. Recalculate the gain or loss on sale.	AC			
35.	Test transactions settled after year-end for recording in the proper period.	CO AC CT			
36.	Select a sample of interest and dividend income due and accrued from Schedule D and DA – Bonds and Short Term Investments. From that sample, verify the collectibility of the interest.	VA			
37.	Consider the reasonableness of due and accrued interest and dividend amounts based upon prior years.	AC CO CT			

		Exam Obj.	Completion Date	Examiner	Work Paper Ref.
38.	From the sample collected in step 34 above, test due and accrued interest and dividend amounts.	AC CO CT			
39.	Ensure that accrued interest is reduced for amounts which have been determined to be uncollectible in accordance with **SSAP No. 34**.	VA			
40.	Trace the above sample of due and accrued interest and dividend amounts to the cash receipts journal.	AC CO CT			
41.	Trace Schedule D and DA – Bonds and Short Term Investments due and accrued totals to the detail investment income exhibit and balance sheet.	AC CO CT			
	Securities Lending, Repurchase and Reverse Repurchase Agreements				
	Securities Lending				
1.	Obtain and review all security lending agreements.	CO			
2.	Obtain a listing of loaned securities as of the most recent quarter and examination date.	EX OB/OW			
3.	Confirm the loaned securities (and associated collateral thereon) with custodian and broker/dealer or lending agent as of the most recent quarter and examination date.	EX OB/OW			
4.	If the insurer administers its own security lending program, ascertain the type and amount of collateral for the security loaned from the securities records.	AC CO CT			
5.	If the insurer fails to maintain sufficient collateral for the loaned securities, ensure the uncollateralized portion is properly nonadmitted in accordance with **SSAP No. 18, paragraph 25**.	VA			
6.	Ensure that the type and fair value of the collateral that is pledged meets the requirements set forth in the NAIC *Purposes and Procedures* of the SVO, state statutes, or regulation.	VA			

	Exam Obj.	Completion Date	Examiner	Work Paper Ref.
7. Select a sample of collateral from the security records. If the collateral is cash, trace the receipt to the cash receipts journal and if the collateral is other than cash, trace the receipt to the confirmation and security lending ledger.	CO AC CT			
8. For loaned securities, identify whether the collateral is restricted or unrestricted. Ensure that unrestricted collateral is recorded as an asset with a corresponding liability to the borrower and that restricted collateral is not recorded as an asset or liability in accordance with **SSAP No. 18, paragraph 25**.	VA			
9. Determine the proper accounting treatment for income associated with loaned securities (investment income or miscellaneous income) in accordance with **SSAP No. 18**.	CO VA CT			
10. Determine whether security lending activities have been presented in accordance with **SSAP No. 18** of the NAIC *Accounting Practices and Procedures Manual* and that disclosure complies with the NAIC *Annual Statement Instructions*.	PD			
Repurchase Agreements, Reverse Repurchase Agreements, and Dollar Repurchase Agreements				
11. Obtain and review repurchase agreements, reverse repurchase agreements and dollar repurchase agreements as of the most recent quarter and examination date.	CO			
12. Confirm and ascertain the type and amount of the underlying collateral of such agreements with the insurer's custodian.	EX OB/OW			
13. Ensure that the type and fair value of the collateral that is pledged meets the requirements set forth in the NAIC *Purposes and Procedures Manual of the SVO*, state statutes or regulation.	VA			
14. Determine the proper accounting treatment for repurchase agreements, in accordance with **SSAP No. 45**, as follows:	VA CO AC CT			

	Exam Obj.	Completion Date	Examiner	Work Paper Ref.
a. Ensure the securities to be resold are substantially the same as the securities purchased. For securities to be substantially the same, the criteria defined **SSAP No. 45, paragraph 14** must be met.	VA			
b. Ensure the amount paid for the securities is reported as a short term investment in accordance with **SSAP No. 45, paragraph 4**.	AC VA			
c. Determine that the difference between the amount paid for the securities and the amount at which the securities will subsequently be resold is reported as interest income, calculated on the straight-line method or the scientific interest method, over the term of the agreement, in accordance with **SSAP No. 45, paragraph 4**.	VA CO CT			
15. Determine the proper accounting treatment for reverse repurchase agreements, in accordance with **SSAP No. 45**, as follows:	VA CO CT			
a. Ensure the securities to be repurchased are substantially the same as the securities sold. For securities to be substantially the same, the criteria defined in **SSAP No. 45, paragraph 14** must be met.	VA			
b. Ensure the amount received for the securities is reported as a liability in accordance with **SSAP No. 45, paragraph 7**.	AC VA			
c. Determine that the difference between the proceeds for the securities and the amount at which the securities will be subsequently reacquired is reported as interest expense, calculated on the straight-line method or the scientific interest method, over the term of the agreement, in accordance with **SSAP No. 45, paragraph 7**.	VA CT			

	Exam Obj.	Completion Date	Examiner	Work Paper Ref.
16. Determine whether repurchase, reverse repurchase, and dollar repurchase securities lending activities have been disclosed in accordance with **SSAP No. 45** of the NAIC *Accounting Practices and Procedures Manual* and the NAIC *Annual Statement Instructions*.	PD			
Insurer Investment Pools				
1. Access the qualifications and independence of the pool manager.	EX OB/OW			
2. Determine whether the pool agreement complies with the guidelines prescribed by the state investment code or insurance department.	CM			
3. Obtain the listing of securities held in the investment pool.	EX OB/OW			
4. Determine that the securities held in the investment pool are in accordance with the pooling agreement and state statutes or regulations.	CM			
5. Confirm the securities held in the investment pool with the investment pool custodian.	EX OB/OW			
6. Ascertain whether the investment pool acquires securities issued by the insurance company or an affiliate, and determine the legality of such practice under state law.	VA CM			
7. Ascertain whether the investment pool enters into borrowing transactions, and determine the legality of such practice under state statute.	VA CM			
8. Determine whether securities have been presented in accordance with **SSAP No. 18** of the NAIC *Accounting Practices and Procedures Manual* and disclosure complies with the NAIC *Annual Statement Instructions*.	VA CM			
Cash on Hand and on Deposit				
1. Obtain an understanding of the check issuance and cash receipts procedures.	EX			

	Exam Obj.	Completion Date	Examiner	Work Paper Ref.
2. Obtain a listing of individuals authorized to sign checks and any limits associated with their signing authority.	CM			
3. From the above listing, send bank confirmations directly to the depositories.	EX OB/OW			
4. Agree the bank confirmation to the bank reconciliation.	EX OB/OW			
5. Count the petty cash fund and reconcile that amount to the balance sheet date.	EX OB/OW			
6. For five days before and after the balance sheet date, verify the proper recording of transfers between bank accounts.	EX OB/OW			
7. Trace deposits in transit, which are included in the bank reconciliation, to the subsequent bank statement.	CO AC			
8. Trace outstanding checks, which are included in the bank reconciliation, to the subsequent bank statement.	CO AC			
9. Investigate the subsequent month's bank statement for cleared checks dated before the balance sheet date but not included in the bank reconciliation.	CO AC			
10. Trace a sample of daily totals from the cash receipts journal to the initial control total over daily cash receipts.	CO AC			
11. Trace a sample of individual withdrawals recorded on the bank statement to cancelled checks and to the cash disbursement journal.	CO AC			
12. Trace a sample of disbursements from the cash disbursements journal to individual check vouchers and supporting documentation.	CO AC			
13. On the sample of cancelled check vouchers from above, examine the check for unauthorized signatures, alterations, irregular endorsements,and date paid.	CO AC			

	Exam Obj.	Completion Date	Examiner	Work Paper Ref.
14. Trace total receipts and disbursements from the cash receipts/disbursements journals to the general ledger.	CO AC			
15. Scan the cash receipts/disbursements journal and bank statements for unusual debits or credits.	CO AC			
16. Test whether account balances and disclosures comply with the NAIC *Accounting Practices and Procedures Manual* and NAIC *Annual Statement Instructions*.	PD			
17. Review the Notes to the Financial Statements and General Interrogatories and evaluate the completeness of information.	PD			
18. Consider the reasonableness of accrued interest and interest received during the year based upon prior years.	VA			
19. Select a sample of interest payments included on the bank statements. Trace those amounts to the cash receipts journal.	CO AC			
20. Trace the total accrued interest to the detailed investment income exhibit and balance sheet.	CO AC			
21. Trace the total interest received to the detailed investment income exhibit.	CO AC			
22. Ensure that the net amounts of all cash accounts are reported jointly. If in the aggregate the insurer has a net negative cash balance, ensure that the amount is reported as a negative asset and not recorded as a liability, in accordance with **SSAP No. 2, paragraph 5**.	AC VA			
<u>**Derivative Instruments**</u>				
Other Invested Assets				
1. Review investment committee minutes and determine whether investment transactions have been properly authorized.	EX			
2. Review available independent audit reports and management letters for evidence of inappropriate hedge accounting practices.	AC			

	Exam Obj.	Completion Date	Examiner	Work Paper Ref.
3. Review available independent audit reports and management letters for joint ventures, partnerships, and limited liability companies in which the insurer has an interest.	AC			
4. Make inquiries to ascertain any conflicts of interest or improprieties affecting the directors, officers, or employees of the company. (Review conflict of interest statements.)	CM			
Derivative Instruments				
5. Obtain contracts which the insurer has entered into and agree them to the documentation provided in the insurer's records and Schedule DB.	EX OB/OW			
6. Obtain direct confirmation of all derivative instruments held at acustodian or a broker.	EX OB/OW			
7. Review hedging transactions to determine that they are consistent with the category hedged, in accordance with **SSAP No. 86, paragraph 18:**	VA			
a. Fair Value Hedges (**SSAP 86, paragraph 19**);				
b. Cash Flow Hedges (**SSAP 86, paragraph 20**);				
c. Forecasted Transaction Hedges (**SSAP 86, paragraph 21**);				
d. Foreign Currency Hedges (**SSAP 86, paragraph 22-31**).				
8. Determine that the appropriate accounting method was applied based upon the type of derivative (e.g., swaps, options, forwards, etc.), in accordance with **SSAP No. 86**.	VA			
9. Review the hedging transactions to determine that ineffective hedges have been accounted for at fair value with changes in the fair value recorded as an unrealized gain/loss in accordance with **SSAP 86, paragraph 15**.				

	Exam Obj.	Completion Date	Examiner	Work Paper Ref.
10. Select a sample of market values from Schedule DB and verify compliance with the guidelines set forth in **SSAP No. 86** of the NAIC *Accounting Practices and Procedures Manual* and the *Purposes and Procedures Manual* of the NAIC SVO.	VA			
11. Review the state investment statutes related to derivative instruments for compliance.	VA			
12. Verify that the insurer has properly documented derivative instruments opened during the year, derivative instruments terminated, expired, or exercised during the year, and derivative instruments open at quarter-end in accordance with **SSAP No. 86, paragraphs 34-36**.	PD			
13. Select a sample of transactions and test whether all significant terms (e.g., maturity, expiration or settlement date, contractual payments, purchase and sale price) were specified and documented, and whether the amounts and terms are consistent with those established by the insurer's hedging techniques.	CO AC			
14. Select a sample of values from Schedule DB and trace to appropriate source documents.	CO AC			
15. Test transactions settled after year-end for recording in the proper period.	CT			
16. Verify that disclosure requirements for derivative contracts in accordance with **SSAP 86, paragraph 53** have been met.	PD			
Joint Ventures, Partnerships, and Limited Liability Companies				
17. Obtain a listing of joint ventures, partnerships, and limited liability companies in which the insurer has invested. From the listing, select a sample to confirm with the administrator of the investment.	EX OB/OW			
18. From the sample above, review the agreement for proper signatures and legitimacy.	EX OB/OW			

		Exam Obj.	Completion Date	Examiner	Work Paper Ref.
19.	Obtain financial reports of joint ventures, partnerships, and limited liability companies, and compare reported amounts of dividends, net rentals, etc. to the insurer's records.	VA			
20.	Determine the insurer's percentage of ownership interest in these investments.	VA			
21.	Determine that joint ventures, partnerships (with the exception of limited partnerships with a minor ownership interest), and limited liability companies are recorded using the statutory equity method, in accordance with **SSAP No. 48, paragraph 7**. Limited partnerships with a minor ownership interest (e.g., less than 10%) shall be recorded using the audited GAAP equity method, in accordance with **SSAP No. 48, paragraph 8**.	VA			
22.	Review the state investment code related to joint ventures, partnerships, and limited liability companies for compliance.	VA			
23.	Review joint ventures, partnerships, and limited liability companies for possible impairment. Ensure that other than temporary impairments are properly recorded in accordance with **SSAP No. 48, paragraphs 10 and 11**.	VA			
24.	Reconcile Schedule BA as of the examination date to the previous examination date.	CO AC			
25.	Trace the values in Schedule BA to the general ledger control accounts. Investigate significant discrepancies, any unusual reconciling items or material charge-offs.	CO AC			
26.	Trace the original amount contributed by the insurer to the investment agreement, cash disbursements journal, and canceled check. This procedure should only be performed on those investments acquired since the last examination.	CO AC			
27.	Select a sample of additions to the investment and trace to the cash disbursement journal.	CO AC			
28.	Select a sample of income recorded in Schedule BA and trace to the cash receipts journal.	CO AC			

	Exam Obj.	Completion Date	Examiner	Work Paper Ref.
29. Test transactions after year-end for recording in the proper period.	CT			
30. Test whether account balances and disclosures comply with **SSAP No. 48** of the NAIC *Accounting Practices and Procedures Manual* and NAIC *Annual Statement Instructions*.	PD			
31. Review the Notes to the Financial Statements and General Interrogatories and evaluate the completeness of information.	PD			
<u>Policy Loans and Premium Notes</u>				
1. Obtain a detailed listing of policy loans:	AC CO EX VA			
a. This listing should include: name of policyholder, policy number, date of policy, interest rate, original loan value, principal, and interest received to date and outstanding loan balance. From the listing, select a sample of loans to confirm with policyholders. Request the outstanding loan balance and perform the following procedures.	CO			
b. Verify that the policy number was included in the in-force records.	EX			
c. Verify that the unpaid balance of the loan is not in excess of the cash surrender value. If the amount is in excess of the cash surrender value and is considered uncollectible, it shall be written off as a reduction of investment income, in accordance with **SSAP No. 49, paragraph 5**. Ensure all other amounts in excess of cash surrender value are properly nonadmitted.	AC VA			

	Exam Obj.	Completion Date	Examiner	Work Paper Ref.
d. Trace the original loan value from the detailed listing to the cash disbursements journal and canceled check. Verify the signature on the policy and loan application to the endorsement of the check.	EX			
e. Test due and accrued interest as follows: Verify that interest income that is past due 90 days or more is properly reclassified from Investment Income Due and Accrued and included in the unpaid balance of the policy loan, in accordance with **SSAP No. 49, paragraph 8**.	VA AC			
f. Trace principal payments from the detailed listing to the cash receipts journal.	CO EX			
2. Trace the detailed listing of policy loans to the general ledger and balance sheet.	CO AC			
3. Trace due and accrued interest to the cash receipts journal.	CO AC			
<u>**Real Estate, Mortgage Loans and Collateral Loans**</u>				
1. Make inquiries to ascertain any conflicts of interest or improprieties, related to the mortgage property or loans, affecting the directors, officers or employees of the company. (Review conflict of interest statements.)	EX OB/OW			
2. Review investment committee minutes and determine whether mortgage transactions and loans have been authorized on a timely basis.	EX			
3. Ascertain whether the use of servicing agents has been properly authorized.	CM			
4. Review servicing agreements to determine compliance with the agreements' provisions. If available, examine any audits of the servicing agents.	CM OB/OW			
5. Obtain affidavits from company management that the mortgages and loans held are free and clear.	OB/OW			

	Exam Obj.	Completion Date	Examiner	Work Paper Ref.
Real Estate				
6. Determine if reappraisals are necessary by assessing the date of valuation and the reasonableness of the appraised value compared to the carrying value, in accordance with **SSAP No. 40, paragraphs 11 and 12**. *Note: Properties occupied by the company and properties held for the production of income shall be carried at depreciated cost less encumbrances unless events or circumstances indicate the carrying amount of the asset may not be recoverable.*	VA			
7. Review the company's procedure for handling a decline in a property value. Ensure that circumstances which indicate that the carrying amount of the asset may not be recoverable are properly assessed, in accordance with **SSAP No. 40, paragraph 9**.	CM			
8. Examine title deeds to ensure they are registered in the insurer's name.	OB/OW EX			
9. Examine evidence of insurance and property tax payments.	OB/OW EX			
10. Review the insurance policies for adequacy of coverage.	OB/OW EX			
11. For properties that were acquired in satisfaction of debt, trace the total capitalized value from the mortgage ledger to the real estate ledger.	OB/OW EX			
12. For properties that were acquired in satisfaction of debt, examine foreclosure records and documents to verify that the foreclosure has been consummated.	OB/OW EX			
For Properties Owned and Occupied by the Company and Properties Held for the Production of Income:				
13. Compare the cost recorded in the investment ledger to supporting documents (e.g., sales contract, deed, cash disbursements journal, cancelled checks). This procedure should only be performed on real estate acquired since the last examination.	VA			

	Exam Obj.	Completion Date	Examiner	Work Paper Ref.
14. Compare the original cost to the appraised value for reasonableness.	VA			
15. Select a sample of capitalized improvements from Schedule A Real Estate. Trace those improvements to the real estate ledger, cash disbursements journal, and canceled checks.	VA			
16. Verify that the actual cost on Schedule A – Real Estate is the sum of the original cost plus total capitalized improvements or additions.	VA			
For Properties Acquired in Satisfaction of Debt:				
17. Identify and trace foreclosure costs, real estate taxes, insurance premiums, and any other costs from the mortgage loan ledger to the cash disbursement journal and canceled checks.	VA			
18. Select a sample of capitalized improvements, which were incurred subsequent to foreclosure, from Schedule A – Real Estate. Trace those improvements to the real estate ledger, cash disbursements journal, and canceled checks.	VA			
For all Real Estate:				
19. Identify encumbrances from the real estate ledger and detailed records. Select a sample of the encumbrances and trace to Schedule A – Real Estate, the cash disbursements journal, and canceled checks.	VA			
20. Verify the reasonableness of the insurer's depreciation methods and test calculations, in accordance with **SSAP No. 40, paragraph 8**.	VA			
21. Verify the insurer's capitalization practices for compliance with **SSAP No. 40, paragraphs 7, 13 and 14**.	VA			
22. Trace real estate sales from Schedule A – Real Estate to the cash receipts journal and detailed records (e.g., original sales contract, authorization records, mortgage loan inventory).	CO AC			
23. Verify that real estate sold was deleted from Schedule A – Real Estate.	CO AC			

Step	Procedure	Exam Obj.	Completion Date	Examiner	Work Paper Ref.
24.	Recompute the gain or loss on real estate sales. Ensure that any profit is recognized only when real estate is sold, provided (a) the profit is determinable and (b) the earnings process is virtually complete, in accordance with **SSAP No. 77, paragraphs 3 and 4**.	AC			
25.	Trace payments on real estate held under sales contract from the cash receipts journal to the real estate ledger. Confirm significant balances with purchasers.	CO AC			
26.	Trace real estate expenses capitalized from Schedule A – Real Estate to expense journals and the real estate ledger.	CO AC			
27.	Test transactions settled after year-end for recording in the proper period.	CO AC			
28.	Test whether disclosures comply with **SSAP No. 40** of the NAIC *Accounting Practices and Procedures* Manual and NAIC *Annual Statement Instructions*.	PD			
29.	Review the Notes to the Financial Statements and General Interrogatories and evaluate the completeness of information.	PD			
30.	Select a sample of rental income due and accrued from Schedule A – Real Estate. From that sample, verify the collectibility of the income.	VA			
31.	Consider the reasonableness of due and accrued rental income based upon prior years.	CO AC			
32.	Compare the rent that the company includes in both its income and expense to the building occupancy and to rental rates of like property located in the same area. Verify compliance with **SSAP No. 40, paragraph 15**.	CO AC			
33.	From the sample collected in step 30, recalculate due and accrued rental income.	CO AC			
34.	Trace the above sample of due and accrued rental income to the cash receipts journal.	CO AC			
35.	Verify that rental income paid in advance is recorded as Unearned Investment Income.	CO AC			

	Exam Obj.	Completion Date	Examiner	Work Paper Ref.
36. Trace Schedule A – Real Estate due and accrued rental income totals to the detailed investment income exhibit and balance sheet.	CO AC			
Mortgage Loans				
37. Obtain a detailed listing of mortgage loans that includes, name of mortgagor, loan number, closing date, current unpaid principal, original principal amount, any premium or discount, yield to maturity, maturity date, amount and timing of contractual payments, interest paid to date, status and date of last payment, amounts held in escrow, any service fees and name of servicing agent and interest due and accrued.	EX OB/OW			
38. Obtain direct confirmation of mortgage loans with mortgagors, mortgage service agents, or state officials.	EX VA OB/OW			
a. Request from mortgagors, the unpaid principal balance, contractual payments and interest.	OB/OW			
b. Request from servicing agents, the number of loans, unpaid principal balance, escrow amounts, status of taxes, adequacy of hazard insurance and any unremitted payments.	OB/OW			
c. Request confirmation from state officials of any mortgages pledged or deposited with the state insurance department.	EX VA			
39. From the mortgage loan inventory on site, select a sample of mortgage loans.	EX OB/OW VA AC CO			
a. Examine the mortgage note to ensure it is registered in the insurer's name.	OB/OW EX			
b. Examine evidence of insurance and property tax payments. In addition, review the insurance policies for adequacy of coverage.	EX			

	Exam Obj.	Completion Date	Examiner	Work Paper Ref.
c. Verify that the mortgage loan balance is recorded and reported at its unpaid principal balance, net of any amounts deferred under the provisions of **SSAP No. 37, paragraphs 5 and 6**.	AC VA			
d. For mortgage loans acquired at a discount or premium, test the amortization calculation using the constant effective yield method, in accordance with **SSAP No. 37, paragraph 9**.	AC VA			
e. Review the mortgage loan file for possible impairment of either principal or interest and ensure that any impairment is properly recorded, in accordance with **SSAP No. 37, paragraph 16**.	VA AC			
f. Verify that the proper postings were made to the escrow accounts.	CO			
g. Test the calculation of interest income due and accrued.	AC			
40. For mortgage loans in default, being voluntarily conveyed, or being foreclosed, evaluate the appropriateness of the accounting method used in valuation, in accordance with **SSAP No. 37, paragraph 17**.	VA			
41. Ascertain compliance with state investment statutes.	CM			
42. Reconcile Schedule B – Mortgage Loans as of the examination date to the previous examination date.	CO AC			
43. Compare unpaid principal balances and interest in Schedule B – Mortgage Loans to the insurer's mortgage loan inventory and general ledger control accounts. Investigate significant discrepancies, any unusual reconciling items or material charge-offs.	CO AC			
44. For mortgage loans issued since the last examination, select a sample of mortgage loans from the mortgage loan inventory.	CO AC			

	Exam Obj.	Completion Date	Examiner	Work Paper Ref.
a. Trace the original principal and any discount or premium from the mortgage inventory to the mortgage note, deed of trust, amortization schedule and county records.	CO			
b. Trace the original principal to the cash disbursements journal and canceled check.	CO			
c. Compare the original principal with the appraised value and evaluate the adequacy and existence of hazard insurance coverage.	AC			
d. Verify payments were distributed accurately between principal and interest.	AC			
e. Examine the current tax status and title policy or abstract and attorney's opinion.	AC CO			
45. Ensure that disclosures and presentation guidelines comply with **SSAP No. 37** of the NAIC *Accounting Practices and Procedures Manual* and the NAIC *Annual Statement Instructions.*	PD			
46. Review the Notes to the Financial Statements and General Interrogatories in the Annual Statement and evaluate the completeness of the information.	PD			
47. Ensure those mortgages which are in foreclosure are properly classified.	PD			
48. Verify that any payments received in advance of due dates are properly classified as follows:	VA PD			
a. Payments received in advance of due dates that represent prepayments of principal shall be recorded as a reduction in the mortgage loan balance, in accordance with **SSAP No. 37, paragraph 10**.	VA PD			
b. Prepaid interest shall be recorded as a liability, Unearned Investment Income, in accordance with **SSAP No. 37, paragraph 10**.	VA PD			

	Exam Obj.	Completion Date	Examiner	Work Paper Ref.
49. Consider the reasonableness of due and accrued interest amounts based upon prior years.	CO AC			
50. Ensure that due and accrued interest which is 180 days past due and collectible is properly nonadmitted and due and accrued interest which is uncollectible is properly written off, in accordance with **SSAP No. 37, paragraph 14**.	VA			
51. Agree Schedule B – Mortgage Loans due and accrued totals to the detailed investment income exhibit and the balance sheet.	CO AC			
Collateral Loans				
52. Obtain a detailed listing of collateral loans. The detailed listing should include: name of borrower, description and value of collateral, original loan value, date of loan, maturity of loan, interest rate, interest accrued and received to date, outstanding loan balance and mode of payment.	EX VA OB/OW AC			
a. From the listing, select a sample of loans to confirm with borrowers. Request the unpaid balance and payments of principal and interest to date.	EX			
b. Verify that the loan agreement was properly signed and the pledged investment was properly assigned to the insurer.	VA OB/OW			
c. Verify that any pledged investment that is not sufficient to cover the collateral loan balance or that does not qualify as an investment is properly nonadmitted, in accordance with **SSAP No. 21, paragraph 4**.	VA			
d. Test due and accrued interest and trace to the cash receipts journal.	EX AC			
53. Reconcile the collateral loans Schedule BA as of the examination date to the previous examination date.	CO AC			

	Exam Obj.	Completion Date	Examiner	Work Paper Ref.
54. Compare outstanding collateral loan balances and interest in Schedule BA to the insurer's collateral loan listing, general ledger control accounts and balance sheet. Investigate significant discrepancies, any unusual reconciling items or material charge-offs.	CO AC			
55. Consider the reasonableness of due and accrued interest based upon prior years.	CO AC			
Other Loan Procedures				
56. Make inquiries to ascertain any conflicts of interest or improprieties related to real estate property affecting the directors, officers or employees of the company. (Review conflict of interest statements.)	OB/OW EX			
57. Review investment committee minutes and determine whether real estate transactions have been authorized on a timely basis and determine whether the use of investment managers and advisors have been properly authorized.	EX			
58. Obtain and review loan agreements with managers, consultants, advisors and intermediaries and compare to the Annual Statement.	CO			
59. Obtain affidavits from company management indicating that real estate held is free and clear.	OB/OW			
<u>**Separate Accounts (Life Companies Only)**</u>				
1. Obtain an understanding of the general nature and characteristics of the various kinds of separate accounts business conducted by the insurer.	EX			
2. Review separate account agreements and verify that investments are handled according to the agreement.	CM			
3. Obtain direct confirmation(s) signed by an authorized signatory of the custodian holding securities on deposit directly or indirectly through a securities depository. (Inspect and count such securities when confirmation is not obtained.)	OB/OW EX CO			

	Exam Obj.	Completion Date	Examiner	Work Paper Ref.
a. Request securities confirmation by location (e.g., security depository, federal book-entry system, bank held).	EX			
b. Confirm existence of borrowed money or any other form of indebtedness to the custodian.	EX			
c. Ascertain whether securities deposited are subject to any liens, claims, or held as collateral for any loans made to an officer, director, or employee of the company.	OB/OW			
d. Ascertain how securities are registered (e.g., company name, company's nominee name, or custodian's nominee name).	OB/OW			
e. Compare confirmed securities listing (e.g., description, par value, number of shares, cost) with Schedule D and investigate discrepancies.	CO			
4. Verify that assets are valued at their fair market value on the date of valuation.	VA			
5. Verify that the reserve or liability established in the separate account is determined on the basis of the fair value of the assets in the separate account.	VA			
6. Review the state investment statutes related to separate accounts for compliance.	VA CM			
7. Verify that transfers between the general and separate account are correctly recorded in accordance with **SSAP No. 56**.	CO AC			
8. Perform a reconciliation since the last examination of transfers between the separate account and general account.	CO AC			
9. Test whether account balances and disclosures comply with **SSAP No. 56** of the NAIC *Accounting Practices and Procedures Manual* and NAIC *Annual Statement Instructions*.	PD			
10. Review the Notes to the Financial Statements and General Interrogatories and evaluate the completeness of information.	PD			

	Exam Obj.	Completion Date	Examiner	Work Paper Ref.
Interest Maintenance Reserve / Asset Valuation Reserve				
Interest Maintenance Reserve (IMR)				
Note: These examination procedures apply only to life insurers.				
1. Obtain the IMR workpapers, including an inventory of investment gains and losses grouped by year of amortization, used to compute the reserve for the period under review.	CM			
2. Trace the IMR inventory, obtained above, to the appropriate investment schedules and exhibits.	AC			
Note: All of the capital gains and losses included in this reserve should be interest-related.				
Generally, a Separate Account only requires an IMR if the assets are valued at book value. If an IMR is required, it is reported in the separate accounts statement. Thus, an examiner may need to review both the separate accounts and general accounts Annual Statements.				
3. Trace the capital gains/losses and the related tax amounts to the appropriate exhibits in the Annual Statement.	OB/OW			
4. From the workpapers obtained above, select a representative sample of IMR inventory and calculations to test the accuracy and completeness of the reserve.	CO			
Listed below are items that should be tested, however, the list is not all-inclusive and the examiner should use his/her judgement in selecting the sample.				
5. Capital gains/losses—Validate the following items:	AC			

	Exam Obj.	Completion Date	Examiner	Work Paper Ref.
a. Bonds and Preferred Stocks—the NAIC/SVO rating classification at the beginning and at the end of the holding period for debt securities and mortgage backed securities on which there was a gain or a loss. If the rating has not changed by more than one rating classification, then the capital gain/loss is interest related and is charged to IMR. However, if the rating was "6" at any time during the holding period or for preferred stock was "4 to 6", then the capital gain/loss is credit related and is charged to AVR.	AC			
b. CMO Negative Yield Adjustments—losses on loan-backed bonds or other structured securities that have a negative effective yield at the time of valuation are included as realized losses.	AC			
c. Mortgage Loans—the status of mortgages on which there was a gain/loss. If the mortgage is in good standing and is not restructured during the last two years, the gain/loss is interest-related and is charged to the IMR.	AC			
d. Derivative Instruments—gain or loss on derivative transactions that have been entered into solely for the purpose of altering the interest rate characteristics of the insurer's assets and/or liabilities have been included and are amortized over the life of the hedged assets and/or liabilities.	AC			
6. Liability Gains/Losses—When reviewing the adjustment for current year's realized liability gains/losses released from the reserve, validate the following items:	AC CO			

	Exam Obj.	Completion Date	Examiner	Work Paper Ref.
a. The calculation to determine the liabilities transferred as a result of the sale, transfer, or reinsurance of a block of liabilities as a percentage of an insurer's general account liabilities. If the transfer represents more than 5% of an insurer's general account liabilities, and the transaction is irrevocable, to a non-affiliate, and completed within the current year, then it must be charged to the IMR and amortized into income;	CO			
b. The calculation to determine the materiality from market value adjustments on policies and contracts backed by assets that are valued at book. If the adjustment is in excess of both .01% of liabilities and $1,000,000, then it must be credited to the IMR. The amortization schedule should be determined in a manner consistent with the determination of associated market value adjustment.	AC CO			
7. Exemptions—Ascertain that interest related gains or losses which arise from the sale of investments required to provide cash flow to meet "excess withdrawal activity" are excluded from the IMR and reflected in net income.	CO			

	Exam Obj.	Completion Date	Examiner	Work Paper Ref.
8. Amortization—Two acceptable methods for accumulating and calculating the amortization schedule, seriatim and grouped, are described in the NAIC *Annual Statement Instructions*. Note that in using the grouped method, the amortization for the current year is the sum of the gains and losses by maturity groupings multiplied by the appropriate factor for the current year. The presence of sinking fund payments, amortization schedules, expected prepayments, and adjustable interest rates must be considered in determining the number of calendar years to expected maturity. For loan-backed bonds and other structured securities that are valued using currently anticipated prepayments, use the remaining weighted average life of principal and interest payments consistent with the prepayment assumptions that would have been used to value the security had the security been repurchased at its sale price. For negative yield adjustments, use the weighted average life consistent with the valuation of the security at the time of loss recognition.	CO			
9. Trace the IMR totals from the workpapers to the balance sheet and summary of operations.	AC			
10. Trace the change in IMR to the liability account.	AC			
11. Test whether account balances and disclosures comply with **SSAP No. 7** of the NAIC *Accounting Practices and Procedures Manual*, *Annual Statement Instructions* and *Purposes and Procedures Manual* of the SVO.	PD			
12. Review the Notes to the Financial Statements and General Interrogatories and evaluate the completeness of information.	PD			
Asset Valuation Reserve (AVR)				
Note: These examination procedures apply only to life insurers.				
13. Obtain the AVR workpapers, including an inventory of investments grouped by subcomponent type, used to compute the reserve for the period under review.	AC CO			

	Exam Obj.	Completion Date	Examiner	Work Paper Ref.
14. Trace the AVR inventory, obtained above, to the appropriate investment schedules and exhibits.	AC CO			
Note: Often, insurer's report mortgages from real estate joint ventures to Schedule B and the related partnership interest on Schedule BA. In these instances, the amount of the mortgage is added to the BA statement value and should be deducted from the statement value of mortgage loans reported in Schedule B.				
A Separate Account only requires an AVR if the insurer suffers the loss in the event of asset default or market value loss. An exception to the above is when specific state regulation provides an alternative to the AVR. If an AVR is required, it is combined with the general account AVR and reported in the general account statement.				
15. Trace the capital gains/losses and the related tax amounts to the appropriate exhibits in the Annual Statement.	AC CO			
16. From the workpapers obtained above, select a representative sample of AVR inventory and calculations to test the accuracy and completeness of the reserve.	AC CO			
Listed below are items that should be tested, however, the list is not all-inclusive and the examiner should use his/her judgement in selecting the sample.				
17. Capital gains/losses—Validate the following items:	AC CO			
a. The NAIC/SVO rating classification at the beginning and at the end of the holding period for debt securities and mortgage backed securities on which there was a gain or loss. If the security changed by more than one rating classification or was rated "6" at any time during the holding period or for preferred stocks was "4 or 6", then the gain/loss is credit related and is charged to AVR.	AC CO			

	Exam Obj.	Completion Date	Examiner	Work Paper Ref.
b. The status of mortgages on which there was a gain or loss. If the mortgage was not in good standing or was restructured within the last two years, the gain/loss is credit related and is charged to AVR.	CO			
c. Whether derivative transactions on which there was a realized or unrealized gain or loss was interest-related. Only gains and losses on hedging instruments that are not interest-related should be reported in the AVR with the hedged instrument.	AC			
18. Transfers—Ensure that transfers between components and sub-components are properly made.	AC CO			
a. If the balance before transfers of any subcomponent exceeds the maximum for that subcomponent and the balance of its "sister" subcomponent is below the maximum for that subcomponent, then the excess must be transferred to the sister subcomponent.	AC CO			
b. If the combined amount of the subcomponent exceeds its respective combined maximum reserve, the excess may be transferred between components or released to surplus.	AC CO			
c. If the amount of the subcomponent is negative, and the amount of its "sister" subcomponent within the same component is positive, the negative amount should be transferred to the "sister" subcomponent. This transfer must not reduce the positive balance of the "sister" subcomponent to less than 50% of its balance prior to the transfer.	AC CO			

	Exam Obj.	Completion Date	Examiner	Work Paper Ref.
19. Reserve Factors—the maximum reserve factor used for mortgage loans is calculated based on the insurer's experience ratio and the industry's experience ratio. The factor is commonly referred to as the Experience Adjustment Factor (EAF). The insurer and industry data should relate to the same time periods.	CM AC CO			
a. A look through treatment for affiliated investment subsidiaries is used in calculating the insurer's maximum AVR reserve. Schedule BA assets are treated in this way.	CM			
b. The maximum reserve for unrated structured securities acquired by conversion is calculated as the lessor of 100% of the maximum reserve for the entire pool associated with the unrated security or the statement value of the unrated security.	AC CO			
c. The maximum reserve factor used for unaffiliated publicly traded common stock is based on a company's weighted average portfolio beta. The portfolio beta is calculated using either the Individual or Aggregate Method. If an insurer does not want the administrative complexity of calculating the beta factor, then the maximum AVR factor of 30% is used.	AC CO			
20. Trace the AVR totals from the workpapers to the balance sheet and summary of operations.	AC CO			
21. Trace the change in AVR to the surplus account.	AC CO			
22. Test whether account balances and disclosures comply with **SSAP No. 7** of the NAIC *Accounting Practices and Procedures Manual*, *Annual Statement Instructions*, and NAIC *Purposes and Procedures Manual* of the SVO.	PD			
23. Review the Notes to the Financial Statements and General Interrogatories and evaluate the results of this information.	PD			

	Exam Obj.	Completion Date	Examiner	Work Paper Ref.
<u>**Receivable/Payable for Securities**</u>				
1. Obtain a listing of receivables/payables for securities as of the examination date.	OB/OW EX			
2. From the above listing, select a sample of receivables/payables and verify the receipt or disbursement of cash after year-end.	OB/OW EX			
3. Verify that receivables/payables for securities are valued in accordance with the NAIC *Accounting Practices and Procedures Manual*.	VA			
4. Review the listing of receivables not received after year end, for possible impairment, in accordance with **SSAP No. 21, paragraph 7**. Ensure that receivables for securities not received within 15 days from the settlement date are properly nonadmitted in accordance with **SSAP No. 21, paragraph 8**.	VA			
5. Review the state investment code for compliance.	VA			
6. From the sample obtained in step 2, verify that the broker advice matches the amount recorded in the insurer's records.	CO AC			
7. Verify that the receivable represents securities that were sold before year-end but the proceeds were not received. This security should not be included in the investment exhibits.	CO AC			
8. Test transactions settled after year-end for recording in the proper period.	CT			
9. Trace the listing of receivables/payables for securities to the general ledger and balance sheet.	CO AC			
10. Test whether account balances and disclosures comply with **SSAP No. 21** of the NAIC *Accounting Practices and Procedures Manual*, NAIC *Annual Statement Instructions* and NAIC *Purposes and Procedures Manual* of the SVO.	PD			
11. Review the Notes to the Financial Statements and General Interrogatories and evaluate the results of this information.	PD			

	Exam Obj.	Completion Date	Examiner	Work Paper Ref.
Aggregate Write-Ins for Invested Assets				
Note: The following examination procedures are very general. Therefore to the extent that examination procedures for other accounts apply to this write-in account, those examination procedures should be utilized.				
1. Obtain an understanding of the nature of the account.	EX			
2. Reconcile the account as of the examination date to the previous examination date.	AC CO			
3. Trace the account balance in the Annual Statement to the general ledger and detailed records.	AC CO			
4. Test the account balance for accuracy and completeness.	AC CO			
5. Verify the proper classification of the account balance in the Annual Statement.	PD			
6. Test the account balance for proper valuation.	VA			
7. Test transactions settled after year-end for recording in the proper period.	CT			
8. Obtain evidence of the insurer's ownership interests in the asset.	EX OB/OW			
9. Verify the existence of the asset.	EX OB/OW			
10. Test whether account balances and disclosures comply with the NAIC *Accounting Practices and Procedures Manual* and NAIC *Annual Statement Instructions*.	PD			
11. Review the Notes to the Financial Statements and General Interrogatories and evaluate the completeness of information.	PD			

SECTION K — OPERATING CYCLE: OTHER ASSETS

The procedures included within this document should be completed if deemed necessary by the examiner in accordance with the overall risk assessment. Each of the items referenced in this document may not be present in every company under examination. The examiner should clearly identify the sections that are pertinent and remove or mark out the remaining sections.

Annual Statement Blank Line Items

Health Care Delivery Assets
Electronic Data Processing (EDP) Equipment and Operating Software
Furniture, Fixtures, and Equipment and Leasehold Improvements

Relevant SSAP's Include:

#16, Electronic Data Processing Equipment and Software
#19, Furniture, Fixtures, and Equipment; Leasehold Improvements Paid by the Reporting Entity as Lessee; Depreciation of Property and Amortization of Leasehold Improvements
#20, Nonadmitted Assets
#73, Health Care Delivery Assets - Supplies, Pharmaceuticals and Surgical Supplies, Durable Medical Equipment, Furniture, Medical Equipment and Fixtures, and Leasehold Improvements in Health Care Facilities
#79, Depreciation of Nonoperating System Software – An Amendment to SSAP No. 16 – Electronic Data Processing Equipment and Software

SPECIFIC RISK ANALYSIS WORKPAPERS

Risk Analysis Prepared By/Date ______________________________

Planning Exam Analysis Prepared By/Date ______________________________

Reviewed By/Date ______________________________

EXAMINATION OBJECTIVES:

1. The assets existed and were the legal property of the reporting entity as of the examination date. (Existence and Ownership)

2. The assets comply and are valued in accordance with the NAIC *Accounting Practices and Procedures Manual* and state laws and regulations. (Compliance and Valuation)

3. The assets have been accurately accounted for, reported in the appropriate accounting period, and reported in the reporting entity's records. (Accuracy, Cut-off and Completeness)

4. The assets are presented in accordance with the NAIC *Annual Statement Instructions* and the NAIC *Accounting Practices and Procedures Manual*. (Presentation and Disclosure)

INHERENT RISKS

INTERNAL AND EXTERNAL ENVIRONMENTAL CONDITIONS/FACTORS

RESULTS OF DETAIL ANALYTICAL REVIEW PROCEDURES

CONTROL RISK — OPERATING CYCLE: OTHER ASSETS

This questionnaire is designed to assist the examiner in assessing control risk for other assets operating cycles. Part 1, Section III and Part 3 of this *Handbook* provides guidance in consideration of a reporting entity's internal control structure for use when designing substantive examination procedures.

This questionnaire includes examples of internal control procedures and policies that are commonly utilized by reporting entities to achieve internal control objectives. For each control procedure listed below, indicate by placing a check mark in the yes or no box whether or not the reporting entity employs such a procedure, or other similar practice (include a description of the similar procedure). To the extent the control procedure is not applicable, indicate N/A. If other relevant control procedures are in place, list them in the space that follows. Control procedures that are tested by the examiner should be documented by including the workpaper reference in the comment section and the examiner's initials in the reliance column.

For each individual control procedure there is a control objective listed that satisfies the procedure.

If the examiner initially assesses control risk as low or medium for a particular account balance, then those controls must be tested. The controls should be tested to determine whether the procedure is operating as expected, applied throughout the entire period of reliance, performed on a timely basis, encompassing all transactions and identifying errors. Some examples of testing procedures are inquiry, observation, re-performance and examination of documents. The level of reliance, if any, should be indicated in the applicable column along with any comments the examiner may have regarding the procedure.

Based upon the testing results, the examiner should determine whether the preliminary control risk assessment is confirmed or should be revised.

CONTROL OBJECTIVES

Authorization (AU) – All transactions recorded were reviewed and approved by designated personnel.

Completeness (CO) – All transactions that occurred are initially entered into the accounting records, accepted for processing, and generated data files and reports reflect that all transactions have occurred.

Accuracy (AC) – Transactions are initially recorded correctly, timely and accurately.

Asset Protection (AP) – Adequate safeguards over access to and use of assets and records, including the appropriate segregation of duties among company personnel.

	Control Obj.	Y	N	Work Paper Ref.	Reliance
General Control Procedures					
The examiner should determine the amount of documentation necessary for each control procedure. If the examiner intends to place substantial reliance on the established controls, the examiner should explain the control procedure in a workpaper and document the individual responsible for supervising the control activity as well as the frequency of the control activity.					
1. Does management review assets for compliance with the classification, valuation and regulatory requirements or limitations?	AU AC				
2. Are changes that are made to the equipment inventory data reviewed to ensure that changes are authorized and that approved transactions are updated to the inventory on a timely basis?	AU CO				
3. Are the equipment control records periodically inspected and reconciled to asset ledgers by an individual independent of the custodial function?	CO AC				
4. Do procedures exist to prevent unauthorized individuals from purchasing or selling assets?	AP AU				
5. Is access to asset records limited to authorized personnel?	AP AC				
6. Is there a separation of duties between employees accounting for assets and those employees authorizing asset decisions?	AP AU				
7. Does management have safeguards in place to prevent unauthorized access to equipment?	AP				
8. Does management review the depreciation calculation and verify that the calculations are in accordance with guidelines established by the NAIC *Accounting Practices and Procedures Manual*?	CM				
9. Does the board of directors or authorized personnel approve all major equipment acquisitions?	AU				

	Control Obj.	Y	N	Work Paper Ref.	Reliance
10. Are reviews completed for those purchases and other asset transactions settling after year-end?	CO AC				
11. Do controls exist to verify that quoted prices on asset transactions are compared periodically to purchase/sale prices by persons independent of those executing and approving transactions?	AC				
12. Does management periodically evaluate the financial condition and capabilities of suppliers and property managers or owners and others with whom the reporting entity has established business relationships?	AP				
13. Are assumptions for future cash flow projections on leaseholds and major purchases, which are on an installment basis, periodically reviewed and monitored by management?	AU				
14. Are equipment and supplies including pharmaceutical supplies, which cannot be located, promptly written off?	CO AC				
15. Does management perform periodic asset reviews to identify and record other than temporary impairments?	AC				
<u>Health Care Delivery Assets</u>					
Note: *These specific procedures under Health Care Delivery Assets are only applicable for reporting entities that directly provide health care services to subscribers, members, or policyholders.* ***Those entities with Health Care Delivery Assets should also complete the general control procedures.***					
1. Has management adopted specific guidelines for the classification of health care delivery assets?	AU				
2. Is there an asset control system that provides for the identification of quantities on hand and valuation of lower of cost or market (e.g., supplies, pharmaceuticals and surgical supplies, and durable medical equipment) as required by **SSAP No. 73, paragraph 5**?	AU AP				

	Control Obj.	Y	N	Work Paper Ref.	Reliance
3. Are daily inventory supply reports reviewed by someone independent of the processing of the transactions?	AU AP				
4. Are there procedures to write off pharmaceutical supplies in accordance with an established policy, such as by expiration date?	AC				

OTHER KEY CONTROLS EXISTING FOR THIS CONTROL OBJECTIVE:

SUMMARY EVALUATION OF CONTROL RISK:

EVALUATION OF INDEPENDENT CPA'S WORK FOR THIS EXAMINATION (CPA REVIEW CHECKLIST):

OVERALL RISK ASSESSMENT

Balance Sheet Evaluation of the Likelihood of a Material Adjustment to Surplus:

The evaluation of the likelihood of a material adjustment to surplus should be based on the following criteria:

- Inherent Risk
- Internal & External Environmental Factors
- Control Risk
- Materiality Consideration

The examiner should rate each item as to the likelihood of a material misstatement. All items are assumed as 'High' prior to any examiner evaluation. A 'High' assessment requires the examiner to perform substantive examination procedures over that account area. A lower assessment allows the examiner to perform analytical or fewer substantive procedures to satisfy the examination requirements. If an assessment other than 'High' is selected for any of the accounts, the examiner needs to document the basis for the assessment. If the assessment is based on control testwork, the documentation should include results of control procedures and related workpaper references.

"Health Care Delivery Assets"

___________ High ___________ Medium ___________ Low

Basis for Assessment:

____

____

____

"Electronic Data Processing (EDP) Equipment and Operating Software"

___________ High ___________ Medium ___________ Low

Basis for Assessment:

____

____

____

3) "Furniture, Fixtures, and Equipment and Leasehold Improvements"

___________ High ___________Medium __________Low

Basis for Assessment:

____

____

____

PRELIMINARY EXAMINATION APPROACH — OPERATING CYCLE: OTHER ASSETS

Listed below are the corresponding Annual Statement line items that are related to the procedures contained in this Operating Specific Risk Analysis:

Health Care Delivery Assets
Electronic Data Processing (EDP) Equipment and Operating Software
Furniture, Fixtures and Equipment and Leasehold Improvements

The actual examination procedures selected to be performed are a matter of considerable judgment by the examiner. The following "Examination Program" includes examples of procedures commonly used.

To the extent that the examiner judgmentally determines that it is appropriate to use one or more of the following procedures, that selection can be documented by checking the space next to the appropriate procedure, with modifications noted in the margin. The examiner may determine that alternative or additional procedures are required. If so, those procedures can be added on a supplemental sheet. The examiner performing the procedure should indicate satisfactory completion by initialing and dating in the space provided, and referencing the workpapers where the procedures and findings are documented.

The examiner may chose to apply the examination procedures to less than 100% of the items comprising an account balance. Guidance for audit sampling and control and substantive procedures can be found in Part 3 of the NAIC *Financial Condition Examiners Handbook.*

After each examination procedure, the examination objective that the procedure satisfies is indicated. The examination objectives are accuracy, completeness, compliance, cutoff, existence, obligation and ownership, valuation and presentation and disclosure.

EXAMINATION OBJECTIVES

Accuracy (AC) – Recorded transactions and account balances are mathematically accurate, are based on correct amounts and have been classified into the correct account.

Completeness (CO) – All transactions and account balances that should be recorded in the annual financial statement were recorded.

Compliance (CM) – Business transactions and affairs have been conducted in accordance with state insurance codes, other state laws or department directives.

Cutoff (CT) – All transactions are recorded in the correct accounting period.

Existence (EX) – Recorded transactions occurred and are not fictitious and recorded assets and liabilities existed as of the balance sheet date.

Obligation (OB) and Ownership (OW) – Recorded liabilities are obligations of the company and recorded assets are the rights of the company at the balance sheet date.

Valuation (VA) – Assets and liabilities are valued in accordance with state statute and NAIC accounting guidance.

Presentation and Disclosure (PD) – The elements of the Annual Statement are properly classified and all disclosures are accurately included in the Annual Statement.

	Exam Obj.	Completion Date	Examiner	Work Paper Ref.
EXAMINATION PROCEDURES				
General Procedures				
1. Obtain affidavits from reporting entity's management that equipment is held free and clear. Verify that encumbrances on equipment subject to liens or loans are properly reflected. Verify that equipment is held in the name of the reporting entity.	OB/OW			
2. Review Board of Directors or committee minutes and determine whether large equipment purchases have been properly and timely authorized.	OB/OW CO CT			
3. Review independent audit or other reports on the system of internal control and assess financial stability of the reporting entity (e.g., SAS 70 report).	CM VA			
4. Make inquiries to ascertain any conflicts of interest or improprieties affecting the directors, officers, or employees of the reporting entity. (Review conflict of interest statements.)	OB/OW			
5. Review arrangements with suppliers and dealers, to assess their qualifications and independence. Contracts should be under the terms that would be considered "arms-length" transactions. Consider the reasonableness of prices for services and supplies.	AC PD			
Health Care Delivery Assets				
Equipment and Inventory				
1. Obtain the inventory listing for health care delivery assets. Agree this schedule to the company's general ledger and Annual Statement.	AC EX			
2. Verify that the classification of health care delivery assets complies with the categories specified in **SSAP No. 73**:	AC PD			

	Exam Obj.	Completion Date	Examiner	Work Paper Ref.
a. Furniture, medical equipment, and fixtures used in connection with the direct delivery of health care services are admitted assets, in accordance with **SSAP No. 73, paragraph 4**.	AC PD			
b. Pharmaceuticals, surgical supplies and durable medical equipment (such as wheelchairs, crutches and braces, etc.) which are used in the direct delivery of healthcare to fulfill policyholder obligations are admitted assets, in accordance with **SSAP No. 73, paragraph 4**.	AC PD			
c. Furniture, fixtures and equipment that are not used in the direct delivery of health care (e.g., for administrative activities including claims processing, billing and maintenance of medical records) are nonadmitted assets, in accordance with **SSAP No. 73, paragraph 4**.	AC PD			
d. Supplies (except pharmaceuticals and surgical supplies noted above) such as linens, uniforms, garments, food, housekeeping, maintenance and office supplies are nonadmitted assets, in accordance with **SSAP No. 73, paragraph 6**.	AC PD			
3. Review the fluctuation of admitted health care delivery asset supply balances from the prior year. Investigate significant fluctuations.	EX AC			
a. Obtain invoices for equipment and inventory purchases made during the examination period. Review the documentation and agree the vendor and payment amount to the inventory listing.	EX AC			
b. Review documentation for equipment or inventory reductions. For inventory used to provide treatment of claims, reconcile the decrease in assets to claim requests. For assets sold or disposed, verify proceeds received to payment remittance as well as any gains or losses recorded on the transaction.	EX AC			

	Exam Obj.	Completion Date	Examiner	Work Paper Ref.
4. Physically locate equipment or inventory kept on company premises and agree it to the asset detail. Investigate any discrepancies.	EX CO			
5. Verify the reporting entity maintains a control system that provides for the identification of quantities on hand and appropriate valuation (lower of cost or market) of supplies, pharmaceuticals and surgical supplies, and durable medical equipment in accordance with **SSAP No. 73, paragraph 5**. The control system should include the following aspects:	EX AC VA			
a. Physical inventories are taken on a regular basis;	EX AC			
b. Expired pharmaceutical supplies and obsolete items are written down or expensed; and	EX AC VA			
c. Inventory items that are lost or stolen are properly expensed.	EX AC VA			
6. Verify that the depreciation for health care delivery assets is in accordance with **SSAP No. 73, paragraphs 8-9** and **SSAP No. 87 paragraph 6.**	VA			
a. Durable medical equipment - when used by policyholders or members and returned, the diminution in value as a result of such use should be recognized.	VA			
b. Furniture, medical equipment, and fixtures - depreciated over their estimated useful lives, not to exceed three years.	VA			
c. Medical supplies, pharmaceuticals, and surgical supplies, durable medical equipment, furniture, medical equipment, and fixtures, and leasehold improvements capitalized prior to January 1, 2001 – depreciated over the shorter of its useful life or three years.	AC			

	Exam Obj.	Completion Date	Examiner	Work Paper Ref.
d. In accordance with **SSAP No. 87 paragraph 6**, amounts less than a predefined threshold of medical supplies, pharmaceuticals, and durable medical equipment may be expensed when purchased.	VA			
7. Inquire whether the company is subject to state and/or federal laws. Verify compliance with these regulations.	CM			
a. Inquire about recent audits or reviews conducted by any other federal or state agencies.	CM			
b. Review the findings of any such review for the potential financial impact on the reporting entity.	CM			
Leasehold Improvements				
1. Obtain a detailed listing or relevant files on leasehold improvements classified as health care delivery assets. Agree the detail to the company's general ledger and Annual Statement.	EX AC			
2. Ascertain that the leasehold improvements classified as health care delivery assets are used for the direct delivery of health care services and are properly recorded as admitted assets in accordance with **SSAP No. 73, paragraph 4**.	EX AC PD			
a. Leasehold improvements not used for the direct delivery of health care services should be nonadmitted in accordance with **SSAP No. 19, paragraph 5**.	EX AC PD			
3. Identify any significant fluctuations in leasehold improvements from the prior year. Trace significant increases to invoices and payment documentation.	EX AC			
4. Verify that the amortization of leasehold improvements is properly recorded in accordance with **SSAP No. 73, paragraph 9**.	AC VA			

	Exam Obj.	Completion Date	Examiner	Work Paper Ref.
a. Leasehold improvements should be amortized against net income over the shorter of its estimated useful life or the remaining life of the original lease excluding renewal or option periods using methods detailed in **SSAP No. 19**.	AC VA			
EDP Equipment and Software				
1. Obtain the detailed listing of EDP equipment and operating system software. Agree the listing to the company's general ledger and Annual Statement.	EX AC			
2. Verify that the admitted asset portion of EDP equipment is limited to 3% of the reporting entity's capital and surplus in the entity's most recently filed statutory financial statement adjusted to exclude EDP equipment, net deferred tax assets, and net positive goodwill in accordance with **SSAP No. 16, paragraph 4**.	VA CM PD			
a. Nonoperating system software is nonadmitted in accordance with **SSAP No. 16, paragraph 2**.	VA PD			
3. Verify that the depreciation methods for the different categories of EDP equipment and software are calculated in accordance with **SSAP No. 79 and SSAP No. 87 paragraph 7.**	EX AC VA			
a. EDP equipment and operating system software should be depreciated over the lesser of its useful life or three years.	EX AC VA			
b. Nonoperating system software should be depreciated over the lesser of its useful life or five years.	EX AC VA			
c. EDP equipment and software capitalized prior to January 1, 2001 are depreciated over the lesser of their remaining useful life or three years.	EX AC VA			
d. In accordance with the reporting entity's capitalization policy, amounts less than a predefined threshold may be expensed as incurred.	EX AC VA			

	Exam Obj.	Completion Date	Examiner	Work Paper Ref.
4. Verify compliance with the required disclosures in accordance with **SSAP No. 16, paragraph 5**.	CM PD			
Furniture, Fixtures and Equipment and Leasehold Improvements				
1. Obtain a detailed listing of furniture, fixtures and equipment and leasehold improvements. Reconcile the listing to the company's general ledger and Annual Statement.	EX AC			
2. Verify that the depreciation methods for furniture, fixtures and equipment follow methods described in **SSAP No. 19, paragraphs 7-13**. Verify that the leasehold improvements have been properly amortized in accordance with **SSAP No. 19, paragraph 5**. (Amounts less than a predefined threshold of such assets can be expensed when purchased in accordance with **SSAP No. 87, paragraph 4**.)	AC VA			
3. Verify that furniture and equipment (unless used in the direct delivery of healthcare) are properly classified as nonadmitted assets in accordance with **SSAP No. 19, paragraph 2**.				
a. Automobiles, airplanes and other vehicles are also considered nonadmitted assets in accordance with **SSAP No. 20, paragraph 4**. The accounting for these items should follow the accounting for furniture, fixtures and equipment included in **SSAP No. 19**.	AC VA			
4. Verify compliance with the required disclosures in accordance with **SSAP No. 19, paragraphs 14 and 15**.	CM PD			

SECTION L — OPERATING CYCLE: TAXES

The procedures included within this document should be completed if deemed necessary by the examiner in accordance with the overall risk assessment. Each of the items referenced in this document may not be present in every company under examination. The examiner should clearly identify the sections that are pertinent and remove or mark-out the remaining sections.

Note: SSAP No. 10, Income Taxes, was adopted by the NAIC effective for years beginning on or after January 1, 2001. Prior to January 2001, the NAIC *Accounting Practices and Procedures Manual* specifically rejected the recognition of deferred income taxes. Under **SSAP No. 10**, company's are now required to compute federal deferred income tax amounts and admit a deferred tax asset subject to an admissibility test or to establish a deferred tax liability.

Note: To assist companies and regulators in implementing SSAP No. 10, the NAIC adopted a Question & Answer Guide in December 2001. It was attached to SSAP No. 10 as Exhibit A in the March 2002 *Accounting Practices and Procedures Manual.* The examiner should become familiar with the requirements of SSAP No. 10 and the Q&A before attempting to examine deferred income taxes. Further assistance can be found in Issue Paper No. 83, which contains excerpts of Statement of Financial Accounting Standards No. 109 (FAS 109) (the GAAP pronouncement **SSAP No. 10** was based upon).

Annual Statement Blank Line Items

Federal and Foreign Income Tax Recoverable and Interest Thereon (Including $...Net Deferred Tax Asset)
Federal and Foreign Income Taxes (Including $...on realized capital losses) (Including $.... Net Deferred Tax Liability)
Taxes, Licenses and Fees (Excluding federal income taxes) *(Property & Casualty Companies)*
Taxes, Licenses and Fees Due or Accrued (Excluding federal income taxes) *(Life Companies*)
General Expenses Due or Accrued *(Health Companies)*
Amounts Withheld or Retained for Account of Others *(Applicable for P&C and Health Company payroll taxes)*

Relevant SSAP's Include:

#10, Income Taxes
#25, Accounting for and Disclosure about Transactions with Affiliates and Related Parties
#35, Guaranty Fund and Other Assessments
#67, Other Liabilities
#70, Allocation of Expenses

SPECIFIC RISK ANALYSIS WORK PAPERS

Risk Analysis Prepared By/Date____

Planning Exam Analysis Prepared By/Date__________________________________

Reviewed By/Date____

EXAMINATION OBJECTIVES:

1. Federal income tax recoverable; federal or foreign income taxes are recorded correctly as to account, amount and period. (Accuracy, Completeness and Cutoff)

2. Provisions for taxes, licenses and fees are recorded correctly as to account, amount and period. (Accuracy, Completeness and Cutoff)

INHERENT RISKS

____

____

____

____

INTERNAL AND EXTERNAL ENVIRONMENTAL CONDITIONS/FACTORS

____

____

____

____

RESULTS OF DETAIL ANALYTICAL REVIEW PROCEDURES

____

____

____

____

CONTROL RISK — OPERATING CYCLE: TAXES

This questionnaire is designed to assist the examiner in assessing control risk for tax cycles. Part 1, Section III and Part 3 of this *Handbook* provides guidance in consideration of an insurer's internal control structure for use when designing substantive examination procedures.

This questionnaire includes examples of internal control procedures and policies that are commonly utilized by insurers to achieve internal control objectives. For each control procedure listed below, indicate by placing a check mark in the yes or no box whether or not the insurer employs such a procedure, or other similar practice (include a description of the similar procedure). To the extent the control procedure is not applicable, indicate N/A. If other relevant control procedures are in place, list them in the space that follows. Control procedures that are tested by the examiner should be documented by including the workpaper reference in the comment section and the examiner's initials in the reliance column.

For each individual control procedure there is a control objective listed that satisfies the procedure.

If the examiner initially assesses control risk as low or medium for a particular account balance, then those controls must be tested. The controls should be tested to determine whether the procedure is operating as expected, applied throughout the entire period of reliance, performed on a timely basis, encompassing all transactions and identifying errors. Some examples of testing procedures are inquiry, observation, re-performance and examination of documents. The level of reliance, if any, should be indicated in the applicable column along with any comments the examiner may have regarding the procedure.

Based upon the testing results, the examiner should determine whether the preliminary control risk assessment is confirmed or should be revised.

CONTROL OBJECTIVES

Authorization (AU) – All transactions recorded were reviewed and approved by designated personnel.

Completeness (CO) – All transactions that occurred are initially entered into the accounting records, accepted for processing, and generated data files and reports reflect that all transactions have occurred.

Accuracy (AC) – Transactions are initially recorded correctly, timely and accurately.

Asset Protection (AP) – Adequate safeguards over access to and use of assets and records, including the appropriate segregation of duties among company personnel.

	Control Obj.	Y	N	Work Paper Ref.	Reliance
General Control Procedures					
The examiner should determine the amount of documentation necessary for each control procedure. If the examiner intends to place substantial reliance on the established control, the examiner should explain the control procedure in a workpaper and document the individual responsible for supervising the control activity as well as the frequency of the control activity.					
1. Are applicable taxing authorities identified?	AC				
2. Does management maintain a calendar or other method to ensure that all returns are prepared, filed timely, and that payments made timely?	AU AC				
3. Is the intercompany allocation of provision and settlement of tax liability among members of consolidated groups documented and reviewed?	AU AC				
4. Are the amounts included in federal income tax calculations and premium tax calculations reconciled to recorded provisions in the Annual Statement?	AC				
5. Is the federal and state taxable income reconciled with statutory income?	AC				
6. Are the premiums used in calculating premium taxes reconciled to recorded premiums?	AC				

OTHER KEY CONTROLS EXISTING FOR THIS EXAMINATION OBJECTIVE:

SUMMARY EVALUATION OF CONTROL RISK:

EVALUATION OF INDEPENDENT CPA'S WORK FOR THIS EXAMINATION (CPA REVIEW CHECKLIST):

OVERALL RISK ASSESSMENT

Balance Sheet Evaluation of the Likelihood of a Material Adjustment to Surplus:

The evaluation of the likelihood of a material adjustment to surplus should be based on the following criteria:

- Inherent Risk
- Internal & External Environmental Factors
- Control Risk
- Materiality Consideration

The examiner should rate each item as to the likelihood of a material misstatement. All items are assumed as 'High' prior to any examiner evaluation. A 'High' assessment requires the examiner to perform substantive examination procedures over that account area. A lower assessment allows the examiner to perform analytical or fewer substantive procedures to satisfy the examination requirements. If an assessment other than 'High' is selected for any of the accounts, the examiner needs to document the basis for the assessment. If the assessment is based on control testwork, the documentation should include results of control procedures and related workpaper references.

1) "Federal and Foreign Income Taxes Recoverable and Interest Thereon (Including $...Net Deferred Tax Asset)"

___________ High ___________ Medium ___________Low

Basis for Assessment:

____

____

____

2) "Federal and Foreign Income Tax (Including $...on realized capital losses) (Including $...Net Deferred Tax Liability)"

___________ High ___________ Medium ___________Low

Basis for Assessment:

____

____

____

3) "Taxes Licenses and Fees (Excluding federal income taxes) (*Property & Casualty Companies*)"

___________ High ___________ Medium ___________Low

Basis for Assessment:

4) "Taxes, Licenses and Fees Due or Accrued (Excluding federal income taxes) (*Life Companies*)"

___________ High ___________ Medium ___________Low

Basis for Assessment:

5) "General Expenses Due or Accrued (*Health Companies*)"

___________ High ___________ Medium ___________Low

Basis for Assessment:

6) "Amounts Withheld or Retained for Account of Others (*Applicable for P&C and Health Company payroll taxes*)"

___________ High ___________ Medium ___________Low

Basis for Assessment:

PRELIMINARY EXAMINATION APPROACH — OPERATING CYCLE: TAXES

Listed below are the corresponding Annual Statement line items that are related to the procedures contained in this Operating Specific Risk Analysis:

Federal and Foreign Income Tax Recoverable and Interest Thereon (Included $...Net Deferred Tax Asset)
Federal and Foreign Income Tax (Including $...on realized capital losses) (Including $.... Net Deferred Tax Liability)
Taxes, Licenses and Fees (Excluding federal income taxes) *(Property & Casualty Companies)*
Taxes, Licenses and Fees Due or Accrued (Excluding federal income taxes) *(Life Companies)*
General Expenses Due or Accrued *(Health Companies)*
Amounts Withheld or Retained for Account of Others *(Applicable for P&C and Health Company payroll taxes)*

The actual examination procedures selected to be performed is a matter of considerable judgment by the examiner. The following "Examination Program" includes examples of procedures commonly used.

To the extent that the examiner judgmentally determines whether it is appropriate to use the following procedures, that selection can be documented by checking the space next to such procedure, with modifications noted in the margin. The examiner may determine that alternative or additional procedures are required. If so, those procedures can be added on a supplemental sheet. The examiner performing the procedure should indicate satisfactory completion by initialing and dating in the space provided, and referencing the work papers where the procedures and findings are documented.

The examiner may choose to apply the examination procedures to less than 100% of the items comprising an account balance. Guidance for audit sampling and control and substantive procedures can be found in Part 3 of the NAIC *Financial Condition Examiners Handbook.*

After each examination procedure, the examination objective that the procedure satisfies is indicated. The examination objectives are accuracy, completeness, compliance, cutoff, existence, obligation and ownership, valuation and presentation and disclosure.

EXAMINATION OBJECTIVES

Accuracy (AC) – Recorded transactions and account balances are mathematically accurate, are based on correct amounts and have been classified into the correct account.

Completeness (CO) – All transactions and account balances that should be recorded in the annual financial statement were recorded.

Compliance (CM) – Business transactions and affairs have been conducted in accordance with state insurance codes, other state laws or department directives.

Cutoff (CT) – All transactions are recorded in the correct accounting period.

Existence (EX) – Recorded transactions occurred and are not fictitious and recorded assets and liabilities existed as of the balance sheet date.

Obligation (OB) and Ownership (OW) – Recorded liabilities are obligations of the company and recorded assets are the rights of the company at the balance sheet date.

Valuation (VA) – Assets and liabilities are valued in accordance with state statute and NAIC accounting guidance.

Presentation and Disclosure (PD) – The elements of the Annual Statement are properly classified and all disclosures are accurately included in the Annual Statement.

	Exam Obj.	Completion Date	Examiner	Work Paper Ref.
EXAMINATION PROCEDURES				
*Note: The following examination procedures apply to all of the above annual statement line items. This is in accordance with the nature of the line items and the examination procedures necessary to properly analyze these areas. By completing the following procedures, the examiner should ascertain compliance of the above annual statement line items with **SSAP No. 10** and the domiciliary state's insurance code.*				
Federal and Foreign Accrued Income Taxes				
1. Obtain a schedule by tax jurisdiction of income tax asset and liability accounts (including deferred tax accounts) showing beginning and ending balances, current-year payments and refunds, adjustments, and current-year provisions for income tax expense or benefit, and perform the following:	CO AC EX CT			
a. Obtain assurance regarding the completeness of the tax jurisdictions by:	CO			
i. Making inquiries of knowledgeable management as to any new tax jurisdictions in which the company operates and whether any notices have been received from tax authorities concerning potential, proposed or agreed adjustments of prior-period taxes;	CO			
ii. Considering any evidence of additional tax jurisdictions obtained through examination procedures such as documents supporting subsequent cash disbursements; and	CO			
iii. Considering the company's potential tax exposure in the various local, municipal, state and foreign tax jurisdictions in which the company conducts business.	CO			
b. Obtain and review copies of prior-year (and current-year, if available) tax returns;	AC EX			

	Exam Obj.	Completion Date	Examiner	Work Paper Ref.
c. Make inquiries of the appropriate personnel as to the existence of any unasserted income tax contingencies, update the list of expiration dates open under the statute of limitations, and determine whether all open years have been considered in identifying and accruing unasserted income tax contingencies; and	CO AC EX CT			
d. Test the summarization of the schedule and agree the ending balances and current-year provisions to the general ledger.	AC			
2. Make a selection of current-year payments shown in the schedule obtained in Step 1, and perform the following for each payment selected:	CO AC EX CT			
a. Agree the amount of the payment to the appropriate income tax return, and, if the payment is for a prior-year liability, to the amount of the accrued liability shown in prior-year work papers;	CO AC EX CT			
b. If the payment is a current-year estimated payment, agree the amount to the appropriate form filed with the taxing authority, and determine that the amount of estimate is likely to be sufficient to avoid penalty or, if a penalty will be incurred, that the company has recorded such penalty appropriately;	CO AC EX CT			
c. If the payment is for an adjustment of prior-period tax liabilities made by the tax authorities, agree the amount to the *Notice of Adjustments* or other appropriate documents, and determine whether the company has adequately considered the potential effect of settled issues for all open years and for the treatment of similar transactions in the current year; and	CO AC EX CT			
d. Agree the amount to the paid check and examine it for unusual features.	AC EX			

	Exam Obj.	Completion Date	Examiner	Work Paper Ref.
3. Determine that tax payments recorded near year-end are supported by cash disbursements prior to year-end.	AC EX CT			
4. Document in the working papers the company's procedures for identifying the issues and obtaining the relevant facts regarding unasserted income tax contingencies and the company's methodology for accruing unasserted income tax contingencies. The examiner should review these methods and document a conclusion over the established procedures and methodology. Further guidance on tax contingencies can be found in **SSAP No. 10, Exhibit A, Question 9**.	AC EX			
5. Review appropriate documentation for and discuss with tax management as necessary, the unasserted income tax contingencies individually estimated to be probable of loss and, regarding pooled contingencies, compare the company's accrual for unasserted income tax contingencies with independent (done by state or consultant) estimate of probable loss, and state a conclusion regarding the reasonableness of the accrual.	AC EX			
6. If the company filed for tax refunds for prior periods, determine that such refunds were received and agree the amounts to the related returns and, if applicable, to cash receipts records.	AC EX CT			
a. Inquire as to the status of refunds filed for and/or recorded as assets in prior periods but not received.	AC EX CT			
b. Agree refunds received to the amounts shown in the schedule obtained in Step 1.	AC EX			
7. Agree the amounts of the provisions for current income taxes to the amounts tested in Step 1.	AC EX			

	Exam Obj.	Completion Date	Examiner	Work Paper Ref.
8. For items in the schedule obtained in Step 1 that represent an adjustment to update the prior-year tax provision to the prior-year tax return, gather and evaluate the evidence in support of the adjustment by reference to the prior-year tax provision and Schedule M-1 items in the prior-year tax return.	CO AC EX CT			
9. For other items in the schedule obtained in Step 1, gather and evaluate the evidence in support of the adjustment or reclassification in light of the procedures performed in testing the current-year tax provision (see Steps 10-12) and deferred tax items (see Steps 13-23).	CO AC EX CT			
Current Federal and Foreign Income Taxes				
10. Obtain or prepare a schedule showing the calculation of the current-year provision for income taxes. This schedule may be prepared in conjunction with the schedule required for Steps 13-23 (e.g., showing the calculation for deferred taxes). For each tax paying component in each tax jurisdiction, perform the following:	AC EX CO VA			
a. Agree pretax income to the Annual Statement.	CO AC EX			
b. Review Schedule M-1 in the company's prior-year (and current year, if available) tax returns, and consider using appropriate checklists (e.g., lists of income not subject to taxation, nondeductible expenses, and items for which the proper period of recording in the financial statements and in the tax returns is different) to test that all significant differences between financial statement income and taxable income are included in the schedule.	CO AC EX			
c. Agree the amounts of significant differences between statutory income and taxable income to the current year activity as tested in Step 16.	CO AC EX			

	Exam Obj.	Completion Date	Examiner	Work Paper Ref.
d. Obtain a worksheet from the company detailing the permanent and temporary differences from taxable income. Determine that items representing differences between current taxable income and financial reporting pretax income that do not give rise to temporary differences have resulted from events recognized in the financial statements that do not have tax consequences (e.g., revenues that are exempt from taxation and expenses that are not deductible).	CO AC EX			
e. Test the summarization of the computation of taxable income.	AC			
f. Recompute the amount of income tax expense or benefit, based on taxable income for tax purposes (e.g., taxable income with timing differences), considering, as applicable:	VA AC			
i. Tax rates, which should be agreed to the rates in the instructions to the tax returns issued by the tax authority or to another independent source;	VA AC			
ii. Tax credits, which should be tested as to propriety and amount based on the relevant tax law and the underlying data; and	VA AC			
iii. Relevant prior-year tax returns, as to any operating loss or tax credit carry forwards that are offset against current-year taxable income or income taxes or are used to obtain a current benefit.	VA AC			
g. Review any relevant revenue agent reports (RARs.)	AC			
11. Agree the provision for current taxes to the schedule obtained in Step 1.	AC EX			

	Exam Obj.	Completion Date	Examiner	Work Paper Ref.
12. For occurrences in which the company files a consolidated income tax return with an affiliate, determine if income tax transactions have been properly recognized in accordance with **SSAP No. 10, paragraph 12**. As indicated in **SSAP No. 10, paragraph 13**, amounts owed to reporting companies under intercompany tax transactions should be accounted for in accordance with **SSAP No. 25**. Guidelines for recognizing income tax transactions with affiliates include:	AC			
a. Transactions are economic transactions in accordance with **SSAP No. 25**;	AC			
b. Transactions are pursuant to a written income tax agreement; and	AC			
c. Income taxes incurred are accounted for in a manner consistent with FAS 109 as modified by **SSAP No. 10**.	AC			
Deferred Federal and Foreign Income Taxes				
13. Obtain or prepare a schedule of items that give rise to temporary differences, segregated by future taxable or deductible amounts, showing prior-year, current activity and end-of-year balances for each of the following:	AC EX			
a. Balance-sheet items on a financial reporting basis and on a tax basis and the calculation of taxable or deductible amounts;	AC EX			
b. Income statement items representing deferred taxable income or tax deductions that have balances only on an income tax balance-sheet and therefore are not identified with a particular balance-sheet item for financial reporting purposes;	AC EX			
c. Net operating loss carry forwards for tax purposes;	AC EX			
d. Tax credit carry forwards for tax purposes; and	AC EX			
e. For Items c and d above, the updated carry forward periods and limitations.	AC EX			

	Exam Obj.	Completion Date	Examiner	Work Paper Ref.
14. Test the completeness of "temporary" differences (e.g., differences between the financial statement basis and tax basis of the company's assets and liabilities) shown in the schedule, as follows:	CO AC			
a. Consider the findings of Step 10 b.	CO AC			
b. Consider, based on evidence obtained in performing other exam procedures, whether there are other assets or liabilities for which the basis is different for tax and financial statement purposes or deferred taxable income or tax deductions.	CO AC			
15. Agree beginning balances to prior-year tax returns as applicable.	CO			
16. Test current-year activity as follows:	CO AC			
a. Agree the current-year activity for financial reporting balances to the general ledger;	CO AC			
b. Recompute the current-year activity for balances on a tax basis based on current enacted tax law;	CO AC			
c. Agree current-year activity representing adjustments to amounts tested in Steps 8 and 9, as applicable; and	CO AC			
d. Agree ending balance to the current-year general ledger.	CO AC			
17. Ensure that the tax rates used to calculate or measure deferred items (e.g., "temporary" differences and NOL carry forwards) represent the rate(s) expected to apply to taxable income in the years that the liability is expected to be settled or the asset recovered.	AC			
18. Recompute the total deferred tax liability for future taxable amounts using the applicable tax rate.	AC EX VA			

	Exam Obj.	Completion Date	Examiner	Work Paper Ref.
19. Recompute the total deferred tax asset for future deductible amounts relating to temporary differences, and NOL and tax credit carry forwards, using the applicable tax rate.	AC EX VA			
20. Determine that the effects of the following, if any, have been properly considered in the deferred tax liability or asset accounts:	AC EX			
a. Alternative tax systems;	AC EX			
b. Enacted changes in tax laws or rates;	AC EX			
c. Changes in tax status;	AC EX			
d. Business combinations; and	AC EX			
e. Other items that may affect deferred taxes.	AC EX			
21. Determine that the exceptions to recognition of deferred taxes have been properly considered in accordance with **SSAP No. 10, paragraph 7**.	AC EX			
22. A deferred tax asset must first be recognized for all deductible temporary differences and net operating loss and tax credit carry forwards and then nonadmitted in accordance with **SSAP No. 10, paragraph 10**. Recompute the nonadmitted deferred tax asset. See **SSAP No. 10, Exhibit A** for further guidance on admission test.	AC EX VA			
23. Recompute the net change in deferred tax included in the surplus section as the change during the period in the deferred tax liabilities and assets.	AC EX VA			

	Exam Obj.	Completion Date	Examiner	Work Paper Ref.
Presentation of Income Taxes				
24. Determine in a statement of financial position that the deferred asset and liability are offset and presented as a single amount and that the current provision for income taxes are presented either as a recoverable or a payable in accordance with **SSAP No. 10, Exhibit A, Question 12**. Also determine that the company has properly reported changes in net deferred income taxes, unrealized gains and losses net of tax and the change in nonadmitted deferred tax assets in the surplus section of the income statement.	AC EX PD			
25. Determine that the provisions of **SSAP No. 10, paragraphs 18-22** are properly disclosed in the Notes to the Financial Statements. (Further guidance can be obtained from **SSAP No. 10, Exhibit A, Question 12.**)	PD			
26. In the case of a reporting company that files a consolidated income tax return with one or more affiliates, income tax transactions (including payment of tax contingencies to its parent) between the affiliated parties shall be recognized if:	AC EX			
a. Such transactions are economic transactions as defined in **SSAP No. 25**; are pursuant to a written income tax allocation agreement; and income taxes incurred are accounted for in a manner consistent with the principles of FAS 109.	EX			
b. Determine that amounts owed to a company pursuant to a recognized transaction are treated as a loan or advance, and nonadmitted, pursuant to **SSAP No. 25**, to the extent that the recoverable is not settled within 90 days of the filing of a consolidated income tax return, or where a refund is due the reporting company's parent, within 90 days of the receipt of such refund.	AC EX			

	Exam Obj.	Completion Date	Examiner	Work Paper Ref.
27. In the case of a company that files a consolidated income tax return with one or more affiliates, determine that the disclosure required by **SSAP No. 10, paragraph 23** is properly included in the Notes to the Financial Statements. (Further guidance is available in **SSAP No. 10, Exhibit A, Question 12**.	EX AC			
28. Ensure compliance with the state of domicile's insurance code with regard to the above annual statement line items.	CM			
TAXES, LICENSES AND FEES				
1. Review the company's accounting system and verify that all taxes, licenses and fees are properly included in this account.	AC			
2. Trace total year end accruals for all taxes, licenses and fees from the records and work papers to the general ledger and balance sheet.	AC			
Real Estate Taxes				
3. Determine that all real estate holdings in Schedule A are included in tax records and work papers.	AC			
4. Select a sample of real estate tax bills and payments and verify the following:	AC EX			
a. Determine that bills and payments cover the proper time period; and	AC			
b. Verify that payments were made in the proper amount.	AC			
State Taxes on Premiums				
5. Verify the premium tax base by reconciling Schedule T (premium revenues by state) with the general ledger and income statement.	AC			
6. Select a sample of states from the records, files and work papers and recompute the premium tax due or accrued.	AC			

	Exam Obj.	Completion Date	Examiner	Work Paper Ref.
7. Review the state insurance regulation governing taxes on premiums to determine:	CM			
a. Premiums to be taxed; and	CM			
b. Amount or rate of taxation.	CM			
8. Select from the records a sample of payments and trace amounts to the cancelled checks.	AC EX			
State Insurance Department Licenses and Fees				
9. Select a sample of payments from the records and work papers of state insurance department licenses and fees:	AC EX			
a. Trace the amount and date of payment to the invoice and tax return.	AC			
10. Select a sample of license and fee invoices that had not been paid as of the balance sheet date and verify that:	AC EX			
a. The correct amount was listed as a payable on the work papers and records; and	AC			
b. Payment was made subsequent to the balance sheet date or the payable is still on the records for the current year.	AC			
11. Perform procedures to verify that the property and casualty guarantee fund assessments are appropriate and properly included in taxes, licenses, and fees as required by **SSAP No. 35, paragraph 4**.	AC VA			
12. Verify tax payments and amounts due and accrued for state and federal payroll taxes.	AC EX VA			
a. For sample periods, trace salary amounts paid from the payroll tax records to the corresponding tax returns.	AC			
b. Further trace payments from the tax returns to cash disbursements and cancelled checks.	AC			

	Exam Obj.	Completion Date	Examiner	Work Paper Ref.
c. Recalculate amounts due or accrued at year-end by examining payroll records and work papers.	VA			
d. Trace amounts accrued or due to payments made subsequent to the balance sheet date.	AC			
13. Compare amounts due or accrued with those for previous period and account for any significant differences.	AC			
14. Verify the accuracy of the amounts due or accrued for other miscellaneous taxes.	AC			

SECTION M — OPERATING CYCLE: AFFILIATE & OTHER RELATED PARTY TRANSACTIONS

The procedures included within this document should be completed if deemed necessary by the examiner in accordance with the overall risk assessment. Each of the items referenced in this document may not be present in every company under examination. The examiner should clearly identify the sections that are pertinent and remove or mark-out the remaining sections.

Annual Statement Blank Line Items

Receivable (Amount Due from) Parent, Subsidiaries and Affiliates
Payable (Amount Due to) Parent, Subsidiaries and Affiliates

NOTE: Transactions resulting from related party tax sharing and reinsurance agreements are to be reported on the appropriate tax and reinsurance financial statement line items.

Relevant SSAP's Include:

#15, Debt and Holding Company Obligations
#25, Accounting for and Disclosures about Transactions with Affiliates and Other Related Parties
#64, Offsetting and Netting of Assets and Liabilities
#67, Other Liabilities

SPECIFIC RISK ANALYSIS WORKPAPERS

Risk Analysis Prepared By/Date______________________________

Planning Exam Analysis Prepared By/Date______________________________

Reviewed By/Date______________________________

EXAMINATION OBJECTIVE:

1. Related parties are identified and all transactions of related parties are reviewed for propriety, recorded accurately on a timely basis, and terms are fair and reasonable. (Existence, Completeness, Compliance and Accuracy)

INHERENT RISKS

INTERNAL AND EXTERNAL ENVIRONMENTAL CONDITIONS/FACTORS

RESULTS OF DETAIL ANALYTICAL REVIEW PROCEDURES

CONTROL RISK — OPERATING CYCLE: AFFILIATE & OTHER RELATED PARTY TRANSACTIONS

This questionnaire is designed to assist the examiner in assessing control risk for affiliate and other related party transactions. Part 1, Section III and Part 3 of this *Handbook* provides guidance in consideration of an insurer's internal control structure for use when designing substantive examination procedures.

This questionnaire includes examples of internal control procedures and policies that are commonly utilized by insurers to achieve internal control objectives. For each control procedure listed, indicate whether or not the insurer employs such a procedure, or other similar practice (include a description of the similar procedure). To the extent the control procedure is not applicable, indicate N/A. If other relevant control procedures are in place, list them in the space that follows. Control procedures that are tested by the examiner should be documented by including the workpaper reference in the comment section and the examiner's initials in the reliance column.

For each individual control procedure there is a control objective listed that satisfies the procedure.

If the examiner initially assesses control risk as low or medium for a particular account balance, then those controls must be tested. The controls should be tested to determine whether the procedure is operating as expected, applied throughout the entire period of reliance, performed on a timely basis, encompassing all transactions and identifying errors. Some examples of testing procedures are inquiry, observation, re-performance and examination of documents. The level of reliance, if any, should be indicated in the applicable column along with any comments the examiner may have regarding the procedure.

Based upon the testing results, the examiner should determine whether the preliminary control risk assessment is confirmed or should be revised.

CONTROL OBJECTIVES

Authorization (AU) – All transactions recorded were reviewed and approved by designated personnel.

Completeness (CO) – All transactions that occurred are initially entered into the accounting records, accepted for processing and generated data files and reports reflect that all transactions have occurred.

Accuracy (AC) – Transactions are initially recorded correctly, timely and accurately.

Asset Protection (AP) – Adequate safeguards over access to and use of assets and records, including the appropriate segregation of duties among company personnel.

	Control Obj.	Y	N	Work Paper Ref.	Reliance
General Control Procedures					
The examiner should determine the amount of documentation necessary for each control procedure. If the examiner intends to place substantial reliance on the established control, the examiner should explain the control procedure in a workpaper and document the individual responsible for supervising the control activity as well as the frequency of the control activity.					
1. Are all contracts between related parties reviewed to determine that the terms are fair and reasonable?	AU AC				
2. Does management review the accounting of related party transactions to verify that the company has utilized the proper valuation method required in **SSAP No. 25, paragraph 14**?	AU AC				
3. Are affiliate transactions/agreements, which are subject to the Holding Company Act, reported to the commissioner on a timely basis?	AU				
4. Does the company maintain records so that individual balances are easily identifiable in the aggregate intercompany balances?	AC CO				
5. Does management periodically review settlements to ensure the settlements comply with the approved provisions of the agreement?	AC CO				
6. Does the company appropriately exclude amounts resulting from tax sharing and reinsurance agreements from Receivable/Payable to Parent, Subsidiary and Affiliate accounts?	AC				

OTHER KEY CONTROLS EXISTING FOR THIS EXAMINATION OBJECTIVE:

SUMMARY EVALUATION OF CONTROL RISK:

EVALUATION OF INDEPENDENT CPA'S WORK FOR THIS EXAMINATION (CPA REVIEW CHECKLIST):

OVERALL RISK ASSESSMENT

Balance Sheet Evaluation of the Likelihood of a Material Adjustment to Surplus:

The evaluation of the likelihood of a material adjustment to surplus should be based on the following criteria:

- Inherent Risk
- Internal and External Environmental Factors
- Control Risk
- Materiality Consideration

The examiner should rate each item as to the likelihood of a material misstatement. All items are assumed as "High" prior to any examiner evaluation. A "High" assessment requires the examiner to perform substantive examination procedures over that account area. A lower assessment allows the examiner to perform analytical or fewer substantive procedures to satisfy the examination requirements. If an assessment other than "High" is selected for any of the accounts, the examiner needs to document the basis for the assessment. If the assessment is based on control testwork, the documentation should include results of control procedures and related workpaper references.

1) "Receivable (Amount Due from) Parent, Subsidiaries and Affiliates"

___________ High ___________ Medium ___________Low

Basis for Assessment:

____

____

____

2) "Payable (Amount Due to) Parent, Subsidiaries and Affiliates"

___________ High ___________ Medium ___________Low

Basis for Assessment:

____

____

____

PRELIMINARY EXAMINATION APPROACH — OPERATIONS CYCLE: AFFILIATE AND OTHER RELATED PARTY TRANSACTIONS

Listed below are the corresponding Annual Statement line items that are related to the procedures contained in this Operating Specific Risk Analysis:

Receivable (Amount Due from) Parent, Subsidiaries and Affiliates
Payable (Amount Due to) Parent, Subsidiaries and Affiliates

The actual examination procedures selected to be performed is a matter of considerable judgment by the examiner. The following "Examination Program" includes examples of procedures commonly used.

To the extent that the examiner judgmentally determines whether it is appropriate to use the following procedures, that selection can be documented by checking the space next to such procedure, with modifications noted in the margin. The examiner may determine that alternative or additional procedures are required. If so, those procedures can be added on a supplemental sheet. The examiner performing the procedure should indicate satisfactory completion by initialing and dating in the space provided, and referencing the workpapers where the procedures and findings are documented.

The examiner may choose to apply the examination procedures to less than 100% of the items comprising an account balance. Guidance for audit sampling and control and substantive procedures can be found in Part 3 of the NAIC *Financial Condition Examiners Handbook.*

After each examination procedure, the examination objective that the procedure satisfies is indicated. The examination objectives are accuracy, completeness, compliance, cutoff, existence, obligation and ownership, valuation and presentation and disclosure.

Note: Although year-end financial statement balances pertaining to affiliates and other related parties may be under the tolerable error threshold established for the examination and considered immaterial, the examiner should utilize this specific risk analysis to investigate the affiliate and other related party contracts and transactions that were conducted throughout the year for compliance with statutory guidelines.

EXAMINATION OBJECTIVES

Accuracy (AC) – Recorded transactions and account balances are mathematically accurate, are based on correct amounts and have been classified in the correct account.

Completeness (CO) – All transactions and account balances that should be recorded in the annual financial statements were recorded.

Compliance (CM) – Business transactions and affairs have been conducted in accordance with state insurance codes, other state laws or department directives.

Cutoff (CT) – All transactions are recorded in the correct accounting period.

Existence (EX) – Recorded transactions occurred and are not fictitious and recorded assets and liabilities existed as of the balance sheet date.

Obligation (OB) and Ownership (OW) – Recorded liabilities are obligations of the company and recorded assets are the rights of the company at the balance sheet date.

Valuation (VA) – Assets and liabilities are valued in accordance with state statute and NAIC accounting guidance.

Presentation and Disclosure (PD) – The elements of the Annual Statement are properly classified and all disclosures are accurately included in the Annual Statement.

Procedure	Exam Obj.	Completion Date	Examiner	Work Paper Ref.
EXAMINATION PROCEDURES				
<u>General Procedures</u>				
1. Identify related parties in accordance with the listing and characteristics provided in **SSAP No. 25, paragraphs 2-5**.	AC EX			
a. Obtain a list of all related parties from management. In addition to other recognized affiliates and related parties, this list should include pension funds and other trusts established for employees, major borrowers and lenders, and significant agents, brokers, producers and providers.	AC EX			
b. Request and review the conflict of interest questionnaires for officers, directors and key employees.	AC EX			
c. Obtain and review the organization chart of the company and related affiliates.	AC EX			
d. Review the Annual Statement Filing, including the General Interrogatories, Notes to Financial Statements and Schedule Y.	AC EX			
e. Review the board of director minutes for disclosure and approval of affiliate contracts.	AC EX			
f. Review the holding company filing for disclosure and approval of affiliate contracts.	AC EX			
2. Obtain and review the significant contracts between the company and its affiliates. Verify that the company is operating in accordance with approved contract terms.	AC EX			
3. Review the general ledger accounts for unreported transactions with affiliates.	EX CO			

	Exam Obj.	Completion Date	Examiner	Work Paper Ref.
4. Review material investment transactions during the period under examination to determine whether the nature and extent of investments during the period create related parties. **SSAP No. 46** provides guidance on investments in subsidiaries, controlled and affiliated entities (SCAs).	AC EX CO			
5. Review tabulations, if any, that summarize the volume of business with various customers or agents to assist in identifying situations that may involve related parties.	AC EX			
6. Review accounting records for large, unusual or nonrecurring transactions or balances, paying particular attention to transactions recognized at or near the end of the accounting period.	EX CO			
7. Refer to financial publications, trade journals, credit agencies and other sources of information if it is suspected that any related party, with which material amounts of business have been transacted, may lack substance.	EX CO			
8. Review the financial statements and related disclosures of the affiliate companies. If permissible, ascertain the affiliate company's methods to report related party/affiliate transactions.	PD			
Receivable (Amount Due from)/Payable (Amount Due to) Parent, Subsidiaries and Affiliates				
Note: *Although the year-end receivable/payable balance pertaining to affiliates and other related parties may be under the tolerable error threshold established for the examination and considered immaterial, the examiner should investigate the affiliate and other related party contracts and transactions that were conducted throughout the year for compliance with statutory guidelines.*				
1. Obtain detail of the receivables (amount due from) and payables (amount due to) parents, subsidiaries, and affiliates and agree to the company's general ledger.	EX AC			

		Exam Obj.	Completion Date	Examiner	Work Paper Ref.
2.	From the detail obtained, review the related party transactions and the respective related party contracts. Identify whether the balance includes receivables/payables for services or loans and/or advances made by the company.	EX AC			
3.	Review the related party transactions and determine whether they are arm's-length and properly reported as economic or non-economic in accordance with **SSAP No. 25, paragraphs 10-13**.	AC			
4.	Verify that the accounting for the related party transactions have been properly reported in accordance with **SSAP No. 25, paragraph 14**.	AC			
5.	Review settlements between related parties to determine reasonableness and consistency. Perform subsequent procedures to verify collectibility and the reported liability.	EX AC			
6.	Identify any offsets between affiliates and related parties and verify that the required conditions necessary to permit the offset have been met in accordance with **SSAP No. 64, paragraph 5**.	EX AC			
7.	Perform examination procedures to ascertain and verify the assets and liabilities that have been offset.	EX AC			
8.	Verify that all necessary disclosures have been properly reported in accordance with **SSAP No. 25, paragraphs 17-18**.	PD			
	Loans or Advances				
9.	Obtain documentation supporting any outstanding loans or advances between related parties. Determine whether the loans or advances were between the company's parent or affiliate, or other related parties.	EX AC			
10.	Perform procedures to determine if the outstanding loan or advance is properly recorded as admitted or non-admitted in accordance with **SSAP No. 25, paragraphs 6-9**.	AC			

	Exam Obj.	Completion Date	Examiner	Work Paper Ref.
11. For loans or advances to related parties perform subsequent receipt procedures and send confirmations to verify amounts and collectibility of reported loan balances.	EX AC			
12. For loans or advances payable to related parties perform a search for unreported liabilities to verify the established liability.	EX AC			
13. Verify required disclosures have been properly reported in accordance with **SSAP No. 25, paragraphs 17-18**.	PD			
Transaction Involving Services				
14. Obtain documentation supporting any receivables or payables pertaining to services provided between related parties.	EX AC			
15. Verify that the amounts charged for services is considered an arm's-length transaction in accordance with **SSAP No. 25, paragraph 15**.	AC			
16. For those service transactions that are not deemed to be arm's-length, verify that the financial statements have been properly adjusted to correctly reflect the transaction in accordance with **SSAP No. 25, paragraph 16**.	AC			
17. Consider whether service transactions are occurring but are not being given accounting recognition, such as receiving or providing accounting, management or other services at no charge to a related party. Determine the materiality of such transactions and the impact on the company.	EX AC			
18. For receivables from related party service transactions, perform subsequent receipt procedures and send confirmations to verify the amount and collectibility of the reported balances.	EX AC			
19. For payables from related party service transactions, perform a search for unrecorded liabilities to verify the established liability.	EX AC			
20. Verify that all necessary disclosures required by **SSAP No. 25, paragraphs 17-18** have been properly reported.	PD			

SECTION N — OPERATING CYCLE: OTHER EXPENSES

The procedures included within this document should be completed if deemed necessary by the examiner in accordance with the overall risk assessment. Each of the items referenced in this document may not be present in every company under examination. The examiner should clearly identify the sections that are pertinent and remove or mark-out the remaining sections.

Annual Statement Blank Line Items

Other Expenses

SPECIFIC RISK ANALYSIS WORK PAPERS

Risk Analysis Prepared By/Date____

Planning Exam Analysis Prepared By/Date___________________________________

Reviewed By/Date____

EXAMINATION OBJECTIVE:

1. Other expenses are authorized and recorded correctly as to account, amount and period.

INHERENT RISKS

INTERNAL AND EXTERNAL ENVIRONMENTAL CONDITIONS/FACTORS

RESULTS OF DETAIL ANALYTICAL REVIEW PROCEDURES

CONTROL RISK — OPERATING CYCLE: OTHER EXPENSES

This questionnaire is designed to assist the examiner in assessing control risk for other expenses operating cycles. Part 1, Section III and Part 3 of this *Handbook* provides guidance in consideration of an insurer's internal control structure for use when designing substantive examination procedures.

This questionnaire includes examples of internal control procedures and policies that are commonly utilized by insurers to achieve internal control objectives. For each control procedure listed below, indicate by placing a check mark in the yes or no box whether or not the insurer employs such a procedure, or other similar practice (include a description of the similar procedure). To the extent the control procedure is not applicable, indicate N/A. If other relevant control procedures are in place, list them in the space that follows. Control procedures that are tested by the examiner should be documented by including the workpaper reference in the comment section and the examiner's initials in the reliance column.

For each individual control procedure there is a control objective listed that satisfies the procedure.

If the examiner initially assesses control risk as low or medium for a particular account balance, then those controls must be tested. The controls should be tested to determine whether the procedure is operating as expected, applied throughout the entire period of reliance, performed on a timely basis, encompassing all transactions and identifying errors. Some examples of testing procedures are inquiry, observation, re-performance and examination of documents. The level of reliance, if any, should be indicated in the applicable column along with any comments the examiner may have regarding the procedure.

Based upon the testing results, the examiner should determine whether the preliminary control risk assessment is confirmed or should be revised.

CONTROL OBJECTIVES

Authorization (AU) – All transactions recorded were reviewed and approved by designated personnel.

Completeness (CO) – All transactions that occurred are initially entered into the accounting records, accepted for processing, and generated data files and reports reflect that all transactions have occurred.

Accuracy (AC) – Transactions are initially recorded correctly, timely and accurately.

Asset Protection (AP) – Adequate safeguards over access to and use of assets and records, including the appropriate segregation of duties among company personnel.

	Control Obj.	Y	N	Work Paper Ref.	Reliance
General Control Procedures					
The examiner should determine the amount of documentation necessary for each control procedure. If the examiner intends to place substantial reliance on the established control, the examiner should explain the control procedure in a workpaper and document the individual responsible for supervising the control activity as well as the frequency of the control activity.					
1. Are the receiving documentation, purchase approvals, and invoices matched before recording a liability?	AC				
2. Are invoices registered immediately upon receipt? Are duplicate invoices identified?	AC				
3. Is the account distribution reviewed when recording a liability or signing a check?	AU AC				
4. Are unmatched invoices investigated for inclusion into the estimated liability at the close of a period?	AC				
5. Do procedures exist for reporting isolated events (e.g., insolvency pool / guaranty fund assessments) to accounting personnel for approval?	AU				

OTHER KEY CONTROLS EXISTING FOR THIS EXAMINATION OBJECTIVE:

SUMMARY EVALUATION OF CONTROL RISK:

EVALUATION OF INDEPENDENT CPA'S WORK FOR THIS EXAMINATION (CPA REVIEW CHECKLIST):

OVERALL RISK ASSESSMENT

Balance Sheet Evaluation of the Likelihood of a Material Adjustment to Surplus:

The evaluation of the likelihood of a material adjustment to surplus should be based on the following criteria:

- Inherent Risk
- Internal & External Environmental Factors
- Control Risk
- Materiality Consideration

The examiner should rate each item as to the likelihood of a material misstatement. All items are assumed as 'High' prior to any examiner evaluation. A 'High' assessment requires the examiner to perform substantive examination procedures over that account area. A lower assessment allows the examiner to perform analytical or fewer substantive procedures to satisfy the examination requirements. If an assessment other than 'High' is selected for any of the accounts, the examiner needs to document the basis for the assessment. If the assessment is based on control testwork, the documentation should include results of control procedures and related workpaper references.

1) "Other Expenses"

___________ High ___________ Medium ___________Low

Basis for Assessment:

____

____

____

PRELIMINARY EXAMINATION APPROACH — OPERATING CYCLE: OTHER EXPENSES

Listed below are the corresponding Annual Statement line items that are related to the procedures contained in this Operating Cycle Specific Risk Analysis:

Other Expenses

The actual examination procedures selected to be performed is a matter of considerable judgment by the examiner. The following "Examination Program" includes examples of procedures commonly used.

To the extent that the examiner judgmentally determines whether it is appropriate to use the following procedures, that selection can be documented by checking the space next to such procedure, with modifications noted in the margin. The examiner may determine that alternative or additional procedures are required. If so, those procedures can be added on a supplemental sheet. The examiner performing the procedure should indicate satisfactory completion by initialing and dating in the space provided, and referencing the work papers where the procedures and findings are documented.

The examiner may choose to apply the examination procedures to less than 100% of the items comprising an account balance. Guidance for audit sampling and control and substantive procedures can be found in Part 3 of the NAIC *Financial Condition Examiners Handbook.*

After each examination procedure, the examination objective that the procedure satisfies is indicated. The examination objectives are accuracy, completeness, compliance, cutoff, existence, obligation and ownership, valuation and presentation and disclosure.

EXAMINATION OBJECTIVES

Accuracy (AC) – Recorded transactions and account balances are mathematically accurate, are based on correct amounts and have been classified into the correct account.

Completeness (CO) – All transactions and account balances that should be recorded in the Annual financial statement were recorded.

Compliance (CM) – Business transactions and affairs have been conducted in accordance with state insurance codes, other state laws or department directives.

Cutoff (CT) – All transactions are recorded in the correct accounting period.

Existence (EX) – Recorded transactions occurred and are not fictitious and recorded assets and liabilities existed as of the balance sheet date.

Obligation (OB) and Ownership (OW) – Recorded liabilities are obligations of the company and recorded assets are the rights of the company at the balance sheet date.

Valuation (VA) – Assets and liabilities are valued in accordance with state statute and NAIC accounting guidance.

Presentation and Disclosure (PD) – The elements of the Annual Statement are properly classified and all disclosures are accurately included in the Annual Statement.

	Exam Obj.	Completion Date	Examiner	Work Paper Ref.
EXAMINATION PROCEDURES				
<u>Other Expenses</u>				
1. Identify the detailed ledgers and payroll records that account for all general expenses for each vendor or employee. Perform procedure to verify the accuracy and completeness of these ledgers and payroll records.	AC EX			
2. Review the company's treatment of all expenses and verify that all head office and branch office general expenses are properly included in the account.	AC EX			
3. Check expense payments made after the "as of" date to the expenses included in the liability.	AC EX CO			
4. Determine the reasonableness of due and unpaid expenses by comparing this year's amounts in prior years. Compare major components of expenses with prior periods and budget estimates.	AC EX CO VA			

SECTION O — OPERATING CYCLE: BORROWED MONEY AND SURPLUS

The procedures included within this document should be completed if deemed necessary by the examiner in accordance with the overall risk assessment. Each of the items referenced in this document may not be present in every company under examination. The examiner should clearly identify the sections that are pertinent and remove or mark-out the remaining sections.

Annual Statement Blank Line Items

Borrowed Money
Capital and Surplus

Relevant SSAP's Include

#72, Surplus and Quasi-reorganizations

SPECIFIC RISK ANALYSIS WORKPAPERS

Risk Analysis Prepared By/Date______________________________

Planning Exam Analysis Prepared By/Date______________________________

Reviewed By/Date______________________________

EXAMINATION OBJECTIVES:

1. Borrowed money is properly stated and interest expense and accrued interest are proper. (Accuracy)
2. Surplus and equity are properly stated and reflect adjustments from related accounts. (Accuracy and Existence)

INHERENT RISKS

INTERNAL AND EXTERNAL ENVIRONMENTAL CONDITIONS/FACTORS

RESULTS OF DETAIL ANALYTICAL REVIEW PROCEDURES

CONTROL RISK — OPERATING CYCLE: BORROWED MONEY AND SURPLUS

This questionnaire is designed to assist the examiner in assessing control risk for borrowed money and capital cycles. Part 1, Section III and Part 3 of this *Handbook* provides guidance in consideration of an insurer's internal control structure for use when designing substantive examination procedures.

This questionnaire includes examples of internal control procedures and policies that are commonly utilized by insurers to achieve internal control objectives. For each control procedure listed below, indicate by placing a check mark in the yes or no box whether or not the insurer employs such a procedure, or other similar practice (include a description of the similar procedure). To the extent the control procedure is not applicable, indicate N/A. If other relevant control procedures are in place, list them in the space that follows. Control procedures that are tested by the examiner should be documented by including the workpaper reference in the comment section and the examiner's initials in the reliance column.

For each individual control procedure there is a control objective listed that satisfies the procedure.

If the examiner initially assesses control risk as low or medium for a particular account balance, then those controls must be tested. The controls should be tested to determine whether the procedure is operating as expected, applied throughout the entire period of reliance, performed on a timely basis, encompassing all transactions and identifying errors. Some examples of testing procedures are inquiry, observation, re-performance, and examination of documents. The level of reliance, if any, should be indicated in the applicable column along with any comments the examiner may have regarding the procedure.

Based upon the testing results, the examiner should determine whether the preliminary control risk assessment is confirmed or should be revised.

CONTROL OBJECTIVES

Authorization (AU) – All transactions recorded were reviewed and approved by designated personnel.

Completeness (CO) – All transactions that occurred are initially entered into the accounting records, accepted for processing and generated data files and reports reflect that all transactions have occurred.

Accuracy (AC) – Transactions are initially recorded correctly, timely and accurately.

Asset Protection (AP) – Adequate safeguards over access to and use of assets and records, including the appropriate segregation of duties among company personnel.

	Control Obj.	Y	N	Work Paper Ref.	Reliance
General Control Procedures					
The examiner should determine the amount of documentation necessary for each control procedure. If the examiner intends to place substantial reliance on the established control, the examiner should explain the control procedure in a workpaper and document the individual responsible for supervising the control activity as well as the frequency of the control activity.					
Borrowed Money					
1. Does the company regularly review and adequately document debt compliance?	AU				
2. Are significant debt arrangements reviewed and approved by the board of directors or a management team appointed by the board of directors?	AU				
3. Are significant debt contracts reviewed for unusual terms?	AU AC				
4. Are cash flow projections performed to determine adequacy of flows to service the debt?	AC				
Capital and Surplus					
1. Are surplus and related equity accounts reconciled between periods?	AU AC				
2. Are stock registers properly controlled and is stock outstanding reconciled to the general ledger?	AU AC				
3. Are stock issuances reviewed to be in compliance with statutory requirements?	AU CM				
4. Are surplus note registers reconciled to the general ledger and are repayments of notes reviewed for authorization and agreed to terms permitted statutorily?	AU AC				

OTHER KEY CONTROLS EXISTING FOR THIS EXAMINATION OBJECTIVE:

SUMMARY EVALUATION OF CONTROL RISK:

EVALUATION OF INDEPENDENT CPA'S WORK FOR THIS EXAMINATION (CPA REVIEW CHECKLIST):

OVERALL RISK ASSESSMENT

Balance Sheet Evaluation of the Likelihood of a Material Adjustment to Surplus:

The evaluation of the likelihood of a material adjustment to surplus should be based on the following criteria:

- Inherent Risk
- Internal & External Environmental Factors
- Control Risk
- Materiality Consideration

The examiner should rate each item as to the likelihood of a material misstatement. All items are assumed as "High" prior to any examiner evaluation. A "High" assessment requires the examiner to perform substantive examination procedures over that account area. A lower assessment allows the examiner to perform analytical or fewer substantive procedures to satisfy the examination requirements. If an assessment other than "High" is selected for any of the accounts, the examiner needs to document the basis for the assessment. If the assessment is based on control testwork, the documentation should include results of control procedures and related workpaper references.

1) "Borrowed Money"

____________ High ____________ Medium ____________ Low

Basis for Assessment:

____

____

____

2) "Capital and Surplus"

____________ High ____________ Medium ____________ Low

Basis for Assessment:

____

____

____

PRELIMINARY EXAMINATION APPROACH — OPERATING CYCLE: BORROWED MONEY AND SURPLUS

Listed below are the corresponding Annual Statement line items that are related to the procedures contained in this Operating Specific Risk Analysis:

Borrowed Money
Capital and Surplus

The actual examination procedures selected to be performed is a matter of considerable judgment by the examiner. The following "Examination Program" includes examples of procedures commonly used.

To the extent that the examiner judgmentally determines whether it is appropriate to use the following procedures, that selection can be documented by checking the space next to such procedure, with modifications noted in the margin. The examiner may determine that alternative or additional procedures are required. If so, those procedures can be added on a supplemental sheet. The examiner performing the procedure should indicate satisfactory completion by initialing and dating in the space provided, and referencing the workpapers where the procedures and findings are documented.

The examiner may choose to apply the examination procedures to less than 100% of the items comprising an account balance. Guidance for audit sampling and control and substantive procedures can be found in Part 3 of the NAIC *Financial Condition Examiners Handbook.*

After each examination procedure, the examination objective that the procedure satisfies is indicated. The examination objectives are accuracy, completeness, compliance, cutoff, existence, obligation and ownership, valuation and presentation and disclosure.

EXAMINATION OBJECTIVES

Accuracy (AC) – Recorded transactions and account balances are mathematically accurate, are based on correct amounts and have been classified into the correct account.

Completeness (CO) – All transactions and account balances that should be recorded in the annual financial statement were recorded.

Compliance (CM) – Business transactions and affairs have been conducted in accordance with state insurance codes, other state laws or department directives.

Cutoff (CT) – All transactions are recorded in the correct accounting period.

Existence (EX) – Recorded transactions occurred and are not fictitious and recorded assets and liabilities existed as of the balance sheet date.

Obligation (OB) and Ownership (OW) – Recorded liabilities are obligations of the company and recorded assets are the rights of the company at the balance sheet date.

Valuation (VA) – Assets and liabilities are valued in accordance with state statute and NAIC accounting guidance.

Presentation and Disclosure (PD) – The elements of the Annual Statement are properly classified and all disclosures are accurately included in the Annual Statement.

	Exam Obj.	Completion Date	Examiner	Work Paper Ref.
EXAMINATION PROCEDURES				
Borrowed Money				
1. Obtain the detailed inventory of outstanding liabilities for loans secured by mortgages on company real estate and verify the following:	AC EX			
a. Original amount of money borrowed;	AC EX			
b. Date money borrowed;	AC EX			
c. Maturity date of note or agreement;	AC EX			
d. Interest date;	AC EX			
e. Interest accrued and owed to date;	AC EX			
f. Loan balance outstanding;	AC EX			
g. Mode of payment; and	AC EX			
h. Status (current or in arrears).	AC EX			
2. Confirm balances with lenders.	AC CO			
3. Check minutes and other records of board of directors, executive, investment or finance committee for proper authorization.	AC			
4. Make inquiries to ascertain any conflicts of interest or improprieties affecting the directors, officers or employees of the company.	EX			
5. Reconcile the total outstanding borrowed money in the borrowed money inventory with the year-end general ledger.	AC EX			
6. Trace total amounts of borrowed money from the general ledger to the annual statement.	AC EX			

	Exam Obj.	Completion Date	Examiner	Work Paper Ref.
Capital and Surplus				
Capital Stock				
1. Reconcile stock ledger with general ledger and verify outstanding shares.	AC EX			
2. Investigate distribution of stock holdings, especially as to control held by small group.	AC EX			
3. In case of issuance of company stock where statute requires a permit, ascertain that such issuance is in conformity with terms of permit.	AC EX CM			
4. If the dollar amount of capital stock issued and outstanding is greater than the multiple of the par value times the number of shares outstanding, explain the basis and method by which such increment was added.	AC VA			
Guaranty Fund				
5. Determine amount, validity and legality.	AC CM VA			
Outstanding Contribution Certificates or Other Advances to Surplus				
6. Determine legality, including compliance with any state permits.	CM			
7. Verify amount outstanding.	AC VA			
8. Ascertain that such advances have been properly shown in the annual statement.	PD			
9. Set forth in the report the significant terms of contract under which such advances were made.	AC			

SECTION P — OPERATING CYCLE: FINANCIAL REPORTING

The procedures included within this document should be completed if deemed necessary by the examiner in accordance with the overall risk assessment. Each of the items referenced in this document may not be present in every company under examination. The examiner should clearly identify the sections that are pertinent and remove or mark-out the remaining sections.

Annual Statement Blank Line Items

Accounts and Records
Commitments and Contingent Liabilities
Management and Control
Fidelity Bonds
Territory and Plan of Operation
Risk-Based Capital
Privacy of Non-Public Financial Information
Privacy of Non-Public Health Information

Note: The procedures included in this cycle relative to Privacy of Non-Public Financial Information and Privacy of Non-Public Health Information were designed to be utilized by the examiner in performing an abbreviated review of said areas, to the extent deemed necessary. If the examiner determines that additional regulatory attention should be given to the company's policies and procedures for privacy, that determination should be communicated to the appropriate market conduct personnel in their state. The NAIC has adopted several sets of privacy requirements, and examiners should be aware of which requirement(s) their state imposes before performing these procedures. Information regarding these requirements can be found in the NAIC *Market Conduct Examiners Handbook.*

SPECIFIC RISK ANALYSIS WORK PAPERS

Risk Analysis Prepared By/Date______________________________

Planning Exam Analysis Prepared By/Date______________________________

Reviewed By/Date______________________________

EXAMINATION OBJECTIVES:

1. Financial information is recorded accurately, reported on a timely basis and is representative of the conditions at the reporting date.

2. Non-public financial and health information is properly protected.

INHERENT RISKS

INTERNAL AND EXTERNAL ENVIRONMENTAL CONDITIONS/FACTORS

RESULTS OF DETAIL ANALYTICAL REVIEW PROCEDURES

CONTROL RISK — OPERATING CYCLE: FINANCIAL REPORTING

This questionnaire is designed to assist the examiner in assessing control risk for financial reporting cycles. Part 1, Section III and Part 3 of this *Handbook* provides guidance in consideration of an insurer's internal control structure for use when designing substantive examination procedures.

This questionnaire includes examples of internal control procedures and policies that are commonly utilized by insurers to achieve internal control objectives. For each control procedure listed below, indicate by placing a check mark in the yes or no box whether or not the insurer employs such a procedure, or other similar practice (include a description of the similar procedure). To the extent the control procedure is not applicable, indicate N/A. If other relevant control procedures are in place, list them in the space that follows. Control procedures that are tested by the examiner should be documented by including the workpaper reference in the comment section and the examiner's initials in the reliance column.

For each individual control procedure there is a control objective listed that satisfies the procedure.

If the examiner initially assesses control risk as low or medium for a particular account balance, then those controls must be tested. The controls should be tested to determine whether the procedure is operating as expected, applied throughout the entire period of reliance, performed on a timely basis, encompassing all transactions and identifying errors. Some examples of testing procedures are inquiry, observation, re-performance, and examination of documents. The level of reliance, if any, should be indicated in the applicable column along with any comments the examiner may have regarding the procedure.

Based upon the testing results, the examiner should determine whether the preliminary control risk assessment is confirmed or should be revised.

CONTROL OBJECTIVES

Authorization (AU) – All transactions recorded were reviewed and approved by designated personnel.

Completeness (CO) – All transactions that occurred are initially entered into the accounting records, accepted for processing, and generated data files and reports reflect that all transactions have occurred.

Accuracy (AC) – Transactions are initially recorded correctly, timely and accurately.

Asset Protection (AP) – Adequate safeguards over access to and use of assets and records, including the appropriate segregation of duties among company personnel.

	Control Obj.	Y	N	Work Paper Ref.	Reliance
General Control Procedures					
The examiner should determine the amount of documentation necessary for each control procedure. If the examiner intends to place substantial reliance on the established control, the examiner should explain the control procedure in a workpaper and document the individual responsible for supervising the control activity as well as the frequency of the control activity.					
1. Does management review the financial reporting package and identify/follow-up on unusual items?	AU				
2. Does management communicate with counsel on a regular basis, identify all outstanding potential litigation and assess the need for accounting consideration and in addition assess compliance with state regulators?	AU AC				
3. Are consolidating/eliminating entries reviewed for reasonableness and consistency?	AC				
4. Is the clerical accuracy of reported financial data tested (manually or electronically)?	AC AU				
5. Does management regularly identify and quantify relationships with related parties?	AC AU				
6. Does management identify all significant subsequent events and consider the accounting implications?	AC				
7. Does management review all significant contracts entered into and consider accounting implications?	AC				
8. Has the company established formal privacy policies and procedures to ensure against the unauthorized release of non-public financial information?	AU				

OTHER KEY CONTROLS EXISTING FOR THIS EXAMINATION OBJECTIVE:

SUMMARY EVALUATION OF CONTROL RISK:

EVALUATION OF INDEPENDENT CPA'S WORK FOR THIS EXAMINATION (CPA REVIEW CHECKLIST):

OVERALL RISK ASSESSMENT

Balance Sheet Evaluation of the Likelihood of a Material Adjustment to Surplus:

The evaluation of the likelihood of a material adjustment to surplus should be based on the following criteria:

- Inherent Risk
- Internal & External Environmental Factors
- Control Risk
- Materiality Consideration

The examiner should rate each item as to the likelihood of a material misstatement. All items are assumed as 'High' prior to any examiner evaluation. A 'High' assessment requires the examiner to perform substantive examination procedures over that account area. A lower assessment allows the examiner to perform analytical or fewer substantive procedures to satisfy the examination requirements. If an assessment other than 'High' is selected for any of the accounts, the examiner needs to document the basis for the assessment. If the assessment is based on control testwork, the documentation should include results of control procedures and related workpaper references.

1) "Accounts and Records"

__________ High __________ Medium __________ Low

Basis for Assessment:

____

____

____

2) "Commitments and Contingent Liabilities"

__________ High __________ Medium __________ Low

Basis for Assessment:

____

____

____

3) "Management and Control"

___________ High ___________ Medium __________Low

Basis for Assessment:

____

____

____

4) "Fidelity Bonds"

___________ High ___________ Medium __________Low

Basis for Assessment:

____

____

____

5) "Territory and Plan of Operation"

___________ High ___________ Medium __________Low

Basis for Assessment:

____

____

____

6) "Risk-Based Capital"

___________ High ___________ Medium __________Low

Basis for Assessment:

____

____

____

7) "Privacy of Non-Public Financial Information"

___________ High ___________ Medium ___________Low

Basis for Assessment:

____

____

____

8) "Privacy of Non-Public Health Information"

___________ High ___________ Medium ___________Low

Basis for Assessment:

____

____

____

PRELIMINARY EXAMINATION APPROACH — OPERATING CYCLE: FINANCIAL REPORTING

Listed below are the corresponding Annual Statement line items that are related to the procedures contained in this Operating Specific Risk Analysis:

Accounts and Records
Commitments and Contingent Liabilities
Management and Control
Fidelity Bonds
Territory and Plan of Operation
Risk-Based Capital
Privacy of Non-Public Financial Information
Privacy of Non-Public Health Information

The actual examination procedures selected to be performed is a matter of considerable judgment by the examiner. The following "Examination Program" includes examples of procedures commonly used.

To the extent that the examiner judgmentally determines whether it is appropriate to use the following procedures, that selection can be documented by checking the space next to such procedure, with modifications noted in the margin. The examiner may determine that alternative or additional procedures are required. If so, those procedures can be added on a supplemental sheet. The examiner performing the procedure should indicate satisfactory completion by initialing and dating in the space provided, and referencing the work papers where the procedures and findings are documented.

The examiner may choose to apply the examination procedures to less than 100% of the items comprising an account balance. Guidance for audit sampling and control and substantive procedures can be found in Part 3 of the NAIC *Financial Condition Examiners Handbook.*

After each examination procedure, the examination objective that the procedure satisfies is indicated. The examination objectives are accuracy, completeness, compliance, cutoff, existence, obligation and ownership, valuation and presentation and disclosure.

The examiner should determine whether it is necessary to review the company's privacy policies and procedures for compliance with applicable state laws and regulations. For example, if a market conduct examination were being performed concurrently with the financial examination, such review would likely not be necessary. If the examiner concludes that a review of the company's privacy policies and procedures is not needed, that conclusion should be documented in the examination workpapers.

EXAMINATION OBJECTIVES

Accuracy (AC) – Recorded transactions and account balances are mathematically accurate, are based on correct amounts and have been classified into the correct account.

Completeness (CO) – All transactions and account balances that should be recorded in the Annual financial statement were recorded.

Compliance (CM) – Business transactions and affairs have been conducted in accordance with state insurance codes, other state laws or department directives.

Cutoff (CT) – All transactions are recorded in the correct accounting period.

Existence (EX) – Recorded transactions occurred and are not fictitious and recorded assets and liabilities existed as of the balance sheet date.

Obligation (OB) and Ownership (OW) – Recorded liabilities are obligations of the company and recorded assets are the rights of the company at the balance sheet date.

Valuation (VA) – Assets and liabilities are valued in accordance with state statute and NAIC accounting guidance.

Presentation and Disclosure (PD) – The elements of the Annual Statement are properly classified and all disclosures are accurately included in the Annual Statement.

	Exam Obj.	Completion Date	Examiner	Work Paper Ref.
EXAMINATION PROCEDURES				
<u>**Accounts and Records**</u>				
1. Prepare a trial balance for each year covered by the examination and verify with the annual statement.	AC EX			
2. Verify with the company's records, to the extent deemed necessary, all schedules and exhibits in the annual statement.	AC EX			
3. Test check posting from books of original entry.	AC			
4. Verify receipts of premiums to the extent and in the manner deemed desirable.	AC EX			
5. Account for the numerical sequence of policies issued and compare with premiums recorded.	AC			
6. To the extent deemed necessary:	AC EX			
a. Verify the income on investments and ascertain interest and dividends due and accrued; and	AC EX			
b. Ascertain and report how profits and losses on sale of investments are treated.	AC EX			
7. Verify the receipt of rents from tenants or real property owned by the company.	AC EX			
8. Examine expense vouchers, claims paid and other disbursements:	AC EX CM			
a. For life companies, note any allocation of expenses and ascertain if properly distributed; and	AC			
b. For fire and casualty companies, check compliance with Uniform Accounting Instructions.	CM			
9. Inquire of management as to significant current year/subsequent events.	EX			

	Exam Obj.	Completion Date	Examiner	Work Paper Ref.
10. Obtain most recent management letter issued by the independent CPA firm and review for significant items.	AC			
11. Perform a reconciliation of detail to control accounts at or near year-end.	AC			
Commitments and Contingent Liabilities				
Identifying Commitments and Contingent Liabilities				
1. Request from company management and attorneys (outside and in-house) a list of nonpolicy-related commitments and contingent liabilities incurred through the examination date. Each item on the list should include a description of the item, present status and opinion of the amount and probability of ultimate payment. This list should include the following:	EX			
a. Unfulfilled purchase agreements that are in excess of normal requirements, or at prices materially in excess of prevailing prices;	EX			
b. Contractual obligations for purchase or sale of property, plant and equipment or other permanent investments;	EX			
c. Lease commitments;	EX			
d. Mergers or acquisitions pending;	EX			
e. Additional income tax payable;	EX			
f. Discounted receivables with records;	EX			
g. Pension or retirement plans;	EX			
h. Endorsements and guarantees;	EX			
i. Contractual arrangements with officers, employees, retirees and consultants;	EX			
j. Individual identification of all securities loaned; and	EX			

	Exam Obj.	Completion Date	Examiner	Work Paper Ref.
k. Individual identification of all reverse repurchase agreements.	EX			
2. Review legal fees for a possible indication of unreported items.	AC EX			
Detecting Commitments and Contingent Liabilities Inappropriately Handled				
3. Determine how each item identified above was reflected in the balance sheet.	AC			
a. No provisions;	AC			
b. Adjustment to a line item; and	AC			
c. Separate line item (liability or segregation of surplus).	AC			
4. Evaluate the company's treatment of each item, given probability and amount of eventual loss or payment resulting from the item. Determine compliance with statutory regulation and investment program authorized by management for securities loans, reverse repurchase agreements and securities held under other financing or leveraging arrangements. Review for authorization to engage in such transactions with specific brokers and banks.	AC VA			
Management and Control				
1. Ascertain if provisions of charter and bylaws are complied with and determine if all changes made during the period of examination were properly authorized and approved.	CM			
2. Read the policyholders', stockholders', directors' and Executive, Finance, etc. Committee minutes for period under examination and report any act inconsistent with the charter or bylaws. Also note:	CM			
a. Attendance at meetings;	CM			
b. Approval of investments;	CM			
c. Authorization of salaries;	CM			

	Exam Obj.	Completion Date	Examiner	Work Paper Ref.
d. Names and business connection of directors; and	CM			
e. Names and duties of executive officers.	CM			
3. Ascertain compliance with provisions of laws, rules and regulations. Also note:	CM			
a. Compliance with laws, rules and regulations covering proxies;	CM			
b. Compliance with laws, rules and regulations covering "insider trading"; and	CM			
c. Nature and effectiveness of provisions for disclosures of conflicts of interest to board of directors or trustees.	CM			
Fidelity Bonds				
1. Ascertain whether all officers and employees are appropriately bonded whose duties and responsibilities require the carrying of such coverage.	EX CM			
2. Review all other insurance policies to determine if adequate coverage is in-force covering the hazards to which the company is exposed, including coverage for the company's various buildings and their contents.	EX CM			
Territory and Plan of Operation				
1. Review state files and examine certificates of authority.	CM			
a. Prepare listing of states and jurisdictions where company is licensed to write business as of the examination date.	CM			
b. Note exceptions.	CM			
c. Interview company personnel regarding the same.	CM			
2. Determine lines and kinds of business written by the company.	CM			

	Exam Obj.	Completion Date	Examiner	Work Paper Ref.
3. Determine company's plan for acquisition of business.	CM			
a. Review company's agency system.	CM			
b. Determine number of agents employed or licensed by company at examination date.	CM			
4. Review company's budgets and forecast.	AC			
a. Compare actual results to budgeted amounts. Obtain explanation of large variances within budgets.	AC			
b. Review company's forecast and projected marketing plan. Review assumptions with management.	AC			
<u>**Risk Based Capital**</u>				
The following are suggested RBC examination procedures intended to be used on companies whose financial condition warrants tests of the company's RBC calculation. For example, if material changes are reflected in the examination report then the examiner should determine the effect of those changes on the RBC calculation. These procedures are optional for an examination of a company whose financial condition is not likely to be considered potentially troubled.				
Risk-Based Capital (RBC) Examination Objectives				
1. Verify that relevant annual statement balances (e.g., invested assets, reinsurance recoverables, premiums and reserves) and other components of the RBC calculation are properly classified within the categories of risk.	AC EX			
2. Determine impact of examination changes on the RBC calculation.	EX VA			

	Exam Obj.	Completion Date	Examiner	Work Paper Ref.
Risk-Based Capital (RBC) Examination Procedures				
3. Obtain and review the insurer's supporting workpapers to test whether material reported values in the RBC report were properly classified, accurately valued and appropriately included. This procedure need only be completed for those values included in the RBC report that are not obtained directly from the Annual Statement and not subject to the NAIC RBC crosscheck procedures. For example, the asset concentration factor, mortgages, real estate, interest rate risk, separate accounts and affiliated investments are all values that are not subject to crosschecks for life company's. For property and casualty company's, the list includes: credit risk reinsurance, affiliated transactions and excessive premium growth. (Note: These lists are not meant to be all-inclusive, therefore, the examiner must exercise judgment when selecting values to test. The NAIC Risk-Based Capital Report instructions indicate which values are not subject to crosschecks.)	AC EX VA			
4. Review the NAIC RBC crosscheck letter from the insurer or NAIC, if applicable and response letter from the insurer to determine the completeness and accuracy of the company's RBC Report. Contact the NAIC Quality Assurance department if such correspondence are unavailable.	EX			
5. Inquire with the insurer whether any amendments to the RBC report or Annual Statement have been filed. If amendments have been filed, ascertain the nature and extent of changes made and examination impact.	AC EX			
6. Review the independent auditors workpapers related to RBC.	AC			
7. If material errors are discovered in the RBC report and/or account values change as a result of the examination, determine the impact on the RBC action levels.	AC VA			

	Exam Obj.	Completion Date	Examiner	Work Paper Ref.
8. Determine from the insurer's Total Adjusted Capital whether the company has triggered a RBC action level (e.g., Company Action Level RBC, Regulatory Action Level RBC, Authorized Control Level RBC and Mandatory Control Level RBC).	EX VA			

SECTION Q — OPERATING CYCLE: SALARY, WAGE AND EMPLOYEE BENEFITS

The procedures included within this document should be completed if deemed necessary by the examiner in accordance with the overall risk assessment. Each of the items referenced in this document may not be present in every company under examination. The examiner should clearly identify the sections that are pertinent and remove or mark-out the remaining sections.

Annual Statement Blank Line Items

Welfare and Pension Plans

Relevant SSAP's Include

#8, Pensions
#11, Postemployment Benefits and Compensated Absences
#12, Employee Stock Ownership Plans
#13, Stock Options and Stock Purchase Plans
#14, Postretirement Benefits Other Than Pensions

SPECIFIC RISK ANALYSIS WORKPAPERS

Risk Analysis Prepared By/Date ______________________________

Planning Exam Analysis Prepared By/Date ______________________________

Reviewed By/Date ______________________________

EXAMINATION OBJECTIVES:

1. Salary, wage and employee benefit expenses are incurred only for work authorized and performed. (Existence)

2. Benefits are calculated at the proper rates; recorded correctly as to account, amount and period. (Accuracy, Completeness and Cutoff)

INHERENT RISKS

INTERNAL AND EXTERNAL ENVIRONMENTAL CONDITIONS/FACTORS

RESULTS OF DETAIL ANALYTICAL REVIEW PROCEDURES

CONTROL RISK — OPERATING CYCLE: SALARY, WAGE AND EMPLOYEE BENEFITS

This questionnaire is designed to assist the examiner in assessing control risk for salary, wage and employee benefits cycles. Part 1, Section III and Part 3 of this *Handbook* provides guidance in consideration of an insurer's internal control structure for use when designing substantive examination procedures.

This questionnaire includes examples of internal control procedures and policies that are commonly utilized by insurers to achieve internal control objectives. For each control procedure listed below, indicate by placing a check mark in the yes or no box whether or not the insurer employs such a procedure, or other similar practice (include a description of the similar procedure). To the extent the control procedure is not applicable, indicate N/A. If other relevant control procedures are in place, list them in the space that follows. Control procedures that are tested by the examiner should be documented by including the workpaper reference in the comment section and the examiner's initials in the reliance column.

For each individual control procedure there is a control objective listed that satisfies the procedure.

If the examiner initially assesses control risk as low or medium for a particular account balance, then those controls must be tested. The controls should be tested to determine whether the procedure is operating as expected, applied throughout the entire period of reliance, performed on a timely basis, encompassing all transactions and identifying errors. Some examples of testing procedures are inquiry, observation, re-performance and examination of documents. The level of reliance, if any, should be indicated in the applicable column along with any comments the examiner may have regarding the procedure.

Based upon the testing results, the examiner should determine whether the preliminary control risk assessment is confirmed or should be revised.

CONTROL OBJECTIVES

Authorization (AU) – All transactions recorded were reviewed and approved by designated personnel.

Completeness (CO) – All transactions that occurred are initially entered into the accounting records, accepted for processing and generated data files and reports reflect that all transactions have occurred.

Accuracy (AC) – Transactions are initially recorded correctly, timely and accurately.

Asset Protection (AP) – Adequate safeguards over access to and use of assets and records, including the appropriate segregation of duties among company personnel.

	Control Obj.	Y	N	Work Paper Ref.	Reliance
General Control Procedures					
The examiner should determine the amount of documentation necessary for each control procedure. If the examiner intends to place substantial reliance on the established control, the examiner should explain the control procedure in a workpaper and document the individual responsible for supervising the control activity as well as the frequency of the control activity.					
1. Are payroll registers reconciled to the general ledger?	AC				
2. Is the distribution of hours to departments reviewed and approved by supervisory personnel?	AU				
3. Are comparisons of actual payroll amounts to budgeted amounts regularly reviewed by management?	AU AC				
4. Is the allocation of payroll costs among affiliated companies periodically reviewed for reasonableness?	AC AU				

OTHER KEY CONTROLS EXISTING FOR THIS EXAMINATION OBJECTIVE:

SUMMARY EVALUATION OF CONTROL RISK:

EVALUATION OF INDEPENDENT CPA'S WORK FOR THIS EXAMINATION (CPA REVIEW CHECKLIST):

OVERALL RISK ASSESSMENT

Balance Sheet Evaluation of the Likelihood of a Material Adjustment to Surplus:

The evaluation of the likelihood of a material adjustment to surplus should be based on the following criteria:

- Inherent Risk
- Internal & External Environmental Factors
- Control Risk
- Materiality Consideration

The examiner should rate each item as to the likelihood of a material misstatement. All items are assumed as "High" prior to any examiner evaluation. A "High" assessment requires the examiner to perform substantive examination procedures over that account area. A lower assessment allows the examiner to perform analytical or fewer substantive procedures to satisfy the examination requirements. If an assessment other than "High" is selected for any of the accounts, the examiner needs to document the basis for the assessment. If the assessment is based on control testwork, the documentation should include results of control procedures and related workpaper references.

1) "Welfare and Pension Plans"

___________ High ___________ Medium ___________Low

Basis for Assessment:

____

____

____

PRELIMINARY EXAMINATION APPROACH — OPERATING CYCLE: SALARY, WAGE AND EMPLOYEE BENEFITS

Listed below are the corresponding Annual Statement line items that are related to the procedures contained in this Operating Specific Risk Analysis:

Welfare and Pension Plans

The actual examination procedures selected to be performed is a matter of considerable judgment by the examiner. The following "Examination Program" includes examples of procedures commonly used.

To the extent that the examiner judgmentally determines whether it is appropriate to use the following procedures, that selection can be documented by checking the space next to such procedure, with modifications noted in the margin. The examiner may determine that alternative or additional procedures are required. If so, those procedures can be added on a supplemental sheet. The examiner performing the procedure should indicate satisfactory completion by initialing and dating in the space provided, and referencing the workpapers where the procedures and findings are documented.

The examiner may choose to apply the examination procedures to less than 100% of the items comprising an account balance. Guidance for audit sampling and control and substantive procedures can be found in Part 3 of the NAIC *Financial Condition Examiners Handbook.*

After each examination procedure, the examination objective that the procedure satisfies is indicated. The examination objectives are accuracy, completeness, compliance, cutoff, existence, obligation and ownership, valuation and presentation and disclosure.

EXAMINATION OBJECTIVES

Accuracy (AC) – Recorded transactions and account balances are mathematically accurate, are based on correct amounts and have been classified into the correct account.

Completeness (CO) – All transactions and account balances that should be recorded in the Annual financial statement were recorded.

Compliance (CM) – Business transactions and affairs have been conducted in accordance with state insurance codes, other state laws or department directives.

Cutoff (CT) – All transactions are recorded in the correct accounting period.

Existence (EX) – Recorded transactions occurred and are not fictitious and recorded assets and liabilities existed as of the balance sheet date.

Obligation (OB) and Ownership (OW) – Recorded liabilities are obligations of the company and recorded assets are the rights of the company at the balance sheet date.

Valuation (VA) – Assets and liabilities are valued in accordance with state statute and NAIC accounting guidance.

Presentation and Disclosure (PD) – The elements of the Annual Statement are properly classified and all disclosures are accurately included in the Annual Statement.

	Exam Obj.	Completion Date	Examiner	Work Paper Ref.
EXAMINATION PROCEDURES				
1. Review pension plans or profit sharing systems or bonus plans for employees.	AC CO CM			
a. Obtain a copy of the company handbook for employees, pension plans, profit sharing systems or bonus plans for employees.	AC CO			
b. Determine if pension plans meet requirements of the Internal Revenue Service.	CM			
c. Determine if any non-recognized liabilities exist.	AC CO			
2. Review deferred compensation or incentive plans.	AC			

PART 3—
AUDIT SAMPLING AND CONTROL AND SUBSTANTIVE TESTING PROCEDURES

TABLE OF CONTENTS

PART 3 — AUDIT SAMPLING AND CONTROL AND SUBSTANTIVE TESTING PROCEDURES

INTRODUCTION

(Note: Much of the material in this chapter is based on the *Audit and Accounting Guide – Audit Sampling*, as published by the American Institute of Certified Public Accountants. In addition, SAS 39 – *Audit Sampling* is a valuable source of information concerning audit sampling. It is suggested that each Department obtain copies of these texts for their reference.)

Audit sampling involves the application of examination procedures to less than 100% of the items comprising an account balance or class of transactions for the purpose of evaluating some characteristic of the balance or class. Audit sampling is frequently used to obtain examination evidence and involves testing an account balance or series of transactions, and identifying items that relate to specific examination objectives. By applying proper examination sampling procedures, the examiner in many instances will be able to improve efficiency and effectiveness in his or her examination. In addition, the use of certain audit sampling methods allows the examiner the ability to mathematically evaluate any errors or misstatements found.

Basic to audit sampling is sampling risk – the risk that the examiner's conclusion based on a sample might be different from the conclusion they would reach if they examined each item in the population. In selecting items from a population using sampling, examiners may often utilize a statistical sampling method. Statistical sampling uses the laws of probability to measure sampling risk and allows the examiner to use the results from the examination of the sample items to be evaluated, so the examiner may form a conclusion about all population items. The two statistical sampling methods discussed in this part are attribute sampling used in the performance of control testing and probability-proportional-to-size (PPS) sample selection used in substantive testing of details.

Examiners should also be cognizant of the fact that statistical audit sampling may not always be appropriate. For instance, the examiner may utilize a non-representative selection method, commonly known as judgmental selection, to perform examination testing. In using judgmental selection, an examiner, using his or her professional judgment, will judgmentally select certain items from a population based on their characteristics or size. For example, an examiner may determine that five large balances within an account comprise 80% of the account balance. Due to their size and significance, the examiner may decide to 'judgmentally' select these items and examine them. As judgmental selection does not measure sampling risk and the results of the sample cannot be used to make inferences about the population as a whole, judgmental selection is not considered a true "sampling" method, but is a valid selection method and may provide the examiner with sufficient examination evidence. The results of a non-representative, judgmental selection are used to obtain assurance about the selected items only and are not used to make inferences about the population as a whole. The remaining population items not selected in a non-representative, judgmental selection would then be subject to some other substantive testing procedure or ignored if immaterial individually and in the aggregate, as determined by the examiner's professional judgment. In addition, examiners may determine that it is easier and/or more efficient to subject 100% of an account balance to testing procedures. For example, if an account balance is comprised of only a small number of high dollar items, the examiner may determine it is simply more efficient to test each of the items within the account. In addition, examiners may choose to use analytical procedures to evaluate an account balance or to use inquiry, reperformance and observation to obtain evidence. In any event, examiners should always use professional judgment in the selection of examination procedures and in determining whether audit sampling is appropriate.

The information contained herein, is designed to provide an explanation of the major aspects of examination sample selection as well as other examination procedures that do not utilize audit sampling. This information should provide a guide for the examiner when it is appropriate to apply sampling techniques in the examination process and what types of sampling methods are considered appropriate. This information will also help the examiner in evaluating his or her examination results when either audit sampling or some other method is used.

I. CONTROL TESTING

A. Introduction to Control Testing

Control tests are intended to provide assurance that control procedures are operating as prescribed. The control environment and the various control procedures are assessed and evaluated through the completion of the Specific Risk Analysis workpapers discussed in Part 1 and 2 of this *Handbook*. Based on the evaluation of the control environment, the examiner will test those controls on which he or she intends to place reliance and use those results in determining the nature and extent of substantive testing. In general, if reliance is placed on a specific control and the testing supports this reliance, the extent of substantive testing the examiner is required to perform relating to that account balance may be reduced. In those situations where the examiner determines that control reliance is not appropriate, testing of controls typically should not be performed unless the examiner has a valid reason for performing such tests.

Although control testing may be performed for any accounting area, control testing by examiners frequently will be relevant to the following areas:

- Premium Recording and Collections
- Claims Expenses and Cash Disbursements

Control testing is generally performed using one of the following methods: corroborative inquiry, observation, reperformance, or examination of documents. Each of these methods may provide the examiner with examination evidence regarding the effectiveness and reliability of the control procedures utilized by the company, and the ultimate choice of which method to use is based on the professional judgment of the examiner, the nature of the control procedure, and the planned reliance the examiner wishes to place on that control.

The use of corroborative inquiry, observation or reperformance in control testing, due to their nature and the fact that these control procedures do not usually provide a documentary trail of evidence, will typically not require the use of sampling methods. For instance, an examiner may obtain reliable evidence that a specific control is operating effectively by making an inquiry into the company operations with various employees or observing various procedures being performed. If an examiner desires to rely on a control tested through one of these procedures, the examiner must use his or her professional judgment to determine the extent of testing which is considered appropriate.

Control procedures performed through the examination of documents, which does leave a ready trail of documentary evidence, will in many cases lend itself to sampling procedures known as attribute sampling. For example, a company may require that all checks are signed by the controller of the company. The control procedure in place would be the signature of the controller on company checks, while the documentary evidence of this control would be the canceled checks of the company. If such documentary evidence of a control exists, and the examiner decides to place reliance on that control, attribute sampling (which is discussed further herein) with a minimum sample size can and should be used to the extent that it is applicable.

In many instances, an examiner may focus his or her control testing procedures on one or several high-level controls that can be supported through the use of corroborative inquiry and/or observation. Typically, the use of inquiry and observation control testing procedures are easier to develop and implement than are control tests of documentary evidence. Accordingly, by focusing on these high level controls, an examiner may be able to limit the amount of time that must be afforded to control testing. As always, the extent to which a particular control procedure should be tested, if at all, is based on the professional judgment of the examiner.

B. Corroborative Inquiry, Observation, and Reperformance

Inquiry consists of questions or interviews held with company personnel regarding the implementation and performance of internal control procedures. Examiners may either inquire of those individuals who are directly responsible for the performance and monitoring of internal controls, those individuals indirectly associated with the performance and monitoring of internal controls (i.e., the users of the information), or a combination of the two. Although the questions that an examiner may ask can and will vary from examination to examination, these questions will frequently revolve around how controls are maintained; how errors are detected, monitored and corrected; who performs the control reviews; and how often these reviews are performed.

Observation of the performance of internal control procedures may provide an examiner with reliable evidence regarding the internal control's effectiveness. For instance, a control procedure relating to cash receipts might include the restrictive endorsement of incoming premium checks by the mail clerk upon receipt. To confirm that this control is operating as prescribed, the examiner may wish to observe the mail clerk opening the morning's mail and restrictively endorsing all incoming checks for that day. This would then lend support to this particular control assertion.

Although competent evidence may be obtained from the observation of, or inquiry into, the internal controls of a company, an examiner should be cognizant of the fact that observation or inquiry alone may not provide sufficient evidence. This is due to the fact that the individuals performing the control tasks may realize that they are being observed and perform the controls more attentively or answer the inquiries of the examiner with the way controls should be operating rather than how they are operating. Because of this, inquiry in conjunction with observation is often required to obtain sufficient evidence.

Reperformance of internal controls involves the actual repeating of an internal control procedure that was performed by the company's personnel or the company's computer system. The reperformance of internal controls is frequently associated with the testing of programmed controls (e.g., computer application controls). In some instances, the examiner may decide to work with the personnel of the insurance company and perform limited reperformance procedures associated with a company's programmed controls. For example, an examiner may wish to evaluate a programmed control relating to batch totaling. To do this, the examiner might utilize the company's software and re-enter a prior day's data and verify that the batch totals are properly calculated and reported, or enter incorrect data and verify that the computer correctly flags this error. Manual reperformance of procedures also may be used by examiners such as footing, or recomputing various account balances, trial balances or other such detail listing.

Determining the effectiveness of a control procedure, and the extent of testing required, using the above testing procedures requires the examiner to use his or her professional judgment. The examiner should evaluate the evidence obtained both qualitatively, as well as quantitatively, to the extent applicable, in reaching his or her determination regarding the reliability and effectiveness of the control procedure.

C. Attribute Sampling

Attribute sampling involves the examination of transaction documents for the presence or absence of specific attributes. Attributes are testable characteristics relating to a specific control on which the examiner wishes to place reliance. By utilizing this sampling method, the examiner is able to reach a conclusion about a population in terms of the rate of occurrence. Attribute sampling, used in the performance of the testing of controls, allows an examiner to analyze whether controls are operating effectively and as prescribed. An examiner will identify specific control attributes and test those attributes to determine the rate of deviation from that attribute. The absence of an attribute indicates a deviation from a prescribed control policy or procedure. As control procedures are expected to be applied to all transactions subject to that control, the dollar value of the transaction selected for testing is irrelevant. Each occurrence of, or deviation from, a prescribed attribute is given equal weight in the examiner's evaluation, regardless of the dollar amount of the transaction. As a rule, as deviations increase, the risk of material misstatement increases, and the reliance the examiner may place on that control is reduced. If the number of actual deviations exceed the number of deviations expected, the examiner may not place reliance on the control and must adjust the level of substantive testing accordingly or find other alternative controls to achieve the control reliance objectives.

The process of performing an attribute sample selection is generally as follows:

- Define the attribute(s) to be tested
- Define what constitutes a deviation
- Define the population
- Determine the sample size
- Select the sample
- Examine the evidence and evaluate the results

1. Define Attribute/Deviation

The first step in attribute sampling selection is to clearly define what attributes are to be tested and what constitutes a deviation. For example, if an issued check requires the signature of the controller of the company, the attribute would be the controller's signature and a deviation would be defined as an issued check that does not contain the controller's signature. By defining the attributes and deviations, this allows for an accurate assessment of whether controls are operating effectively and ensures that the selection process is performed efficiently.

To define attributes and deviations, the examiner must have a thorough understanding of the control environment, the potential errors that might occur, and the controls in place to eliminate or detect those errors. This is accomplished through the completion of the Specific Risk Analysis worksheets discussed in Part 1 and 2 of this *Handbook*. In completing this analysis, the examiner should be alert for any changes in the control environment, relating to the area under examination, during the latest calendar year. If controls have substantially changed during the year under examination, the examiner should determine whether a control reliance strategy is appropriate as two control systems were in place during the year. If control reliance is still deemed appropriate, the examiner should have an understanding of each control environment and the applicable control procedures that were in place under both control environments. The examiner would then test those controls for both periods. If the controls relating to the examination objective under both periods are considered reliable, the examiner may adopt a control reliance strategy. It is not considered appropriate for an examiner to adopt a control reliance strategy and identify, test and evaluate controls that were in place for only a portion of the calendar year and ignore the control procedures and environment that existed for the remainder of the year. To do so may cause the examiner to reach the wrong conclusion regarding the control effectiveness for the entire period, as the controls tested were not operating for the entire year. Likewise, if controls during one period are deemed unreliable, the examiner should not adopt a control reliance strategy and instead perform more focused substantive tests.

2. Define Population

Having defined the attributes to be tested, the examiner must then define the population. Typically, the total population is comprised of individual sampling units and is represented by a series of documents, computer listings or other physical items. The population is, of course, dependent on the attributes to be tested. The importance of accurately defining the population cannot be overstated, as the results of the testing may only be inferred to items included in the population. The population should include all transactions related to the test objective. In addition, the examiner should consider such factors as the period to be covered and the completeness of the physical representation. Generally, the population should include all items from the period under examination, which would typically be the latest calendar year under examination. For instance, in our above example regarding the controller's signature required on all checks, the population would include all checks issued by the company for the year-ended 12/31/XX. The examiner should also ensure that the population is complete and contains all sampling units subject to testing. One such method might include accounting for the numerical sequence of prenumbered documents.

3. Determine Sample Size

The next step in the sampling process is to determine the sample size. In determining the sample size, the examiner must first consider the sampling risk associated with the reliance on internal accounting controls. This sampling risk is the risk that the examiner may over rely or under rely on the effectiveness and operation of the internal controls being tested, based on the results of the sample selected. Over-reliance on internal controls occurs when an examiner determines that controls are operating effectively based on the sample of controls selected, when in fact the population as a whole would not support this level of reliance. Under-reliance occurs when an examiner determines that controls are not operating effectively based on the sample selected, when in fact, the entire population does support the control procedure. Generally, examiners should be concerned about the risk of over-reliance on accounting controls as improper reliance on ineffective controls may work to reduce the level of substantive testing and cause the examiner to reach an improper conclusion regarding the company's financial position. Conversely, examiners should not be as concerned with the risk of under-reliance as the examiner will not rely on controls, which will typically result in more substantive testing. Although varying levels of assurance may be obtained by an examiner, as a general recommendation, the examiner should be willing to accept no more than a 10% risk of over-reliance relating to control testing, which translates to a 90% confidence level which is the basis for the sample selection matrixes below. By accepting a 90% confidence level, the examiner is saying that he or she has a 90% assurance that the conclusions about the application of the control procedure, based on the sample of transactions subject to the control procedure, would not differ from the conclusions that would be reached if the test were applied to all transactions.

In addition to the risk of over-reliance, examiners should be cognizant of the desired level of the allowable error rate that is considered acceptable within the testing application. The allowable error rate is the maximum rate of deviation from control procedures that the examiner is willing to accept. As a general rule, the level of the allowable error rate has an inverse relationship with the sample size. As the allowable error rate decreases, the sample size required to be selected will increase and vice versa. During the Specific Risk Analysis, the examiner is responsible for identifying and determining whether the control environment and the various control procedures in place result in a high, medium or low risk that material errors may exist. Generally, the higher the degree of risk that a material error may exist, the lower the allowable error rate the examiner should be willing to accept. Likewise, as the degree of risk decreases, the allowable error rate may be set at a higher level. The allowable error rate determination is also dependent on the examiner's planned reliance on the actual internal control procedure. This planned reliance differs from the over-reliance and under-reliance, discussed above, which dealt with the issue of sampling risk. This reliance refers to the significance or importance that an examiner will place on a control procedure in determining the level and extent of testing necessary. By their very design, some control procedures are more significant and effective in preventing errors than are other controls, and examiners may wish to rely on these controls more than low level controls. This fact, coupled with the desired level of testing and the overall determination of the risk for material misstatement within the account, will determine the examiner's planned degree of reliance. Although the level of allowable error, as with the level of assurance, varies depending on the level of risk and the degree of reliance the examiner places on that control, for practical purposes, the examiner may use the general recommendations as set forth in the matrixes below.

Another consideration when determining the sample size is the number of deviations expected to be found by the examiner. This expectation is determined by the examiner's professional judgment based on a number of factors including the procedures performed during the Specific Risk Analysis, past errors noted by the examiner, and any past and current errors noted in the examiner's review of the CPA's workpapers. The sample sizes presented in the matrix below have been determined allowing for the discovery of one or no deviations in the sample. If the examiner anticipates no deviations and one is discovered, reliance on that control may not be appropriate and the examiner should reassess this effect on the planned examination approach. However, if the examiner still believes the control is reliable, and no additional deviations are expected to be found, the examiner may expand the sample size under the two-step sample size method discussed herein. If the sample is designed with the initial expectation of detecting one deviation, the examiner should use the one-step sample size. If more than one deviation is noted under either method, the examiner should not rely on that control. Although valid samples may be developed with the expectation that deviations will exceed more than one deviation, the resulting size of the sample that would be required would normally be such that no efficiencies would be gained from performing tests of controls. As such, the detection of two or more deviations by the examiner should preclude the examiner from concluding that controls may be relied upon. However, an examiner should always qualitatively review the reasons for any deviation, and if the reason for that deviation may be isolated as the result of unusual or unique circumstances, it may be appropriate for the examiner to disregard this deviation from his overall assessment of the reliability of the internal control procedures. For example, in the check signing example, assume that the controller was absent for a week as a result of illness. In his absence, the head accounting clerk signed the checks, one of which was selected by the examiner for control testing purposes. Although the check was not signed by the controller, and thus would appear to be a deviation, the fact that he was ill and out for the week in which this check was signed would appear to be an usual situation, and in actuality, does not represent a true control breakdown because the disbursement was approved by a responsible individual with the proper authority to authorize such a transaction in the controller's absence. Accordingly, the examiner may identify and document it as such, and disregard this deviation from his overall control assessment. This allows the examiner some flexibility in evaluating his or her control testing results and prevents the evaluation of the effectiveness of control procedures from being unduly influenced by unusual transactions which may be readily and reasonably explained.

Generally, the examiner should utilize the following recommendations as outlined in the tables to achieve the planned degree of reliance associated with the internal accounting control procedures. The Attribute Sampling Selection Matrix tables assume a 10% risk of over-reliance on internal control procedures (i.e., 90% confidence level) and one or no expected deviations for each of the various levels on which the examiner intends to rely on the controls. In addition, sample size is not greatly affected by the population size and the table assumes a large population size for conservatism. As such, the number of sample selections needed to be chosen is applicable for all sample sizes.

Attribute Sampling Selection Matrix

Intended Reliance on Internal Controls - Low				
		# of Sample Selections		
Level of Risk Identified	**Allowable Error Rate**	**0 Deviations**	**1 Deviation (Two Step)**	**1 Deviation (One Step)**
Low	20%	11	20	18
Medium	15%	15	28	25
High	10%	22	42	38

Intended Reliance on Internal Controls - Medium				
		# of Sample Selections		
Level of Risk Identified	**Allowable Error Rate**	**0 Deviations**	**1 Deviation (Two Step)**	**1 Deviation (One Step)**
Low	12%	20	39	35
Medium	10%	22	42	38
High	8%	28	53	48

Intended Reliance on Internal Controls - High				
		# of Sample Selections		
Level of Risk Identified	**Allowable Error Rate**	**0 Deviations**	**1 Deviation (Two Step)**	**1 Deviation (One Step)**
Low	7%	32	60	55
Medium	5%	45	84	77
High	3%	76	142	129

In certain situations the actual number of items comprising the population may be such that the number of items required to be selected, using the above matrix, is not practical or possible. For example, an examiner may identify a control relating to monthly account reconciliations for a specific account balance. As an account balance would have no more than 12 monthly reconciliations in any given calendar year, it would clearly be impossible to select a minimum sample of 25 items. In most cases, it would also not be practical to select all 12 items, which defeats the purposes of sampling. In this case, the examiner would judgmentally determine the number of selections desired and randomly select that number. As such, the examiner should utilize professional judgment in the determination of the number of items to be selected in situations where the selection of a minimum sample using the matrix above is not applicable or appropriate.

4. Select the Sample

Once the population has been determined and the sampling plan designed, the examiner selects and examines the applicable items to determine if any deviations are found. The selection of sample items may be used to test more than one attribute as considered applicable by the examiner. For example, if an examiner selects a sample of in-force policies, the examiner may use the policies selected to test control objectives relating to both accuracy and completeness. The selection of individual items should typically be performed using a random selection process. This may be accomplished through the use of random number generators, which may be found in most spreadsheet software packages or through the use of audit software containing a random number generator. If random selection is not possible or practical, an examiner may haphazardly select the sample. Haphazard selection is a manual selection method that approximates random selection as the examiner selects the sample without bias. An illustrative example of haphazard selection would be an examiner randomly pulling invoices out of a file drawer that contained all invoices received by the company during the year.

5. Evaluate the Results

After selecting the sample items, the examiner examines the items to determine if the controls are operating as prescribed. If documents relating to the sampling unit cannot be found or the examiner is otherwise unable to examine the document, it must be considered a deviation unless alternative supporting documents can be found — for example a duplicate invoice. Voided or unused documents selected for testing should be reviewed to ensure that they are not a deviation from the prescribed control, and if such determination is made, the examiner should randomly select another item. The examiner may wish to include several additional or extra selections in his or her initial random selection process.

Generally, if deviations are found early in the testing process, testing for that particular control may be discontinued as the results do not support the planned reliance. In this case, the examiner should reassess his or her planned level of control reliance and its effects on the amount of substantive testing to be performed. In most cases, if reliance cannot be placed on the internal controls, the examiner should increase the level of substantive testing to be performed. In addition, even though the presence of deviations indicate that controls may not be relied upon, it is still important for the examiner to evaluate and analyze the deviations detected. Specifically, the examiner should evaluate and analyze the nature and cause of the deviation detected and include this analysis in his or her overall assessment of examination risk and include this assessment in the planned level of substantive testing to be performed.

If no deviations are found, or one deviation is found as allowed in the selection process, the examiner may conclude that the particular control tested may be sufficiently relied upon for the level of assurance provided.

II. SUBSTANTIVE TESTING

Substantive testing, or tests of details, involves the use of examination procedures by the examiner to obtain assurance regarding examination objectives applicable to individual account balances. Substantive testing is primarily interested in reaching a conclusion about an account balance in dollar terms. The level of substantive testing necessary to obtain the desired level of assurance is dependent to a large degree on the examiner's assessment of inherent and control risk. Frequently, substantive testing procedures are accomplished through the use of the sampling and selection methods discussed herein. However, not all substantive testing procedures need to involve the use of sampling procedures. For instance, an examiner may choose to use analytical procedures to substantively test an account balance or to confirm the existence of a legal liability through a confirmation letter with the company's lawyer. Whether the use of sampling or some other selection method is appropriate depends on the examiner's test objective, the nature of the account balance, the degree of assurance desired and professional judgment.

A. 100% Testing

In certain situations, an examiner may determine it is both effective and efficient to test 100% of the items comprising the account balance. As 100% of the items are selected for testing, this is not a 'sampling' procedure, although the examiner obtains maximum assurance regarding the examination procedure. These tests are only considered appropriate in situations where the account balance is comprised of only one or relatively few highly significant items. 100% testing may also be considered appropriate in situations where the entire balance is easily confirmed (e.g., confirmation of investments with trustee).

B. Non-representative Selection

Non-representative selection, or judgmental selection, does not attempt to select a sample of items which are representative of the population as a whole. Instead, certain account balances are selected that have certain characteristics which draws the examiner to select that item. The most common characteristic would be the size of the balance (i.e., high dollar items), although other characteristics may also exist (for example, the selection of all receivables from a specific agent). As judgmental selection is a non-representative selection method, the examiner is unable to use the results from the items selected to make inferences to the population as a whole. The number of selections required in a judgmental selection is, of course, determined by the examiner through the use of professional judgment, although individual items that exceed planned tolerable error for the account should always be selected. Additionally, as the examiner only obtains assurance about the items selected, the remaining items within the population must be tested through some other substantive procedure unless the items are insignificant individually or in the aggregate.

The benefit of using judgmental selection over a representative sampling method such as probability proportional to size method, discussed below, is primarily the time savings which may be afforded by using this method. For example, if an examiner is able to scan an account summary and is quickly able to determine that approximately 80% of the account balance subject to testing is comprised of four items out of a population detail of over 100 items, he or she may decide to judgmentally select these items and eliminate the steps involved in developing and implementing a statistically based sample.

Judgmental selection may also be appropriate in situations where the examiner desires to concentrate his or her testing to a specific group of items where there is a high risk of material error or where some other uncertainty exists. In these situations, an examiner will typically be required to perform a high level of detail testing to ensure that a material error does not exist. Statistical sampling, as discussed below, is usually not appropriate in these situations due to the inherent nature and limitation of the statistical sampling design. As such, judgmental selection may be used by the examiner, and the extent of testing would be determined through the examiner's use of professional judgment.

C. Representative Sampling - Probability Proportional to Size (PPS)

PPS sampling is a sampling method that utilizes attribute sampling theory to select and evaluate a sample based proportionately to the dollar value of the items comprising the population. In effect, PPS sampling breaks the account balance down into individual $1 transactions for sampling purposes and the entire transaction balance containing the selected $1 item is examined in total by the examiner. For instance, during an examination of agent balances receivable, the examiner using the PPS sampling method selects $1 which is included in a total receivable of $10,000. The entire $10,000 balance would then be subject to selection and examination. Thus, in effect, each item comprising an account balance has a chance of selection proportionally equal to its size. In the above example, the $10,000 item effectively has 10,000 chances of selection (i.e., $10,000 balance divided by $1) while a $500 item would have 500 chances of being selected. Accordingly, PPS correctly skews the sample selections to the large dollar items or balances, which theoretically is where the examiner would desire to direct his or her examination efforts.

The benefits to using probability proportional to size are numerous. Chief among these is the ease in which PPS can be administered. In addition, the sampling method stratifies the sample, and individually significant items that exceed the selection interval will be automatically selected. Another benefit, which is discussed below, is that the determination of the sample size is dependent in part to the materiality level determined during the planning period and the extent of control testing performed by the examiner.

One area of limitation, which examiners should be aware of, relates to testing of accounts (generally credit balances) for understatement. Due to the objective of an understatement test, it is not considered acceptable to sample directly from the account balance (e.g., the general ledger or detail schedules within the Annual Statement). Instead, items should be selected from an independent or reciprocal population as a test of completeness which will indicate whether items have been properly recorded in the correct period. To illustrate this concept using an extreme example, assume that a company had recorded a $0 balance for its accounts payable balance at year-end, implying that the company had no outstanding payables at year-end. As the payable balance is a liability balance, the examiner is primarily concerned with the potential understatement of this balance. However, it would be impractical, not to mention impossible, for the examiner to use PPS sampling directly on this account balance as 1) there are no items with which to sample and 2) the examiner is more concerned with what is not recorded as opposed to what is recorded. Accordingly, an examiner would be forced to utilize a reciprocal or independent population to test the account balance. If this independent or reciprocal population is monetary in nature, PPS sampling is considered appropriate. In our example, the examiner may decide to use disbursements made subsequent to year-end to test the accounts payable balance. If this were the case, the examiner could then utilize PPS sampling to select an appropriate sample of these disbursements. However, an examiner should be aware that if the independent population is not monetary in nature (e.g., policies issued after year-end, identified by policy number), PPS sampling should not be used and some other form of selection such as judgmental selection should be used.

Examiners should also be cognizant of zero and negative value items (e.g., credit balances) which may be found within a natural debit (e.g., asset) account balance under examination. Similar to the payable example discussed above, the examiner is concerned that these zero or negative balances may be understated, which indirectly leads to an overstatement of the asset account balance. Accordingly, it is not considered appropriate for an examiner to include these balances in the selection of a PPS sample of an asset account, and these balances should be excluded from the sample population. To exclude these balances, the examiner would simply ignore, or skip over these balances, during the PPS process which effectively grosses up the asset balance. The zero and negative value items would then be evaluated separately by the examiner and the extent of testing required would be determined based on the number and value of the zero and negative value items noted, the nature of these items, and the examiners professional judgment.

Additionally, examiners may also find PPS sampling difficult and time consuming to implement in regards to tests of certain income statement account balances due to the volume of transactions and the difficulty in obtaining sufficient, detailed information with which to sample. In these situations, examiners may find it easier and more beneficial to use some other form of substantive testing such as analytical reviews.

The PPS sampling process can generally be described as follows:

- Determine the sample selection interval
- Determine sample size
- Select the sample
- Examine the evidence, evaluate the results and extrapolate any errors detected

1. Determine Sample Selection Interval

To utilize PPS sampling, an examiner must first determine a selection interval. The selection interval is a function of overall planning materiality and the assurance or reliability desired by the examiner.

The selection interval is determined as follows:

$$\text{Selection Interval} = \frac{\text{Tolerable Error}}{\text{Reliability Factor}}$$

The determination of the selection interval is very important in the PPS selection process as the selection interval considers both tolerable error, which is a function of overall materiality, and the reliability or confidence level desired by the examiner. Tolerable error refers to the tolerable error as determined by the examiner during the planning process and which is described in Part 1, Planning Examinations, Section C-6. The reliability factor refers to the confidence level desired by the examiner and is based on the examiner's consideration of sampling risk. These reliability factors are represented numerically and relate to the level of assurance that the examiner desires for that specific test and his or her decision on whether to rely on controls. The following matrix represents reliability factor guidelines which the examiner may wish to use in the development of his or her testing procedures. The control reliance adopted by the examiner (e.g., high, medium, low or no reliance) refers to the extent of control testing performed by the examiner which was discussed earlier. The assessed level of risk of material misstatement again refers to the examiner's risk assessment relating to that particular account and is determined by the examiner through the completion of the SRA workpapers. The reliability factors below relate to varying levels of substantive testing assurance, which, when combined with the reliance on and extent of control testing performed, give the examiner an overall examination assurance of approximately 95%.

Reliability Factors [1]			
	Risk of Material Misstatement		
Control Reliance	Low	Medium	High
High Reliance on Controls	.7	.7	1.0
Medium Reliance on Controls	1.0	1.4	1.9
Low Reliance on Controls	1.4	1.9	2.3
No Reliance on Controls	1.6	2.3	3.0

2. Determine Sample Size

Once the selection interval has been determined, the examiner may then determine the sample size. The number of sample selections required to be made is determined by dividing the recorded amount of the population by the sample interval discussed above.

$$\text{Sample Size} = \frac{\text{Recorded amount of population}}{\text{Selection interval}}$$

For example, if the account balance to be tested is $152,000, tolerable error is 10,000, and the reliability factor is determined to be 1.0 (based on a medium control reliance strategy as a result of control testing and a low risk of material misstatement associated with the account balance), the sample size using a PPS sample is calculated as follows:

Selection interval	=	10,000/1.0	=	10,000
Sample Size	=	152,000/10,000	=	15.2 say 15 or 16 selections

Thus, in the above example, the examiner's sample would consist of either 15 or 16 selections. In situations such as the one above where the number of selections required does not result in a whole number, implying that a partial selection is required, the actual number of selection may be rounded up or down depending on the random start utilized by the examiner (which is discussed further in the following section). Unfortunately, the exact number of selections cannot be determined until the actual sample is performed. However, the sample size exercise above will alert the examiner that he or she will have at least a minimum of 15 selection in his or her sample.

3. Select Sample

Once the sample size has been determined, PPS sampling is easy to utilize. To begin, an examiner randomly selects a number that is less than or equal to the selection interval. This number is then subtracted from zero and entered as a negative number. The examiner then begins to add the population items, ignoring negative value items, until the cumulative total becomes positive (exceeds zero). This item is considered a selection. The examiner would then subtract the selection interval, determined above, from the cumulative total until it becomes negative again and repeats the process. Anytime the balance becomes positive, a selection is made. For example, if an examiner determines that the selection interval for a particular account balance is $500, a random start of $300 is selected, and the first 4 items in the detail account summary are valued at $200, $300, $75 and $250, the determination of the items selected would be as follows:

[1]For reference to the assurance level associated with the reliability factors, as well as further discussion regarding reliability factors and PPS sampling, see the AICPA Accounting and Audit Guide "Audit Sampling."

	Item Values	Cumulative Total	Selection
Random Start		$(300)	
Item #1	$200	$(100)	
Item #2	$300	$200	Yes
	Subtract selection interval of $500	$(300)	
Item #3	$75	$(225)	
Item #4	$250	$25	Yes

Another method that could be used is the cumulative dollar method. Under this method, the examiner would also select a random start that is less than or equal to the selection interval. The examiner then begins to add the recorded values of the items within the population maintaining a cumulative total. The first item selected is the one that corresponds to the random start number. The examiner then selects each item that corresponds to every *n*th dollar thereafter (with *n*th being the selection interval). For example, using the same numbers as above, if the selection interval was determined to be $500 and the examiner had a random start of $300, the sample selections would include those items found in the $300th dollar (random start), the $800th dollar ($300 + $500), the $1,300th dollar ($300 + $500 + $500), and each succeeding $500th dollar until the entire population is selected.

The choice of which PPS method to use is up to the examiner's discretion and will largely be dependent on which method is easier to use. As you can see from the above examples, as each dollar has an equal chance of selection, large dollar items have a higher chance of being selected than do smaller dollar items. In addition, due to the nature of the selection design, all items which are equal to, or exceed, the selection interval will be selected. If the recorded value of the item selected exceeds the selection interval, it could theoretically be selected more than once. For instance, in the cumulative selection method above, if an item valued at $1,000 is the first item in the account summary, it would actually cover the first two selections (e.g., the $300th and $800th dollars). If this happens, the examiner should ignore the repeat selection and consider the item as only one selection when evaluating the sample results. No additional selection would be required for the repeat selection (e.g., only the $1,000th dollar would be selected in the above example). However, because some items may be "selected" more than once, the actual physical number of items selected may differ from the sample size number computed using the above formula.

In the event that the determination of the sample size indicates that less than 5 items must be selected, a judgmental or haphazard selection may be utilized due to the small number of selections required. In addition, if the items comprising the account balance are of similar value, the number of items required to be selected should be determined using the PPS sample size equation, while the actual selection of those items may be done utilizing a random selection process.

Once the examiner has sampled through the account summary, the examiner should reconcile or prove the accumulated totals, as per the examiner computations, to the control total of the recorded balance (e.g., the ledger balance, etc.). This ensures that the sample has been properly developed and executed. This may be accomplished by utilizing the following formula:

Selection interval multiplied by the number of times selection interval was subtracted + beginning negative balance + negative value items - ending balance = recorded population total.

4. Evaluate Results and Extrapolate Errors

Once the sample items have been selected, and the applicable evidence obtained, the examiner should evaluate the results of his or her sample. As PPS sampling is a statistical sampling method, the results of a PPS sample may be projected, or extrapolated, to the population as a whole. If errors are found, the examiner needs to project or extrapolate that error to the population as a whole. From the known errors noted, the examiner is then able to compute the probable, or likely, misstatement error. This error can be computed as follows:

Projected Probable Misstatement = SI x (Stet OE - UE) + sum of misstatement in sample items exceeding the selection interval where:

SI is the selection interval

OE is the amount of overstatement in an item as a proportion of its recorded value (excluding the overstatement of errors from items which are equal to, or exceed, the selection interval)

UE is the amount of understatement in an item as a proportion of its recorded value (excluding the understatement of errors from items which are equal to, or exceed, the selection interval)

For instance, if an examiner uses PPS sampling to test an account balance using a selection interval of $10,000 and found an overstatement of $750 in a sampling item which exceeded the selection interval; overstatements of $50 and $75 in two sample items with recorded book values of $300 and $250, respectively, and an understatement of $35 in a sample item totaling $100, the projected probable misstatement would be calculated as follows:

OE (excluding error found in sample item exceeding selection interval):

Recorded Value	Exam Value	Overstatement	Proportion
300	250	50	.167
250	175	75	.3
		OE Total	.467

UE:

Recorded Value	Exam Value	Understatement	Proportion
100	135	35	.35
		UE Total	.35

The projected probable misstatement is computed as follows:

= $10,000 (Selection Interval) X (.467 - .35) + $750

= $1,920 - which includes both the known misstatement of $840 ($750 + $50 + $75 - $35) and the likely misstatement of $1,080 ($1,920 - $840).

If no errors are noted from the sample the known and projected error would of course be zero.

As with any error evaluation, the examiner should qualitatively evaluate the nature and implication of the errors discovered. The examiner should be particularly alert for highly unusual or suspicious errors which may indicate that the financial statements may be misleading or contain fraudulent information.

The examiner should also be alert for any unusual and infrequent errors which may not be representative of the entire population. In certain instances, the extrapolation of an error to the population as a whole may not be appropriate as the error may be highly unique and isolated in nature. As such, the extrapolation of these errors would tend to distort the calculated projected errors and may not provide an accurate representation of the true error rate found throughout the population. In these instances, the examiner would account for the error as a known error but would not project the error to the population as a whole.

If the examiner believes that a material misstatement exists within an account balance prior to selecting a sample, the examiner should utilize other examination procedures in lieu of, or in complement to, the PPS process. This is primarily due to the fact that sampling of an account balance where a specific risk exists is usually inefficient due to the large sample size generated. In addition, if the testing confirms that significant errors do exist, the extrapolation of the errors may result in significant errors that may seem unusual and are extremely hard to substantiate to the management of the insurance company.

D. Documentation of Errors

Errors detected as a result of substantive testing may take many forms, including both known and likely errors as demonstrated in the PPS sampling discussion. In addition to these, examiners may note classification errors or have disagreements with an insurance company's management regarding various accounting estimates used by the company.

One of the overriding objectives of the examiner is to determine whether the company's surplus or solvency position is materially misstated. Frequently, the examiner adjusts for the error within his or her examination report. In addition, examiners may also encounter individually small misstatements that are not considered material to the company and are so insignificant as to not require adjustment within the examination report. The determination of which errors to include in the examination report is up to the professional judgment of the examiner in charge. Often, the examiner may wish to exclude clearly immaterial misstatements in the exam report. Where an adjustment is not made, the examiner must ensure that these individually immaterial misstatements are not material in the aggregate or do not involve violations of law. The examiner must be able to summarize the exam results of each individual account balance and perform an overall error evaluation on unadjusted errors. Accordingly, to gauge the effect of each of the various errors, the examiner should prepare a summary of unadjusted errors worksheet to be placed within the examiners' workpapers which summarizes the aggregate effect of all uncorrected errors. Errors that the examiner has adjusted in the exam report should not be included in this summary, although the examiner should maintain a separate summary which shows those adjustments which will be included in the examination report. An illustrative example of one method of summarizing unadjusted errors is presented as follows:

Summary of Unadjusted Errors (SUE)					
W/P Reference		**Net Admitted Assets**	**Liabilities**	**Surplus**	**Income Stmt.**
	Known Errors:				
	Likely Errors:				
	Aggregate Effect				

The above worksheet separately identifies each error as to whether it is a known error or a likely error and summarizes its effect on the components of the financial statements. This allows the examiner to review the effects of the errors on the various financial statement components and to assess whether the aggregate effect of these errors is close to, or exceeds planned tolerable error, which may indicate whether certain unadjusted errors should be included in the examination report.

Examiners should always include both known and likely errors. Known errors are those errors which are quantifiable as a result of the testing procedures performed. For example, in performing substantive tests on premiums receivable, an examiner may determine from the evidence that a receivable listed as $10,500 on the company's books should have been recorded at $5,500. As such, premium receivables, and thus premium income, would be overstated by $5,000. This would be considered a known error as the evidence clearly indicates. Likely errors may also be identified by the examiner, although the amounts cannot be exactly identified. These errors are identified through the extrapolation of misstatements found in a statistical sample or are based on the professional judgment and opinion of the examiner. An example of a likely error would be a disagreement over an accounting estimate, such as IBNR reserves for a property/casualty company.

Having summarized the uncorrected misstatements, the examiner should consider the effects of the errors against planned tolerable error. If the aggregate known and likely unadjusted errors exceed, or are close to planned tolerable error, the risk that surplus may be materially misstated is great. If this situation occurs, the examiner should typically: 1) make adjustments in the exam report for some or all of the known misstatements, and/or 2) have the company assist the examiner in evaluating the likely errors noted to determine if the actual evidence supports the examiner's assessed likely error. By utilizing one, or both of these procedures, the examiner should reduce the aggregate summary of uncorrected misstatements so that the number is acceptably small such that the examiner may conclude that the exam report is not materially misstated.

III. USE OF CPA WORKPAPERS RELATING TO CONTROL AND SUBSTANTIVE TESTING

As discussed in Part 1, Planning Examinations Section C-10, an examiner may consider the work of the insurance company's independent auditor as a supplement, or substitute, to the work required to be performed by the examiner. This would include procedures associated with the testing of internal controls and substantive tests of details. If the examiner determines that the work performed by the CPA may aid in the examination, the examiner may use the CPA's work to reduce the extent of control or substantive testing required.

The first step in determining whether the CPA workpapers may be used is to evaluate the work performed by the CPA. The examiner will typically evaluate the CPA workpapers as part of the planning procedures through the completion of the CPA Checklist. By completing this Checklist, the examiner will develop a thorough understanding of the scope of the CPA audit engagement and the audit procedures utilized by the CPA. The examiner will then look for those areas in which his or her examination effort and planned testing procedures may overlap with those of the CPA. For those areas where overlap exists, examination efficiencies in many instances may be obtained by utilizing the work performed by the CPA.

In areas where overlap does exist, the examiner should evaluate the quality, adequacy and results of the CPA's work. The ultimate determination of whether the work performed by the CPA may be used is dependent on the professional judgment of the examiner and the nature of the testing being evaluated. Generally, if the CPA's workpapers relating to control testing for a particular attribute indicate that significant control deviations exist as a result of testing, the examiner should reassess his or her own planned reliance relating to the applicable control procedure.

If significant substantive testing errors are noted within the CPA's workpapers, the examiner should evaluate the total of the known identified errors in relation to planning materiality and reassess the planned scope of substantive testing for the applicable account balance. Depending on the frequency, size and nature of the errors identified by the CPA, the examiner may or may not wish to use the CPA's work. However, the examiner should always evaluate and consider known errors that have been identified by the CPA and adjust the extent of his or her testing accordingly.

If the CPA's workpapers indicate that they may reasonably be used by the examiner to gain examination efficiencies, the examiner should then evaluate the work of the CPA. The examiner should consider the purpose of the testing procedures and ensure that the CPA's audit objectives, relating to the applicable testing procedures, meet the examination objectives of the examiner. The examiner also should assess the overall quality of the CPA's work focusing primarily on the quality of the documentation of the audit procedures and the results obtained.

The examiner also should consider the nature of the test design, including the number of items selected for testing and the method in which those items were selected. The extent of testing by the CPA, as well as an evaluation of the method of selection, will largely determine the degree to which an examiner may supplement the required amount of testing by the examiner on a stand-alone basis. The determination of the extent to which the CPA's work may be utilized as a substitute for testing performed by the examiner is based on the professional judgment of the examiner. However, as a general rule, as the sophistication of the selection and testing procedures performed by the CPA increase, the less work the examiner will be required to perform. For instance, if a CPA has substantively tested 90% of an account balance without exception, the examiner could reasonably utilize the work performed by the CPA. Likewise, if a CPA has performed internal control testing procedures on a selected number of transactions, which would be sufficient to satisfy the attribute sample requirements which would be required by the examiner, the examiner may choose to utilize the CPA's work to perform control testing. In situations where the CPA has performed an extensive amount of work, the examiner may wish to utilize solely the work performed by the CPA. The examiner may wish to select a limited number of additional items, independent of the CPA selections to ensure that examination objectives are met. The number of additional selections, if any, should be determined based upon the professional judgment of the examiner. However, the examiner should not solely utilize the work of an independent auditor, if in the examiner's professional judgment, the extent of testing performed by the CPA is less than what the examiner deems sufficient.

The extent to which reperformance of the CPA's work, if any, should be performed is dependent on the examiner's professional judgment based on a number of factors including the risk associated with the area of testing and the errors noted by the CPA.

APPENDIX A — CASE STUDY USING PPS SAMPLING

The following case study is intended to show how PPS is performed. It is a simplistic example and is shown for informational purposes only.

Situation

An examiner desires to substantively test the agent balances receivable of ABC Insurance Co. as of the year-end date. The examiner has scanned the account summary and has decided that PPS testing is the most appropriate examination procedure.

Agents balances receivable per the Annual Statement total $600,000 and consist of $800,000 in gross receivables due from agents, net of ceded reinsurance payables of $200,000. The examiner has determined that both balances are material to his or her evaluation of the agents balances receivable account balance and determines that testing will need to be done on both the receivable and payable balances. As the examiner is concerned that the gross receivable balance is overstated and the reinsurance payable balance is understated, the examiner would segregate these populations into two distinct populations and would test these balances separately as explained herein.

The following additional facts are relevant:

- During preliminary planning, the examiner determines overall examination materiality as $140,000. Tolerable error was set at $70,000 ($140,000/2).
- The examiner decided to rely on controls relating to premium billings, cash receipts and cash disbursements. Controls relating to these accounting systems were believed to be highly effective and had a low risk of material error. Accordingly, control testing was performed using a confidence level of 90%. Based on the testing performed controls were found to be reliable, and accordingly, a basic level of substantive testing using a reliance factor of .7 will be used.

Testing of Gross Agent Balances Receivable

The receivables due from agents balance totaled $800,000 and was comprised of 15 items. Included in the receivable balance is a $10,000 credit balance (e.g., a return premium credit) which would not be subject to PPS sampling and which would be excluded from PPS testing as noted below. The credit balance would be subject to testing using some other method of substantive testing unless the examiner determines that the balance is immaterial. Excluding such credit balances from the agents balances receivable results in a gross receivable balance of $810,000.

As the gross agent balances receivable is an asset account, PPS sampling is considered appropriate and is easy to implement as shown below:

Selection Process

The selection interval would be determined as follows:

Selection Interval = Tolerable Error/Reliance Factor

= 70,000/.7

= 100,000

Based on the selection interval computed, the estimated number of selections can be computed as follows:

Estimated Selections = Account Balance (excluding negative value items)/Selection Interval

= 810,000/100,000

= 8 selections

The random starting point as determined by the examiner using a random number generator was determined to be $44,200.

To perform the sampling process, the examiner would perform the following:

1. Subtract the random number to be used, in this case (44,200).
2. Add the recorded amounts of the individual balances, obtaining a subtotal after the addition of each succeeding individual balance. The first individual balance that makes the subtotal positive is selected as part of the sample.
3. After each selection, subtract the selection interval as many times as necessary to make the subtotal fall negative again.
4. Continue adding the individual balances as described in step #3, again selecting all items that cause the subtotal to become positive.

The following table illustrates this process:

Item Number	Item Valuation	Subtotal	Selection
	Random Start	(44,200)	
1	$40,000	(4,420)	
2	55,000	50,800	Yes
		(49,200)	
3	(10,000)	negative item ignored	
4	165,000	115,800	Yes (considered top-stratum)
		15,800	
		(84,200)	
5	45,000	(39,200)	
6	50,000	10,800	Yes
		(89,200)	
7	45,000	(44,200)	
8	60,000	15,800	Yes
		(84,200)	
9	60,000	(24,200)	
10	50,000	25,800	Yes
		(74,200)	
11	65,000	(9,200)	
12	55,000	45,800	Yes
		(54,200)	
13	45,000	(9,200)	
14	45,000	35,800	Yes
		(64,200)	
15	30,000	(34,200)	

Based on this example, the examiner's selection would include items 2, 4, 6, 8, 10, 12, 14. Note that item 4 is considered a "top-stratum" selection as the value of the item, $165,000, exceeds the selection interval of $100,000. Accordingly, despite the fact that only seven physical selections were made, the examiner would consider the $165,000 item as two selections and thus has theoretically made eight selections for sampling purposes. As a general rule, the examiner should add up the number of times he or she is required to subtract the selection interval after going positive. This number will then represent the number of items selected for sampling purposes.

To "prove" the selection process, the examiner would perform a reconciliation as follows:

Random Start		=	44,200
+	# of selections * selection interval (8* 100,000)	=	800,000
+	Ending selection balance	=	(34,200)
+	Negative value items	=	(10,000)
Ending balance		=	800,000
Balance per G/L		=	800,000

Performing the Test and Evaluating the Results

Having selected the seven items using the process above, the examiner would then subject these items to whatever testing procedure is considered appropriate. In this example, the examiner may determine that confirmation of the receivable balances with the various agents is the most effective method in testing the receivable balance. Accordingly, the examiner would send confirmation requests to each of the seven agents in question.

Having sent the confirmations, assume that the examiner receives responses from six of the seven agents, with one confirmation not being returned. Further assume that for four of the confirmations that were received, the agent agreed with the receivable balance existing at year-end as reflected on the confirmation. Based on this information, the examiner concludes that these sampled receivable balances are correct and no further testing is necessary with regard to those balances.

In addition to the four received with no exceptions, two of the confirmations were returned with exceptions or differences (we'll assume that the two are items 4 and 14). For illustrative purposes, assume that item 4 was confirmed by the agent as having a balance of $150,000 (a difference of $15,000) and item 14 was confirmed as having a balance of $40,000 (a difference of $5,000). Having noted these differences, the first thing the examiner must do is to try to determine the reason for the differences, and based on that determination, determine whether the insurance company's financial records are misstated. In this example, we will assume that the examiner has looked into the differences and has determined that the insurance company's records are misstated with regard to these receivables. Having determined this, the examiner would then need to extrapolate these errors along with any other agent balance receivable errors noted during testing to determine the projected probable misstatement within the account balance. This procedure is performed below.

With regard to the confirmation that was not received, the fact that the confirmation was not returned does not indicate that this is not a valid receivable balance. There could be several reasons why the confirmation was not returned including the agent simply not taking the time to return it. Accordingly, the examiner must perform some other alternative procedures to provide assurance that the receivable is valid. In this case, the examiner may wish to examine the invoice that was generated for this receivable and mailed to the agent. In addition, the examiner may wish to trace the receivable to a cash receipt received subsequent to year-end. In this example, we will assume that the examiner is able to perform sufficient alternative procedures to enable him or her to satisfy themselves that the balance is correctly stated.

Of the seven confirmations sent, two contain misstatements that will require further evaluation. As noted when the sample was initially taken, Item 4 is considered a "top-stratum" selection meaning the value of this balance exceeds the determined selection interval. Accordingly, the $15,000 error associated with Item 4 should not be extrapolated to the population. However, it is a known error and will be included in the total projected error associated with this account balance.

Item 14 is not considered a top-stratum selection as the recorded balance does not exceed the selection interval, and accordingly, this error should be extrapolated to the population as a whole. As noted above, Item 4 has a misstatement of $5,000 which represents 11% of the recorded balance (e.g., $5,000/$45,000).

Using the following formula, we can then determine our projected probable misstatement as follows:

Projected probable misstatement	=	(Selection interval times overstatement percentage + misstatements in top stratum items)
	=	($100,000 times 11% + 15,000)
	=	11,000 + 15,000
	=	(comprised of known errors of $20,000 and likely errors of $6,000)

Having determined the projected probable misstatement, the examiner should either adjust the agent receivable account balance in the examination report or post the misstatements to the summary of unadjusted misstatements. In addition, the examiner also should evaluate the error against tolerable error in determining whether the account balance and/or financial statements are materially misstated. In this case, the estimated error of $26,000 is significantly less than the $70,000 tolerable error. However, if the projected error associated with this account, or in combination with errors noted within other accounts, approach or exceed planned tolerable error, the examiner should perform additional examination procedures to ensure that the financial statements are not materially misstated.

Reinsurance Balances Payable

As mentioned above, the examiner in evaluating ceded reinsurance payables primarily would be concerned with the understatement of the payable balance that would indirectly lead to an overstatement of the net agent balance receivable. While the examiner could use alternative testing methods to evaluate the payable balance (for instance, analytical review procedures), the examiner has decided that PPS sampling would be the most efficient method to use. However, as the ceded reinsurance payable balance is a credit balance, and the primary direction of the test is a test of understatement, it would not be considered appropriate for the examiner to sample through the general ledger detail of the payable balance because any item that was understated would not be fully represented in the detail and thus would result in a flawed PPS sample selection. For example, assume that a company had not recorded a $1,000,000 payable on its books. This balance would clearly be material in the above example; however, as the balance is not recorded, it would have no chance of selection using the PPS sampling method and the general ledger detail. To counter this, the examiner would need to sample from an independent or reciprocal population to evaluate reinsurance payables. To accomplish this, an examiner may wish to use PPS sampling to test reinsurance payments subsequent to year-end to determine whether the payment was properly included or excluded from the payable balance at year-end. To do this an examiner would have to determine the typical payment cycle of reinsurance payables (for instance, it may be company policy to pay all ceded reinsurance payables within 30 days after the policy is billed to the policyholder) and then determine the total value of the ceded reinsurance disbursements made during this period. Having determined this, the examiner would then be able to sample through this detail using the PPS sampling method as discussed above.

APPENDIX B — ANSWERS TO COMMONLY ASKED QUESTIONS

Questions:

Attribute Sampling

Q: Is attribute control testing with a minimum sample size required to be performed?

A: No, attribute control testing with a minimum required sample size is not required to be performed. Attribute control testing with a minimum sample size is performed when documentary evidence of a control that is to be relied upon exists. If no reliance on such a control is planned, the examiner should typically not perform any type of testing. In addition, if the total population of an item is sufficiently small, an examiner may determine that attribute testing with a minimum sample size is inefficient or not practical. In these situations, if the examiner still wishes to rely on this control, he or she should judgmentally select an appropriate sample size. Additionally, an examiner may obtain reliable evidence using alternative methods such as observation and inquiry when non-documentary controls exist.

Q: If we expect to find more than one control error, is attribute testing of controls still appropriate?

A: Generally, if the examiner expects to find more than one deviation in his or her sample, attribute testing of internal controls should not be used. Although a valid sample could be constructed with the expectation of finding two or more expected errors, the number of selections required is usually prohibitive to the performance of efficient examination procedures and is beyond the scope of this material.

Q: How are selections of items made for control testing?

A: Having determined the number of selections necessary, the examiner may select the items randomly from among the total population under examination using a random number generator or some other tool. If random selection is not available, the examiner may make his or her selection using a manual haphazard selection process that approximates randomness.

Q: Does the dollar value of the items selected for control matter in the determination of the control effectiveness?

A: The dollar value of the item selected for control testing should not matter in the examiner's evaluation of control effectiveness. Control procedures should be expected to be applied to all transactions in the same manner on a consistent basis. As such, the dollar value of the transaction selected for testing is considered irrelevant and each occurrence of, or deviation from, a prescribed control is given equal weight in the examiner's evaluation.

Q: How is the level of risk of material error determined?

A: The risk of material error (i.e., high, medium or low) is determined by the examiner through the completion of the SRA workpapers and is discussed further in Section 2 of the *Handbook*.

Q: How is the intended reliance on internal controls determined?

A: The intended reliance that an examiner wishes to place on an internal control is largely dependent on the professional judgment of the examiner. Among the factors to be considered by the examiner relating to the intended reliance placed on the control procedure would include the degree to which substantive testing within a particular area might be reduced, the ease with which the control might be tested, the effectiveness and degree of importance of the control procedure to the company, the extent to which alternative controls exist that may be tested more efficiently, as well as a number of other factors.

Q: How should lost or otherwise unavailable documents selected for control testing be handled? How about voided documents?

A: If documents selected for control testing are unable to be found by the company, or the examiner is otherwise unable to examine the document, the examiner should consider it a deviation unless alternative supporting documents can be utilized and provide the same degree of comfort (for example, a duplicate invoice). Voided or unused documents should be examined to ensure that they are not a deviation from the prescribed control, and if such a determination may be made, the examiner should randomly select another item.

Substantive Testing

Q: What are the primary benefits of PPS sampling?

A: There are a number of benefits to be gained from using PPS sampling methods. Among these is the fact that PPS sampling is generally easier to utilize than other variable sampling methods. In addition, PPS sampling results in a stratified sample (i.e., higher dollar value items have greater chance for selection than do lower dollar value items) and individually significant items that are greater than the sampling interval will be automatically selected for testing.

Q: Is PPS sampling required?

A: PPS sampling methods are not required to be used by an examiner. An examiner has a wide variety of test selection methods available to him or her, of which PPS sampling is one. An examiner should carefully evaluate the account balance to be tested to determine which method is considered most appropriate. Generally, PPS sampling is most effective when testing an account balance for overstatement and thus works well with the testing of admitted assets. In addition, PPS sampling may be used to test certain liability accounts, as long as the examiner pays particular attention to the design of the testing procedure and selects his or her sample from an independent or reciprocal population (for example, using PPS sampling on subsequent disbursements to test accounts payable).

Q: Can PPS sampling be used to test for understatement of credit balances?

A: Due to the design of the PPS sampling process, PPS sampling directly from the population of examination interest should generally not be used for understatement testing. This results from the fact that PPS sampling is designed to select a sample with each item having a chance of selection proportional to its size (i.e., the higher the balance, the more chance for selection and vice versa). Intuitively, if a balance is understated its recorded value is less than its actual value and the item would not have a chance of selection proportional to its actual size. For example, if a company failed to record a payable at the end of the year and the examiner was using the general ledger detail at year-end, this payable would have no chance of selection as its recorded value would be zero.

However, testing of credit balances using PPS sampling may be performed if the examiner is able to use an independent or reciprocal monetary population. Such a population would be one that includes valid transactions which should be included (or excluded as considered appropriate) in the population of examination interest. An example of an independent or reciprocal population would be sampling disbursements made after year-end as a test of payables. By sampling subsequent disbursements, an examiner would be able to determine whether these disbursements were properly included or excluded from the payable detail at year-end.

Q: The asset account subject to testing has numerous credit balances within the detail. Is it still appropriate to use PPS sampling?

A: One of the disadvantages of PPS sampling is that PPS sampling is not considered appropriate for the testing of zero or negative value (e.g., credit) balances found within an asset account balance for the reasons discussed above dealing with understatement testing. Accordingly, an examiner should segregate that part of the population that consists of zero or negative value items and evaluate these balances separately using some other method. However, an examiner may still utilize PPS sampling on the "remaining" asset or debit balances within the account balance recognizing that the balance of these remaining items will be grossed up by excluding the zero and negative value items.

APPENDIX C — GLOSSARY

Audit Sampling – the application of audit procedures to less than 100 percent of the items within an account balance or class of transaction for the purpose of evaluating some characteristic of the balance or class.

Sampling Risk – the risk that the examiners' conclusion based on a sample might be different from the conclusion they would reach if they examined each item in the population.

Population – the total sum of all items which are subject to selection.

Statistical Sampling – audit sampling which quantitatively measures the sampling risk and allows the examiner to extrapolate any errors to the population.

Attribute Sampling – sampling which is used to reach a conclusion about a population in terms of a rate of occurrence. Typically used to test the rate of deviation from a prescribed control procedure.

Probability Proportional to Size (PPS) Sampling – a form of variables sampling in which each item within a population has a chance of selection proportional to its size in relation to the entire population.

Substantive Tests of Detail – test procedures designed to obtain evidence about the validity and propriety of the accounting treatment of transactions and balances or to detect errors. Primary interest in substantive tests of details is a conclusion as to dollar terms.

Control Testing – test procedures designed to obtain evidence regarding the effectiveness of accounting controls.

Non-representative Selection – the selection of items that are not representative of the population as a whole. An example of non-representative selection is judgmental selection.

Haphazard Selection – the manual selection of items using a method that approximates randomness (for example, the random pulling of invoices out of a file drawer). This type of selection is considered appropriate when random selection using computer software is not practical or efficient.

Judgmental Selection – the selection of items based on some judgmental evaluation of individual characteristics.

Risk of Overreliance on Internal Control – the risk that an examiner will incorrectly conclude that internal controls are operating effectively based on the sample selected when in fact the true population would not support this reliance.

Risk of Underreliance on Internal Control – the risk that an examiner will conclude that internal controls are not operating effectively, and thus no reliance will be placed on those controls, based on the sample selected, when in fact the true population would support control reliance by the examiner.

Allowable Error Rate – the maximum rate of deviation from a prescribed control procedure that an examiner is willing to accept without altering planned reliance on that control.

Tolerable Error – the amount of error which may exist with the financial statements, or within a specific account, without causing the examiner to believe that the financial statements taken as a whole are misstated.

Projected Probable Misstatement – represents the total estimated misstatement as determined based on the results of the sample selected. Typically will include provisions for both known errors and estimated errors.

PART 4 — REINSURANCE

TABLE OF CONTENTS

PART 4 — REINSURANCE

I. REINSURANCE OVERVIEW

Reinsurance transactions in the insurance industry are occurring more frequently and are increasingly complicated. This part of the *Handbook* has been dedicated to providing a general understanding of the various reinsurance aspects present in the insurance industry and among the diverse lines of business.

Companies may employ numerous reinsurance transactions with a variety of specific details, but typically, there are six basic reasons why companies desire to engage in reinsurance:

1. Expand the Insurance Company's Capacity – Insurance company capacity is the maximum amount of risk the insurer can undertake in relationship to its surplus. By engaging in reinsurance transactions, companies are able to write more policies and obtain premium income while transferring a portion of the liability risk to assuming companies.

2. Stabilize Underwriting Results – Significant individual losses have the capacity to endanger the insurance company's overall underwriting results. By engaging in reinsurance, the insurance company has the capability to level out yearly fluctuations of losses on its overall underwriting results by transferring a portion of the risk to other companies.

3. Financing – Statutory accounting rules prohibit the amortization of acquisition expenses. Although the revenue from the insurance policy is earned over the policy term, the commissions paid to agents for new or renewed insurance policies must be recognized immediately. This puts a financial strain on an insurance company's surplus so reinsurance is sometimes used as a vehicle to share or transfer this surplus strain.

4. Provide Catastrophe Protection – Insurance companies may provide insurance for various types of perils in which one event may significantly impact numerous insurers for extensive amounts. It is vital for insurance companies to remain solvent by minimizing the financial impact of a single catastrophic loss occurrence.

5. Withdraw from a Line or Class of Business – Insurance companies may decide to stop writing a particular line or class of business. The insurer can transfer, or cede, risks to reinsurers who will assume the obligations of the primary insurer.

6. Spread of Risk – Reinsurance permits companies to lessen surplus strain and improve their capacity levels. It also enables companies to increase the amount of risks assumed and policies written as well as provides opportunity to engage in various types of risks among classes and businesses. This provides the company with the opportunity to improve the stability of underwriting risks and overall performance.

The remaining guidance included in this part of the *Handbook* will provide additional information over the reinsurance industry and will elaborate the reinsurance fundamentals pertinent to financial examiners.

II. FUNDAMENTALS OF REINSURANCE

A. Fundamentals of Reinsurance

Reinsurance, simply defined, is the process by which one insurer, the reinsurer, agrees to indemnify another insurer, the reinsured, or cedent, either entirely or partially, against loss arising from an insurance policy previously issued by the reinsured. The existence of reinsurance does not alter or diminish the liability of the reinsured, under the terms of the original insurance policy, to the policyholder.

Long-term continuity is usually an element of great importance in reinsurance relationships. The reinsurance agreement entered into today is quite likely to have a financial impact on both parties that may persist over many years. The ultimate underwriting result on the contract may not become fully apparent until long after the agreement itself has expired or been terminated.

Reinsurance, reduced to fundamentals, is therefore a contractual promise to pay, which in many instances will not be presented for collection until long after the contractual obligations are created. Close attention must be paid to the nature and structure of the company's reinsurance arrangements, since they can have a substantial impact on the company's operating results and overall financial condition. Evaluation of the quality of reinsurance security and the degree to which the company's surplus is leveraged by reinsurance recoverables should be given a high priority in every examination. Uncollectible reinsurance has been a major element in a number of past insolvencies.

B. Reinsurance Contracts and Terminology

The reinsurance agreement is a contract between the insurance company that transfers risk to a reinsurance company (the cedent), and the insurance company(s) that assumes all or part of a ceding company's insurance risk (the reinsurer). Reinsurance agreements may also be arranged directly with the reinsurer or through a reinsurance broker or intermediary. A reinsurance broker is an individual who represents a ceding company in placing business with a reinsurer and is not a party to the reinsurance contract. This is considered significant because in most reinsurance agreements the arbitration clause lets the parties to the contract resolve differences or disputes among themselves without resorting to formal litigation. On the other hand, disputes between the broker and the company, or reinsurers (or both), cannot usually be delegated to an arbitration panel without the mutual agreement of all parties. Traditionally, such differences have been resolved between the affected parties via direct negotiation and compromise, but should that approach prove ineffective in a specific case, formal litigation would probably be the only remaining recourse.

Reinsurance agreements are contracts of indemnity in that the reinsurer's obligation arises only when the company's liability under its original insurance policy has been incurred. The extent of that obligation is defined by the specific terms and conditions of the applicable reinsurance agreement. Absent specific agreement to the contrary (for example, a "cut-through" provision in which the obligations of the reinsurer will be paid directly to the insured or claimant under the original policy), there are no privities of contract between the reinsurer and any party other than the company defined as the "reinsured" in the reinsurance agreement. Some states prohibit cut-through provisions because specific policyholders may receive preferential treatment if the cedent were to become insolvent.

Reinsurers also buy reinsurance protection, principally for the purpose of spreading risk and reducing the impact of catastrophic loss events. A cession, or transfer, of obligations from one reinsurer to another is a "retrocession," the first reinsurer being the "retrocedent" and the second the "retrocessionaire."

(The terminology of the reinsurance industry and contracts is oftentimes complex. In order to improve the utilization of the included guidance, some of the more prominent terms included in reinsurance contract clauses have been defined in Appendix A.)

III. TYPES OF REINSURANCE

While reinsurance arrangements may be structured in a variety of ways and serve a number of possible purposes, reinsurance comes in only two basic types.

A. Property/Casualty Reinsurance

1. Treaty Reinsurance

Reinsurance treaties are usually automatic arrangements in that the company does not have to make specific cessions in order to activate reinsurance protection. Exceptions to this general rule are special acceptances, a procedure by which risks that do not qualify for coverage under the terms and conditions of the treaty may be submitted to the reinsurer for specific underwriting evaluation and determination of any additional premium charge.

Treaties are also usually obligatory in that the cedent is obligated to cede all business defined by the reinsurance agreement, and the reinsurer is obligated to accept all such business, subject to the terms and conditions of the contract. Surplus treaties are sometimes non-obligatory from the company's standpoint, as the company may elect not to cede a specific risk, or to cede something less than the maximum cession permitted under the contract provisions.

Treaty reinsurance usually applies to a broad segment of the company's overall book of business (e.g., all Workers' Compensation business, all Commercial Property business, all Accident & Health business, all Aviation business). All sorts of segregations are possible, but the idea is to group together entire lines or classes of business. As long as the business to be reinsured is reasonably homogeneous in nature or exposed to loss arising from a common cause, and written in sufficient volume, it can be considered for treaty reinsurance. A sufficient volume of reinsurance is necessary in order to satisfy the reinsurers' need to collect reinsurance premiums that bear a reasonable relationship to the assumed liabilities. Treaty reinsurance is considered to be the most efficient and least expensive way of arranging for such transfers.

2. Facultative Reinsurance

Facultative transactions, by their nature, are not obligatory with respect to either the cedent or the reinsurer. Facultative reinsurance involves the reinsurance of the exposures covered by a single policy, or sometimes only specific portions of a policy. The nature of the underwriting process and the kind and amount of data that are usually required by the facultative underwriter make this approach far less efficient and much more expensive to handle than treaty reinsurance.

Nevertheless, facultative reinsurance often plays a significant role in a company's overall reinsurance program. It is commonly used to enable the company to write risks that may be excluded under its reinsurance treaties, to generate additional capacity needed that is not fully accommodated under its treaties, or to accept risks requiring technical underwriting expertise beyond that which may be available in-house.

It is also possible to arrange reinsurance protection on a "hybrid" basis that contains obligatory and non-obligatory elements.

Two commonly encountered facultative arrangements are:

a. Facultative Obligatory Reinsurance

Facultative obligatory reinsurance, or "open cover," is an arrangement pursuant to which the cedent may, at its option, cede certain defined risks to the reinsurer, which the reinsurer must assume, subject to the cedent's retention. This arrangement has both treaty and facultative elements. It is normally used to provide cover for risks that are irregular in incidence or to supplement a treaty that has limited capacity.

b. Semi-automatic Facultative Reinsurance

Semi-automatic facultative reinsurance requires the reinsurer to accept certain defined risks of the reinsured, subject to the right of the reinsurer to reject liability for any of such risks within a stated period after submission. Like facultative obligatory reinsurance, semi-automatic facultative reinsurance is also a hybrid of both treaty and facultative reinsurance.

B. Life, Accident & Health Reinsurance

1. Automatic

Automatic life reinsurance is similar to property/casualty "treaty" reinsurance. In automatic reinsurance, the ceding company is able to bind the reinsurer on a risk without submitting an application for reinsurance provided certain conditions are met. These conditions vary by agreement, but typically obligate the ceding company to keep a retention on the life, limit the amount of insurance on a life that may be ceded, and limit the overall amount of insurance that may be in force on the life in all companies. The ceding company may be required to notify the reinsurer of the automatic reinsurance agreements through specific cessions (i.e.,"cession reporting"), otherwise it is called "bordereau reporting." This type of reinsurance will be typically offered to broad segments of a company's business, such as all issues of a specified policy form.

2. Facultative

Life facultative reinsurance is similar to property/casualty facultative reinsurance or to "special acceptances" reinsurance under treaty reinsurance. However, "facultative obligatory" reinsurance and "semi-automatic" reinsurance will rarely be encountered in the life and health market.

C. Health Reinsurance

Reinsurance transactions for health companies typically follow the reinsurance practices of property/casualty companies. Recently, new guidance has been adopted for health companies and risk sharing receivables. Information on risk sharing receivables is provided in **SSAP No. 84** in the NAIC *Accounting Practices and Procedures Manual.*

IV. FORMS OF REINSURANCE

Whether on a treaty basis or a facultative basis, there are two forms of reinsurance, Proportional (also often referred to as pro-rata reinsurance) and Non-proportional (often referred to as excess of loss reinsurance).

A. Property/Casualty Reinsurance

1. Proportional Reinsurance

Under proportional reinsurance the company and the reinsurer share in an agreed ratio all premiums, losses and loss expenses arising out of the original business covered under the reinsurance agreement. There are two forms of proportional reinsurance: Quota Share and Surplus Share.

a. Quota Share Reinsurance

This type of reinsurance was the earliest form of proportional reinsurance and is still widely used. Quota share reinsurance agreements represent a sharing of all business in a fixed ratio, or proportion. A 50% quota share agreement is one in which premiums, losses, and loss expenses of a policy are shared equally, half being retained by the company and half being ceded to the reinsurer. A 70% quota share would involve a 70% share ceded to the reinsurer, with the remaining 30% retained by the company.

> *In Practice* – A $500,000 insurance policy remitting annual premiums of $1,000 under a 50% quota share agreement, would entitle the insurer and reinsurer to $500 of the annual premiums, and liability of up to $250,000 on a claim.

The company's needs and objectives, and the amount of proportional capacity available in the reinsurance marketplace at the time of placement, will determine the percentage share it will retain for its own account.

Quota share treaties are invariably obligatory contracts. The contract will contain a stipulated limit of liability with respect to any single original policy. There will ordinarily be certain forms of coverage or classes of business that are excluded under the terms of the contract. These may not be ceded to the reinsurer without prior review and approval (usually referred to as a special acceptance) by the reinsurer.

The reinsurance premium is simply the reinsurer's proportional share of the company's original premium for all business ceded. The reinsurer's share of the company's acquisition costs and general operating expenses associated with the ceded business is recovered by the company via the ceding commission allowance, which is a deduction from the reinsurer's share of the gross original premium.

b. Surplus Share Reinsurance

This type of proportional reinsurance is a variation on the quota share concept. Instead of sharing the premiums, losses and loss adjustment expenses on every policy on the basis of a first dollar fixed ratio, a surplus agreement permits the company to cede varying amounts or percentage shares in excess of a specified retention of each original policy to the reinsurer. The amounts ceded are still subject to a stipulated minimum retention and maximum cession.

In Practice – In a three-line surplus agreement, the insurer would transfer three times the amount of liability retained. On a $40,000 policy, the insurer would retain $10,000 (1/4) of the liability and the reinsurer would assume $30,000 (3/4). In the event of a total or partial liability claim, the insurer and reinsurer would maintain the same percentages for claim resolution. *(The percentages and amount assumed and ceded may differ among reinsurance contracts.)*

Once a cession has been made to the surplus treaty, premiums, expenses and losses will be shared proportionally between the company and the reinsurer.

2. Non-Proportional Reinsurance

Non-proportional reinsurance occurs when the reinsurer indemnifies the ceding entity against the amount of loss in excess of the cedent company's specified retention for a predetermined percentage of premiums. Non-proportional reinsurance, as the name implies, does not contemplate the sort of sharing of premiums, losses and loss expenses that occurs under proportional structures. Instead, the reinsurer assumes liability for only such loss as exceeds the company's stipulated net retention (or, in the case of a layered excess structure, loss which exceeds the combined limit of liability of all underlying layers of reinsurance plus the company's retention). The three types of non-proportional reinsurance include:

a. Excess Per Risk

This reinsurance method provides indemnification to the ceding company for each covered risk up to a predetermined limit. The ceding company is required to meet the obligations of the claim up to a preset dollar amount before the reinsurer becomes liable.

In Practice – A company that utilizes the excess per risk reinsurance method may cede amounts exceeding the first $100,000 of claim liability on a policy to a reinsurer. That reinsurer agrees to accept this risk, but limits their total liability for this policy to $900,000. In effect, a claim on this policy for $850,000 would be settled from $100,000 from the original insurer and $750,000 from the reinsurer.

b. Aggregate Excess of Loss Reinsurance (Stop-Loss)

This method provides reinsurer indemnification to the ceding company for the aggregate amount of losses during a specific time frame up to a predetermined limit or percentage.

In Practice – A company decides to cede all insurance losses that exceed 75% of the company's subject premiums for the calendar year ended 12/31/XX. The reinsurer agrees to assume this liability, but limits responsibility at $2,500,000. In effect, if the reinsurer incurred losses totaling 80% of the subject premiums, the reinsurer would be liable for 5% of the losses up to $2,500,000. (*For these situations, the ceding company will be expected to provide documentation to the reinsurer of the premiums collected and the losses sustained.*)

c. Per Occurrence (Catastrophe) Excess of Loss

This reinsurance method is identical to the 'Excess Per Risk of Reinsurance' indicated above, except that the policies are designed to account for an accumulation of losses from a single catastrophic event.

In Practice – A company may decide to cede all insurance losses exceeding $4,000,000 that result from a natural catastrophic event. One reinsurer who accepts the risk may limit liability at $25,000,000. In the event of an earthquake that causes losses of $29,000,000, the original insurer would be responsible for the first $4,000,000 in losses and the reinsurer would be responsible for $25,000,000. As catastrophic events can result in a significant loss, the insurer may find it necessary to cede parts of the risk to different reinsurers, or the assuming reinsurer may cede some of the assumed risk to others (retrocession).

In non-proportional reinsurance the reinsurer does not assume responsibility for a proportional share of all losses. Therefore, the distribution of premium will not be on a proportional basis but is determined on a contract basis in accordance with the amount of retention by the ceding company. Non-proportional reinsurance is commonly arranged in a series of layers, the first of which attaches immediately to the excess of the company's retention, followed by as many additional layers as are necessary to generate the required total amount of capacity (per risk) or to afford such catastrophe (per occurrence) aggregate (net retained loss) protection as deemed prudent and sufficient, given the size, geographic distribution and nature of the company's portfolio of business.

B. Life & Health Reinsurance

There are two forms of life reinsurance: proportional and nonproportional.

1. Proportional Reinsurance

As a general rule life insurance companies establish limits of retention as a matter of general practice. These limits, which may vary by age at issue, plan or substandard classification, are the amounts which the company has decided it can safely retain at its own risk with respect to newly issued policies. A schedule of limits of retention also includes limits for supplemental benefits such as disability and accidental death. These limits may or may not be independent of the limits for life insurance benefits. With these limits of retention established for all the forms of coverage issued, a company makes reinsurance arrangements with one or more reinsurers to take care of those applications on which the amounts are in excess of the established retention.

Using the above methodology, proportional life reinsurance may be written on:

a. Yearly Renewable Term (YRT) or Risk Premium Reinsurance Basis

Reinsurance agreements written on this basis transfer the mortality risk to the reinsurer. For every age, plan and policy year, there is a certain reserve per $1,000 of insurance. In calculating the company's statutory surplus, this is the liability that is deducted from assets to arrive at the company's surplus. Since this reserve amount is already in the company's liabilities, it is clear that if the company is called upon to pay more than this amount, only the excess over the reserve needs to be taken from the company's surplus. In the event of a death claim, assets are reduced by the face amount paid, liabilities are reduced by the reserve amount, and the excess of the face amount over the reserve comes from its surplus. This excess is called the "policy net amount at risk." In the reinsurance agreement the ceding company and the reinsurer agree upon how the policy net amount at risk will be apportioned between them.

In Practice - The ceding company would prepare a schedule of the net amounts at risk for each policy year. The reinsurer would develop a schedule of yearly renewable term premium rates for reinsurance on the ceding company's schedule.

The ceding insurer would pay the reinsurer the established premiums for the appropriate net amounts at risk each year. In the occurrence of a claim, the reinsurer would remit payment for the assumed portion of the policy's net amount at risk.

Although the policy net amount at risk will decline over time as the policy reserves increase, it is common for the parties to agree to make adjustments only at agreed intervals to ease administration and lower processing costs. This reinsurance method is widely used because it reduces reinsurance to its fundamentals and provides a very flexible mechanism for satisfying the company's reinsurance needs.

b. Coinsurance Basis

This type of reinsurance is considered to be the most comprehensive basis since it usually involves transfer of a portion of all the risks inherent in the original business on a quota share or excess of retention basis from the ceding company to the reinsurer.

In this type of reinsurance, the ceding company and the reinsurer share a portion of the risks under the original insurance policy. The reinsurer receives a portion of the gross paid policy premiums based on the amount of risk assumed and establishes a correlating reserve. In addition to fulfilling the assumed portion of the claim, the reinsurer is also required to reimburse the ceding company for any other benefits provided under the policy (i.e., policy dividends, commissions, premium taxes, etc.). The reinsurer also provides the ceding company with a commission to cover the marketing, underwriting and distribution aspects of the policy.

In Practice – If the ceding company desired to cede 50% of a $500,000 life insurance policy with annual premiums of $1,000, the reinsurer would receive $500 (50%) of the premiums collected. The reinsurer would establish an adequate reserve on its books and pay the ceding company for the share of commission costs and benefits provided. In the event of the death of the policyholder, the reinsurer would be required to remit $250,000.

- Coinsurance with funds transferred

  A slight variation of this reinsurance method may occur if assets are transferred between the ceding company and reinsurer. Under this method, assets supporting the reserves on the ceded portion of the business are transferred to the reinsurer. Typically, unless otherwise stated, any investment gains and losses arising on these assets belong to the reinsurer.

  In some circumstances, the ceding company may wish to retain control of the funds arising from its own policies either to maximize its own investment returns, or as security against the event that the reinsurer's ability to discharge its obligations to the ceding insurer becomes impaired. (The latter may also be a concern to regulators in the ceding company's state of domicile.) In response to such considerations, the modified coinsurance (a variation of the coinsurance reinsurance method) method to account for reinsurance was developed.

c. Modified Coinsurance Basis

Modified coinsurance, or "modco," differs from coinsurance agreements in that the portion of policy assets normally entitled to the reinsurer are actually retained by the ceding company. In addition to the transactions required in a coinsurance arrangement, a "reserve adjustment" must be calculated. For each accounting period, the change in reserves is first determined. If these have increased, the amount of the increase, less interest on the reserve for the period, will be payable to the ceding company. If reserves have decreased, the amount of the decrease, plus interest on the reserve, will be payable to the reinsurer.

In Practice – (Using the same example for the coinsurance method) If the ceding company desired to cede 50% of the $500,000 life insurance policy with annual premiums of $1,000, the ceding company and reinsurer would each receive $500 (50%) of the premiums collected. The ceding company would establish the full portion of the reserve for this policy and retain all funds held to support the reserve. Each year, the reserve basis would be determined, and after considering the impact of interest on the funds held by the ceding company, the reinsurer would remit or receive payment to cover the increase/decrease in reserve. In the event of the death of the policyholder, the reinsurer would be required to remit $250,000 less amount funds withheld.

The rationale for this procedure is that the ceding company holds the policy reserves and the corresponding assets of the reinsured business and, therefore, is responsible for the portion of the reserve increase derived from interest on the policy assets. Any other fluctuations in the reserve would be the responsibility of the reinsurer. Establishing the reserve adjustment interest rate is a complex part of the treaty negotiations. The formula for calculating the interest rate is typically set forth in the reinsurance agreement.

2. Non-proportional Reinsurance

Non-proportional reinsurance provides for aggregate losses rather than indemnification on individual policies. Typically, these reinsurance policies are written annually to protect from excessive losses.

Non-proportional Life & Health Reinsurance may be written as:

a. Catastrophe Reinsurance

This provides for payment by the reinsurer when the ceding company's aggregate net retained claims resulting from a single accidental event exceed the company's retention under the reinsurance agreement. Commonly, the reinsurer pays something less than 100% of such excess, the balance being retained by the company, and a limit is placed on the amount the reinsurer will pay on any one catastrophe. An annual limit may also be placed on the total amount to be paid by the reinsurer. The coverage may be purchased on the ceding company's entire portfolio of retained risks or on any readily definable category, such as all retained individual risks, a particular group case, a category of group cases, etc. Normally, both the regular life insurance risk and the accidental death risk will be included.

In Practice – The ceding company cedes to a reinsurer 100% of aggregate, entire portfolio claims caused by a natural catastrophic event that exceed $5,000,000. The reinsurer agrees to accept the risk with a limit of 2 claims per year and an annual dollar limit of $10,000,000. In the event of an earthquake that resulted in life claims totaling $7,500,000, the insurer would be responsible for $5,000,000 and the reinsurer would be responsible for $2,500,000. If a second natural catastrophe occurred throughout the same calendar year, the reinsurer liability would be limited to $7,500,000.

b. Stop-Loss Reinsurance

The term stop–loss reinsurance is commonly used to describe coverage for a collection of insurance risks under which, once the ceding company pays the total amount of all claims in a specified period, usually a calendar year, up to a total aggregate limit determined in advance for the period, the reinsurer will reimburse a specified proportion (e.g., 90%) of the amount in excess of the aggregate retention for the period, subject to a maximum reinsurance limit. In practice, the maximum amount of claim on any one life is usually "warranted" by the ceding company. Any policy amounts issued in excess of the warranted maximum are reinsured conventionally.

In Practice – The ceding company wishes to cede the risk that life insurance claims may exceed $2,000,000 for the calendar year. The reinsurer agrees to accept the risk, and agrees to pay 90% of all claims that exceed the $2,000,000 threshold. At the end of the calendar year, the reinsurer would receive documentation of the current-year paid claims from the ceding company, and remit any required amounts based on the stated liability.

C. Heath Reinsurance

Managed care reinsurance contracts have generally operated on a per risk excess of loss basis with an aggregate limit per year on each risk and aggregate limit on the life of the member covered. Reinsurance premiums paid are based upon the number of members reinsured and are generally paid on a per member per month basis with options by the reinsurer to adjust the premium with notice based upon certain agreed upon terms. There is normally a minimum reinsurance premium owed by the ceding company independent of the number of members covered.

Generally, the reinsurer will reimburse an agreed upon percentage (i.e., 90%) of claims once the ceding company has satisfied its retention on network claims. (A network is a group of providers under a managed care plan that has agreed to administer health care services to covered persons with the expectation of receiving payment, other than co-payments or deductibles, directly or indirectly from the health maintenance organization.) The reinsurer normally reimburses a lesser percentage (i.e., 70%) for out-of-network claims. Given that out-of-network claims are typically not subject to the discounts accorded to in-network claims, the reinsurer is less eager to participate in out-of-network claims.

A different retention level for hospital claims (i.e., $100,000) vs. physician claims (i.e., $15,000) is also common in a managed care reinsurance contract. These multiple retention levels exist to protect the company as well as the reinsurer. The company is protected from retaining too much risk for claim expenses that are traditionally lower (physician) and the reinsurer is protected from participating too heavily in claim expenses that are normally higher (hospitals).

V. FUNCTIONS OF REINSURANCE

A. Capacity

The term "capacity" has two commonly used meanings in the context of insurance and reinsurance. It may be used to describe the maximum amount of liability that the company is prepared to accept on any individual risk or policy (or, with respect to a reinsurer, under any one reinsurance agreement or on any one reinsurance program, such as all reinsurance agreements relating to an individual cedent). It may be used to describe the maximum overall volume of premium income that an insurer or reinsurer may absorb without leveraging its surplus to an unreasonable or hazardous extent.

Capacity, as set forth in the first definition above, can be generated via a variety of possible reinsurance arrangements. For example, a company with only $10,000,000 in policyholder surplus may need to be able to issue policies with a $1,000,000 limit of liability in order to compete effectively in the marketplace, yet might be very uncomfortable with the idea of retaining that much liability. The company may prudently decide to limit its retention to $250,000 and look to reinsurers for assistance and support.

The amount of liability that an insurer may prudently retain on any one risk is obviously dependent upon the company's capital base, (or in statutory terms, upon the level of policyholder surplus), RBC requirements and the degree of underwriting risk to which the company's management is willing to expose its surplus. In most states there are statutory limitations relating to property/casualty reinsurance which typically require the company to limit the amount of net liability it assumes on any one risk to no more than 10% of statutory surplus. Those restrictions may make it difficult for smaller companies to compete effectively in a marketplace environment that requires the ability to offer higher limits of liability. Conversely, management may only be comfortable with a net retention level substantially lower than the statutory provision, depending on the actual level of the company's surplus and the nature and composition of its book of business. Proportional life and health arrangements (coinsurance or modified coinsurance) permit the cedent to issue policies with higher face amounts than could comfortably be retained net.

Also, while management may be quite comfortable with a given net retention on certain established lines or classes of business, entering new lines or classes of business might require a more cautious and conservative approach. The company may require use of a lower level of retention until enough experience has been developed in the new area to permit better evaluations and judgments.

The following alternatives are the principal methods of generating the required gross line capacity (for the sake of simplicity, the illustration assumes that facultative reinsurance is never utilized, and ignores the effect of ceding commission under the proportional structures — quota share and surplus share).

	QUOTA SHARE (75% OF $1,000,000)	SURPLUS SHARE (3 LINE SURPLUS)	EXCESS OF LOSS
Company Retention	25%	1 line, not less than $100,000 not to exceed $250,000	$250,000
Reinsurer Share	75%	Up to 3 lines, not to exceed $750,000	$750,000
Gross Line Capacity	$1,000,000	$1,000,000	$1,000,000

Under the quota share approach, reinsurers would get 75% of the company's original premium income for business covered under the treaty, and would be responsible for 75% of all losses and loss adjustment expenses, irrespective of the dollar value of the loss, subject to the contract limit of $1,000,000.

Under the surplus share arrangement, the company may vary its retention on any specific cession between $100,000 and $250,000, and may vary the number of lines (multiples of the company's retention) ceded to reinsurers on a specific cession. In the three-line surplus share agreement illustrated above, the reinsurers' limit is not to exceed the maximum of three lines. Once the company has determined what its retention will be and a cession has been made to the treaty, then premium, losses and loss adjustment expense will be shared proportionally, either 50/50, 33.33/66.67 or 25/75, depending on whether one, two or three lines have been ceded. The distribution is not automatic or necessarily uniform as it would be under the quota share structure.

If instead of a proportional approach the company chose a non-proportional, or excess of loss arrangement, the distribution of premium, losses and loss adjustment expenses would be quite different. Since reinsurers would have no responsibility for any loss unless it was greater than the company's retention of $250,000, they would clearly not be entitled to a proportional share of the company's original premium income for business covered under the treaty. The reinsurer usually calculates a premium for the layer of excess protection being afforded which is a function of its attachment point (which in a first excess layer situation such as this will be identical to the company's retention), the limit of liability under the reinsurance contract ($750,000 in this illustration), the anticipated level of the company's original premium income for business subject to the treaty, the reinsurer's judgment with respect to the frequency with which the company's losses individually are likely to exceed the company's retention and thus become recoverable under the reinsurance treaty, and the reinsurer's evaluation of expected total losses recoverable under the treaty.

Proportional reinsurance structures also serve to expand the cedent's capacity in the other sense of the term (i.e., the ratio of net premium writings to policyholder surplus). A temporary augmentation of surplus arises as a result of the effect of the ceding commission allowance on the cedent's balance sheet, which can be simply illustrated by noting the surplus impact of a 50% quota share cession with a ceding commission of 25%.

Before Reinsurance

Written Premium	Unearned Premium Reserve	Assets	Liabilities	Surplus
$2,000,000	$2,000,000	$5,000,000	$2,000,000	$3,000,000

After Reinsurance

Written Premium	Unearned Premium Reserve	Assets	Liabilities	Surplus
$1,000,000	$1,000,000	$4,250,000	$1,000,000	$3,250,000

Because the reduction in assets (the ceded reinsurance premium, net of ceding commission) of $750,000 ($5,000,000 less $4,250,000) is less than the reduction in liabilities (the ceded unearned premium reserve) of $1,000,000 ($2,000,000 less $1,000,000), surplus is increased by an amount equal to the difference between the two, or $250,000.

Managed care entities determine their capacity in much the same way as life and health insurers. The initial determination would be made based upon the total surplus of the entity, the number of members covered by the plan, and how long the entity has written this business. For example, a managed care entity may issue a policy to its members with a maximum annual coverage of up to $1,000,000 per year with a lifetime limit of $2,000,000. The amount of liability that the managed care entity may retain on any one risk will be based upon the above factors.

B. Stabilization

Apart from the impact of accumulation of individual losses arising from a single event, which can be addressed via catastrophe excess of loss reinsurance, a company will wish to limit the impact of individual large losses on its overall underwriting results. Proportional covers will obviously serve to limit the volatility of overall underwriting performance, since all loss not otherwise reinsured will be shared between the company and reinsurers. Also, by virtue of the surplus augmentation, which occurs in all proportional reinsurance arrangements, the company will be able to write a greater volume of business and thus potentially achieve a better spread of risk with attendant benefit in terms of stabilization of incurred loss levels. The most common technique, however, for limiting the impact of large individual losses is the use of Per Risk Excess of Loss reinsurance.

The potential sources of large "per risk" losses are numerous, varied and have increased substantially over time as insurable values have increased, technology has become more complex, and concepts and standards of negligence and liability have been expanded in the industrialized countries, especially the United States. Both the frequency and the dollar value of large losses have grown dramatically in nearly all areas of property and casualty insurance, leading to an increased dependence upon per risk excess of loss reinsurance as the principal vehicle to limit and contain the impact of large single risk losses upon overall operating results.

While stabilization of year-to-year experience is itself a legitimate purpose to which reinsurance can be directed, arrangements that entail the use of multiple year retrospectively rated agreements must be carefully scrutinized to determine whether the arrangement, viewed as a whole, transfers sufficient risk to the reinsurer to warrant reinsurance accounting treatment. Additionally, examiners will need to determine whether liabilities arising out of any contractual obligations to reimburse the reinsurer for any portion of recoveries previously made have been appropriately disclosed and accrued for in the company's financial statements. SSAP No. 62 of the NAIC *Accounting Practices and Procedures Manual* provides guidance on the accounting and reporting procedures applicable to multiple years retrospectively rated reinsurance agreements.

Another method of achieving stabilization of the company's underwriting results is the use of Aggregate Excess of Loss reinsurance, often referred to as "stop-loss" reinsurance. Under this arrangement the reinsurer agrees to indemnify the ceding company for all losses incurred during the reinsurance period, which exceed a stipulated aggregate amount to be retained by the company, subject to a maximum limit on the reinsurer's obligation. Both the company's retention and the reinsurer's limit of liability may be expressed either as dollar amounts, or in terms of loss ratios (the ratio of incurred losses to earned premium).

In reviewing aggregate excess covers, the examiner should pay close attention to any contract provisions that effectively serve to defer the reinsurer's obligation to reimburse covered losses. These would include such elements as aggregating multiple year retentions, or periodic recalculation of the company's retention based on subsequent development of earlier accident year incurred losses, and "experience accounts" into which premium, net of the reinsurer's margin, is deposited, to be subsequently returned with accumulated interest to the company upon eventual commutation of the reinsurance agreement. When present, such provisions may be indicative of an absence of genuine transfer of risk, in which case the arrangement would properly be accorded deposit-type accounting treatment.

The examiner should also bear in mind that current accounting procedures require a clear distinction to be made between prospective and retroactive reinsurance agreements. Traditionally, aggregate excess contracts have often covered losses that occurred prior to the inception date of the reinsurance agreement. The examiner should utilize SSAP No.62, Property and Casualty Reinsurance, from the NAIC *Accounting Practices and Procedures Manual*, to determine whether any special accounting treatment for these instances is required.

C. Catastrophe Protection

Protection against catastrophic loss is one of the most important forms of property and casualty reinsurance protection that a company can buy. Many causes of insured loss can be controlled, or at least mitigated to a certain extent, via various loss prevention techniques employed by insurers and their policyholders.

Companies inevitably accumulate substantial aggregations of exposure to loss arising from natural perils (and certain man-made perils, e.g., riot, civil commotion, vandalism) when they write forms of insurance that provide protection against damage or destruction caused by such perils. This accumulation of exposure usually can be limited to levels which management considers to be reasonable and prudent through Per Occurrence Excess of Loss reinsurance, more commonly referred to as Catastrophe protection. Catastrophe reinsurance, like most other reinsurance products, is intended to protect the company's net position, and therefore applies only after recoveries have been made from all other applicable reinsurance (other than aggregate excess of loss protection), whether proportional or non-proportional, treaty or facultative. For this purpose, other reinsurance is usually deemed to have been recovered by the cedent, whether or not recoveries have actually been made. In order to ensure that the settlement of individual claims is carefully controlled, reinsurers usually insist that a participation, or co-reinsurance, be retained by the ceding company.

The amount of catastrophe protection required is a function of the amount and the geographic spread of business written by the company, and can vary from relatively modest limits of a few million dollars to very substantial programs with limits in the hundreds of millions. Protection is almost always arranged in a series of layers or bands, and depending upon the total capacity required, frequently involves extensive use of international markets in addition to domestic reinsurers.

In reviewing the company's catastrophe reinsurance arrangements attention should be directed to the methods employed by the company to determine estimated aggregate exposure (i.e., total insured values on policies in force) by geographic zone or region. If the aggregate exposure for any zone exceeds the maximum amount of reinsurance recoverable with respect to any single loss occurrence, the examiner should consider the probable impact on the company's financial condition and determine whether a contingency plan has been established. In order to understand the company's aggregate exposure and risk, the examiner should review the company's completed 'General Interrogatories' included in the company's filed Annual Statement. This indicates the company's maximum net liabilities and determination of concentrations of insured exposure to catastrophic loss events.

The examiner should also determine whether any of the catastrophe contracts contain provisions that obligate the company to reimburse any amounts recovered from the reinsurer, or which reduce coverage for future events commensurate with prior loss payments made by the reinsurer. Such arrangements, often referred to as "funded covers," are no longer encountered very frequently, since statutory accounting rules now require timely disclosure and accrual by the ceding company.

"Clash" covers are essentially the casualty equivalent of property catastrophe reinsurance. This type of reinsurance protects the company against the accumulation of net retentions that would otherwise arise when more than one insured or policy is involved in the same loss occurrence, and are designed to respond only in such instances. (The attachment point of the clash cover should be no lower than the company's maximum single policy limit.)

For life and health reinsurance stop-loss and catastrophe covers are used to limit the impact of adverse experience on blocks of in-force business, or of multiple claims arising from a single event.

D. Financing

Statutory accounting rules require that expenses attributable to the production of new and renewal business, the largest element of which is usually agents' commission, must be fully expensed immediately, without recognition of the fact that revenues generated by that business will be earned over the term of the policies issued. This inability to amortize acquisition expenses by matching them to revenues gives rise to a temporary strain on the company's surplus. Although the surplus strain will eventually disappear as written premiums are earned, it can represent a significant financial burden, especially for newer companies that are experiencing rapid growth.

This burden can be substantially alleviated via the use of proportional reinsurance arrangements under which the commission allowances serve to offset the impact of these acquisition expenses, effectively permitting the company to recover what is sometimes referred to as the "equity" in its unearned premium reserve. Although non-proportional reinsurance has usually been transacted on a net basis, it is possible to structure such arrangements so as to provide a commission allowance to the cedent, which would serve to alleviate surplus strain. Regulators sometimes use the terms "surplus aid" or "surplus relief" to characterize this effect.

As long as the level of commission allowed bears some reasonable relationship to the company's actual acquisition expenses, there should ordinarily be no cause for concern on the part of the examiner. On the contrary, if commission allowances are significantly higher than the level of acquisition expenses, it may indicate an arrangement that has been deliberately designed to camouflage an overall expense problem in an effort to avoid or defer regulatory scrutiny.

It is possible to structure the reinsurance agreement commission provision in a way that effectively guarantees a minimum profit margin for the reinsurer. These types of arrangements appear to have become far less prevalent in recent years, as a result of closer regulatory scrutiny. Instances of unusual commission provisions should be subjected to careful review by the examiner.

E. Spread of Risk

By alleviating the surplus strain associated with new business writings and by enabling the company to provide capacity well beyond levels that could be supported on a net basis, reinsurance effectively allows the company to write not only a larger portfolio of business in terms of premium income, but also a more diversified portfolio in terms of kinds and classes of business and geographic locations of business incurred. These factors serve to reduce the volatility of the company's underwriting results from year to year, with attendant benefits in terms of cash flow, investment results and operating income.

F. Further functions of Reinsurance for Life & Health Companies

Typically, the issuance of a life insurance policy causes a drain on the surplus of the life company issuing the policy. This is a matter of simple arithmetic in that the first year reserve plus the commission and other issue expenses exceed the first year premium. This initial investment is usually not recovered for several years. Life insurance depends on the proposition that the present value, at the moment of issue, of all future gross premiums exceeds the present value, at the same moment, of all future expenses and benefits to policyholders, the excess being counted upon as the margin of safety in the premium rate. This margin, if not called upon to meet unexpected future increases in expenses and the cost of benefits, is available for dividends to policyholders and/or stockholders.

Statutory reserving strikes a balance at any point during the life of the policy between the past and the future, by comparing the present values of future income and outflow. Various methods of computing such present values have been devised. The statutory valuation system, however, must be concerned with the company's ability to settle its liabilities immediately as well as in the future, and therefore requires that the company provide enough of a valuation premium in the first year to pay expected claims in that year on a conservative standard.

Business considerations have led to the use of level premiums and substantially higher commissions in the first year than in renewal years. Statutory requirements are conservative in order to protect policyholders under a wide variety of operating philosophies. The net result of the interaction between business considerations and statutory requirements is that the strain on surplus of writing a large volume of new business can be a serious problem for a company. Those ceding companies may seek relief by electing to reinsure on a coinsurance or modified coinsurance basis, under which the reinsurer assumes the surplus strain along with the risk involved on the portions of policies reinsured. Those companies whose surplus problems are particularly acute may choose to retain less and reinsure more in order to obtain additional surplus relief. For the reinsurer providing the surplus relief, the key consideration at the reinsurance inception is the comparison of the present value of future reinsurance premiums to the present value of future reinsurance payments and expenses. Clearly, there are many circumstances under which the transactions are advantageous to both sides.

The reinsurer is, in effect, helping the ceding company to meet its immediate obligations in return for an expected profit in the future. The arrangement differs from a loan in that the return of surplus to the reinsurer together with its profit depends upon future contingencies. The reinsurer must concern itself not only with the quality of the business and the likelihood that future benefits and expenses will be within the range covered by the reinsurance premiums, but also with the viability of the ceding company.

Non-proportional life reinsurance is used for essentially the same purposes as non-proportional property-casualty reinsurance in that it is used to limit the company's aggregate net exposure to losses on a block of in–force business (stop-loss), and to losses arising out of any single event such as an airplane crash, or an earthquake (catastrophe). Premiums for such protection are negotiated between the company and the reinsurer and since expense allowances are not usually contemplated, there is little or no surplus relief effect. Since insurance usually attaches in excess of normal statutory reserves, the cedent is usually not able to take reserve credit on its financial statements for such reinsurance. (See Section VIII Credit For Reinsurance for more detail on this topic.)

VI. THE REINSURANCE MARKETPLACE

A. Reinsurance Brokers

(Guidance over reinsurance broker contracts is included in section XI: Reinsurance Contract Language.)

The total volume of US non-life reinsurance business transacted in recent years has been equally divided between those reinsurers that deal directly with their clients and those which do all or the larger part of their business via reinsurance brokers. It is difficult to say whether the direct writing approach or the broker approach is the "better" one, since there are inherent advantages and disadvantages associated with each.

If the company's reinsurance requirements are fairly straightforward and nothing really unique is necessary in terms of coverage or capacity, there are several advantages for placing the entire reinsurance program with a single direct-writing reinsurer (i.e., "one-stop" shopping). In accordance with this practice, the caliber of security offered is very high, the range of services available from the reinsurer is extensive, communication between the parties is usually simple and efficient, and barring any disagreement or dispute, claims are usually paid by the reinsurer quite promptly.

1. Property/Casualty Reinsurance Brokers

On the property/casualty side, a company that has certain unique requirements unable to be readily satisfied by the direct-writing reinsurers, or that requires capacity substantially beyond that which the direct writer is prepared to commit, may find the brokerage marketplace better suited for its needs. The reinsurance broker acts as the company's advisor and advocate in designing and implementing reinsurance protection on the company's behalf. Brokers have access to the capacity available not only domestically but also in London and other major international reinsurance markets. Since most reinsurance placements via brokers involve participation by a number of reinsurers, the question of relative negotiating leverage becomes less of a potential disadvantage to the company. The broker often represents the company from a position of relative strength. The broker can exert substantial leverage because the volume of business placed by the broker with any single reinsurer in many cases represents a very large share of the reinsurer's total premium income. The reinsurer is thus likely to agree to terms more favorable to the company than might be obtainable from a direct-writing reinsurer. Interposing a broker between the insurer and the reinsurer reduces the likelihood that any of the participating reinsurers will exert undue influence over areas of business conduct that would normally be management's prerogative.

2. Life and Health Reinsurance Brokers

On the life and health side, reinsurance brokers play a much less prominent role than in the property-casualty sector. Most reinsurance is placed directly by the cedent with professional reinsurers or with the reinsurance departments of large life and health insurers. Pools established to handle certain specialty types of business are sometimes used to generate capacity for such business.

Several life insurers may enter into a pool or reinsurance agreement to share certain specified risks. Each insurer functions in the dual role of reinsurer and ceding company. Risks are usually placed on a treaty, or automatic, basis. Usually the insurers will deal directly with each other. Since transfer of new business surplus strain is not normally an objective of pool reinsurance, the yearly renewable term method (YRT form), or some variation thereof, is common. Premiums may be based wholly, or in part, on pool experience and an experience refund provision will usually be a key part of the pool treaty.

Reinsurance is also sometimes ceded to captive reinsurers set up by the company's agents or by certain sources of specialty business in expectation of sharing in the eventual underwriting profits (e.g., automobile dealers may arrange credit life and disability protection for their customers). The examiner should pay close attention in these cases to the collaterization of the cedent's recoverables.

Companies dealing with a reinsurance broker need to pay close attention to the financial strength and long-term solvency prospects of both the reinsurers and the broker. Companies should also monitor the collateralization of amounts recoverable from unauthorized reinsurers. The major US and London reinsurance brokers can usually be expected to carefully scrutinize reinsurers' financials, marketplace behavior and reputation. Both brokers and ceding companies have in recent years become considerably more sophisticated in terms of financial analysis of prospective reinsurers, and in general, are quite security-conscious.

A reinsurance broker operates as the company's representative in dealing with reinsurers. The broker's remuneration comes in the form of a brokerage fee from the reinsurer which usually ranges from 1% of ceded premium on proportional reinsurance to as much as 10% on non-proportional reinsurance. Some reinsurance brokers are also called "intermediaries," but the two terms reflect no difference in function. Some of the larger reinsurance brokers are subsidiaries of large insurance brokerage firms, but in such instances the broker operates autonomously.

In addition to designing protection consistent with the company's requirements and objectives, and negotiating with reinsurers to establish terms and conditions of the agreement, the broker is responsible for proper documentation (fully executed placement slips, cover notes or binders, the reinsurance agreement and any amendments thereto), and transmitting all communications and funds between the company and reinsurers. However, the company selects the reinsurers and determines their respective shares of the placement.

Reinsurance is sometimes placed with, or assumed from, certain voluntary pools or underwriting associations established to provide capacity for unique or unusual risks, or risks with exceptionally high levels of insurable values (e.g., aircraft, nuclear facilities, offshore drilling platforms, etc.). Companies are also common participants in certain involuntary pools established by regulatory authorities to provide coverage for risks not served in the open market, or for risks exposed to certain natural hazards.

Under intercompany pooling arrangements, pool participants enter into a conventional quota share reinsurance agreement under which all of the pooled business is ceded to the pool or lead company. The risks in the pool are then retroceded back to the pool participants in accordance with their stipulated shares. In such arrangements, each pool participant has direct liability to its policyholders or claimants and the other pool participants are liable to the issuing company as reinsurers for their share of the issuing company's obligations. In addition, once the business has been pooled, part of the risk can be ceded to an outside third party. This permits the pool participants to reduce the amount of risk assumed. It should be noted that in addition to the pool participating in reinsurance transactions, the individual companies within an intercompany pool may also engage in reinsurance transactions independently.

3. Health Care Reinsurance Brokers

Most reinsurance is placed directly with the reinsurer. There are a limited number of reinsurers/brokers available to reinsure managed care entities.

B. Special Purpose Reinsurance Vehicles

Special Purpose Reinsurance Vehicles (SPRVs) are entities created exclusively to allow ceding insurers to access alternative sources of risk bearing capital via the securitization of insurance risk. Under a SPRV contract, the ceding insurer would receive an agreed amount from the SPRV for losses incurred if and when a specific event (the "indemnity trigger") occurs. To date, nearly all SPRVs have been formed offshore to provide catastrophic reinsurance, although there have recently been some securitization deals covering other risks. These entities provide capacity to the reinsurance marketplace; diversifying the risk related to catastrophic occurrences or other securitized coverages to the capital markets. This capacity can manifest itself during "hard markets," when the availability and/or the affordability of catastrophe reinsurance is strained. The NAIC Special Purpose Reinsurance Vehicle Model Act authorizes the formation of SPRVs in the United States.

Utilizing SPRVs for insurance securitization involves a number of transactions occurring concurrently. The SPRV obtains proceeds through the issuance of securities (generally bonds) in the capital market. In addition to the proceeds from the sale of securities, the ceding insurer(s) pays a premium to the SPRV for the insurance coverage provided. The payment from the ceding insurer(s) is used to pay administrative costs related to the SPRV and enhance the return to the investors who purchased the securities and represents the yield the investors receive for assuming the insurance risk embedded in the securities. The SPRV holds the proceeds from the investors and the ceding insurer(s) in trust to secure obligations the SPRV has with the investors and/or the ceding insurers. The SPRV is required to have a separate trust account for each ceding insurer and maintain the trust account at fair value. The obligation of the SPRV to return the full initial investment to the security holders is contingent on the funds not being used to compensate the ceding insurers under the SPRV contract. If the specific event or condition under the SPRV contract does not occur, the security holders would receive the principal plus interest on their investment.

SPRVs are limited to the services they perform and are not allowed to enter into contracts outside of SPRV contracts for the assumption of risk or the indemnification of losses. SPRVs must also be fully funded; that is the entire amount of the coverage they provide to ceding insurers must be placed in the trust, whether or not the triggering event has occurred. The security assets must be held in trust in accordance with the SPRV trust guidelines.

1. Requirements and Business Practices of SPRVs Organized in the United States Pursuant to the NAIC Special Purpose Reinsurance Vehicle Model Act

In order to operate as an SPRV, the organization is required to obtain a limited certificate of authority from the Commissioner. In order to obtain this certificate, the SPRV must complete and submit a detailed application to the Commissioner that contains various information and representations on the organization including: the names and biological affidavits of the proposed officers and directors and organizers of the SPRV, the SPRV's plan of operation and proposed contract, investment strategy, and source of the $5,000 minimum cash capital. The Commissioner must determine that the SPRVs proposed plan of operation has reasonable expectations, is not hazardous to ceding insurers or policyholders, and is compliant with specified regulations. In addition, the domiciliary Commissioner of the ceding insurer has an opportunity to object to the transaction; if he/she does not disapprove the transaction in writing and the proposed plan of operation is compliant with the statutory requirements, the Commissioner may issue the limited certificate of authority.

Once the certificate has been issued, the SPRV may conduct business by entering into SPRV contracts and receiving premiums from ceding insurers. These contracts must require the SPRV to indemnify the ceding insurers for covered contract losses. Additionally, potential SPRV obligations under the SPRV contract must be entirely securitized and funded with assets held in trust. Although the SPRV is restricted from performing services for the assumption of risk or the indemnification of losses outside of SPRV contracts, the SPRV is entitled to engage in transactions and enter into agreements to fulfill its obligations and administrative duties related to the securities issued and the SPRV contracts. This may include managing the credit or interest rate risk of the investments held in trust in order to mitigate the risk that would lose value over time and not be adequate to fund obligations under the insurance securitization transactions.

In order to maintain the "SPRV" status, the organization must comply with several specific requirements. Although many of the initial SPRV requirements have been indicated above, the "Special Purpose Reinsurance Vehicle Model Act" should be consulted to determine complete compliance with all requirements.

2. SPRV Contract and Credit for Reinsurance

In general, a ceding insurer that enters into a SPRV contract shall be entitled to a credit for reinsurance due to the fact that the SPRV contract qualifies as a reinsurance contract and any liabilities under the agreement will be held in a trust that qualifies for credit under the NAIC Credit for Reinsurance Model Act. These credits are permitted since the structure and guidelines of the SPRVs provide reasonable assurance that the ceding insurers would be indemnified for losses incurred under the SPRV contracts. In order to receive a credit for reinsurance or other offsets, the assets held by the SPRV must be held and maintained in the stipulated trusts and in the manner required by the Specific Purpose Reinsurance Vehicle Model Act and the NAIC Credit for Reinsurance Model Act.

C. Protected Cell Company

1. Summary Description

A protected cell company is a domestic insurer with one or more protected cells organized pursuant to the NAIC Protected Cell Company Model Act. A protected cell company can only be established with the prior written approval of the Commissioner of a plan of operation or amendments thereto submitted by the protected cell company with respect to each protected cell in connection with an insurance securitization.

Protected cell company insurance securitizations provide domestic insurers the opportunity to access alternative sources of capital and achieve the benefits of insurance securitization.

An insurance-linked security can be issued by the insurer through a protected cell for purchase by investors. A protected cell is retained within the insurance or reinsurance company and is used to insulate the proceeds of the securities offering from the general business risks of the insurer, granting an additional comfort level for investors of the securitized instrument. The insurance exposures that have been securitized by the insurance-linked security are attributed to the protected cell.

Under the terms of the security, the principal may be paid to the investor on a specified maturity date, with interest, unless a trigger event occurs. The proceeds of the security offering will collateralize (i) the issuer's obligation under an insurance or reinsurance agreement if a trigger event occurs and (ii) the issuer's obligation to repay the security if a trigger event does not occur.

If the trigger event takes place before a specified date, the issuer is relieved of some or its entire obligation to repay the securityholders, and the investor incurs a loss of some or all of its investment. The security must be issued with an indemnity trigger.

In an insurance-linked security, the insurer that originated the transaction has hedged its portfolio of insurance risks by transferring certain of those risks to the securityholders. Should the triggering event occur, the issuer would incur a loss that would be partly offset by the amount of liability to securityholders from which it is relieved.

2. Assets and Liabilities of a Protected Cell

Protected cells are intended to insulate the assets and liabilities from the protected cell company's other assets and liabilities not identified in accounting records as attributable to the protected cell. Protected cells are analogous to separate accounts that are typically utilized by life insurers. Protected cell accounts are specifically identified bank or custodial accounts established by a protected cell company to segregate the assets of one protected cell from those of other cells and the company's general account. The protected cell company must transfer all assets attributable to a protected cell to one or more separately established and identified protected cell accounts bearing the name or description of the protected cell.

Assets may be allocated only in accordance with a plan of operation approved by the Commissioner of the domiciliary state and must equal at least the insurance liabilities related to that protected cell. Protected cell assets must be stated at fair value and held only to fulfill the obligations of that protected cell. The protected cell contracts require that only those established protected cell assets be used for the fulfillment of the related protected cell liabilities. Protected cell assets and liabilities are required to be kept separate and readily identifiable from the company's general account and other protected cell accounts. Assets or liabilities may be transferred among the protected cell account and the company's general account or other protected cells only as expressly stated in the approved plan.

Assets in a protected cell must be valued at fair value. "Fair value" of an asset (or liability) means the amount at which that asset (or liability) could be bought (or incurred) or sold (or settled) in a current transaction between willing parties, that is, other than in a forced or liquidation sale. Quoted market prices in active markets are the best evidence of fair value and shall be used as the basis for the measurement, if available.

3. Protected Cell Insurance Securitization Requirements with Respect to Offsetting Loss Reserves or Booking Receivables

A protected cell company must, in respect of any of its protected cells, engage in fully funded indemnity triggered insurance securitization to support in full the protected cell exposures attributable to that protected cell.

"Fully funded" means that, with respect to any exposure attributed to a protected cell, the fair value of the protected cell assets, on the date on which the insurance securitization is effected, equals or exceeds the maximum possible exposure attributable to the protected cell with respect to such exposures. A protected cell company insurance securitization must be fully funded.

"Indemnity trigger" means a transaction term by which relief of the issuer's obligation to repay investors is triggered by its incurring a specified level of losses under its insurance or reinsurance contracts. A protected cell company insurance securitization that is non-indemnity triggered qualifies as an insurance securitization only after the Commissioner adopts regulations addressing the methods of funding of the portion of the risk that is not indemnity based, accounting, disclosure, risk based capital treatment, and assessing risks associated with such securitizations. Protected cell assets may be used to pay interest or other consideration on any outstanding debt or other obligation attributable to that protected cell. A protected cell company may enter into a swap agreement or other transaction for the account of the protected cell if the agreement or transaction has the effect of guaranteeing interest or other consideration.

Protected cell insurance securitizations meeting these requirements may offset loss reserves and book reinsurance recoverables in accordance with the accounting standards set forth in SSAP No. 74 (Accounting for the Issuance of Insurance-Linked Securities Issued by a Property and Casualty Insurer through a Protected Cell). Other appropriate accounting standards are set forth in SSAP No. 74 and INT 02-06.

4. No Transaction of an Insurance Business

A protected cell company insurance securitization is not deemed to be an insurance or reinsurance contract. An investor whose sole activity is to invest in the protected cell's security is not deemed to be transacting an insurance business. The underwriters or selling agents (and their partners, directors, officers, members, managers, employees, agents, representatives, or advisors) involved in a protected cell company insurance securitization are not considered to be conducting an insurance or reinsurance agency, brokerage, intermediary, advisory or consulting business through their securitization activities.

Although several of the guidelines governing the use of protected cell agreements are outlined above, the examiner should consult the "Protected Cell Company Model Act" when reviewing protected cell agreements or transactions.

VII. REVIEW OF REINSURERS & EVALUATION OF RISK TRANSFER

The examiner should review the procedures followed by the company in accordance with the selection of reinsurers and the ongoing monitoring of their financial condition. It is important to review all reinsurance documentation (placement slips, cover notes, reinsurance agreements and any addenda thereto) for completeness, accuracy and timeliness, and to verify that acceptable forms of collateral (usually funds withheld, letters of credit or trust accounts) have been secured by the company in a timely manner for all amounts recoverable from unauthorized reinsurers.

Risk transfer is by nature an elusive concept. There is a variety of risk transfer agreements ranging from a purely financial arrangement in which no underwriting or timing risk is transferred to the reinsurer to a quota share arrangement in which no limitations on risk transfer other than those inherent in the original policies and the reinsurance agreement, are applicable to the obligations of the reinsurer.

While examples of the "pure financial arrangements" are still to be found in the London market and in some offshore domiciles, recent changes in accounting rules applicable to companies domiciled in the United States have apparently reduced the incidence of "reinsurance" transactions which transfer no significant amount of risk to the reinsurer.

Outside the US, in London and in offshore domiciles, the practice of "financial reinsurance" or "finite risk reinsurance" still exists. Under this practice, the reinsurance contract contains vague terms stipulating that the reinsurance arrangement will have some kind of "financial" impact on the parties to the agreement. Additionally, the reinsurance agreement will contain limitations of one kind or another on the obligations of the reinsurer, in order to strike a reasonable balance between the level of risk assumed by the reinsurer and the consideration received from the cedent.

A. Property/Casualty Reinsurance

For statutory accounting purposes, "risk" is defined in SSAP No. 62, Property and Casualty Reinsurance, of the NAIC *Accounting Practices and Procedures Manual* as consisting of two distinct elements: underwriting risk and timing risk.

- Underwriting risk is the possibility that losses and expenses recoverable by the cedent from the reinsurer will exceed the consideration received by the reinsurer, thus resulting in an underwriting loss to the reinsurer.

- Timing risk exists when anticipated loss payment patterns are not considered during the development of recoverable losses under the reinsurance agreement, and result in a reduction in investment income to the reinsurer as an effect of the accelerated loss payments.

Both of these elements of risk must be present in order to warrant reinsurance accounting treatment. The other elements of risk, including credit risk or yield risk, are inherent in most reinsurance agreements, and result in a reduction in investment income to the reinsurer as an effect of the accelerated loss payments.

There is no defined quantitative level of risk transfer that must be met before the transaction can be accounted for as reinsurance. The language in SSAP No. 62 requires only that the reinsurer assume significant insurance risk (i.e., underwriting and timing risk) and that a reasonable possibility exists that the reinsurer, in so doing, may sustain a significant loss from the transaction. The determination of what amount of risk is "significant" is to be made on a case-by-case basis by the regulator. The term "reasonably possible" is defined in Question #12 in SSAP No. 62 Appendix A as any probability that is "more than remote." A common method for GAAP purposes is that there must exist at least a ten percent probability that the reinsurer could sustain a loss of at least ten percent on the transaction. Transactions that cannot satisfy statutory risk transfer requirements must be accounted for as deposits rather than reinsurance.

In determining how much credit should be allowed it is necessary to examine closely the provisions of the reinsurance agreement. Limitations on the maximum amount recoverable from the reinsurer during any defined period (e.g., contract year) should serve to limit the amount by which gross losses may be reduced on the cedent's financial statements. Such limitations may take the form of loss ratio caps, per occurrence loss limits, loss "corridors" (a band of loss which must be assumed net by the company before the reinsurer becomes responsible for any further losses under the agreement) etc. The amount of credit allowed should be directly related to the amount of loss recoverable (i.e., for a "finite" amount of risk transferred to the reinsurer, no more than an equivalent "finite" amount of statement credit should be allowed).

Provisions in the reinsurance agreement that have the effect of deferring the reinsurer's obligation to reimburse covered losses will generally cause the transaction to fail the timing risk requirement, preventing the application of a credit for reinsurance. Examples of these provisions include "floating" retentions, "last dollar paid" arrangements and multiple-year retentions.

Examiners should determine whether any separate agreements or understandings exist between the reinsurance agreement parties that would serve to reduce, offset or eliminate the reinsurer's obligations. In any such instance, a credit for reinsurance should not be allowed under the reinsurance agreement. For property/casualty companies, the examiner should review the company's responses to the appropriate disclosures in the Annual Statement General Interrogatories to determine whether these type of situations exist.

An analysis of contract provisions is necessary to determine whether, and to what extent, reinsurance accounting treatment should be allowed. Even if the provisions in the reinsurance agreement satisfy risk transfer requirements, it is often necessary to perform an analysis of discounted cash flows, using reasonable assumptions as to the ultimate amount of recoverable incurred losses, loss payment patterns and interest rates, to determine whether there is a reasonable likelihood of a significant underwriting loss to the reinsurer. If this cannot be demonstrated, the transaction should be accounted for as a deposit.

In the simplified illustration that follows, if the probability of a loss ratio of 100% or higher on the business reinsured does not illustrate a greater than "remote" possibility, one would have to conclude that the transaction does not transfer sufficient risk to the reinsurer to warrant reinsurance accounting treatment.

Simplified Illustration of Cash Flow Analysis

Assumptions:

- Ultimate loss ratio will be no lower than 75% and no greater than 125%
- $5,000,000 premium less 20% ceding commission will be paid at inception of the reinsurance agreement
- Interest rate = 5%, compounding annually
- Paid losses will be recovered from the reinsurer at the end of each year as follows:

Year 1	20%
Year 2	35%
Year 3	20%
Year 4	15%
Year 5	10%
	100%

Simplified Illustration of Cash Flow Analysis

Cash flows @ 75% loss ratio

	Paid Losses					
Net Premium:	Year 1	Year 2	Year 3	Year 4	Year 5	Total
$4,000,000	($750,000)	($1,312,500)	($750,000)	($562,500)	($375,000)	($3,750,000)
Present Value						
$4,000,000	($714,286)	($1,190,476)	($647,878)	($462,770)	($293,822)	($3,309,232)

Gain/(Loss) to Reinsurer: $4,000,000 – $3,309,232 = $690,768 = 17% gain

Cash flows @ 100% loss ratio

	Paid Losses					
Net Premium:	Year 1	Year 2	Year 3	Year 4	Year 5	Total
$4,000,000	($1,000,000)	($1,750,000)	($1,000,000)	($750,000)	($500,000)	($5,000,000)
Present Value						
$4,000,000	($952,381)	($1,587,302)	($863,838)	($617,027)	($391,763)	($4,412,311)

Gain/(Loss) to Reinsurer: $4,000,000 – $4,412,311 = ($412,311) = 10% loss

Cash flows @ 125% loss ratio

	Paid Losses					
Net Premium:	Year 1	Year 2	Year 3	Year 4	Year 5	Total
$4,000,000	($1,250,000)	($2,187,500)	($1,250,000)	($937,500)	($625,000)	($6,250,000)
Present Value						
$4,000,000	($1,190,476)	($1,984,127)	($1,079,797)	($771,284)	($489,704)	($5,515,388)

Gain/(Loss) to Reinsurer: $4,000,000 – $5,515,388 = ($1,515,388) = 38% loss

In determining whether reinsurance accounting is allowable, it should be noted that in certain instances the business covered by the reinsurance agreement may be inherently profitable. As long as the provisions of the reinsurance agreement place no limitations on the obligations of the reinsurer, (i.e., the reinsurer's underwriting result can be expected to mirror that of the ceding company) commission impact aside, it would be appropriate to allow reinsurance accounting.

In reviewing the company's reinsurance arrangements it is also important to determine whether any reinsurance agreement that was incepted or renewed on or after January 1, 1994 applies to losses occurring prior to the inception date of the agreement. These agreements must be accounted for as retroactive reinsurance, per the instructions set forth in SSAP No. 62 of the NAIC *Accounting Practices and Procedures Manual*.

B. Life & Health Reinsurance

For life and health reinsurance, the evaluation of risk transfer is quite different from that for property/casualty reinsurance. SSAP No. 61 in the NAIC *Accounting Practices and Procedures Manual,* Deposit-Type and Accident and Health Reinsurance, requires a "transfer of significant risks inherent to the business reinsured." The regulation does not address the probability of loss to the reinsurer at all in defining transfer of risk. "Significant risks" are defined with reference to a table of risks and contract types. The examiner should consult SSAP No. 61 for details concerning the evaluation of risk transfer for life and health reinsurance agreements. The SSAP specifically prohibits the use of side agreements, which differs from the property/casualty treatment of side agreements.

VIII. CREDIT FOR REINSURANCE

A. Credit for Reinsurance Guidelines

Subject to the laws of the various states, credit for reinsurance may be allowed to the ceding company when the reinsurance contract includes a proper insolvency clause and the specific criteria for the appropriate category have been adequately met:

1. Reinsurer is licensed in the ceding company's domiciliary state
2. Assuming insurer has obtained reinsurer accreditation
3. Reinsurer is domiciled in another state
4. Reinsurer maintains trust funds
5. Credit for reinsurance is required by law
6. Assuming insurer is unathorized and not included within the previous categories

1. Reinsurer is Licensed in the Ceding Company's Domiciliary State

Reinsurers who meet this classification must have obtained their licensure status at the time the statutory financial statement credit for reinsurance is claimed or when financial statements indicating the credit have been filed by the ceding company. The reinsurer then must continue to maintain compliance with the licensure status at all times after the credit has been taken. The licensure requirement is considered to be perpetual and not periodic, therefore, appropriate information is required to be included in the company's statements when reinsurers do not comply with the requirements.

2. Assuming Insurer has Obtained Reinsurer Accreditation

An assuming insurer must have obtained reinsurance accreditation in the domiciliary state of the ceding company at the time the financial statement credit is claimed in order for the domestic insurer to receive a credit for reinsurance. In order to obtain the status of an accredited reinsurer, the assuming company must file a Form AR-1 that grants specific authority to the ceding company's state Commissioner (Exhibit B), as well as documentation of licensure to transact insurance or reinsurance and annual statements with the state Commissioner. Additionally, the assuming insurer must maintain a surplus level of $20,000,000. It should be assumed that insurers who maintain a surplus level of less than $20,000,000 may be accredited if approved by the Commissioner. The Commissioner is entitled to revoke reinsurer accreditation if the above conditions are not preserved.

3. Reinsurer is Domiciled in Another State

The reinsurer must be domiciled (and licensed) in a substantially similar state that has adopted the model credit for reinsurance or substantially similar law, and therefore subject to that state's credit for reinsurance standards at the time the financial statement credit for reinsurance is claimed. The reinsurer must also maintain a surplus of at least $20,000,000 and file an AR-1 form with the Commissioner.

4. Reinsurer Maintains Trust Funds

A credit for reinsurance ceded by domestic insurers is available to assuming insurers that maintain trust funds for a requisite amount in a qualified US financial institution. (Actual amount is determined by the classification of the assuming insurer.) The assuming insurer is required to annually report to the Commissioner for determination of the sufficiency of the trust fund. The classifications of assuming insurers are as follows:

a. <u>Single Assuming Insurer</u> – Trust funds must equal or exceed the assuming insurer's liabilities attributable to ceded reinsurance by US domiciled insurers. Additionally, the assuming insurer shall maintain trusteed surplus of at least $20,000,000.

b. <u>Incorporated and Unincorporated Group Underwriters</u> – For reinsurance ceded under reinsurance agreements dated after August 1, 1995, trust funds must equal or exceed the group's liabilities for business ceded by US domiciled ceding insurers. For reinsurance agreements dated before July 31, 1995, trust funds must at least equal the insurance and reinsurance liabilities attributable to business written in the United States. In addition to these trusts, the underwriters must maintain $100,000,000 in surplus for the benefit of US domiciled ceding insurers. The incorporated members of the group are prohibited from engaging in auxiliary business other than underwriting as a member of the group and must be subject to the same regulation and control of the group as the unincorporated members. The group is also required to annually file either a certification of solvency for each underwriter member or independently prepared financial statements for each underwriter to the Commissioner.

A credit for reinsurance will not be granted for reinsurers who maintain trust funds unless the Commissioner of the state where the trust is domiciled has approved the form of the trust. A Commissioner from another state may approve the trust if the Commissioner has accepted responsibility for the regulatory oversight of the trust. The form of the trust is required to be filed with the Commissioner in every state the ceding insurer beneficiaries of the trust are domiciled.

5. Credit for Reinsurance is Required by Law

For those jurisdictions in which reinsurance is required by law, the domestic ceding insurers may take a credit for reinsurance, although the assuming insurer does not meet the requirements set forth in the above sections. Examples of the assuming insurers for which credit may be allowed include state owned or controlled insurance or reinsurance companies, guaranty organizations or residual required market mechanisms.

6. Assuming Insurer is Unauthorized and Not Included Within the Previous Categories

A credit for reinsurance may also be granted to the ceding company even when the assuming insurer does not meet any of the above credit-permitted categories. In these instances, if the ceding insurer holds funds or is exclusively entitled to funds held in a U.S. institution provided as security for reinsurance obligations, the ceding insurer is permitted to take a reduction of liability or record an asset. The reduction is not permitted to exceed the liabilities carried by the ceding insurer. The funds held may take the form of cash, qualifying admitted asset securities as indicated by the NAIC Securities Valuation Office, letters of credit, and any other security that has been approved by the Commissioner. In order for the letters of credit to be accepted they must be clean, irrevocable, unconditional, and issued or confirmed by a U.S. qualified financial institution. Additionally, they must have an "evergreen" clause that indicates the letter cannot expire without 30 day advance notice, and provide notice on what laws the letter of credit is governed by (i.e., state, Uniform Customs and Practice for Documentary Credits of the International Chamber of Commerce, or any other publication). An example letter of credit form is included as Exhibit A.

In addition to the categories addressed above, the ceding insurer may take credit for unencumbered funds withheld by the U.S. ceding insurer that are under the exclusive control and withdrawal of the ceding insurer. However, no credit, asset or reduction from liability will be permitted for reinsurance agreements that do not contain a proper insolvency clause. Additionally, unauthorized assuming insurers must submit and comply with requirements of a US jurisdiction.

Credit will not be allowed to a ceding company for reinsurance cessions under contracts incepting on or after January 1, 1980, where payments are made via an intermediary unless the reinsurance agreement includes a provision whereby the reinsurer assumes all credit risks of the intermediary related to payments to the intermediary.

Certain special requirements must be satisfied before credit for reinsurance may be taken with respect to life and health reinsurance structured on a proportional basis; these requirements are set forth in the NAIC Life and Health Reinsurance Agreements Model Regulation, which has been adopted in one form or another by nearly all of the states.

Reinsurers applying for accredited or authorized status (or, in the case of reinsurers domiciled outside the United States, "trusteed" status) in states which they are not licensed must provide to the Commissioner in such states a properly executed Form AR-1 (Exhibit B) as evidence of their compliance with the requirement to designate the Commissioner as agent for receipt of service of process and to recognize the Commissioner's authority to examine their books and records.

(The examiner should refer to Appendix A-785 in the NAIC *Accounting Practices and Procedures Manual* for additional guidance over Credits for Reinsurance.)

B. Credit for Reinsurance – Lloyd's Syndicates

The credit for reinsurance laws in nearly all states allow credit to be taken for reinsurance cessions to syndicates at Lloyd's, based on the premise that Lloyd's American Trust Fund, maintained in New York and administered by Citibank, contained assets sufficient to collateralize all of the insurance and reinsurance liabilities arising out of business written by such syndicates in the United States, including non-U.S. business denominated in U.S. dollars, plus an amount, to be held on a joint basis, of no less than $100,000,000 over and above the syndicates' total U.S. liabilities.

Beginning with cessions under reinsurance agreements with an inception, anniversary or renewal date on or after August 1, 1995, collateral for U.S. reinsurance liabilities assumed by syndicates at Lloyd's will no longer be afforded on a collective basis via Lloyd's American Trust Fund; each syndicate writing U.S. situs reinsurance business (i.e., reinsurance ceded by an insurer domiciled in the United States) must subscribe a deed of trust under the terms of which the syndicate undertakes to maintain assets in a separate trust account in an amount equal to its total gross liabilities arising out of its assumed U.S. situs reinsurance business. Statement credit for reinsurance ceded to syndicates not participating in the new collateralization arrangement would be allowable only upon demonstration that adequate specific collateral has been provided to the cedent. Additionally, Lloyd's has undertaken to maintain a joint trusteed surplus in the amount of $100,000,000.

The trustee is obligated to file no later than February 28 of the year following the year for which the ceding company has taken credit on its financial statement for reinsurance ceded to a "trusteed" alien reinsurer or to syndicates at Lloyd's maintaining U.S. situs reinsurance trust accounts a statement indicating the balance in such accounts as of the date of the ceding company's financial statement, and describing the assets held in the account. The trustee's statement is to be filed with each state in which a domestic insurer has taken such reinsurance credit.

Information regarding total U.S. assumed reinsurance liabilities of trusteed alien reinsurers and syndicates at Lloyd's maintaining U.S. situs reinsurance trust accounts can be obtained directly from the NAIC database; if assistance is required in that regard, the examiner should contact the Reinsurance Department in the Financial Regulatory Services Division of the NAIC in Kansas City.

IX. REINSURANCE BALANCES RECOVERABLE

Reinsurance balances recoverable from the company's reinsurers should be evaluated on the perceived financial condition of the reinsurer. The examiner should evaluate the likelihood that the company will receive all of the amounts recoverable from that reinsurer in a timely manner. Receipt of receivables from reinsurers should be consistent with the actual payment of claims under the policy's reinsured, in accordance with the reinsurance agreement settlement provisions, and in line with established aggregate or catastrophe reinsurance protections.

An evaluation of the current financial condition of all reinsurers from which material balances will eventually become recoverable should be completed, with the examiner focusing first on the reinsurer with the most assumed risk. Review of the most recent annual statement will provide an overview of all recoverable balances for this purpose. In accordance with the review, the examiner should determine the degree to which the company's statutory surplus may be exposed to erosion in the event of unrecoverable reinsurance.

The introduction of statutory penalties for delinquent property and casualty reinsurance recoverables appears to have had the intended effect of accelerating cash recoveries. If, however, the examiner finds evidence of difficulty in making timely recoveries, the company's overall exposure to potentially unrecoverable balances should be thoroughly investigated. Balances recoverable from reinsurers known to be in liquidation should be viewed with considerable skepticism. The examiner should verify that reinsurance balances deemed uncollectible are properly written off and that reinsurance recoverables from unauthorized reinsurers are reported as an asset and a liability (as necessary) to comply with statutory accounting rules. Additionally, any penalties assessed from authorized overdue reinsurance balances should be recorded as a liability.

X. TERMINATION OF REINSURANCE AGREEMENTS

A. Reinsurance Treaties

Reinsurance treaties may be written either on a "continuous-until-canceled" basis, or for a defined period of time, usually 12 months. Contracts written on a continuous basis will ordinarily contain a termination clause that will indicate which party may initiate termination (usually either party, but in some instances the reinsurer may effect termination only under certain defined circumstances), the date by which intent to terminate must be communicated to the other party (usually at least 90 days prior to the anniversary date of the agreement), and the date on which termination will be effective, assuming that the termination notice has not been rescinded.

It is not unusual for reinsurers to issue a "provisional notification of intent to terminate" prior to the notification date stipulated in the agreement. The reinsurers complete this in order to preserve the right to terminate while awaiting receipt of pertinent updated underwriting information that the reinsurer desires to review in order to determine whether it will continue the existing arrangement, or its participation therein, or whether modifications in current terms and conditions may be appropriate. Upon receipt and review of this data, if the reinsurer decides to continue, the "provisional" notice should be rescinded.

When a continuous agreement is terminated it is necessary to indicate clearly what is to be done regarding business in-force as of the termination date. For reinsurance agreements, there are two methods to terminate in-force business. To address these situations, the contract may indicate use of the "cut-off" basis or use of the "run-off" basis. Under the cut-off basis, the reinsurer remains liable for losses occurring prior to the termination date, but not for losses occurring at any time thereafter. Under the run-off basis, the reinsurer remains liable for losses occurring on policies in-force as of the termination date of the reinsurance agreement, usually until the earliest of the expiration, termination or next anniversary date of the original policies.

If the reinsurance agreement contemplates remittance of reinsurance premium on the basis of written rather than earned premium, termination on a cut-off basis will require the reinsurer to return the unearned premium, calculated as of the termination date, to the ceding company. Reinsurance agreements written for a specific term usually cover only losses occurring during that period and the reinsurance premium is usually based on earned premium, so the issues of run-off protection or return of the unearned premium portfolio do not typically occur.

B. Life Accident & Health Reinsurance

Life reinsurance agreements generally may be terminated with respect to new business. Such termination is effected by either the ceding company or the reinsurer giving advance notice to the other. The reinsurer may also terminate all reinsurance for non-payment of reinsurance premiums or the parties may mutually agree to terminate the agreement for the in-force reinsurance. In the latter case, since such termination is under the control of the ceding company, a commonly encountered provision obligates the ceding company to indemnify the reinsurer for adverse experience ceded and in-force as of the termination date. Some forms of health reinsurance differ from life reinsurance in that they may be annually renewed. With these forms of reinsurance, if reinsurance is not renewed, all reinsurance terminates at the end of the agreement period.

C. Health Reinsurance

Health entities generally require prior notification (i.e., 60 days) before their contracts can be terminated, except for non-payment of premium. Most health contracts have termination language that allows for automatic termination in the event of insolvency or cessation of operations. In the event of either of these events, the continuation of benefits clause should be triggered which requires the reinsurer to be liable for all claims incurred from the date of insolvency through the next 31 days. This prospective of first dollar coverage is not normally found in other types of reinsurance. It may require that the reinsurer be licensed to write direct Accident and Health Insurance in the state(s) that the health entity does business. In addition, continuation of benefits clauses typically require that the reinsurer pay claims from the date of insolvency through the earlier of the date of discharge for a member who is confined to an impatient facility, or the date the member becomes eligible for health coverage under another plan. Continuation of benefits clauses may also contain other limitations as well. The coverage may also provide that the reinsurance company continue benefits for any member for medical services incurred for a service date subsequent to the date of insolvency provided that premium for the members is current. Historically, continuation of benefits clauses have not contained maximum limits. However, more recently, reinsurers have attempted to insert dollar limits to avoid large exposure under the provision resulting from the insolvency of a large health entity. It is imperative that the language included in the continuation of benefits clause match the language in the insolvency clause so there is no gap in coverage for the members covered by the plan.

Some states require 60 days prior written notification to the plan and the Commissioner of insurance for termination for any cause, including the non-payment of premiums.

D. Facultative Certificates

Certificates of facultative reinsurance usually have termination dates that are coterminous. In these situations, the reinsurance agreement terminates automatically with the termination date of the original policy.

E. Commutation

Reinsurance agreements often create obligations, particularly to the reinsurer, which will not be entirely fulfilled until long after the agreement has expired or been terminated. Many agreements contain a commutation clause, which provides a basis upon which the parties can agree on the net present value of estimated future loss payments. The commutation clause basis entails a careful actuarial analysis of reserves for reported and unreported losses as well as expected timing of loss payments by the cedent. Upon payment by the reinsurer of the agreed amount, the cedent will execute an agreement relieving the reinsurer from any further responsibility for such losses.

The commutation arrangement may apply to the entire reinsurance agreement or only to certain elements thereof, (such as to specific claims, or certain types of covered business, e.g., workers compensation, medical malpractice or long term disability), or only to losses attributable to specific accident years. In the event of partial commutation, the balance of the reinsurance relationship and the respective responsibilities of the parties will remain unchanged. Since the net present value consideration received by the ceding company will invariably be less than the ultimate undiscounted value of losses originally ceded to the reinsurer, the company will sustain an immediate reduction in surplus. As a result, the reinsurer will realize an immediate increase in surplus as a result of the commutation. The examiner should ascertain whether all such transactions have been properly accounted for and properly disclosed in the financial statements in accordance with SSAP No. 62, paragraphs 57-60 and SSAP No. 61, paragraph 49.

F. Rescission

The rescission of a reinsurance agreement is effectively the retroactive termination of the contract ab initio. Under this method the respective rights and obligations arising under the contract are entirely voided, and the parties are thereby restored to their respective positions prior to inception of the agreement. This may occur by mutual agreement of the parties, or may be the remedy that is granted, by an arbitration panel or court, in cases where one party, more commonly the reinsurer, is able to demonstrate that it has been irreparably damaged as a result of reliance upon deliberate material misrepresentations made by the other party.

G. Novation (Assumption Reinsurance)

A novation, strictly speaking, does not serve to terminate a contract. It is a legal process whereby one of the original parties is replaced by another person or entity, with the result that all rights and obligations of that original party are assumed, as of the date of the novation, by the new person or entity. Ordinarily, other terms and conditions of the agreement will not be affected by the novation itself, although they may subsequently be amended by mutual consent, consistent with contract provisions and subject, where applicable, to regulatory approval.

In the insurance industry such transactions have generally been characterized as "assumption reinsurance." This is really a misnomer, since in an ordinary indemnity reinsurance arrangement no novation occurs, as the insurer's liabilities to its policyholders are not eliminated or reduced by virtue of the existence of reinsurance protection. However, the term is widely used in both industry and the regulatory community.

While regulatory treatment has historically been somewhat inconsistent from state to state, it is expected that greater uniformity in the future with respect to policyholder notification, disclosure, and prior regulatory approval of transactions will be present as the states adopt the major elements of the NAIC Assumption Reinsurance Model Act. Since long-term, non-cancelable policies are preponderantly found in the life and health sector, assumption transactions are utilized much more extensively there than in the property/casualty sector.

Having disposed of a block of in-force business by means of an assumption by another insurer, the original insurer may still be obligated to fulfill contractual responsibilities to policyholders who have explicitly rejected the transfer of their policies to the new insurer. Additionally, the insurer may have contingent obligations to policyholders whose consent has not been received prior to the established deadline after which the novation will be considered as a matter of law. In such cases, the examiner should determine whether the company has appropriately reflected reserves for residual or contingent exposure in its financial statements. In order to prevent these issues, many companies will 100% coinsure until approval of assumptions by all states are received.

XI. REINSURANCE CONTRACT LANGUAGE

A. Reinsurance Agreement Contract Language

It is not possible to undertake here a detailed discussion of the various clauses that one might expect to find in a "typical" reinsurance agreement. Apart from a certain amount of fairly standardized boilerplate language, reinsurance treaties tend to be "one-of-a-kind" products designed to reflect the needs and intentions of the parties with respect to a specific situation or set of circumstances. A glossary of commonly encountered clauses is included in Appendix A. The best advice is simply to read the entire reinsurance agreement closely and carefully.

By way of a brief overview, the document will identify the parties to the agreement, and will define the subject matter and scope of the agreement, the basis on which reinsurance applies, the duration of the contract and the basis upon which it may be terminated. It will describe the respective rights and obligations of the parties, and will indicate the limits of the reinsurer's obligations and any amounts to be retained net by the company for its own account.

It is important to note that reinsurance contracts must include a transfer of risk. A risk-transfer occurs when the reinsurer agrees to indemnify the insurer for loss or liability under the terms stipulated in the contract. Indemnification requires a reinsurer to assume significant risk from the ceding company while having a reasonably possible chance of realizing significant losses on behalf of the assumed risk. Although reinsurance contracts may exist that do not transfer risk, the transactions under these contracts are not recorded in the same manner as risk-transferring reinsurance transactions. These transactions are required to be recorded under the deposit accounting guidelines.

A reinsurance contract will also define the amount of premium to be paid by the company to the reinsurer, the basis upon which it is to be calculated and, if applicable, adjusted, when it is to be remitted, and indicate what pertinent supporting data must be provided in connection with premium payment or specific cession, where necessary, to the reinsurer. On proportional covers, it will indicate the applicable ceding commission or expense allowance, and describe any applicable profit-sharing mechanism.

Property-casualty contracts will usually define "loss occurrence" in some manner, and indicate the method by which recoverable losses are to be collected from the reinsurer. A method for resolving differences that may arise between the parties regarding interpretation of contract provisions should be provided, and the contract should indicate what collateralization requirements, if any, will apply as respects amounts recoverable from unlicensed or unauthorized reinsurers.

Contracts which have been arranged by a reinsurance intermediary will usually contain a standard clause dealing with reporting of required information and remittance of funds from one party to the other via the intermediary; a service of suit provision should be included if alien reinsurers are participating on the cover, and an insolvency clause which defines the reinsurer's obligations in the event of financial impairment or insolvency of the company should be present in every reinsurance contract.

It might seem to be self-evident that the contract will clearly define exactly what business is to be covered, how claims will be dealt with, and what happens in the event of cancellation of the treaty. Unfortunately, unintended ambiguities do occasionally arise, and the time and effort needed for close review at the outset is a very worthwhile investment, since it is always a good deal easier to resolve confusion or inaccuracy before a claim has been presented for settlement. It may be the intent of the parties, for example, that the contract cover new or renewal business only, with business in-force as of the inception date of the treaty to be run off under an earlier treaty where it had originally been covered, or the intent may be that such in-force business be covered under the new treaty, in which event there should be a provision dealing with the portfolio transfer of unearned premium associated with that in-force business.

Property-casualty contracts may be designed to cover all losses on subject business which incepted during the term of the treaty (or during a given "underwriting year" in the case of a continuous contract), irrespective of the date on which the loss occurred, or to cover losses which occur during the term of the treaty irrespective of the inception date of the original policy under which the loss arose. These alternative approaches are commonly referred to as "risks attaching" and "losses occurring," respectively, and the applicable method obviously should be clearly defined. Similarly, cancellation may be on either a "cut-off" or "run-off" basis and language used in the cancellation clause and termination addendum should be clear in this regard. Life reinsurance contracts often include a provision for recapture by the company of business previously ceded to the reinsurer.

The drafting of reinsurance contract language is probably more of an art than a science, and will probably always resist the natural desire to reduce everything to totally consistent "standards." Regulators may find this to be a source of frustration, especially as the examiner tries to discern the true intent of the parties with regard to transfer of risk. Unfortunately, there isn't any single rule of thumb that can make the process simple and painless. Ideally, contracts should be drafted in the simplest fashion possible, consistent with the objectives of clarity and completeness. Wherever possible, terms should be used which have a generally accepted meaning in the reinsurance community. Many contracts will be very well drafted, and present no difficulty for the examiner or auditor analyzing the document, but others may be models of obscurity and confusion.

Whether this is the result of inept drafting rather than a conscious effort to camouflage actual intent is sometimes difficult to determine; examiners are encouraged to first consult with their state department's designated reinsurance personnel and then consult with the Reinsurance Department in the Financial Regulatory Services Division of the NAIC regarding interpretation of contract language, evaluation of risk transfer, appropriate accounting treatment, or other matters involving reinsurance practices and procedures.

B. Reinsurance Intermediary Contracts

Reinsurance intermediaries can act either in the role of a reinsurance broker or a reinsurance manager. A reinsurance broker solicits, negotiates, or places reinsurance cessions or retrocessions on behalf of a ceding insurer without the authority or power to bind reinsurance on behalf of the insurer. A reinsurance manager manages all or part of the assumed reinsurance business of a reinsurer (including the management of a separate division, department, or underwriting office) and acts as an agent for the reinsurer. As the responsibilities between the reinsurance brokers and reinsurance managers differ substantially, the contract guidelines for enlisting the assistance of either a reinsurance broker or manager also differ significantly. Specific contract requirements for reinsurance brokers and managers have been developed and are outlined below. Failure to comply with the required contract stipulations may result in Commissioner ordered penalties, revocation or suspension of the reinsurance intermediary's license, and for instances of material non-compliance in which the insurer or reinsurer suffered loss or damage, the Commissioner may maintain a civil action for recovery of compensatory damages or other appropriate relief.

- Reinsurance Brokers

  Prior to contracting with a reinsurance broker, the insurer shall verify that the Commissioner has granted the intermediary a reinsurance broker license as either a licensed producer in the state or a licensed non-resident reinsurance intermediary. The Commissioner may choose not to grant licenses to applicants deemed untrustworthy, or those who have failed to comply with the prerequisites. If the reinsurance broker is a nonresident, the Commissioner may require the broker to designate the Commissioner as an agent and furnish the Commissioner with the name and address of a resident of the state to whom the Commissioner may send notices or orders.

Contracts between insurance companies and reinsurance intermediaries shall be in writing and clearly indicate the responsibilities of each party. Specific guidelines for contracting with reinsurance brokers have been established in the Reinsurance Intermediary Model Act to promote the solvency and prudent business practices of the ceding insurance companies. Those guidelines that must be included in the reinsurance broker contract and other requirements promoted by the model act are illustrated below:

1. The reinsurance broker is licensed by a Commissioner with a reinsurance broker license or a non-domestic reinsurance intermediary license and has provided evidence of this licensure to the insurer prior to engaging services.

2. The insurer does not employ the reinsurance broker, other than in the context of this contract, unless the reinsurance broker is under common control with the insurer and subject to the Holding Company Act.

3. The reinsurance broker will annually provide a copy of its financial statements to the insurer.

4. The insurer may terminate the reinsurance broker's authority at any time.

5. Reinsurance broker will render accounts to the insurer detailing all material transactions, including information necessary to support all commissions, charges and other fees received by or owing, to the reinsurance broker, and remit all funds due within 30 days of receipt.

6. The reinsurance broker will hold all funds collected for the insurer's account in a fiduciary capacity in a bank that is a qualified US financial institution.

7. The reinsurance broker will maintain complete records of each transaction for at least 10 years. Information maintained by the reinsurance broker shall include:

    a. The type of contracts, limits, underwriting restrictions and risks;

    b. Period of coverage, including effective and expiration dates, cancellation provisions and notice required of cancellation;

    c. Reporting and settlement requirements of balances;

    d. Rates used to compute reinsurance premium;

    e. Names and addresses of assuming reinsurers;

    f. Rates of all reinsurance and retrocession commissions;

    g. Related correspondence and memoranda;

    h. Proof of placement;

    i. Details of retrocessions handled by the reinsurance broker including the identity of retrocessionaires and percentage of each contract assumed or ceded;

    j. Financial records, including but not limited to, premium and loss accounts; and

k. In instances when the intermediary produces a reinsurance contract from a licensed ceding insurer:

i. Directly from any assuming reinsurer, the reinsurance broker will provide written evidence that the assuming reinsurer has agreed to assume the risk;

ii. Placed through a representative of the assuming reinsurer, other than an employee, the reinsurance broker will provide written evidence that such reinsurer has delegated binding authority to the representative.

8. The insurer will have access and the right to copy and audit all accounts and records maintained by the reinsurance broker related to its business in a form useable by the insurer.

9. The reinsurance broker will comply with the written standards established by the insurer for the cession or retrocession of all risks.

10. The reinsurance broker will disclose to the insurer any relationship with any reinsurer to which business will be ceded or retroceded.

11. The reinsurance broker is subject and agrees to examination by the Commissioner. The Commissioner shall have access to all books, bank accounts and records of the reinsurance intermediary in a form usable to the Commissioner.

- Reinsurance Managers

Prior to contracting with a reinsurance manager, the insurance company shall verify that the Commissioner has granted the intermediary with a reinsurance manager license as either a licensed producer in the state or a licensed non-domestic reinsurance intermediary. The Commissioner may choose not to grant licenses to applicants deemed untrustworthy, or those who have failed to comply with the prerequisites. The Commissioner may require the reinsurance manager to file a bond and maintain an errors and omissions policy prior to receiving a license. If the reinsurance manager is a nonresident, the Commissioner may require the manger to designate the Commissioner as an agent and furnish the Commissioner with the name and address of a resident of the state to whom the Commissioner may send notices or orders.

Contracts between insurance companies and reinsurance managers shall be in writing, clearly indicate the responsibilities of each party and be approved by the reinsurer's board of directors. A copy of the approved contract must be filed with the Commissioner for approval at least 30 days before the reinsurance manager assumes or cedes business. Specific guidelines for contracting with reinsurance managers have been established in the Reinsurance Intermediary Model Act to promote the solvency and prudent business practices of the reinsurance assuming company. Those contract guidelines that must be included in the approved contract and other requirements promoted by the model act are illustrated below:

1. The reinsurance manager is licensed by the Commissioner with a reinsurance manager license or with a non-resident intermediary license and has provided evidence of this licensure to the reinsurer prior to engaging services.

2. The reinsurance manager will annually provide the reinsurer a copy of statements indicating financial condition that have been prepared by an independent certified accountant in a form acceptable to the Commissioner.

3. The reinsurer may terminate the contract for cause upon written notice to the reinsurance manager. The reinsurer may immediately suspend the authority of the reinsurance manager to assume or cede business during the duration of any dispute regarding the cause for termination.

4. The reinsurance manager will render accounts to the reinsurer accurately detailing all material transactions, including information necessary to support all commissions, charges and other fees received by, or owing to the reinsurance manager, and remit all funds due under the contract to the reinsurer on not less than a monthly basis.

5. The reinsurance manager will hold all funds collected for the reinsurer's account in a fiduciary capacity in a bank that is a qualified U.S. financial institution. The reinsurance manager may retain no more than three (3) months estimated claims payments and allocated loss adjustment expenses. The reinsurance manager shall maintain a separate bank account for each reinsurer that it represents.

6. For at least ten (10) years after expiration of each contract of reinsurance transacted by the reinsurance manager, the reinsurance manager will keep a complete record for each transactions showing:

   a. The type of contract, limits, underwriting restrictions, classes or risks and territory;

   b. Period of coverage, including effective and expiration dates, cancellation provisions and notice required of cancellation, and disposition of outstanding reserves on covered risks;

   c. Reporting and settlement requirements of balances;

   d. Rate used to compute the reinsurance premium;

   e. Names and addresses of reinsurers;

   f. Rates of all reinsurance commissions, including the commissions on any retrocessions handled by the reinsurance manager;

   g. Related correspondence and memoranda;

   h. Proof of placement;

   i. Details regarding retrocessions handled by the reinsurance manager, including the identity of retrocessionaires and percentage of each contract assumed or ceded;

   j. Financial records, including but not limited to, premium and loss accounts; and

   k. For instances when the reinsurance manager places a reinsurance contract on behalf of a ceding insurer:

      i. Directly from any assuming reinsurer the reinsurance broker will provide written evidence that the assuming reinsurer has agreed to assume the risk;

ii. Placed through a representative of the assuming reinsurer, other than an employee, the reinsurance broker will provide written evidence that such reinsurer has delegated binding authority to the representative.

7. The reinsurer will have access and the right to copy all accounts and records maintained by the reinsurance manager related to its business in a form usable by the reinsurer.

8. The reinsurance manager is prohibited from assigning the contract either in whole or in part.

9. The reinsurance manager will comply with the written underwriting and rating standards established by the insurer for the acceptance, rejection or cession of all risks.

10. Rates, terms and purposes of commissions, charges and other fees which the reinsurance manager may levy against the reinsurer are set forth.

11. If the contract permits the reinsurance manager to settle claims on behalf of the reinsurer, the reinsurance manager will report all claims to the reinsurer in a timely manner and a copy of the claim file will be sent to the reinsurer at its request or as soon as it becomes known that the claim:

    a. Has the potential to exceed the lesser of an amount determined by the Commissioner or the limit set by the reinsurer;

    b. Involves a coverage dispute;

    c. May exceed the reinsurance manager's claims settlement authority;

    d. Is open for more than six months; or

    e. Is closed by payment of the lesser of an amount set by the Commissioner or an amount set by the reinsurer.

12. All claim files will be the joint property of the reinsurer and reinsurance manager. However, upon an order of liquidation of the reinsurer the files shall become the sole property of the reinsurer or its estate; the reinsurance manager shall have reasonable access to and the right to copy the files on a timely basis.

13. Any settlement authority granted to the reinsurance manager may be terminated for cause upon the reinsurer's written notice to the reinsurance manager or upon the termination of the contract. The reinsurer may suspend the settlement authority during the duration of the dispute regarding the cause of termination.

14. If the contract provides for a sharing of interim profits by the reinsurance manager, interim profits will not be paid until one year after the end of each underwriting period for property business and five years after the end of each underwriting period for casualty business (or a later period set by the Commissioner for specified lines of insurance) and not until the adequacy of reserves on remaining claims has been verified.

15. The reinsurer shall periodically (at least semi-annually) conduct an on-site review of the underwriting and claims processing operations of the reinsurance manager.

16. The reinsurance manager will disclose to the reinsurer any relationship it has with any insurer prior to ceding or assuming any business with such insurer pursuant to this contract.

17. Within the scope of its actual or apparent authority the acts of the reinsurance manager shall be deemed to be the acts of the reinsurer on whose behalf it is acting.

18. The reinsurance manager shall not:

   a. Cede retrocessions on behalf of the reinsurer, except that the reinsurance manager may cede facultative retrocessions pursuant to obligatory facultative agreements if the contract with the reinsurer contains reinsurance underwriting guidelines for such retrocessions. The guidelines shall include a list of reinsurers with which automatic agreements are in effect, and for each such reinsurer, the coverages and amounts or percentages that may be reinsured, and commission schedules;

   b. Commit the reinsurer to participate in reinsurance syndicates;

   c. Appoint any producer without assuring that the producer is lawfully licensed to transact the type of reinsurance for which he is appointed;

   d. Without prior approval of the reinsurer, pay or commit the reinsurer to pay a claim, net of retrocessions, that exceeds the lesser of an amount specified by the reinsurer or one percent of the reinsurer's policyholder's surplus as of December 31 of the last complete calendar year;

   e. Collect any payment from a retrocessionaire or commit the reinsurer to any claim settlement with a retrocessionaire, without prior approval of the reinsurer. If prior approval is given, a report must be promptly forwarded to the reinsurer;

   f. Jointly employ an individual who is employed by the reinsurer unless such reinsurance manager is under common control with the reinsurer subject to the Holding Company Act; or

   g. Appoint a sub-reinsurance manager.

19. If a reinsurance manager establishes loss reserves, the reinsurer shall annually obtain the opinion of an actuary attesting to the adequacy of loss reserves established for losses incurred and outstanding on business produced by the reinsurance manager. This opinion shall be in addition to any other required loss reserve certification.

20. Binding authority for all retrocessional contracts or participation in reinsurance syndicates shall rest with an officer of the reinsurer who shall not be affiliated with the reinsurance manager.

21. Within 30 days of termination of a contract with a reinsurance manager, the reinsurer shall provide written notification of termination to the Commissioner.

22. A reinsurer shall not appoint to its board of directors, any officer, director, employee, controlling shareholder or sub-producer of its reinsurance manager. This subsection shall not apply to relationships governed by the Holding Company Act or equivalent state laws to the Broker Controlled Insurer Act.

23. A reinsurance manager shall be subject to examination by the Commissioner. The Commissioner shall have access to all books, bank accounts and records of the reinsurance intermediary in a form usable to the Commissioner.

24. A reinsurance manager may be examined as if it were the reinsurer.

APPENDIX A
COMMON REINSURANCE AGREEMENT CLAUSES/DEFINITIONS

Accelerated Death Benefits * – Defines the extent to which the reinsurer is obligated to participate in any accelerated death benefit provision included in policies covered under the reinsurance agreement.

Access to Records – Stipulates that the reinsurer shall be granted access to company records pertinent to business covered under the reinsurance agreement.

Arbitration – Stipulates that differences or disputes between the parties are to be resolved via arbitration, and outlines the procedure to be followed.

Business Covered – Specifies the lines and classes of business to be reinsured.

Cancellation – Specifies the basis upon which a continuous reinsurance agreement may be terminated.

Commencement and Termination – Specifies the inception date and termination date, if any, of the reinsurance agreement.

Commission – Indicates the amount of ceding commission to be allowed to the company (on proportional contracts) and the basis of subsequent adjustments, if any, thereof.

Commutation – Permits the parties to settle outstanding claims on a net present value basis.

Continuations * – Defines the respective rights and obligations of the parties with respect to the policies covered by the reinsurance agreement which have been substantially modified, or replaced by another policy, subsequent to the date on which the reinsurance coverage originally attached.

Conversions * – Defines how coverage under the reinsurance agreement applies with the respect to the policies covered thereunder which have been converted to a different policy form.

Currency – Defines the basis for conversion, where premium is paid and losses settled in more than one currency.

Cut–through – Stipulates that in the event of the insolvency of the ceding company, obligations of the reinsurer with respect to the business covered under the reinsurance agreement will be paid by the reinsurer directly to the insured or claimant under the ceding company's original policy.

Disability Benefits * – (Sometimes combined with Accidental Death Benefits) Defines the extent to which the reinsurer is obligated to participate in disability or, if applicable, accidental death benefits afforded under policies covered under the reinsurance agreement.

Errors and Omissions – Stipulates that inadvertent errors or oversights will not affect obligations of the parties, provided that correction is made as soon as possible.

Excess of Policy Limits – Defines the extent to which the reinsurance agreement will indemnify for awards in excess of original policy limits.

Exclusions – Specifies the lines and classes of business to be excluded under the reinsurance agreement.

Experience Refunds * – Provides a mechanism by which a stipulated portion of the reinsurer's profits on the business ceded under the reinsurance agreement will be returned to the ceding company.

Extended Term Coverage * – Defines the reinsurer's obligations with respect to the policies covered under the reinsurance agreement which have lapsed where coverage is being continued under an extended term or reduced paid–up insurance provision.

Extra–contractual Obligations – Defines the extent to which the reinsurance agreement will indemnify for judgments against the cedent arising from its handling of a claim.

Federal Excise Tax – Stipulates that FET will be deducted from premium remitted to alien reinsurers domiciled in countries not signatory to U.S. tax treaties.

Funding – Requires unlicensed or unauthorized reinsurers to provide collateral for obligations to the ceding company.

Increasing Death Benefits * – Defines the reinsurer's obligations with respect to the policies covered under the reinsurance agreement which provide for an increase in the amount of the death benefit at a date subsequent to the original issue date.

Indexation – Defines the manner in which the ceding company's retention and/or the amount of reinsurance coverage afforded will be adjusted to reflect changes in some agreed upon index of inflation, e.g., the *Consumer Price Index.*

Insolvency – Defines the reinsurer's obligation in the event the ceding company becomes financially impaired or adjudged to be insolvent.

Intermediary	–	Identifies the intermediary, if any, involved in the placement of reinsurance and defines fiduciary responsibilities.
Joint Life *	–	Defines the manner in which reinsurance applies to policies insuring more than one life.
Jumbo Limit *	–	Defines the maximum amount of insurance that may be in–force or applied for before any additional reinsurance must be submitted on a facultative basis to the reinsurer.
Loss and Loss Adjustment Expense (Ultimate Net Loss)	–	Defines the reinsurer's obligation to indemnify the ceding company for losses covered under the reinsurance agreement, and the basis upon which loss adjustment expenses will be handled.
Loss Occurrence	–	Defines what constitutes a single loss occurrence, for purposes of establishing the ceding company's retention and the reinsurer's liability.
Mod–co Reserve Adjustment *	–	Describes the manner in which a cash settlement will be made periodically to compensate the reinsurer for loss of investment income on reserves/assets held by the ceding company.
Net Retained Lines	–	Stipulates that the reinsurer will be responsible for only that portion of covered business which the ceding company retains net for its own account, i.e., the reinsurance applies net of any other applicable reinsurance whether or not collectible.
Offset	–	Permits setting off of mutual debts between the reinsurer and the ceding company.
Persistency Bonus *	–	Defines the basis on which the reinsurer will compensate the ceding company for policies covered under the reinsurance agreement which meet or exceed a stipulated persistency rate.
Policy Dividends *	–	Defines the extent to which the reinsurer will participate in policy loans on policies covered under the reinsurance agreement.
Policy Surrender Values *	–	Defines the extent to which the reinsurer will participate in the cash settlement of surrendered policies covered under the reinsurance agreement.
Preamble	–	Identifies the parties to the contract.
Premium	–	Specifies the amount of premium to be paid to the reinsurer, the basis of calculation, and the timing of and method of subsequent adjustments, if any.

Recapture * – Defines the basis on which business ceded to the reinsurer may be recaptured by the ceding company.

Reductions * – Defines the reinsurer's obligations with respect to the policies covered under the reinsurance agreement on which the amount of insurance has been reduced.

Reinstatement – Defines the basis on which the reinsurer's limit of liability will be reinstated if depleted or exhausted by a loss, recoverable under the reinsurance agreement.

Reinsurance Rates * – Defines the basis on which rates applicable under the reinsurance agreement to in–force policies may be modified by either the reinsurer or the ceding company.

Reports and Remittances – Specifies the information which must be provided to the reinsurer, and the intervals at which information and premium payable must be remitted to the reinsurer.

Retention and Limits – Defines the ceding company's retention, the reinsurer's limit of liability, and the basis upon which loss adjustment expense will be handled. (LAE is sometimes addressed in the separate Ultimate Net Loss clause.)

Service of Suit – Requires unlicensed or unauthorized reinsurers to appoint an agent for receipt of service of process, and to submit to the jurisdiction of any U.S. court of competent jurisdiction.

Special Acceptances – Provides a method by which otherwise excluded business may be submitted for consideration by the reinsurer.

Surplus Aid or (Surplus Relief) – A term commonly used to describe reinsurance transactions designed primarily to alleviate surplus strain arising from the statutory accounting requirement that acquisition expenses be recognized immediately rather than amortized over the policy term.

Taxes – Stipulates that the ceding company is responsible for all taxes, other than Federal excise tax, and agrees not to deduct reinsurance premium when making tax returns other than income or profits tax (i.e., premium tax must be based on gross premium income).

Territory – Defines the geographic limitations, if any, of the reinsurance agreement.

*Indicates clauses ordinarily applicable to Life/A&H reinsurance agreements.

EXHIBIT A — EXAMPLE LETTER OF CREDIT FORM

(Name of Bank)
(Address)

FOR INTERNAL IDENTIFICATION PURPOSE ONLY

Date ____________________ ID No. ___________ Issuing Bank No. ____________________

Clean, Irrevocable, Unconditional Letter of Credit No.:____________________

Account Holder (Reinsured):____________________

Issuing Bank:____________________

Beneficiary (Reinsured):____________________

Amount:____________________ Expiration Date:____________________

Date ________________

Clean, Irrevocable Unconditional Letter of Credit No.:____________________

To Beneficiary: (Name)____________________

(Address)____________________

Dear Sir or Madam:

We have established this clean, irrevocable, and unconditional letter of credit in your favor for drawing up to U.S. $______________ effective immediately and expiring at our (bank address) with our close of business on ______________. Except when the amount of this letter of credit is increased, this credit cannot be modified or revoked without your consent.

We hereby undertake to promptly honor your sight draft(s) drawn on us, indicating our credit No. ______________, for all or any part of this credit upon presentation of your draft drawn on us at our offices prior to the expiration date hereof.

The term "Beneficiary" as used herein includes any successor by operation of law of the named Beneficiary including, without limitation, any liquidator, rehabiliatator, receiver or conservator.*

Except as stated herein, this undertaking is not subject to any requirement or qualification. Our obligation under this letter of credit is the individual obligation of the Bank, in no way contingent upon reimbursement with respect thereto, or upon our ability to perfect any lien or security interest.

This letter of credit expires on ______________, but will automatically extend without amendment for one year from the expiration date or any future expiration date, unless thirty days prior to such expiration date, we notify you by Registered Mail that this letter of credit will not be renewed.

This letter of credit is subject to the Uniform Customs and Practice for Documentary Credits (1993 Revision) International Chamber of Commerce publication No. 500. Notwithstanding Article 17 of said publication, in the event that one or more of the occurrences specified in Article 17 of said Publication occurs, then the bank hereby specifically agrees that this letter of credit shall be extended so as not to expire during such interruption of business and shall extend for ten days after such resumption of business.

______________________________ ______________________________

Signature Title

*If the named Beneficiary is a California domestic insurer, this paragraph should be deleted and replaced by: "The term Beneficiary as used herein includes and is limited to the court appointed domiciliary receiver, conservator, rehabilitator or liquidator."

EXHIBIT B — EXAMPLE FORM AR-1 CERTIFICATE OF ASSUMING INSURER

I, ______(name of officer)______ ______(title of officer)______

of ______(name of assuming insurer)______ the assuming insurer

under a reinsurance agreement with one or more insurers domiciled in

______(name of state)______ hereby certify that

______(name of assuming insurer)______ ("Assuming Insurer"):

1. Submits to the jurisdiction of any court competent jurisdiction in ______(ceding insurer's state of domicile)______

for the adjudication of any issues arising out of the reinsurance agreement, agrees to comply with all requirements necessary to give such court jurisdiction, and will abide by the final decision of such court or any appellate court in the event of an appeal. Nothing in this paragraph constitutes or should be understood to constitute a waiver of Assuming Insurer's rights to commence an action in any court of competent jurisdiction in the United States, to remove an action to a United States District Court, or to seek a transfer of a case to another court as permitted by the laws of the United States or of any state in the United States. This paragraph is not intended to conflict with or override the obligation of the parties to the reinsurance agreement to arbitrate their dispute if such an obligation is created in the agreement.

2. Designates the Insurance Commissioner of ______(ceding insurer's state of domicile)______

as its lawful attorney upon whom may be served any lawful process in any action, suit or proceeding arising out of the reinsurance agreement instituted by or on behalf of the ceding insurer.

3. Submits to the authority of the Insurance Commissioner of ______(ceding insurer's state of domicile)______

to examine its books and records and agrees to bear the expense of any such examination.

4. Submits with this form a current list of insurers domiciled in ______(ceding insurer's state of domicile)______

reinsured by Assuming Insurer and undertakes to submit additions to or deletions from the list to the Insurance Commissioner at least once per calendar quarter.

Dated: ______________ ______________
(name of assuming insurer)

By: ______________
(name of officer)

____
(title of officer)

EXHIBIT C — GENERAL REINSURANCE CHECKLIST

The examiner should complete the following checklist in accordance with the overall review of the reinsurance transactions incurred by the company.

	Yes	No	N/A	Done By	Date
General Reinsurance Checklist					
1. Does the company conduct a review at least annually to monitor the suitability of the ceded reinsurance program with regards to:					
a. Company's overall business plan?					
b. Changes in the company's underwriting or marketing operations?					
c. Changes on its territorial operations?					
2. Does the company maintain centralized oversight over its ceded reinsurance program:					
a. Are signed copies of all placement slips, cover notes, facultative certificates and treaties retained?					
b. Are all treaty documentation finalized and executed by all parties within 9 months of contract inception in accordance with SSAP No. 62, paragraph 23?					
c. Are all reinsurance contracts summarized for reference by company underwriting, claims, accounting and legal staff?					
3. Does the company monitor aggregations of exposure to natural disasters? Document the procedures employed by the company: ________________ ________________ ________________ ________________					

	Yes	No	N/A	Done By	Date
a. Is the total catastrophe reinsurance protection in place sufficient for the company's needs?					
4. Has the company established standards of acceptability for reinsurers, and does the company annually review its reinsurance security? Describe the company's procedures and resources utilized to accomplish this purpose: ______ ______ ______ ______					
5. Does the company conduct audits of reinsurance accounting and claims transactions? Obtain documentation and details of these audits.					
6. Does the company have a monitoring system for timely collection/payment of reinsurance balances? Obtain documentation and details of established systems.					
7. Does the company have an internal quality control program to regularly monitor the accuracy of transactions processed? Obtain documentation and details of established programs.					
8. Does the company regularly review policies issued against reinsurance documents to determine:					
a. Whether policy coverage is consistent with the scope of applicable reinsurance protection?					
b. The extent of net exposure remaining?					
c. How net exposure is likely to impact the company?					
9. Does the company have a formal procedure to communicate with reinsurers, either directly, or via a reinsurance intermediary?					

	Yes	No	N/A	Done By	Date
a. Does the company verify the licensing status of, and the amount of Errors & Omissions coverage maintained by each reinsurance intermediary involved in placement of ceded reinsurance?					
10. Does the company monitor and report to senior management reinsurance collection difficulties?					
a. Is there a formal procedure to determine when unrecoverable balances should be written off?					
b. Have write-offs and commutations been properly accounted for and reported in the company's financial statements?					

EXHIBIT D — CEDED REINSURANCE CONTRACT REVIEW

The examiner should complete the following workpaper in accordance with the review of the company's ceded reinsurance contracts. For those items that are not applicable, indicate N/A:

1. Affiliated Transaction (Y/N)? ______________________________

2. Treaty of Certificated Number: ______________________________

3. Name of Reinsured: ______________________________

4. Name of Reinsurer and Authorization Status (Authorized/Unauthorized):

   ____

   ____

5. Do all reinsurers meet the company's minimum acceptability standards?

   ____

6. Does collateral meet the NAIC standards? Document the collateral provided by the unauthorized reinsurers:

   ____

   ____

   ____

7. Document any reinsurance intermediaries used:

   ____

8. Document the type of the reinsurance contract, the effective date, expiration date and the date the contract was signed by both parties:

   ____

   ____

9. Identify and document the contract termination provisions:

   ____

10. Identify and document whether the following insurance clauses are included in the contract:

    Insolvency Clause: ______________________________

    Arbitration Clause: ______________________________

    Intermediary Clause: ______________________________

    Errors & Omissions Clause: ______________________________

11. Document the classes or line of business reinsured: ______________________________

12. Document any exclusions noted in the contract: ______________________________

13. Does the agreement apply on a "loss occurring" or on a "risks attaching" basis? ______________

14. Document the territory the contract covers: ______________________________

15. Does the agreement cover losses occurred prior to its inception date? If so, verify that the contract has been properly accounted as retroactive reinsurance: ______________________________

____

16. Document the company's retention under the contract: ______________________________

17. Does the contract contain a "loss corridor" provision? ______________________________

18. Indicate the reinsurer's limits under the contract: ______________________________

____

19. Is there an aggregate limitation applicable to a period of coverage, a single loss event, or to the agreement overall? ______________________________

20. Document the premiums stipulations set forth in the contract:

Annual Reinsurance Premium: ______________________________

Minimum Reinsurance Premium: ______________________________

Deposit Premium: ______________________________

Date Premiums are Adjustable: ______________________________

21. Determine whether the reinsurance rate or premiums are adjustable based on loss experience. If they are adjustable, indicate the minimum and maximum level, how often they can be adjusted, whether adjustments have resulted in a deficit or credit carry forward, and that premiums adjustments have been properly accrued: ______________________________

____

22. Identify the contract settlement provisions. Determine the payment schedules, adjustable retention provisions, accumulating retentions from multiple years, or other provisions which serve to defer settlement of the reinsurer's obligations: ______________________________

____

23. Determine whether a managing general agent produced the reinsurance contract. Document the MGAs responsibilities regarding the reinsurance arrangement: ______________________________

____

24. Determine how often are the reports of premiums/losses are to be rendered: ______________

25. Does the agreement contain a "cash call" provisions? ______________________________

26. Is there a significant transfer of risk (underwriting and timing)? If no, has the deposit method of accounting been properly followed? (Refer to Section VI of this document.) Does a cash flow analysis need to be performed? ______________________________

____

27. Is the reinsurance credit taken by the company consistent with the provisions of the contract? __________

____

28. Identify and document any amendments or addendas to the contract: ______________________________

____

PART 5— SAMPLE WORKING PAPERS

TABLE OF CONTENTS

PART 5 — SAMPLE WORKING PAPERS

A.B.C. Life Insurance Company
Outline of Work Done
12/31/X1

		DATE	INITIALS	REF.
1.	Count cash in office and reconcile with accounting records.	1/15/X2	TR	A-7/pg 5
2.	Secure certificates from depositories and reconcile balances with book balances.	1/15/X2 1/16/X2	TR TR	A-7/pg 8 A-7/pg 6
3.	Note any unusual increases at end of year and ascertain if all bank balances are unpledged.	1/16/X2 1/15/X2	TR TR	A-7/pg 6 A-7/pg 8

A.B.C. Life Insurance Company	Tom Rowe
Cash and Bank Deposits (A-7)	1/16/X2
12/31/X1	

Account No.	Description	Work Paper Reference	Balance 12/31/X1
0700	Cash in Office	A-7/p95	$300.00
0701	Cash in Bank	A-7/p96	7,717.36
	Total Cash 12/31/X1		$8,017.36
	Investment Income Due and Accrued	N.L.(e)	150.75~
~ Verified Investment Income Due and Accrued on Savings Account Received 1/10/X2			

A.B.C. Life Insurance Company	Tom Rowe
Cash	1/16/X2
Exceptions, Errors and Problems	
12/31/X1	

No Discrepancies, errors or unusual problems
were noted during the audit work performed.
1/16/X2
T.R.

A.B.C. Life Insurance Company	Tom Rowe
Cash and Bank Deposits – Petty	1/15/X2
Cash Count as of 1/15/X2	
12/31/X1	

Account No. 0700	Petty Cash	Number	Denomination	Amount	Total
	Coins:	35	.01	.35	
		40	.05	2.00	
		18	.10	1.80	
		15	.25	3.75	
	Rolls:	4 @ 50	.01	2.00	
		2@ 1.00	.05	2.00	
		1 @ 5.00	.10	5.00	
		1 @ 10.00	.25	10.00	
	Currency:	48	1.00	48.00	
		5	5.00	25.00	
		3	10.00	30.00	
		2	20.00	40.00	169.90
January Disbursements per tape attached					130.10
	Total Per Count				$300.00N
					To A-1/pg3

January Disbursements

0.+ ✔
229.+ ✔
1,500.+ ✔
2,250.+ ✔
969.+ ✔
1,251.+ ✔
1,344.+ ✔
839.+ ✔
2,345.+ ✔
1,652.+ ✔
581.+ ✔
13,010. *

✔ = Examined invoice or receipt and verified date, payee, purpose and amount

N = Traced to General Ledger

The above cash and cash items total $300.00 were counted in my presence and returned to me intact.

John Doe, Fund Custodian 11:15 a.m. 1/5/X2

A.B.C. Life Insurance Company	Tom Rowe
Cash – Bank Reconciliation	1/16/X2
12/31/X1	

Account No. C701	Account Title Cash – First National Bank – General	
	Balance per bank statement A-1/pg 7	32,023.26 (c)
	Add: Deposit in transit 12/31/X1	837.50 ✔
	Deduct: Outstanding Checks (tape attached)	25,143.40 (n)
	Balance per books, 12/31/X1	7,717.36 (m)
		To A-1/pg 3

Outstanding Checks
12/31/X1

Check No.	
13021	15.36
13025	14,695.73
13026	2,383.45
13027	58.35
13029	7,892.41
13030	30.98
13031	67.12
	25,145.40

c = Balance confirmed

✔ = Traced to cutoff bank statement

n = All checks dated December 31, 20X1 and earlier returned with this statement were traced to the list of outstanding checks as of December 31, 20X1.

m = Examined account balance during year, no unusual increase at year end.

First National Bank	Account Number	Date of Last Payment
A.B.C. Life Insurance Company 18 Oak Street Your State	812 046	11/30/X1
	Date this Statement	Balance Last Statement
	12/31/X1	27,846.21

Date	Checks in Order of Payment	Deposit	Balance
		167.95	
		172.14	
		242.00	18,444.52
12/12		94.64	
		107.19	18,646.35
12/15		133.80	
		174.18	
		137.10	
12/18		151.25	19,242.68
		62.62	
		64.42	
		106.02	19,475.74
12/19		104.94	
		116.17	19,696.85
12/29		123.06	
		8503.29	28,323.20
12/22		142.77	
		149.78	
		145.63	28,761.38
12/26		50.00	
		153.49	
		331.53	29,296.40
		89.75	
12/28		146.21	29,532.36
12/29		62.40	
		151.25	
		141.31	
		152.86	
		1799.34	31,839.52

Explanation of Symbols		Service Charge		Overdrawn	
We have Subtracted Debits		And Added Credits		For a Service Charge of	Resulting Balance
Number	Amount	Number	Amount		
		64	18,931.01		32,023.25
					Total